Otto Preminger

Otto Preminger

The Man Who Would Be King

FOSTER HIRSCH

ALFRED A. KNOPF
NEW YORK
2007

THIS IS A BORZOI BOOK
PUBLISHED BY ALFRED A. KNOPF

Library of Congress Cataloging-in-Publication Data
Hirsch, Foster.
Otto Preminger: the man who would be king / by Foster Hirsch.
p. cm.
Includes bibliographical references and index.
ISBN 978-0-375-41373-5
1. Preminger, Otto. 2. Motion picture producers and directors—
United States—Biography. 3. Motion picture actors and
actresses—United States—Biography. I. Title.
PN1998.3.P743H57 2007
791.4302'33092—dc22
[B]
2007012315

Manufactured in the United States of America
Published October 21, 2007
Second Printing, November 2007

For Kristofer

Contents

List of Illustrations

Acknowledgments

For candid, generous interviews I would like to thank the following: the late Elaine Barrymore; Trumball Barton; Peter Bogdanovich; Donald Bogle; the late Phoebe Brand; William Doran Cannon; Lewis Chambers; Carol Channing; Kathryn Grant Crosby; Christian Divine; Keir Dullea; the late Douglas Fairbanks Jr.; Vera Fairbanks; Nina Foch; Horton Foote; Larkin Ford; Mona Freeman; Rita Gam; Gilbert Gardner; Ben Gazzara; Howell Gilbert; Tony Gittelson; Wolfgang Glattes; Elaine Gold; Paul Green; George Grizzard; the late Kitty Carlisle Hart; Jill Haworth; Bill Hayes; Diana Herbert; Celeste Holm; Robert Hooks; Geoffrey Horne; Harry Howard; Kathleen Hughes; the late Kim Hunter; Olga James; Leslie Jay; Ken Kaufman; the late Marjorie Kellogg; Robert Lantz; Lionel Larner; the late Paula Laurence; Arthur Laurents; John Phillip Law; Beck Lee; Arlene Leuzzi; David Lewin; Nicola Lubitsch; Carol Lynley; Mike Macdonald; John Martello; Virginia McDowall; Biff McGuire; Eva Monley; Rita Moriarty; Don Murray; Patricia Neal; the late Barry Nelson; Hilde Odelga; Wolfgang Odelga; the late Charlie Okun; Jennifer O'Neil; Austin Pendleton; the late Brock Peters; Barbara Preminger; Erik Lee Preminger; Eve Preminger; Hope Preminger; the late Ingo Preminger; Kathy Preminger; Mark Preminger; Victoria Preminger; Harold Prince; the late David Raksin; Val Robins; Bud Rosenthal; Stanley Rubin; Eva Marie Saint; John Saxon; the late Martin Schute; Madeleine Sherwood; Jean Simmons; the late Peter Stone; the late Leon Uris; Michael Wager; the late Ruth Warrick.

For help in locating interviewees: Bruce Goldstein; Jane Klain; Marvin Paige; Sam Staggs; Jim Watters; Joanne Zyontz.

For research assistance: Irene Cohen; Donald R. D'Aries; Samuel Lorca; Janet Lorenz, the Fairbanks Center for Motion Picture Study, Beverly Hills; Piero Passatore; Richard Prolsdorfer, Twentieth Century-Fox.

For help in locating hard-to-find films: Tom Toth; Charles Silver at the Museum of Modern Art.

For photographs: Otto Preminger Films, Inc.; Photofest.

The staff of the Billy Rose Theatre Collection at the New York Public Library for the Performing Arts, Lincoln Center; the staff of the Margaret Herrick Library, Academy of Motion Picture Arts and Sciences, Beverly Hills; the staff of the Theatre in der Josefstadt, Vienna.

At Alfred A. Knopf: Victoria Wilson, my wise and exacting editor.

Otto Preminger

An Encounter

I was in the presence of Otto Preminger only once. Because he was listed as the director, in November 1980 I went to see a play at an acting studio where Preminger was then teaching called The Corner Loft, located at Twelfth Street and University Place in New York City. The play, a routine psychological thriller called *The Killer Thing*, turned out to be beside the point, because during the intermission, with the audience members squashed together in the minuscule lobby, a drama far more enticing than the one onstage erupted suddenly. As if in response to some deep atavistic instinct, patrons parted to make room for the tall, commanding figure—unmistakably Otto Preminger in person—who entered the lobby and began, with purposeful stride, to make his way across the room that seemed almost too small to contain him. With his large, bald, ovoid head, piercing blue eyes, lips that formed a faint half-smile that seemed poised between charm and contempt, and his imperial bearing, Preminger radiated a lifetime of privilege, wealth, fame, and power. There was no disregarding this man's deeply engrained sense of self, his unassailable amour propre. The milling crowd, evidently as pleased as I was to catch a glimpse of a director who at the time was as recognizable as Alfred Hitchcock, looked at him with the respect, and the wariness, that his reputation as a terrible-tempered tyrant seemed to warrant. Such a large man in such a small space seemed pregnant with possibilities for a collision of Grand Guignol magnitude.

And indeed, within a few seconds of his appearance, Preminger's booming voice—"*You always louse things up, don't you?*"—reduced the room to a hushed silence, quickly shattered by another insult delivered in Preminger's thick Austrian accent. *"Lousing things up and getting in the way is your particular specialty, isn't it?"* Evidently trying to wish himself into invisibility, the minion who was the object of the director's blasts crumpled into an almost fetal position as he walked (hobbled?) to a nearby door, fumbled briefly with the doorknob, then disappeared from view. (And from history. No one I talked to who had worked at the Loft in the Preminger era, including its director, Elaine Gold, or John Martello, who starred in the play, was able to identify the unlucky subaltern.)

Frozen, we all waited for Preminger's next move. His half-smile in place and behaving as if the scene we had witnessed had not happened, the director calmly helped himself to coffee and cookies at the refreshment table. In what seemed at the time excruciating slow motion, the room began to fill once again with the murmur of conversation as the audience feebly pretended to do what Preminger had accomplished with such remarkable aplomb—dismiss the scene he had just played.

Was the tantrum for real, or had the maestro favored us with a command performance of "Otto Preminger," the world-renowned filmmaker who was as noted for his outbursts as for his work? Were we privileged witnesses of a reprise of the Hollywood Nazi roles Preminger had played with such conviction that some of his enemies regarded these performances as the real thing? Or had we just observed an aging director losing his grip? The explosion was awesome, but also ambiguous: that secret-sharer smile, the post-tirade ease and obliviousness with which he helped himself at the coffee table. "Real people don't behave this way," I remember thinking at the time. What had the unfortunate young man done, or failed to do, to warrant such withering public abuse? Couldn't the dressing-down have waited until Preminger and the miscreant were discreetly out of sight? Or was a public forum precisely the arena in which Preminger wanted to stage his anger? That night, Preminger certainly stole the show. Over twenty years later I recall nothing of the play, while the memory of those few moments remains vivid.

Little did I suspect that two decades later I would be eager to write the story of Preminger's life and that the high drama of my one encounter with him would be echoed many times over in the recollections of the colleagues and family members I interviewed. Nearly everyone I spoke with had a story about a Preminger outburst, while to the informed moviegoer "Otto Preminger" still connotes an image of a Teutonic tyrant capable in a flash of eliciting fear and trembling among the groundlings.

It has been part of my job to rescue Preminger from his persona, and to present him as the complex, variegated, often endearing, sometimes infuriating person who lurked behind the role of the temperamental titan he played with incomparable vigor. Rages, to be sure, defined one component of Preminger's personality, but conviviality, courtliness, great generosity, loyalty, compassion, and accessibility were other, equally tangible traits, attested to many times over by family, friends, co-workers, and even, sometimes, enemies. With his legendary temper on the one hand, and his dazzling Viennese charm on the other, he was like a character in an epic Russian novel: a man of many parts.

To borrow E. M. Forster's terms for describing fictional characters, Preminger was decidedly "round" rather than "flat." Flat characters can be defined by a few broad strokes, and remain unchanged and unchanging on each appearance; round characters, in contrast, are richly mercurial, perplexing, dense with conflicts, and always capable of surprises. A round character to the ultimate degree, Preminger provoked wildly divided reactions—indeed, the ability to inspire controversy seemed as much a part of his birthright as his rock-solid self-confidence. He was a fine man, a true humanitarian, I was told; no, others claimed, when he played Nazis no acting was necessary. He was a Continental sophisticate, according to some; no, a compulsive philanderer, according to others.

As "himself," abetted by his genius for self-promotion, he had size and flair, and "Otto Preminger" may have been his most successful production. Big-boned, and with a stentorian voice that retained the staccato rhythm and spitting consonants of his native German, Preminger was not only physically but also psychologically and existentially titanic, a force of nature. As the elder son of a prominent Austrian lawyer, Preminger was born into a world of wealth and status which, in living his own life on a grand scale, he never once abandoned. Hotel suites sparkling with Old World opulence, a baronial mansion in Bel-Air, a Manhattan town house of severe modern design, sleek modern offices with large marble desks, and a white marble villa on the French Riviera were among the infernally elegant settings in which he lived and worked. At fashionable restaurants in the great cities of the world, "Mr. Preminger" was an always honored guest. Before he settled down with Hope Bryce, his third wife, and became a devoted husband and father, he was famed as a man-about-town, first as a bachelor in Vienna and then, in New York and Hollywood, as a straying spouse in two long-distance marriages. He gained (unwanted) fame for two of his affairs. The first was a brief liaison with the stripper Gypsy Rose Lee (with whom he fathered a son); the second was a stormy relationship with the beautiful and doomed

Dorothy Dandridge, who became the first black female star in Hollywood history when Preminger cast her in *Carmen Jones.*

Preminger's imperial temperament—he was born to give rather than to follow orders—had a significant impact on the business of filmmaking in America. Chafing under the restrictions of his first job in Hollywood, as a studio employee at Twentieth Century-Fox, Preminger broke away when he could in order to set up in business for himself. Relocating his base from Los Angeles to New York, he became an industry pioneer, the first fully independent producer-director in American films, and in the process created a model for the way motion pictures are produced that endures to the present.

Defenders and detractors agree on only one point: Preminger was a superb producer who completed his films on or even ahead of schedule and who never went over budget. Of his dependability, efficiency, financial common sense, managerial skill, and salesmanship, there was never any question. His artistic legacy, however, has proven to be as polarizing as his personality, and for the most part the jury is still out. When I called to request an interview, Otto's younger brother Ingo asked why I wanted to write the book. "I can see eight, nine, ten books about Bergman or Fellini, but a book about Otto? He was a very good producer and he fought important battles against censorship, but there was no great film!"[1] I answered that I wanted to write the book because I admired many of his films and felt that they had been seriously underrated.

Part of my attraction to Preminger was in the apparent contradiction between his temperament and the cool tone of his most commanding films. The inner demons that pressed him into conducting his ceremonies of public abuse and humiliation are nowhere to be found in the majestic containment of his most representative work. At a casual glance his corpus might seem to lack a distinctive touch, but on closer inspection the films reveal exactly the kinds of insignia by which directors are anointed auteurs. Beneath the formal veneer of his films and the wide variety of genres in which he worked are the traces of an unexpectedly personal filmmaker, a decidedly stealthy auteur.

Preminger's long career has three distinct periods: early, when he was a contract director at Fox, from 1935 to 1936 and from 1943 to 1953; middle, from 1953 to 1967, when he hit his stride as an independent; and late, from 1968 to 1979, when he seemed to lose focus. Preminger bashers often concede only one really good film in the canon, *Laura,* an elegant 1944 film noir glistening with sexual and psychological perversity. But no, the list of the director's victories must be expanded to include at least nine or ten other films. And waiting for critical resuscitation is an almost equal number of "wounded" and often unjustly vilified projects.

Whenever I mentioned that I was writing a biography of Otto Preminger, I elicited an unvarying response: a gasp, a rolling of eyes, an expression of mock pity or mock terror, as if my subject might rise from his grave to berate or scold me. "Wasn't he a terrible man?" I was often asked. "No," I would respond, "he was only difficult." It was the sheer size and scale of that challenging personality, along with my conviction that his often elegant work has been largely misjudged, which drew me to him as a subject. Inevitably in the course of research and writing, a biographer fuses with his subject; and in completing a book the writer in a sense "wins" the struggle and of course claims the final word. Perhaps foolishly, as I reconstructed his life, I began to feel that, had I known him, I would have been able to "handle" Otto, a man who so evidently required special handling. I know I would have been an appreciative audience for his brand of Germanic wit, and I like to think I could have coaxed some laughter from him for some of my own zingers. A Preminger dressing-down would have been incinerating, of course, but I felt in time that I might have been able to see through, and perhaps even to justify, some of his tantrums. No one I spoke with, either friend or foe, accused him of being dull, and, deceased, Otto Preminger, as he had been in life, was good company.

ONE

A Ring from the Emperor

"One set of documents lists Vienna as my birthplace, but another set, equally valid-looking, places my birth at my great-grandfather's farm some distance away," Preminger claimed in his 1977 autobiography.[1] In fact, how-ever, as Otto's younger brother Ingo stated in a tone that allowed for no argument, "Otto was born in Wiznitz, which then was in Poland and later in Romania."[2] Preminger also offered two possibilities for his date of birth: one record claimed December 5, 1906, the other "exactly one year earlier." Although he left the matter hanging ("at my time of life one year more or less makes little difference"),[3] Otto Preminger was in fact born on Decem-ber 5, 1905—in Wiznitz, Poland.

There would have been no reason for Preminger to be coy about his age, but misstating where he was born was an artful subterfuge. "Wiznitz" clearly does not have the same lustrous ring that "Vienna" has—and his attempt to disguise the actual place of his birth revealed class issues endemic to the Austro-Hungarian Empire. The Premingers were Eastern European Jews, *Ostjuden,* an ethnic group scorned by many non-Jews, Viennese and Austri-ans in particular, and by German Jews as well. Eastern Europeans were widely regarded as less refined, less Germanic, than their German-Jewish coreligion-ists. To the always ambitious Preminger, who throughout his career gilded his persona by presenting himself as a native son of Vienna, the imperial capital, his Polish birth was an inconvenient fact about which the less said the better.

Otto's father, Markus Preminger, was born in 1877 in Czernovic, Galicia, at a time when it, too, was part of Poland. (Later it was to be claimed by Romania and then by Soviet Russia.) "Whatever country it may have been attached to, at one time or another, Czernovic was German-speaking, and strictly German in temperament," recalled Ingo, who was born in the city in 1911. "Czernovic was a province of the Austrian Empire, which Germanized these countries: my parents did not speak a word of Polish, and they didn't feel that they *were* Polish in any way. Czernovic had a beautiful German university that my father attended."[4]

Although Markus's father was an impoverished Eastern European Talmudic scholar unable to provide for his wife, his son, and his five daughters,

Otto's father, Markus, as a public prosecutor in Czernovic, Poland: confident, proud, and on the cusp of an extraordinary career defending the interests of the Emperor Franz Josef.

he recognized Markus's inborn drive and was eager for his only son to receive a secular education. When his father died suddenly at a young age, Markus became the sole support of his mother and sisters. He enrolled at the university in Czernovic and, working full time and often going without sleep for days at a time, graduated with highest honors as doctor of law. He was such an extraordinarily gifted student that, on graduation, he received a ring from the emperor on which the initials of Franz Josef are set in tiny diamonds. "A big ring with a lot of jewels, it is not a ring to wear," Ingo observed. "The person who got this ring, and there were only a few given out, had to pass every test with highest distinction. It was an exceptional honor, and even more so in my father's case because he was Jewish."[5] (Tangible proof that Markus Preminger triumphed over the circumstances of his birth, the ring from Emperor Franz Josef remains a Preminger family heirloom, kept in a safe-deposit box in the custody of Ingo's son, James.)

The ring assured Markus a position in the emperor's legal department. His first job was as a public prosecutor in Czernovic. His tenacity, confidence, and keenness of mind, along with an equally important quality— "My father was a charming man," Ingo said—propelled Markus Preminger, a self-made ethnic and religious outsider, into a rapidly ascending career. At twenty-six, poised to attain the worldly success his father had never sought, Markus married a woman seven years his junior, Josefa Fraenkel, who came from a prosperous, nonreligious, assimilated Jewish family. "Her father was the owner of a lumberyard, which in those days, in Poland, was quite an important industry," as Ingo recalled.[6] Josefa's land-rich grandfather owned a large farm where he grew crops and kept herds of horses and cattle. Josefa was an ideal wife for the fast-rising young public prosecutor. Her formal manner, touched with hauteur, and her sense of her own social standing as the daughter of a prominent businessman and now as the wife of a doctor of law who had won a ring from the emperor, refuted the stereotype of Eastern European Jews as vulgar country cousins. "My grandmother, a great beauty, was an incredible snob," Eve Preminger, Ingo's oldest daughter, explained. "She was the one born with money. To her father you only spoke in the third person. Markus, who unlike Josefa came from humble beginnings, was the boy who made good and married the beautiful princess."[7]

In family photos, regarding the camera warily, their unyielding gazes and tight, faint smiles suggesting they would not have suffered fools gladly and that, if wronged, vengeance would be theirs, Markus and Josefa carry themselves with unshakable pride. Traditional Jewish warmth and *menschlichkeit* are not the qualities they offer to the camera. If in public Markus

Otto's parents, Markus and Josefa, on vacation
in Badgastein, Austria, August 1936.

and Josefa seemed formidable, their insisted-upon dignity perhaps a stance
intended to counteract always simmering anti-Semitism as well as widespread disdain for *Ostjuden,* within the family they were affectionate parents
who provided a stable home life for their two young sons. "My father
believed that it was impossible to be too kind or too loving to a child," Otto
recalled. "He never punished me. I don't think my mother agreed completely with this method but she acted, as always, according to his wishes. I
adored him."[8] "He was a very good father," Ingo agreed. "He spoiled us. He
believed children *should* be spoiled."[9]

"I had an affectionate relationship with my mother," Otto said. "[She
was] a wonderful, warm-hearted woman, but she did not really play a large
part in the formation of my character. Intellectually my father influenced
me more than my mother."[10] "I can't say anything about my mother's per-

The handsome young Otto (left), with his brother Ingo and his parents, with a come-hither gaze and a princely carriage, radiates self-assurance.

sonality," Ingo responded.[11] ("Ingo and Otto often ignored nuance," Eve Preminger said, laughing, when she heard of her father's unwillingness or inability to characterize his mother, "but then, in the end, they'd go back to it.")[12] Clearly, in the Preminger household Father always knew best. However, Ingo's son Jim recalled that when he was a youngster, his grandmother Josefa was "a little more formidable as a presence than Markus. Josefa's own family had been very formal, and my mother has described to me the formality in Josefa's house when she visited at the time my father was courting her. There were servants, and my mother remembered that Josefa wore gloves. Markus was formal too, in an Old World way. But I sensed beneath the austere presence that he was really a gentle man, benign and fair."[13] "My guess is that Markus was the warmer of the two parents," Ingo's younger daughter Kathy speculated. "I'd often go with him to the drugstore, a half mile from our house; he would walk there every day, always dressed in a suit and tie, and wearing a hat and carrying a cane. He would raise his cane to express his displeasure with a careless driver. He was dignified but not arrogant—certainly not arrogant toward the family. He was an indulgent, loving father and I have an image of him frequently hugging Ingo and Otto."[14]

Both Markus and Josefa bequeathed their sons a strong sense of self, and a belief that they were expected and entitled to be successful. In a photograph taken in Czernovic the two youngsters radiate astonishing poise. "Yes, we were very sure of ourselves," Ingo said, "and we overrated each other continually."[15] The young Otto, make no mistake about it, is remarkably handsome, his destiny as a renowned ladies' man already clearly imprinted in his beseeching eyes and commanding carriage. Despite their doubly marked outsider status—they were provincial *Ostjuden*—the two boys have princely bearing and oh, the potential for disdain and sardonic wit their young faces already display. "Growing up, my relationship with Otto was flawless," Ingo said. "I loved my brother."[16] "They had a powerful sense of family, I always felt that from my father and uncle," Jim Preminger said. "They were people who were willing to do anything for other members of the family: they always said that, and they lived by that."[17]

Under any circumstances, a man as ambitious as Markus would not have remained indefinitely in a depressed backwater of the Empire, but his exodus from Czernovic was hastened by the cataclysms of a world war. At least since the turn of the century, rumblings for national independence among a number of the subject peoples of the extended Austro-Hungarian Empire, including Serbians, Croatians, Bohemians, Moravians, Galicians, Transylvanians, Hungarians, and Czechs, had been sounding with increasing fervor. Fired at Sarajevo by an enflamed Serbian nationalist, Gavrilo Princip, on June 28, 1914, the bullets that killed the Archduke Franz Ferdinand, the heir apparent to the throne, and his wife, launched a conflict that within weeks escalated into the Great War. Russia entered the war on the Serbian side, and czarist armies began to invade Eastern Europe. Perilously close to Russia, Czernovic was especially vulnerable. "We became refugees escaping the Russians," Ingo recalled.[18] Like other refugees in flight from the armies of the czar, Dr. Preminger looked to Austria as a haven. Because he had been highly regarded for his work in Czernovic, he was able to secure a job as public prosecutor in Graz, capital of the Austrian province of Styria. Here, in the Graz law courts, Dr. Preminger prosecuted nationalist Serbs and Croats who had been incarcerated as suspected enemies of the Empire. To the earnest young lawyer was granted the extraordinary power, as Otto described it, of "sort[ing] out those prisoners who should stand trial and free[ing] those wrongfully arrested."[19]

Dr. Preminger's responsibilities were both enormous and also, considering the fact that he was a Galician Jew in a position of power in a notoriously anti-Semitic and pro-German Austrian city, potentially dangerous. ("Graz was a cradle of anti-Semitism, far worse than it was in Vienna, which was bad enough," Ingo recalled.)[20] Only a man with a firm belief in his own judgment and fearlessness in deciding the fates of other human beings would have been offered, or have taken, the job—or been as successful at it as Markus proved to be. Both his sons spoke proudly of their father's work in Graz without ever questioning the implications of Markus's awesome moral task. If later in life they ever came to suspect their father might have been defending the wrong side, they never said so.

Graz is a city of picture-postcard loveliness—its old quarter remains the best-preserved medieval town in Europe. When the Preminger family relocated from Czernovic to Graz, Otto, nearly nine, was enrolled in a school where instruction in Catholic dogma was mandatory and Jewish history and religion had no place on the syllabus. Ingo, not yet four, remained at home. With his German retaining the trace of a Galician accent and his notable silence during religious instruction and compulsory prayers, Otto was vulnerable to taunts from his mostly Catholic classmates. When he was asked in class one day to identify his religion, Otto, having been taught to do so by his father, answered that he was Jewish. That afternoon on the way home a group of classmates attacked him. Deeply ashamed, and also feeling protective of his father because he felt that in some way the attack had been directed against Markus, Otto explained his cuts and bruises as the result of a fall. But of course the eagle-eyed Dr. Preminger realized what had occurred. "Without mentioning it to me my father went to the school principal to complain," Otto recalled. "He must have been impressed by my father's high rank. Though he said there was nothing he could do, I was not attacked again."[21]

After a year in Graz, the decisive public prosecutor who had to determine the innocence or guilt of hundreds, perhaps even thousands, of Serbian and Croatian prisoners, was summoned to Vienna, where he was offered an eminent position, roughly equivalent to that of the attorney general in the United States. Dr. Preminger was to prosecute insurgents who, in their struggles to gain national recognition, were accused of plotting against the monarchy. Because Markus was young, only thirty-six at the time, and a Jew—in the history of the Empire, then as always heavily Roman Catholic, no Jew had ever been appointed as chief prosecutor—the invitation was indeed exceptional. But as he sat for the interview in the baroque office of the minister of justice, Markus was told that the position would be his only if he converted to Catholicism. Although he had forsaken his father's devoutness, attended synagogue only on the high holy days, and would not give either of his sons a bar mitzvah, Markus nonetheless thought of himself as a Jew. In a gesture of defiance and self-assertion—exactly the kind his famous older son would many times demonstrate in the course of his career—Markus refused. "My father simply would not renounce his Judaism," Ingo said, "and he remained a Jew to the end of his life."[22] Remarkably, Markus was awarded the position anyway.

In 1915 Markus relocated his family to Vienna, the city that Otto claimed to have been born in. The family's first home was on the Strozzigasse, in Vienna's working-class eighth district, respectable enough but not part of the highly prized inner city. "When we arrived in Vienna, we were not wealthy," Ingo noted. "My father was working for the emperor, and so he was a government employee. As a result, we started out with modest quarters."[23] (As Paul Hofmann observes in *The Viennese,* his magisterial history of his native city, "Even today many Viennese will make a point of describing themselves as natives or longtime residents of a certain neighborhood, thereby emitting subtle cultural and social signals that only another Viennese can read.")[24] Otto was enrolled in a Catholic high school located near enough to the family's apartment for him to be able to walk to classes. "In Vienna, which certainly wasn't nearly as bad as Graz, you could still be beaten up if you were Jewish," Ingo recalled. "There had always been anti-Semitism in Austria, but it is not the same brand as in this country, which is *social* anti-Semitism. In Vienna, there was a very different contempt for Jews, for which the church was responsible. It was the church that taught, over and over, that the Jews killed Jesus Christ. Hatred for Jews was always present, in the capital as well as in the provincial towns and cities."[25]

Ingo praised the education he and Otto received in Vienna.

The schooling was unimaginative and quite rigid, which may be the best way to educate children. A ten-year-old child in Vienna knew more than a ten-year-old here, and that was true for France and Germany as well. They believed in drilling, drilling, which builds discipline, a quality Otto and I certainly developed. We had eight years of Latin, six years of Greek, and we also studied French. English wasn't on the syllabus then, and I didn't know English until I was eighteen. Religious studies were included, and in addition to being instructed in Catholicism we were also taught Jewish history, and Hebrew. We had to read classic authors; we were encouraged to read the great books, and we used to read night and day. At night, we even read in bed with flashlights.[26]

In his new post as "attorney general," Dr. Preminger, as he had on a much smaller scale first in Czernovic and then in Graz, became the legal defender of the crown's interests, prosecuting those suspected of instigating or conspiring in nationalist rebellions throughout the Austro-Hungarian Empire. Like Emperor Franz Josef himself, Dr. Preminger was an ideal bureaucrat, unfailingly punctual, industrious, and self-disciplined, qualities he passed on to his sons. Otto also inherited his father's instinctive theatricality—in court Dr. Preminger was noted for his showmanship. As Willi Frischauer, Otto's contemporary and first biographer, and at the time a young journalist, recalled, "[I] covered at least one of the spectacular court appearances of this brilliant lawyer. A determined defender of the status quo, he became a stern prosecutor of all who tried to stab the multinational country in the back while it was still fighting for its life."[27] In court, facing prominent dissidents and would-be secessionists, Dr. Preminger with well-timed retorts and withering glances displayed a seeming delight in going for the jugular. As Frischauer reported, Dr. Preminger was the lead prosecutor of a certain Dr. Kramarz,

which in German rhymes with "arse," a Bohemian member of the Austrian parliament who was indicted for plotting the breakaway of Bohemia from the monarchy. The verbal duel [between the defendant and the prosecutor] was a forensic occasion. Facing the dock, Dr. Preminger stemmed the flow of Kramarz's inflammatory rhetoric: "You ought to be ashamed," he said with an icy voice, "right into the last syllable of your name!" The phrase is still quoted as a unique example of courtroom invective.[28]

"When we moved to Vienna [in 1915] the great days were already gone," Ingo observed. The Great War that Gavrilo Princip's bullets at Sarajevo had initiated was being fought, in part, in an attempt to preserve what was left of Vienna's imperial heritage, its celebrated status as the capital of a vast empire. A long period of swelling discontent among the people it governed had severely tarnished the regime, however, and by 1915 Vienna was on its way to becoming "a museum city, a city that lived on its past," as Ingo said.[29] For centuries, since the rule of the first Hapsburg emperor, Albert II, began in 1438, Vienna had been the seat of the Empire, a cosmopolitan crossroads to which Polish, German, Croatian, Slovenian, Italian, Hungarian, and Bohemian citizens were frequent visitors. Proud of its royal status, Vienna was addicted to pomp and ceremony, and to florid architecture. The Viennese admiration of façade is epitomized by the baroque embellishments of the Hofburg, the sprawling imperial residence located in the heart of the old city, and in the Ringstrasse, the wide boulevard that encircles the inner city. The Ringstrasse, which began to be constructed on May 1, 1865, but was not completed for two decades, was designed as a spectacular civic self-promotion, the myriad architectural references of the buildings that line the boulevard intended to assert Vienna's place in a historical continuum. The university is sheathed in an imposing Italian Renaissance face, the style adopted also for the joined museums of art history and natural history. Parliament is designed with classic Greek simplicity, wrought on a monumental scale. City Hall is intensely Gothic. The Court Opera is French Renaissance. Early Baroque is the style for the Burgtheater. The forced magnitude of the architectural performance, along with the eclectic historical references, betrays a sneaking sense of inferiority. Rather than conjuring strength, the Ringstrasse projects an aura of borrowed grandeur.

Like Otto Preminger, a "native" son destined to achieve international fame, historical Vienna was a city of vivid contradictions, in many ways a city divided against itself. In *The Viennese,* Paul Hofmann quotes a revelatory insight by an outsider, a Dutch conductor-composer named Beernard van Beurden: "The Austrian lives in a two-room apartment. One room is bright, friendly, the 'cozy parlor,' well furnished, where he receives his guests. The other room is dark, somber, barred, totally unfathomable. If the visitors in the friendly parlor are not naïve," Hofmann concludes, "they will nevertheless soon steal glances of the 'other room,' where the ambivalent Viennese personality also dwells."[30] Summarizing the disparity between appearance and reality seemingly endemic to Vienna, Hofmann observes that "the city that inspired Mozart, Beethoven, and Schubert, the capital of *Gemütlichkeit*, of hand-kissing and the waltz, of coffeehouses and wine taverns in the green, of whipped cream and the annual ball, has long had one of the highest suicide rates in the world."[31]

As the site of imperial power and its rituals, Vienna adopted a courtly culture defined by exaggerated deference to women, a love of gossip and intrigue, virtual adulation of titles, jostling for preferment, and a mask of sociability put on to sustain the fiction of "merry Vienna" enacted in the numerous historic coffeehouses. The image of cozy Vienna, a light-minded city engaged in perpetual play, the city of Sachertorte *mit Schlag* and Wiener melange, of perennial productions of *The Merry Widow*, of waltzes eternal on the banks of the blue Danube, is of course sleight of hand concocted to distract the tourist trade from the city's other, darker face. Vienna's relentless self-mythologizing is sometimes easily enough shattered. For one, the Danube is rarely blue (a blank, steely gray is more like it), and further, is nowhere to be seen from within the heart of imperial Vienna. Only the equally drab Danube canal can be glimpsed fleetingly from the outer edges of the Old City. Unlike in Budapest, where the Danube flows through the heart of the city in a stream of majestic width, the fabled river linked to Vienna in song and story is notable for its absence. Like so much else in the city's iconography, the blue Danube is a cunning ruse, an attempt to gild plain reality with a manufactured romantic veneer: Vienna "performed" rather than content to be itself. The Viennese themselves have a word to describe their fondness for pretense: *Schmähe*. The "best translation of this dialect term," as Hofmann writes, is " 'blarney, Viennese style.' "[32] (Otto Preminger's skilled importation of "Vienna" to New York and Hollywood— his deft performance of Viennese courtliness—would help to solidify his reputation as a "personality.")

A far more sobering charge against the city is its history of anti-Semitism. It was during his time in Vienna, in a crucial formative period from 1907 to 1913, that Hitler began to develop his maniacal racial beliefs. In Vienna he heard, and was impressed by, poisonous theories of racial anti-Semitism spouted by Georg von Schönerer, the Austrian pan-Germanist and founder of the German National Party. The city's mayor, the most beloved in its history, was the infamous Karl Lueger, *der Schöne Karl* ("Handsome Karl"), whose Christian Social Party pretended to represent the voice of the common people. Mayor from 1897 until his death in 1910,

Lueger honed his performance of Viennese charm to diabolic perfection. Taking an accurate pulse of his primarily working-class supporters, Lueger was elected on a platform of attacks against Jewish influence in the city's business, industrial, and cultural affairs. "I decide who is a Jew," declared Lueger, a strategic anti-Semite who in fact had a number of Jewish friends. He intuited, correctly, that a relentless rhetoric of anti-Semitism would get him elected and would help to sustain his popularity once he was in office. (On three separate occasions the philo-Semitic Emperor Franz Josef had opposed Lueger's election by the city parliament.) In *Mein Kampf,* Hitler conferred on *der Schöne Karl* the epithet Lueger no doubt deserved: "the most formidable German mayor of all time."[33]

It is surely not merely historical chance that Theodor Herzl, the father of Zionism, was exposed in his formative years to the endemic anti-Semitism of Austrian culture. A Viennese dandy (though born in Budapest, Herzl was raised in Vienna) and an assimilated Jew, Herzl was the victim of numerous anti-Semitic attacks while a law student at the University of Vienna. When, as a correspondent for Vienna's liberal newspaper *Neue Freie Presse,* he went to Paris to cover the Dreyfus affair, French anti-Semitism together with his Viennese experience propelled him toward a momentous Zionist conversion.

If Vienna reveled, then as now, in its status as a "museum city" and vigorously promoted its Old World patina, only a few years before Dr. Markus Preminger and his family arrived, the city, in another of its contradictions, had been a crucible of modernist rebellion. The roll call of Viennese visionaries of the early years of the century includes painters Gustav Klimt, Oskar Kokoschka, and Egon Schiele; architects Adolf Loos and Otto Wagner; composers Gustav Mahler, Arnold Schoenberg, and Alban Berg; and writers Karl Kraus, Arthur Schnitzler, and Robert Musil. Challenging the academic tradition in painting, based in historicism and naturalism, Klimt founded the artistic movement known as the Secession. Schoenberg explored atonality. The artisans working in the Viennese brand of art nouveau known as Jugendstil, and craftsmen of the Wiener Werstätte (the Viennese Workshop, founded by Kolo Moser and Josef Hoffmann in 1903), developed a simple style in furniture, ceramics, jewelry, textiles, and objets d'art that forcibly rejected the baroque overstatement which had always been the city's favored mode. And it was during Vienna's brief period at the cutting edge of modernism that Theodor Herzl developed his Zionist idea and native son Sigmund Freud, finding plentiful data among his fellow citizens for his theories about neurosis, explored the death wish, dreams, and human sexuality.

Ironically, the city's short-lived golden age as a center of avant-garde experiment was also the beginning of the end. As Paul Hofmann observes, by the conclusion of the Great War, in October and November 1918, Vienna "joined the ranks of those once-illustrious cities that have fallen on hard, or drab, times. Like Alexandria, Athens, Istanbul, Lisbon, Naples, Venice . . . Vienna became an urban has-been."[34]

When Markus Preminger relocated his family to Vienna in 1915, the city had already passed through an initial outburst of patriotism that followed the outbreak of war. And though in the thick of the conflict it was not yet possible to foresee the eventual defeat of the Empire, the death tremors, sotto voce, had already begun. Nonetheless, at the time the Premingers arrived, Vienna was still an imperial capital with an array of cultural offerings that tempted Otto, at ten already incurably stagestruck. Often accompanied by his maternal grandfather, Otto made regular visits, sometimes as many as three or four a week, to the Burgtheater on the Ringstrasse, where he saw a wide variety of both classical and contemporary plays.

In retrospect Ingo recalled the Viennese theater of the time as "terrible—the only good stuff came from Berlin." And unlike Otto, "who was basically nonmusical—music bored him, he never went to the opera," Ingo preferred the city's rich musical offerings, even though "the really great days, when Vienna was the center of the musical world, were over by the time I started going to concerts and operas."[35]

From his very earliest days in Vienna, seeing and reading plays was more important to Otto than attending school. The youngster thought nothing of missing class in order to read another great play, by Shaw or Schiller or Shakespeare, in a handsome edition at the National Library. Soon after the family settled in Vienna, a routine visit to a family doctor revealed that Otto had a heart murmur. The doctor's recommendation that the young man should refrain from sports was no hardship—unlike his younger brother, Otto was nonathletic, and being sidelined from exercise gave him more time to read.

Typical of assimilated, well-to-do Jewish families, the Premingers were cultural connoisseurs. Books, theater, concerts, and museums quickly became a part of the fabric of their lives as new arrivals in Vienna. And given Dr. Preminger's prominence ("My father was very well known in Vienna for his work of so-called patriotic indictments," Ingo recalled),[36] attendance at cultural events might also have been a way of attaining social cachet. Markus encouraged Otto's obsession with theater. "I saw everything," Otto recalled. "Shaw was popular then: I saw *Caesar and Cleopatra* 72 times."[37]

Otto's first theatrical ambition was to become an actor. And with his already stentorian voice, his penetrating eyes, and his sturdy build, the young man, who projected a crackling sexual energy, was not deluding himself with dreams of joining the Burgtheater ensemble. In his early teens he could recite from memory many of the great monologues from the international classic repertory, and, never shy, he demanded an audience. At first, most of the burden fell on his grandfather, who regularly filled the young

Otto as a young man on the town, more interested in theater and concerts than in attending classes.

man's ears with praise. Otto began to recruit some of his schoolmates for group readings in his family's apartment of some of the plays he had committed to memory. Emboldened by the success of the readings, he soon sought and gained permission from the stodgy director of the National Library to allow him and his friends to read aloud portions of classic plays in the library's rotunda. Otto's own most successful performance in the rotunda was Mark Antony's funeral oration from *Julius Caesar*.

As he read, saw, and after a fashion began to produce plays, Otto started missing more and more classes at the local Catholic gymnasium. "There were times when I didn't go to school for many weeks, and when it came to light, [my father] stood up for me. He told the school [officials] I [had been] sick and [they] gave me a chance to catch up on what I had missed. [My father and I] had a wonderful relationship, like two brothers. He never punished me."[38]

Austria's failing fortunes in the world war had no impact on the Preminger family's way of life. Indeed, throughout the conflict, Markus flourished professionally as he continued to prosecute dissenters, mostly Czech nationalists. At the end of 1916 he moved his family from the eighth district to Mahlerstrasse 9, fashionably located within the inner city. Throughout the war years, Otto, now often with his younger brother, continued to go to the theater and concerts, museums, and the National Library. His attendance at school remained irregular, with his absences never once eliciting a cross word from his father.

Following Austria's defeat in the autumn of 1918, Vienna's status fell quickly. Inflation escalated. Immigrants from the countries that had been ruled by the former Empire flooded into the already overpopulated city. Famine was widespread. Overnight, with the collapse of the Empire, Austria faced the challenge of becoming a republic, a prospect that roused the skepticism of the Austrians as well as of the international community. "In 1918 and 1919 . . . the Viennese not only doubted the new state's chances for survival but were not even sure how it should be called," as Paul Hofmann notes. "Some proposed German Alpine Land, others Southeast Germany. The name German-Austria (*Deutschoesterreich*) came eventually to be accepted and, for some time, official."[39] With the dissolution of the monarchy Markus, of course, lost his government job, and as erstwhile attorney general he was publicly attacked by leaders of countries that had been newly created in the wake of the Empire's defeat. Under fire, Dr. Preminger, who had believed in the Empire he had worked vigorously to safeguard, bequeathed a valuable lesson to his older son. "One day [my father] found my mother weeping over a cruel editorial [denouncing Markus's work for the Empire]. He comforted her with words that left a deep impression on me," Preminger recalled. " 'Will you never learn, darling?' he said. 'Anyone who acts in public must be prepared for criticism, just or unjust. Only your own conviction and your own judgment of yourself count.' "[40]

Soon after his former employer was out of business, Markus opened his own law practice. Because his clients—bankers, industrialists, and business-men—were drawn from the new ruling class, Dr. Preminger remained on the same side of the political spectrum, with the elite rather than the disen-franchised. And as defender of the well-to-do he proved as adept as he had been in prosecuting enemies of the Empire. But Markus instilled in both his sons a sense of fair play as well as respect for those with opposing view-points, and rather than becoming reactionary conservatives, as their privi-leged upbringing might seem to have foreordained, Otto and Ingo became lifelong liberal Democrats.

"It was when he switched to private practice that my father started mak-ing good money, very good money," Ingo said. "We started out in Vienna in modest quarters, but we ended up on the Ringstrasse." The Premingers' third and last apartment in Vienna was located at Lueger Ring No. 10. (The street was named for Karl Lueger, for whom Ingo expressed respect. "He fol-lowed a 'creative' kind of anti-Semitism, and if a Jew became Catholic the prejudice disappeared," Ingo claimed. "It was well known that, privately, Lueger did not hate Jews.")[41] Directly across the street was the University of Vienna, which Otto would enter soon after the family had moved into their new apartment, and just a few minutes' walk down the Ringstrasse were the Burgtheater and the elegant Café Landtmann. As was customary at the time, Markus's office was in a separate wing of the family apartment.

To provide a suitable setting for Markus's prosperous clients, and no doubt reflecting their own tastes, Dr. and Mrs. Preminger decorated their apartment in a style of traditional Ringstrasse formality. The ornate Bieder-meier furnishings evoked an Old World taste that Markus's sons, and espe-cially Otto, would repudiate. "For both my father and uncle, the Old World style was to be shunned," Eve Preminger remarked. "It was simply a style they could not abide."[42]

As Markus continued to thrive in postwar Vienna, Otto began seriously to pursue a career in the theater. At sixteen, he won the role of Lysander in a production of *A Midsummer Night's Dream* performed in the open-air the-ater, the Burggarten, on the grounds of the old imperial palace. And in 1923, at seventeen, as was often to be the case in his career, timing was on his side. Max Reinhardt, the Viennese-born director who had established his base of operation in Berlin, announced plans to establish a theatrical company in

Vienna in the rundown, 135-year-old Theater in der Josefstadt, located only
steps away from the school Otto was then attending. A stagestruck banker,
Camillo Castiglioni, who had amassed a fortune amid the economic shambles of postwar Vienna, made Reinhardt a princely offer: unlimited funding
for the renovation of the theater in exchange for the best house seats at every
performance. Under Reinhardt's supervision, the Theater in der Josefstadt
was transformed into a baroque bijou. Despite lavish appointments in the
lobby and auditorium, however, the renovated theater had an air of intimacy, as if the grand seigneur himself was welcoming the audience into his
living room. In the beautifully proportioned hall each seat offered a clear
view of the stage. Adding a final personal touch, Reinhardt ordered from
Venice a magnificent crystal chandelier, which "hangs brightly lit in the
middle of the theater as the audience arrives," Otto noted, with the kind of
admiration the maestro had clearly wanted to evoke from his audiences.
"When the performance is about to start its eight hundred electric candles
dim slowly while the huge glittering fixture rises to the ceiling in order to
give the boxes and balconies an unobstructed view of the stage. This beautiful effect creates in the audience a unique mood of expectation."[43]

Interior of the Theater in der Josefstadt, Max Reinhardt's headquarters in Vienna.

Based in Berlin since early in the century, Reinhardt had established a world-renowned reputation as director and theater executive. A man for all theatrical seasons, he had won acclaim for spectacles as well as chamber dramas, and he had proven to be as skillful with Shakespeare as with contemporary dramas and comedies. He had even been a pioneer in Berlin cabaret. As a director of actors he was without peer in the international theater. With the able assistance of his brother Edmund and a protective staff, he presided over a theatrical empire that was to remain unrivaled until the Shubert brothers gained dominance over the American theater in the 1920s.

Max Reinhardt, Otto's first mentor, theatrical impresario second to none.

Reinhardt's announcement that he would be returning to Vienna was good news for the city's stagnant cultural life, and for the ambitious seventeen-year-old Otto Preminger it had the call of destiny. Otto wrote a letter to Reinhardt requesting an audition. "For six weeks I went three times a day to the post office to ask if there was a letter for me," he recalled. "Then I gave up. About a month later I went back—just in case."[44] Waiting for him was a letter from a Reinhardt associate, Dr. Stefan Hock, giving him a date for an audition Otto had now missed by two days. Under cover of being ill, Otto skipped classes as he hovered near the stage door hoping to encounter Dr. Hock entering or leaving. When he finally spotted him, he showed him the letter and beseeched Dr. Hock for another audition. Otto must have made a vivid impression because on the spot Dr. Hock took the eager young man directly in to Reinhardt, surrounded as usual by a phalanx of associates. His nerves on edge but in control of himself, Otto passed the audition—no doubt his strong voice and presence caught Reinhardt's eye. As Otto was able to boast for the rest of his life, he had then and there become "the first apprentice actor of the Viennese Reinhardt Company."[45]

Flushed with a sense of triumph and the belief that he would be spending many hours at the Josefstadt, Otto announced to his father that for him the theater was no longer an avocation. He wanted Markus to understand that his interest in the theater was not a youthful lark or an excuse to miss classes, but a way of life, the only way of life he wanted. For Dr. Preminger, who had risen from poverty to the highest levels in the socially approved profession of law, his son's announcement must surely have come as a thunderbolt. Although he had assumed that his intelligent sons would follow his example and become lawyers, Markus accepted Otto's decision to apprentice with Reinhardt. Yet it is typical of Markus's wisdom as a father, and Otto's obedience as a son, that they worked out a compromise. For reasons of both practicality and social standing, Markus demanded that Otto do the right thing for a young man of his class: finish gymnasium and complete the study of law at the University of Vienna. If at the end of his studies Otto were still intent on pursuing a career as an actor, Markus would give his blessing. Not for a moment did Otto consider defying his father. But it is unlikely that the self-confident young man gave any weight to the practical aspect of their plan. In his own mind Otto was convinced that he would succeed in the theater and that he would never need to depend on the law as a means of earning his living.

As a law student at the University of Vienna Otto was absent even more than he had been during his gymnasium years. Since law students, however, were required only to show up for six exams over a period of four years, truancy was hardly a hanging offense. A student who passed all the exams could conceivably earn the title of doctor of law without ever having set foot in a law class. The format couldn't have been more convenient for Otto. Markus hired tutors to help his son master the intricacies of Austrian law;

and Otto was a diligent student of a subject in which, in fact, he had a great deal of interest.

But his primary commitment was to his new position as a Reinhardt apprentice. Observing the maestro at close hand, the young acolyte received nonpareil on-the-job training. Like all great directors, Reinhardt, in effect, was a lay analyst with keen instincts about how to meet the individual needs of each of his actors. As required, he could become friend, confidant, surrogate father, older brother, or "lover" in a strictly figurative sense—Reinhardt was not predatory. Quite unlike directors who were to be trained in the American Method, Reinhardt would perform scenes for his actors, and his imagination was so fertile that often he played the same action several different ways.

When the theater opened, on April 1, 1924, Otto Preminger appeared as a furniture mover in Reinhardt's commedia dell'arte staging of Carlo Goldoni's *The Servant of Two Masters*. His next, more substantial appearance was as Stephano, one of Portia's servants, in the master's production of *The Merchant of Venice*, which opened on May 26. (Also in the cast, as the Prince of Morocco, one of Portia's suitors, was Wilhelm Dieterle, who, like Otto, was to achieve fame as a director in Hollywood.) In the fall of 1924 Otto had two other small roles. He appeared as a swain, Marc Cèrizolles, in the translation of a French farce, *Schöne Frauen* (*Beautiful Lady*), by Etienne Rey. (Notable in the cast was Mady Christians, who was to commit suicide after having been blacklisted during the McCarthy era in Hollywood, and Nora Gregor, who was to star in Jean Renoir's masterpiece, *The Rules of the Game*, and to marry Prince Starhemsky, an Austrian aristocrat with pronounced Nazi sympathies.) At the end of October Otto was relegated to the role of *ein junger Mann* (a young man) in a translation of a Russian play by Leonid Andreyev, *Du Sollst Nicht Töten* (*The Dead Shall Awaken*).

Reinhardt may have had reservations about Otto's acting but he quickly detected the young man's abilities as an administrator. He appointed Otto as an assistant in the Reinhardt acting school that opened in the theater at Schönbrunn, the former summer palace of the emperor. And he also chose Otto as one of his two dozen assistants at the Salzburg Festival, which Reinhardt had founded in 1920. For the 1924 festival, to Otto's frustration, Reinhardt appointed him to be a chorus leader in a procession of nuns in *The Miracle*, probably the most celebrated of the maestro's superspectacles. In the monumental pantomime it was Otto's job, dressed as a nun, to lead about five hundred society matrons, also masquerading as nuns. Otto in drag superintending a mob of unruly theatrical amateurs: the situation was ripe for an Otto tantrum, but none was ever reported. Otto was unhappy nevertheless. He wanted to act, and even as a theatrical novice he was already a young man in a terrific hurry. Following the summer in Salzburg, Otto was no longer content to occupy the place of a subordinate and he decided to leave the Reinhardt fold. "After a year with the professor, watching and learning, I decided my career would advance better if I joined a company where I would have the opportunity to play important parts," he said.[46]

Otto, in 1924, was a Reinhardt employee, but his penetrating eyes and relaxed yet commanding posture mark him as a born leader.

A more self-effacing person would have stayed on, basking in the reflected glory of Reinhardt's reputation and eager to learn more from the world's foremost director. A more patient fellow would surely have bided his time, content with the insignificant roles and assuming larger roles would eventually follow. But this wasn't Otto. "My brother was tremendously ambitious," Ingo said, recalling Otto's early departure from Reinhardt. "He had great energy, and even then, so early on, he was a first-rate executive. He was also, even then, excitable. There was always yelling, but he also had a good sense of humor that helped to curb the damage inflicted by one of his outbursts."[47] As Willi Frischauer succinctly phrased it, "The top was Otto Preminger's natural habitat."[48] And as it happened, Preminger's departure from Reinhardt at the end of the 1924–25 season turned out to be a cunning career move.

It was the custom for the managers of the many government-supported regional theaters throughout the former Austro-Hungarian Empire, in which every large and mid-sized city boasted a repertory theater along with an opera house, to hold auditions in Vienna and Berlin. Assuming that in the provinces he would have a better chance than in Vienna for securing bigger roles, Otto decided, in the spring of 1925, before leaving for Salzburg for the summer, to audition for a number of German-speaking theaters. His status as a Reinhardt apprentice gave him an edge over much of his competition, and indeed the managing director who hired him, Leopold Karma, had himself served a brief apprenticeship with Reinhardt in Berlin. Karma's German-speaking theater, however, was in Prague, the capital of the new country of Czechoslovakia, governed by men Otto's father had prosecuted during the war. To indemnify himself against his father's enemies, Otto adopted the stage name of Pretori. Nonetheless, he fared little better than he had in Vienna. "I remember I played [only] two parts there," he said. "One was a role in a German farce called *Frei Frankfurt,* which was about the Rothschild family."[49] He attributed his lackluster profile to the fact that, at nineteen, he was already beginning to go bald. But it could also have been that he was an actor of limited resources, as his later screen performances were to confirm.

Quickly bored with Karma's theater and with Prague, in the spring of 1926 Otto successfully auditioned for a place in the company of the Schauspielhaus in Zurich. Here he played young leading roles, often wearing a wig. But at this time Otto made the shrewd self-assessment that his days as a leading man were numbered. In the following spring, still restless, he tried out for a theater closer to home, in the German-speaking Czech city of Aussig an der Elbe, where he "decided not to act anymore, only to direct."[50]

Preminger, losing his hair at an early age, decided
to retire from acting.

Soon after he joined the Aussig theater, Otto began an affair with a
young singer in the company who also happened to be the lover of the manager, Alfred Huttig. Losing his hair and already growing stout, Otto no
longer looked like a matinee idol, but he exuded, as he would for the rest of
his life, a primal sexual force. "The word along Broadway when Otto first
came over from Europe was that he was a good lover," recalled Paula Laurence, a Broadway actress of the time. "It hardly mattered that he was not
movie-star handsome; because he was so charming to women, in that delec-
table Viennese manner he cultivated, and because he had such a relish for
life, Otto really had terrific sex appeal. He also had a great sense of entitle-
ment, and no apparent guilt—you sensed that he felt that sexual pleasure
belonged to him."[51]

As a young man in Aussig an der Elbe wooing and winning his boss's
mistress, Otto was already a bona fide ladies' man, gallant in courtship and
an ardent lover. Knowing that Huttig knew of the affair and charged with
that inborn fearlessness his father had instilled in him, Otto asked if he
could direct *The Chalk Circle,* one of the scheduled plays of the season. The
cuckolded manager gave him the assignment.

At the end of the season, in the early summer of 1928, Otto terminated his affair with the singer and decided to return to Vienna, where, almost as if he were setting himself in competition with the great Reinhardt, he ventured into theater management. With a partner, an actor named Rolf Jahn, he organized a company of players in an intimate, chamber-sized theater called Die Komödie (which, like the Theater in der Josefstadt, is still in operation). Jahn was married to a wealthy woman, Marita Streelen, a countess more beautiful than talented who was willing to fund the enterprise in exchange for playing leading roles. She gave a pallid performance in the company's opening production, Chekhov's *Three Sisters,* which Preminger dismissed as "a miserable failure."[52] That afternoon, as Preminger claimed, he had taken and failed the last of his law school exams.

From the beginning the executive setup at Die Komödie, in which all decisions had to be agreed to by the three directors, played havoc with Preminger's already fully formed autocratic temperament. And surely Preminger would not have remained silent about Countess Streelen's lack of talent. In the early months of his partnership with the Jahns, a young actress in a small role in a touring production of an American import called *Broadway* impressed Otto, who made a point of seeing every play and musical in town. He liked the performer's raw sexuality and recommended Marlene Dietrich to his partners as a possible recruit for their new company. No doubt sensing the young woman from Berlin would threaten her place as the first lady of Die Komödie, Marita Streelen nixed her. Infuriated, Preminger announced that his partnership with the countess would be over at the end of the season.

Throughout the spring of 1929, as it became increasingly clear to him that he would not be able to work well with his partners, he had begun to cultivate potential new ones. An actor of his acquaintance, Jacob Feldhammer, had a sister married to a stagestruck industrialist. With his support, Otto along with the Feldhammers converted a large suburban theater, a former opera house, into a repertory house ostentatiously named Neues Wiener Schauspielhaus (New Vienna Playhouse). Otto promoted the new theater, and himself, vigorously. Not untruthfully, he presented himself as an artistic manager with a "Reinhardt background"[53] and heralded his enterprise as an experimental people's theater. In an attempt to attract young people and workers who could not afford to attend the Burgtheater or the Opera, he scaled tickets at record-low prices. And running a privately funded theater, he promised to present the kind of material, lesser-known classics and challenging contemporary plays, unlikely to be available anywhere else in the city. True to his word, he directed a production of

Wedekind's sexually provocative *Lulu,* and from Berlin he imported *Roar China,* pro-Communist agitprop.

The undertaking revealed Otto's pleasure in discovering new talent and his catholic tastes. But the theater foundered on what were already potential pitfalls to his success—his unruly temper and disdain for collaboration. He became impatient with Feldhammer for his tendency to choose plays solely on the basis of whether they contained juicy roles for himself; and he was disgruntled with Feldhammer's sister for demanding a voice in the selection of material. Nor did Preminger endear himself to his actors, who, according to one of them, Gerhard Hinze, were growing "angrier and angrier" at Preminger's treatment.[54] Following Reinhardt's example, Otto would demonstrate how he wanted a scene to be played; but unlike Reinhardt, who was sensitive to the egos of his performers, Preminger could be brusque. "Imitate me!" seemed to be Preminger's directorial method, an approach that, along with his expectations of instant results, often caused tempers to flare during rehearsals. By the end of the season, yielding to his partners' demands as well as to commercial necessity, Otto presented a light comedy called *The Sachertorte,* which was a big box-office hit but a far cry from his original manifesto for the theater. In June 1930 Otto resigned.

In two seasons, 1928–29 and 1929–30, with the kind of momentum that Ingo described as "Otto's way,"[55] the young man, not yet twenty-five, had cofounded and served as artistic director of two new theater companies. And on a second try he had managed to pass his final law exam. This entitled him to call himself Dr. Preminger, a possibility he was quick to take advantage of in status-conscious Vienna. It was an astonishing record, proof positive of the wünderkind label later to be claimed for him in Broadway and Hollywood press releases. His achievement is especially noteworthy when set against the backdrop of a city beleaguered by unemployment, widespread food rationing, and the deep psychic scars of military defeat. If Vienna at the time had to adjust to a diminished identity, a scaled-down sense of its historical and cultural importance, downsizing was not part of Otto's agenda. Clearly, the young Dr. Preminger could persuade people to back him and to share his passion for the stage. Just as clearly, he had an equally prodigious talent for colliding with colleagues.

Since his return to Vienna in the summer of 1928, like a good son Otto had lived at home in the family's opulent Ringstrasse apartment. The extroverted young man of the theater frequently socialized with a network of mostly Jewish millionaires who were his father's clients. One of these was Reinhardt's patron, the banker Camillo Castiglioni, fat, diminutive, charming, and witty, who in fact had seen and admired some of Otto's productions at Die Komödie and the Neues Wiener Schauspielhaus. As Castiglioni informed Otto, the Theater in der Josefstadt had begun to develop a number of problems, not least the fact that Castiglioni himself, reeling from the effects of the New York Stock Exchange crash in October 1929, could no longer provide the funding Reinhardt was accustomed to. In the past Reinhardt's extravagance had been contained by his practical brother Edmund, the administrator and chief executive of all the Reinhardt theaters; but after Edmund died (in July 1929) and with Castiglioni becoming financially strapped, both Reinhardt and the Theater in der Josefstadt were headed for a fall, as the banker told Otto in March 1930.

Despite warnings from Castiglioni and others of his entourage, Reinhardt was incapable of forsaking the grand style. Like an imperial potentate or rajah of inestimable wealth, Reinhardt continued to hold court in Leopoldskron, his lakeside castle in Salzburg, where dozens of chandeliers sparkled, expensive wines flowed from decanters of silver, over fifty servants catered to the wishes of guests, and two dozen gardeners tended to the formal grounds. And as the maestro of the Theater in der Josefstadt he continued to offer productions of unparalleled opulence. But over the last year, growing bored with Vienna and looking for new territory, Reinhardt had become an increasingly absentee artistic director. In the summer of 1929 he had been lured to Hollywood, where studio moguls gushed over his genius. He allowed himself to believe that they were really interested in turning *The Miracle* into an American-style epic, but he returned empty-handed at the beginning of the 1929–30 season. Reinhardt had been so often absent from the city that he had entrusted the daily operation of the theater to an assistant, Emil Geyer, a workmanlike functionary with no artistic passion.

In short, Reinhardt's theater needed a new leader, a position Castiglioni believed should be Otto's. In Castiglioni, Otto had a crucial champion, but despite Castiglioni's persuasive powers Reinhardt was not inclined to hire him, no doubt having already recognized that he and the young Preminger were not kindred spirits. For all his fabled hospitality at Leopoldskron, the Professor at heart was introspective and deeply private, where Otto was full of chat and bonhomie. Reinhardt was a practical man of the theater but also a theoretician, while Otto, though a passionate lifelong reader, was immune to theory. Reinhardt wrote elaborate notes opposite each page of his script that often detoured on philosophical and intellectual tangents; Otto's scripts were clean and he hardly wrote a letter in his life. Reinhardt was a slow starter; Otto worked quickly. In hesitating about Otto, Reinhardt was surely influenced by his wife, Helene Thimig, who disliked Otto's seductive Viennese style and was not convinced of the young man's talent as either an actor or a director. But Castiglioni, who remained president of the corporation that owned the Theater in der Josefstadt, kept pushing Otto and ultimately prevailed: in the summer of 1930 Reinhardt hired Preminger, although in exactly what capacity was not clear. Reinhardt was still the theater's titular director, with Geyer assuming the duties of day-to-day operation.

Otto's premature baldness, the "calamity" that had put paid to his fledgling acting career, along with his imposing bearing, were decided assets in his new role as a Reinhardt executive. As he oversaw actors' contracts, organized Reinhardt's scripts, conducted seminars at the Reinhardt School at Schönbrunn Castle, and ran interference with technicians, designers, and performers, the young Preminger became, in effect, the Josefstadt's principal troubleshooter. Dealing with often irascible guest stars, including Peter Lorre, Lili Darvas, Elisabeth Bergner, Oskar Karlweis, and Alexander Moissi, Preminger, as he could, became a resourceful diplomat. And as he was busy quelling the divalike tantrums of egocentric stars, he had no time for any of his own.

Although he had been hired as an executive, Preminger of course had his eye on directing. It didn't take him long to land an assignment. Appropriately, the new doctor of law directed a courtroom drama, *Voruntersuchung* (*Preliminary Inquiry*), written by a lawyer from Berlin, Max Alsberg, in collaboration with dramatist Otto Ernst Hesse. The play, a crackling legal melodrama, first and last Preminger's favorite genre, opened on January 20, 1931, only a few months after Otto had returned to the Josefstadt. It was a notable house debut for the new director. Throughout his career, courtroom scenes were to draw forth Preminger's keenest work, and in *Preliminary Inquiry* he handled the courtroom atmosphere—outbursts from wrangling lawyers and recalcitrant witnesses, interruptions of an imperious judge—with verve and an insider's knowing touch. Opening night he took twenty-one curtain calls with his cast and the elated coauthors.

Soon after *Preliminary Inquiry,* a wealthy industrialist from Graz, Heinrich Haas, who, as Preminger recalled, "had an interest in the studios in Vienna,"[56] approached the rising young *homme du théâtre* with an offer to direct a film called *Die Grosse Liebe* (*The Great Love*). Otto felt unprepared. He knew nothing about the technique of filmmaking and, moreover, he didn't have the same passion for the medium as he had for the theater. The plays of Shakespeare and Shaw meant far more to him than the silent film masterworks made by F. W. Murnau, Ernst Lubitsch, or Fritz Lang in Germany, or by D. W. Griffith in America. He accepted the assignment nonetheless, because he recognized an opportunity, because the film was to be made over the summer when he would be freed from his duties at the theater, and because he was attracted to the material Haas was offering him. The screenplay by Siegfried Bernfeld and Arthur Berger was based on a true story about an Austrian soldier returning home from Russia ten years after the end of the Great War who is reunited with a woman who thinks he is her son. Otto liked the ambiguity of the situation and of the characters.

As the "son," he chose a Josefstadt actor, Attila Hörbiger (who, along with his actress wife, Paula Wessely, was to become an ardent Nazi). A Germanic John Garfield, the actor projected a brooding, rough-edged, enigmatic quality just right for the role, a damaged man with a past the film never reveals. Significantly, Preminger introduces the character with his back to the camera as he is looking out a fogged-up train window. As the "mother," Preminger cast Hansi Niese, "a Viennese comedy star, like an Ethel Merman," as Preminger recalled.[57]

Preminger dismissed *Die Grosse Liebe* as a juvenile folly. "I would rather forget it," he said.[58] Ingo called it "unspeakable."[59] But these assessments are too harsh. While an occasionally stilted passage reveals the director's inexperience, there is also evidence of Preminger's good judgment about how and when to move the camera; how to build tension through crosscutting; and how to elicit from theater-trained actors a style of intimate naturalism suited to talking pictures. The film opened at the Emperor Theater in Vienna on December 21, 1931, to strong reviews and business.

Although infernally busy in his new job of jack-of-all-trades at the Josefstadt and with his responsibilities as a first-time film director, Preminger did not forgo a private life. His professional advancement, in fact, only enhanced his status as a man-about-town. However, one day in the spring of 1931, his carefree bachelor's life was threatened when a young woman with a legal problem appeared at his office. A vivacious Hungarian (think Zsa Zsa Gabor), Marion Mill was a would-be actress who had recently performed in a nightclub revue as the Sachertorte Girl. "I appeared posed on an enormous chocolate cake on a plate which revolved to music," she recalled in her revealingly titled memoir, *All I Want Is Everything*.[60] When she came calling, Marion was facing a lawsuit of ten thousand schillings because the nightclub owner was accusing her of breach of contract; to help her out of her legal bind, an actress friend recommended Otto Preminger, a doctor of law as well as a theater impresario. When Marion entered his office, Otto was struck by the young woman's imposing height, her cascading dark hair, and her inviting smile and laugh. As Eve Preminger recalled, "Marion had flair,"[61] and indeed she did. She also had a hyperactive imagination. Marion Mill was a fabulist, particularly about her past. "She was possessed by a spirit of wishfulness that converted the modest house in which she was born into a castle and her middle-class family into rich nobility," as Otto later observed. "Her name was Deutsch but she claimed to be a Baroness Deuth, using Mill as her stage name because her family did not want their aristocratic friends to know that she was an actress."[62] According to Otto's niece Kathy Preminger, the "Hungarian Baroness" came from an all-but-impoverished Jewish family.[63]

The attraction between the young woman "with flair" and the young man who oozed executive as well as sexual authority was immediate. Otto invited her for lunch. "I sat down and changed my life," Marion recalled. "All that I had experienced before I met Otto counted for nothing. I was fascinated by his learning, which surpassed that of any man I had known. He knew all of Goethe, and all of Shakespeare and all the Roman Law by heart, and could quote them at length. He was the most widely-read man I had ever known. He was what few learned men are, exceedingly witty."[64] Marion made Otto laugh, a skill he always appreciated; in this case it was also an aphrodisiac. After Otto succeeded in extricating Marion from her legal problems, the couple began dating regularly. Marion at first neglected to tell Otto that she was already married, though estranged from her husband, and that she also had an ardent beau. Otto didn't think she had any talent as an actress but nonetheless, to improve her chances in auditions, agreed to tutor her in German, which she spoke with a Hungarian accent. Marion claimed that Otto found time to coach her "at least one hour every afternoon."[65]

In the summer of 1932, Otto asked Marion to marry him; Marion, delighted by Otto as both mentor and lover, readily accepted. They were wed in a plain ceremony in Town Hall on the bride's birthday, August 3, only thirty minutes after her divorce from her first husband had been finalized. Following the ceremony Otto had to rush back to the theater for rehearsals of a play Marion said was called *Bigamy* ("This did not seem too good an augury for the marriage," she noted).[66] The irony is indeed delicious, but the truth of the matter was that Marion was off by a year: *Bigamy* had opened the previous August. The play Otto would have been rehearsing the day of their marriage was *Derr Kuss vor dem Spiegel* (*The Kiss Before the Mirror*). Nonetheless her new husband was guilty of a kind of bigamy: Otto's hasty departure from his nuptials to the theater indicated that for the theatrical wünderkind, career came first.

Until his marriage Otto had continued to live at home. After his marriage he and Marion moved into a small apartment that, with almost oedipal defiance, Otto furnished in a style of severe modernism—not a touch of his parents' Biedermeier taste was anywhere to be found. Soon after they were married, Otto informed his wife that she could not pursue a theatrical

Marion Mill, Otto's first wife, a charming fantasist.

career. But Marion readily found a way of earning applause. "Her talent as a party giver helped Otto perhaps more than he realized," Eve Preminger noted.[67] To be sure, the Premingers' elaborate soirées, which always included Castiglioni and other members of the Josefstadt board of directors, were an asset to the up-and-coming impresario. And Marion's entrances on opening nights at the theater—twinkling and flirting at Otto's side she was more vividly Viennese than the natives—also gave a boost to her new husband.

Otto's second directorial assignment at the theater, *Reporter,* a translation of the blockbuster American comedy *The Front Page,* by Ben Hecht and Charles MacArthur, which had opened on Broadway in 1929, continued his lucky streak. The material, about newspaper reporters who speak in a staccato American vernacular, would not seem to have been in Preminger's line, but his production had the necessary snap and was a big success. Reinhardt and his advisers took note. By the beginning of 1932, with a growing sense of foreboding about the Nazis, and still with an eye on Hollywood,

Reinhardt withdrew from active management of his theaters in Berlin. Shortly thereafter he announced that the 1932–33 season would be his last in Vienna. Castiglioni, whose fortune had continued to shrink in the deepening world Depression, remained chairman of the group that owned the Josefstadt and urged Reinhardt to appoint Otto as his successor, pointing out the commercial and popular success of *Preliminary Inquiry* and *Reporter*. Reinhardt, too, had by this time come to appreciate Preminger's abilities both onstage and off. But Madame Reinhardt was still opposed and there was an anti-Otto faction among the maestro's staff. In the end, Castiglioni again won out. "[My appointment] caused quite a sensation in Vienna's theatrical circles," Preminger recalled.[68]

As Preminger was beginning to prepare the next season, Reinhardt approached him with a proposal: Reinhardt wanted to direct four large-scale, all-star productions that would open at the Theater in der Josefstadt before going on European tours. Otto rejected the offer. Helene Thimig, fiercely protective of her husband, stormed into Preminger's office. "She was shocked," Otto recalled. "She and the Professor had thought I would be grateful to have these four Reinhardt productions in the theatre."[69] But Otto, who had won Castiglioni's support in part because the banker was convinced that the young man had the financial prudence Reinhardt lacked, considered Reinhardt's proposal to be unsound. Although it isn't possible now to cite chapter and verse of what took place during the meeting, it's likely that Otto lost his temper with his former boss's wife, who had the kind of haughty, exigent quality he resented, especially in women. Madame Reinhardt, who may well have tried to threaten or intimidate her husband's immovable successor, left the office enraged. "Helene did not approve of me, because I was too outspoken," Preminger admitted. "I never became a member of the close circle [that formed around the Professor]."[70] "Otto did not like Reinhardt's wife—she had a very grand style he didn't approve of— and I'm sure he told her off during that meeting," Ingo said. "The temper ran away from him, but Otto was very shrewd in how he used that temper: ten minutes later he could be charming. Nobody else in the family was like that: this was *not* a family trait. It was part of that executive Germanic style that Otto mastered, even as a young man in Vienna, and this included the lack of respect for other people. That he lost, or used, his temper against Madame Reinhardt—that showed Otto's fearlessness."[71]

Although Otto would not risk the theater's finances to support Reinhardt, he suggested a likely angel, Eleonora von Mendelsohn, a young actress in the company that Reinhardt was then forming who came from one of the country's wealthiest families. After Reinhardt did indeed secure the backing of Eleonora, Preminger agreed to present the Reinhardt season at the Josefstadt as an outside attraction and temporarily moved his own programs to another house. "The four plays and the following tour were a disaster and Eleonora von Mendelsohn lost a small fortune on the venture," Preminger reported.[72]

"Whether it was luck, instinct, or talent [or, perhaps, the kind of financial common sense that led him to reject his mentor's overambitious project], at the end of my first season as head of the Josefstadt the theatre was showing a profit," Otto noted.[73] Preminger's success in rescuing the theater caught the attention of the directors of the Burgtheater. And at the end of his first season Otto was summoned to the office, located in the former Imperial Palace, of the Austrian minister of art and education, who, as head of the Austrian State Theater Administration, was responsible for the opera companies as well as the Burgtheater. The minister offered Otto, then only twenty-eight, the post of director-manager of the State Theater, which at the time was coasting on its illustrious history and in danger of becoming trapped there, frozen in time. The job was his, the minister assured him, if he would honor one small request: Would he convert to Catholicism? Like his father faced with a similar request twenty years earlier, Otto needed no time to consider his answer: No, he replied, in a courteous tone, he would not convert. Otto was not a practicing or observant Jew—religious belief of any kind was never to be of any importance to him—but like his father he was determined to respect the fact of his having been born Jewish. "The Minister made polite conversation for a few more minutes. Then I left and never heard of the contract again. My refusal to convert most likely saved my life," Preminger reflected.[74]

For three seasons, Otto ran the Josefstadt by keeping his eye on the bottom line. Unlike Reinhardt, Otto was by no means a theatrical visionary. The Josefstadt seasons under his management contained no revelatory productions of new plays, no ingenious interpretations of classic plays, and no superspectacles in the Reinhardt mold. Instead, as he balanced revivals of Austrian and world classics with popular contemporary dramas, comedies, and musicals, artistic and economic prudence was the custom of the house. On the whole, Preminger's standards in acting and production were higher than his literary judgment. Otto certainly knew and loved the great classic repertoire, but he also had a perhaps typically Viennese taste for theatrical bonbons, for strictly boulevard fare in the form of light romantic comedies with a naughty twist. Precisely the qualities he demonstrated right from the start in his management of the Josefstadt—his ability to balance the budget, to compromise when necessary, and to cater to popular taste without forsaking artistic standards—were to earn him a place for decades on the Holly-wood A-list. (And it was exactly the absence of these traits in Max Reinhardt that was to ensure the Professor's failure in the American film capital.)

From *Preliminary Inquiry* in January 1931 to his final production at the theater, in October 1935, Preminger directed twenty-six shows. Most were ephemera by Austrian and Hungarian authors tailoring their wares for the local market. Among the strictly bread-and-butter works Preminger directed were *Der Kuss vor dem Spiegel* (*The Kiss Before the Mirror*), by Ladis-laus Fodor; *Eine Himmlische Frau* (*A Heavenly Woman*), by Johannes von Vaszary; *Ende Schlecht, Alles Gut* (*Bad End, Everything Fine*), by Siegfried Geyer; *Der König mit dem Regenschirin* (*The King with the Umbrella*), by Ralph Benatzky; and *Skandal im Konzerthaus* (*Scandal in the Concert House*), by Karl Farkas. Absent from the list, surprisingly, was any play by George Bernard Shaw, Preminger's favorite playwright. Also missing were any works by Shakespeare, Ibsen, Strindberg, or Chekhov. Preminger him-self did not direct the plays with the most exalted literary pedigrees. During his tenure Schiller's *Maria Stuart,* Goethe's *Faust,* and Pirandello's *Six Char-acters in Search of an Author* were directed by others. For his own projects Preminger focused on shows that had been recent hits on Broadway or Lon-don's West End. His well-received production of Sidney Kingsley's hospital melodrama, *Men in White,* for instance, opened at the Josefstadt on Novem-ber 9, 1934, only a year after it had been a huge success for the Group The-atre in New York.

To fill out a season, or to boost sales, Otto was not above reviving an old warhorse such as Wilhelm Mayer-Förster's perennial *Alt-Heidelberg* (*Old Heidelberg*), the play that was the basis of the popular Sigmund Romberg operetta, *The Student Prince.* He was also not too proud to cater to local popular taste by offering an occasional risqué farce or a historical pageant of dubious literary merit. In this vein his most opulent production was *Makart,* a biographical drama about the nineteenth-century Viennese painter Hans Makart, whose lush style was emblematic of Ringstrasse Vienna. Before the production opened, Makart's heirs threatened to sue Preminger for defaming them and their famous relative. While Preminger in his Hollywood years would have transformed the contretemps into a cru-sade for artistic freedom and pumped up the show into a cause célèbre, this time, as a pragmatic impresario, he compromised, agreeing to make some script changes that would smooth over the painter's sexual and moral lapses. A payment of an undisclosed sum to the Makart family bought their silence and allowed the play to open on schedule.

Preminger's most assured work was in the vein of scrupulous realism, of exactly the kind demanded in films. His lifelike scene in an operating room in *Men in White,* for instance, was widely praised. His most notable work was his handling of a tense courtroom drama, *Sensationsprozess (Libel!),* a translation of a West End hit by Edward Wooll. As in *Die Grosse Liebe,* ambiguity of character and motive drives the story—Is a prominent member of the House of Commons who he claims to be, or is he an impostor?

"Otto was especially good in casting," as Ingo observed,[75] and among the performers he hired, a number, including Lili Darvas, Lilia Skala, Harry Horner (who became a production designer on Broadway and in Hollywood), Oskar Karlweis, Albert Bassermann, and Luise Rainer, were to achieve recognition far beyond Austria. Shortly after being directed by Preminger in *Men in White,* Luise Rainer was to win back-to-back Academy Awards, for *The Great Ziegfeld* in 1936 and *The Good Earth* in 1937. Rainer's Hollywood career foundered because her imperious manner offended her boss, MGM chieftain Louis B. Mayer; Preminger, however, admired her self-assurance. And Rainer recalled that working with Preminger she had "not a hint of trouble. Yes, there was talk of Preminger being excitable and inconsiderate . . . [but] I personally never experienced anything of the kind."[76]

Ingo Preminger, who saw all of the productions during his brother's management of the Theater in der Josefstadt, offered a balanced appraisal.

> Otto's work there was very good, very solid. He operated a good, shrewd, commercial theater. Otto had a terrific way of pushing through things; he had a way of convincing people he could do what he said he was planning to do, and then he would come through on his promises, always. And he was a master of publicity: a publicity genius, really. During the few years that he ran the theater he was extremely productive and he kept it on a firm financial footing after Reinhardt's extravagance and neglect. And remember, by the time he left he was only twenty-nine. All in all, it was an amazing achievement.[77]

Preminger left the Josefstadt because, once again, and not for the last time, he was in the right place at the right time. At least since the first decade of the twentieth century, when theater had become big business in America, it had been common practice for theatrical managers to scout European theaters for shows, actors, and directors. With the rise of silent films as a full-length narrative medium in the postwar period, film scouts from Hollywood also began to make regular pilgrimages abroad. Vienna, a

major cultural nexus in addition to its reputation as a tourists' mecca, was a
favorite stopover on the itineraries of American headhunters. Among the
most frequent American visitors was Gilbert Miller, a producer, director,
and theater owner who maintained a notable presence on Broadway and in
the West End for over fifty years. Each time he was in Vienna, Miller made
it a point to attend performances at the jewel-box theater Reinhardt had
refurbished. When he saw Otto's production of *Libel!* in the fall of 1934,
Miller decided to present the play in New York. He also resolved to hire its
young director to re-create his crisp, naturalistic staging. In addition, when
he met Otto backstage—Miller had a serviceable, if rudimentary, command
of spoken German—he was charmed. Miller's wife Kitty was the daughter
of Jules Bache, one of the richest stockbrokers in America, and Miller shared
with Otto a delight in the company and the rituals of high society. (Another
devotee of the well-to-do, Cecil Beaton, had this to say about the Gilbert
Millers: "I don't know if it might be possible to write a symposium of all the
laughs that there have been at the expense of Gilbert and Kitty during the
last forty years. They are a continual source of gossip, of rows, apologies and
outrageous behavior of all sorts. Perhaps a play could be made. Kitty, rich,
worldly to the point of madness, insatiable, full of energy, never tired, never
secure . . . [and] hideous beyond recall. Gilbert, a cad, a beast, with certain
disarming qualities of charm, brashness."[78])

Tight-fisted, Miller did not offer Otto a contract, extending instead a
vague invitation to direct *Libel!* on Broadway in the fall of 1935. Enticed
even so, Otto started at once to learn English. But he might not have gotten
to New York at all if another American scout, this one from Hollywood, had
not taken an interest in his work. In April 1935, about six months after
Miller's visit, as Otto was rehearsing a boulevard farce, *Der König mit dem
Regenschirm* (*The King with an Umbrella*), he received a summons from an
American film producer, Joseph Schenck, to a five o'clock meeting at the
Imperial Hotel. No, the busy director replied, he would still be in rehearsal
at five and could not possibly accommodate the request. A secretary
returned a few minutes later with the announcement that Mr. Schenck
would be "pleased" to see Dr. Preminger at any time during the evening, at
Otto's convenience. As it turned out, at least according to Preminger's testimony (and why not believe him, since the story presents him behaving
entirely true to form?), it was not "convenient" to present himself at the
Imperial until ten o'clock.[79]

Born in Rybinsk, Russia, in 1876, Schenck, along with his brother
Nicholas, born in 1880, had achieved a position of eminence in the still-
young American film industry. Early in their careers—they started out as

owners of amusement arcades—they had come into contact with theater owner and studio mogul Marcus Loew; Nicholas had maneuvered his way into becoming Loew's second in command, and when Loew died suddenly in 1927 Nicholas had been heir apparent. He became president of Loew's, Inc., in 1927, and was to remain on the job until 1955. In effect, Nicholas Schenck ran Metro-Goldwyn-Mayer. Joe had also flourished. After he married the actress Norma Talmadge, he became the producer of her films as well as those of her sisters Natalie and Constance. Joe also produced the films of Natalie's husband, Buster Keaton. In 1924 Joe had become the president of United Artists, and in 1933 had founded a new company called Twentieth Century. Two years later (and only several months before he waited for Otto at the Imperial Hotel), Joe had taken over William Fox's ail-

Darryl F. Zanuck (left) and Joseph Schenck, the cofounders in 1935 of a new studio, Twentieth Century-Fox.

ing studio and with a partner, Darryl F. Zanuck, had set up a new entity, Twentieth Century-Fox. At the new studio, Zanuck was in charge of all film production while Joe Schenck handled the finances. Because he and Zanuck intended to compete with established studios like Paramount and Metro-Goldwyn-Mayer, Schenck was on the lookout for new talent.

Unlike Gilbert Miller, Joe Schenck was not a theatergoer, and he became aware of Preminger only because of a friend of his, Julius Steger. Steger, an Austrian who had been a partner of William Fox, had amassed a sizable fortune in America, where Schenck had met him, and had now returned to Vienna, where he had become a client of Dr. Markus Preminger. Steger knew Otto socially and had watched, with an admiration he communicated to Schenck, the young man's ascending career in the Viennese theater. "It was Julius Steger who introduced Otto to Schenck," Ingo said. "Steger told Schenck, 'There's a good guy here in Vienna named Otto: you should hire him.' "[80]

When Otto entered Joe Schenck's suite at the Imperial, at ten o'clock that evening in April 1935, he encountered a man with a nose that resembled an oversized boiled potato—many people were to claim Schenck was the ugliest person they had ever seen. But Schenck had great warmth, and such was the force of his personality that in a matter of minutes his ugliness seemed magically to be transformed into a quality that was almost its opposite. Otto at that point spoke no English; Schenck, a Jew from Russia, spoke no German. Julius Steger translated. But it hardly mattered. Schenck could recognize that he and Otto spoke the same "language," and within a half-hour he offered Otto an invitation to come to work at the newly hatched Twentieth Century-Fox in Los Angeles. On the spot, Otto accepted. As Ingo recalled, "When Schenck gave Otto a deal on a piece of paper, he didn't know Otto or his work at all; he was simply taking Julius Steger's word for Otto. It was to Steger that Otto owed his great good fortune."[81]

Schenck did not specify the salary Otto was to receive, nor did he mention what he was hiring Otto to do. On his own, without first consulting with Zanuck, who was solely responsible for all creative decisions, Schenck could not have offered Preminger a directing job. It's likely, since Steger had informed him of Preminger's prudential management of the Josefstadt, that Schenck was inviting Otto to come onboard for his administrative rather than artistic ability. The vagueness of Schenck's offer, later to cause Preminger some distress, did not deter him at the time, nor should it have. Otto knew he had been handed the chance of a lifetime.

Schenck asked Otto to wind up his affairs in Vienna and to cable him when he would be ready to leave for America. In the event, Preminger needed six months. He had to give adequate notice to the Theater in der Josefstadt as well as his parents; and, not least, he had to begin in earnest to learn the language of the country he would be moving to. When he told his wife they would be moving to America—to Hollywood!—Marion was ecstatic. For her, the movie colony was a new social domain waiting to be conquered. And besides, though she wouldn't, and perhaps couldn't, admit it to Otto, in Hollywood she might be able to resume the acting career her husband had forbidden her to pursue in Vienna. But Otto informed Marion that he would be going to America on his own and would send for her after he was settled. It was a curious decision, even in light of the fact that the Premingers had a sophisticated European idea of marriage. Otto later claimed Marion "wanted to spend a few weeks with her family in Hungary before joining me."[82] But Marion, no doubt for once speaking the truth, recalled in her memoir that Preminger insisted on going himself and that he had been on his own for "several months" before he sent for her.[83]

Markus and Josefa, who like other wealthy Austrian Jews identified far more with being Austrian than with being Jewish and had not confronted—or had not allowed themselves to confront—the implications of rising anti-Semitism, implored their older son not to leave. Although Otto warned his parents that he was certain Hitler's rise to power in Germany would have dark consequences for Austria, he did not, as he was later to wish he had, insist on taking them with him. Throughout Preminger's rise to prominence, Vienna had suffered periods of political and economic turbulence, but in October 1935, unlike in Berlin, it was still possible to maintain an illusion that a place at the table would continue to be made for Jews. The elder Premingers held onto this belief, which their departing son could not dislodge.

Certainly anti-Semitism, which had always been part of Austrian culture, had been on the rise for more than a decade before Hitler was to annex Austria in 1938. Most Austrian Jews belonged to the Social Democrats, the leaders of Red Vienna, because the other two major parties, the Christian Social Party (the Blacks) and the Pan-German Nationalists (the Blues), were tarred with overt anti-Semitism. But Red Vienna, which had held a dominant position in the postwar period, lost control of the masses on July 15, 1927, in a mob uprising quelled by rightist militia. "That Friday started an ominous chain of events that in little more than a decade would lead to Hitler's triumph in Vienna and ultimately to the horrors and ashes of World War II," as Paul Hofmann observes.[84] With the virtual elimination of the Social Democratic Party in 1927, Austrian Jews had no party or leader to protect them against a swelling tide of hatred.

In 1932, when a Christian Social cabinet member named Engelbert Dollfuss, nicknamed "Millimetternich" because of his height of five feet, became federal chancellor, he confronted enormous challenges in keeping Austria from economic and political ruin. On March 7, 1933, in a desperate measure to ensure his ability to govern, he suspended the National Assembly, which had become virtually paralyzed by political schisms. And he won the support of Mussolini, not yet in league with Hitler, against the Nazis. Fearful of the increasingly inflammatory displays of Nazi agitators, Dollfuss declared the Nazi Party illegal. On May 1, 1934, he enacted a new constitution that, in effect, banned all political parties. On July 25 the "illegal" Nazis responded with a putsch led by a core group of 144 brownshirts against the tottering government. The putsch was unsuccessful, and Mussolini sent military support to ensure the defeat of the insurgents. But the Nazis assassinated the scrappy, diminutive chancellor who had turned them into outlaws.

That same evening, on July 25, the Austrian president, Wilhelm Miklas, appointed Kurt von Schuschnigg, Dollfuss's minister of justice and education, as the new chancellor. With the Nazis repelled, at least for the moment, and with von Schuschnigg providing an illusion of stability, Austrian Jews like the Premingers were lulled into thinking peace had been maintained. But the reality, of course, was that the tiger was at the gates. An Austro-Fascist like Dollfuss, von Schuschnigg lacked his predecessor's populist appeal as well as his relish for a fight. And as history would tragically prove, neither he nor Austria had the resources or the will to resist a Nazi takeover.

The Preminger family may have been complacent because of their history of good fortune. Even in his last months in Vienna, Otto's luck held. Civil war had been stilled for the moment. And his management of the Theater in der Josefstadt ended on a high note. Although his tenure at the theater ended officially in July 1935, Otto's successor, a playwright named Ernst Lothar, offered him a farewell production of his own choosing, to be staged in the fall. Otto not surprisingly selected an American play, *The First Legion,* by Emmett Lavery, in which a priest regains his faith after a crippled boy who believes in miracles is healed. Preminger's choice of material, perhaps intended as a placatory gesture toward the staunchly Catholic regime that was governing the country, was another example of his executive cunning. The opening night audience, which included the archbishop of Vienna, Cardinal Theodor Innitzer, who was to collaborate with Hitler, and Chancellor von Schuschnigg, making a rare public appearance, was filled with Catholic dignitaries representing both church and state. To forestall a possible riot by Nazi sympathizers, who despite the ban were increasing at an alarming rate in both number and aggressiveness, the theater was guarded by police, while inside the house officers in plain clothes kept a watch on the crowd. "We received a threat that a bomb would explode during the performance," Preminger recalled.[85] That night the theater resembled an armed camp, but the only demonstration was that of the audience at the curtain call, when the Jewish director of a drama about a priest's renewal of faith joined his cast onstage to acknowledge tumultuous applause. As Preminger boasted, "*The First Legion* was one of the most successful plays ever presented in Vienna and had one of the longest runs in theatrical history there."[86]

While the omens for Austria's future may have been malignant, Preminger himself could look forward to a double victory. Over the summer, when he learned that Otto would be coming to America at the expense of the munificent Joe Schenck, Gilbert Miller finally hired the young man to direct *Libel!* on Broadway. Miller's confidence in a director who barely spoke English was extraordinary—and so certain was he of Preminger's ability that, in advance of his director's arrival in New York in late October, Miller arranged for the show to open on December 20 at the Henry Miller Theatre (named for Miller's father, a prominent actor).

On October 16, only six days after the opening night of *The First Legion,* Otto was at the train station in Vienna, set to begin the first leg of his journey to the New World. Seeing him off were his parents, still not reconciled to his departure; his brother Ingo; Marion, perhaps a bit unsettled because Otto was leaving without her; and some well-wishers from the Josefstadt, including the budding Nazi, Attila Hörbiger, the actor who had appeared more often than any other in Preminger's productions. Thickset and looking older than his twenty-nine years, Otto was a young prince whose crown had remained remarkably untarnished. Nothing so far in his young and already crowded life had made him feel that the world offered him anything other than opportunities for proving he was a winner—a conquistador.

Unlike many Jewish émigrés forced to flee for their lives from Nazi persecution, Otto Preminger departed on his own terms and by his own choice. To be sure, he left with bitter feelings about Austria and Austrians that he was never to renounce, and with the conviction that catastrophe was about to engulf the country. But in October 1935, rather than skulking away under cover of night like a desperate refugee, Otto was accorded a hero's farewell. Certainly both Otto and his father would have been justified in the belief that they led charmed lives. Markus had defended a dying Empire and yet attained far greater wealth after the Empire had been dismantled; Otto had risen swiftly to a position of cultural power during a period when his country was on a collision course with political annihilation. As he was saying good-bye to his family on the day of his departure for America, why should the young man have suffered a moment of self-doubt or anticipated anything but a triumphant future?

TWO

Rise and Fall

Otto's trip to America was first-class all the way. Traveling on the same train with him from Vienna to Paris was the future film producer Sam Spiegel, whom Otto met for meals in the wood-paneled dining car. From Paris, Otto on his own took another train to Le Havre, where he joined up with Gilbert and Kitty Miller, who sailed with him to New York on the *Normandie*. Under the wings of the socially voracious producer and his heiress wife, Otto was assured a seat at the captain's table each evening and entrée to parties hosted by the wealthiest passengers. He attended affairs given by an Indian maharani and a grand duke, "a stupendously tall and boring personage" from a country he couldn't remember.[1] When Otto wasn't hobnobbing with grandees, he remained in his stateroom committing *Libel!* to memory in both German and English.

The *Normandie* arrived in New York on October 21, 1935, a sparkling autumn morning, one of those days (New Yorkers know there are about a dozen each year) when the city's climate attains an unrivaled perfection. Gilbert Miller proposed lunch at one of his favorite spots, "21," located then as now at 21 West Fifty-second Street just off Fifth Avenue. Co-owner Jack Kriendler gave the Gilbert Millers and their foreign guest a personal tour of the restaurant beginning with the wine cellar in the basement and ending with a look into the host's apartment on the top floor. For the rest of his life, "21" remained Otto's restaurant of choice in Manhattan. After lunch, Miller

accompanied Otto to a suite he had reserved for his director at the St. Regis
Hotel, at Fifty-fifth Street and Fifth Avenue. Preminger's ornate new home
recalled his parents' apartment on the Ringstrasse.

Within a few days of his arrival Otto encountered Viennese author
Franz Werfel in the hotel elevator. In New York to collaborate with Max
Reinhardt and Berlin émigré Kurt Weill on *The Eternal Road,* a biblical ora-
torio, Werfel, a sourpuss, regaled Otto with a list of complaints about the
city, calling it a cultural backwater populated by barbarians. Otto, however,
who thereafter avoided Werfel, had formed a quite different opinion: from
the moment he had seen the Statue of Liberty and the thrusting Manhattan
skyline, he knew that New York was the city he would always want to live in.
"I fell in love with New York on October 21, 1935," as he told columnist Earl
Wilson more than twenty-five years later.[2]

Ten days after his arrival, Preminger on November 1 began rehearsals for
Libel! Gilbert Miller, assuring his director that Americans were enamored of
titles, introduced Otto to the cast as "Dr. Otto Ludwig Preminger from

Joan Marion on the witness stand in *Libel!,*
staged by "the distinguished Viennese director
Otto Ludwig Preminger" in his Broadway debut.

Vienna" and immediately launched a campaign to promote Otto as a new theatrical luminary. A November 2 press release from Miller's office announced that on December 20, when *Libel!* would have its premiere, "one of Europe's most distinguished directors will [be making] his bow." Under the headline "Preminger Happy to Be in America," a November 3 article in the *New York World-Telegram* offered a charming portrait of the new arrival. An anonymous scribe observed that only with "difficulty" could Preminger be persuaded to recall anything about "the Old World and the Vienna he has left behind." About the hazards of communicating in his new language, Otto was more loquacious:

> The worst for me is the telephone. One day I asked my hotel to move the telephone from the desk to the table beside my bed. The next morning, very early, the phone rang; I was still half asleep and could not understand one word which a lady was shouting at me. I listened for a few minutes, and then hung up. Ten minutes later, there was a great knocking and three enormous men marched in and began shoving me around. The noise became terrific; I didn't understand a word they said, so I hid my head under the covers and prayed in my native tongue. Some time later, when the noise subsided, I peered out and found my telephone had been moved.

In an interview a week before the play was to open, Preminger was still reluctant to talk about the past. "You want to know about my theatre in Vienna? Well, it is not really very exciting," he offered. "It is the best theatre in Vienna . . . built only a few years ago [*sic*], in the best baroque style. When I took it over it was in very bad financial condition; when I gave it up, a few months ago, it was a great financial success, although conditions in the Vienna theatre are very bad." Preminger was equally terse about *Libel!* "I cannot tell you anything of the way I have directed it. Better you come and see it," he said, and with a flourish added that in Vienna the show had been "an enormous success, one of the best we ever had."[3]

Despite his struggles speaking and understanding English, Preminger remained confident about himself and the play and throughout rehearsals behaved with exquisite tact. When it opened on December 20, after out-of-town tryouts in Philadelphia and Boston, the show received enthusiastic notices. "Preminger's direction proves that courtrooms can bristle with theatre," Brooks Atkinson observed in his review in the *New York Times.* Robert Coleman in the *New York Mirror* called *Libel!* "the last word in melodrama, one of the most exciting of recent seasons, an aristocrat of its kind."

With *Libel!* set for a good run (the show would play for 159 performances), Otto took a train to Los Angeles on January 2, 1936, to report to
Joseph Schenck, his second American benefactor. At the Pasadena train station, Otto was met by Schenck's chauffeur and driven in a long black limousine to a suite at Hernando Courtright's Beverly Wilshire Hotel. Was
Marion with him? In some accounts, she was, Otto claiming to have summoned her to join him for the opening night of *Libel!* But he later told at
least one interviewer that he went to Los Angeles by himself and that "my
first wife joined me there about the middle of January."[4] In Hollywood,
where Schenck was as well connected as Gilbert Miller in New York, Otto
received a conqueror's welcome. Schenck introduced the Premingers to local
royalty, including Irving Thalberg, Norma Shearer, Gary Cooper, Joan
Crawford, and Greta Garbo. For Otto, the most memorable party was at
Pickfair, Mary Pickford's hilltop mansion in Beverly Hills, where he met
Charlie Chaplin. At all the gatherings, the Premingers—Otto with his egg-
shaped head, now as bald as it would be forevermore, and Marion flashing
her "million-dollar" smile—exhibited extraordinary savoir faire.

Although his original good looks were eroding under his advancing
fleshiness, Otto at thirty radiated vigor, wit, and sex appeal. He had the
great gift of drawing out his interlocutors, male as well as female, while
seeming to pay them his undivided attention. No matter his inexact command of English; no matter that his prominence in the Viennese theater had
rested primarily on his executive acumen rather than his artistry; no matter
even that he had been brought to Hollywood under Schenck's patronage
not as a star director but more as an apprentice and observer—Preminger
projected the aura of a man poised for success. His strongly accented voice
exuded authority, and, changing color from bright blue to slate gray, his
already heavy-lidded eyes were alight with curiosity.

As in New York, Preminger was touted as "one of Europe's youngest and
most distinguished stage producers." And as he became accustomed to the
rituals of American publicity, more forcibly and volubly than he had in New
York he began to play up to the role that had been created for him. In one of
his first interviews in Los Angeles, in January 1936, he pontificated about
American theater. "Los Angeles needs a civically endowed theatre," he said.
"And with Hollywood so overflowing with talent . . . such a theatre needs to
be established. With your national government encouraging the theatre
financially, Los Angeles should take the lead in pointing the way to the rest
of the nation by building a civic theatre which could be the model for the
world."[5]

Clearly, Preminger had won Schenck's favor, but it was Schenck's partner, Darryl F. Zanuck, who would determine Otto's destiny at Twentieth Century-Fox. The two men could hardly have been more unlike. Zanuck was a hayseed from Nebraska who spoke in a flat Plains accent. While Otto as a young man had memorized many of the works of the great playwrights, Zanuck from his earliest years had been a literary lowbrow entranced by pulp mysteries and adventure yarns. The only Gentile to run a major studio during Hollywood's Golden Age, Zanuck was as coarse-grained and hard-driving as Harry Cohn at Columbia, Adolph Zukor at Paramount, Louis B. Mayer at Metro-Goldwyn-Mayer, and Jack and Harry Warner. Zanuck began his career as a scriptwriter at Warner Bros., turning out scenarios for war films, biblical epics, tearjerkers, dog stories, and musicals so quickly that in addition to his own name he wrote under three pseudonyms: Gregory Rogers, Mark Canfield, and Melville Crossman. Recognizing a live wire, the Warner brothers hired him as a producer. In 1927 Zanuck supervised the seminal *Jazz Singer.* In 1931 he both adapted and produced *Little Caesar,* the prototype of the gangster saga. Later that year he produced the equally influential *Public Enemy.* In 1932 he adapted and produced *I Am a Fugitive from a Chain Gang.* And in 1933, his last year at Warner Bros., he produced *42nd Street,* which redefined the movie musical as decisively as his gangster sagas had etched a new formula for crime pictures. To enact his populist fables he championed a new kind of movie star, urban, fast-talking, imperfect-looking actors such as James Cagney, Edward G. Robinson, and Joan Blondell, who injected a proletarian energy into the early American sound film.

When he left Warner Bros. in 1933 to form his own company, Twentieth Century, Zanuck's taste became somewhat more elevated. His slate included period dramas—*The Affairs of Cellini* (1934), *Clive of India* (1935), *Cardinal Richelieu* (1935)—and movies with a Gallic touch like *Moulin Rouge* (1934) and *Folies Bergère* (1934). He also presented stories with a literary pedigree: *Advice to the Lovelorn* (1933) was based on Nathanael West's *Miss Lonelyhearts; Call of the Wild* (1935) was drawn from a Jack London novel; and *Les Misérables* (1933) was an adaptation of Victor Hugo's classic tale. Not entirely overlooked was the raffish urban fare that had been Zanuck's specialty at Warner Bros. *The Bowery* (1933) starred the terminally thuggish George Raft; *Broadway Through a Keyhole* (1933) was based on a story by tough guy New York newspaper columnist Walter Winchell. On the whole, however, in his opening salvos running Twentieth Century, Zanuck seemed consciously to be trading upward. His biggest in-house star was the stentorian-toned and now largely forgotten British actor George Arliss, whom Zanuck presented in *The House of Rothschild* (1934), *The Last Gentleman*

Darryl F. Zanuck, Otto's first American boss and first American adversary, a gruff Nebraska native who ran Twentieth Century-Fox with an iron will.

(1934), and *Cardinal Richelieu*. Joining up with Schenck early in 1935 to form Twentieth Century-Fox, Zanuck offered a collection of films that have left no imprint: *Metropolitan* (1935), *Thanks a Million* (1935), *Show Them No Mercy!* (1935), *Professional Soldier* (1936), and *It Had to Happen* (1936).

Beneath their obvious differences—Zanuck's no-frills, populist American manner as against Preminger's lordly Continental air—the two men did share a number of common traits. Like Preminger, Zanuck was a wünderkind whose rise to the top had been achieved with remarkable speed. Both men also had hyperactive libidos. Zanuck, a short fellow, chomped on large cigars and seemed to be attached to a croquet mallet he would swing and stroke as he stalked around his office during interviews. Any bargain basement Freudian would surely be justified in interpreting the ever present cigar and mallet as "registers" of their owner's ever ready phallus. "Zanuck was a tit man," as Celeste Holm, a Fox contract player in the 1940s, bluntly recalled. "And he was known to make passes," she added. "The only time I was in his office I was dressed up to the neck. He made a snappish comment that I was dressed for New York rather than Los Angeles; but I had dressed to make a point of not being available."[6] "Otto was a gentleman; Zanuck was scummy," recalled actress Ruth Warrick. "He was known to be lecherous, and you had to run pretty fast to stay clear of him. It was also known that he would make Marilyn Monroe service everyone at the Fox board meetings. Once Zanuck felt me up at a dinner party in his home, with his wife present; I was too embarrassed to do anything."[7]

Above all, both Zanuck and Preminger were born leaders. Zanuck, wanting to be able to call all the creative shots himself, had left Warner Bros. because he no longer wanted to report to the meddling brothers who owned the store. At the shop he had just set up with Joe Schenck, he was to have complete sovereignty over all artistic matters. If Preminger was to have a chance to direct he would therefore have to pass Zanuck's inspection. Recognizing that Zanuck rather than Schenck ruled the studio, Otto was a little apprehensive about his initial interview with the pint-sized, cigar-chomping mogul, and when he entered Zanuck's green office for the first time he was uncharacteristically muted. Otto's voice and bearing may not have had quite the same attack as when he felt he was in full command of the field, but the savvy Zanuck marked the newcomer as a winner. Rather than handing him an A-list directing job, however, he asked Otto to become an observer so he could familiarize himself with how Americans made movies. Otto, aware of how much he had to learn, readily accepted the assignment.

By 1935 the assembly-line formation of the studio system, one that Zanuck had helped to refine, was firmly in place. Each studio had its own roster of directors, writers, editors, cinematographers, and designers, in addition to its own repertory company of stars and character actors. Typically, talent was signed up for a seven-year period, during which employees were expected to do as they were told and to report to work on pictures assigned to them by the front office. At the top of the hierarchy was the studio boss, who was answerable only to the business office, typically located in New York. In 1935, when Otto began to report for work, no studio captain had more autonomy than Zanuck, nor could any of the others match Zanuck's track record for anticipating or molding popular taste.

Otto quickly adapted to the role of observer, suppressing his ego and his arrogance. From early in the morning until late at night he scrutinized the rites of Hollywood moviemaking: the way rehearsals were conducted; the procedures for setting up shots and for shooting multiple takes; the protocol during the viewing of dailies. He explored the mammoth, set-filled sound stages; mechanically challenged, he regarded the technological wonderland of cameras, lighting, and sound equipment with mingled awe and incomprehension. In effect, Otto was an exchange student with special privileges. But he was a more diligent student than he had been in Vienna.

Early on, Zanuck assigned Preminger to observe *Sing, Baby, Sing,* a routine musical directed by Sidney Lanfield, a minor contract director. The film starred the Ritz Brothers, now forgotten lower-rung vaudevillians; newcomer Alice Faye, whom Zanuck was grooming for stardom; and Gregory Ratoff, a high-strung Russian émigré who was a top Zanuck toady and was to become a lifelong Preminger pal. Lanfield, who may have suspected that Otto was sent to spy on him, or to replace him, took an immediate dislike to the Viennese observer. "He couldn't stand the sight of me," Preminger recalled. "Everything I did irritated him. One day I was standing with my hands in my pockets just as he was about to start a scene. He turned to me in a fury. 'You're making a noise!' he shouted. 'You're playing with the coins in your pockets!' My pockets were empty."[8] Shrewd, practical, and biding his time, Otto said nothing, but continued to watch Lanfield at work for the rest of the shoot.

Preminger's apprenticeship lasted for nearly eight months, long enough for him to begin to worry that Zanuck had either forgotten him or perhaps was planning to dismiss him. During this time, he and Marion continued to be socially active. They were frequent guests at Hollywood gatherings, and reciprocated with parties of their own, at which, despite Otto's humble salary, both the amount and quality of the food and drink were exceptional. Then one day near the end of July Otto was summoned to the boss's office, where, croquet mallet in hand and cigar in mouth, Zanuck told Otto he would be directing a film in Sol Wurtzel's unit. Having familiarized himself with the studio chain of command, Otto knew well what the assignment meant. Wurtzel, more interested in listening to baseball games than in supervising scripts or productions, was the resident king of the B's, the man in charge of all the studio's low-budget program pictures targeted for the bottom half of then-ubiquitous double features.

Preminger's assignment, to direct a vehicle for Lawrence Tibbett, a renowned opera singer Zanuck wanted to get rid of, was problematic. In effect Zanuck was hiring Otto as his hatchet man, a role for which Zanuck no doubt sensed the Teutonic Otto was well suited. The first picture released by Zanuck and Schenck's Twentieth Century-Fox, in 1935, had been *Metropolitan*, a high-budget star vehicle for Tibbett, who had enjoyed a quiet success in four Metro-Goldwyn-Mayer musicals in 1930 and 1931 and had then returned to the stage. With plans of creating a movie musical bonanza as he had with *The Jazz Singer* and *42nd Street*, Zanuck had lured Tibbett back to films with a generous contract. But *Metropolitan* fizzled.

Zanuck's initial interest in Tibbett had not been misplaced, however. A forerunner in opening the opera stage to American-born and -trained singers like himself, Tibbett was also an important crossover artist who regularly included popular songs in his concert performances and was dedicated to rescuing opera from its elitist isolation. Good-looking, likeable, unpretentious, and with a large popular following, Tibbett seemed a prime candidate for joining the short list of motion picture singing stars headed by Jeanette MacDonald and Nelson Eddy. But on-screen Tibbett was pallid— a strictly B-movie personality. Zanuck had signed him for two films, but after *Metropolitan*'s failure he wanted to close the books on the singer. "We're stuck with the son of a bitch," a boiling Zanuck reported to Preminger and added, "There's no chance he'll ever be a success in films so you go ahead and practice on him."[9]

Metropolitan was a flattering, made-to-order story in which Tibbett was presented as an American performer, slighted by the Met's European bias, who triumphs as the headliner of a rival company of native-born singers. In contrast, *Under Your Spell*, the film Otto was to direct, had a decidedly unfriendly premise. Tibbett appears as a singer with crossover appeal who happily retires, giving up his career for love. Fully aware of Zanuck's intentions and not blaming Otto for accepting the job, Tibbett was an affable colleague throughout the shooting in August and September 1936. At the end of the day Tibbett would frequently sing for the cast and crew, accompanying himself on a piano. Otto, appreciating the tough spot the singer was in, also behaved beautifully. In a typical press release (on September 23, 1936), Otto was depicted as "the embodiment of Continental courtliness" and so extraordinarily generous that the cast and crew were reluctant to admire "any of the doctor's possessions." When Arthur Treacher (playing Tibbett's butler) admired a striped tie Preminger was wearing, the director took it off on the spot and handed it to the nonplussed actor. When Gregory Ratoff (playing the singer's agent) admired Preminger's sweater, Otto pleaded with him to take it. Only once did a trace of Preminger willfulness surface. When Tibbett was scheduled to perform an aria from Gounod's *Faust* at the Los Angeles Philharmonic Auditorium, Otto refused the request of a group of Tibbett's opera fans to be cast as audience members.

Instead, Tibbett sang "Le veau d'or" to an audience of expensive dress extras hired by the director.

As he always would, Otto worked efficiently, completing the film well under budget and well before the scheduled deadline. *Under Your Spell* opened to tepid notices on November 6, 1936, on the bottom half of the bill at the RKO Palace on Broadway. "The direction by Otto Ludwig Preminger is spotty, not overcoming any of the story's shortcomings," *Variety* huffed.[10] "Tibbett's manifest weakness as a screen artist has always been his essential incongruity in the conventional romantic context, and if 20th Fox has not discovered it by this time it deserves the consequences," Bosley Crowther wrote in his November 6 review in the *New York Times,* as if on Zanuck's orders.

Although intended as Lawrence Tibbett's swan song, *Under Your Spell* was also Otto Preminger's debut, in effect his graduation thesis. The film is a low-grade screwball comedy, a knockoff of *It Happened One Night* performed by a troupe of lackluster road-company players, and Preminger's direction is no more than routine. Any competent, second-string studio

"We're stuck with the son of a bitch," Zanuck told Otto about Lawrence Tibbett, the star of *Under Your Spell,* Preminger's first directing job in America.

Preminger provides a proscenium-like frame for the singing star Lawrence Tibbett (Arthur Treacher plays the butler) in *Under Your Spell.*

employee could have done as well. Toiling at the bottom of the Fox factory after having headed the prestigious Theater in der Josefstadt, Preminger may have experienced a twinge of identification with the plight of his star, a celebrated opera singer stuck in a trifling B movie. But if Otto did feel he was working beneath his station, he wisely never let on. He recognized what Zanuck wanted from him: proof that the "distinguished Dr. Preminger from Vienna" could play by the rules of the Hollywood system.

Surely, however, Zanuck took notice that in two sequences the novice director demonstrates a rapport with a new medium. The first is a long tracking shot that opens the film in which an inquisitive moving camera surveys a recording studio. The scene begins with a close-up of a record playing on a turntable, after which the camera begins a slow, circular movement around the room. It focuses first on an orchestra, then on the reactions of two listeners, the agent and the butler of the singer, and settles finally on the source of the sound, the singing star himself, in the process of recording the title song. Here, as he will throughout his career, Preminger favors camera movement—the gliding, peering camera in one unbroken stride binding together all the elements of the scene—over montage, a succession of separate shots. The second sequence in which the film snaps briskly to attention is in a courtroom, which Preminger presents as a beehive of overlapping dialogue. Lawyers argue back and forth as an exasperated judge bangs his gavel. It's clear that for Preminger a courtroom is a privileged place, and the scene has a vibrancy unmatched by anything else in the film.

Otto, proving to Zanuck's satisfaction that he was not a rebellious European hotshot, graduated. Zanuck promoted him to the A-list, assigning him a story called *Nancy Steele Is Missing,* which was to star Wallace Beery, who had recently won an Academy Award for *The Champ* and had had major roles in two recent hits, *Grand Hotel* and *Tugboat Annie.* But Beery never showed up. Zanuck's emissary, Gregory Ratoff, brought Otto the bad news: "Beery won't do the picture with you. He says he won't make a film with a director whose name he can't pronounce."[11] Preminger surely was spared. There was no way he could have gotten along with the famously cantankerous Beery.

Zanuck bumped Otto back to the B unit to direct a fast-talking comedy called *Danger—Love at Work.* If there had been a certain logic in Zanuck's choice of the cultivated young European to direct a film starring an opera singer, this assignment was a mismatch. With his still tentative command of English, Otto couldn't hope to get the hang of the script's fast-paced, vernacular idiom. Compounding the damage was Zanuck's puzzling choice for leading lady: Simone Simon, just arrived from Paris, with an accent as thick as her director's. Preposterously, Simon would be playing an American character (it was Zanuck's intention to account for her accent with the alibi that she had been educated in Paris). Although Otto politely challenged Zanuck's casting, the mogul, with a lifelong soft spot for French starlets less enticing on screen than in his boudoir, would not relent. Preminger tried to smooth the rough edges of Simon's fractured English, but surely this was a case of the blind leading the blind. After watching the first few days' rushes Zanuck had to face facts: Simone Simon was lost in translation.

According to Preminger, Zanuck dismissed the actress with the kind of zinger Otto himself was to become famous for: "You have no talent whatever. Go back to Paris."[12] (Before returning to France, however, Simon in 1936 and 1937 made four minor films at Twentieth Century-Fox. She was to have a second chance in Hollywood in the 1940s at RKO, where her most famous roles were in *The Cat People* [1942] and *The Curse of the Cat People* [1944].)

Otto wasn't quite as lucky as Simon: Zanuck kept him on the job, with

Ann Sothern replacing the French actress. As he was filming over the summer, Markus and Josefa visited Otto, who was an attentive host, inviting his parents to see him at work on the set at Fox and showing them the sights of Los Angeles. He took them to the finest restaurants and on trips to Palm Springs and Lake Arrowhead, all the while imploring them to leave Vienna. Otto was more certain than ever that it would soon be impossible for any Jew to survive in Austria. He urged his parents to obtain immigration visas, but Markus refused. "He was convinced that I was mistaken, and [he] felt that it was wrong and unpatriotic for a prominent Austrian to show such lack of confidence in the future of his country."[13] Refusing to give up, Otto promised his parents a good life in America, but Markus was as stubborn as his son; for prominent Jews, he assured Otto, life in Vienna would continue to be safe. When his parents left after a visit of three weeks, Otto was fearful that he might not see his beloved father or mother again.

It was hard for Otto to give his full attention to the minor film he was working on. But professional as ever, he persevered. *Danger—Love at Work* has a slight but workable premise—a lawyer must persuade eight members of an eccentric rich family to agree to hand over land left them by their grandfather to a corporation for development. However, instead of exploring the potentially engaging social themes implicit in the material— capitalist excess, the growing division between haves and have-nots in Depression America—the film reduces its focus to the oddball family. Held up for light comic ridicule are a tiny, meek paterfamilias, his dithering wife, a son who paints on windows, a child prodigy, two maiden sisters who ward off intruders with a shotgun rigged to go off when their doorbell rings, and an uncle who lives in a cave and dresses in early Cro-Magnon.

Reviews of this disposable boulevard fare, released on September 30, 1937, were surprisingly pleasant. "Not important enough to be a main feature but a very good dualer," *Variety* noted, adding that "it is old farcical stuff but well executed and well directed so that it is still very funny."[14] In a clear-eyed postmortem, however, Preminger dismissed the film as "just part of my schooling. My English was so spotty I didn't know whether the actors were speaking their lines or talking politics with me." He recognized that he "needed to know more about America before he tried to interpret it on the screen."[15]

Darryl Zanuck, however, had a different reaction. Appreciating Preminger's handling of group shots in which characters jabber at the same time and a beautifully lighted scene in which the romantic couple are

From early on, as in this nine-character setup in *Danger—Love at Work,* the group shot was a Preminger specialty.

caught in a barn during a rainstorm, he offered Otto a new two-year contract. From Zanuck's point of view, Preminger had twice proven to be a willing foot soldier. And on a personal level, Zanuck enjoyed Preminger's European flair. He began to favor Otto and Marion with invitations to parties in his homes in Santa Monica and Palm Springs, and at the studio he frequently asked Preminger to join him for lunch or dinner in the executive dining room. Other studio employees, as alert as Otto to the politics of power that fueled the system, also read the signs: clearly the newcomer had become a court favorite.

In November 1937, Zanuck's perennial emissary Gregory Ratoff brought Preminger the news that Zanuck had chosen him to direct *Kidnapped,* the most expensive feature to date in the studio's history. Zanuck himself had adapted the Robert Louis Stevenson novel, set in the Scottish Highlands, and was also planning to produce. Otto had never heard of the novel, and after he read Zanuck's script he knew he was in trouble. Once again, Zanuck's pairing of director to material was odd, and in this case perverse. Could his reasoning have been that a foreign director would have an affinity for a story with a foreign setting? Otto informed Ratoff that he could not possibly accept the assignment—"all I knew about the Scots was that they wore kilts," he claimed.[16] But Ratoff warned him that if he turned Zanuck down, he risked demotion, even possible banishment. When Otto wouldn't budge, the excitable Ratoff broke down in wrenching sobs, pounding his chest as he pleaded with Otto to accept the job. Reluctantly, Otto yielded.

With less time for preparation than he had had on either of his first two films, Preminger started to shoot a story set in a backlot re-creation of Scotland that he simply did not understand or have any feeling for. It was Zanuck's practice to watch the dailies on every production, but because he was in New York for a stockholders' meeting when Otto began filming *Kidnapped,* several days of dailies had accumulated. When he screened Otto's footage as soon as he returned, he was unhappy. The work was stilted, and it was clear to Zanuck that Preminger had not been able to win the trust of the child actor, Freddie Bartholomew, who was playing Stevenson's young hero. Zanuck called Otto to his office, where he accused the director of making changes in a scene between Bartholomew and a dog. Otto, composed at first, said he shot the scene exactly as it was in the script. Zanuck, insisting he knew his own script, disagreed. Otto repeated that he had made no changes whatever. The argument escalated. Zanuck raised his voice and his height, pulling himself up to confront his massive adversary. And then, perhaps for the first time in America, Otto had one of his tantrums. The veins in his neck started to throb; his head and face were overtaken by a fire-alarm red; his voice rose to ear-splitting volume. In recalling the incident Preminger liked to speculate that Zanuck's anger rose as "he began to suspect he was mistaken."[17] Zanuck, who was certainly no slouch in a temper roller derby but probably could not have matched Preminger, commanded his employee to leave the office. Otto, fuming, left quickly, slamming the door to Zanuck's office on his way out. "If you don't patch this up with Zanuck you'll never again work anywhere in Hollywood," Gregory Ratoff warned, again bursting into tears.[18] Otto at first was unconcerned, choosing to regard Ratoff's predictions as the ravings of a natural-born hysteric.

In the hermetic studio enclave, news of Preminger's encounter with Zanuck spread quickly, and Otto began to notice a rapid change in the temperature. Beginning to feel uneasy, he turned to his mentor, Joe Schenck, who had professed lifelong devotion, assuring Otto that he regarded him as the son he didn't have. Otto called Schenck's office, fully assuming that his "father," who was also the cofounder of the studio, would intercede on his behalf. But Schenck did not return any of the more than a dozen calls that Otto made. Banned from the executive dining room, Otto ate alone in the commissary, shunned by colleagues. Ratoff would speak to him only outside

the studio. The lock to Otto's office was changed and his name was removed
from the door. After his parking space was relocated to a remote spot, he
stopped going to the studio. At that point, a Zanuck intermediary offered
Preminger a buyout deal, which he rejected: he wanted to be paid for the
eleven months remaining on the two-year contract he had signed. He began
to look for work at other studios, but received no offers. In the winter of
1937, two years after his arrival in Los Angeles, Otto Preminger had to confront the fact that he had become unemployable.

Rebuffed for perhaps the first time in his life, Otto did not cave in. As
he continued to collect his salary he enrolled in courses in American history
at UCLA. Under an assumed name he also began to audit a drama course,
but when the teacher discovered who Otto was he "threw me out because he
thought I was spying," as Preminger recalled.[19] He also began to explore
opportunities in local theater. In this winter of his discontent, he asked
Luise Rainer, then at the peak of a remarkably short-lived Hollywood career,
to appear in a play he would direct. "All I remember is that I did not want to
do it," Rainer recalled. Assessing the man who had directed her in Vienna in
Men in White only three years earlier, Rainer did not care for what she saw.
"Some people are what they look like. What did he look like? He looked like
a man with a certain amount of hardness. A man who wants to get what he
wants to get."[20]

At the time, Max Reinhardt was also in Hollywood, but there is no evidence that Preminger sought out his former mentor, who also was not thriving. After he had codirected, with his former Josefstadt protégé Wilhelm
Dieterle, a 1935 film of his favorite play, *A Midsummer Night's Dream*, Reinhardt had had no further offers. And as both he and his slightly embarrassed
American hosts were only too well aware, in Hollywood the great impresario of the European theater was out of his element. With no other visible
means of support, Reinhardt had opened a school, the Max Reinhardt
School for the Theatre, where conceivably Preminger could have been
employed. But the proud and temporarily humbled young man did not,
and perhaps could not, ask for a job there.

If by temperament and artistic inclination Reinhardt and Luise Rainer
were ill suited to Hollywood, Preminger decidedly was not. He was tough
and practical in ways that the industry both understood and rewarded, and
unlike his former Viennese compatriots he disparaged neither the products
nor the business practices of the commercial American filmmaking establishment. But the scene in Zanuck's office had sidelined him, at least for the
moment. After months of batting his considerable head against tightly
closed doors—at one low point he even offered his services as a director of

screen tests—he realized that his only chance for rehabilitation would be in the place where he had launched his career in America: on Broadway.

But before he was free to relocate to New York he had to face another crisis, one far more threatening than his interrupted career. On March 12, 1938, an event occurred that Otto had foreseen but that many Austrian Jews including his parents and his brother had failed to anticipate: Hitler, a native son, invaded Austria. Following the Anschluss, Austria was subject to the same racial laws as Germany, which meant that every single Jewish person was in immediate mortal peril. When he was unable to reach his family for a forty-eight-hour period following the Anschluss, Otto became alarmed. Finally receiving a phone call from his father—the elder Premingers, having barely managed to escape, were in Zurich—Otto was profoundly relieved. By means of prominent connections Markus had been able to secure two seats on a train from Vienna to Italy; but the borders were already closed and the train was rerouted back to Vienna. Desperate, and now finally and fully aware that he and Josefa were facing extermination, Markus, as Otto recounted the events, "appealed for help to an old friend, the Chief of Police in Vienna, Otto Skubl. At great risk to himself he put my parents on a plane to Zurich."[21]

Ingo amplified the narrative of his parents' escape. "My father was stupid enough to think he could stay on after March 12, 1938," he recalled. "He had a foolish optimism: 'It won't be so terrible,' he said. He felt, because of his position, 'it was going to be all right.' But of course it wasn't going to be all right." With his wife Kate and young daughter Eve, Ingo, who at the time of the Anschluss was a successful lawyer living on the same street as Freud, made a hasty and narrow escape from Vienna to Zurich. "I spent hours crying on the phone, begging my father to leave Vienna, and even then, he said he wouldn't leave." Eventually Ingo prevailed, and "at the last moment that it was possible for Otto Skubl to help them," Markus and Josefa left Vienna to join Ingo and his family in Zurich.[22]

When the Premingers were reunited in Switzerland they had to confront the fact that they were unlikely to find a safe haven anywhere in Europe. Otto, of course, wanted his entire family with him in America. "Everybody wanted to go to the United States," Ingo recalled.

Some European Jews went to China and to Australia, but it was the United States—New York in particular—that had the greatest attraction. How to get there in 1938, after the Anschluss, was going to be a problem, however. American immigration laws had quotas.

The fact that my father and I had been born in Romania was an obstacle: Romania had a small quota in 1938, and it was already overfilled by the time we would have applied. In fact, I was thrown out of Zurich: the immigration quota was full. There was also a visitor's visa, but if the consul interviewing you thought you would want to remain in the United States he wouldn't give you a visa. I was turned down because I was considered a possible immigrant. From Zurich we went to Paris. My wife and daughter had no problem getting an immigrant visa, and along with my parents were able to leave Paris for the United States, but I was forced to stay behind.[23]

In Paris, Julius Steger, who had been instrumental in urging Joe Schenck to hire Otto, once again became a Preminger benefactor. At a party given by Steger, Ingo met

a guy called Mascovitch who said he could help me when I told him I couldn't get a visa. He told me to go to Nice and see a man named Szabo who ran a travel office. "He has special connections. He will get you a visitor's visa within twenty-four hours." Of course I went to Nice immediately to see this Mr. Szabo, who was young, charming, and good-looking. Yes, he could help, but of course he needed money. Desperate, I gave him what he wanted. "You have to become a resident of Nice: get a driver's license and rent an apartment." Two days later I had both. "I need a few more dollars," he told me. Again, I gave it to him. "Go to the American consulate, there's a young lady there who is my girlfriend." The consul signed the visa form, and I was on the next boat to New York.[24]

Once the Premingers were reunited in New York the problem of the temporary visitors' visas that Ingo and his parents were holding had to be resolved. Otto always claimed that the father (then speaker of the U.S. House of Representatives) and uncle (a U.S. senator) of Tallulah Bankhead were the family saviors because they introduced an emergency bill that granted immigrant status to holders of visitors' visas regardless of quotas. Ingo, however, disputed this. "It is true that Miss Bankhead's father proposed a law, but it was never used. What actually happened was that at the expiration of our visitors' visas my father and I went to Canada for a day, to Windsor, where we applied for and received a visa, and by this means we were able to reenter the United States as full-fledged immigrants."[25]

Through connections, resourcefulness, hair-trigger timing, and the good luck that seemed to favor the family, the tightly knit Preminger clan managed to survive the Holocaust.

In the spring of 1938, when his parents and Ingo and his family joined him in New York, Otto was at the lowest point in his career. His contract at Twentieth Century-Fox had run its course, and so far he had been unable to find work in the theater. Because he was addicted to the high life, even now when he could scarcely afford it, Otto once again had taken a suite in the St. Regis Hotel. He and Marion continued to be avid hosts as well as party-goers and were seen frequently at Manhattan nightspots like El Morocco and the Stork Club. Although Otto often encountered the equally social Gilbert Miller, his former producer had no job offers. When Preminger was unable to pay his hotel bill, the manager, Colonel Serge Obolensky, charmed by Otto and believing in his prospects, allowed him and Marion to remain in the half-filled hotel—so long as they did not use room service. Otto, confident he would succeed, rejected an offer of help from his father, who, as Otto noted, had "a modest amount of money, some of it from a Swiss bank account he had maintained and some of it derived from the sale of jewels my mother had managed to hide on her body during the flight from Vienna."[26]

Zanuck's blacklisting would not have had an impact on Broadway, but still Otto was having a hard time finding work. Weeks of pavement pounding yielded no possibilities, until, once again, Otto acquired an influential patron: Lee Shubert, the producer and theater owner who had cofounded a theatrical empire with his brothers Sam and J.J. and for over four decades was the single most powerful man in the American theater. Like others before him, the canny and hard-as-nails Lee Shubert saw promise in the now beleaguered young Preminger. He offered Otto an office, rent-free, in the Shubert-owned Sardi building (named for the ground-floor restaurant that is in business to this day) located on West Forty-fourth Street in the heart of the theater district. All that Lee asked in return was a first look at any production Otto would undertake.

As much as Hollywood, Broadway conducted business according to a clear-cut caste system, and the fact that Otto, who in fact was too broke even to afford a secretary, was in a Shubert building gave him legitimacy. Soon after he moved into his office above Sardi's, Otto, through his almost nightly socializing, met a stagestruck heiress named Jean Rodney who offered to work for him for free. In association with William Brady, who owned the Playhouse Theatre, Rodney was in the process of forming a group called the Playhouse Company, whose goal was to present a season of plays in rotating repertory. As their inaugural production they selected a revival of a 1923 play by Sutton Vane called *Outward Bound,* a potboiler that takes place on a mysterious ship filled with passengers who discover that, having died, they are "outward bound" to eternity. Although Rodney was working for Otto, her first choice to direct was Bramwell Fletcher, who also played one of the passengers. It was only after Fletcher stepped down early in rehearsals that Rodney approached Preminger. Otto accepted immedi-

One of the great challenges of Preminger's career, directing Laurette Taylor (here with Vincent Price and Bramwell Fletcher) in her return to the stage after a ten-year absence, in *Outward Bound.*

ately, even knowing that he would be facing the same problem that had caused Fletcher to depart—Laurette Taylor, a beloved star making a comeback after ten years' absence from the stage, who was also a troublesome alcoholic. (Although Otto was later to claim that he had insisted on casting Taylor, in fact Rodney and Brady had cast her before they hired him.) Taylor had quarreled with every suggestion Fletcher had made, and when Otto took over she continued to be snappish, distant, and wary.

Preminger realized that the fate of the show, and probably his career, depended on his overcoming Taylor's suspicion. He took her to lunch, speaking candidly about the concerns of the producers, and about what he had heard about her from Gilbert Miller and others in the theatrical community. "His frankness brought forth her own," Taylor's daughter Marguerite Courtney wrote in her biography of her mother.[27] Taylor confided to her director how unhappy she was over the fact that Grace George, a well-known actress and the wife of coproducer William Brady, had been hired as her understudy and was watching her from the balcony at every rehearsal. The actress expressed her fear that the producers had hired her only for the publicity value and that they were planning to replace her with George. When Laurette "admitted [to Preminger] she was bitterly disillusioned, licked," Otto responded sympathetically. He assured his star that he would dismiss George; that there would be no understudy for her; that she had his full support and confidence. Then, aware that Taylor was always shaky with lines, he asked her to go home and memorize her (short) part as a self-effacing scrubwoman, and told her not to return until she had. Although Preminger's insistence on early memorization was to earn him the scorn of many Method-trained actors, for Laurette Taylor it proved to be exactly the right approach. After three days at home memorizing her lines, Taylor returned to a company of actors still reading from their scripts. "It was a psychological boost of inestimable importance," as Courtney noted.[28]

"It would have been quite hopeless to approach her with a promise-me-you'll-be-a-good-girl," Preminger recalled. "There was a demon in her that would not be boxed like that. It was in part what made her so weird on the stage—surprising you with unexpected phrasing and accent; the fluid, the unexpected, this was the nub of her inspiration. To approach her with a program of being good, of never touching another drop, was to try and box her demon. She would never allow it. I knew this at once."[29] Sensing their common traits—a high-strung perfectionism and an outspoken manner that could easily rub others the wrong way—Preminger handled Taylor adroitly. During private lunches and dinners he welcomed her suggestions, shared behind-the-scenes production details with her, made her laugh, and above all gave her a feeling of security. To support his unstable star he subdued his own temperament and approached her with deep patience and tact that earned him the respect of the cast.

On opening night, December 22, 1938, when Laurette Taylor made her entrance in a pork-pie hat, a black alpaca cape with a fur collar, and holding a knitting bag, she was greeted by a prolonged ovation. For ten minutes the audience cheered and stomped and whistled. After the applause finally receded she performed with conviction. The pauses and hesitations with which she embellished the character's sparse dialogue and the detailed behavior she had worked out—"she knit in a way that was both humble and commanding, humorous and apologetic," as Marguerite Courtney wrote[30]—were wonderfully lifelike.

During her twenty-two curtain calls, the star made, or attempted to make, three short speeches expressing her gratitude. Taylor's triumph was also, of course, Preminger's; and in post-opening interviews the actress gave generous credit to her director. It's likely that if her return to the stage had not gone well, seven years later she would not have been able to create the role of the mother in Tennessee Williams's *Glass Menagerie*—Taylor's Amanda Wingfield has been widely cited as the single finest performance in the American theater of the twentieth century. *Outward Bound* became such a box-office success that the producers ran the play until the following November, abandoning their original intention of presenting a season of repertory.

The show's success gave Preminger a second chance. His no-nonsense, straightforward treatment of *Outward Bound* justified Lee Shubert's faith in him. Now the phone in Preminger's office in the Sardi building rang frequently; he could at last afford a secretary; and a line of people in the outer office waited patiently to see him. Soon he would even be able to pay Colonel Obolensky, his understanding landlord at the St. Regis. On January 30, 1939, President Roosevelt's birthday, the company was asked to present the play at the National Theatre in a benefit performance for the March of Dimes, to be followed by dinner with Mr. and Mrs. Roosevelt at the White House. Although meeting powerful figures had been part of his legacy as the son of Dr. Markus Preminger, Otto was not blasé. He had great admiration for FDR, and was thrilled to be meeting the president. Laurette Taylor, also a fervent Roosevelt supporter, was nervous at the prospect of supping with her idol, and her agitation only increased when she discovered that the president had requested her to be seated next to him. While Preminger needed no warming up—he was a voluble guest—Taylor, as the president was quick to spot, was tongue-tied, and in a down-to-earth style he regaled her with stories that soon put her at ease. "Of all the people I have met in my life the two who impressed me most were Franklin Roosevelt and Jawaharlal Nehru," Preminger recollected. "[Roosevelt] had the gift to make you feel he cared about you and was truly interested in what you had to say. . . . You felt he would remain your friend for life."[31]

The first offer Otto accepted following *Outward Bound* was from Cheryl Crawford, who in 1930 had been one of the cofounders of the idealistic Group Theatre, which she had left in 1937 to pursue a career as an independent Broadway producer. Crawford was offering Otto a starring vehicle for Ina Claire, the first lady of drawing-room comedy, at the time a popular genre. Preminger had first begun discussing the project (originally called *Generals Need Beds* and later changed to the more palatable *Yankee Fable*) with Crawford in the fall of 1938. From the first, he and Crawford, a severe-looking woman who had none of the social animation Otto appreciated and lived by, were not a good match. The producer was tight-fisted, as stingy with money as with smiles and affability. But Otto persevered because, like everyone else in the theater, he admired Ina Claire and because he thought the comedy, by Lewis Meltzer, had real promise. The star's role, that of a witty young matron of the Revolutionary War era who influences the course of history by her romantic intrigue with a British general, was enriched by the kind of droll turns of phrase that were Claire's specialty. For Preminger, who kept his dislike of Crawford to himself, rehearsals were joyful: Claire, disciplined and well prepared, was as effervescent offstage as on and like her director she enjoyed the beau monde.

The honeymoon came to an abrupt halt, however, when the company went to Boston for a two-week tryout and, to everyone's surprise, Claire could not remember her lines. She was unable to get through a single performance without substantial help from a prompter. As he had been with Laurette Taylor, Preminger was patient. Every day he would take his star for long walks in the Boston Common during which he would guide her through her entire part, and she would never miss a line. But then onstage at night her concentration would be shot. "I was very sorry for her because she was a very good actress and tried very hard. We had no choice but to close the play," Otto said.[32] Trumball Barton, who had a role in the play as a soldier (and later worked for a year as Otto's secretary), recalled that the director "had a flirtation with Ina Claire. Ina, who thought Otto was rather ridiculous, was somehow under the impression that he didn't speak English. Maybe that's why we closed after two weeks out of town."[33]

Preminger's problems with Laurette Taylor and Ina Claire, however, were as nothing compared to those presented by his next star. Shortly after

Yankee Fable folded, coproducers Richard Aldrich and Richard Myers approached Otto to direct John Barrymore, returning to the stage after seventeen years making films, in a slight comedy, *My Dear Children,* about a renowned stage actor with three hard-to-handle daughters. Anticipating that Barrymore's Broadway comeback would command as much attention as Laurette Taylor's and sensing the possibility of a box-office hit, Otto accepted at once and moreover asked to become a coproducer as well. With the last of his Hollywood salary already spent and *Outward Bound* bringing in only a meager stipend, Otto needed cash, especially as he and Marion continued to live it up at the St. Regis.

The impetus for Barrymore's theatrical comeback came from his young wife Elaine, who had met him when as a student she had managed to nab an interview for the Hunter College newspaper. The two had had an instant rapport. Like Barrymore, Elaine was a voracious reader, and an opinionated live wire who gave as good as she got. "I hated Hollywood, and I convinced John to go back to Broadway," the New York–born Mrs. Barrymore recalled. "We'd been looking for a play for ages. In Los Angeles we met a couple of screenwriters, Catherine Turney and Jerry Horwin, who offered John a comedy they had just written called *My Dear Children.* John liked it because he saw it was a piece where he could ad-lib and nobody would know the difference. John didn't memorize lines anymore—in pictures he had been using cardboards. Cathy and Jerry weren't great writers, and nobody thought it was Shakespeare, but what they had was moderately amusing."[34] (Not incidentally the play also contained a role for Elaine.) When Aldrich and Myers, who "were looking like mad for a play," were dinner guests at the Barrymores' one night early in 1939, Elaine showed them the script. "They snapped up the rights immediately," Elaine recalled,

> and in their next breath said they wanted Preminger, who had quite a reputation in New York at the moment because of what he had done for Laurette Taylor, to direct. Otto's response was as quick as the producers'. They had him fly out to Los Angeles to meet John and me and the coauthors, and it was instant antipathy. I was chilled. I was really against him from the start because in New York I had known Marion Mill, who was so bubbly and so tremendously charming, and Preminger was a notorious womanizer who had hurt her so badly.

For his part, Preminger sized up Elaine as "a woman of little acting ability."[35]

When rehearsals began in New York in March 1939, there was every prospect of fireworks between Preminger, who demanded that his actors be word-perfect early in the rehearsal process, and Barrymore, who had signed on with the express intention of *not* memorizing his lines and who regarded the script, moreover, the way a jazz artist looked at notes—as a chance to riff. But Preminger treated Barrymore gingerly. "Otto was much too self-serving to yell at John," Elaine felt,

> and he handled John with deference and respect because John, after all, was a big star and also because Otto was afraid of him. But Otto made up for it with how he treated everyone else: he was dreadful. He treated the authors like dirt, as if they had nothing to do with the play. He would sit in the audience shouting directions—he didn't give a damn whether you felt anything, and he wasn't interested in drawing us out. He didn't know how to. He just dictated. He wouldn't listen to anyone, not even to John. He was so Germanic that I felt he was more a nation than a human being. John, who was afraid of no one except perhaps himself, called Preminger "Otto" while I called him "Dr. Preminger."[36]

During rehearsals Otto several times invited the star and his young wife to the St. Regis. "Oh, but he could be charming then," Elaine said. "He would lay it on. And Marion was such a darling hostess. He lived at the hotel to impress: he did things in a large way. But he had a brutal streak that was barely concealed by good manners. In a certain sense, things had come too easily to him, and this had given him a smug attitude. His charm was an act and if you were at all sensitive you knew it was an act. Deep down, I was a little afraid of him; he represented a sort of hidden danger." In one scene, Barrymore had to spank Elaine, who was playing one of his daughters, and during rehearsals Preminger seemed to take a particular delight in showing the actor how to deliver the proper whack. "Otto was a little fresh in his slapping when he had me over his knee," Elaine recalled.

> John needed direction to fit into the rest of the play, and this Otto couldn't give him. John knew what Preminger was *not* giving him, but he was never sharp with him: John only acted up in performance, not during rehearsals. He even thought that Preminger was basically a good director, just not for this kind of trifle, which required someone who could handle nothingness. The show needed a champagne touch not in Otto's line, and I felt Otto really had very

little humor and no gift for this kind of comedy. If directed improperly, the show fell apart, which is what happened. But John recognized Preminger's talent and intelligence and he saw, as even I did, that Preminger loved the theater. But they didn't become buddies and go out drinking. They were such different personalities. I had the feeling that Preminger didn't much like John.[37]

Otto and his coproducers, confident of the market value of Barrymore's name and determined to avoid the taint of the scathing notices they expected to receive in New York, planned a lengthy pre-Broadway tour confined for the most part to cities outside the theatrical loop. Hence the anomaly of *My Dear Children* opening in Princeton, New Jersey, in the presence of Albert Einstein. "People stood and cheered, delighted with Barrymore's broad mockery of himself," as Preminger recalled. In his curtain speech the actor acknowledged his director, thanked the cast and the backstage crew, and then pretended to forget the names of his producers. "Has someone got a program?" he asked. The audience laughed, but according to Preminger the coproducers "were not amused. They were both able men but they were unfortunately somewhat afraid of Barrymore and it gave him perverse pleasure to torment people who were intimidated by him."[38]

Elaine Barrymore recollected the Princeton opening in a very different light. "John was letter-perfect but it was a dull and empty performance," she said. "John was aware that Einstein was in the audience and he tried too hard; he was afraid of missing lines. He would have been better off forgetting a few lines but getting a little life into the play. Einstein greeted John like he was a world leader: they were instant friends. That night no one paid any attention to Preminger."[39]

Barrymore's good behavior was short-lived. As the tour moved on from Princeton to other theatrical backwaters, the actor began to improvise with increasing recklessness. Each night he would disrupt the play in a different way and at different points, addressing the audience with peppery asides. His send-ups—of himself and of the show—became an expected part of the performance: the spectacle audiences had paid to see. "The audience adored the little ad-libs," Elaine recalled. "When he would tell someone off, or growl to a latecomer, 'Where the hell have you been?' or say seductively to a matinee lady, 'You're a little late, darling,' the spectators were thrilled. When John was on good behavior, when he was doing the ad-libs in the *right* way, the show was entertaining and he was really irresistible."[40] But there were nights when alcohol had overtaken him, and what the audience saw was not a star in expert control of his "misbehavior" but a drunkard stumbling

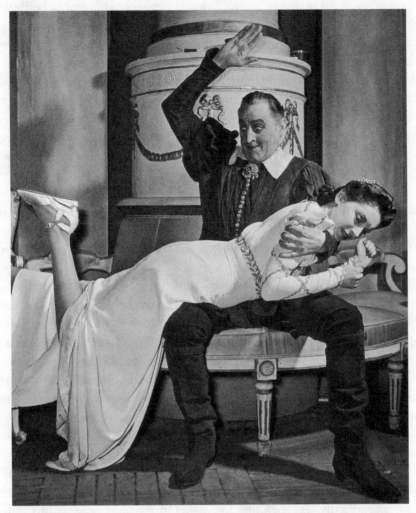

John Barrymore as a ham actor in the notorious *My Dear Children*, taking delight in spanking one of his three daughters (played by Elaine Barrymore, John's young wife).

through a performance that was painful to observe. On these nights the actor's self-contempt was palpable.

Preminger stayed on with the show through the early weeks of the tour, giving notes after each performance. "Later on, he realized there was no point," Elaine said. When Preminger left, however, Barrymore began to deteriorate. "John began to drink more, and we had so many fights," Elaine recalled. "In Detroit and Dayton we weren't talking at all, except onstage, but he still spoke to my mother. Mama would put in a good word for me, and when she was in the audience John would ad-lib to her."[41] At a luncheon given in his honor in Joliet, Illinois, John kicked his wife, a headline-making incident quickly followed by the news that Barrymore wanted to divorce Elaine and have her removed from the show. Otto flew in from New York and was met at the airport by Barrymore and a towering male nurse who had been hired to keep the star from drinking. But, as Otto noted, "Each of them had a bottle sticking out of his coat pocket."[42] That night Preminger, stunned, watched a performance in which the actor proceeded to dismantle the show. As the director observed, "Most of the time [Barrymore] sat, sagging, on a bench placed center stage. He remained there whether he was supposed to be onstage or not, sometimes asleep."[43]

The director traveled with the cast by train to St. Louis, the next stop on the tour. During the night, Elaine and her stout mother, Mrs. Jacob, climbed onto Otto's Pullman bed and sat on his chest, urging and then threatening him not to fire Elaine. "Mrs. Jacob said she would tell the newspaper that Barrymore had repeatedly tried to rape her. 'Who would believe you, Mrs. Jacob?' " Otto, in vintage put-down mode, inquired, before ordering the frantic women off his chest. The midnight visit did not save Elaine's job. She would be paid for the run of the show but would leave the cast after playing out the week in St. Louis. During the week Otto rehearsed a new actress, Doris Dudley, in the role. Preminger told Barrymore he was dismayed by the opening night performance in St. Louis and that the actor was going to have to shape up "or else"; chastened, the star asked his director to return the following night. "Impeccable," Otto responded. "Jack, why can't you do this every night?" For many years afterward Preminger enjoyed quoting Barrymore's answer: "B-o-r-e-d, my dear boy, bored."[44]

At the end of the St. Louis run, Preminger and Elaine returned (separately) to New York. Otto became alarmed by reports from Chicago, where the star reportedly was spending his nights in a whorehouse. "Otto really adored and respected the theater and the fact that the tour was a mess wasn't easy for him, as it wasn't easy for Aldrich and Myers either," Elaine said. "They stuck it through, however, because the show was making money on John's name."[45] To be sure, Barrymore's misconduct was proving good for business, and advance sales for the Broadway engagement swelled after each account of a new mishap on the road. Dorothy McGuire, a genteel young woman who played one of Barrymore's daughters and would go on to a major film career, did not want to make her Broadway debut under these circumstances and resigned at the end of the tour, a decision that earned her Preminger's lifelong respect.

On January 30, 1940, opening night in New York, Barrymore was up to speed and, on the whole, reviews were positive. "Although he has recklessly played the fool for a number of years [Barrymore] is nobody's fool in *My Dear Children,* but a superbly gifted actor on a tired holiday," Brooks Atkinson wrote in the *New York Times.* On opening night Elaine paid a visit backstage.

> John was thoroughly sober, but he told me to "get the hell out of here." Diana [John's daughter] stretched her arms across the door. But he invited me to the cast party at El Morocco, where Preminger tried to prevent me from entering. John embraced me, and asked if he could go back with me to the Hotel Navarro, where I was staying—John was staying in Long Island with the company manager. John promised he'd be good. The next day the newspapers flooded the hotel: it was pandemonium. John announced to the reporters: "Since when is it illegal in the state of New York for a man to sleep with his wife?" We were back together, and he wanted me back in the show. With John, it was all-encompassing, and when it was going right it was delirious.[46]

Elaine was back, and she remained in the show for the rest of the run.

Barrymore continued his unsteady course. On sober nights, tweaking his image he served skillfully carved portions of ham on wry and the show was exactly the kind of shipshape commercial enterprise that Preminger had directed it to be. On sodden nights, however, Barrymore and the play were in ruins. Although business warranted a longer run, Barrymore, at last irreversibly bored, closed the show after 117 performances. Two years later, he died. "John was so terribly unhappy," Elaine Barrymore said.

Over twenty years after *My Dear Children* closed, Elaine had an appointment to see Preminger about a part in an upcoming play. "I dreaded the meeting and I knew nothing would come of it. What had happened between us was much too overloaded. When I entered his office he looked me up and down and said, 'You're getting fat.' But when he spoke of his young wife and showed me photos of his two young children, you could feel he was human. His feelings for his new family were genuine, and I couldn't help liking him after all."[47] (Elaine Barrymore, who died in New York in 2003 at eighty-nine, never remarried. Photos of her husband, the man she had never stopped loving, lined the walls of her modest studio apartment on East Fifty-seventh Street.)

While Barrymore had been cutting up on the road, Otto was in New York reading through dozens of scripts. The one that he decided on as his next project was *Margin for Error,* a play by Clare Boothe set in the New

York office of the German consul, a Nazi. Otto had no trouble persuading his partners, Aldrich and Myers, to coproduce. He felt the script needed work, however. He generally liked Act I, in which Boothe sets up the Nazi consul as the kind of character everyone in the show has a motive for killing; and at the end of the act, under mysterious circumstances, the odious German is bumped off. Act II is an investigation of the murder conducted by a Jewish policeman (were there ever any?). When the crime is finally solved, to everyone's relief the killer is not prosecuted. Otto felt that the second act needed extensive surgery. Boothe agreed to work with him and while Aldrich and Myers were often on the road ministering to John Barrymore, she met with the director every afternoon in his suite at the St. Regis.

At first the collaboration was amicable, with the playwright following a number of Otto's suggestions. Most days Boothe's husband, Henry Luce, the founder of *Time* and *Life,* joined them for dinner. But relations between Preminger and the writer were destined to turn sour. Trumball Barton, who was Otto's secretary at the time, remembered Boothe as being "very grand, and just like Otto she wanted to do things her own way. She really didn't like Otto very much, but then she didn't like anybody very much."

As he took his morning bath, Otto would dictate daily script changes to Barton.

He always called me "Trambull," and I always called him "Dr. Preminger." In his bath he would also give me his orders for the day. He was always very clear about what he wanted. With Otto there was never, never, any doubt or hesitation, just the way it was with Clare Boothe: that's why trouble started. When she wouldn't budge about a point in the script where he was sure he was right and she was wrong, Otto began to yell. I dismissed his temper—a lot of that was a put-on, he'd lose it to make a theatrical impact, and he would cope by laughing at his temper. He paid me five dollars a week, but he would take me to dinners and sometimes to shows, and through him I met Miss Garbo. Oh, he could be charming: devastatingly so. Bending low, he'd kiss my mother's hand. He was colorful. And Marion was *very* exotic. She'd come swanning out of their bedroom dressed in an expensive robe, and she often wore a sailor's coat. But he was a terrible man with the women, a devil really, and so seductive in that Continental way he had. He was crazy about women, but he wasn't crazy about Boothe: who could be?[48]

Despite the changes Boothe had made, when rehearsals started Otto remained dissatisfied with Act II. Publicly he was polite to the playwright, hoping to persuade her to agree to further alterations. But he began to lash out at some of the cast. "He took a violent turn against a young actress," as Trumball Barton recalled. "He would just yell and scream at her in front of the entire company. I supposed at the time that she had turned him down. He also screamed at Sam Levene [who played the Jewish policeman], but when Levene yelled back, Otto backed down." Levene also made Preminger laugh—a sure recipe for putting paid to an Otto tantrum. "They became friends," Barton noted.[49]

During the second week of rehearsals, the actor playing the German consul, whom Otto had known in Vienna, suddenly departed. "Dear Otto, I'm going home to rejoin Adolf. Love, Rudolf Forster," he informed his director.[50]

Preminger quickly read a number of actors for the role, but, as he noted, "There seemed to be a shortage of Nazis in New York at the time."[51] When Clare Boothe suggested that Otto himself play the part, a resounding "No!" was his initial response. He hadn't acted since he was nineteen and he no longer thought of himself as a performer. Boothe persisted, assuring him that no one else in New York could possibly be as effective in the role. Preminger relented, no doubt realizing the publicity value of his doing double duty. "It is not precisely without precedent that a director should also act a part, but by no means common," the *Brooklyn Daily Eagle* reported on October 22, 1939. "A product of the finest theatres of Europe . . . Otto Ludwig Preminger is satisfied with no halfway measures. [For the role] he had his hair [*sic*] clipped in the best Prussian tradition, went to a make-up expert to take up such matters as putting a scar on his face, and bought a monocle."

Preminger informed Boothe that he would play the consul on Broadway only if he received good notices in the out-of-town tryouts. As it happened, he got raves, while for good reason reviewers were less sanguine about the play itself. When Preminger attempted to address persistent second-act problems, Boothe no longer even pretended to listen. "Oh, there were rows," Barton recalled. "And this time Otto was not putting on an act. He was really mad. He yelled at her, but it did no good."[52] "I told her what I thought of her unprofessional arrogant behavior," Preminger said. "But she had apparently given up on her play."[53]

As *My Dear Children* was wending its way across the country in advance of its scheduled Broadway opening in January 1940, *Margin for Error,* directed by and starring Otto Preminger, opened in New York on November 2, 1939. Second-act knots were still in place, but Preminger's acting was praised. "Barring a certain monotony of attack, Mr. Preminger plays an excellent, bald-headed, wrinkle-necked villain. His [German consul] is the

Preminger in his Broadway acting debut in *Margin for Error* as the
Nazi consul, a shiny-domed villain.

most odious character on any New York stage at the moment," Brooks
Atkinson observed in his *New York Times* review.

As a piece of theater carpentry *Margin for Error* has even less merit than
My Dear Children. Because Clare Boothe's thematic stakes, however, are
much higher than the harmless trifle concocted for John Barrymore, her
failure is much greater. Boothe wrote the play as an anti-isolationist battle
cry; and when it was presented in 1939, before America had entered the war,
her work had a certain propaganda value. But Boothe's thin, smart-aleck
writing, her drawing room quips, and her sub-vaudevillian treatment of the
Jewish policeman (Yiddish shtick clumsily conceived by a Gentile) are
grotesquely mismatched to the gravity of her subject. *Margin for Error* is
arrogantly trivial.

Nonetheless, for Preminger, the play was good news. His vivid, comic-
opera Nazi turned him into a bona fide Broadway celebrity, a new status
that gave him a platform from which to make serious comments about
events in Europe. And in interviews after the opening he spoke with a

rhetorical power nowhere to be found in Boothe's manufactured playmaking. "The Nazis are a sardonic jest of cosmic proportions, the Gargantuan gag of the ages, and the incredibly cruel joke is on the world," he announced in a November 29, 1939, interview in the *New York Post*. "The great tragedy of Germany is that German youth is being turned into a giant band of nihilists," he continued. "Superficially, we regard 1939 as the start of the war, but actually, there has been war on the continent since 1914. . . . One thing is certain . . . Europe is committing suicide."

A week after *Margin for Error* opened, Preminger was offered a teaching position at the Yale School of Drama. And in addition to performing eight shows a week and overseeing Barrymore in *My Dear Children,* Otto began to commute twice a week to Yale to lecture on directing and acting. His social life continued at a robust pace as well, and he remained a frequent patron, sometimes with Marion, sometimes solo, at most of Manhattan's elite nightspots.

Preminger was certainly busy, but in artistic heft his résumé came up short. *My Dear Children* was the swan song of a fallen star; *Outward Bound* and *Margin for Error* were claptrap. Shows like these could not sustain the illusion of "young European genius" that was still attached to Preminger's name. Where were the brilliantly reimagined classic dramas? Where were the pathbreaking new plays directed with a rigor that would justify Preminger's wünderkind label? Where, in short, was evidence of "genius"? What Preminger's track record so far clearly enough indicated was that, as he had proven in Hollywood, he could conform to the rules of the game. There was no question of his competence and his ability to handle difficult personalities. But there was also no hint that he was more than a journeyman laborer in the commercial theater. His next four plays would only reinforce that impression.

After *Margin for Error* closed on Broadway (its 264-performance run, judged by the standards of the day, represented a moderate success), Preminger re-created his role on the strawhat circuit in the summer of 1940. The tour was less an artistic comedown than a financial necessity. While on the road Otto looked for a show to produce and direct on Broadway the following season. Was it merely by chance that he chose a script about bad behavior in Hollywood? *Beverly Hills,* cowritten by Lynn Starling and Howard J. Green, presents the movie colony as a Darwinian organism composed of petty, greedy, oversexed scavengers. Darryl Zanuck's name is taken in vain, along with those of Elsa Maxwell, Louella Parsons, Hedda Hopper, and many others. Otto enjoyed rehearsals because of two of his actresses. Ilka Chase, a specialist in playing catty characters, had the leading role, that of an ambitious wife who schemes to land a screenwriting job for her namby-pamby husband. Trumball Barton claimed that "Otto was having a heavy affair with Ilka, who was oh so wicked, and quite, quite charming."[54] The other actress Otto fell for, but in a different way, was the delightful Doro Merande, who was to have a long career playing snippy spinsters and gossips. Merande, who in *Beverly Hills* played a long-suffering nurse to two Hollywood brats, touched Otto's funny bone; onstage and off she made him laugh and over the years he was to cast her in many small, juicy roles.

Beverly Hills opened to poisonous notices on November 7, 1940. The show expired after twenty-eight performances, but Preminger already had another project in place for the same season. As he prepared his new show, he continued to teach at Yale for a second year; he also became a popular lecturer at women's clubs, where his savoir faire (lots of hand kissing and courteous phrases uttered in his spicy accent), his quick-wittedness, and his erudition were appreciated. *Cue for Passion* by Edward Chodorov and H. S. Kraft was a whodunit littered, like *Beverly Hills,* with particularly ornery characters. The premise: a tart-tongued columnist tries to disguise as a suicide the murder of her disagreeable husband, a celebrated novelist. Rehearsals went suspiciously well. Then on December 16, 1940, three days before the play was scheduled to open at the Royale Theatre, Otto received a bombshell from a lawyer, Louis Nizer.

> I was calling to tell Otto that he could not proceed with the production. The two principal characters, a columnist and a Nobel Prize–winning novelist, were not named but in the way they were described it was about as difficult to guess who they were as it would have been to answer the question, who fought the Spanish-American War? Clearly the characters were based on Dorothy Thompson, the only famous female columnist in those days, and her husband at the time, Sinclair Lewis. Dorothy was a friend and at that time also a client and she was outraged that she and Sinclair Lewis should be identified in a murder mystery. She pleaded with me to get an injunction.[55]

When Nizer called, Preminger was "flabbergasted" and asked if there was any way to avoid the injunction. Nizer suggested as the only possible remedy "changing the play so that it is the same play without the identification, even indirectly, of the two principal characters." Otto, as Nizer remembered, was "delighted" at the idea. When they met for the first time that night the two men took an immediate liking to each other as they

Directing Frank Albertson and Grace Macdonald in *The More the Merrier.*

worked till dawn scrubbing the play of any obvious references to Thompson or Lewis. The hastily revised play opened on schedule, on December 19, 1940, received middling reviews, and closed twelve days later. But Preminger and Nizer had started a friendship that endured for the rest of their lives.

Throughout the spring of 1941, Preminger issued a stream of press releases about upcoming projects, all of them to sink without a ripple. In the summer he was back on the summer stock circuit, this time appearing as Professor Metz with Moss Hart in the beloved comedy by Hart and George S. Kaufman, *The Man Who Came to Dinner.* That summer Otto for the last time also reprised his signature role in *Margin for Error.* By the end of the summer Preminger had two shows lined up for the new season.

The More the Merrier, a murder melodrama laced with farce, was about a Colorado newspaper tycoon who wants to be elected governor as a first step toward running for the presidency—until a corpse is discovered in his mansion. It opened on September 15 and closed after sixteen performances.

Preminger thought he could reverse his string of bad luck with his next play, *In Time to Come,* an ambitious drama about President Wilson's fight for peace cowritten by Howard Koch and John Huston. But when the show opened on December 28, 1941, a scant three weeks after the Japanese attack on Pearl Harbor had led to America's belated entry into World War II, its implicitly antiwar sentiment was mistimed. *In Time to Come* closed after forty performances.

As always seemed to be the case, whenever he needed a break Otto got one. Nunnally Johnson, a Hollywood writer impressed by Preminger's performance in *Margin for Error,* called to ask if he would be interested in playing another Nazi, in a film called *The Pied Piper* that Johnson was writing and producing. Based on a novel by Nevil Shute, the story was set in France in June 1940 on the eve of the advancing German occupation. Otto accepted on the spot. He certainly needed the money, but far more important was the fact that the film was to be made by Twentieth Century-Fox, the studio that he had been banished from. A fainter-hearted man might have had some qualms about revisiting the scene of his "crime," but not Otto. Even though Darryl Zanuck was not running the studio—after Pearl Harbor he had joined the Army and was in London overseeing training films—when Otto reported to Twentieth Century-Fox in the early spring of 1942 he was not expecting to remain in Hollywood. He rented a small furnished apartment, a bachelor's pad, while Marion stayed on in New York at the St. Regis.

On the set, Otto, who knew he was being watched, was a model citizen, following Irving Pichel's direction without a single grimace or raised eyebrow. He also knew his reemergence at Fox was newsworthy, and he agreed to every request for an interview. "I think these Nazi roles do something to help defeat the Germans, because the more the people dislike my Nazi portrayals the harder they will work against the real enemy," Otto offered, adding that "for a gentle soul like me, playing heavies is a form of release."[56]

In *The Pied Piper* a British fuddy-duddy (Monty Woolley), "too old to be employed in the war," as he says, is forced to lead a group of dispossessed children across Nazi-infested France to safety in England. Prevented by German soldiers from entering the boat that will carry them across the Channel, they are taken to the large office of a Major Diessen, the ranking Nazi: Otto, seated at a desk beneath a large swastika, his bald pate gleaming, his nostrils flaring, his lips curled disdainfully. However, in this sentimental Hollywood confection designed to soothe rather than agitate wartime American audiences, it turns out that the Nazi has a heart. "Could my niece find refuge in America?" Major Diessen, a concerned uncle, asks. "In Amer-

Another Preminger Nazi, this one with a heart: Major Diessen in
The Pied Piper.

ica, I don't believe they'd turn down any child, even a German one," the
pied piper answers, endorsing the film's idealized version of the American
Way. The Nazi's about-face is absurdly abrupt, and Otto isn't a resourceful
enough actor to be able to make it convincing.

After collecting a sizable salary for his work, Preminger was preparing to
return to New York when he received a call from his agent, Ned Marin,
informing him that Fox wanted him to reprise his role of Karl Baumen in
the upcoming film of *Margin for Error.* Marin assured him of star billing

and a generous paycheck, but Otto hesitated. Taking on another Nazi role, he realized, would be useful only for the short haul; and as he would often quip in the coming years, explaining his retirement from acting, "How many Nazis can you play?" What he wanted, and what he sensed might be attainable, was the chance to return to directing. Ernst Lubitsch was set to direct, and in an April 15 letter to his friend, the prominent Hollywood agent Paul Kohner, Otto asked Kohner to offer his services as an artistic adviser on the film. "Since I played the role 300 times and know how each scene works, I could be of help to Lubitsch."[57] After Lubitsch, having second thoughts about the script, withdrew, Otto moved into high gear. He went directly to Charles Feldman, the head of the agency Marin worked for, demanding to know why he couldn't be trusted to direct material that he had handled successfully on Broadway. Feldman dismissed the idea, reminding Preminger that Zanuck's decree against him as a director was still in force. Feldman tried to impress on Preminger the fact that he was lucky to have been offered any kind of Hollywood job. Otto, not in a grateful mood, refused to back off. He took his case to the top: to William Goetz, Louis B. Mayer's son-in-law, who was running Fox in Zanuck's absence. Before his meeting with Goetz, Charles Feldman warned Preminger that there was no chance he would be hired as a director and that he should be content with an acting job. But bowing and scraping was hardly Otto's style. He sensed that Goetz was malleable, and he also calculated that in any showdown with Goetz, Preminger rather than Goetz would be the likely victor. When Goetz spurned his offer to direct, Otto persisted, presenting Goetz with a creative counteroffer: he would direct the film for free, and if at the end of the first week Goetz was unhappy with the dailies, Preminger would step down as director but stay on to play the role of the German consul. Operating in cutthroat mode, Otto was counting on his hunch that Goetz might hire him, a known enemy of Zanuck, as a way of declaring his independence from Zanuck. (Before his departure for the Army, Zanuck had treated Goetz condescendingly.)

Goetz took the bait. And when he called the morning after the meeting to tell Otto that he was accepting his offer, Otto knew his fortunes had changed. After eight disappointing years in America, during which he had been banned from Hollywood and seen his prospects in the theater dwindle, Preminger realized he had finally won the opportunity to turn himself into a Hollywood insider, a full-blown American success.

THREE

Seizing the Day

"It was awful," Preminger said about the screenplay of *Margin for Error* that Fox was planning to film.[1] He was certain that if he shot the script he had been handed his second chance in Hollywood would fizzle. At his own expense and without the knowledge of the film's inexperienced producer, Ralph Dietrich, Otto hired a writer to help rework the entire script. Lucky Otto found a novice named Samuel Fuller, at the moment on leave from the Army, who was to write and direct a series of idiosyncratic low-budget films that were to earn him the admiration first of French and then of American cinephiles. Fuller, with his omnipresent cigar and guttural voice, was a quirky tough guy who shared Darryl Zanuck's taste for hard-boiled pulp fiction. The screenwriter and his employer would appear to have had nothing in common except their hair-trigger tempers. Yet they worked together in the summer of 1942 without a hint of friction.

"I remember Fuller in uniform used to come to the little apartment I had on El Camino Drive," Preminger recalled. "I remember seeing him from the window arriving in his car carrying a huge typewriter. I didn't pay him much."[2] Preminger and Fuller realized the material needed a new framework—onstage in 1939 *Margin for Error* had been a call to arms; in 1942 it had to be recast as a morale booster for a country at war with an evil empire. The cowriters decided to present the story as a flashback set before America's entry into the war, narrated by the Jewish policeman, representing

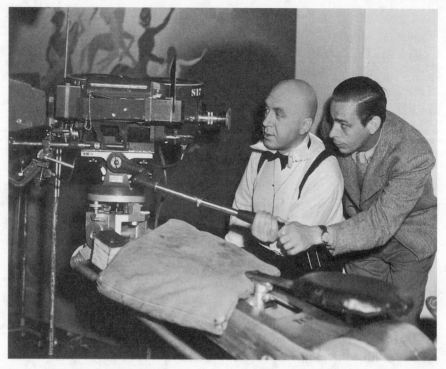

Directing *Margin for Error* (with unidentified man).

in word and deed the spirit of American democracy. In either version, however, the disproportion between history and fable was in bad taste.

It isn't clear whether Ralph Dietrich or William Goetz ever became
aware of Preminger's covert operation. Once shooting started, on September 28, 1942, Goetz, like Zanuck, viewed the dailies each night; but he
revealed nothing to Preminger about his assessment of their quality. As
agreed, at the end of the first week Goetz summoned Otto to his office to
render his decision. Otto knew this was a make-or-break meeting. If Goetz
gave him the go-ahead, he had a chance at a Hollywood career as a filmmaker. If Goetz was displeased and took him off the picture, word would
spread quickly, and he was likely to be washed up: the European "genius"
twice fired by studio chieftains. Uncharacteristically, Otto was worried.
Although he felt the first week's shooting had gone well, walking into the
meeting he thought he was going to be axed. Goetz, however, announced he
was pleased with Otto's dailies; moreover, he offered Preminger a seven-year
contract calling on his services as both director and actor. An emboldened
Preminger, taking full measure of the temporary studio czar and realizing he

had won him over, asked for, and received, a clause that gave him producing rights as well. "I felt it was very difficult for a director to get along if he didn't produce his own film. This contract, with certain changes, was the contract I worked under (except that I always got more and more money) until I left Fox to become an independent producer."[3]

"Five years ago Otto Preminger left Fox under the kind of cloud which hovers only over directors whose pictures have not been fringed with gold," Virginia Wright wrote in an article in the *Los Angeles Daily News* on October 12, 1942. "Today Otto Preminger is holder of a Fox contract that acknowledges his talents as actor/producer/director. Goetz offered him a contract before *Error* was completed, and Otto Preminger added a clause that he be allowed to present *The Seventh Cross* on Broadway."

Contract in hand, Preminger completed production on schedule, on November 5. Although the original budget was $321,753, the final budget was a little higher, $379,489—the increased expenditure was standard operating practice at the studio and no reflection on Preminger's efficiency. When the film was released on February 10, 1943, reviews were dismissive. "The timing has been bad with *Margin for Error*," Howard Barnes wrote in

Otto's Nazi consul in *Margin for Error* fixes his unhappy wife (Joan Bennett) with a sadistic leer.

the *New York Herald Tribune.* "Three years ago, the anti-Nazi accents of a tricky murder mystery made it something of a stage event. At this point it is remote and even a bit ridiculous. . . . Both in his acting and staging, Otto Preminger holds the piece to a ponderous pace."

Preminger's direction, to be sure, is lackluster. His static approach fails to reconceive the stage-bound material in cinematic terms, and as a director of actors he seems all but helpless. He was unable to wean Joan Bennett, who plays the consul's wife, from zombielike paralysis, or to smooth the coarse edges of Milton Berle's strictly Borscht Belt approach to the policeman-narrator. And in directing himself he was equally uninspired: his Nazi is a dead-eyed, one-trick pony barking his lines in a monotone.

In a career spiked with good fortune and good timing, Preminger's receiving a pass from William Goetz after seven days' shooting on *Margin for Error* may well have been his luckiest moment. His by-the-numbers direction had earned him not only a go-ahead on the film but a lucrative seven-year contract as well. Why? Preminger himself surmised that in hiring him Goetz was punishing Zanuck, who had treated Goetz as a mere care-taker, a second-rate interloper. That may have been true, but it may also have been possible that Goetz was not a shrewd critic; unlike Zanuck, Goetz had no creative instincts or ambitions, and he may genuinely have felt that Otto's first-week dailies represented solid work. Like Zanuck, in fact, he may have regarded the *absence* of temperament in Preminger's direction as proof of Otto's willingness to adhere to the style expected of a contract director. Although stillborn and deservedly forgotten, *Margin for Error* is a crucial work in Preminger's career: it's the movie that got him back into the business.

After finishing the film, Otto summoned Marion from the St. Regis. He moved out of his apartment on El Camino and with Marion relocated to a baronial house at 333 Bel-Air Road, located in a colony of other German-speaking refugees doing well in Hollywood. His immediate neighbors were Ernst Lubitsch and writer Walter Reisch. Among the expatriates there was a round of dressy dinners and cocktail parties and, on Sunday afternoons, informal coffee klatches most often hosted by Reisch. "Marion took a passionate interest in these events and returned our social obligations with imaginative flair," Preminger recalled.[4] Otto encouraged his wife's party giving at least in part because he did not want her to pursue an acting career. "He said I had no talent, and that I established no connection with the audience," Marion was to recall in her autobiography. "I accepted his judgment, even though I could not believe this was true. Today, when I am the most booked woman lecturer in the United States, and have been called by all the women's organizations of the country, 'The Platform Sensation of America,' I know how wrong he was."[5]

Marion's parties were also compensation for another agreement the couple had struck: Otto was free to go out with other women so long as Marion could retain the name of Mrs. Otto Preminger and the appearance of having a stable marriage. Since Otto conducted his affairs with discretion, the arrangement was to endure for some years after his reinstatement in Hollywood. Otto professed to be bored by the unending social rituals, but his skill and Marion's in working a room was a great help in reclaiming his place in the film community.

"I began to learn about Hollywood protocol, which is stricter than pro-

Otto with his wife Marion on the town in Hollywood, early 1940s.

tocol in Washington," Marion observed. "Directors outrank writers and artists. Producers outrank directors. Executives form an unchallenged aristocracy. Stars may be sprinkled through all three ranks, but always with strict regard to their box office value and to the importance of their lovers."[6]

The still-standing house at 333 Bel-Air Road from which the Premingers launched their comeback emanates prestige. Behind a gate a formal garden slopes down to a Tudor-style mansion. An oversized wood-carved front door confronts the visitor with mock-medieval grandeur. As Marion reported, the entrance hall led to "a little salon which I furnished in French Empire pieces which formerly had belonged to the Archduke Francis Ferdinand who was murdered at Sarajevo." In the salon hung a painting of the school of Boucher that "showed a lady in a white crinoline swinging in a rose bower and losing her slipper which an adoring cavalier stood ready to catch." Next came a salon in which everything was gray, "including the piano. It looked divine, and a part of the room—as so many pianos do not." The sole painting in the gray salon was "a small exquisite Renoir . . . a nude woman seated on a red carpet." Two large Cocteau paintings "let into mirrors" encircled "the only dining-room in America with two tables—one for the host, one for the hostess," Marion boasted. "On gala occasions the tables had gold lamé cloths, and the napkins were of gold satin, and each was decorated with a tiny yellow orchid. One must have two butlers to serve dinner in this fashion, and a major domo in the center of the room to direct them," as Marion pointed out. The walls of the adjoining bar were decorated with murals depicting scenes from the life of the hostess. "The dinners and luncheons I gave became talked about and were always written up in the press," claimed Mrs. Otto Preminger, on her way to becoming Hollywood's premier "hostess with the mostess."

The bedrooms were also designed as stage sets. In the master bedroom were exquisitely bound rare books, two Rodin watercolors of dancers, and a royalty-sized bed made of leather with two matching leather chairs. In one corner was a table from a medieval church sacristy (an odd point of pride for a woman rumored to have been born Jewish) on which were placed lamps of seventeenth-century globes. All the textiles in the room were of the finest silk made to match the leather, "the color of old parchment." The house had twenty "perfumed" telephones. Marion's private phone emitted a gardenia scent while the other nineteen phones released the less rarefied aroma of pine. Despite the mise-en-scène, Marion claimed that she was not happy in the house, nor was she able to reverse the neighborhood rumor that 333 "had a curse on it."[7]

In offering these descriptions of her House Beautiful ("it was all mine, and expressed my personality") Marion, according to Otto, was up to her usual embroidery. "Not a single room or piece of furniture [in her account] is recognizable," he asserted. "She speaks of white carpets. They did not exist. She says we had twenty telephones. We had four. She describes a painting by Renoir hanging over the piano. We had a piano but never owned a Renoir."[8] Marion's imaginative house tour nonetheless revealed the fact that, as Mrs. Otto Preminger, she was a far more accomplished performer than her husband ever gave her credit for. And at this turning point in Otto's career, when he was still chafing under Zanuck's fatwa, Marion with her vivacity and her almost childlike desire to be admired was a valuable partner.

After finishing *Margin for Error* and before getting another directing assignment at Fox, Otto was hired by Sam Goldwyn to appear as—what else?—a Nazi in a 1943 Bob Hope comedy called *They Got Me Covered.* Otto was not eager but recognized that an alliance with Goldwyn might be further ammunition against the day when Zanuck returned from military duty. Preminger made a point of befriending Goldwyn and, on the set, accepted direction from David Butler without a fuss. Like *Margin for Error* and *The Pied Piper, They Got Me Covered,* set in wartime Washington, is a light treatment of a grave topic. A reporter (Bob Hope, playing his usual cowardly, bumbling, fast-talking role) uncovers a ring of Axis spies in Washington hatching plans to blow up the city. Although in historical retrospect a story of enemies working secretly in the nation's capital on a terrorist agenda might seem to have been proscribed subject matter for a comedy, evidently this was not the case at the time. The war taking place when the film was made is used as a backdrop for a divertissement in which Hope's American ingenuity triumphs over a nest of Nazi vipers. Otto, of course, is cast as the head Nazi, named Otto Fauscheim. At thirty-nine but looking much closer to fifty-nine, Preminger rolls out his by-now signature Nazi persona, this time in a purely light comedy version. He is given no close-ups or one-shots, yet he is the dominant focus in the group scenes. In this Bob Hope romp, Otto comes off as a good sport, but it is clear that he knows how to intimidate everyone within the sound of his voice.

For the Jewish moguls who ran the film industry, references to the Holocaust, like most issues of Jewish concern and self-identity, were off-limits. Otto Preminger, however, a Jew from a country overtaken by Hitler and a man with a strong social conscience, felt some responsibility to address the subject, and in the summer of 1943 he began to prepare a script that he hoped would refute the industry's silence. *Ambassador Dodd's Diary,* as Preminger explained, is the story of "an American family who goes to

Germany at the beginning of the Hitler regime. It is the story of that family's reactions to the Nazis; it's the story of the rise of the Nazi party, as seen through the eyes of an American family. It will be the first time that all the prominent members of the Nazi party will be presented on the screen."[9] To ensure authenticity Preminger began working with Martha Dodd, the daughter of the former ambassador. Otto regarded the project as a socially responsible work that would also give him the kind of validation he knew he could not attain by being associated with entertainments like *Margin for Error* or *They Got Me Covered.*

Preminger's commitment to the project was sharpened because that summer he was applying for his American citizenship. Unlike many émigrés who grumbled about their new homeland, decrying American taste, manners, and morals, Preminger from the instant of his arrival had been an American enthusiast, a patriot and a booster. He had a profound respect for his new country's democratic government and its guarantee of free speech. And in return for being a vocal supporter of the American Way, Preminger, unlike a number of émigrés in the film community, was to remain untouched in the witch hunt for Communists that Senator Joseph McCarthy was to conduct later in the decade. On August 27, 1943, one of the proudest days of his life, Otto Preminger became an American citizen. Throughout the ceremony, with Marion at his side, he beamed. That night, on the sweeping grounds of 333 Bel-Air Road, the Premingers hosted one of their most bountiful parties.

Otto hoped to get *Ambassador Dodd's Diary* into production before Zanuck returned from armed service, but to his regret he could not persuade Goetz, or anyone else at Fox, to finance the film. Nonetheless, with Goetz's encouragement Otto regularly read books and plays and scripts on file in the story department hoping to find possible properties he could develop before Zanuck came back. Two stories caught his attention. One was an original screenplay by Arthur Kober and Michael Uris called *Army Wives,* with a contemporary wartime setting; the other a suspense novel called *Laura,* by Vera Caspary, set in the kind of New York beau monde Otto had become familiar with during his time at the St. Regis. Goetz quickly gave his approval to both projects.

Preminger was intrigued by the basic premise of Vera Caspary's story: after presumably having been found dead in her apartment, Laura reappears and becomes a prime suspect in a murder case. "That was the good part of the novel," Otto said, claiming that "everything else, including the characters, was newly created for the film."[10] Untrue. The major characters—the detective who investigates the "murder" of the bewitching young woman and who becomes obsessed with her portrait; Laura's older, epicene mentor who wants to control her and is enraged when she threatens to marry a young man—are fully etched in the novel. Also richly depicted is an atmosphere of sexual perversity among the upper crust.

Preminger's reluctance to give proper credit to Caspary may have stemmed from personal antipathy—from the time they first met in New York in the late 1930s their relationship had been rancorous. At that time, Caspary's agent, Monica McCall, offered the first draft of a play called *Ring Twice for Laura* to Preminger, then shopping for theater projects. Preminger responded to the poisoned high-society setting and to the twist of the heroine's surprising reappearance, but felt the working out of the story required major revision. He offered to collaborate with the playwright. "He provided all of his Middle European charm, along with an elegant lunch of blini and caviar," as Vera Caspary recalled. But the two could not agree on how to shape the material. "He wanted to make it a conventional detective story; I saw it as a psychological drama about people involved in a murder. We fell

Vera Caspary, author of the novel *Laura* and no friend to Otto.

out over this and [writer] George Sklar worked with me instead. Marlene Dietrich expressed an interest in playing the title character. This beautiful woman came closer to the independent girl who earned her living and pampered her lovers than anyone who has yet played the part," Caspary recalled. "We wanted her to tour with it. And we were bombarded with rejections. There were no Broadway takers."[11]

After the play script failed to sell, Caspary wrote two novels, *Ring Twice for Laura* and *Laura,* which McCall sent to film studios. Only two showed any interest: Metro-Goldwyn-Mayer, which wanted to turn it into a B mystery "if they could buy the story cheaply enough,"[12] and Fox, which in the end bought the play and the two novels for $30,000. It was at this point that Preminger reentered the *Laura* saga. Remembering their original disagreement, Preminger, as he was developing a screenplay with three writers, Jay Dratler, Samuel Hoffenstein, and Betty Reinhardt, did not welcome any contributions from Caspary. He felt he knew the smart Manhattan milieu at least as well as she, and he was certain he knew far more than she did about what was needed to turn the material into a film. Early decisions suggest his confidence was well founded. In *Laura,* the basic source from which Preminger and his writers were working, Caspary's conceit had been to tell her tale with multiple narrators, each of whom has only a partial perspective. Preminger vetoed the device as too literary for the popular suspense film he was envisioning. Point of view, he realized, would have to be simplified and aligned with the Hollywood convention in which objective, "invisible," third-person narration is always preferable to first-person. And Preminger sensed, correctly, that the most important character was not the mysterious Laura but her mentor, Waldo Lydecker, the imperious, obsessive, decadent dandy who sponsors her rise to prominence in New York society. A homosexual fearful of losing Laura to a heterosexual rival, it is Waldo who has murdered the wrong woman (a weekend guest in Laura's apartment) and who attempts in the end to kill Laura. Working closely with his writers, Otto turned Waldo into the lead.

When he completed a first draft, Preminger invited Vera Caspary to the studio. "It was not a peaceful visit," she remembered. She objected to the way Preminger had worked out the ending, in which Waldo hides the gun he plans to kill Laura with in a baroque standing clock in Laura's apartment.

> In the novel Waldo's gun is hidden in his cane, [Caspary observed]. This is not merely a murder story device . . . but a symbol (Freudian) of Waldo's impotence and destructiveness, actually the theme of the novel. Preminger argued that a gun that could destroy

a woman's face could not possibly have been contained in a walking stick and he said no one would get the symbolism. "Would a man as elegant and self-conscious as Waldo Lydecker, himself an authority on murder . . . be so dumb as to carry a shotgun through the streets of New York on his way to a murder?" Preminger argued.[13]

In this case Caspary was right: the phallic symbolism of the gun concealed in the impotent man's walking stick is revelatory, whereas the ending Preminger proposed is merely a narrative device.

Caspary also felt that Preminger misread her heroine. " 'In the book, Laura has no character and no sex,' Preminger said to me. I howled. 'Then why did she have to pay a gigolo?' he asked. I could have been struck down by an inch of celluloid. 'Laura gives everything with her love. Perhaps you don't know anything about love, Mr. Preminger?' I said, and made a haughty exit."[14]

Just after finishing the first-draft screenplay, Otto received word that Zanuck was about to return to work. At his own request Zanuck had been on leave from the studio since April 29, 1942; on May 31, 1943, again at his own request, he asked to be released back to civilian duty and was planning to report to Fox at the end of July. Goetz resigned, but would remain at the studio over the summer to finish up several projects. Goetz had taken the job knowing it was to be only on an interim basis, but as Louis B. Mayer's son-in-law and astute in the ways of front office politics, he did not think of himself as either a caretaker or a mere functionary. His hiring of Preminger behind Zanuck's back was one indication that he was determined to be his own man; his complete refurbishing of Zanuck's office, from which every trace of Zanuck's favored green had been removed, was another. Goetz in fact was an able superintendent, a businessman who focused on contracts and internal organization while leaving creative decisions to others. Under his watch, Twentieth Century-Fox did not lose money. (After he left Fox, Goetz, backed by his father-in-law, founded International Pictures, which would merge with Universal, as Twentieth Century had combined with Fox.)

On his return Zanuck lost no time reclaiming his power. His first order of business was to condemn the entire slate of films Goetz had overseen in his absence. The Goetz-era films, he contended, "would make the public vomit . . . if we make the mistake of showing them."[15] With Goetz gone and Zanuck reinstated, Preminger suddenly was on shaky ground. When the mogul ordered him to his beachfront house in Santa Monica, Otto knew he would be facing an adversary far cagier and far more ruthless than Goetz. As he was driving along Wilshire Boulevard to the showdown with Zanuck, Otto tried to prepare himself for the worst. He was certain he was going to be banned once again, his hopes for *Laura* and for a major career smashed by a vengeful czar's need to reassert his omnipotence. Arriving at Zanuck's house, Otto was escorted by a butler out to the pool, where Zanuck sat with his back turned to his anxious visitor. Without getting up from his low-lying lounge chair, he issued a decree. "I see you are working on a few things. I don't think much of them except for one, *Laura.* I've read it and it isn't bad. You can produce it but as long as I am at Fox you will never direct. Good-bye."[16] Speaking to his host's back Preminger claimed to have uttered his own "good-bye" in a tone as deadpan as Zanuck's. Leaving quickly, Otto was immensely relieved. He would still be on the studio payroll, after all, and he would have a producer's credit on a film he was sure would be successful.

Although it makes a compelling narrative, one that Preminger always relished telling, the poolside meeting with Zanuck cannot have transpired exactly as Preminger claimed. Yes, Zanuck did grant Preminger permission to produce *Laura,* but at the same time he also gave Preminger the green light on his other project, *Army Wives.* And on this minor film he was allowing Preminger to direct as well as produce. Far from having to fight his way back to directing, then, Otto was "forgiven" almost as soon as Zanuck had returned to the studio. He would produce as well as direct *Army Wives,* and at the same time he would continue working on the screenplay of *Laura,* which he would produce but not direct. As both producer *and* director, Otto Preminger was back in business.

Both assignments were for the B unit, run by Byrnie Foy, as diffident a boss as his predecessor Sol Wurtzel. Like Wurtzel, Foy didn't bother to read scripts and had no desire to be a hands-on creative producer in the DFZ mold. Foy was a company functionary with his eye on the bottom line. Assignment to the B's did not diminish Otto's enthusiasm, however: he had two projects to engage him, and after all he had managed to contradict the Cassandras. Zanuck had rescinded his ban against him.

He prepared and filmed *Army Wives* first. As he recalled, it was "a small story I had acquired before *Laura;* then it stuck with me and I had to do it, a minor film."[17] He had no illusions about the importance of the material. Yet the setting, a U.S. Army camp, and the story's homespun patriotism—the film is a morale booster for a country at war that celebrates the sacrifices made by women as they send their husbands off to the front—appealed to Otto, a newly naturalized American citizen. He regarded the film as an expression of gratitude to his new country.

Jeanne Crain as a spoiled young woman who has a lot to learn in Preminger's wartime morale booster, *In the Meantime, Darling*.

Otto had no firsthand experience with the subject—as Willi Frischauer asked, "What did Preminger know of life in the American army? He had never worn a uniform except the Nazi insignia on stage and screen."[18] But he responded to the heroine, Maggie Preston, a spoiled young newlywed from a wealthy family who learns to overcome a bad case of noblesse oblige and by the end is ready to participate in the common cause. The film was a showcase for Jeanne Crain, an actress the studio was grooming for A-list stardom. To her foreign director, Crain's wholesome, beauty queen veneer (her other vehicle the same year was *Home in Indiana*) had an exotic appeal. Otto handled her gently, appreciating her serene temperament, her lack of inner fire—exactly the quality that was to drive Elia Kazan to distraction in 1950 when he directed Crain as a light-skinned Negro in *Pinky*. While his relations with his star were unblemished (he was to work with Crain, happily, on two later films), he had a significant blowup with the actor who played Crain's father, gravel-voiced, portly Eugene Pallette, one of Fox's stable of reliable character actors. Preminger claimed Pallette was "an admirer of Hitler and convinced that Germany would win the war." As if that weren't enough, Pallette refused to sit down at the same table with a black actor in a scene set in a kitchen. "You're out of your mind," he hissed at Preminger. "I won't sit next to a nigger." Infuriated, Preminger canceled production for the day, and informed Zanuck, who fired the actor, most of whose scenes had already been shot. "We wrote him out of what was left," Preminger recalled.[19]

Preminger began shooting *Army Wives* on December 20, 1943, and wrapped on March 7, 1944—a longer-than-usual schedule for a modestly budgeted (about $450,000) B movie. Given a new, meaningless title, *In the Meantime, Darling,* the film opened on September 22, 1944, a month before *Laura.* The film is conservative Hollywood propaganda, which, in effect, defines the "proper" roles for women and men during wartime, and it would be silly to make too much of it. But it is directed with a far greater fluency than Preminger's previous films. And it is suffused with good will.

Perhaps because little was at stake, Preminger found producing and directing *In the Meantime, Darling* easy on his nerves. Producing *Laura,* in contrast, was filled with hurdles. His first obstacle was Byrnie Foy, who hadn't read the script but was prepared to table it on the recommendation of his chief reader, who had reported, "This is not suspense; it's not a thriller. There is not one scene with the police. It has got to be completely rewritten." Otto cajoled Foy into reading the screenplay. "After all, I get $1500 a week, and your reader gets only $50," Preminger argued. The next day Foy informed Otto that after reading the script he was prepared to support his reader's opinion: the material was not worthy and they would be shelving it. Otto of course would not retreat. Moreover, assessing his opponent closely as he always did, Preminger was convinced he could clobber Foy. He insisted that Foy send the script to Zanuck; Foy countered that he wouldn't do that because he was certain Zanuck would reject anything Otto would submit. He urged Preminger to play it safe, to bide his time, to collect his paychecks, and "maybe we'll even pick up your option."[20] Foy's plea confirmed his decency—in his own way he was trying to protect Otto—as well as his second-rateness. It also revealed his critical misreading of both Preminger and Darryl Zanuck.

Finally yielding under Preminger's insistence, Foy agreed to send the script to Zanuck. A few days later Zanuck called them to his office (restored to its original green). Cigar and croquet mallet in place, and clearly prepared to play "DFZ" to the hilt, he began by asking Foy his opinion of the script. The unwary subaltern, not quick enough in interpreting the signals and trying to protect his pal (he and Otto played gin rummy together), said it was not a viable property but that Preminger was in no way to blame. As Zanuck began grilling Foy as to why he didn't like the script, Foy became flustered. "It turned out he really hadn't read the script to the end," as Otto recalled, and as he must have suspected all along. Drawing himself up to his full height, Zanuck informed Foy that he thought the script was "potentially terrific," and that he was upgrading the project to the A unit and would be supervising the film himself. Preminger, he informed Foy, would remain as producer but now would report to him rather than Foy. "It was a great victory," Otto recalled.[21]

Once he came on board, Zanuck began to function as a script doctor. "The only chance this picture has of becoming a big-time success is if these characters emerge as real outstanding personalities," he wrote Preminger in an early memo. "Otherwise it will become nothing more than a blown-up whodunit."[22] Zanuck had sharp insights about how each of the principal characters should be developed. The title character, who he felt in the present version was "flat and uninspired," should "come into the story like a breath of spring, like something out of this world. . . . Where the others are Park Avenue cutthroats she should be as fresh as a child." "There ought to be more of Cagney about the detective [Mark]," he urged. He felt that Waldo should speak with "the biting flavor of the man who came to dinner" and be "likable and charming so that Mark can tolerate having him around." Zanuck had one (wrong-headed) idea for Waldo that smacked of his pulp-fiction background: the character should be a secret morphine addict with "subtle hints of this secret vice" used to prepare the audience for "the revelation of Waldo as the murderer."[23]

Although he worked well with Preminger on the script and even though Preminger at the time was directing *In the Meantime, Darling,* Zanuck was not willing to appoint Otto as the director of an A-list project. It was Preminger's bittersweet responsibility as producer of *Laura* to find a director. Yet no one on the lot appeared to be interested. It may have been that a number of contract directors shied away from the project because of Preminger, whose place in the studio pecking order was not yet clear—he was still widely viewed as the man Zanuck had exiled. Preminger was grateful when Lewis Milestone's turndown took the form of a generous note to Zanuck: "Preminger probably knows what to do with the script. He should direct it; I won't." Finally, Rouben Mamoulian, although he did not particularly care for the characters or the milieu, reluctantly accepted the assignment. "He wanted the money" was Preminger's unsporting estimation.[24]

Mamoulian, who could be as high-handed as Otto, also had a troubled history with Zanuck, having clashed with him during the production of *The Mark of Zorro* in 1940. Born to wealth (his father was a bank president) in Russia in 1898, Mamoulian was raised in Paris and then trained for the stage at the Moscow Art Theater, where he became a protégé of Vakhtangov, a Stanislavski disciple. For the Theatre Guild Mamoulian had directed the original play of *Porgy* in 1927 and the landmark Gershwin folk opera, *Porgy and Bess,* in 1935. In March 1943, only a few months before Otto approached him about *Laura,* he had directed another important Broadway musical, Rodgers and Hammerstein's *Oklahoma!* In film his track record was equally distinguished. With their fluent use of a mobile camera, Mamoulian's *Applause* (1929) and *City Streets* (1931) had none of the rigor mortis that afflicted most early sound films. His *Love Me Tonight* (1932), with a sparkling score by Rodgers and Hart, swirling camera movement, and intermittent rhyming dialogue, remains to this day one of the most inventive of all musical films. Mamoulian directed Garbo's exquisite performance in *Queen Christina* (1934) and the beautifully designed *Becky Sharp* (1935), the first three-color Technicolor movie made in Hollywood. For Mamoulian, *Laura* would seem to have been the right project at the right time.

Once he accepted the job, however, Mamoulian began to misbehave. "Ignoring" his producer, as Preminger bitterly recalled, Mamoulian began to rewrite the script. Although Preminger had no complaint about the two young contract players, Gene Tierney and Dana Andrews, whom Zanuck and Mamoulian had hired for the romantic leads, he balked at their choice for Waldo: Laird Cregar, who had just made a splash playing Jack the Ripper in *The Lodger* (1943). In a private meeting with Zanuck, Otto said, "Look, this whole thing is wrong if you have Laird Cregar. You must have a man who either is unknown or has never played heavies before."[25] Preminger argued that if the audience could immediately identify Waldo as the villain, which he felt they would with Cregar in the role, suspense and ambivalence—exactly the qualities Otto and his writers had striven for— would be sacrificed. Zanuck was not persuaded.

Violating studio protocol and acting daringly, since he was still working in a kind of limbo, Preminger bypassed Zanuck and tentatively offered the part to an actor he knew would be ideal for it: Clifton Webb, then appearing at the Biltmore Theatre in downtown Los Angeles in Noël Coward's *Blithe Spirit.* Unlike Cregar, Webb was not a known film personality. He had made a few forgettable appearances in silent pictures of the mid-1920s, but film audiences hadn't seen him since; he had achieved his success on the stage, mostly in musical comedies and revues. Preminger's choice of Webb to play Waldo Lydecker was inspired: with a large, pointed nose that seemed to twitch in perpetual disapproval, and a voice lined with upper-crust refinement and world-weariness, the actor, himself a homosexual dandy, was the incarnation of Caspary's character.

When Otto mentioned Webb at a casting session, however, he encountered stiff resistance. "I was at Metro when Webb made a test there, and he 'flies,' you can't have him on this film," said Rufus LeMaire, a Fox casting director. To be sure, Webb was unmistakably fey—just the quality Preminger was looking for. Against the advice of his neighbor and friend Ernst Lubitsch, who urged him to climb down from the battlements, Otto persisted. "You have a chance to produce this big picture," argued Lubitsch. "You have Mamoulian. Why do you fight? Why do you have to be so difficult? You will cut your throat again. They threw you out once; they'll throw you out again."[26] But fighting was Otto's way. Even after Zanuck made crude remarks about Webb's homosexuality Otto persuaded his boss to look at the test that Webb had made at Metro. Yet again fortune smiled on Otto Preminger, because through a friend at Metro he discovered that Webb had never made a test. Armed with this knowledge, he challenged Rufus LeMaire in front of Zanuck. "This test was never made," Otto thundered. "You just don't like Clifton Webb, you don't want him in the part, and you're sabotaging him, that's all."

As Otto observed with admiration, Zanuck "once again proved to be a very interesting man." He ordered a screen test of Webb and, since Mamoulian was out of town, granted Otto permission to direct it. Zanuck also arranged for Gene Tierney to play opposite Webb in the test. But then Webb, a prima donna (he said he had never heard of "this Miss Tierney"), refused to make the test. The actor did agree, however, to perform a monologue from *Blithe Spirit* on the Biltmore Theatre stage, and although Zanuck had specifically requested a scene from *Laura,* Otto decided to override him. Placing Webb onstage in a dramatic half-light, Otto filmed the test carefully; Webb, according to Preminger, "knew what Zanuck's objection to him might be and avoided all that completely: he didn't 'fly.' "[27] After viewing the test, and with the objectivity and fair-mindedness that had helped to keep him in the room at the top, Zanuck concurred with Preminger that the urbane actor was indeed born to play Waldo Lydecker.

One battle won, Preminger soon faced another. Mamoulian, no fool after all and doubtless suspecting that Otto was lying in wait, had the producer banned from the set. Mamoulian then proceeded to misdirect most of the cast. He allowed Judith Anderson, a classically trained stage actress playing a society doyenne, to ham it up rather than trying to rein her in. He did not give Gene Tierney and Dana Andrews, relative newcomers with limited strings to their bows, the attention they needed. He and the snippy Clifton Webb were at a standoff because the actor had heard that Mamoulian did not want him in the film. After viewing the rushes in New York, where he was meeting with the Fox business office, Zanuck fired off a blistering telegram to Otto. "This Dana Andrews whom you sponsored is an amateur without any sex appeal, and Clifton Webb is 'flying.' Judith Anderson should stay on the stage, and you should have stayed in New York or Vienna, where you belong."[28]

When he returned from New York, Zanuck called Preminger and Mamoulian to his office. Mamoulian defended his approach and blamed the script; Preminger argued that the acting needed to be less arch, more casual and contemporary—more like film acting. Having committed every line of the script to memory, Otto proceeded to perform some scenes in the understated style he was lobbying for. Impressed, Zanuck encouraged Mamoulian to direct "in the Preminger style." Doubtless infuriated by the boss's suggestion and perhaps already beginning to see the handwriting on the wall, the following day the irascible Mamoulian handed in inferior work. At lunch on Friday, "in front of eighteen people," as Otto recalled, Zanuck asked him if Mamoulian should be replaced. "I said 'yes.' Just like that." And because Preminger was able to say " 'yes' just like that," he proved once again that he had the constitution for playing according to the rules of the Hollywood game. On the walk back from the dining room to the administration building Zanuck uttered the single most important sentence Preminger was ever to hear in the course of his sixty-year career: "You can start directing."[29] (Mamoulian was to live for nearly forty-five years after being removed from *Laura,* but was to direct only two more films, *Summer Holiday* in 1948 and *Silk Stockings* in 1957. In 1958 he was fired as the director of *Porgy and Bess* and replaced by . . . Otto Preminger. And in 1961 he was removed from *Cleopatra* and replaced by Joseph Mankiewicz.)

Preminger started from scratch. He hired a new cameraman, Joseph La Shelle, a new designer, and a new portrait of Laura—Mrs. Mamoulian had painted the original one. (As Gene Tierney recollected, "Otto felt that [the portrait] lacked the mystic quality he insisted on having. He sent me instead to pose for Frank Polony, the studio photographer. . . . Otto had [the photo] enlarged and lightly brushed with paint to create the effect he wanted. So the 'portrait' of Laura was, in truth, a blow-up of a photograph."[30] When Otto began rehearsals, except for the deeply grateful Clifton Webb, he faced a resentful company—as a parting shot Mamoulian had told them Preminger was displeased with their work. As Vincent Price, playing a gigolo, recalled in a 1989 interview, his memory no doubt sweetened by the passage of time, "During the six weeks we had worked together with Rouben, we all thought we had been doing well. We loved Rouben and each other—we all got along wonderfully well with Rouben, a very dignified and very lovely man."[31]

On the fateful first morning, Judith Anderson confronted Otto. Mispronouncing his name, she said she had heard he was disappointed with her work and she asked him to show her how to play the part. "That is exactly what I am going to do, Miss Anderson, and you will do it exactly like this. Then I will take you to see the rushes tomorrow, and you will be the first one to agree that I was right." That first day the cast did as he instructed, and when he showed them the results "they were convinced." "I had no more difficulties," he maintained.[32] "Otto had an idea about the material, and he was right," Vincent Price said. "The New York society depicted in the film are all darlings, sweet and charming and clever and bright—on the surface. But underneath they're evil. And Otto understood this in a way that Mamoulian did not. 'Mamoulian is a nice man, isn't he Vincent?' Otto asked me. And I said, 'Yes, he is a nice man.' Otto said, 'I'm not, and most of my friends are these kind of people.' I think it was true: Otto was very given to the sort of society group of people who basically are really kind of evil people underneath."[33]

If the atmosphere with Otto at the helm wasn't exactly "lovey-dovey," as Price claimed it had been on Mamoulian's set, nonetheless a cooperative spirit prevailed. "I think Otto had a crush on Gene, but then who didn't?" Price observed. "I did five pictures with her and every director went 'ahahhhh.' So did the leading men and everybody else. She had a charm very few actresses have. Otto couldn't really shout at Gene; he couldn't shout at Clifton because he was inventing Clifton really; and he certainly couldn't shout at Judith Anderson—one doesn't shout at Judith Anderson, because one's likely to get shouted back at. And Dana Andrews was really very easygoing. So once we got used to Otto, we had a pretty easy time."[34] Price himself had goodwill toward Preminger because, having appeared in *Outward Bound* on Broadway, he remembered with admiration the way Otto had handled Laurette Taylor.

Gene Tierney represented the greatest challenge for Preminger. Although she had starred in some major Fox productions, including *Tobacco Road* in 1941 and *Heaven Can Wait* in 1943, she remained unsure of her ability. And as she herself recalled, she was not excited by the role. "The time on camera was less than one would like. And who wants to play a painting?" She also knew that she had been a second choice. "If Jennifer Jones doesn't want it, why should I?" Tierney recalled inquiring of Darryl

Zanuck. "The role is right for you, Gene. You'll be good in it. And, you'll see, this one will help your career," Zanuck had assured her.[35] Fortunately, Tierney appreciated Otto's take-charge approach. "Only [he] had absolute faith in the project," she said. "He drove himself, and us, so hard. . . . He was simply tireless. When the rest of the cast seemed ready to drop from exhaustion, Otto would still muster as much vigor as when the day began." Although to the actress Preminger "looked the part of a fencing instructor at a Prussian military academy" and "could charm and intimidate you at the same time" with his "basset-hound eyes" and "egg-shaped dome," she thought him "a gentleman. Unlike certain other directors of that period, he had no insecurity and did not feel obligated to attempt the seduction of his leading ladies."[36] Otto, who could be an astute psychoanalyst when he took the time, recognized Tierney's anxiety (the actress would suffer numerous nervous breakdowns in the coming years) and treated her with special consideration.

Under Mamoulian's direction, following several weeks of rehearsal and preproduction *Laura* had started filming on April 27, 1944, with a projected budget of $849,000. After Preminger took over, the film continued to shoot until June 29, and the final budget was just over one million dollars. Working with an initially uneasy cast and a new cinematographer who worked slowly, Otto still was able to finish within the projected timetable. Zanuck took note.

Once principal photography had been completed, Preminger hired David Raksin to compose a score. The first time he watched the dailies Raksin saw

> a long scene in Laura's apartment. When it was over, Zanuck turned to Otto and said, "I'm going to cut the scene down severely." "Don't do that, Mr. Zanuck," I spoke up. "The music I'll write can take care of the scene, don't cut it!" Because of what I said, they did not cut the scene. I saw Otto the next day at Alfred Newman's [Newman was in charge of the music department at Fox], where he told me he was going to use Duke Ellington's "Sophisticated Lady" as the theme song and work it around the original music that I would be composing. I told him it would be wrong for the movie. We argued; we both raised our voices. He said the song would be right because "Laura's a whore." I said, "According to who?" "Where did you get this fellow?" Otto asked Newman. Al said to Otto, "Listen to Dave." Otto did, and he gave me the weekend to come up with a song to replace "Sophisticated Lady." It was very generous of him.

That weekend I watched the movie several times and it inspired me. Coincidentally, that Saturday, I received a letter of farewell from a lady I was in love with. I put the letter on my piano on Sunday evening and "Farewell, buddy" was in my mind as I began to compose. The tune came to me. It sounds corny, but it's true. The melody of our theme song needed to evoke melancholy, and I had just been given a heavy dose.

When Raksin played the "Laura" theme to Preminger and Newman, they reacted favorably. "There was no further talk about 'Sophisticated Lady,' " Raksin said. "Otto saw what the theme did for his movie: the guy who wrote that melody deserved respect, and Otto gave it to me. I worked for him on four later films, and each time he trusted me completely. I did things my way, and he appreciated that."[37]

When Preminger showed Zanuck his first cut of *Laura,* the mogul and his coterie of yes-men sat through the film in silence. Afterward, Zanuck's pronouncement was devastating: "Well, Byrnie was right. We missed the bus on this one." A flurry of memos then passed between Zanuck and his minions about how the picture could be saved. Zanuck hired a studio writer to reshape the third act—Zanuck had the notion of telling the story within the framework of a dream. In the new ending, written in less than a week, Laura in a voice-over narration says that "nothing was true, it had all been in Waldo Lydecker's imagination." "What they came up with was just unbelievable," Otto recalled. At a screening of the Zanuck-inspired ending the influential New York newspaper columnist Walter Winchell happened to be present. Winchell, to Otto's relief, responded volubly throughout the film. "For the first time in the film's history, at last there was a [moviegoer's] reaction," as Otto recalled. Seated in his customary spot in the front row of the screening room Zanuck kept turning around to look at Winchell whenever the columnist laughed. Winchell's words of praise at the end were as if Otto himself had scripted them: "Big time, Darryl. Big time. But the ending. I didn't get it. You've got to change it."[38]

Yet again, as Preminger noted, Zanuck "proved that his success is deserved, because he's a very flexible man. He's not stubborn when it comes to admitting a mistake." In front of Winchell, Zanuck asked Preminger if he wanted to reinstate the original ending. Zanuck's final words to Preminger on *Laura:* "This is your success. I concede."[39]

"It should clean up," *Variety* accurately predicted after the film opened on October 17, 1944. Reviews were favorable yet tempered ("When the lady herself appears upon the scene, she is a disappointment," Thomas M. Pryor noted in the *New York Times*). But business was brisk. At Twentieth Century-Fox and throughout the industry *Laura* was perceived as an unqualified hit. Otto Preminger, after nearly a decade in America, had finally justified his erstwhile wünderkind reputation. For his immaculate work, he would receive an Academy Award nomination as best director. (Clifton Webb won a best supporting actor nomination; the three writers Otto had worked closely with won a best screenplay nomination; Lyle Wheeler, who would work with Otto many times in the future, was nominated for best art direction/interior decoration [black-and-white]; and Joseph La Shelle won the Academy Award for his ravishing black-and-white noir cinematography.)

After *Laura* opened, Otto had one final encounter with Vera Caspary—at the Stork Club, where Preminger, as Caspary recalled, was

in triumph over the film's success . . . and he stated that I had been wrong on every point. "It wasn't the same screenplay," I said. "Remember, I read the version *before* Sam Hoffenstein and Betty Reinhardt had done the rewrite. I was not responding to the final version, Otto, and you know that." Whereupon Otto drew himself up to his full *Margin for Error* height and said . . . I was not telling the truth. Two Southern gentlemen began stripping off their coats and [Stork Club owner] Sherman Billingsley rushed to our table. Otto made a Central European bow and said he had meant no insult.

"I still believe it would have been a better picture if the melodrama at the end had been equal to the mood of the beginning, if Waldo's character had remained consistent, if the weapon had been contained in the cane," Caspary recalled in 1971, claiming the last word.[40]

The contemporary reviews didn't (and after all couldn't) predict that *Laura* was to become one of the most beloved and enduring films of the 1940s, a landmark in the emerging genre of film noir. For decades this sleek, elegant suspense film has had a secure place in the affections of filmgoers, and even Preminger detractors, who condemn the work as well as the man, concede that on at least this one occasion he did a commendable job. A small cadre of die-hard antagonists, however, likes to stoke the flames of old rumors that the bulk of this universally admired film represents the work of its original director, Rouben Mamoulian. But no, *Laura*, as Zanuck himself acknowledged, is Preminger's success, and in it, for all who care to take a close and fair-minded look, are the essential ingredients that would define the director's style for the rest of his career.

The film begins, unforgettably, with the kind of flowing camera movement Preminger would always favor. The effete, offscreen voice of Waldo Lydecker, eminent gossip columnist and Manhattan insider, whines about the terrific heat of a New York summer as the camera surveys glass figurines and objets d'art on display in his apartment. The detached camera, an eyewitness with a mind of its own, places the spectator as a privileged observer of a fetish-laden private world. At the end of its tour the camera makes a sudden lunging movement as it "discovers" an alien presence, indeed a bull in the china shop: the detective Mark, a man's man evidently ill at ease in the feminine mise-en-scène of Waldo's aerie, come to question Waldo about Laura's "death." The initial confrontation between the detective and Waldo, which takes place in Waldo's mirrored, marbled bathroom as he takes a bath, evocatively sets up the entire film: the two

Rivals for the absent Laura, a woman in a painting: an effete homosexual (Clifton Webb) and an emotionally wounded man's man (Dana Andrews), in *Laura*.

Setting up for a smooth Preminger tracking shot in *Laura*.

men are to become oddly unequal sexual rivals for the absent figure of Laura.

In Preminger's deliciously perverse salon noir, sexual masquerade is omnipresent. Waldo, who has mistakenly killed a woman he presumed to be Laura, is a pretend heterosexual—the character's glass figurines and his prissy aura signal the truth of his possible sexual "difference" in an era when the homosexual, who could not be named as such, was invariably represented as effeminate. Flashbacks tell the tale: as he discovered and then sponsored Laura in her successful career as an advertising executive, Waldo took a proprietary rather than sexual interest in his protégée. But when Laura became engaged to Shelby Carpenter, a young rake available to the highest bidder, Waldo felt his ownership rights were threatened. As Shelby,

A deviant couple in heterosexual masquerade, played by
Judith Anderson and Vincent Price, in *Laura*.

Vincent Price is hardly more convincing in heterosexual garb than Clifton
Webb. Laura, a single career woman and the pawn in a sexual competition
between two "gay" men, may well be suspected of harboring some sexual
surprises of her own. Adding to the atmosphere of sexual repression and
uncertainty is Judith Anderson as Laura's aunt, an habitué of the beau
monde who becomes Shelby's sponsor and would-be lover. Anderson, best
known as the crypto-lesbian housekeeper obsessed with the title character in
Rebecca, projects a more assertive, more "masculine" presence than either
Webb or Price.

An impulse that could not speak its name in 1944, as indeed it could not
for decades to come in mainstream American films, homosexuality in *Laura*
is covert, disguised. "This is the way very wealthy Manhattanites might be
expected to behave" is the film's assumption about its aberrant, supposed
heterosexuals. The desires of the three not-quite-straight characters played
by Webb, Price, and Anderson (each of whom, not incidentally, was gay) are

Steeped in noir shadows, the detective (Dana Andrews) grills Laura (Gene Tierney), a supposed murder victim who has become a suspect.

thwarted. And to ensure a conventional happy ending of heterosexual closure for Laura and Mark, the three disruptive figures must be eliminated. Hardly politically correct in contemporary terms, the film's oblique handling of the characters' sexuality gives *Laura* intriguing noir shadings, a wicked aroma that in part accounts for the film's continuing appeal. Viewers sense that beneath the manicured surface something ambiguous and provocative is going on.

Preminger confines forbidden love to the film's subtext and directs the actors to perform in a matte style—the somnambulistic mode customary for 1940s psychological thrillers. The restrained performances of Webb, Price, and Anderson add to the mysterious mood, the sense of unspoken desire that hovers over the film. As the hard-boiled detective who falls in love with Laura's portrait, Dana Andrews appropriately projects a confident masculinity. The sexual as well as social outsider in a nest of society vipers, the detective steals little sidelong, disbelieving glances at the two fey men he must investigate. But in subtle ways Andrews suggests that the detective isn't quite right either; after all, Mark falls in love with a woman he presumes to be dead. He is bewitched not by a real woman but by a painting. Beneath the character's stoical veneer Andrews suggests (and only that: Preminger would not have allowed for anything more) traces of the character's wounds, his potentially coiled inner life.

A catalyst for unhinging other characters, Laura herself, as Gene Tierney realized, is primarily an image in a painting, a figure encased in aloofness who arouses melancholy and desire in others. Gene Tierney can seem mannequinlike, especially in roles requiring her to be animated; but as Laura her ethereal presence is ideal. Her Laura seems indeed like a figure conjured in a dream.

Preminger's purring direction is wonderfully understated. Working with Joseph La Shelle, he makes spare but potent use of such noir inflections as chiaroscuro lighting, occasional neurotic camera angles, and mirror and ceiling shots that entrap the characters. He permits himself only a few scenes of full-blown noir virtuosity. As the detective becomes enamored of Laura's portrait, the mise-en-scène slowly acquires an Expressionist intensification: shadows overtake Laura's living room, as Mark, transfixed by the portrait, seems to become stranded in a space that grows larger and emptier. In the climax, shadows loom ominously as Waldo, with murder on his mind, climbs the stairs leading up to Laura's apartment. In the showdown between the killer and his intended victim, Waldo is photographed from a disfiguring low angle. Throughout, David Raksin's haunting theme song, one of the most memorable in Hollywood history, adds a dose of yearning that warms up Preminger's cool touch. His stately, contained approach may seem to be impersonal, a refusal of authorial presence, but his work vibrates with autobiographical overtones. The filmmaker knew at first hand, in Vienna and New York, the society world the film is set in, a world governed by strict codes of public behavior. *Laura's* decorum reflects the director's European formality and his inborn sense of etiquette. A less confident filmmaker might have spent the remainder of his career trying to find another *Laura,* and while Preminger, to be sure, made other psychological thrillers, pictures that perhaps inevitably recalled his first great success, he was to spend far more time on projects of an altogether different stripe.

As they continued to live together at 333 Bel-Air Road, Mr. and Mrs. Otto Preminger became more and more estranged. Otto's triumph with *Laura* seemed to spark his always enflamed libido, and he stepped out frequently. But dutifully he appeared by his wife's side at parties at their home and sometimes at social gatherings elsewhere. And as hosts they continued to be renowned. It was an open secret, however, that they had an arrangement. So long as he promised not to seek a divorce, Otto was free to see other women, and in effect he lived like a bachelor. "His reputation for sexual appetite and prowess which had followed him from Vienna was enhanced when he was seen with some of Hollywood's prettiest faces and best figures," as Willi Frischauer noted. Otto would spend weekends away from town in the company of "slim, tall, long-legged" young women, many of them would-be actresses on the make, and some, Frischauer reported, "turned out to be pretty dumb, which is the occupational hazard of an amorous man with a big turnover."[41] He may have been voracious, but Otto was also careful: he knew that scandal could endanger his restarted career, and as much as possible he also wanted to spare Marion, whom in his own way he cared for.

His caution is apparent in his keeping secret the one serious affair he had during this period of sexual restlessness. As he was in preproduction for *Laura,* at a party early in 1944 he met Gypsy Rose Lee, then in Hollywood filming *Belle of the Yukon.* Born Rose Louise Hovick in 1914, Gypsy had been appearing onstage, first in vaudeville and then in burlesque, since the age of four. By the time Otto met her, for many years she had been the most famous stripper of the day, a queen of burlesque second to none. Gypsy had the long-legged look Otto favored, but was decidedly not the empty-headed type he was then casually dating. Although she had had no formal education to speak of, Gypsy was well read and interested in a broad range of subjects. With no apparent talent whatsoever—she was no beauty and as an actress she was a hopeless amateur—she had managed to carve out a prominent show business career, sustaining her masquerade with notable skill. Her entire career was a clever con job. "Gypsy found a gimmick: she was the 'so-called' intelligent stripper, and I stress 'so-called,' " said Arthur Laurents, who wrote the book of *Gypsy,* the classic 1959 musical based on Lee's 1957 memoir. "It was all a tease: she did not have a good body. But she was street-smart, she was amusing, you had to like her. She was fun. She had an over-bite that caused her to speak in a funny way; some people thought it was classy. And indeed, Gypsy herself thought she was classy: when she poured tea, she had her pinkie out. There was about her a certain gaucheness and also a naïveté, and she was allergic to the truth. Her memoir was mostly invention."[42]

At first and perhaps even at second or third glance, Dr. Otto Ludwig Preminger of Vienna and Gypsy Rose Lee, the ecdysiast from Seattle, would seem to have been a colossal mismatch. Coming from a hardscrabble back-ground and raised by the ultimate stage mother from hell, Gypsy had an unmistakable common touch. Otto's privileged background left very differ-ent tonal imprints. They met at the home of William Goetz, Otto's mentor at Fox. Since leaving Fox in the summer of 1943, Goetz had formed and was now the head of International Pictures, and he had hired Gypsy to costar in a Randolph Scott western.

This was not Gypsy's first crack at movies. After having seen her onstage in the 1936 edition of *The Ziegfeld Follies,* Darryl Zanuck had offered her a contract. But Will Hays, who was the chairman of the Hollywood self-censorship board, was affronted by the prospect of a stripper appearing on the screens of America and assured Zanuck that no film featuring Gypsy would ever be shown in theaters. Zanuck reached a compromise with Hays: Gypsy would appear under her own name, as Louise Hovick. But without the marquee lure of "Gypsy" her career could not possibly take off; and no doubt when he saw her on-screen Zanuck realized that she would never be able to carry a film. He quickly assigned her to the B unit, where she appeared in five less-than-minor movies before her one-year contract expired.

For Goetz, she was to appear under her stage name, but her second chance at Hollywood prominence also capsized. Released about the same time as *Laura, Belle of the Yukon* fared poorly at the box office. Gypsy returned to burlesque, and for the rest of her life made only rare guest appearances in unimportant films. In burlesque, Gypsy was a lively pres-ence; on film she was vacant.

While she was shooting *Belle of the Yukon,* Otto dated Gypsy on the sly. She had recently separated from her husband, Alexander Kirkland, who, according to Arthur Laurents, was "gay. And so, for that matter, was Gypsy, and Gypsy's mother too, the infamous Mama Rose. Lesbians make the best hookers because they don't get emotionally involved. They can work a guy over, control him and play him." Whatever designation might best apply to her, Gypsy was certainly sexually versatile, and at least for a while she was able to hold the attention of the sexually demanding Preminger. Was it only sex that drew them together? "Otto liked to be amused by people, and Gypsy amused him," Laurents suggested. "But he couldn't have taken her seriously."[43]

Preminger, who recalled his Hollywood liaison with Gypsy as fleeting and casual, was "surprised to discover one day that she had returned to New York without saying good-bye to me."[44] He did not see or speak to her again until he was in New York in early December, when he called her to ask why she had departed so abruptly. He discovered she was in New York Hospital, where, on December 11, 1944, she gave birth to their son, Erik. A family man at heart, and instinctively generous, Otto was delighted, and eager to accept his fatherhood both emotionally and financially. But Gypsy spurned his help. "I can support my son myself," she announced when Otto arrived at her bedside at the hospital. "I want to bring him up to be my son only." "Her statement was firm but without hostility," as Preminger recalled.[45]

Gypsy elicited a vow of silence from Otto: he was not to reveal his paternity to anyone, including their son. As a man of honor Otto observed her request scrupulously—it's doubtful that he mentioned Erik even to Marion. Gypsy called her son Erik Kirkland, and allowed him to believe that Alexander Kirkland was his father. She did not banish Otto, however, but encouraged him to visit her and Erik, under the guise of being a good friend, whenever he was in New York. For about the first three years of his son's life, Otto, with pleasure, made ritualistic visits to Gypsy's overdecorated townhouse on East Sixty-third Street. After she remarried in 1947 (her new husband was a Spanish painter, Julio de Diego), Otto's visits, as he recalled, "became awkward and eventually stopped."[46] Periodically, but to no avail, he would petition Gypsy to tell Erik the truth. He did win one victory over Gypsy's resistance, however, when he got her to state in her will that he was Erik's father "so that in case she died before me [the boy] would know whom to turn to."[47] Nonetheless, for nearly twenty years Otto disappeared from his son's life. The two were not to see each other again until 1966, when Otto was sixty and Erik twenty-two. But this time, with Gypsy's consent, they were to meet finally as father and son.

There were a number of possible explanations for Gypsy's choice. In her own way Gypsy was a feminist before the fact, determined to claim her

The two sides of Gypsy Rose Lee: as the prim author of a mystery, *The G-String Murders,* and as a burlesque queen in *Belle of the Yukon.*

independence from her gay ex-husband, Alexander Kirkland, as well as her transcendently heterosexual lover, Otto Preminger. Her own mother, a demon of cheapness and devouring possessiveness who lived vicariously through the show business careers she enforced on Gypsy and her sister, June Havoc, was hardly a model of maternal nurturing, and Gypsy's resolve to take control of her son's life may have been a replay of the way Mama Rose had dominated her own childhood. But her wanting to raise Erik on her own could also have been her way of making sure, without anyone interfering with her, that she would be the wise and nurturing parent she had never had. Too, Gypsy may simply have been unwilling to share her son's love with anyone else.

Why did Otto, who could be insistent in pursuit of what he wanted, withdraw his offer of fatherhood so readily, with a beneficent smile, abundant good wishes, and an enormous floral bouquet? It's possible that, at thirty-nine and on the cusp of a rejuvenated career, he was not entirely prepared to become a parent. By his own design, after all, his marriage to Marion was childless. He also may not have wanted to hurt Marion by presenting to her a son he had conceived with another woman. And then he may simply have recognized that since Gypsy was as stubborn as he was, her intentions were unshakable and under the circumstances a civil retreat was his best available option.

FOUR

On the Job (1)

Preminger expected that acclaim for *Laura* would promote him to the Fox pantheon, but as he quickly discovered, his status remained that of a contract director whose professional fate was subject to the will of Darryl Zanuck. For his next assignment, instead of the kind of plum he was certainly justified in expecting, Zanuck accorded him a dubious honor. He would replace Ernst Lubitsch, who had recently suffered a heart attack, on *A Royal Scandal*, a remake of Lubitsch's own 1924 silent *Forbidden Paradise*, starring Pola Negri as Catherine the Great. Otto was safely out of the B unit, it's true, but he was being forced to step into a project where he would be following another director's blueprint. Before his heart attack, Lubitsch had already cast the film (starring Tallulah Bankhead) and spent several months on preproduction.

The kind of team spirit that the assignment demanded of Preminger was part of the routine for a studio employee, and it was a lucky quirk of Otto's paradoxical temperament that despite his independence he was able to bend to the "genius" of the system. It was never easy for Otto, a born bully, to follow orders, but he could force himself to be compliant if that is what he had to do to survive. In many ways, however, the administrative as well as artistic conservatism of studio filmmaking practice was congenial to him. The film factory's need for punctuality, discipline, and financial prudence matched his personality to a T. And Otto was also temperamentally

suited to the highly regularized approach of the so-called classical Hollywood style, defined by objective, centered compositions, "invisible" continuity editing, and unobtrusive camera work. For Preminger, having to
remain within the parameters of the studio-imposed style was no hardship—he was not an artistic renegade determined to dismantle the system's
visual codes. Quite the opposite, having to conform to studio practice
helped him to refine his own essentially mainstream sensibility.

As Willi Frischauer speculated, "In Zanuck's eyes one foreign director
was as good as another. Lubitsch, Preminger—what was the difference? Preminger, currently unemployed, was assigned."[1] According to Otto, however,
Zanuck turned to him at Lubitsch's instigation. The claim is credible. Preminger and Lubitsch were neighbors on Bel-Air Road, and along with Walter Reisch, the Berlin-born director William Wyler, producer Alexander
Korda (then married to the actress Merle Oberon), and Max Reinhardt's son

Marlene Dietrich on the set of *Angel* (1937) with the famously affable Ernst
Lubitsch. In any contest with Lubitsch, whether judged on friendliness or
artistry, Otto seemed destined to lose.

Gottfried, also a producer, they formed a close-knit group alert to job opportunities for one another. At his best in such social gatherings, Otto charmed his landsmen. "Otto was very generous," Lubitsch's daughter Nicola said. "I remember that he took my father and me downtown to see *Rosalinda,* the American version of *Die Fledermaus.* We were driven in a big limousine, and he took us to a big dinner beforehand. I thought he was avuncular." (Nicola recalled Otto's fellow Viennese Billy Wilder, a frequent guest at the Reisches' Sunday afternoon get-togethers, as "not a nice man: vulgar. My mother didn't want him for dinner. He had terrible table manners, unlike my father, who had no vulgarity whatsoever. My father was *not* the ill-spoken Jew that Herman Weinberg depicted in his book on my father. Otto had no vulgarity either. He and Reisch, who looked like a ferret and was very warm, were both wonderful hosts.")[2]

This was not the first time that Preminger had been asked to step in for Lubitsch. Immediately following Lubitsch's heart attack, Zanuck had asked Otto to work on a comic script Lubitsch had been preparing with Henry and Phoebe Ephron called *All Out Arlene.* From the results of that collaboration, however, Zanuck might have taken heed that Preminger was not a promising Lubitsch surrogate. The Ephrons found Otto "unbearable." They complained that he spent too much time on the phone "quarreling with his cook over Saturday night's menu or arguing with his tailor," and unlike Lubitsch, Otto did not laugh at their jokes. "Where was that wonderful, free Lubitsch laugh that filled you with enthusiasm and made you try harder and be even funnier?" Phoebe Ephron asked.[3] As displeased with the Ephrons as they were with him, Otto had the writers replaced. But the new, Preminger-supervised script of *All Out Arlene* was shelved.

To be sure, Preminger and Lubitsch had different styles personally and professionally. Where Lubitsch smiled and laughed, on the job and off, Preminger's good humor tended to fade in working situations. "Although my father was terribly spoiled [like Preminger, Lubitsch came from a well-to-do family] and his own father was very choleric, he never raised his voice," Nicola Lubitsch recalled. "He was moody, and he certainly didn't like being challenged; once he didn't speak to me for two weeks when I had questioned him. But he *never* screamed."[4] Lubitsch was renowned for his light touch— the ineffable grace notes he bestowed on his comedies of sexual peccadilloes that, in other hands, might have become coarse-grained. Preminger's more literal, essentially realist style was decidedly heavier, tending to the ponderous. Preminger didn't have Lubitsch's whimsical point of view or his bemused slant on sexual misbehavior. Otto Preminger could not have made any of Lubitsch's sparkling comedies of seduction and masquerade—and Ernst Lubitsch could not have made *Laura.*

The subject of *A Royal Scandal*—the Empress Catherine seduces a naive young officer who is protecting her from a palace revolt—was vintage Lubitsch. Of much less moment to Lubitsch than the political furor cooking in the wings was the Empress's boudoir deportment; for Preminger, however, the political background was more enticing than *l'amour* and *la ronde*. Moreover, in a fundamental way Otto misunderstood Lubitsch's approach to comedy. "The characters would do anything for a laugh," he contended, "whether it was in keeping with what they represented or not. . . . the Empress of Russia behaved like no Empress of Russia ever would behave in order to produce laughs."[5] "Seldom has anybody missed the essence of the joke—any joke with such certitude," Lubitsch's biographer Scott Eyman commented.[6] As he began directing the film Preminger felt "the era of 'the Lubitsch touch' was coming to an end. It was a change that Zanuck was not yet prepared to understand. Of course, Lubitsch was a first-rate filmmaker, but in his films the humor was based on situations and not on character. . . . A big change had slowly taken place. Audiences wanted more than the chance to laugh. They wanted to see characters on the screen who behaved consistently."[7] As an analysis of either Lubitsch or a supposed change in film comedy, this is preposterous—and if this is how he really felt about Lubitsch's work, Otto should not have taken the job.

"Lubitsch will rehearse the master scenes each day with Preminger and the actors and thereafter Preminger will take over as the sequence goes before the camera," the *New York Times* reported on July 10, 1944. Clearly, Preminger would be working with his hands tied. He may well have wondered if this was his "reward" for *Laura*.

The inevitable clash between director and producer occurred in late July just before the first day of rehearsals. Flushed with excitement, Lubitsch announced that Garbo was interested in playing Catherine. Along with everyone else, Preminger had enormous admiration for Garbo, but he also was deeply indebted to the already cast Tallulah Bankhead, who had tried to help Otto get his family out of Nazi Austria. He made it clear that he would not "participate in anything that would hurt her" and assured Lubitsch that he would have to withdraw if Tallulah were replaced. "Lubitsch refused to listen to me. He insisted there would be some way to get around the situation. He took me to see Zanuck."[8] But Zanuck was not convinced that Garbo was a stronger box-office lure than Tallulah, who had just appeared in a major hit, Hitchcock's *Lifeboat*, whereas Garbo's last film, in 1941, had been a flop called *Two-faced Woman*.

Preminger, of course, won the first round—Garbo was never to make a comeback. But he felt that an aggrieved Lubitsch began to treat Tallulah

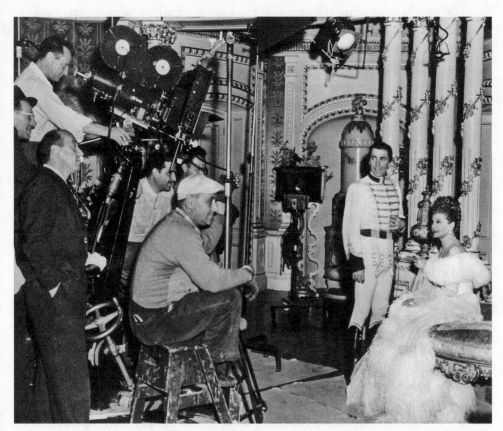

Otto (left) looks at Tallulah Bankhead, a good friend, on the set of *A Royal Scandal.*

with disdain. "He behaved rudely whenever he met her," Otto claimed.[9] Insulted, Tallulah threatened to quit, but Otto, who admired her bawdy humor, her liberal politics, and her talent, talked her out of it. He also had to deal with her terror of the camera. When the actress insisted that she could only be photographed from one side, Preminger and his cameraman Arthur Miller appeased her by placing a light on the camera (Miller called it "the Bankhead") just above the lens that would compensate for Bankhead's lopsided profile. A further bond between director and star was formed because of the hearty dislike they both developed for Anne Baxter, cast as a lady-in-waiting and the Empress's romantic rival. A phony both on-screen and off, Baxter assumed a grand manner that rubbed them the wrong way. When Baxter asked if her grandfather, architect Frank Lloyd Wright, a conservative Republican and a noted anti-Semite, could visit the set, liberal Democrats Otto and Tallulah were incensed. With his star's collusion, Otto devised a ruse. When Wright came to watch, Otto only pretended to shoot a scene between Bankhead and Baxter. He discovered "picayune problems" and stopped shooting ten times. Wright grew bored, as he was meant to, and left, as Otto flashed him a smile that had all the charm of a surgeon's incision. Tallulah winked at her director. "I'll never understand those stories about Otto, because he was awfully sweet to me," she told the *New York Times* twenty years later, on December 6, 1964.

"Tallulah wasn't right for the role," recalled costar Vincent Price, by now a Preminger veteran. "If she had had Lubitsch directing, maybe she could have been. But not with Otto. It was difficult for all of us making the film because Otto really didn't have a huge sense of humor, at least not in the way the material needed. Whereas Lubitsch had this particular humor the script needed. He could take three doors and make you roar with laughter just with people walking in and out of the doors."[10]

Is it any surprise that the film was not well reviewed? "One for the jay-birds," sniffed Otis L. Guernsey Jr. in the *New York Herald Tribune* on March 27, 1945. "Ernst Lubitsch, who produced, should blush," Bosley Crowther grumbled in the March 27 *New York Times*. The box office was wan: $1.5 million against a cost of $1.7 million. For Tallulah, the tepid response spelled doom; for Otto, the lackluster film was merely an assignment he could, and did, shrug off with his customary sangfroid. "Someone said I was quite brave to accept the assignment," he recalled. "I don't worry about these things. I am not brave. It is part of my philosophy not to worry about what other people think of me. . . . I directed the film my way and if people felt that Lubitsch would have done it better, that is their opinion."[11]

Lubitsch certainly would have done it better. For a boulevard comedy about sexual mischief Preminger's approach was much too stodgy. And he seemed to have no ideas about how to give the talky script cinematic momentum. For example, after a scene in which courtiers have gabbed about the Empress, setting the stage for a shimmering entrance (perhaps Catherine might appear in deep focus, then walk forward through a series of doors), Preminger settles for introducing his star in a static long shot in which she is seated at her desk in the right corner of the frame. He allows Tallulah's distinctive voice to carry the show, and she doesn't betray his confidence. Her famed basso with its lascivious ripples and her distinctively clipped rhythm whip the piece into shape. Barking orders, casting sidelong glances at handsome young attendants and barbed looks at the dreaded Anne Baxter, Tallulah's Catherine is a take-charge woman. As Lubitsch intended, Tallulah's Empress understands that the art of seduction demands a royal performance. (Although she had many of the characteristics of Bette Davis, Bankhead lacked Davis's brio as a movie star. Perhaps it was her too deep voice, her sexual ambiguity, her strangely ungiving eyes, the whiff of the stage that always hovered over her screen acting, which blocked her from attaining film star status. For all the rhetorical force of her performance, *A Royal Scandal* proved to be the end of the line for Tallulah as a film personality. There was to be only one other movie twenty years later, a cheap horror show called *Die, Die, My Darling*.)

Zanuck was grateful to Preminger for having completed the project on schedule. The relationship between Otto and his employer seemed now to be fully healed. Otto ate with Zanuck frequently in the executive dining room.

A lady-in-waiting (Anne Baxter) is reprimanded by Catherine the Great (Tallulah Bankhead) in *A Royal Scandal*. Baxter's high-flown manner irritated Tallulah and Otto.

He and Marion received invitations to the Santa Monica beach house. He had immediate access to Zanuck by phone and in his office. And the Zanucks were frequent guests at 333, where, as another frequent guest, composer David Raksin, recalled, "Zanuck appreciated Marion as a Viennese babe who gave great parties, and he also saw that she knew how to cope with Otto."[12]

As a favor to his friend Gregory Ratoff, who was directing, Otto appeared in a cameo in a musical fantasy with a score by Kurt Weill and Ira Gershwin called *Where Do We Go from Here?* (1944). Playing a comically autocratic Hessian officer in an episode set in the Revolutionary War, once again Otto was being a good citizen. But where was the payoff? When would he get the compensation due him as the director of *Laura*? "Freedom of choice was in rather short supply at Twentieth Century-Fox under Darryl Zanuck," he grumbled. "I had to turn out a string of films following rules and obeying orders not unlike a foreman in a sausage factory."[13]

Preminger did not like to repeat himself, but as he became an increasingly sophisticated decoder of Hollywood rituals he recognized that repetition was one of the pillars of the system. If you had a big hit with a particular kind of film, you were obligated to return to the scene of the killing. And so Preminger presented the boss with a story conceived in the *Laura* mold, a psychological suspense film with the potent noir title of *Fallen Angel*. Zanuck gave him an enthusiastic go-ahead.

In *Fallen Angel* an archetypal noir drifter, a con man and a womanizer, ends up by chance in a small California town, where he romances a sultry waitress and a well-to-do spinster. When the waitress is killed, the drifter becomes the prime suspect. As in *Laura,* appearances are deceiving and sex is twisted. To adapt the source material, a novel by Marty Holland, Preminger hired Harry Kleiner, a student of his at Yale in 1939. "Not one of my pupils succeeded," Otto recollected in 1945. "This irked me, so I looked up Harry Kleiner, one of my best pupils, when I was in New York last year for the opening of *Laura*. I read a play he was working on, liked it, and brought him to Hollywood to do the script. His work on *Fallen Angel* vindicated me as a teacher."[14] As always, Preminger worked closely with the writer, supervising every line, and by the time the script was finished and ready to go into production he had committed it to memory.

After approving the script Zanuck gave Otto the task of convincing Alice Faye, the studio's top musical star of the late 1930s and early 1940s, to play the role of the spinster. Faye was a strong-willed young woman who had often stood up to Zanuck. At the moment Zanuck and Faye were feuding again, but the mogul was eager to bring Faye back to the studio—she hadn't worked in over two years—because she had a large and loyal following. Zanuck was hoping that Faye's appearance in a straight role, her first, would boost the film's box-office appeal. "I knew Alice had turned down sixteen or seventeen stories, and I also didn't think she'd want the part [of June, a repressed, organ-playing spinster]," Preminger said. "It was different from anything she had ever done. It wasn't glamorous, or the part of a pretty girl, or a very young one. But I knew it was real and down to earth, more like Alice's own personality than the other roles she had played."[15] To his surprise Faye said yes.

The obvious choice for the role of Stella, the doomed, come-hither waitress, was the studio's resident sexpot, raven-haired Linda Darnell. For Eric, the brooding drifter, Preminger was certain that Dana Andrews, his sad-eyed leading man in *Laura,* would be ideal. Shooting started on May 1 and finished on June 26. Remarkably, Preminger exceeded the original budget of $1,055,136 by less than $20,000—a rare achievement. He enjoyed working with Faye, who may have been truculent with Zanuck but not with him. Otto regarded Andrews as "a director's delight. He always knows his lines, arrives on time [the two essential criteria for survival on a Preminger set], and knows what he wants to do with a part."[16] The film's composer David Raksin recalled Andrews as "a man's man, a great guy really, and so easy to work with. At Fox he was one of Otto's favorites."[17]

If Faye and Andrews were Preminger-proof, Linda Darnell was not. Eager to prove that she could do more than decorate the set, Darnell worked at the studio coffee shop to prepare for her role. But off the set she had already begun what was to be a lifelong battle with alcohol. "She was so scared she was almost always drunk," recalled Celeste Holm, who was under contract to the studio at the same time.[18] In either preventing or defending herself against an Otto tirade, Darnell proved to be helpless. "My impression was that Linda was learning her profession as she went along," David Raksin noted. "I realized she was there not because she was a schooled actress—she was not—but because she was beautiful. That meant there would be a more or less sophisticated competition for her in the studio, which apparently developed. Little girls like that were sort of fair game. She tried very hard, but she couldn't give Otto what he wanted on the first take, and he got very impatient. She would tremble, then he would scream."[19]

Raksin wrote a song, "Slowly" (with lyrics by Kermit Goell), to be sung by Alice Faye.

Otto liked the song, but thought it wasn't right for the character Alice was playing. Instead, he wanted to use my tune for the opening [in which the antihero rides into town on a bus], but I said it was wrong there too. "Don't you like your own tune?" he asked me. "Of course I do, but it's too sentimental for an opening where a guy on a bus is about to be thrown off because he has no money." It would have made the picture start out in the wrong way. "It should open with a sense of urgency," I told him. I said the song was right for Linda's character. I was right, and he knew I was right. I respected him in turn: Otto was a smart son of a gun.[20]

Heard on the jukebox in the diner where Stella works, "Slowly" becomes the character's theme song, its melancholy refrain carried by a wailing trombone whenever Stella appears.

After his discomfort with the palace intrigue in *A Royal Scandal*, Preminger returns to form in *Fallen Angel*. His command of noir's visual idiom is apparent in the arresting title sequence. Headlights from a bus pierce the infinite darkness of the open road as titles designed in the form of highway signs come into view. Throughout, the settings ripple with apprehension and instability, the imminence of mischance. The walls of the seaside diner where Stella works are crisscrossed with striped shadows cast by venetian blinds. Stella lives in an apartment at the top of a rickety staircase which, shot on the diagonal, becomes an augury of her dark fate. A rundown hotel room with a relentless blinking neon sign outside the windows reeks of the protagonist's ill fortune. To underline his antihero's entrapment, Preminger with his ace cinematographer Joseph La Shelle frames the character in low-angle ceiling shots in which space seems to be closing in on him.

As in *Laura* and many other noir thrillers, the narrative is riddled with suggestions of pathology. The spinster, June, plays the organ in a joyless-looking church, a crucible for sexual repression, and shares a house with her older, unmarried sister Clara (the frostbitten Anne Revere), who has an incestuous attachment to June that the film can only hint at. In June's capitulation to Eric, an "homme fatale," there is more than a hint of masochism. "Walk all over me," she seems to say to the man who leaves her on their wedding night. A detective (played by Charles Bickford) who hangs out in the diner and has it bad for Stella is a sadist who administers a brutal beating (off screen) to a man he pretends to suspect of having killed Stella. (In a last-act twist, the crazed-with-jealousy detective is identified as the murderer.)

Dana Andrews's masked style strikes all the right notes for his ill-starred loner thrust into a noir whirlpool. Linda Darnell is equally fragrant as the small-town siren. When she makes her entrance at the café door, after having been missing for three days (shades of *Laura*), her allure is palpable. Fixing her stocking, and with a flower in her hair, she's a fallen angel all right—a sweet girl with a tough veneer who seems forever destined to choose the wrong guy. Preminger failed only with Alice Faye, whose ineradicable common touch clashes with the well-born spinster she is playing. Her matte performance ended her starring career; many years later she was to appear again in small roles in which she is equally inexpressive.

For all its visual and stylistic victories, *Fallen Angel* did not match the achievement of *Laura*—an accusation Preminger was to face for the rest of his career. The problem, as it was often to be for the director, was narrative structure, getting the story right. "There are three stories in this one screenplay, but none of them is brought into sharp focus," observed Otis Guernsey Jr. in the *New York Herald Tribune* on November 8, 1945. The finale, with the detective revealed as the murderer, feels like a last-minute rewrite. And the happy ending, with June reunited with Eric, also seems manufactured. It's no wonder that Preminger could never remember how the film ended. "I was dressing for dinner one night and *Fallen Angel* was on television," he recalled. "I watched it and I got quite involved; then we had to go out and I never saw the ending. I still cannot recall the ending."[21]

Post-*Laura*, Preminger was becoming indoctrinated into the factory lineup. First he was a substitute for Lubitsch, a thankless task because he was being set up against a director with a far longer track record and vastly higher critical standing than his own. Then, with *Fallen Angel*, he slipped into the trap of trying to make a movie in the mold of his big hit. Neither project advanced his reputation in or out of the studio, and Preminger was in danger of becoming a company functionary marching in step with front-office orders.

His next project, a musical with an original score by Jerome Kern, at least offered the change of pace that Otto always relished. But the project held little intrinsic interest for him. "I took it because it was available; it was something Zanuck asked me to do, and at the time I was in no position to turn him down. And I didn't want to: Zanuck ran the show, as I had learned."[22] "Today [1971] I would not be capable of spending three or four months on *Centennial Summer*—neither the story nor the characters would interest me. At that time it probably served some purpose in my life and in my career."[23] In fact, it is easy to see why the material "at that time" appealed to him. "Preminger's thinking is strictly American," a September 5, 1945, Fox press release announced. "He is Hollywood's outstanding exception to the general rule that foreign-born directors prefer to make films with foreign settings." The release then quoted Preminger: "For me, Europe is the past, America is the future. As Carl Sandburg once wrote, 'The past is a bucket of ashes.' Never having gone back to Europe I would hardly have a new view-

Frames within the frame in *Fallen Angel*: (above) June (Alice Faye) in a mirror shot caught between a photograph of her possessive sister Clara (Anne Revere) and Clara herself; (below) Stella (Linda Darnell) enclosed by a doorway and a low ceiling and watched by her boss (Percy Kilbride) as the noir antihero (Dana Andrews) eavesdrops.

point about things European. But as a new American intensely interested in every facet of American life I might just possibly have something new to offer to stories with American settings."

Centennial Summer, set in Philadelphia in the summer of 1876 and presenting an idealized view of an all-American working-class family, is one of those stories. Ordinary problems confront the Rogers clan. Mr. Rogers's job on the railroad is imperiled. Two sisters become rivals for the same dreamboat. Family routine is interrupted by the sudden arrival of Mrs. Rogers's elegant, gallivanting sister, who has had an amorous career among European royalty and who brings with her the handsome nephew of her late husband, a French duke. The homespun Rogers household is contrasted favorably with the representatives of European worldliness. Glazed with nostalgia for an American Arcadia, the slight narrative with its evocation of a vibrant young nation reflects the spirit of a country newly victorious in the world war.

Zanuck was itching to put the project on the studio slate because he was hoping to duplicate the success of the 1944 MGM musical *Meet Me in St. Louis*—for a while he even thought of calling his film *See You in Philadelphia.* Fox had already released one Americana musical, *State Fair* (1945), featuring an original score by Rodgers and Hammerstein; and rural dramas, perhaps a reflection of Zanuck's own country-boy origins, had been a staple of the studio since its founding. His enlistment of Preminger for the project made sense on two counts. Zanuck was well aware of Otto's patriotic fervor, and he knew he could count on the director completing the film quickly so that it could be released while the upbeat postwar mood was still ripe. Because of the elaborate production values, the film had a longer than usual shooting schedule (a full two months, from September 5 to November 9, 1945), but as Zanuck expected, Otto kept costs down. The final budget was a little over $2,200,000, as against an initial projection of two million dollars— almost any other director on the lot would have ended up spending far more of the studio's money.

At first Otto welcomed the chance to work with Jerome Kern, the Broadway composer whose score (with Oscar Hammerstein) for *Show Boat* in 1927 had altered the course of the American musical theater. But Kern, volatile and impatient, was not an easy collaborator. And in a fundamental way their artistic temperaments were not compatible: Kern's sentimentality collided with the aura of reserve that was an innate part of Preminger's style. During production Kern was more ill-tempered than usual because he was working with a lyricist, Leo Robin, who was slow-moving. Kern was eager to return to New York to supervise the upcoming Broadway revival of *Show*

Boat, for which he and Oscar Hammerstein had written a new song, as well as to begin working with Hammerstein on a musical about Annie Oakley. Finally fed up with Robin, and refusing to wait any longer for him to finish the lyrics on a few numbers, Kern returned to New York in mid-October before the score had been completed. Before decamping he offered Preminger (appalled by Kern's lack of professionalism) two songs he had written with other lyricists. ("All Through the Day," with words by Oscar Hammerstein, and "Cinderella Sue," with lyrics by E. Y. Harburg, are performed in the film as interpolated specialty numbers.) In early November Kern collapsed while walking in the theater district and on November 11, 1945, he died. *Show Boat* opened, as scheduled, on January 25, 1946; the Annie Oakley musical, *Annie Get Your Gun,* opened on Broadway on May 16, 1946, with a score written with remarkable speed by Irving Berlin.

Zanuck opened *Centennial Summer* in July to tepid reviews and box office. Preminger got much of the blame. "Obviously the script was weak, but Preminger did little to snap it up," Bosley Crowther observed in the *New York Times* on July 18, 1946. Ideally, the warm-hearted story and Kern's robust, all-American songs need a cozy style not in Otto's line. *Centennial Summer* doesn't invite the audience in, as the equally fragile *Meet Me in St. Louis* does; and the rich sense of family and home that illuminates Vincente Minnelli's direction of the MGM classic is missing.

Though *Centennial Summer,* Preminger's first film in color (he was working with cinematographer Ernest Palmer), is hardly the equal of *Meet Me in St. Louis,* it is sturdier than its obscure reputation suggests. Preminger's characteristic stateliness gilds the story with an appropriately ceremonial touch, and throughout, there are graceful set pieces—a smooth tracking shot around the outside of the Rogers house; craning, pirouetting camera movement in a ball scene. Preminger's direction of the musical sequences is sensitive. Since the characters are not performers, he is careful to bind the songs to the story rather than to isolate them in a separate realm—music doesn't interrupt the action but grows out of it, and to reduce the "taint" of performance Preminger often interrupts songs before they are over. Clustering around a piano, the family sings a ditty called "The Railroad Song," which Preminger stages naturalistically as a spontaneous activity: this is something an American family of the period might do.

Only one song, "Cinderella Sue," is entirely unmotivated—and it's the best moment in the film, an inspired interruption. Into an Irish bar where two of the characters go for a drink, a black singer (Avon Long, who played Sportin' Life in *Porgy and Bess*) and a group of black children enter suddenly and begin to sing the song. The camera moves in for a close-up as Long

Parade for the world premiere of *Centennial Summer* in Philadelphia.

Preminger emerges from a cab at the premiere of *Centennial Summer*.

Musical numbers in *Centennial Summer:* the Rogers family singing "The Railroad Song"; Avon Long performing the showstopping "Cinderella Sue."

strums a banjo and one of the kids plays a harmonica; then during a dance break the camera retreats to a discreet distance. At the end of the number the kids pick up coins the white spectators toss at them, and then, as quickly as they entered, the performers exit. From a contemporary viewpoint the number—black performers performing "blackness" for the amusement of a white audience—certainly violates political correctness. But "Cinderella Sue" is showstopping in the best sense. To watch Avon Long's strutting turn is to catch a glimpse of his Sportin' Life. And in its irresistible melody and rhythm the number has echoes of the great Negro songs Kern composed for *Show Boat.* Anticipating his landmark all-black musicals of the 1950s, *Carmen Jones* and *Porgy and Bess,* Preminger films the interlude with evident respect and delight.

By now Preminger had become one of a small cadre of directors Zanuck knew he could trust absolutely. And Preminger, on his side, had developed great respect for DFZ. "I think he is basically one of the fairest men I have ever met," he said. "He inspires a certain loyalty and following. He has a group of people, and I'm one of them, who would do anything for him. When we had an argument, there was nothing malicious about it. In spite of, or because of, everything, I have a warm feeling for him."[24] By 1946 Preminger also had one of the plushest contracts on the lot: $7,500 a week, a princely sum at the time.

As his position at Fox solidified, however, complications bedeviled Otto's private life. He and Marion had been estranged for years, and in the sense that Marion had never quite received his full attention, the couple had been estranged from the beginning of their marriage. In Hollywood social circles their open marriage had long been an open secret. Otto was surprised, however, when in May 1946 Marion asked for a divorce. On a trip to Mexico she had met a fabulously wealthy (married) Swedish financier named Alex Wennergren who, as reported in an article in the *Los Angeles Times* on May 27, 1946, had been "blacklisted by the Allies during the war." Agreeing to Marion's petition for a speedy divorce, Otto consented to go to the Mexican consul in Los Angeles to sign papers. "Two days later I received a letter from Marion full of affectionate Hungarian farewells," he recalled. "She would never forget our happy years together but she knew that I did not love her anymore and there was a man who loved her very much. She didn't want anything from me except a few personal belongings that would be picked up in a few days by her fiancé's private plane."[25] The plane never arrived, but Marion did. Mrs. Wennergren, apparently, was not willing to grant a divorce—more than that, she was madly jealous of her rival and began to stalk Marion. One afternoon in a post office in Mexico, Marion claimed that Mrs. Wennergren attempted to shoot her.

If Marion was a poor actress onstage, there was no question of her skill as the flamboyant leading lady of her own life. Whether or not the attempted shooting took place, or whether, as Otto speculated, it was "just a figment of Marion's Hungarian imagination,"[26] she lived her life with panache. A bit sheepishly but essentially unbowed, Marion returned to 333 Bel-Air Road in June 1946 to resume her appearances as Otto's wife and to lunch regularly at all the industry favorites, including the Polo Lounge at the Beverly Hills Hotel, Romanoff's, Chasen's, and the Brown Derby. Marion persevered, despite the fact that the charade of being Mrs. Otto Preminger had worn thin—Otto was enjoying his escapades as a freewheeling man-about-town and had begun dating Natalie Draper, a niece of Marion Davies and one of the extras on the Fox lot. Marion Preminger was on borrowed time and no doubt she knew it.

Long before Marion asked for a divorce, Otto often went on his own to parties at Zanuck's Santa Monica beach house or for weekends in the desert at Ric-su-dar, Zanuck's Palm Springs estate named for his three children, Richard, Susan, and Darrilyn. However, one weekend invitation, in June 1946, a few weeks after Marion's request for a divorce, was a ruse. Zanuck, as always keeping daily watch on every production at the studio and aghast at the rushes on *Forever Amber,* based on Kathleen Winsor's infernally popular novel, had decided to remove the director, John Stahl. To protect his investment—Zanuck had already spent over two million on the production, by far the most expensive undertaking in the studio's history—Zanuck turned to the reliable Preminger to bail him out. When Otto arrived, solo, at Ric-su-dar on Friday afternoon, Zanuck informed him that he was to leave after breakfast the next morning, drive directly to the studio to view all the footage that Stahl had shot during the six weeks the film had been in production, and on Monday offer a candid assessment of what he saw. "Monday, you will tell me what you want to do," Zanuck said.

"I'll tell you now what I want to do," Preminger shot back. "I want not to do *Forever Amber.* I read the book when it was sent round by the story department and I thought it was terrible." He told Zanuck he was adapting *Daisy Kenyon,* another best seller aimed at a female audience, and did not want to interrupt the good progress he was making with his scriptwriter, David Hertz.

"You're a member of the team," Zanuck said sternly. "You must do it. I won't blame you if it doesn't turn out well."[27]

Otto told Zanuck that if he agreed to work on "this trashy story" there would certainly be a reprise of the kind of argument they had had on *Kidnapped* and that Zanuck would end up firing him.

"You must help me," the czar persisted. Then he assured Otto, who

knew it to be a subterfuge, that as director he would be allowed to do whatever he wanted with the material.

"It was very difficult," Preminger later recalled. "You wanted to get
along with him when he talked like this."²⁸ In the end, as he had perhaps
realized all along, Otto knew he had "no choice."²⁹ Daisy Kenyon, a heroine
he believed in, would have to wait until he had rescued the lusty Amber, a
heroine he despised.

Peggy Cummins (as Amber) and Peter Whitney in scrapped footage of *Forever Amber*,
directed by John Stahl, replaced by Preminger. The actors were replaced by Linda Darnell
and John Russell.

Preminger drove back to Los Angeles Saturday morning, looked over
Stahl's footage, and on Monday rendered his judgment. To proceed, he
must have a completely new script, and the leading lady, Peggy Cummins, a
young British blonde Zanuck had signed up and whom Preminger found
"amateurish beyond belief," would have to be replaced. Otto said he would
need at least two months to prepare a script, and in the meantime production would have to be halted. In all his demands Preminger omitted a

request for a producing credit—he was only too relieved that William Perlberg would have that burden. Zanuck agreed to the provisos, adding that as
the script was being prepared they would "think about [Cummins's] replacement."[30] Only later did Preminger discover that Zanuck had already hired
Fox contract player Linda Darnell.

Demanding the right to choose his own writer, Otto turned to Ring
Lardner Jr., who, uncredited, had written some of Waldo Lydecker's dialogue in *Laura*. Although like everyone else Lardner thought the novel was
"junk," he accepted because he liked working with Preminger. "Otto was
extremely bright and curious about almost everything," he recalled. "He was
also very good company, and when we worked together, we tended to spend
as much time talking about the world in general as we did about the movie
at hand."[31] Philip Dunne, who had written the first draft, was relieved,
thinking he was now free of "the whole sorry mess. It was an amateur book
that somehow caught on. It was a dollar catcher. It was supposed to be
raunchy, and of course here were the censors looking at us: 'Don't you dare
make a move.' I wanted to make a spoof of it. But Zanuck said, 'No. It's a
best seller. Let's go with it.' "[32] Curbing his desire to transform Winsor's rib-
ald story into a comedy, Dunne had turned in "a dreary, dutifully sanitized
script."[33] Zanuck, however, wanted Dunne to remain on the project. As
Lardner recalled, "I was now supposed to collaborate with Phil on a
rewrite—a touchy situation, or rather, it would have been if he had been any
less of an exemplar of graciousness and professionalism. As it was, the three
of us, Otto, Phil, and I, established a strong bond based, in part, on a fervent common desire to be working on almost any property other than the
one Zanuck had foisted on us."[34]

Zanuck was risking a king's ransom because he believed the novel's popularity ensured a large audience. At 972 pages, Winsor's chronicle of the fortunes of a poor country lass who sleeps her way into the court of Charles II
in Restoration England is a monumental bodice ripper. Vixen, whore, royal
consort, and sometime actress, Amber for all her erotic cunning fails to
secure the affection of the one man she really loves, Bruce Carlton, a fortune
hunter who in the end goes off to the new colony of Virginia with another
woman by his side. Winsor draws on mountainous research to evoke a
tapestry of the period: teeming with a Brueghelesque density of detail, her
accounts of a historical plague and fire, of the decadent court of Charles II,
and of the brothels and theaters where Amber works at various points in her
career, provide bravura literary set pieces. Winsor, to be sure, is occasionally
naughty, her passages about her heroine's amorous exploits calculated to tit-
illate her mostly female 1940s readers. But at the same time that she had her

Preminger, a photo of FDR, one of his heroes, on his office wall, with the script of *Forever Amber*, a film he was to direct under protest.

eye squarely on the box office, Winsor was also a real writer, and Preminger and his team should have been able to see that there was a terrific movie to be sculpted out of her saga.

Only after turning in his revised script did Preminger learn that Zanuck had already cast Linda Darnell. Otto had nothing against the actress (he never knew how much she had already grown to dislike him), and quite rightly thought she had done good work for him on *Fallen Angel* and *Centennial Summer*. But Winsor's heroine was blonde and he couldn't see the raven-haired Darnell in the role. He wanted a real blonde, Lana Turner, who was under contract to MGM. Zanuck protested. He was convinced that whoever played Amber would become a big star, and as he told Otto, he did not intend to give that kind of break to another studio's "property." Even after Zanuck decreed that Amber would be played by Linda Darnell, Otto, thinking he had an advantage—he had agreed to direct only as a favor to the boss—and confident of his rising place in the studio hierarchy, continued to promote Turner. He invited Zanuck and Turner to a lavish dinner at 333, and to prepare her for the meeting Otto coached Lana about how she should play up to the mogul. "She did her best," he recalled. "She flirted shamelessly with Zanuck, at one point even sitting on his legs."[35] But Zanuck remained adamant, and Preminger, checking his audacity at this point, backed off, realizing he had no choice other than to proceed with an actress he could not envision in the role.

For her part, Linda Darnell stifled her anxiety about working with Preminger once again because she knew Amber was a star-making role. "I thought I was the luckiest girl in Hollywood," she said at the time.[36] Indeed, right after Zanuck announced that Darnell would play the coveted part she was given a major star buildup. Six weeks before filming was scheduled to resume in mid-October, Darnell was subjected to a routine as rigorous as that of an athlete in training for a championship event. She was placed on a severe diet. She began intensive daily studies with a vocal coach, British actress Constance Collier, in order to transform her Texas twang into a simulation of mid-Atlantic "movie speech." In successive stages her brunette hair was dyed blond and twisted into a variety of shapes in preparation for the thirty-four different hairstyles Amber would have. She had to endure hundreds of costume fittings. And as a rising "star of tomorrow" she was required to give interviews in which, coached by the studio public relations department, she was expected to underline the similarities between her own humble background and Amber's. None too flatteringly, in building a bad-girl image for Darnell, press releases reminded fans that Darnell was estranged from her husband, cameraman Peverall Marley, and like many other Hollywood brunettes had had an affair with Howard Hughes. In forging a link between the actress and her role, the studio was suggesting that a slut had been chosen to play a slut. Insecure and not remotely divalike, Darnell submitted without a whisper of discontent to her preproduction regimen.

However, her costar Cornel Wilde, cast as the unattainable Bruce Carlton, wanted to bail. Wilde had already suffered through the aborted Peggy Cummins version, had rancorous memories of working with Preminger on Centennial Summer, and shared the writers' conviction that the material was rubbish. But Wilde was a big star at the time, the kind of heartthrob the role demanded, and both Zanuck and Preminger wanted him to remain. When Wilde's agents negotiated a sizable salary increase, the actor stayed on, grudgingly.

With no one except Linda Darnell excited about the project, Otto began filming on October 24. Darnell, whose days began at 4:30 a.m. with hair and costume fittings and often continued until eight at night, was under enormous pressure, and Preminger did nothing to bolster her confidence. Suffering her director's almost daily explosions, Darnell, as she confided to her sister, became "convinced that Preminger was holding her back in the

Showing a bemused Cornel Wilde how to make love to
Linda Darnell in *Forever Amber*. The actress feared and
loathed Preminger's autocratic methods.

part. Linda was not one to dislike many people . . . but Preminger she
couldn't tolerate. He was a good director, but a mean SOB. She hated
him."[37] (During the filming of *A Letter to Three Wives* in 1949, when he
needed a look of disgust from Darnell, director Joseph Mankiewicz placed
as a prop a portrait of Preminger in a Nazi uniform.[38]) Exhausted, and
demoralized by her director's outbursts, Darnell midway through the
seventeen-week ordeal collapsed and under doctor's orders remained away
from the set for ten days.

Other mishaps followed. To create a semblance of English fog that Otto
wanted for an early-morning duel scene, a spray called Nujol was used. "It
was a laxative," Cornel Wilde recalled, "and half the cast and crew got diar-
rhea breathing and swallowing it."[39] The most harrowing incident occurred

during the shooting of the Great Fire. After meticulous preparation—no traffic was allowed within a mile of the Fox lot—the sequence was shot at 3 a.m., with a battalion of fire trucks at the ready if something were to go wrong. Something did. The star was burned. "Linda Darnell just escaped death, because during the Great Fire a roof caved in," recalled the film's cinematographer Leon Shamroy. "I pulled the camera back and just got her off the set in time. She was terrified of fire, almost as though she had a premonition."[40] (Darnell was to die in a fire in 1965.)

The only member of the production who enjoyed working on the film was the composer, David Raksin, who hadn't read the novel but felt the screenplay was

> terrifically good for such a piece of trash. Phil Dunne and Ring were first-rate writers. As soon as I read their work I knew I wanted the score to have a symphonic sweep. I worked on it steadily for about six weeks. The picture has a helluva lot of music, and needs it. It has more themes than you would believe. I already knew a lot about the music of the period, but you can't be too accurate to the period: it won't work. Your aim is to simulate the music of the time. Otto didn't touch a note of my score, because he recognized he had something extraordinary. Very few scores are like that. Zanuck sent down a note to Alfred Newman, who was to conduct, saying the score was magnificent in every respect.[41]

(Raksin earned an Academy Award nomination for his score.)

Filming dragged on until March 11, 1947. "It was the longest shooting schedule I ever had," Preminger grumbled. "Zanuck was determined that this would be the biggest and most expensive and most successful film in history."[42] After principal photography was completed, however, another round of problems ensued. Zanuck had bought the book because its scandalous reputation promised big box-office returns. Yet he and Preminger realized that the story of a promiscuous heroine who has a child out of wedlock and who seems, until she receives her comeuppance at the end, to be rewarded for her turpitude, would need to be toned down. As Preminger recalled, "We were very careful to stay well within the rules of the industry's own censoring body," known as the Hays Office, named for Will Hays, a former U.S. postmaster who was the first head of the Motion Picture Producers and Distributors Association.[43]

The Hays Office did indeed pass the film, but the more austere (and at the time more powerful) Catholic Legion of Decency condemned it. In an effort to avert the financial disaster that a C rating from the Legion then represented, Spyros Skouras, the high-strung president of Twentieth Century-Fox, summoned Preminger and three priests from the Legion to a meeting in his New York office. Determined to protect the company's $5 million investment, a near record at the time, Skouras proceeded to behave in a way that Otto would long remember. When the youngest priest, the chief spokesman for the Legion, began by chastising him for having dared to film Winsor's banned book in the first place, Skouras with increasing agitation started twisting his yellow worry beads. After he saw that pleading with the irate priest to rescind the C rating had no effect, Skouras got down on his knees and began to cry, quietly at first but then with mounting fervor until his body was wracked with heaving sobs. At the high point of his aria, Skouras began to pound the floor furiously. Otto, no slouch in putting on a show to get what he wanted, was nonplussed. At that point the young priest, perhaps a little frightened by Skouras's display, suggested that the Legion's objection might be withdrawn if Fox changed the title. Skouras shrieked, as if in mortal pain: the title was the selling point of the film, and could not possibly be changed, he assured the priest in a voice shaking with indignation. Skouras promised the Catholic delegation, however, that the studio would make any changes they might request. "Just show [Mr. Preminger] what you want cut and he'll cut it," he announced.[44] And proving once again that he could be a good citizen, Otto sat patiently with the priests in the Fox screening room in New York, listening to their concerns scene by scene. Perhaps because he had no faith in the project, he readily agreed to make strategic cuts in all the kissing scenes, and promised to schedule retakes to reduce the amount of the star's cleavage in certain shots. After viewing Preminger's sanitized version, with all the nips and tucks in place, the Legion bestowed its approval on the film. Preminger was to remember the "pathetic scene" in Skouras's office a few years later, when he would have his own run-ins with the Legion of Decency and the Production Code Administration office. And with Skouras's behavior as a negative model, he would refuse to capitulate.

On October 10, 1947, *Forever Amber* opened to big business, with Zanuck and Skouras making a quick and handsome profit on their expensive investment. The film even garnered some decent reviews. Bosley Crowther in the *New York Times* saluted Preminger's "lush theatricalism" and noted that "although the film does not picture the details of Amber's amours with such boldness as did Miss Winsor, it doesn't spare the innuendoes, chum!"

In an interview with the *New York Times* ten years after the film's release, Preminger recalled that *Forever Amber* was "by far the most expensive picture I ever made and it was also the worst."[45] He couldn't have been more wrong. Closer to the mark was David Raksin's assessment: "Otto sure did a hell of a good job with it."[46] Even more than *Laura,* the unfairly maligned *Forever Amber* confirms Preminger as a maestro of mise-en-scène. Working closely with Leon Shamroy (Preminger called him "a brilliant cameraman and a marvelous friend"),[47] he assembled a procession of images that have the rhetorical power of master paintings. The Puritan dwelling where Amber was raised, shot with looming shadows and figures in silhouette lit ominously from below, is quickly established as a place of stultifying repression, the joyless rooms seeming almost to incite Amber's amorous career. After examining herself in a mirror—Amber is always a self-conscious "performer"—she enters a packed, smoke-filled tavern where she waits on tables, mixing with a crowd of rollicking peasants in a mise-en-scène that oozes a primal vitality. Amber's early career as a London cut-purse takes place in settings—dark, narrow lanes, dank rooms with threateningly low ceilings—roiling with underworld menace. Three scenes set in the theater where Amber is to become a successful actress are suffused with Preminger's love of the stage. In the first, the heroine is mesmerized at

Preminger's love of the stage is displayed in the theater scenes in *Forever Amber.* Amber (Linda Darnell), far right.

a performance of *Romeo and Juliet.* In the other scenes she is herself onstage, having become a leading player in the company of Sir Richard Killigrew. The richly detailed theater setting with its horseshoe-shaped auditorium filled with obstreperous patrons milling in the pit among women selling apples (and what else?) as the gentry primp and ogle each other in the boxes would surely satisfy the most exacting historian. A duel between Bruce Carlton and a jealous captain, shot in elegant horizontal compositions, takes place in a pearly, Corot-like early morning light. The decrepit house where Amber saves Bruce from the plague radiates an aura of disease and decay. Preminger and Shamroy shoot the scenes of the Great Fire in a chiaroscuro that has the virtuosity of a Georges de la Tour painting. And for the elaborate processions and dances at the worldly court of Charles II, they use a vibrant palette.

Preminger's Old World formality is exactly what the material needs—Zanuck was astute in assigning him to be the rescue man—and not for a moment does Otto reveal his distaste for the story. Maintaining narrative momentum for over two hours and twenty minutes, his direction achieves genuine epic sweep. Shaping his star's performance, however, he was less successful. Perhaps because he didn't believe she could offer more, he presents Linda Darnell as an object to be looked at: a mannequin on display in period costumes and hairdos. As Amber she is no more than a virtual actress, a Restoration figurine with a small and inescapably contemporary-sounding voice. Under Preminger's careful (perhaps too careful) direction, Darnell is never less than adequate. But the director gives her no chance to make a stab at the potentially bravura acting moments, as for instance when Amber saves Bruce from the plague, which a spirited, intuitive performer could have brought to roaring life. Preminger even subdues Darnell's trademark sultriness. Her Amber is coquettish, but unlike Winsor's heroine she is never allowed to be sexually threatening or to be consumed by lust.

Throughout the five-month shoot on *Forever Amber* Otto maintained a bruising schedule. Putting in ten-hour days on the troubled production, he also worked regularly with writers on scripts for two upcoming projects, *Daisy Kenyon* and *The Dark Wood;* read or at least scanned dozens of novels circulated by the Fox story department; and saw every film and play that opened in Los Angeles. He boasted that he took no vacations, claiming that once he completed a film he would "go to bed for three days" before launching into his next project. Because *Amber,* a film he did not want to make, took so long, Preminger hardly took his customary three days before plunging into preproduction on a film he very much wanted to make.

FIVE

On the Job (2)

After being cooped up with Amber, Preminger was relieved to be working on Daisy Kenyon, an ambivalent character of the kind he was always drawn to. Based on a best-selling 1945 novel by Elizabeth Janeway, the undertaking also offered him the chance to prove himself in a new genre, the regulation woman's film of the 1940s. Daisy is a successful magazine illustrator facing a romantic conflict: Will she choose a prominent, married lawyer or an unmarried neurotic veteran? (At the time a sympathetic heroine would, of course, end up with the single veteran rather than the married lawyer, but against the odds Preminger sustains suspense by refusing to play favorites. His impartial response to the characters keeps the viewer guessing.)

For different reasons, the film's star, Joan Crawford, was as enthusiastic as Otto about making Daisy Kenyon. At forty-three, Crawford was old by the standards of Hollywood, and in fact too mature to play Janeway's troubled heroine. Yet as Ruth Warrick, cast as the lawyer's wife, recalled, "She begged on her knees to get the role. She had recently won an Academy Award for Mildred Pierce, in which she played her first mother part, and now she wanted to prove to the industry that she still could be convincing in a younger role. She was determined to fight the Hollywood 'rule' that a woman had claim to real beauty only for as long as the seven-year contract the studios then offered. To achieve this, she'd have done anything Preminger asked her to."[1]

With his *Daisy Kenyon* stars, Dana Andrews, Joan Crawford, and Henry Fonda. Andrews didn't want to be in the film.

Weeks before filming was to begin, at Crawford's request Preminger met with her for daily conferences in which they went over the script page by page, working out the blocking and motivation of each scene. "They got on very, very well," Ruth Warrick observed. "Joan was a thorough professional, a good screen actress who was probably *too* disciplined. And when she didn't want to be difficult, she wasn't. Otto had enormous respect for the very concentrated way she worked and also for her great dedication to being a movie star.

"With Otto and Joan, we had two tyrants on the set," as Warrick commented,

> and that may have kept both of them in line. I think each of them sensed the potential ferocity of the other. Quite unlike Otto, Joan was very secretive. You could never quite tell what she was thinking, although you felt she had an underlying anger at the world. Quite *like* Otto, however, she was used to being in command. She *demanded* deference, and she insisted on protocol because she came

In *Daisy Kenyon*, a woman's film saturated with male as well as female neuroses, an unfaithful husband (Dana Andrews) is more attentive to his daughters (Peggy Ann Garner and Connie Marshall) than to his wife (Ruth Warrick), standing next to her protective father (Nicholas Joy).

from such desperately low circumstances. She was polite to the men in the company, as you would be to a maid, but she didn't acknowledge I was alive; we were like boxers across the room, and I was just as glad because I didn't want to tangle with her.[2]

Crawford had an exceptional clause in her contract: because she was suffering from change of life and experiencing hot flashes, the temperature on the set had to remain at fifty degrees. "She was always in tennis shorts and a thin blouse because she was so hot, while I had to wear a fur coat to keep warm," Warrick recalled. "Otto said not one word about the temperature." (As Warrick commented, "A subject of talk every morning was Joan's mistreatment of her children, whom she had adopted when she was menopausal and an alcoholic; she couldn't have children of her own because she had had so many abortions. She wanted the publicity of photo ops with her children. I actually heard her say to her children, 'You *must* say, "I love you, Mommie dearest." ' ")[3]

Because all the actors were as reliable and hardworking as Crawford—like the star, Dana Andrews (as the lawyer), Henry Fonda (as the former soldier), and Warrick knew their lines, arrived on time, and followed instructions—Preminger was on cruise control throughout the shooting. "It was all as serene as a mill pond," Warrick remembered.

> I was surprised, because Otto already had quite a reputation for yelling. He had two styles, actually, the courtly and the tyrannical, but I felt he really preferred the courtly one. When he was in his courtly mode, in a most dignified manner he would announce to the cast, "Ladies and gentlemen, may I have your attention, please?" "Ladies and gentlemen, will you please join me in the commissary for luncheon?" Otto also was known as a ladies' man. But he was a gentleman and he was gallant to me, almost the way Orson [Welles] had been on *Citizen Kane* [in which Warrick played Emily Norton, Kane's first wife]. Like Orson, Otto respected actors, and he was very patient with me.
>
> Nonetheless, I have to say he carried himself like an army officer, and behaved like a general moving the troops. There were no fishing expeditions with Otto. No one, including Joan, *ever* argued with him; we all trusted his intelligence. But I think we all sensed he could cut you down to size.[4]

The trouble-free production, shot from June 16 to August 12, 1947, wrapped two days ahead of schedule with the final budget less than one hundred dollars over the original budget of $1,852,000. On the first day of shooting, as a thank-you for all the time he had spent with her working through the script, Crawford had presented Preminger with a set of garden furniture for 333 Bel-Air Road. On the final day she presented him with gold cuff links. Flattered, Otto later learned that "she always gave her director cuff links at the conclusion of shooting. Once at a party there were four of us wearing identical sets."[5]

Preminger and his first-rate cinematographer Leon Shamroy give the romantic melodrama a moody film noir undertow. Low-angle ceiling shots seem to trap the characters, and doors and windows enclose them in frames within the frame. Eve Preminger, who was visiting her uncle while he was shooting, said the sets were dark "to hide Joan Crawford's wrinkles."[6] That may well be true. But the four principal characters suffer from the kind of emotional wounds that Preminger had explored in his psychological thrillers, and the pools of darkness that seem to be lying in wait ready to

Magazine illustrator Daisy Kenyon (Joan Crawford) has an ambiguous, undeclared attraction to one of her models (Martha Stewart).

engulf each of them are thematically apt. Grieving over the death of his wife in a car accident five years ago, the vet is plagued by nightmares. The lawyer's brittle, unloved wife is a sexual hysteric who beats her daughters. In less obvious ways the lawyer and Daisy are also unstable. The lawyer's treatment of his wife is sadistic, and to win Daisy he's prepared to give up his children. And Daisy, too old to be as indecisive as she is about her romantic choices, befriends a fetching female model who becomes her roommate.

Daisy Kenyon was a project Preminger himself initiated, and at the time he was more engaged by it than by any of his other post-*Laura* films. As the years passed, however, he claimed that the film was simply an "assignment" about which he remembered nothing. (Similarly dismissive was the film's composer, the busy David Raksin. "I don't recall a goddamn thing about it. I was trying to get it done on time; the way we worked it's a miracle we

Fond brothers, Otto and Ingo, in 1947, when Ingo and his family moved from New York to Los Angeles.

remember anything. All I remember is that I had about four hours of sleep a night. I had to write to deadline, and I could.")[7] To be sure, *Daisy Kenyon* is no more than a well-wrought commodity that demonstrates yet again Preminger's ability to play by the rules. Rather than trying to reinvent or to deconstruct a 1940s woman's film, Preminger treats the material with respect, and his irony-free approach, along with the restrained performances he draws from his cast of pros, honors the genre.

As *Variety* proclaimed, the film is "high powered melodrama surefire for the femme market. It is a *True Confessions* yarn with a *Vogue* sheen. Producer-director Otto Preminger hasn't missed a trick in endowing 20th-Fox's version of the successful Elizabeth Janeway novel with glittering box office accoutrements."[8]

In the fall of 1947, as Otto was in postproduction on *Daisy Kenyon,* Ingo moved his family and the elder Premingers to Los Angeles from New York, where they had remained since their arrival from Austria in 1938. After Otto's film career had been reignited in 1942 he had continued to visit New York regularly and to remain a loving son, brother, brother-in-law, and uncle. But since he lived like a bachelor even before his marriage to Marion had begun to deteriorate, it had fallen to the solidly married Ingo to take care of Markus and Josefa. (Wed in 1936, Ingo and Kate remained a devoted couple until Ingo's death in 2006.) Although Ingo had a law degree from the University of Vienna, he never worked as a lawyer in America. Until he moved the family to Los Angeles, Ingo had "bought and sold job lots, which was a very good business during the war. Merchandise was hard to get, and I struck up friendships with manufacturers and sold to people who couldn't get any merchandise. After the war I saw there was no future in it."[9] Notably lacking his brother's talent ("I have no artistic gifts," he claimed), Ingo was a steady paterfamilias able to adjust quickly to life in a new country. It was simply not the Preminger style to grumble or to reflect nostalgically on the past—for Markus Preminger's two sons, the present was the only tense that mattered.

The elder Premingers had also managed to adjust. "My grandparents had smaller living quarters in the United States, in New York as well as Los Angeles, than what they had been used to in Austria," Eve Preminger recalled.

For one thing, they no longer had the same number of servants. Here, my grandmother had to cook instead of directing the servants to cook. I gather they still had money but they had to accept a change of status, which they did quite gracefully. It was harder for me to adjust than it was for them. During the war, when I was five, six, and seven, people did not distinguish between Germans and Austrians who had escaped from Hitler, and being a Nazi. I hid my parents because of their accents; but since I was so little I couldn't hide them that much. Having a German accent was a problem at that time, a real problem. Otto played Nazis in films, and I remember I would stand up in school and say he wasn't really that way.[10]

Eve, who had looked forward to Otto's visits during the time her family was in New York, recalled him as "a doting uncle who would take me to lunch at the Stork Club." In the summer of 1945, "when my mother was going to give birth, Otto offered to take me back with him to Hollywood. I went out to Los Angeles with Otto on the *Super Chief*—and Otto saw to it that I had a fabulous month. He built a swimming pool for me, he bought a dog and had a doghouse built, and he hired Miss College America, who had been on the cover of *Life,* to be my companion. Meals were served in a formal style, quite unlike at my parents' home. A butler would serve you, and then remove the plate."[11] Preminger's extravagance was second nature, but his gift giving was in no sense a substitute for affection: Otto adored his eldest niece, and all the presents were supplements to rather than surrogates for his feelings for her.

Otto's niece Eve with her beloved uncle.

Eve's glowing reports to her parents of her summer with Otto may have influenced her father to relocate to Los Angeles two years later. Also influencing Ingo's decision was his brother's professional prominence. As Ingo said, "Hollywood is a snobbish place, and when I first arrived there, Otto was an important director. That gave me cachet." Because he was skilled in meeting and greeting, Ingo decided to become an agent. And with the help of his established older brother—"I owe Otto more than he owes me," Ingo said—he quickly began to sign up clients, his famous brother among them. Otto gave Ingo access to industry figures, but Ingo had the temperament necessary to sustain a career as an agent. "I made an honest impression, and people trusted me," he admitted.[12] And there was one other factor: unlike his brother, Ingo did not yell. "My father always made a point of being calm," Eve said.[13] And in a way having a famously hot-tempered brother worked to Ingo's advantage. "Many people began to say that I was the nice Preminger," he said.[14] Ingo may not have screamed as part of his way of conducting business, but blessed with the strong sense of self he inherited from his father, he was also no pushover. With his sharp wit and sarcastic quips ever at the ready, Ingo was every bit as capable as his brother of putting malingerers in their place.

Ingo's first job was with the Nat Goldstone Agency on Sunset Boulevard. "When my father went to work for Nat Goldstone, he told him it would be for a year and that after that year he would open his own agency," Jim Preminger, now also an agent, recalled. "And that is exactly what he did, when nobody thought he could or would. Otto introduced Ingo to a lot of people, including Ring Lardner Jr. and Dalton Trumbo, who became his clients; and then, near the end of his life, I also repped Lardner."[15] "Agenting is such a good business," Ingo said. "Unlike in my previous line, you didn't have to buy the product; you acquire actors as clients and get 10 percent or more. How can you do better than that?"[16]

As Ingo and his family were settling into their new life in Los Angeles in the fall of 1947, *Forever Amber* (on October 10) and *Daisy Kenyon* (on November 27) opened to good business and reviews. Otto was at the top of his game as a trusty contract director. On his next assignment, however, he stumbled. Once again he was called on to replace Ernst Lubitsch, in uncertain health since he had been unable to complete *A Royal Scandal* in 1945. In 1946, Lubitsch had successfully directed *Cluny Brown,* but shortly after that film's release he had suffered another heart seizure—at a party Otto was hosting at 333 Bel-Air Road for one of the leading jurists of the Nuremberg trials. Nonetheless, during the following spring and summer Lubitsch felt well enough to begin working with his favorite screenwriter, Samson Raphaelson, on adapting the kind of frothy operetta that had enjoyed a vogue in Hollywood in the 1930s but by 1947 had become a back number. For the project that he was calling *That Lady in Ermine,* a fable about a countess who saves her small (mythical) country when she seduces the Hungarian colonel in charge of the occupation, Lubitsch cast Betty Grable, Fox's top wartime musical comedy star. "Daddy? How could you? Why Betty Grable?" Lubitsch's daughter Nicola remembered asking her father in consternation. "He didn't like being challenged and he was upset that his own daughter questioned him. But I thought, and still think so many years later: How could he ever have chosen her? She couldn't sing or dance or act. I felt his career must have been in trouble, and that hers must have been also. Had he been forced to accept her? I thought she was just awful, so common and ordinary."[17]

If Nicola Lubitsch could not see Betty Grable in the role, neither could the star herself. "It's very witty, but is it me?" Grable remarked to Darryl Zanuck after she read the script. "And, more to the point, will my fans buy it?" Zanuck told her to have confidence in Lubitsch and assured her that the change of venue ("not a footlight in sight") would be a wise career move.[18]

Once Grable began working with Lubitsch in early November, the director's delight in his own material charmed her and helped to still her doubts. Like Preminger a former Reinhardt actor, Lubitsch "loved acting all the parts," recalled costar Douglas Fairbanks Jr., cast as the invading Hungarian. "He was very good, actually. He had such vitality; he was tripping over himself with ideas. During rehearsal he'd laugh with pleasure and sometimes he'd even ruin his own takes."[19]

For the first two weeks of shooting Lubitsch was a buoyant presence. On Saturday, November 29, seemingly in good health, he spent the day setting up master shots for a scene with Fairbanks and Cesar Romero. On Sunday, along with Otto, Billy Wilder, and Marlene Dietrich, Lubitsch was to attend a screening of a new film, *Le diable au corps,* at the home of the William Wylers. Before the screening, however, following a tryst with a woman he was seeing casually, Lubitsch suffered a massive seizure. His terrified date called Otto, who rushed across the street to find that his friend was near death. Otto phoned Lubitsch's doctor, on whose advice he then called for an ambulance; but by the time help arrived Lubitsch had died. To avert a scandal, and before friends and the police arrived, Otto took the hysterical young woman to his own house.

Later that night, during an informal wake, Mrs. William Wyler reported that she overheard a phone call Otto made to Darryl Zanuck in which Preminger claimed that Lubitsch had asked him to complete the film if anything should happen to him. Preminger was "an avid careerist and saw *That Lady in Ermine* as an opportunity," as Lubitsch's biographer Scott Eyman maintained.[20] But at this point in his career, with *Forever Amber* and *Daisy Kenyon* bringing in a lot of money for the studio, Otto surely did not need the reflected glory of completing the work of another director. In addition, he had not enjoyed making *A Royal Scandal,* and he certainly would not have relished the "opportunity" of working with Betty Grable. Preminger was always to claim that it was Zanuck who had asked him to finish the film, and it is only fair and probably accurate to take Otto at his word. Besides, Scott Eyman's demonizing portrait of Preminger as an insensitive "careerist" angling for preferment at a moment of tragedy is out of character. Taking on Lubitsch's film was for Preminger an act of friendship and a professional obligation, another example of his being a cooperative employee.

On December 5, 1947, only five days after Lubitsch's death, he was compelled to resume shooting. However, once Otto took over, the mood on the set changed. Lubitsch had laughed at the jokes he had written and loved performing all the roles; Otto, in contrast, thought the script was "uninteresting."[21] The shoot was no longer fun. Between Preminger and his two leading players there was a total absence of rapport. Early on, after Otto blew up at an electrician, Douglas Fairbanks Jr. walked off the set and refused to return unless the director apologized. "Douglas could not and would not tolerate rudeness of any kind," Vera (Mrs. Douglas) Fairbanks recalled. "He was not a saint—he could be severe—but he could *not* be rude; politeness was inherent in his nature, and he could not bear to see rude behavior in others. He could not have continued unless Preminger apologized."[22] Otto did as Fairbanks demanded, but the actor continued to be unhappy. When Fairbanks mentioned a point of interpretation he had discussed with Lubitsch, Preminger was offended. "Mr. Lubitsch is dead. *I* am the director of this picture," he said.[23] "We did not get along," Fairbanks succinctly remembered.[24]

Douglas Fairbanks Jr. in a scene from *That Lady in Ermine*. He didn't get along with Preminger or his costar Betty Grable (depicted in the painting).

Where Lubitsch had treated Betty Grable with a fetching whimsy and showered her with reassurance, Preminger was brusque. Grable felt he was "too heavy-handed in his approach to the story"[25] and, justifiably, she was dismayed when Preminger eliminated some of the musical numbers Lubitsch had shot. The company's esprit de corps was further undermined by a rising tension between the two stars, who seemed to be acting out a real-life version of *The Prince and the Showgirl* minus the sexual attraction. According to her biographer, Tom McGee, Grable "thought Fairbanks acted more regally than the King of England. She felt that Fairbanks denigrated her fame, regarding her as a chorus girl who got lucky."[26] Well? "Douglas did not think Grable was a mental giant, but he would never have been less than polite to her," Vera Fairbanks said.[27]

Preminger, regarding himself as no more than a hired hand, completed the film on January 5, a few days ahead of schedule. But the joyless atmosphere on the set is reflected in the film, easily the most leaden in the Preminger canon. The original fault, however, must be attributed to Lubitsch. Under his direction the film certainly would have been jauntier, slyer, and the rites of seduction would have been conducted with a greater playfulness. Preminger, to be sure, does what he can to drain the material of vivacity, but it's hard to see how the film could ever have been a winner. In casting all-American Betty as a patriot who outsmarts foreign invaders, Lubitsch may have intended his romp as a metaphor for the recent American victory in the war, but if so he chose the wrong star. Grable with her tinny, vapid voice and slovenly diction exudes a common touch that trounces Lubitsch's famously refined one. When the film opened to moderate business on July 15, 1948, it received better notices than it deserved as reviewers scrambled to discern traces of Lubitsch's hand. But Nicola Lubitsch had the right idea: "Grable was terrible, the film was terrible, and it should have been abandoned after my father died."[28] Otto's assessment of *That Lady in Ermine* was that he "finished it—that was it."[29]

On January 12, 1948, a week after Otto completed *That Lady in Ermine*, gossip columnist Louella Parsons reported in the *Los Angeles Herald Examiner* that Preminger had asked Marion for a divorce. "Last year, Mrs. Preminger in Mexico asked Otto for a divorce so she could marry Alex Wennergren, but his wife refused," Parsons wrote, bringing her readers up to date. "A few months later Mrs. Preminger returned to Hollywood and Otto and nothing more was said about the divorce," Parsons continued. "The pending divorce will be amicable. Mrs. Preminger several months ago went to Budapest to visit her family. They have all gone to Romania, where she has a home."

At the same time that Preminger was formally ending his marriage, his affair with Natalie Draper also unraveled, in an encounter at Le Papillon, a fashionable restaurant on Sunset Boulevard. There were conflicting reports about what took place, but apparently Otto became jealous when he saw Natalie at the restaurant with a date, screenwriter Ivan Goff. In an interview in the *Los Angeles Herald Examiner* on January 13, Natalie recalled that "on this occasion Otto came over to the bar, kissed my hand, then slapped Ivan without a word." "There was no such incident," Preminger contended. Goff's recollection was that "there were a few hot words, but no blows were struck. We cooled off." The next day in the same newspaper Goff offered another version of the encounter. "I rose from my seat and propelled my fist three times into what might have been a face." "Natalie is embarrassed," her mother reported in the same article. "She told me Ivan had hit Mr. Preminger in self-defense, and that Ivan acted like a perfect gentleman." "Otto Preminger and I went together for a long time," Draper herself explained. "He wants me to marry him and has asked his estranged wife for a divorce. But I don't want any part of him. He's enraged with jealousy. He doesn't like anyone I go out with." Summoning an Old World gallantry after the fact, Otto, who never claimed to have proposed to Natalie, said he refused "to take the matter seriously. I wish to make no statement that would involve a lady, and particularly a lady that has been my friend." After the incident, however, whether or not blows had been struck, Natalie was a friend no longer.

When Marion returned from Romania in February, the Premingers didn't bother to keep up appearances. As divorce proceedings dragged on— the divorce was not final until August 25, 1949—they continued to reside at 333 Bel-Air Road but did not cohost parties or go together as a couple to restaurants and industry gatherings. Their estrangement was final, but it was not bitter. And, as always, Otto had the support of his family, who had appreciated Marion's "flair" and her social skills but had never fully accepted her. For a family man like Otto, surrounded by the enduring marriages of his parents and his brother, this was a difficult time. Now in his mid-forties, he may well have wondered if he would ever have other children besides the son he had had with Gypsy Rose Lee, or if, with his volatile temperament, he would ever be able to sustain a lasting relationship.

Meanwhile, his professional status also seemed to be coming apart. For many months after he finished the Lubitsch assignment, Otto, preoccupied with negotiating the terms of his divorce, seemed to flounder, his name attached to a number of projects that were never produced. Finally, in late spring he began to work on a screenplay that would make it into production, an adaptation of Oscar Wilde's 1897 play *Lady Windermere's Fan,* about a woman with a past, the mysterious Mrs. Erlynne, who is redeemed when she prevents her married daughter Lady Windermere (who does not know that Mrs. Erlynne is her mother) from running off with a roué. Preminger's standing was still secure enough for him to be able to persuade Zanuck to let him produce and direct a period piece based on a literary classic that could not possibly have seemed at the time to be a good commercial bet. That Zanuck approved not only attests to his artistic integrity, it also reveals the flexibility of the studio system itself. Built into the factory production mode was the possibility of making the occasional coterie project such as the version of Wilde's play that Preminger was planning.

To help him with the adaptation Otto selected an odd duo, his Bel-Air Road neighbor Walter Reisch, noted for his generosity and goodwill, and Dorothy Parker, the acidulous New York wit. Added to the mix was Ross Evans, a studio writer. Preminger's intention was to transform Wilde's brilliant but unstable play, part nineteenth-century melodrama, part coruscating drawing-room comedy of manners, into a fluent, modern film. He and his writers faced major challenges. Despite his epigrams and his apparent insouciance, Wilde was dedicated to the importance of being earnest about preserving the British class system—for the playwright, as for most of his characters, a frivolous surface conceals a conservative heart. As a result, Wilde's wit is devoted to keeping in place a system of values most audiences in "classless" America would be unlikely to embrace. Further, with its manifold contrivances, Wilde's playmaking exudes a musty aroma that any contemporary film would have to dispel. Was Preminger once again, as with *That Lady in Ermine,* taking on a project certain to fail?

As he hammered out a screenplay with his three able writers, Otto approached Oscar Wilde fearlessly, without any regard for the sanctity of the original text. His goal, however, was not to dismember a work he greatly admired but rather to ease its transition into a new medium. Over the spring and early summer of 1948 he was renovating Oscar Wilde's *Lady Windermere's Fan* into *The Fan,* a film to be produced and directed by Otto Preminger, take it or leave it.

At this point in his career, Wilde's play was a strategically unwise and perhaps even perverse choice for Preminger. Since Ernst Lubitsch in 1925 had directed a brilliant silent version of *Lady Windermere's Fan,* Otto for the third time would be setting himself up in a contest with Lubitsch he was destined to lose. Preminger respected Lubitsch's straight-faced treatment of the play as a high melodrama that endorses the strict social codes by which the British upper crust secures its power. But with justice he felt that a silent version of Wilde could hardly be the last word, and he was convinced that his was a fresh approach rather than a reworking of Lubitsch's.

Otto began production with his usual ebullience, certain that the screenplay he had supervised had conquered all the obvious obstacles. As Virginia McDowall (cast as Lady Agatha, the daughter of an acid-tongued society dowager) recalled, Preminger

> behaved himself and there was a good feeling on the set. It wasn't the family feeling I had while working on *How Green Was My Valley* with John Ford, but it was a nice experience for all of us. I wasn't afraid of Otto—I had worked for Cecil B. DeMille for five years and I hadn't been afraid of him either. The way Otto worked was that we had rehearsals before the shots, rather than before the film started shooting. It was a good cast, and though Otto's relations with Martita Hunt, who played my mother and who had a "rep," as Otto certainly did, were sometimes strained, there were no explosions. The only real tension came from George Sanders [playing the disruptive rake, Lord Darlington, who tries to seduce Lady Windermere away from her husband], who was a strange man and not friendly to anyone. He was bored, and seemed so lonely. Otto was always kind to him, however. And he was really lovely with Jeanne Crain [Lady Windermere], who had a natural elegance that was right for the part, and Madeleine Carroll [Mrs. Erlynne]—I remembered her with Ronald Colman in *The Prisoner of Zenda:* heaven![30]

Preminger shot quickly, from July 7 to August 18, 1948, and brought the film in several hundred dollars under the $1.5 million budget. But about halfway through, for the only time in his career, he lost his confidence. He began to question both his screenplay and his direction. He didn't think he had the right touch for mixing the work's disparate tones of melodrama and comedy of manners, and he was convinced the film would be poorly reviewed and attended. "It was a mistake on my part to have remade the play," he said, looking back. "Whatever I did to the film was wrong. It is one of the few pictures I disliked while I was making it."[31] Virginia McDowall agreed.

> I felt at the time, and I still think so, that Zanuck was out of his mind to allow Otto Preminger to direct Oscar Wilde. Otto didn't have the delicacy for it. But if he had doubts as we were shooting, he never let on. Not for a moment. He always behaved professionally. And at the end, when he hosted a party for us at a swank restaurant, he kept up the pretense. He was oh so charming that night, and

Martita, with whom he had had some friction, was charming too. She was terribly ugly, but that night she was being very hostessy, she was dressed beautifully, and she was delightful. If Otto thought the film was not a success—and he must have known, we all felt it—he did not let on.[32]

As Preminger fully expected, *The Fan* opened to withering notices. "Except for a wonderful portrayal of the Duchess of Berwick by Martita Hunt, the work has been drained of all Wilde's wit, style, and period color, and all of Wilde's defects as a dramatist are rudely underlined," huffed Howard Barnes in the *New York Herald Tribune* on April 7, 1949. Apart from Preminger's early B projects, *The Fan,* branded with a malodorous reputation, remains the most obscure work of the director's career. It is also Preminger's most underrated film and richly deserving of reassessment.

As Lubitsch had, Preminger emphasizes Wilde's melodrama over his social comedy and refuses to regard Wilde's conservative ideology as either quaint or irrelevant. Having decided to tell Wilde's story as a memory piece set in a frame within the frame, Preminger opens the film in postwar London at an auction where the incriminating fan that Lady Windermere left at Lord Darlington's the night she almost ran off with him is to be sold. An elderly woman, Mrs. Erlynne, comes forward to claim the fan, and a kindly auctioneer allows her twenty-four hours to prove that the fan is hers. When she revisits Lord Darlington's residence, Mrs. Erlynne encounters the elderly roué and the two survivors begin to reminisce (we learn that Lord and Lady Windermere died when a bomb ripped through their town house during the Blitz). At that point the film segues into the past, adhering to the general outlines of Wilde's play. Tampering with Wilde's structure may have been literary heresy (of a kind Preminger never hesitated to commit), but the framing device proves effective—presented as memory, Wilde's old-fashioned storytelling is softened. Setting the action in the past, in effect a "foreign" country with a set of social rules different from those of the present, endows it with an almost Proustian poignancy.

Throughout, Preminger and his *Laura* cinematographer Joseph La Shelle indicate transitions from present to past by elegant, sweeping pan shots. For the crowded party scenes, they use deep focus and swirling camera movement. But the visual ingenuity would be no more than bric-a-brac if Preminger's actors were not up to the challenge of giving Wilde a fair shake. Ham-resistant as ever, the director permitted Madeleine Carroll none of the florid gestures and vocal overemphasis with which stage actresses are often tempted to play a woman with a past. Carroll's subtle performance is

Maternal sacrifice in *The Fan,* Preminger's overlooked adaptation of Oscar Wilde's *Lady Windermere's Fan.* Mrs. Erlynne (Madeleine Carroll) (right) tries to save her married daughter Lady Windermere (Jeanne Crain) from ruining her reputation.

attuned to the intimacy of film. Preminger helped Jeanne Crain, the sole American in the cast (who speaks in a mid-Atlantic diction), to eliminate any trace in her voice or body language of a casual contemporary quality. Her Lady Windermere, surely her finest performance, is graceful and touching. George Sanders as a world-weary Lord Darlington; Martita Hunt as the choruslike Duchess of Berwick, her every syllable dripping with venom; and Virginia McDowall as the Duchess's idiotically compliant daughter ("Yes, Mamá," are the only words she utters) are pitch perfect. More than any of his Fox films *The Fan* evokes a sense of the Viennese Otto, the stagestruck young man who skipped school in order to devour the world's great plays amid the Baroque splendor of the National Library.

After completing *The Fan,* Otto seemed again to be at loose ends. He was incapable of not working, but he had no exciting new projects to engage him. His seven-year contract would be coming up for renewal or revision in a year, in the summer of 1950, and he began to wonder if Zanuck would ask him to sign. He also wondered whether he would want to continue working at the studio. As Preminger had to have seen, his track record was uneven.

After *Laura* there had been no other triumphs. *Fallen Angel,* his second psychological thriller, was only spottily effective. *Forever Amber* may have been one of the finest rescue missions in recent Hollywood history, but Preminger himself had no respect for it. His completion of the two projects begun by Lubitsch had yielded two stillborn talkfests. The well-made *Daisy Kenyon* was a work in a minor key, *Centennial Summer* a not altogether fluent musical. And then there was *The Fan:* supremely intelligent, "Viennese," and, both at the time and ever since, completely dismissed. Although Preminger's refusal to repeat *Laura* represented a praiseworthy effort to defy typecasting, there was still reason for the director and for Zanuck to feel dissatisfied, to regard the career as floating on a promise as yet unfulfilled. Prestige projects seemed to be handed out to other directors.

As Preminger's fortunes at the studio in 1949 and 1950 seemed to be dipping, the top director on the lot was Joseph Mankiewicz, who won Oscars for both writing and directing *A Letter to Three Wives* (in 1949) and *All About Eve* (in 1950). It was Mankiewicz's impression that Otto's personality was holding him back. "I felt that Otto was angry at the position he was in," Mankiewicz observed forty years later.

> In Vienna he had been a man of power, and got all those things a man of power should get. Otto played a Nazi too well; he became too good a villain and I was sorry for him because nobody would let him off the hook. He looked like a villain: Otto was *not* handsome—and he became defensive very quickly. He did not want to be disliked. I think it puzzled him, and made him sad. But I don't think he ever quite understood that the American ego is different from the Germanic ego. In Vienna Otto could say "It stinks" to a writer and the writer would say, "Yah! Herr Preminger, you are right." The Germans are used to being more loud. I worked with Fritz Lang, another German who was hated. The grips had rigged a light and they were going to drop it on Fritz, who made many violent enemies. Oh, how that man was reviled! But Fritz was more sophisticated than Otto for some reason and he did make friends, mostly actors. I guess Otto didn't. Fritz kept very quiet, lived a very quiet life, and Otto didn't. Otto was in a strange country, he had a strange look, and if it had been me I'd have played it cool. But that wasn't Otto's way.[33]

For what were to be the three final films under his original Fox contract, Preminger, perhaps yielding to the pull of the system, returned to the noir terrain of *Laura.* In quick succession he produced and directed *Whirlpool* (1949), *Where the Sidewalk Ends* (1950), and *The Thirteenth Letter* (1950).

As José Ferrer, *Whirlpool*'s costar, recalled, "Otto and Zanuck hoped that the film, which is like a sequel to *Laura*—it had the same star, the same mood and atmosphere—would have the same success."[34] Like *Laura*, *Whirlpool* is a sleek thriller about the well-to-do. Ann Sutton (Gene Tierney), the fashionable, neurotic wife of a prominent psychoanalyst, is a kleptomaniac. When she is arrested at an upscale department store for stealing a broach, she is saved by Korvo (José Ferrer), an astrologer and hypnotist who specializes in separating gullible rich women from their money. Korvo convinces Ann that he can cure her; his real goal, however, is to implicate her in the murder of his ex-mistress, a patient of Ann's husband. At the end, Korvo is gunned down in front of the large portrait of the woman he has killed.

Working with experienced screenwriters like Ben Hecht and Andrew Solt, Preminger could not get the convoluted plot to gel. But his shrewd casting of the two leads helped to offset the damage. As the unstable heroine Gene Tierney, who had already suffered periods of mental illness and in later years was to have a harrowing history of breakdowns followed by fragile recoveries, is startlingly effective. Korvo's comment to Ann, that she has become imprisoned in her role as a pampered, dressed-to-perfection housewife, is also a comment on Tierney's own "perfection" as a well-behaved Hollywood mannequin. As Korvo (*kuervo* in Yiddish is a male prostitute, an apt description of the character's gigolo manner), José Ferrer offers the enticing spectacle of a phony actor playing a phony actor. The hamminess that was to curdle almost all Ferrer's work is exactly the point here: Korvo is an out-and-out charlatan. For the other major role, that of the society therapist with a trophy wife, Preminger made a rare casting flub: in a tuxedo Richard Conte looks and sounds like a thug. "Conte was a big mistake," Ferrer said. "We all felt it while we were shooting the film. He suggested a New York street type rather than a well-educated psychiatrist."[35]

The director and his cinematographer Arthur Miller gild *Whirlpool* with many visual pleasures. Mirror shots of the troubled heroine in her well-appointed home—as in *Laura* the objects of the rich are made to glisten—underline the character's duality. In a brilliant sequence of noir iconography, under hypnosis and performing the script Korvo has provided, Ann leaves her house and drives to the house of the murdered woman. The camera is placed at odd, transfiguring angles; diagonal shadows cover the walls of Ann's house and of the hilltop house of the dead woman whose portrait looms over her living room like a malevolent deity. The shot in which Gene Tierney stands before the portrait is an obvious homage to *Laura* and a rare

Imitating *Laura:* Gene Tierney in a scene from *Whirlpool.*

moment of self-quotation in Preminger's oeuvre. David Raksin's theme song ("nice, but not great," as the composer recalled)[36] evokes the heroine's descent into a vortex.

After finishing the thriller (shot from June 6 to July 22, 1949, with Otto's final budget again several hundred dollars under the original estimate), the director was thrown into a whirlpool of his own as he finalized his divorce from Marion. In court, playing fast and loose with the facts in her usual way, Marion charged her husband with desertion, claiming he had left 333 Bel-Air Road on January 17, 1946, and "never came back." The truth was that, as she had begun to travel more frequently, it was Marion herself who had hardly been at home. In her 1957 autobiography Marion contradicted her courtroom testimony. "While the lawyers were busy with our case we went on living in the Bel-Air house exactly as if we intended going on that way indefinitely," she wrote. "We talked over our affairs quietly and so dispassionately that I had the feeling none of it was real. Surely, two people did not plan to terminate a relationship of nearly twenty years with so little emotion. But we did." Marion added that friends who came for lunch or dinner and "to swim in the pool among the white gardenias did not suspect that all this was the final scene of the last act of a play."[37]

Although she was wrong about the date of her husband's departure, Marion was indeed accurate about his desertion. For many years Otto had not been a loving or faithful spouse, and for his abandonment Marion exacted stiff reparations. In an interview in 1958, however, Marion in her highly colored way claimed that she walked out of 333 virtually empty-handed. "I left a closet of clothes and a great art collection."³⁸ Otto's recollection was quite different. "Marion got the best lawyers [who] got for her all they could, according to California law. It was expensive but it felt good to be free."³⁹ Ultimately, the divorce was to cost him the Bel-Air house, for which he admitted he had "overspent." "I had a lot of financial obligations, and I hadn't paid my taxes [when] my business manager [early in 1951, when Otto was in New York] called and said, 'the Government has attached your house.' I said: 'Sell it.' I never saw it again. Never saw that house, which I loved . . . or its paintings and furniture. I never cared because I felt I must be able to detach myself from material things and live."⁴⁰

The divorce was good news for both Otto and Marion. Otto won his freedom and Marion's life took a completely unexpected turn. "One outgrows things," Marion said. "The world I knew was suddenly meaningless and without purpose." Not long after leaving Bel-Air Road, Marion met Dr. Albert Schweitzer. "Since I was a schoolgirl I have been fascinated with the teachings of Dr. Albert Schweitzer," Marion claimed. "I earned my Dr. of Philosophy degree at the University of Vienna on a thesis written on Dr. Schweitzer." (Marion did not even graduate from high school, and at the time she was supposedly writing her thesis she was appearing as a chorus girl posed on an enormous replica of a chocolate cake that revolved to music.) She began to spend several months each year at Dr. Schweitzer's hospital in an African jungle. Here, in a remote outpost in Lambaréné, Gabon, the ex–Mrs. Otto Preminger, former doyenne of New York and Hollywood society, put in long hours as a nurse. "I have dedicated my life to the work of the greatest man who ever lived," she said in a 1958 interview.⁴¹

Whenever she returned to New York from her yearly visit to Africa, Marion sought contributions from rich people she had met during her marriage to Otto. Against his will, Otto also became one of Dr. Schweitzer's benefactors. In August 1953, Marion took Otto to court, claiming that her ex-husband owed her $48,000 under the terms of their 1949 separation agreement. She accused Otto of living on "a very grand scale" and entertaining "with lavishness" while ducking payments to her. Otto maintained that the 1949 agreement was void because at the time it was executed Marion had concealed that she had obtained a divorce in Mexico, a charge Marion denied. On September 30, 1953, California Supreme Court Justice Edgar J.

Nathan Jr. upheld Marion's claim that Preminger had failed to live up to his agreement and ordered him to pay his former wife $48,000.[42] Marion used her back alimony to buy medical and surgical supplies for Dr. Schweitzer's clinics. For many years Marion worked tirelessly to raise money for the clinics, and in the 1960s she served as the honorary consul in New York for the Republic of Gabon.

Marion published two books. In her 1957 autobiography, *All I Want Is Everything,* she "stars" as Mrs. Otto Preminger. "A goulash sadly lacking in paprika," reported the *Library Journal.*[43] "Outstandingly vapid," huffed Helen Lawrenson in *McCall's.*[44] However, Marion's second book, *The Sands of Tamanrasset,* is another matter altogether. In it she recounts the story of Charles de Foucauld (1858–1916), a dissolute Parisian aristocrat who as a hussar in North Africa fell under its spell and experienced a spiritual conversion. Exchanging the high life in Paris for a regime of poverty and prayer, Foucauld established a Christian sanctuary in a remote Saharan location. At the time that Marion's book was published, in 1965, Foucauld, who was killed by Arab brigands, was being considered for sainthood. Tracing her hero's evolution from flesh to spirit, Marion seemed to be writing a disguised autobiography that evoked her own journey from Bel-Air to Lambaréné. Despite some amateurish passages of invented dialogue, the book achieves a depth of feeling that belies Marion's self-created image as an airhead, the woman with "the million-dollar smile."

In the last decade of her life, Marion settled on Park Avenue rather than the African jungle. But her marriage in 1962 to a wealthy New York industrialist, Albert Mayer, did not end her good works and she continued to raise money for Schweitzer. Because the name was useful for her social standing as well as her fund-raising endeavors, even after her remarriage Marion continued to identify herself as Mrs. Otto Preminger. In 1960, after he had married for the third time, which meant that there were three women who were called Mrs. Otto Preminger, Otto attempted to prevent Marion from continuing to use his name. Reaching Marion's secretary, he asked if his former wife could be known as Marion Preminger-Mayer. "The secretary's reaction was amazing," Otto recalled. " 'You should be ashamed of yourself,' she said furiously. 'Do you know of whom you are speaking? You are speaking of a saint!' "[45]

In 1971, Willi Frischauer received a chilly reception when he tried to interview Marion for the biography he was writing about Otto. "I have forgotten [Preminger]. I do not remember he ever existed. I do not want to hear his name," she said. When Frischauer pointed out that she had written about Otto in her memoirs, she snapped that she "repudiated" the book, which besides was "years ago." Frischauer continued to challenge her, reminding her that she was still using the Preminger name. "I am Your Excellency now, Consul-General of Gabon!" she snapped before hanging up.[46] Marion, who knows at what age, died suddenly of a heart attack in April 1972. "All in all, Marion always meant well," Otto recalled in his autobiography. "She was a decent human being without any malice."[47] In the end, she was much more than that. As the first Mrs. Otto Preminger, she was a crucial partner in her husband's rise to Hollywood prominence. After her life with Otto, first as an ambassador-at-large for Dr. Schweitzer and then as the chronicler of Charles de Foucauld, her "spiritual lover," she

Dana Andrews plays a police officer with an explosive temper in Preminger's psychological thriller, *Where the Sidewalk Ends.*

became a person of real substance. In her own way, Marion's strength of will and her determination to accomplish something of value were reflections of the powerful men she was drawn to. To be sure, she was often an artful fabricator, vain and frivolous; yet she was also good-hearted, and in her devotion to Dr. Schweitzer she attained a stature that would not have been available to her as Mrs. Otto Preminger.

As he was negotiating divorce terms with Marion and her lawyers, Otto worked on *Where the Sidewalk Ends,* which he shot from December 27, 1949, to March 3, 1950. Unlike *Laura* and *Whirlpool,* set in a world of wealth Otto knew at first hand, *Where the Sidewalk Ends* takes place on the mean streets. Preminger may have been in alien territory but surely he identified with the film's protagonist, Lieutenant Mark Dixon, a police investigator with an ungovernable temper. After Dixon accidentally kills a suspect in a murder case he is investigating, he is charged with the job of finding the killer, and as he attempts to conceal what he did he begins to act and think like a criminal. Falling for the estranged wife of the man he murdered and horrified when her father is arrested for the crime, Dixon is caught in a noir whirlpool. He may be unruly but Dixon is decent, and to save the widow and her innocent father he is willing to sacrifice his life. In the end, however, through the kind of tortuous plotting that stains Preminger's Fox-period noirs, Dixon survives. As the divided antihero, Preminger cast one of his favorite players, tight-lipped minimalist Dana Andrews.

Preminger and his cinematographer, Joseph La Shelle, transform Times Square (part location, part studio re-creation) into a setting twitching with menace. A place where good things do not happen, the film's Times Square, something of a dress rehearsal for the famous New York-at-night location shooting of *Sweet Smell of Success* seven years later, is a neon playground of frenetic movement. In the title sequence, Dixon and his partner listen to dispatches on their car radio as they drive by the flashing lights of the city at night, a cauldron waiting to explode. There is no title music; the only sounds are the buzzing radio and the muffled cacophony of street noises. The settings resemble noir-city prints by Martin Lewis or Reginald Marsh. Dixon works in a bare office with barred windows. The suspect he kills hides out in the kind of rooming house often found in film noir; outside, elevated trains in the deep-focus distance provide a rumbling undercurrent.

On June 28, 1950, a week before the film opened, Otto was offered, and decided to sign, a new contract with Fox. Under his original seven-year contract, the studio had had exclusive claims on his services, but now at his own request his obligations were reduced. He would produce and direct one film a year for four years, and beyond that he was free to work on whatever projects he wanted. In return for release time, Otto's salary was cut. When Preminger had originally approached his agent, Charles Feldman, to negotiate the contractual terms he would be demanding—release time and half pay—Feldman refused to represent him and warned his client that he would be committing professional suicide. "You'll wind up directing plays on Broadway again," he predicted.[48] Yet returning to the theater was exactly what Preminger had been itching to do throughout the seven years in which he had been bound to the studio. More crucially, he also wanted time off so that he could set himself up as an independent filmmaker—the industry was about to undergo a seismic change, and unlike his recalcitrant agent, Otto was among the first to recognize it.

In 1947, the federal government had accused the major studios of restraint of trade—in addition to producing and distributing their films, the majors exhibited them in their own theater chains—and invoked an antitrust suit in the form of a consent decree, under the terms of which the studios would gradually have to sell their theaters. Since exhibition would be divorced from production and distribution, the stranglehold the studios had had over the American film industry would begin to be loosened. It was to take about a decade for the process to be completed, but the consent decree signaled the beginning of the end for the old system. Theater owners, freed from the time-honored practice of block booking, could bid for films on a competitive basis. And as Preminger noted, with the new arrangement "independent producers could at last make pictures and have them exhibited. I was one of the first to take advantage of the opportunity."[49]

Since he had been given a second chance at Fox in 1942, Otto had indeed behaved himself, but privately he often bristled at the kind of compromises that being a studio employee in good standing had required. If he hadn't been a contract director, for example, he wouldn't have had to make *Forever Amber;* he wouldn't have been forced to use contract players and writers who might not have been the best people for the job; he might have had a wider—and better—choice of material. As he assessed his status in the industry in 1950, Otto was not satisfied. To become "Otto Preminger," master filmmaker, he knew he needed to strike out on his own. And his new contract, marking an important transition not only for him but also for the business of filmmaking, gave him the chance to do that.

When he re-signed with Fox, however, Preminger was at work for the studio on *The Thirteenth Letter* and had no independent project lined up. In July and August he worked with Howard Koch on the screenplay, an adaptation of *Le Corbeau* (*The Raven*), a 1943 French film directed by Henri-Georges Clouzot about an epidemic of poison-pen letters in a rural community. Clouzot's *Corbeau,* set in France during the German occupation, is an allegory about the treachery of collaboration with the enemy; Preminger and Koch set the story in French Canada, divesting it of its original political subtext and turning it into a noir vision of male menopause. An aging doctor, Paul Laurent, is driven mad by the fear that he's losing his potency. When he suspects his wife Cora of having an affair with Dr. Pearson, a young newcomer to the community, Laurent forces her to write anonymous letters attacking his supposed rival. As in other Preminger noirs, sexual repression and perversity are everywhere. Dr. Pearson is a prim gynecologist with an obsessive attachment to clocks. Cora's older sister Marie, a nurse who long ago was in love with Dr. Laurent, is an embittered spinster. Denise, one of Dr. Pearson's patients, is an oversexed clubfoot who tries to seduce the aloof doctor. Denise's sister Rochelle wears thick spectacles and plays with a paddleball. Until the last-act revelation of Dr. Laurent's guilt, each of the sexual neurotics is implicated as the potential author of the letters. Though it isn't the major point, the script has echoes of the blacklist

On location in a small town in Quebec for *The Thirteenth Letter.* From left: Constance Smith, Michael Rennie, Charles Boyer, and Otto, sitting on a step above his actors.

Michael Rennie, mid-1950s, with Mary Gardner, the second Mrs. Otto Preminger.

just beginning to infiltrate the film industry. As Dr. Laurent announces, "In times of hysteria the accusation itself is enough to establish guilt."

Preminger was determined to shoot all the exteriors on location, and over the summer, together with his art directors Lyle Wheeler and Maurice Ransford, he scouted a number of small towns in Quebec, including St.-Hyacinthe, St.-Denis, St.-Charles, St.-Hilaire, and St.-Mare. He appreciated the odd regional architecture and the landscape, and he planned to shoot in September and October when he could take advantage of the dim light of a Canadian fall and bare trees would enfold the story in a wintry chill. On his return from Quebec, Preminger had to persuade Zanuck that location shooting would give the film a texture that could not be matched in the studio. At the time studio heads typically regarded location shooting as a sure way to swell a film's budget, but Preminger argued his point so persuasively that Zanuck authorized him to shoot some of the interiors on location as well. Otto knew that he had to prove himself, and he completed principal photography in five packed weeks in September and October, going only sixty dollars above the original $1,109,000 budget.

Far from home in an isolated location, cast and crew developed the kind of camaraderie probably not attainable in studio shooting. And for

Preminger the enforced intimacy had an unexpected dividend. Several times during filming leading man Michael Rennie (who played Dr. Pearson) had a visitor from New York, a tall, striking, but perilously thin young blonde named Mary Gardner, whose attention, as Otto noticed, "gradually switched from [Rennie] to me."[50] A romance developed quickly. Mary, "a knockout all her life," as her half-brother Howell Gilbert recalled,[51] was a successful fashion model with artistic aspirations. At sixteen she had won a scholarship to the Kansas City Art Institute, and with money earned from her modeling career she continued to study painting and sculpture.

After completing principal photography in Quebec on October 20, 1950, Otto returned to Hollywood for postproduction and Mary returned to her modeling career in New York. As soon as he finished editing *The Thirteenth Letter*, Otto was planning on going to New York as well—before he had begun shooting in Quebec he had acquired the rights to two plays. On a Sunday morning in late August, a week before he was to leave for Canada, he had read a comedy by Joseph Kesselring, the author of *Arsenic and Old Lace,* about the sex life of Osage Indians. By lunch he knew he wanted to produce and direct *Four Twelves Are 48,* and the next day he bought the rights. After returning from Quebec in late October, he summoned the author to Los Angeles, and as he supervised editing on his film he also met daily to work with Kesselring. By mid-November, satisfied with the revised script, he flew to New York for a breakfast meeting with his former coproducers Richard Aldrich and Richard Myers. By noon they reached an agreement to produce the play, in association with Julius Fleischmann. Within two weeks Preminger had a cast, was ready to begin rehearsals, and had booked two out-of-town theaters for tryouts as well as a theater on Broadway. The show would bow at the 48th Street Theatre on January 17, 1951.

Calling on actors he knew or had already worked with, Otto precast the show, but he was required by Equity rules to hold open call auditions. Biff McGuire, one of the auditioners, recalled that "there was a line of actors winding from the lobby of the Empire Theatre upstairs to where Otto was seated. He would look at the picture of the actor standing in front of him but not at the actor. I was determined to get him to look up at me. I said, 'I am required only to give my name, rank, and serial number.' I know I took a terrible chance—I was certainly familiar with his reputation for yelling—but he enjoyed the humor of it. 'What is it?' he said, looking up and laughing. He had a wonderful humor with a cutting edge. He remembered me, and cast me as a replacement lead in his next show."[52]

"I was lucky," Preminger said in a pre-opening interview with the *New York Post* on January 16, 1951. "Anne Revere wanted to do a play and she liked this one. And [theater veterans] Hiram Sherman and Ernest Truex, the people I first visualized, were also interested. Everything just fell into place. I wanted to present a comedy that has something to say. People right now need to laugh, and we made them laugh in Wilmington and Philadelphia, but New York is the last and highest court." New York, however, did not laugh. The show received blistering notices: "vulgar" and "tedious" were the adjectives most frequently used to describe the play, while "heavy-handed" seemed the label of choice about Preminger's direction.

"As of tonight we are through with the multiplication tables and are taking up differential calculus," the four coproducers wired the cast.[53] They closed the show after the second performance. Two days later, *The Thirteenth Letter* opened to indifferent notices. Preminger's interpretation may be less corrosive or politically pointed than Clouzot's—on its release in wartime France *Le Corbeau* had created the kind of scandal the French delight in—but it is solid work nonetheless. Preminger directs in a style as severe as the setting. The characters work in a hospital with empty rooms and corridors and live in sparsely furnished houses that seem infested with cobwebs. In the virtuoso opening shot, a man with a cane, the impotent Dr. Laurent, his back to the camera, stands on a barge as it moves toward the small town he is returning to. The composition ripples with premonitions of the character's isolation from the city he is approaching as well as of his dark influence over it. The film is beautifully cast. The aging roué Charles Boyer, no longer the heartthrob he had been in the 1930s and 1940s, turns Paul Laurent, gripped by terror at the prospect of losing his allure, into a moving figure. And Linda Darnell, at the end of her tenure as siren-in-residence at Fox, is equally touching as the crippled woman struggling to seduce Michael Rennie's frigid gynecologist. Preminger, for good reason, trusted Darnell in the role, and on the set there were no flare-ups between them.

Despite a failed play and film, Preminger was in a buoyant mood. His relationship with Mary was blossoming, and he and his theatrical partners were ready to begin production on a new comedy they had great confidence in. Before Kesselring's play had even begun its tryout tour, Preminger and his coproducers had already worked out a schedule for their next show. They set the first rehearsal for the Monday after *Four Twelves Are 48* was to open on Broadway. They booked theaters in Wilmington and Boston for the pre-Broadway tour. And they set a Broadway opening at the Henry Miller Theatre on March 8, 1951. The play, called *The Moon Is Blue,* was a frothy comedy about sex; yet this boulevard divertissement was to prove the single most important property in Otto Preminger's career.

SIX

The Declaration of Independence

F. Hugh Herbert, the author of *The Moon Is Blue,* was Viennese by birth but had been raised in England. He and Preminger, neighbors in Bel-Air, had met when they were both under contract at Fox. The two became good friends who took frequent walks in the hills and canyons near their homes. In the summer of 1950, at the point when Preminger had extracted release time from Fox and was actively seeking film and theater properties, Herbert on one of their jaunts around Bel-Air mentioned a play he had just written about a would-be young actress, a virgin, who flirts with an all-American young bachelor and an older continental rake. No doubt reminded of the Viennese naughty-but-nice romantic comedies he had presented at the Theater in der Josefstadt whenever he had needed a quick box-office fix, Preminger was enticed.

Since 1926 Herbert had been writing frolicsome screenplays with such semi-risqué titles as *The Demi-Bride, Adam and Evil, Tea for Three* (all 1927), *The Cardboard Lover* (1928), *He Knew Women* (1930), *The Secret Bride* (1935), and *As Good as Married* (1937). But like Preminger, Herbert also had a keen interest in the theater. He made his Broadway debut in 1940 with *Quiet Please,* an unsavory comedy about a film star who teaches her straying husband a lesson about fidelity by having an affair with a gas station attendant. In 1943 Herbert had a commercial hit with *Kiss and Tell.* The queasy premise: in order to protect her secretly married brother a fifteen-year-old must pretend she is pregnant. "Although my father wrote material that had a 'sexy' touch, he was anything but a roué," Diana Herbert remarked. "He was not a sophisticated man, but an innocent really, and he wrote about innocence. When he wrote about roustabouts, that was his dream of what he might have wanted to be. He and Otto shared an Old World sensibility. They were both formal and very proper. Otto was so austere that when we saw him my sister and I practically curtsied; we felt we had to."[1]

When he put Herbert's comedy into rehearsal in January 1951, Preminger had a lot at stake. He knew he couldn't afford a second theatrical flop after *Four Twelves Are 48,* and since *The Moon Is Blue* was another slight piece about sexual mores, a bout of insecurity might have been understandable. But Otto had no such twinges, and throughout rehearsals, as his romance with Mary Gardner continued to thrive, he was in an upbeat mood. His major concern was a third act he felt needed reworking. He

Two Old World fuddy-duddies, Preminger and F. Hugh Herbert, the author of *The Moon Is Blue,* confer with their Broadway leading lady, Barbara Bel Geddes.

wanted the author to "rewrite it no matter what the reviews said or how well the audiences liked it out of town."[2] Herbert agreed, but he may have been unnerved by the fact that the conversation took place as Otto lay in a large bathtub filled with soapsuds. "My father told me that he tried to keep a straight face, but it was hard for him because he was so proper," Diana Herbert recalled. "He told me that Otto would often hold court in his tub, and it would always disconcert my father."[3]

Act Three aside, Otto believed in the play and in a cast he felt was made to order for it. As the professional virgin Patty O'Neill he chose the winsome and appealing Barbara Bel Geddes. To play Don Gresham, the eligible bachelor who picks up Patty on the observation deck of the Empire State Building, he selected an expert light comedian, Barry Nelson. And as Gresham's upstairs neighbor David Slater, a middle-aged sybarite with a prize-winning manner, he tapped Donald Cook, a veteran of drawing room comedy. "I was punctual, I knew my lines, I knew I could do the part, Otto knew I could do it, and there wasn't a moment's trouble," Nelson recalled. "The play was a joy to work on, and Otto was a pleasure to work with."[4] When Biff McGuire replaced Barry Nelson, Preminger directed him in four intense days. "Otto was sometimes hard to decipher," McGuire recalled.

But he knew what he wanted. "More champagne, less beer," he would say—and that is what he got. His staging was very natural; he didn't force anything. He directed us so that we got all the laughter that was involved, and I was surprised at how much there was. But sometimes I thought he was *playing* the role of the director rather than really being one. He did something that would embarrass the cast. He had an assistant, Max Slater, whom he had known in Vienna and whose real name was Schultz (Max changed his name to Slater, after the character named David Slater in the play). Max had a smile Otto enjoyed. He would call Max to the stage and say, "Smile, smile at Otto." Max would come out, dutifully smile, then leave the stage.[5]

During rehearsals, Preminger, through numerous press releases, tried to create a naughty image for the show. "We have to get a bishop to condemn us," Preminger said, according to Biff McGuire.

When *The Moon Is Blue* opened in Wilmington to a delighted reception, Preminger remained convinced that a rewritten third act was still mandatory. During the Boston tryout the cast performed the original third act each night, while during the day they rehearsed the new third act in bits and pieces as Herbert was reworking it. When the show opened at the Henry Miller on schedule on March 8, 1951, with a revised final act, it received a warm welcome. Detailing the play-by-play choreography for a tryst that never occurs—the dangling question throughout the evening is whether Patty will lose her virginity—Hugh Herbert's slight comedy became Otto Preminger's one major success in the American theater.

Taking advantage of his new contract with Fox, which allowed him to remain in New York for six months during the height of the theater season, Otto settled into an apartment in a converted mansion at 40 East Sixty-eighth Street. He saw virtually every show that opened on Broadway and he would often travel to see shows out of town. After the theater, often in the company of Mary Gardner and sometimes with Mary's son Sandy along as well, he was a frequent patron at the Stork Club and El Morocco. Emboldened by the success of *The Moon Is Blue,* he announced that his next venture would be *The Greatest Story Ever Told,* featuring a cast of one hundred. "None of the actors will receive billing," Preminger promised, "and because of the nature of the story they will not be identified with the parts they play. Our plan is to take the show on the road for six months, and then into New York," he told the *New York Herald Tribune* on February 12, 1951. He promised other productions: *The Devil's General,* by Carl Zuckmayer; *From Left Field,* a play about baseball in a small town, a most unlikely choice for a man who had no interest whatever in either watching or participating in sports; and *The Chameleon Complex,* another light sexual rondelay in the *Moon Is Blue* vein. With producer Ben Marden, Preminger operated the Playhouse Theatre and booked its attractions. Over the summer as he scouted stock productions for possible tenants for the Playhouse, he was elated to have the job of casting and booking the second and third national companies of *The Moon Is Blue* and of directing Chicago and London productions as well. (*The Moon Is Blue* would run for 924 performances on Broadway and for a year in Chicago and London.)

When Otto had to return to Hollywood after six months, he managed to duck any commitments to Zanuck. He had already decided that a film of *The Moon Is Blue* would be his first independent production, for a company called Carlyle that he was setting up with Hugh Herbert. From a number of angles *The Moon Is Blue* was a shrewd choice. Since he was not planning to open up the play, Otto could produce on a low budget. And he was counting on a censorship brouhaha to give the project notoriety. He did not want to rush into production, however, but would make the film only when the Broadway and touring companies had run their course.

After an abbreviated visit to Hollywood, Preminger returned eagerly to

New York and to Mary, quickly adding two more plays to his portfolio of promises: another light comedy, *The Brass Ring,* and *The Koenig Masterpiece,* a drama by novelist Herman Wouk. Of all the shows during this period that Preminger had announced, Wouk's was the only one that he staged. He began rehearsals at the Playhouse Theatre at 2 p.m. on December 4, 1951. That morning, he and Mary were wed in a brief civil ceremony, after which Otto dashed to the theater with his bride. Mary's honeymoon was watching her new husband rehearse Wouk's play (which had been given a new title, *A Modern Primitive*). "Otto was beaming and delighted, and Mary, blonde, very beautiful, and very charming, was in a bridal state of bliss," recalled Paula Laurence, who had a principal role in the play. "They both had an aura of radiant joy. Otto would take all of us out to extravagant lunches at which Mary was worshipful. Otto told stories and she laughed and applauded, as did the rest of us. At that moment they were clearly happy with each other. Otto was in a benign mood and remained so throughout rehearsals. Maybe he should have gotten married more often!"

As it turned out, Otto needed to be patient because Wouk's promising play about a painter who embezzles money and flees to Mexico required major renovations. "Wouk was shy and serious," as Paula Laurence remembered. "There was no friction between him and Otto at rehearsals, at least in front of us; I don't think Otto would have allowed it. But I knew that Otto was asking for rewrites and Wouk was not doing them. Wouk had a good reason for resisting, however. He could say, in good faith, 'I don't want to rewrite because I haven't yet seen what I have written.' " The problem was that the leading actor, Murvyn Vye, couldn't remember his lines.

> Otto was enormously patient with Murvyn, trying to get a perfor-
> mance out of this bewildered man [Laurence said]. He thought
> Murvyn would get the lines eventually and he would not fire him.
> Because he remained focused on Murvyn, however, the rest of us
> didn't get much attention. At one rehearsal Otto turned to me and
> said, "Paula, you're so charming in life and so boring in this scene."
> All of us shrieked with laughter. I was playing a journalist who had
> come down to interview the artist, and I *was* boring because
> Murvyn would scramble the lines and I had no idea what he was
> talking about.

The show opened for a pre-Broadway run in Hartford, Connecticut, right after Christmas, and closed almost immediately. "We barely opened in Hartford, and some of us felt that we never really did open," Laurence recalled. "Over the years I was to hear mean, scandalous things about Otto, fierce stories that were almost hard to believe. But I was a witness to the fact that there was a decent person there. And with that Viennese charm, which was like a show, a performance, though I wouldn't say it wasn't sincere on his part, and his well-known skill as a lover, he was certainly a 'character' and so regarded in the New York theater."[6]

Diana Douglas, who played the artist's mistress, had a different reaction to Preminger. Douglas felt that Vye was insecure because he knew he had been Preminger's second choice for the role, tapped after Anthony Quinn had turned it down.

> Knowing he was second choice didn't help his confidence. Otto picked on him unmercifully during rehearsals, which only made him falter more. Otto would scream at poor Murvyn, the veins standing out on his forehead, literally foaming at the mouth. I had never seen such terrifying rage in anyone. He had Murvyn trembling and incoherent. It was sickening. I am sorry now that I was too chicken to challenge Otto directly over his cruelty toward a fellow human being, but I was craven and determined not to jeopardize my job.[7]

As Douglas reported, Vye "had what we found out later was a complete nervous breakdown. . . . he was carted away to spend the next four months in a sanitarium."[8] Before Preminger closed the show Saturday night, he asked if Diana would ask her husband, Kirk Douglas, to take over the role. The actress refused to honor the request.

Two weeks after closing *A Modern Primitive,* Otto received a call from his friend Billy Wilder asking him to play the commandant of a Nazi prisoner-of-war camp in *Stalag 17.* Preminger, newly married and still busy superintending *The Moon Is Blue,* said no, but Wilder insisted he read the script. After he did, Otto changed his mind. Wilder offered him $45,000 for three weeks' work. Wilder and Preminger had much in common. Six months younger than Otto, Billy Wilder was born Jewish in Vienna and like Otto had enrolled as a law student at the University of Vienna. Unlike Otto, however, he quit after one year in order to pursue a career as a journalist. As a quite young man he moved to Berlin, where he continued to write for newspapers and where, as he was to admit, he also became a taxi dancer (in other words, a gigolo) at a hotel. In 1933 Wilder fled from Germany to Hollywood, where he arrived with none of the entrée or welcome that had been extended to Preminger. A crude, bitter man, over the years Wilder was to make as many enemies as Preminger, but despite a long downhill slide after 1960 his work was to be far more appreciated. In collaboration with Charles Brackett, Wilder wrote a series of highly regarded comedies, including *Midnight* (1939), *Ninotchka* (1939), and *Ball of Fire* (1941). In 1944 he cowrote and directed a canonical film noir, *Double Indemnity.* The next year he won Academy Awards for writing and directing *The Lost Weekend,* a portrait of an alcoholic. And with Brackett he won another Academy Award in 1950 for the screenplay for *Sunset Boulevard,* the best film ever made about Hollywood. Wilder had just received ecstatic reviews for *Ace in the Hole* (1951), a smug melodrama about a cynical journalist that failed commercially. Over the years the friendship between Wilder and Preminger was marked by fiery episodes—they weren't on speaking terms for the last decade of Otto's life—but when Wilder called Preminger in early 1952 to offer him a role, they were in a period of accord.

Wilder's script for *Stalag 17,* cowritten with Edwin Blum, transformed a sentimental play about a German camp for Allied prisoners of war that Wilder had seen on Broadway in the spring of 1951. Wilder and Blum turned the material into a hard-boiled comedy about a group of prisoners who wrongly accuse the mercenary protagonist, a prisoner who operates a thriving black market business and runs bets on rat races, of being the camp informer. To enhance the biting tone he wanted, Wilder invented the character Otto plays, the witty, acidulous camp commandant. Happily married (Otto was living with Mary and his stepson Sandy in Anatol Litvak's palatial pink house on the beach in Malibu), Otto reported to work in an ebullient mood and from the first day made it clear that he was there to take direction rather than to give it.

His well-being was shattered during the first week of shooting, however, when his beloved father died of cancer at seventy-five. Dr. Preminger had never spoken about the cancer that had caused him to waste away quickly and he had refused to submit to any surgery that might have prolonged his life. Otto was aggrieved. But his profound sense of loss was tempered by pride in the way his father had adjusted to life in America. Sixty-one when he had fled from Austria, Markus had felt that qualifying as a lawyer in an unfamiliar language was out of the question, so he decided, as Otto reported, "to invest the modest amount of money he had brought with him in the stock market." After studying the American market and the financial histories of major corporations, Markus had proceeded to make sound investments. And as Otto boasted, Markus was "wealthier when he died than when he arrived here. In the meantime, he had lived well for over fourteen years, buying a house for himself and one for my brother as well."[9]

(Although in 1942 Josefa had suffered a severe stroke that left her almost completely paralyzed, she survived her husband. "She was bedridden when I knew her, and needed round-the-clock care, and in those days she was not encouraged to seek rehabilitation," Kathy Preminger remembered.[10] Even as his own health declined rapidly in the six months before his death, Markus had maintained a vigilant watch over his wife. At the time, Ingo and Kate and their three children lived across the street from the elder Premingers, and ironically Kate, the young woman the snobbish Josefa had disdained in Vienna, became her greatest friend. "Kate behaved beautifully," Otto testified.[11] "My mother was so reliable and attentive that both my grandparents grew to love her," Kathy said. "My mother told me that in her illness Josefa became sweeter."[12] When Ingo and his family moved into a larger house a year after Markus's death, Josefa moved in with them. "She lived for several years in a room that later became our den," Jim Preminger said. "I was very young, and she seemed very elderly to me, but she was still

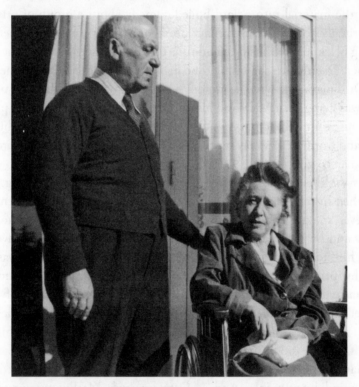

Markus's concern for his paralyzed wife Josefa, who suffered a stroke in 1942, is evident in this 1950 family photo.

a more formidable presence than my grandfather had been."[13] After Josefa began to require more attention than Ingo and Kate and their three children could provide, she was moved to a nursing home. Kate went to see her on a daily basis, bringing food and flowers. Josefa outlived her husband by five years.)

When Otto returned to filming after overseeing funeral arrangements for Markus, he was subdued but never for a moment other than completely professional. He admired Wilder's methods. "Even though he came from Vienna, [Wilder] directed like a Prussian officer," Preminger commented, as if talking about himself. "What he wanted with his words was rigid, absolutely rigid. Billy was a stickler for every word, because they were *his* words."[14] Surprisingly, however, Otto regularly messed up his lines. "When I hired him I told him every time he got his lines wrong, he owed me a jar of caviar," Wilder recalled. "He may not have been the greatest actor, especially when it came to getting his lines right, but he was the world champion payer of debts. He missed a lot of lines, but he never missed sending a jar of caviar. He sent only the very best caviar. Now, *that* he did not have to do."[15] "I was happy to send [Billy] the caviar and the expense I didn't mind, but the real price I paid was Billy directed me too well, and many people thought I was the part I played."[16]

Preminger appears in three scenes. In the first, as underlings put down boards to protect his boots from contact with the muddy ground, the commandant makes a grand entrance as the American prisoners stand at attention. When the commandant speaks, his inflections laced with sarcasm and threat, he addresses the prisoners as if they were guests at a party of swells: "*Guten Morgen,* sergeants. Nasty weather we are having, eh? And I *so* much hoped we could give you a white Christmas, just like the ones you used to know. With Christmas coming on I have a special treat for you. I'll have you all deloused for the holidays."

In his second scene, entering the barracks to conduct a search, Preminger speaks again in a mock-gracious tone, as if holding court in a Noël Coward drawing room. "Curtains would do wonders for this barracks. You won't get them." His final scene has a visual gag Preminger appreciated. "The colonel wants to report to Berlin that an American officer suspected of espionage has been captured," Otto recalled. "He has his orderly put on his boots for the phone call. During the call, he clicks his heels for his superiors. After the call, he has the orderly take off the boots. That's a good joke, but I don't know how many people got it."[17]

Otto's pungent performance in a hit film gave him the kind of fame few directors ever attain. But as he recognized and at least pretended to regret, it

also provided ammunition to his growing list of enemies, who over the
years would describe his acting in *Stalag 17* as lifelike, or as an example of
Otto on a good day. His work is certainly vivid, but it also reveals Preminger's limitations. His eyes lack the liveliness of the natural screen performer, and, missing variety and shading, his vocal delivery slides toward
monotony. Popping the character into the film for what are, in effect, three
cameo appearances, Wilder himself seemed to be aware that a little of Otto's
Nazi goes a long way.

After completing his scenes in *Stalag 17*, Preminger had to report to Fox,
where he was still contractually obligated to deliver a film a year. Dutifully
he read scripts and stories, hoping to find a property he could take an interest in, but a few months passed without his finding a suitable vehicle. One
afternoon, as he was reading a story synopsis, Zanuck called him to his
office to inform him that Howard Hughes, the more-than-eccentric air-
plane billionaire who owned RKO, had requested Otto's services. Zanuck
told his startled employee that he had already accepted the assignment on
Otto's behalf: because Hughes needed a director who could work fast,
Zanuck had recommended Otto. "[Zanuck] was indebted to Hughes for

Serving the master: Preminger as the commandant of a German camp for Allied prisoners of
war in Billy Wilder's *Stalag 17*.

many favors financially and otherwise and wanted to show his gratitude by making him a friendly gift of me," as Otto recalled.[18]

The assignment was a psychological thriller called *Murder Story,* starring Jean Simmons, under personal contract to Hughes. Since the British-born actress had arrived in America in 1949 to promote a film called *The Blue Lagoon,* Hughes had become a silent admirer. According to Hughes's biographer Robert Brown, Simmons "awakened one morning in early 1951 to learn her contract with the British-based J. Arthur Rank Organization had been purchased by Hughes."[19] "Hughes bought me," as Simmons herself recalled. "You can't do that anymore, or you'd hear about it in the papers. He *owned* me, and I had to make four pictures for him."[20] The actress went to court to free herself from what she had come to regard as her indentured servitude to Hughes, and the upcoming film, for which she was contractually committed for no more than eighteen days of shooting, was to end her association with the billionaire. For the new film, because Hughes had already decreed that her hair was to be long, the enraged actress "whacked off the front of [her] hair with scissors. It had to be cut very, very short, which is absolutely what Hughes didn't want."[21] In order to satisfy Hughes's infatuation with long hair, Simmons throughout the filming would have to wear wigs.

Aware that he would be dealing with a disgruntled actress and leery of having to take orders from Hughes, Preminger was reluctant to proceed. After he read the script, he informed Zanuck that he refused to accept the assignment. That night in the witching hours Otto received a call from Hughes demanding a conference that, he was told, was to be held in a half-hour in Hughes's battered Chevrolet. Promising Otto complete control of the project and assuring him that if he didn't like the script he could have it rewritten by writers of his own choosing, Hughes pleaded with the director to take the job. "I'm going to get even with that little bitch, and you must help me," he cajoled Preminger, who by the end of the postmidnight ride agreed—or was forced into agreeing—to direct.[22]

Preminger hired Oscar Millard, one of Ingo's clients, to help him rewrite *Murder Story.* "My brother tells me you are a genius: let me see proof!" Otto exclaimed to his new writer. "Relations with Otto steadily deteriorated," Millard recalled.[23] To assist Millard, Otto hired Frank Nugent, an experienced screenwriter with a number of John Ford films on his résumé. Working quickly, with Otto providing daily supervision, they prepared a heavily revised version of *Murder Story* now entitled *Angel Face.* The original script may well have been a collection of genre clichés—the familiar story is about a femme fatale who ensnares a vulnerable man into a

Circe nailing her prey: Diane (Jean Simmons) gives Frank (Robert Mitchum) a look that promises trouble ahead in *Angel Face*.

web of passion and murder—but, reworked as *Angel Face,* it is Preminger's most deliriously perverse excursion into noir.

The Tremayne family, enclosed in a hilltop mansion in Beverly Hills, is pure Hollywood Gothic. Charles, the paterfamilias, is a writer who has been unable to write since his late-in-life marriage to Catherine, wealthy, quivering with resentment and repression, and emasculating. The two characters are so wedded to their neuroses that they fail to register the lethal intentions of Tremayne's daughter Diane, incestuously attached to her father and itching to get her hands on her stepmother's fortune. To secure both the money and her father she is prepared to murder her stepmother. When Frank Jessup, an ambulance driver responding to an emergency call, enters the house radiating sex and indolence, Diane enlists him as a conspirator. With Frank's help Diane rigs the family car so that it shifts into reverse when the driver intends to go forward. The plan misfires when Diane's father by chance enters the car with her stepmother and both are killed. (It was Preminger, a very bad driver, who suggested the death-car motif.) Charged with murder, Diane hires a lawyer who concocts a scheme to exonerate her: if she marries Frank, they cannot testify against each other in court. After she's released from jail Diane tries to confess to the lawyer but he silences her, assuring her that she can shout her guilt from the rooftops but she is protected by the law and cannot be tried again for a crime of which she has been acquitted. At the end, with Frank beside her, Diane plunges the car off the steep cliff next to the Tremayne house.

In this glacial salon noir, none of the principal characters survives, and family love, romantic love, justice, and the law are poisoned beyond redemption. Otto and his writers conjured a fallen world in which even the Tremayne servants, who snap at each other in Japanese (the wife is aggressively ungeishalike), and Frank's normal-seeming fiancée, who turns out to be a tough cookie, provide no comfort.

Otto, for good reason pleased with the script, began filming at record speed on June 16, driving to work down Sunset Boulevard from his house in Malibu to the Lewis estate in Beverly Hills, which RKO rented to serve as the Tremayne mansion. In his autobiography Preminger, without once

The conspirators on trial for murder in *Angel Face*. In the foreground, the defective car engine that caused the deaths of Diane's father and stepmother.

referring to her by name, recollected that the lead actress "was most cooperative. I enjoyed working with her."[24] That is decidedly not how Jean Simmons remembered the shooting. "Ah, Mr. Preminger . . . I'm sorry you mentioned his name," Simmons said. "He was . . . *very* unpleasant. Talented, yes, and socially charming; but I was told he always picked a patsy, and on this film *I* was the one. I only got through it because of my costar, Robert Mitchum."[25] In a scene in which Mitchum was to strike Simmons, Preminger made the actor "slap her for real" and insisted on a number of retakes before an enraged Mitchum turned to the director and smacked him. Preminger left the set screaming for Mitchum to be replaced. But as a hired hand he was not able to get his way and he had no choice but to return to work. "Well, do you think we can be friends?" he asked his mutinous actor. "Otto, we're all here for you," Mitchum responded.[26] There were no other incidents, but Simmons remained wary. She felt that following the orders of Howard Hughes, Preminger was treating her in a needling, disrespectful way. (On her next film, *The Actress,* she was directed by George Cukor. "He was everything Preminger was not. He was so kind and helpful. We rehearsed for two weeks, then shot for three. When we started to shoot, we were prepared.")[27]

Mona Freeman played Robert Mitchum's strong-willed fiancée. She recalled:

> I had only one scene with Jean, who was such a nice, cute gal, and there weren't any problems that I could see. I wasn't aware that Jean was unhappy or that she didn't want to do the film. Otto was certainly nice to *me.* He was very open to discussion. If I had any concerns I went to him; I felt I *could* go to him. It was Otto's set—Hughes was never there—but there was no discord at all whenever I was there. We shot the whole thing in about twenty minutes, and frankly, it didn't seem important. I've heard that it now has a huge reputation, especially in France, but I can tell you that at the time we didn't think what we were doing was masterful: just the opposite. Mitchum, who was very easygoing, certainly didn't take it too seriously. And neither did I. I've never seen the film. I'm glad to hear I was unlikable, though; I always played such likable characters.[28]

Working with Harry Stradling, known as the fastest cinematographer in town, Otto shot the entire film in twenty-one working days. He finished editing and postproduction by the end of September, and on December 11,

1952, RKO released the film. For a story about psychopathic behavior in a wealthy family, Preminger was exactly the right director. By this point in his career he was a master delineator of sexual derangement and of the noir set piece—and *Angel Face* has a number of the most memorable in the canon.

Early on, in his first visit to the mansion on the hill, Frank is bewitched when he hears a piano being played. Drawn by the music, he walks into the living room where Diane, a Circe nabbing her prey, is seated at the piano, her dark eyes emitting fire and ice. The film has a memorably bizarre marriage scene. With shadows forming crisscross patterns on the wall behind her, Diane, a bedridden inmate in a prison hospital, marries Frank as prisoners who look like they have dropped in from *The Snake Pit* joylessly serenade the newlyweds.

Near the end, her parents dead and her husband about to forsake her, Diane takes one last walk through the deserted mansion, its shadowed rooms and corridors moaning with absence as Dimitri Tiomkin's score—all wailing strings—mirrors the character's unfulfillable desire. Here, in this climactic passage of operatic noir, and in contrast to his usual restraint, Preminger brings the film's festering atmosphere to full boil. At the end of her walk Diane enters Frank's room, sits in his oversized chair, and wraps herself in his big hound's-tooth jacket, a moment that comes as close to a love scene as the film offers. After Frank in the finale tells Diane that he's leaving for good, she asks to drive him to the train station. Frank, careless as ever, once again submits to her. In a moment that epitomizes the film's fleeting gallows humor, Diane produces a bottle of champagne; seated in the car that is about to become an engine of death, the two former lovers toast each other. Then, shooting one last dark glance at Frank, Diane steps on the gas. Preminger and his scenarists offer a final turn of the screw. Before he had accepted Diane's invitation, Frank had called a taxi, which arrives a few moments after Diane has driven the car off the cliff. His engine idling in front of the now vacant mansion, the taxi driver waits, as the film ends on "a moment of haunting emptiness like nothing else in the American cinema," as Robert Mitchum's biographer, Lee Server, commented.[29]

Jean Simmons may have thought he was brutal and Mitchum went after him, but under Preminger's guidance the two performers were never better. Fueled by anger toward her "owner" and her "unpleasant" director, Simmons takes the bait. Her femme fatale, loaded with venom beneath a lacquered surface, is one of the most poisonous in noir, half-cocked and ready to shoot from her first scene at the piano. As the luckless antihero, the prey ensnared in the spider lady's web, Mitchum oozes ambivalence. Neither Diane (nor the viewer) is ever quite certain about Frank's motives. Is he attracted to, repelled by, or merely indifferent to Diane? Is he using her or allowing himself to be used by her? Is he on to her from the start, or is he so self-involved that he doesn't really see what she is up to?

Unusual in withholding sympathy for any of its characters and marbled with astringent ironies, Preminger's compact, fierce film is one of the masterpieces of the American *cinéma maudit*. American critics, by and large, were uncomfortable with the film's seemingly un-American amorality, its refusal to conform to sentimental notions about family or justice. In the *New York Times* on December 11, Bosley Crowther derided "the absurdly dismal finale" and warned "paying customers out for sense and sensibility to hang onto the brief appearances of Mona Freeman as the spunky realistic little nurse." Otis Guernsey in the *New York Herald Tribune* bemoaned the film's apparent detachment "from any real association with crime and punishment." Parisian cinephiles, however, were quick to recognize Preminger's achievement. Jean-Luc Godard placed *Angel Face* high on the list of his ten all-time favorite American films.

Racing through postproduction on *Angel Face* in the fall of 1952, Preminger began to prepare for the screen adaptation of *The Moon Is Blue,* his debut as an independent producer-director. While Hugh Herbert worked on the script, Otto began casting. On Broadway he had been delighted with Barbara Bel Geddes, the original Patty O'Neill, but he was concerned that on film she would not look young enough. Instead he chose Maggie McNamara, wonderfully fresh-looking at twenty-four, a former teenage model who had played the role in the Chicago company. To reassure his investors, Preminger needed to cast an A-list star to play the bachelor, Don Gresham. His first choice was William Holden, whom he had met while filming *Stalag 17*.

Offstage, Holden seemed like the man in the gray flannel suit, but as Otto sensed, the actor had a defiant streak. Holden, who accepted right away, relished the possibility of the censorship dustup he thought the film might provoke, and he also saw that starring in an independent film could be a possible financial bonanza. The contract that Carlyle Productions worked out with him—Holden would receive no salary up front but would take a percentage of the profits—established a financial model that was to become standard in the poststudio era.

Once Herbert's screenplay was finished, Preminger submitted it to Joe Breen, who for nearly twenty years, as chief enforcer of the Motion Picture Production Code, had been the de facto guardian of screen morality. Breen did exactly what Otto expected and hoped he would: he rejected *The Moon Is Blue*. Twice. (Written and formally adopted by the Association of Motion Picture Producers [California] and the Motion Picture Association of America [New York] in March 1930, the Motion Picture Production Code had had no force until 1934, when Breen devised an economic sanction. Any film in violation of the Code and given a condemned rating—the dreaded "C"—by the Catholic Legion of Decency would be subject to a widespread Catholic boycott. Since its inception, as Breen had intended, the C rating had hovered like the sword of Damocles over filmmakers. In league with the fearsome Legion of Decency, Breen had thus been able to force the studios to comply with the Code.)

Preminger claimed that Breen's objections focused on the use of such then taboo words as "virgin," "seduce," and "pregnant," but in fact Breen's disapproval was more far-reaching. He cited a provision in the Production Code that specifically interdicted seduction as "a subject for comedy" and assailed *The Moon Is Blue* for exuding "an unacceptably cavalier approach toward seduction and illicit sex."[30] Fearing Breen's power, Paramount and then Warner Bros., Otto's first two choices, turned down the project; it was only at that point that Otto approached Arthur Krim and Robert S. Benjamin, two young lawyers who had taken over United Artists in February 1951. In record time they had managed to convert the ailing studio's red ink into black by attracting independent producers with promises of creative autonomy. United Artists had no studio of its own, but rented space from other studios. Krim and Benjamin quickly agreed to support Otto, pledging front money, distribution, and almost complete artistic freedom.

Krim and Benjamin, however, tried to talk Otto out of hiring David Niven to play the third principal role, David Slater, a potentially sleazy character who, in effect, pimps for his daughter while making a play for his downstairs neighbor's virginal pickup. The lawyers thought Niven was out of fashion. But when he had seen Niven on Broadway in December 1951 as a debonair lover in a short-lived boudoir farce called *Nina,* Otto knew he had found the actor for Slater. Preminger went to bat for Niven with the same persistence he had shown in his campaign to cast Clifton Webb in *Laura.* "Otto is an immensely determined individual, and what Otto wants, he usually gets. He got me—bless him!" Niven recalled.[31]

The lawyers backed down, and Preminger thought he was ready to go when, late in 1952, the screenplay received yet another blistering rejection from the Production Code Administration office. Jack Vizzard, Breen's associate, attacked the movie Preminger was planning to make as "unclean." "The story was saying that 'free love' was something outside the scope of morality altogether, was a matter of moral indifference," Vizzard protested. "What came into contention was the Code clause that stated, 'Pictures shall not infer that low forms of sex relationships are the accepted or common thing.' Philosophically this was one of the most important provisions in the entire Code document." According to Vizzard, what "made the hackles rise on the back of Joe Breen's neck" was the way the script seemed to trump virtue in favor of sin. "To the devotees of sexual continence, the figure [Patty O'Neill] . . . is made to seem eccentric for being 'clean,' an oddball for clinging to her virtue in the midst of this 'characteristically' loose [and, by inference, preferable, more enjoyable] way of life."[32]

In early January Preminger met with Vizzard and his colleague Geoffrey Shurlock for lunch at "21," where Otto made it clear that he intended to shoot the script he had submitted to the Production Code Administration office. "As a token concession, [Preminger] offered to add dialogue at the end . . . condemning the 'immoral philosophy of life' expressed by Slater; beyond that, he would not budge," as Leonard Leff and Jerold L. Simmons reported in their history of film censorship, *The Dame in the Kimono*.[33] Dartmouth-educated and at that time Breen's second in command, Geoffrey Shurlock was more modern than his boss. He had seen *The Moon Is Blue* onstage and thought it was "swell. A lot of fun." He also believed that the Code prohibition against comic seduction was "idiotic."[34] Because of Shurlock's conciliatory tone, by the end of the lunch Preminger modified— or at least pretended to—his defiant stance, and in principle even agreed to review Breen's original list of objections as well as to submit the completed film to the Code office.

Preminger sensed that in Geoffrey Shurlock he had an ideological ally. Perhaps carelessly, Shurlock privately shared with Otto his dismay that just the week before Breen had approved the screenplay based on *From Here to Eternity*, James Jones's "near-scandalous" novel. As a result Shurlock felt that Breen's outrage over Preminger's "harmless comedy of manners" seemed "not only irony but hypocrisy."[35] Preminger may well have felt that, with a "mole" like Shurlock in the Production Code Administration office, Joe Breen's tenure had a termination date. Nonetheless, he was resolved not to make any changes in the script in order to pacify Breen, and he fully expected that his film would not be given the Production Code Administration Seal of Approval.

Krim and Benjamin were not as fearless as Otto. They began to express concern that if the film did not receive the Code Seal, as it surely wouldn't if Otto shot it as he was planning to, they would be unlikely to find any theaters in which to show it. They were reluctant to cancel their contract with Preminger, however, because to do so would seriously tarnish the image they had been working to build of United Artists as a place uniquely welcoming to independent producers. They hesitated, but by the end of January, allotting Preminger a modest $250,000 budget, they decided to go ahead: Otto could film his comedy exactly as he wanted. After deleting a clause from Preminger's contract that "required delivery of a Code-approved" product, they negotiated a production loan from the Chemical Bank of New York and thereby, as Leff and Simmons reported, "committed UA to a frontal assault on Joseph L. Breen."[36]

Otto moved quickly. He assembled his small cast and began three weeks of rehearsals. With his two male leads, Preminger was home free. David Niven had exactly the right touch. He tickled his lines as if delivering bons mots in a Noël Coward drawing room and raised his eyebrows at an expressive slant that suggested civilized wickedness. Not only was Niven tough enough to weather any Preminger assaults, in a way he even welcomed them. "Many actors don't like working with Otto because he shouts even louder than Goldwyn [to whom Niven had been under contract] and can be very sarcastic. I love it. Actors have a certain amount of donkey blood in them and need a carrot dangled in front of them from time to time. The directors I dread are the ones who say, 'You've played this sort of thing before—do anything you want.' Otto dangles carrots."[37] William Holden was a little too solemn for the material and didn't seem to be having as much fun as Niven. Nonetheless Holden had an intuitive sense of how little the camera needs—to Preminger's delight, his star seemed incapable of overacting. Maggie McNamara, however, provoked a few Preminger tantrums. Although she had played the role in Chicago and then in New York ("I know she had trouble during the New York run," Biff McGuire recalled),[38] she was a jittery newcomer with a fragile ego (McNamara was to commit suicide in 1978). When, unlike her costars, she was unable to give him what he wanted on the first take, Otto would roar that her flubs were costing him time and money. McNamara brought out both the best and the worst aspects of the director's temperament. As with all of his young discoveries in the future—the performers he would pluck from obscurity because he believed he could develop them into screen stars—Otto was alternately cranky and caring. After one of his flare-ups, which would pulverize his protégée, he would shower her with reassurance. He knew that McNamara, pert and appropriately dignified, indeed "virginal," had the right qualities for the role, and like everyone in the company, he genuinely liked her. "Maggie was dear and sweet," as Biff McGuire said, "but she wanted desperately to be an intellectual—to be someone other than who she was."[39]

Preminger shot the film in twenty-one days, an impressive achievement considering the fact that he also filmed a German-language version on the same sets in the same time frame, getting two films for the price of one. For

With his insecure young discovery, Maggie McNamara, on the set of *The Moon Is Blue*.

the German version, called *Die Jungfrau auf dem Dach* (*The Virgin on the Roof*), Preminger cast Hardy Krüger and Johanna Matz, both with major careers in German theater and films. "When the American actors would leave the set, we would go in and do the same," Matz recalled.

> I had to do exactly like Maggie, which was hard, but she was very nice. It was very quick and very disciplined work. Not everybody likes this kind of work—it was unique. But I liked to do it. Otto was a little bit nervous—we worked so fast. He was sometimes a little bit loud, but Germans are loud anyway. I like to have "temperament," and he had it! So what? It was very modern, very simple: he says what he wants and we do it. Only one thing was hard: in German you need more words than in English. So sometimes there were complications.[40]

By early April Preminger sent a completed film to the Production Code Administration office. He had made a few minor concessions to Breen, but he received exactly the response he wanted: Breen denied certification to *The Moon Is Blue* because of its "unacceptably light attitude toward seduction, illicit sex, chastity and virginity."[41] Fully prepared, Preminger went into attack mode, writing a letter of defense in which he claimed that his film was highly moral. "Our picture . . . is a harmless story of a very virtuous girl, who works for her living, who neither smokes nor drinks, who is completely honest and outspoken, who resists temptation and whose one aim in life is to get married and have children. . . . There are no scenes of passion . . . no scenes of crime or vice."[42] Breen was immovable. As a last resort Preminger and United Artists decided to appeal his decision to the board of the Motion Picture Association in New York. The lawyer representing the Production Code Administration office argued that *The Moon Is Blue* would be "highly offensive to many parents to whom virginity of their daughters is still a matter of greatest concern, and who do not consider this a matter to be laughed at."[43] Headed by Nicholas Schenck, the president of Loew's and the brother of Otto's original American mentor, Joe Schenck, the Motion Picture Association upheld Breen's condemnation. Nicholas Schenck maintained that he wouldn't "let [his] daughter see it. It's true that the girl is not seduced in the time she spends with the boy, but other girls in a similar situation might get closer to the flame."[44]

For Preminger and United Artists, the moment of reckoning had arrived. Had they been bluffing all along? Had their defiance been an act of bravado that would now crumble? Would they—indeed, *could* they—release *The Moon Is Blue* without a Production Code Administration Seal of Approval? Many industry pundits predicted that no major theater chains would book the film. But working arm in arm with United Artists, Preminger persevered and in a short time secured a few key theaters in Los Angeles, Chicago, and San Francisco. In Los Angeles, Preminger was fortunate in booking the Four Star, a sedate house on Wilshire Boulevard in the then fashionable Miracle Mile district. The theater had a distinguished history and only recently had presented a lengthy, reserved-seat engagement of MGM's *Julius Caesar.* An exclusive booking at this location would give Preminger's film a touch of class.

When Otto saw the ad that the studio's publicity department had designed—a half-nude young woman gazing up at the moon—he was apoplectic. "The ad suggest[ed] that the movie after all was pornographic," he maintained.[45] In another decision that was to have historic reverberations, he hired a New York graphic designer, Saul Bass, to prepare a new ad. Preminger and Bass set to work under terrific time pressure. "We were like Samurai warriors, and always going up in smoke," as Bass recalled.

Oh, the screaming, and we threw things. He really taught me how to fight. Otto, you see, liked to fight. It was half-serious and half ritual; he was tough, autocratic, he jealously guarded his prerogatives: he was the boss. But there was also such generosity of spirit, and he was so accessible—it was always so easy to get an appointment. He was the best client I ever had—and the most difficult. He brought out the best in me and at times I really wanted to throttle him. He was very critical, very difficult to satisfy, but what I discovered is that with all the conflict and the yelling the work was better at the end than at the beginning. And that was a powerful realization. Ours was a richly volatile relationship. Eventually, I learned to love the guy.[46]

Although Bass judged his first important work with Preminger to be the ad he designed in 1955 for *The Man with the Golden Arm,* his whimsical design for *The Moon Is Blue*—a drawing of two pigeons perched on a windowsill—is also noteworthy. "Suggestive" in the mildest way—no one could possibly have read the design as "pornographic"—it evoked the film's light tone. And in focusing on one image it represented an entirely new approach to film advertising. "Otto and I made a commitment to one central idea to promote a film, rather than the potpourri stew notion that was customary at the time, in which you threw everything into the advertisement on the theory that there will be something in it for everyone."[47]

Long before it opened on June 3, 1953, *The Moon Is Blue* was a cause célèbre. For weeks prior to the premiere, Preminger held dozens of press conferences during which he defended his film's morality while deriding Breen's "hypocritical interpretation of an antiquated Code." "Nobody's character can possibly be corrupted by this harmless little comedy," Otto asserted repeatedly. "Why did nobody object to the play when it ran in theatres across the country?"[48] Indeed, the whole point of the piece is that nothing sexual happens. A young professional man picks up a perky young actress and takes her home, where they talk and flirt and make plans for a cozy dinner. When she meets her new beau's dashing upstairs neighbor, the young woman flirts with him, chattering gaily about her virginity. In the end, after all the palaver about seduction, and with the young woman's chastity undefiled, a once-in-a-blue-moon event occurs: a pickup blossoms into romance, and the bachelor and his date decide to get married.

Preminger opened the discussion to concerns that went far beyond his "little comedy." He contended that his refusal to cut any "offending" words from the film was not because he believed the excisions would inflict irreparable damage but because he was opposed to censorship. "It is an evil institution, and if we give in to it on small matters this is the first step toward the kind of totalitarian government that destroyed my country, Austria," he thundered with impressive conviction.[49]

"A middling and harmless little thing, speciously risqué," opined Bosley Crowther in the *New York Times* on June 3, setting the terms in which the film was received. "The film is not outstanding as a romance or as film," he noted, adding that "at times it gets awfully tedious and the talk is exceedingly long." "There are bubbles in this film but champagne is mixed with baser stuff in about 50-50 proportions," Otis Guernsey commented in the *New York Herald Tribune*. "The action has little more area than it did on the stage, but mostly Preminger has filmed the script as a photographed play. The farce is so fragile, so pleasantly evanescent, that it might not have stood the strain of ordinary movie emphasis."

But as Preminger had hoped, the reviews didn't matter. Opening business was brisk, and when the Legion of Decency, always working hand in glove with the Production Code Administration office, gave the film a C rating, calling it "an occasion of sin, sophisticated smut," it got even brisker. "I didn't negotiate with the Catholic Legion of Decency," Preminger said. "If they wanted to instruct Catholics not to see the film, fine. They had every right to do so. But I am not Catholic and they could not tell me what to take out of my picture."[50] State censorship boards joined in the attack. Three states—Ohio, Maryland, and Kansas—banned it outright. Preminger and United Artists took the case to a Maryland court. On December 7, 1953, Judge Herman Moser, describing the film as "a light comedy telling a tale of wide-eyed, brash, puppy-like innocence routing or converting to its side the forces of evil it encounters," reversed the State Censor Board, ordering it to grant a license to the film.[51] The Supreme Court of Kansas, however, unanimously upheld the decision of the state board of review to ban the film. Refusing to be silenced, Preminger and United Artists, at considerable cost, took their case before the United States Supreme Court—and won. On October 24, 1955, the U.S. Supreme Court overturned the finding of the Supreme Court of Kansas.

In early July, after the film had broken box-office records at the Four Star in Los Angeles and in the other, carefully selected houses in the tryout cities, three theater chains, United Paramount, Stanley Warner, and National Theatres (by now divorced from the studios that had originally owned them), made the momentous decision to book *The Moon Is Blue*. By July 15 the film that had opened without the industry's Seal of Approval was playing in two thousand large theaters across the country and was on its way to grossing $3.5 million, a considerable sum at the time. Preminger, Hugh Herbert, William Holden, and United Artists made a substantial amount of money.

"*The Moon Is Blue* sounded the death rattle of the Legion of Decency and the Production Code," conclude Leonard Leff and Jerold Simmons in their history of Hollywood censorship.[52] Joe Breen's battle with Preminger was the censorship czar's "last great orchestral flourish," as Breen's lieutenant Jack Vizzard commented.[53] Not surprisingly, on the eve of his downfall Breen was awarded an honorary Oscar at the Academy Awards ceremony on March 25, 1954. (That night, *The Moon Is Blue* was nominated for three awards, including a best actress nod for Maggie McNamara.) On October 15, 1954, Geoffrey Shurlock succeeded Breen. On June 28, 1961, Shurlock personally issued a Certificate of Approval to *The Moon Is Blue,* and at that point United Artists rejoined the Motion Picture Association. The Production Code Administration operated with diminished impact, a situation Shurlock himself approved of, until November 1, 1968, when a system of classification replaced it and the former enforcers of the Code became the honchos of the Code and Rating Administration.

In what was the decisive battle of his professional life, Preminger once again had the advantages of both good timing and good luck. As Otto had suspected and counted on, after twenty years of exerting an inordinate influence over the moral and visual content of mainstream American films, both the Production Code Administration office and Joe Breen himself—flamboyant, feisty, and personally likable—were ripe for a fall. All they had needed to push them off their pedestal was a David with the courage to sling a strategic stone at the Goliath of an outmoded document of censorship. Dr. Otto Ludwig Preminger of Vienna cast himself in the role, which he played with unstoppable conviction. His motives were a blend of idealism (Preminger's objection to censorship in both its immediate and long-range consequences was genuine) and financial common sense (he knew in his bones that a public confrontation with the enforcers of the antediluvian Code could be worth its weight in box-office gold). As a spokesman for free speech, a defender of freedom in artistic expression, and an adversary of the straitlaced Code, Otto demonstrated redoubtable stamina and style.

Amid the hullabaloo, the film itself seemed to be almost beside the point, a mere parenthesis. The narrative of the film's reception in 1953 provides important insights into the moral codes of Eisenhower's America— only a deeply puritanical society could have regarded this talky, innocuous comedy as sophisticated smut, a cause for alarm. The characters do indeed discuss the protocols of seduction with a "modern" insouciance unusual for the era, but the deeply conservative film in no way threatens the social or sexual status quo. "Now of course it all seems so innocent and even sweet, and so very old-fashioned," Hugh Herbert's daughter Diana said. "But in those days you did not hear words like 'virgin' and 'seduced' and 'pregnant' on stage or screen. Today you'd have to add strange sex scenes to get the same kind of reaction. In London critics and audiences weren't as shocked; if anything they were amused by the American reaction. For many years now the primary market for the play has been high schools."[54]

Preminger's direction reinforces the material's fundamental tameness. When he submitted as part of his defense of the film's morality the argument that "there is not a moment of passion," Otto wasn't kidding. Never for an instant do the characters or, for that matter, the director, lose their cool. Working in a strict minimalist vein of straightforward continuing editing, objective camera movement, and centered compositions, Preminger transfers his hit play into the more durable form of celluloid with unimaginative competence. His approach indemnifies the material against any possible charge of licentiousness, but it also suppresses a liberating comic spirit, precisely the qualities of spontaneity and friskiness that might have been teased out of the show's premise.

Preminger expands the action to include scenes in the shopping concourse of the Empire State Building; Don Gresham's office; a taxi; the hallway, elevator, and fire escape in the building where Don lives; and the living room and bathroom of David Slater's apartment. Throw in some fog and rain briefly glimpsed outside the windows, and that's about it for scenic amplitude. "Don't spoil the customers" might have been Preminger's mantra to his art directors, Nicolai Remisoff and Edward Boyle. As a result the story unfolds in an airless environment, a world apart that is curiously unpopulated. When Don and Patty meet on the observation deck of the Empire State Building, for instance, no one else is there. (In the rhyming scene at the end, however, Preminger in a nice touch includes tourists—the stars of the German version of the film.) However, the film's two major settings, the apartments of the swinging bachelor and his suave upstairs neighbor, are intelligently designed. Don's modern bachelor pad, with abstract art on chaste white walls (a décor reflecting Otto's regard for the International Style), is meaningfully contrasted with the Continental luxury (heavy drapes, museumlike representational paintings, Old World furniture, a decadent bathroom with a marble-lined tub) of Slater's apartment.

On its own merits, rather than as a specimen in a censorship furor, *The Moon Is Blue* long ago failed the test of time. Even so, regarded with patience and generosity, it has an antique charm. In the short term the film made Otto money and established his bona fides as a cunning independent filmmaker. But in the long term this ephemeral comedy that happened to light a spark in an age of innocence drove another nail into the director's always precarious critical standing. Unfairly, Preminger bashers have taken it as a paradigm of the director's entire portfolio: not-so-good films on currently controversial topics that have no resonance once their "hot" subject matter ages.

As he was starting his career as an independent producer-director, Preminger was also getting adjusted to a new wife and to an unaccustomed role as a stepfather to Sandy. Because of Otto's six-month annual release from Fox, the Premingers were peripatetic. The new couple, however, had different preferences about where to live. Otto favored New York and wanted to spend as much time there as he could; Mary, who liked Los Angeles, wanted to stay in one place and in a house of her own where she could paint and sculpt. "Otto was a big hotel liver," as Sandy, now known as Gilbert Gardner, recalled,

and at the beginning of the marriage we were with him in suites at the Carlyle, the St. Regis, and the Ambassador. Later Otto had an apartment at 40 East Sixty-eighth Street; basically, nobody but me lived there. I was studying acting with Stella Adler at the time. The first time Otto brought my mother to Los Angeles, after they were married, he rented a small house overlooking the Bel-Air Hotel. And something happened that worried her. Gregory Ratoff stayed there for five days and played cards the whole time; Sam Spiegel was there much of that time too. It was all part of Otto's Hollywood buddy system, which my mother didn't understand.

After a period of moving around, Otto rented Anatol Litvak's pink palace in Malibu—Litvak had built it in 1936 for Miriam Hopkins, his lady friend at the time. Litvak began to rent out the house in the early 1950s, and after a while that was Otto's and my mother's base when they were in Los Angeles. The house had an intercom system that was state-of-the-art. Otto employed a couple who ran the house. In my time Otto gave five or six major parties, sometimes with as many as three hundred people gathered on the huge deck and in the dining room. Cars would be lined up by valets. And there were a huge number of caterers. These were gatherings of people of great worth and value: Chaplin, who became a special friend of mine; Cole Porter—I met him four times, but he never remembered me; Tyrone Power; the Henry Fondas; the David

Selznicks; James Stewart. I was kind of shocked by the excess, the ostentatiousness. Rock stars now run their lives in that fashion. This was the Old Hollywood, a very insular way of life.[55]

At the beginning, as Gardner recalled,

my mother and Otto were really fond of each other and Otto was fatherly to me. He wanted me to be a part of his business, and while the marriage lasted I worked in some fashion on all his projects. He spent time with me; he *wanted* to spend time with me. He would always ask me to go to the theater with him. There was very little of the temper at home. That was reserved for younger actors, for business dealings, and with production people. Mostly, I thought the temper was an act. At home he really was not that way, but he *was* patriarchal, and he was European. He liked to have his butler take care of his clothes, and he expected his wife to run his household, to arrange dinners in the proper way. Fortunately, Mary was a good party giver. She had the grace and upbringing to be a good hostess.[56]

With (left to right) French actress Suzanne Dadelle, Mrs. Gary Cooper, Kirk Douglas, and Otto's stepson Sandy Gardner, New York, December 1955.

From the start, however, the marriage had a shaky foundation. Increasingly preoccupied with the hubbub over *The Moon Is Blue,* Otto was a long-distance husband, and although Gardner did not know it at the time, from early in the marriage his mother and stepfather were not faithful to each other. In a basic way the marriage was a business arrangement. Otto wanted a hostess for his A-list Hollywood parties, and Mary, who had already weathered three failed marriages, wanted financial security.

Since he had signed his new contract with Fox, Preminger had managed to avoid making any commitment. But when Darryl Zanuck called Otto when he was in New York preparing for the June opening of *The Moon Is Blue,* asking him to direct a western with a nifty pulp title, *River of No Return,* he realized the time had come to pay the piper. Understandably, "after the complete freedom I had enjoyed making *The Moon Is Blue* as an independent and the almost-freedom Howard Hughes had given me in order to take revenge on an actress," Otto was reluctant to return to a factory job.[57] Because for good reason he had trouble picturing himself out on the open range, he was not thrilled at the prospect of directing a western.

Preminger wasn't the only one who questioned Zanuck's assignment. Stanley Rubin, the film's producer, was also doubtful. "I wanted Richard Fleischer, who had just done such a terrific job on *Narrow Margin* [a first-rate film noir Rubin had produced the previous year at RKO], but he wasn't available," as Rubin recalled. "It was at that point Zanuck mentioned Otto Preminger. I was familiar with his work, of course: I loved *Laura* and I felt he was talented but not the man for our piece of Americana. At a meeting with Zanuck's assistant Lou Schreiber, I said Otto was wrong, his skill was in contemporary sophisticated melodrama and comedy. I saw Wild Bill [William] Wellman or Raoul Walsh or Henry King instead. When I found that Preminger had a pay-or-play commitment, I realized I was fighting a losing battle."

Once Preminger read the screenplay, however, his attitude changed. He liked the story, which Rubin had developed with a series of writers.

A friend of mine, Louis Lantz, [Rubin recalled,] had a great idea. He wanted to steal the premise of *Bicycle Thief,* in which the hero finds that after his bicycle is stolen he has no way to support himself and his son, and transport it to the American West. When our hero in the West has his horse and gun stolen, he too can't support or protect himself and his son. Lou wrote a good treatment and first draft, and I hired Frank Fenton for the final draft. Originally, the plan was to make the film on a modest budget; but as we were working on the first draft, Fox got "married" to CinemaScope [the first two Fox films in the new wide-screen process, *The Robe* and *How to Marry a Millionaire,* had been released in the fall of 1953]. "Your movie lends itself to CinemaScope, and your budget is going to go up," Zanuck, delightful and stubborn, a boss in the days when there really was a boss, told me.[58]

Preminger welcomed the chance to shoot in CinemaScope, and he approved of the stars Zanuck and Rubin had already cast: Robert Mitchum for the horseless hero (Otto had forgiven, or more likely forgotten, their fracas during *Angel Face*) and Marilyn Monroe for the role of a saloon singer who hooks up with the hero and his son. Zanuck, famously ambivalent about Monroe, had resisted when Rubin pushed for her. "He was suggesting others. He mentioned Anne Bancroft in particular, but Monroe had the combination of qualities—sexiness, beauty, vulnerability—I wanted in the part. She was the only one I wanted," Rubin said, "and I prevailed."

When Otto flew in from New York, Rubin took him to lunch at the Fox commissary. "I made the mistake of youth—at thirty-six I was the youngest producer on the lot, and I was honest," Rubin recalled. "I told Otto he was not the director I was looking for. What did that candor gain me? It put Otto on edge from our first meeting." But as they began to confer about the songs Monroe would sing and about the production schedule, and after they traveled to Canada to scout locations at Banff and Lake Louise, Rubin grew fond of Preminger. "I felt he really wanted to do the picture, and that it was not just a contractual obligation." Before production was scheduled to begin in the late spring, Zanuck made a change in the script that neither Rubin nor Preminger agreed with. "It wasn't anything major, as I recall, but we felt we had to address it with Zanuck," Rubin said. "I set up a meeting, expecting Otto to join me in the battle, and more likely, to lead it. But his behavior totally surprised me: he did not open his mouth. It was the only time I ever saw Otto fade into the wallpaper. I won the battle, but I won it alone." It was only afterward that Rubin learned of Preminger's long-past falling out with Zanuck: "Could Otto have been afraid of starting up again with Zanuck? I did not feel any tension between them, however, and fifty years later I still don't know why Otto clammed up as he did in that meeting."[59]

For his big-budget CinemaScope western Rubin was able to schedule twelve weeks of preproduction, during which Marilyn Monroe rehearsed and recorded her musical numbers, and a forty-five-day shooting schedule. Location scenes in Canada were shot first. At the end of June (only weeks after *The Moon Is Blue* had opened), Preminger and the cast flew to Calgary from Los

Angeles. As a publicity gimmick, the cast traveled eighty miles on a specially commissioned train from Calgary to the Banff Springs Hotel. Crowds lined up along the route to catch a glimpse of Monroe, who as the star of the recently released *Niagara* and *Gentlemen Prefer Blondes* and the upcoming *How to Marry a Millionaire* was on the verge of becoming the world's most famous blonde. Traveling with Monroe was her acting coach Natasha Lytess, "passing herself off as a Russian, for reasons of her own," according to Otto, who was certain that in fact she was "a German."[60]

Under any circumstances, Preminger and the always tardy Monroe, who also seemed unable to memorize lines, could never have gotten along. But Natasha, hovering over Monroe's every line and gesture, stoked Otto's temper to the boiling point. Before and after each scene Monroe would be locked in private conference with Lytess, the star's self-appointed codirector as well as her surrogate mother. According to instructions from Lytess, Monroe would either request or refuse to do another take. Maddeningly, Lytess had convinced Monroe that her reputation as a dramatic actress would rest on her ability to enunciate each syllable of every line of dialogue with exaggerated emphasis. "She rehearsed her lines with such grave ar-tic-yew-lay-shun that her violent lip movements made it impossible to photograph her," Preminger complained. "I pleaded with her to relax and speak naturally but she paid no attention. She listened only to Natasha."[61]

The circumstance of Otto Preminger taking his marching orders from a pretentious acting guru and a desperately insecure actress surely conforms to at least two of Aristotle's criteria for tragedy, capable as it is of eliciting both pity and terror. But the harassed director won little support from the crew. "Otto was a complete pain in the ass," according to Paul Helmick, the assistant director and unit manager. "[He was] vicious, impatient, very crude to people."[62] When he could no longer tolerate the Marilyn-Natasha onslaught, Preminger called Stanley Rubin in Los Angeles to demand Natasha's removal. After her coach was dismissed, Monroe called Zanuck to demand her reinstatement and the next day Lytess was back on the set. "Otto had the power to get Natasha off the set, and Marilyn had the power to get her back," Rubin recalled.[63] Zanuck phoned Otto to commiserate, but also to reinforce the fact that Monroe's box-office pull was, in effect, paying his $65,000 director's salary. Flummoxed and humiliated, and realizing he was stuck with Natasha, Otto began to turn his rage onto Monroe. "Deriding her talent as an actress and recalling [her] days as one of Sam Spiegel's 'house girls,' he advised her to return to her 'former profession,' " Monroe's biographer Barbara Leaming claimed.[64] As Paul Helmick observed, "It was the biggest mismatch I'd ever seen. [Monroe and Preminger] absolutely detested each other."[65]

Preminger survived because his erstwhile adversary, Robert Mitchum, was equally impatient with Monroe. Immune to his costar's sex appeal—she wasn't his type—Mitchum more than once called her bluff. "He would slap her sharply on the bottom and snap, 'Now stop that nonsense! Let's play it like human beings,' " as Preminger recalled.[66] Before a number of scenes Mitchum was able to startle Monroe into speaking in her own voice, delightfully slurred and intimate. In the finished film it's possible to see the shots where Mitchum got to her and the ones where he failed to.

Monroe and Preminger were both soothed by the presence of Tommy Rettig, a delightful eleven-year-old cast as Mitchum's son. "Marilyn loved the boy, and they had a sweet, warm relationship," Rubin said. "Otto respected Tommy's professionalism; when Marilyn would go up in her lines, and a scene might have to be shot over twenty times, the boy would be word-perfect every time."[67] Tommy's confidence, however, faltered after Natasha repeatedly told him that child actors were in danger of misplacing their talent unless they took lessons and "learned to use their instrument." Tommy began to forget his lines and then, several times, burst into tears. It didn't take long for Preminger to locate the source of the boy's discomfort. Infuriated, he once again demanded Natasha's banishment. And once again, at Monroe's insistence, Natasha reappeared. Preminger, however, spoke to the cast and crew about Natasha's abuse of Tommy and as he gleefully reported, "Everyone in the company [except, of course, Marilyn] cut her dead."[68]

Preminger also had to contend with rainy weather and dangerous stunts on the Bow River. For the most hazardous scenes, stunt doubles stood in for the stars, who worked only on a raft tied securely to the riverbank. Still, Mitchum's heavy nightly intake of alcohol and Monroe's perpetual distraction rendered them unsuited for scampering on rocks made slippery by rushing water. Near the end of the location shooting Monroe suffered a serious twist to her leg that kept her off the set for a few days. When she returned to Los Angeles in early September to shoot the interior scenes at Fox, she was on crutches.

Tensions did not ease once the company began working in the studio. "At that point I was on the set every day, and I saw Otto bully Marilyn and some of the crafts people, some of the lower ones," Rubin said.

I never saw him scream at Natasha, but in speaking to Marilyn he would be just below yelling—in front of everybody. It was a frontal assault. I saw her in tears near the end of shooting. When we were scheduled to do close-ups on the raft on the tank stage and she knew she was going to be drenched, with water pouring all over her, she wouldn't come out of her dressing room. Otto was enraged. He

Location shooting in Canada for *River of No Return,* Preminger's first film in CinemaScope.

started screaming at his full lung power and he pounded the back of his chair, demanding Marilyn's immediate appearance on the set. I talked Marilyn down—she may have been frightened. When she came out Otto was seething, and he continued to hurl insults, berating her for being selfish and unprofessional. He wouldn't let up; everyone could see that he despised her, and it seemed to be personal as well as professional. Marilyn and I got on nicely because we had a common enemy: Otto Preminger.

Rubin's examination of the dailies confirmed his original belief that Preminger had been the wrong choice. "An aura that would have been natural for a Raoul Walsh, who was steeped in Western lore, wasn't there," Rubin concluded. "A feeling, a tone I was looking for, and that was in the script, wasn't there. Otto and I had a bad fight about a scene with Monroe and Mitchum in the woods. Otto said it would work fine; I felt an element had been lost. In the first and final analysis, Otto and I were not meant for each other—our personalities were not attuned. Otto was bigger than life, and I am life-sized."[69]

Despite the embattled atmosphere Preminger finished on schedule, on September 29, and within Rubin's original budget. Once shooting was completed, Otto began to edit with Lou Loeffler, whom he trusted, but before the end of postproduction he left for Europe; working alongside Loeffler, Rubin finished the film. "We made some changes and a few retakes were shot by Preminger's friend, Jean Negulesco," Rubin said.[70] As Otto recalled, "After *River of No Return* I decided not to work ever again as a studio employee. I paid Fox $150,000 to cancel my half-year contract."[71]

Otto's leaving before the final cut was completed was a declaration of independence, but during filming he had been engaged by the project. The story of a father, just released from prison, who learns to love a son he has not known no doubt caused Otto to reflect on his own unknown son Erik, now nine and being raised by his mother. The scenes between father and son tentatively reaching out to each other are the strongest in the film, beautifully played by Robert Mitchum and Tommy Rettig.

Preminger discovered that shooting in CinemaScope supported his usual preferences for long shots and minimum intercutting. "It is actually more difficult to compose in this size," he said. "Few painters have chosen these proportions, and somehow it embraces more, we see more widely, and it fits into long takes better. On the wide screen, abrupt cuts disturb audiences."[72] On a first outing in the wide-screen format in which he was to become a master, Preminger and his cinematographer Joseph La Shelle revel in panoramic vistas: high-angle shots of the raft floating on the river between canyons of massive rock; low-angle shots of Indians massed threateningly on the tops of high cliffs. The opening scene, which Preminger and La Shelle design as a fluid tracking shot that follows Mitchum as he rides through a tent community buzzing with activity, reveals the increased possibilities in CinemaScope for long takes and deep focus.

There is no way, however, that as a director of a western Otto Preminger could ever be mistaken for John Ford. A fight scene, in which two roughnecks suddenly appear, without a horse, in the middle of the wilderness and begin to attack the hero, is perfunctorily staged and edited. An Indian attack is only marginally more convincing. (The film's reactionary, reflexive treatment of faceless Indians on the warpath is standard for the era. Their individuality erased, their grievances never addressed, their cameo appearances cued by dissonant chords on the sound track, the Indians function as pure motiveless malignity, a threat to the white man's hegemony.) Problematic, too, is the occasionally faulty match between studio and location shots. A scene in a cave smells of studio artifice, and repeated process shots of the characters on the raft fall well below the technical standards of the time.

Tommy Rettig (eleven years old) helped Marilyn Monroe, who detested Preminger and her role as a chorus girl, through the ordeal of filming *River of No Return*.

Otto stumbled with Monroe. The actress herself frequently claimed that *River of No Return* was her worst film. It isn't, but it's easy enough to see why she was unhappy. Aside from her dislike of the director, the role of a saloon singer longing for love and respectability reinforced stereotypes she was already determined to resist. And in a story of masculine rituals, her whore with a heart of gold is not only a cliché, she is also largely irrelevant. In most of her scenes with Tommy Rettig, in which she speaks in her natural voice, and in her musical numbers, Monroe is captivating in ways that only a born movie star can be. But in the far more numerous scenes with adult males, she delivers her lines in the style demanded by Natasha. Otto's failure to knock the affectation out of his misguided star is a notable lapse in his careerlong assault on overacting.

For years after *River of No Return* was released, Preminger spoke bitterly about Monroe. "If I was offered a million dollars tax free I wouldn't make another picture with her," he stated in a March 3, 1957, interview with Art Buchwald. "It's okay for a star to be late one time, and two, but when she's late fifty-four or fifty-six times it's too much. It's beneath the dignity of any director or any other star." "If Miss Monroe should ask me to do another picture—and I think she won't—I will not do it because life is too short," he announced in an interview in the *New York Post* on August 22, 1958. Yet over time, as the memory of his bruising encounters with Monroe and her sorceress began to recede, Preminger struck a more gallant tone. And after Monroe acquired the kind of mythic standing he could never have anticipated when locked in battle with her in the summer of 1953, he began to express praise for her abilities and compassion for her torment. "She tried very hard, and when people try hard, you can't be mad at them," he reflected in a January 28, 1980, interview in the *New York Daily News*.

SEVEN

Lightning Strikes Twice

Otto's haste to be done with Monroe and Fox was due to his eagerness to launch into his second independent production, an opera with an all-black cast. He was counting on the likely fact, as he had with *The Moon Is Blue,* that no major studio would take the risk of making *Carmen Jones,* an adaptation by Oscar Hammerstein II of Georges Bizet's 1875 opera *Carmen* that had been an unexpected hit on Broadway in 1943. Otto was convinced he could transform Bizet's perennially popular opera, with its ravishing melodies, sex-driven characters, and compelling story, into a realistic film that had every chance of stirring up controversy. It was not an easy sell, however.

From the moment Oscar Hammerstein had heard Bizet's opera in concert at the Hollywood Bowl in 1934, he had seen its potential as a musical play—a show for Broadway rather than the opera house. In his adaptation, set in North Carolina and Chicago during World War II, Bizet's fiery heroine becomes Carmen Jones, a worker in a parachute factory who seduces and abandons Joe, a soldier, before moving on to her next conquest, a prizefighter, Husky Miller. Joe, driven mad by Carmen's desertion, strangles her. Hammerstein eliminated recitative, noting that the composer and his collaborators "originally wrote *Carmen* with spoken dialogue scenes between the arias. The work was not converted to 'grand opera' until after Bizet's death [with music written by Ernest Guiraud]."[1] Nonetheless, Hammerstein had difficulty finding investors. Billy Rose, a scrappy impresario with deep pockets, decided to take a chance on the show, which he presented on Broadway on December 2, 1943, to a warm reception. *Carmen Jones* had a substantial run of 502 performances followed by an eighteen-month national tour.

When he had seen it, Preminger was impressed more by the idea of the show than what Hammerstein had done with it. Inaccurately, he dismissed the Broadway *Carmen Jones* as a series of "skits loosely based on the opera" and recalled that the score had been "simplified and changed so that the performers who had no operatic training could sing it."[2] In fact, *Carmen Jones* adheres closely to the opera's structure and was sung operatically. In his film, Preminger was intending to disregard "Hammerstein's revue" as well as the opera's libretto by Meilhac and Halévy and to return to the original source, the 1845 novel by Prosper Mérimée. To write the script he hired Harry Kleiner, his former student at Yale, instructing him to open up the material beyond the limited settings of both the opera and Hammerstein's adaptation. (In the "revue," Hammerstein sets Act I in a parachute factory and improbably squeezes Act II onto the terrace of a black country club.) "I had decided to make a dramatic film with music rather than a conventional film musical," Preminger said, and to maintain movie realism he intended to shoot as much of the film as he could on location.[3]

After his success with *The Moon Is Blue,* Preminger was counting on the support of Arthur Krim and Robert Benjamin at United Artists. But at a lunch at "21," the two men, having examined the financial history of all-black films and concluding that the project was not economically viable, declined. "Sorry, Otto, but this is too rich for our blood," they said.[4] Surprised by their reaction, Preminger quickly offered the project elsewhere. Again the response was negative.

As he continued to search for backers, Otto did something he had never done before and would never attempt again. In October 1953, he directed an opera for the New York City Opera, the American premiere of a work by Gottfried von Einem based on *The Trial,* by Franz Kafka. For Preminger the material was a radical departure: Kafka's novel, a nightmarish allegory of a man accused of a nameless crime, is not concerned with the realistic kind of trial and the real-world legal issues that were Preminger's usual bailiwick. But Otto welcomed the challenge of directing an opera for the stage as a way of preparing for *Carmen Jones.* "Mr. Preminger, being a believer in the work of the New York City Opera, is charging a considerate fee, but it would nevertheless be higher than any previous fee paid to a stage director by the City Opera," an article in the *New York Times* on September 21, 1953, noted. On the whole, Otto's production received stronger reviews than the opera itself.

Olin Downes in his *New York Times* review on October 23 praised "a carefully prepared and extremely capable performance" but expressed disappointment in the opera. "Its musical substance is of the slightest. . . . Could any librettist, any composer, have turned this work of Kafka into a compelling music drama? One might, the Alban Berg of *Wozzeck*. But he has gone, and it is doubtful if the future will produce another like him."

Despite many turndowns, Otto continued to believe in *Carmen Jones*. Salvation came finally from a perhaps not unexpected source: Darryl Zanuck, who had heard of Preminger's difficulties placing the project and asked to see the script. After reading it, he promptly offered financing. Fox would be providing the funds, but Preminger would operate as an entirely independent filmmaker.

Zanuck believed *Carmen Jones* had blockbuster potential. But Joseph Moscowitz, the head of Fox's business affairs in New York, did not, and for weeks he avoided meeting with Preminger. When Zanuck finally forced him to complete the deal, Moscowitz refused to offer more than a meager $750,000. After finally signing a contract in December 1953, Preminger began what was to be a prolonged preproduction process. He started to scout possible locations, always one of his favorite activities. He hired his crew. Veteran Sam Leavitt would shoot the film. The musical director would be Herschel Burke Gilbert, who had composed the score for *The Moon Is Blue*. Herbert Ross would choreograph. All the while Otto continued to huddle with Harry Kleiner on refining the script, making sure drama rather than music remained the focus.

And then, on April 19, 1954, six weeks before he was scheduled to begin shooting, Preminger had another run-in with Joe Breen, who in his final months at the head of the Production Code Administration office seemed determined to even the score over Otto's victory with *The Moon Is Blue*. After he read the script, Breen was livid. His objections to *The Moon Is Blue* had been entirely in what the characters said, in their *mental* attitude toward sex, whereas his complaints about *Carmen Jones* were visual as well as verbal. Carmen lives by her erotic skills, titillating her men with seductive body language and verbal come-ons—there was no question that as written, the character was intended to be sexually provocative in ways that violated contemporary Hollywood standards. Breen to his horror fully grasped that Otto, capitalizing on the racist stereotype of blacks as sexually superior to pale Anglo-Saxons, was intending to produce one hell of a hot-blooded movie. Breen cited the script's "over-emphasis on lustfulness," lodging particular complaints against Carmen sliding down Joe's body after he has lifted her up; Carmen adjusting her stockings as Joe watches; and Joe waking up in Carmen's bed. "We cannot see our way clear to approve detailed scenes of passion, in bedrooms, between unmarried couples," Breen fulminated. Breen overall was outraged by the film's apparent neutrality, "the lack of any voice of morality properly condemning Carmen's complete lack of morals."[5]

Because he had made his point in the fight over *The Moon Is Blue;* because he was relieved at last to have found backing; and because, unlike the comedy, which had needed a fracas to put it over, *Carmen Jones* had far more than some sexy images to entice mid-1950s moviegoers, Preminger agreed to make some minor adjustments. But he drew the line at Breen's objection to a lyric, "Stand up and fight like hell," sung by the prizefighter Husky Miller. Here he would not budge. Neither would Breen. A flurry of memos flew back and forth between Fox and the Production Code Administration office. Preminger applied to the board of the Motion Picture Association of America and won his case. But at the same time he agreed to shoot two versions of two scenes Breen had found offensive—in both cases, Preminger's original versions survived.

Otto was unfazed about violating sexual taboos, but in 1954, at a time when blacks had virtually been written out of mainstream American films, he was sensitive to issues of racial representation. Aware of the value of providing employment to performers who had been overlooked, he was at the same time alert to the possibility that the all-black world of the film could reinforce prejudice. He was concerned, too, that black characters speaking in dialect and impelled by atavistic sexual urges could be potentially offensive to some black viewers. "*Carmen Jones* was really a fantasy, as *Porgy and Bess* was," Preminger said. "The all-black world shown in these films doesn't exist, at least not in the United States. We used the musical-fantasy quality to convey something of the needs and aspirations of colored people."[6]

At Zanuck's urging, Preminger sent the script to Walter White, president of the NAACP. White's response, recorded in a memo from Preminger to Zanuck, was reassuring. "While White indicated that he principally is opposed to an all-Negro show as such, because their fight is for integration as opposed to segregation in any form, he likes this particular script very much and has no objection to any part of it."[7]

Preminger assembled his cast quickly. For Joe, the male lead, he signed Harry Belafonte, a good-looking folk singer who had recently popularized calypso and in 1953 had made his film debut in *Bright Road* and won a Tony Award for *John Murray's Almanac.* In the supporting role of Frankie, Carmen's good-time, smart-talking friend, he hired Pearl Bailey, who had appeared in two minor films but had become popular as a band singer and on Broadway in 1945 in *St. Louis Woman.* As the prizefighter Preminger chose Joe Adams, a strapping Los Angeles disc jockey.

For Diahann Carroll, then a nineteen-year-old singer from New York, auditioning for Preminger was a terrifying experience. "I had never before encountered power on such a grand scale," she recalled. "Otto Preminger was seated behind the longest desk I had ever seen . . . his office was the size of a hotel ballroom."[8] Preminger, catching her off guard, asked her to read for the title role. On the spot she was to prepare a scene in which Joe (read by James Edwards, who only a few years earlier had seemed about to become the first black leading man in American films) paints Carmen's toenails. Stunned by Preminger's order for her to remove her shoes and stockings, she could barely focus on rehearsing with Edwards, "one of the most seductive men I have ever met." When Preminger returned, she stumbled through the scene.

> Nothing in my young life had prepared me for this kind of heavy sexuality, and I couldn't begin to handle it, even on the level of "let's pretend." Sensing my discomfort, Preminger asked, blaring at me with his full force (but with a glint in his eyes), "Who ever told you you were sexy?" "No one! No one! I swear!" I answered quickly, looking him straight in the eye, somehow recognizing that both of us knew this was outrageous, and that a friendship had just begun. And then Otto Preminger, the bully extraordinaire, threw back his head and roared with laughter.[9]

Diahann Carroll didn't get the part. But Preminger, who always appreciated people who could make him laugh, found a small role in the film for his new friend (she was to play Frankie's sidekick Myrt), and he was to cast her in two future films as well.

Brock Peters, who, unlike the other performers Preminger had cast so far, was operatically trained, remembered "a surprisingly easy interview. I knew Preminger's reputation, we all did. But when I saw him, in New York, he couldn't have been more polite and gracious. He did not ask me to sing, but I could feel he was looking me over very closely. His blue eyes looked at me intently; I had the feeling those eyes could see right through you. My first impression was that here was a man who was all-knowing, and from that came the terrific power that he radiated." At the end of the meeting Preminger cast Peters in the unsympathetic role of Sergeant Brown, a troublemaker attracted to Carmen and resentful of Joe. Peters was thrilled. "Film to a black performer back then seemed a long way away—the very thought of Hollywood was so remote, and so unattainable for black youngsters. We all felt we needed some kind of magic to make it happen."[10]

As he was casting, Preminger scheduled a rehearsal period beginning on June 3 and planned to start shooting on June 24. But well into April two

Dorothy Dandridge in a cameo appearance as herself, a sophisticated nightclub singer, in *Remains to Be Seen,* a year before *Carmen Jones.*

principal roles remained unfilled: Joe's small-town gal Cindy Lou, and the star-making title role. In retrospect Otto's casting of Dorothy Dandridge, a striking beauty and a performer with a lengthy résumé, would seem to have been a foregone conclusion. Born in 1923, Dandridge had been working professionally since the age of four. She appeared regularly in nightclubs, was on television in *Beulah,* and had had occasional roles in movies, beginning with a bit part in the Marx Brothers' *A Day at the Races* in 1937. Type-cast as an "exotic," she had been seen in such minor films as *Bahama Passage* (1941), *Drums of the Congo* (1942), and *Tarzan and the Jungle Queen* (1951). However, in 1953 her appearance as a high school teacher in *Bright Road* had given her a new stature in the film community, and her career as a sultry chanteuse was flourishing. Preminger certainly knew about her; he had even seen her in a nightclub appearance in New York. But he thought she was too self-contained to play Carmen. He was looking for an actress with a drop-dead, come-hither sex appeal he did not feel Dandridge projected. Dandridge's agents at MCA, who also thought she was the wrong type, were promoting another client, Joyce Bryant. But Dorothy wanted the role and was determined to get it.

Preminger agreed to see her only because of the intervention of his brother, Ingo, whose office at 214 South Beverly Drive was located in the same building where Dorothy's personal manager, Earl Mills, also had an office. Mills showed Ingo a file of Dandridge's photos and clippings and pleaded with him to get his client an interview. Ingo spoke to his brother, but when Otto called Mills to arrange a meeting he stated frankly that he didn't think Dandridge was Carmen. "She's too much like Loretta Young," he told Mills.[11]

When Earl Mills and his anxious client arrived for the interview, Dorothy was too beautifully dressed, almost as if she had been compelled to confirm Preminger's preconception of her. Perhaps being a little wicked, Otto suggested right off that she audition for the role of Cindy Lou, "a sweet, yielding girl,"[12] which in fact is how he saw Dorothy. He wanted to give her the script, have her study the part of Cindy Lou, and then come back to audition. As Dandridge recalled, Otto was quite definite. "You cannot act the Carmen role. You have a veneer, my dear. You look the sophisticate. When I saw you I thought, How lovely, a model, a beautiful butterfly . . . but not Carmen, my dear."[13]

Dorothy exploded. "Mr. Preminger, I'm an actress. I can play a whore as well as I can play a nun. If I could only convince you. I'm not a Cindy Lou. You don't know what I've gone through." Mills, sensing that Preminger liked Dorothy and "even wanted to help her," silenced his client.[14] He grabbed the script Otto was offering because he knew this would give them the chance for a second meeting.

Mills and Dorothy resolved to play their second act with Otto Preminger in a different key. At Max Factor's, Dorothy and her manager borrowed a "messy looking black wig," "an off-the-shoulder low cut black peasant blouse without a bra," "a black satin skirt with a slit to the thigh without a girdle," and "black high-heeled pumps."[15] Then Dorothy applied "sexy" makeup and began to practice a hip-swaying walk. To top off her impersonation Dorothy thought she needed "a tired look as if I had worn out a bed. I went to the gym and deliberately tired myself before I went to

For her *Carmen Jones* screen test, Dandridge transformed herself from a ladylike chanteuse into Bizet's rough-and-ready siren.

the audition."[16] As Mills commented, "She felt she might not get the role of Carmen but she was sure as hell certain that she wouldn't be asked to do the role of Cindy."[17]

When for the second time she and her manager entered Preminger's office, by design just a shade late for their appointment, Dorothy with a provocative look in her "tired" eyes sashayed across the large room. "My God, it's Carmen!" Preminger exclaimed, caught off guard by Dandridge's transformation. "I had ceased to be the saloon singer, the lady, the sophisticate," Dorothy exulted.[18] Clearly delighted and no doubt realizing he had found his Carmen, Preminger asked her to move about the office, to open and close drawers, all the while gauging her gestures and body language on the sexual Richter scale. At the end of the meeting, he told her he wanted to shoot a screen test. To accommodate Dorothy's nightclub schedule—she had a contract to appear at the Chase Hotel in St. Louis on May 3—he scheduled the test for mid-May.

When Dandridge was out of town, Otto found his Cindy Lou, Olga James, a Juilliard School of Music graduate with an operatic vocal range. "When I sang an aria for Preminger at the Alvin Theatre in New York, everybody applauded," as James recalled. "It wasn't a stretch for me. I was that character, a country-looking girl. I was just a little ingenue."[19]

Dorothy's test scene was the same one that Preminger had asked Diahann Carroll to perform. Playing opposite James Edwards, Dandridge gave a riveting performance, sexy and fearless. Preminger, who had already shot tests of Joyce Bryant and Elizabeth Foster in the same scene, was convinced, and on May 21 he announced that Dorothy Dandridge would play Carmen Jones.

At first Dorothy was exhilarated by having won the showiest leading role ever offered to a black performer in an American film. But a few days later she began to feel she wouldn't be able to play it. "Too much stress. I feared my emotional system couldn't handle it," she recalled.[20] Despite her veneer, Dorothy Dandridge was deeply troubled. She had had numerous affairs, often with white men who she felt had betrayed her, and she was guilt-stricken about her daughter, brain-damaged from birth. Eager to be taken seriously as an actress and frustrated by the kinds of roles she was offered, in the late 1940s she had studied at the Actors Lab, run by veterans of the 1930s Group Theatre. "The studios often sent young players to us, but Dorothy came on her own," recalled Phoebe Brand, a Group actress who taught at the Lab.

> She was very serious about acting. We taught Stanislavski, and unlike Marilyn Monroe, who also studied with us at the time and did not understand me, Dorothy absorbed our approach quickly. Morrie [Morris Carnovsky, Brand's husband] cast Dorothy as Kukachin in our production of O'Neill's *Marco Millions,* and she was marvelous—we would have cast her in that role on Broadway. Dorothy was beautiful, startlingly so, but very fragile. She was a loner who didn't make chums and was not easy to know. I remember once that she brought in her daughter; she carried her in. It was clear that she was crazy about her, but that she also felt so sorry and responsible for the child's illness. There weren't many blacks studying with us, though I wished there had been, but at that time the studios were not using black actors. We were surprised when she was cast as Carmen: who would have thought of casting her that way?[21]

Now, at thirty-one, not young by Hollywood standards, Dorothy had been handed the chance to act that she had long wished for, and she was panic-stricken. Her anxiety grew when a number of black friends cautioned her against playing a part that could reinforce negative preconceptions. "The Negro community is plagued by fears of its image," Dorothy observed. "It has been so much the victim of stereotypes that it has developed an understandable sensitivity. I couldn't bear to think I might turn in a performance that would be injurious to that perennial spectre, race pride, the group dignity."[22] After several agonizing days in seclusion, she delegated Earl Mills to inform Preminger that he would have to continue his search for Carmen.

As soon as he heard, Otto drove over to Dorothy's apartment on the Sunset Strip. He assured her, as Dorothy recalled, that she was indeed "a good actress . . . uninhibited, [with] natural free motions. By the middle of the evening I called him Otto." By the end of the evening, Dorothy not only agreed to play Carmen, she "became [Otto's] girl."[23] Dorothy's biographer Donald Bogle was not certain that the affair began "at the beginning, as Dorothy claimed—you can't trust everything in Dandridge's autobiography. But it certainly started during the filming."[24]

"Black women fascinated Otto," as Willi Frischauer reported,[25] while Dorothy had a decided preference for Caucasian men. For Otto, Dorothy personified a sexual ideal, the incarnation of his enduring, fetishistic devotion to black women. For Dorothy, Otto "was physical, all male—no problem there." Aside from mutual racial and sexual attraction, however, there was much that would have drawn them together. Dorothy was enticed by Otto's cultivated background and found his paternalistic attitude toward her wonderfully comforting. Her own father had abandoned her and her sister Vivian and she despised her mother, Ruby, an actress whose sadistic lesbian lover regularly beat both young women. Otto's complexity, his combination of "both hardness and sensitivity," also appealed to her.[26] To Otto, the young woman's vulnerability was as magnetic as her beauty. He knew he could draw a powerful Carmen from her, in the process transforming a damaged bronze Venus into a bona fide movie star, the first dark-skinned female star in Hollywood history. But he also sensed he would be able to exert control over her private life.

Beginning an affair with his star violated Preminger's strict policy of separating church and state, but he succumbed this one time because his attraction to Dorothy was oceanic. "There was no doubt that he cared enormously about her," Donald Bogle said. "Just as there was no doubt that Dorothy cared deeply for him. They were in love; on both sides, the feelings were overpowering. Both Otto and Dorothy, however, were concerned about race and the effect on their careers, and so there were no public or open displays, although there were rumors."[27] When they began their affair Preminger told Dorothy that he and Mary continued to live in the same house and cohosted parties but "were not exactly husband and wife." "I think he had said we would be lovers 'for the duration of the picture,' but if so I ignored it," as Dorothy recalled.[28]

As the last cast member to be signed, Dorothy had little time to collect herself. Music recording sessions in which she and Harry Belafonte were to be dubbed, respectively, by Marilyn Horne and LaVerne Hutchinson, were scheduled for June 1. (Neither Dandridge nor Belafonte could sing in the operatic range the score required.) Following three weeks of intensive rehearsals, shooting was now scheduled to begin June 30. "Otto knew he was dealing with people who had not been well treated by the industry, and he was fatherly and respectful," recalled his stepson Sandy, hired to work on the film. (At the time Sandy did not know of Otto's affair with Dorothy.) "Pearlie May [Pearl Bailey], respected by everybody, would joke and keep it light, and that also helped to take the heat off. She joked with Otto, who was just crazy about her. She was a doll."[29] "Preminger treated people like

On the *Carmen Jones* set with Dorothy Dandridge, Harry Belafonte, and visitor Robert Mitchum. The rapport between Otto and Dorothy is apparent.

professionals," Olga James maintained. "He rode a few people, yes, but that had nothing at all to do with race. There was no kind of fake camaraderie, or any kind of condescension whatsoever."[30]

Preminger proceeded at a breakneck pace. Working from early morning until late at night, he put in longer hours than anyone else. Although still living with Mary and Sandy in Malibu, he spent some evenings at Dorothy's apartment. The demands of a highly compressed shoot that moved between exterior locations in El Monte, California, doubling for the Southern locales, and interiors, including "Chicago," filmed at the Culver Studios in Culver City, took their toll on the filmmaker, and perhaps inevitably he exploded a few times. The first episode occurred with a tense Brock Peters, "the new kid on the block," who felt other cast members were "more sophisticated and experienced" than he was. "In one scene, Otto wasn't getting what he wanted from me and he began to pressure me," Peters recalled.

> He was haranguing me, "You're a New York actor, I expect better," in front of everybody, in this terribly competitive environment. I was already insecure, and I thought his comment meant that somebody in Los Angeles should be playing my part. I was angry, and I lost it. I moved in on him. I didn't know what I was going to do, but Pearl and somebody else held me back. Pearl said, "Hold your temper, or you will never work again." I subsided quickly. We got past that, but then I was worried I'd be fired. A little later on—Otto was an equal opportunity haranguer—he went after Olga James, a glorious singer. The orchestra was assembled and she was to record her aria. He wanted *Sprechgesang*—he wanted it to sound more like speaking and less operatic, and when Olga didn't immediately do what he felt he had clearly explained, he began to say terrible things to her out in the open. He just began to berate her in front of the full orchestra and all the singers; it was uncomfortable for everybody, and he didn't seem to care or to notice.[31]

Olga James, as she remembered,

> shouted back. "Don't you yell at me," I said. "How dare you?" When he lost his temper with me a second time, I snapped back at him again. He wanted to get a shot on location before he lost the light, and when I wasn't quite ready he started in. But he was right and I was wrong: a professional would have understood about getting the light. He took charge, as he had every right to. "This is my

picture," he told me. Most of the time, however, Otto really was charming to all of us. Many people were afraid of him, though, and I noticed that he appreciated the ones who were not. In one rehearsal I remember Preminger saying with a big smile to Diahann Carroll, "You're not intimidated by me at all, are you?" She wasn't, and he enjoyed that.[32]

Vague rumors of an affair between Otto and Dorothy were floated within the cast ("I didn't believe it when someone hinted about it," Brock Peters said).[33] But on the set the relationship remained strictly professional. "Preminger treated Dorothy very, very carefully, we all saw that, but once he did say something that made her cry," Olga James recollected. "She went to her dressing room and cried like a lady."[34] Working under enormous pressure—she had to awake each morning at five, and was on call for almost every scene—Dorothy kept to herself. By nature she was reclusive and untrusting, and relations between her and the other performers remained distant. "Harry was much more accessible," Brock Peters said. "At first, Dorothy was extremely unfriendly to me, and I wondered if she thought I was a bad actor. I could see she was having a hard time, though, and that she was terribly insecure."[35]

Dorothy's retreats were also prompted by tensions with Pearl Bailey. "It was obvious to all of us that Pearl was jealous of Dorothy," James said. "Most of us were theater trained, including Pearl, and Dorothy was from a different tradition. She was a very fine actress for film—she let the camera come to her. But Pearl didn't think Dorothy was a good actress or singer. I don't want to say anything disparaging about Pearl, however, who was a wonderful performer of a particular kind. White people loved her."[36] According to Donald Bogle, Bailey was "a pill, a holy terror like Ethel Waters and Bill 'Bojangles' Robinson. She was very competitive, and very jealous. She thought *she* should have played Carmen, as later she thought she should have played Bess [in *Porgy and Bess*]."[37]

After completing principal photography at the beginning of August, Preminger and the Fox publicity department gave Dorothy an all-out star buildup. Otto arranged for Philippe Halsman to photograph Dorothy for an article in *Ebony* magazine entitled "The Five Most Beautiful Negro Women in the World" (the others were Lena Horne, Hilda Simms, Eartha Kitt, and Joyce Bryant). He booked Dorothy, dressed in a Carmen costume of red skirt and black blouse, to sing two songs on October 24 on a live television spectacular, "Light's Diamond Jubilee," produced by David O. Selznick. On October 25, dressed in the same Carmen costume, she

Preminger and Pearl Bailey, one of his favorite actresses, on the set of *Carmen Jones.*

appeared on the cover of *Life,* again photographed by Philippe Halsman. To attend the world premiere at the Rivoli Theatre on October 28, Dorothy flew East with her sister Vivian. On opening night the klieg lights illuminating the sky were red, a tribute to the burning rose shimmering in fire, which was the image Preminger and Saul Bass had designed as the film's logo. When Dorothy, alone, stepped out of a limousine to a barrage of flashing lightbulbs, she smiled radiantly. "If ever Dorothy looked happy, it was this night," Donald Bogle noted.[38]

Her reviews were sensational. "She comes close to the edge of greatness," Archer Winsten proclaimed in the *New York Post.* "Incandescent," *Newsweek* hailed. According to *Time,* "she holds the eye—like a match burning steadily in a tornado." "Dorothy Dandridge lights a blazing bonfire on the screen," wrote Otis Guernsey in the *New York Herald Tribune.* Hedda Hopper raved that she "got so excited she burned a big hole in the front of [her] dress. Yes, the film is *that* hot."[39]

Creating a sizzling Carmen in collaboration with his lover, a frightened actress, Preminger achieved one of the triumphs of his career, and over fifty years later Dorothy's performance remains vibrant, and beyond either stereotype or vulgarity. For the first time in a mainstream American film Preminger had revealed a black woman's potent sexuality. And in 1954 the erotic force that he helped Dorothy to unleash gave the film a tingle of danger, a shivering, "forbidden" undertow. Dorothy's Carmen, sexually restless, forever on the prowl and forever dissatisfied, knows and controls her value in the sexual marketplace. She's cunning in her ability to manipulate male desire, but unlike a man (Otto Preminger, for instance), for whom sexual conquest is a natural right, a way of seizing and maintaining power, Carmen is doomed: she's too sexy to live. Drawing on his intimate knowledge of her, Preminger directed Dorothy to line Carmen's sensuality with an underlying melancholy, and her performance is infused with the actress's own wounds, her history as a black woman both rewarded and bruised, lionized and punished, for her beauty.

Knowing instinctively how to "let the camera come to her," Dorothy with her director's help pitches her acting precisely for film rather than the opera house or the Broadway stage. When she sings (with Marilyn Horne's voice), the show, as Preminger intended, doesn't stop for vocal display. For this down-to-earth Carmen singing is only one of her modes of seduction.

In 1954, in addition to being sexually and racially transgressive, *Carmen Jones* was also an artistic gamble. Preminger's goal, turning an opera into a realistic dramatic film, was all but unprecedented at the time and, at least in prospect, insurmountably paradoxical. To make the film conform to the visual codes of movie realism he had to declare war on the conventions of both musical films and opera. Although he could have chosen to protect the unreality of musical performance by embedding the songs in artificial settings, he reasoned that a tinseled mise-en-scène that would be appropriate for light material would be jarring for a dramatic story. And it might alienate or puzzle the general moviegoing public he was hoping to reach.

To translate *Carmen* into a full-fledged film with popular appeal, he had to find ways of "naturalizing" Bizet's score. The wisdom of his approach is revealed in Carmen's first aria, "Dat's Love" ("Habañera" in the opera), performed in an unmusical setting, the cafeteria of the parachute factory where Carmen works. As she sings, Carmen places food on her tray, exchanges greetings and insults with co-workers, and cozies up to Joe, her next quarry. Preminger's direction, treating singing as a realistic, casual activity, an extension of speaking, significantly closes a breach between the imperatives of movie realism and those of musical performance.

Although Preminger was everywhere prepared to sacrifice musical purity for dramatic impact, he nonetheless filmed musical performance tactfully, refusing to allow the language of film—editing, camera movement, lighting—to compete with or to artificially enhance the score. His restrained approach works beautifully for the intimate songs; for the big production numbers, however, Preminger's invisible movie realism is occasionally too tame. In a scene in a café, for instance, when Pearl Bailey launches into a rousing rendition of "Beat Out Dat Rhythm on a Drum" ("Gypsy Song" in Bizet), the camera remains on a group of characters at the bar as dancers are glimpsed in deep focus. In the absence of intercutting or reframing the audience is never allowed to appreciate the energy of the dancers. Preminger handles "Stan' Up and Fight" ("Toreador Song" in Bizet), the entrance song for the prizefighter, in a similarly sedate way, with the camera placed at a distance from the action. But the number calls for a touch of razzle-dazzle, a bit of cinematic bravura in which at least momentarily the film itself should spin along with the musical rhythm.

Preminger's staging of Joe's aria, "Dis Flower" ("Flower Song" in Bizet)—the music expresses the character's passion for the woman who has

Carmen (Dorothy Dandridge) sings "Dat's Love" ("Habañera") in a realistic setting, the cafeteria of a parachute factory, in *Carmen Jones*.

already seduced and abandoned him—is also too becalmed, another instance of the filmmaker seeming to resist the lure of Bizet's music. Working on a chain gang, Joe, shirtless, performs the number against a panoramic mountain vista that could have been imported from *River of No Return*. But the implied connection between the deep sexual longing conveyed in the song and the spectacular setting is obscure. Filmed in one unbroken take, the number has a static quality reinforced by Harry Belafonte's febrile performance—there isn't enough going on in his face and body to hold the audience's interest for the duration of the shot.

In "My Joe" ("Micaela's Air" in Bizet), as Cindy Lou searches for Joe in empty locales (a boxing club, a rickety stairway, a grim city street) that foreshadow her bereavement, the correlation between song and setting is far more potent. This time, treating the aria (magnificently sung by Olga James) as a miniature drama with a structure all its own, Preminger effectively uses intercutting for visual variety. He also stages Joe's final aria in a dramatically charged setting, a dark basement room in which the character strangles Carmen. In the number, his face suffused with passion, Harry Belafonte, who throughout the film is too guarded for a character gripped by lust, is more expressive than at any other point.

Preminger makes some strong visual choices in opening up the story beyond the limited settings of Hammerstein's "revue." An unedited scene early on in a car, as Carmen goes to work on Joe, has become a celebrated early use of CinemaScope composition. Initially, the two characters are separated by a window divider, but as she moves in on her prey, Carmen moves from her side of the car to Joe's. Preminger inserts a lively action sequence in which Carmen hurls herself out of the car, jumps onto the top of a moving train, and then leaps off the train onto a hillside—a cinematic way of representing the character's impulsive physicality. When Carmen returns with Joe to her family house in a small black community overrun with hanging moss and sweltering with humidity, the atmosphere oozes sex, and Carmen, grinding her body against Joe's, slowly takes off his belt. (Was Joe Breen looking the other way?) A boxing ring scene (shot in Olympic Stadium in downtown Los Angeles) explodes with a pent-up violence that reflects Joe's growing rage.

"For a whole generation of blacks, *Carmen Jones* was *the* film," historian Donald Bogle recalled.

> It is still an important film, as is Dandridge's performance. It is still one of the great black films. For many blacks, the film and Dorothy remain alive, passed on from one generation to another, without the larger white culture acknowledging it. What makes it so compelling

to audiences still—and surely Preminger understood this—is that it is a film in which an African-American woman is not only at the center, but she is making her own choices and is in control, unlike the way Hollywood had previously depicted black women, as in *Cabin in the Sky* and *Pinky.* Carmen lives in a world where men are calling the shots, and yet she matches them. And there is an intimacy between Dandridge and Belafonte that was new for black audiences. Their romantic scenes still have a contemporary kick and edge.[40]

In the weeks before the world premiere of *Carmen Jones,* Otto personally attended to every detail of advertising and promotion and monitored Dorothy's extensive publicity campaign. At the same time he was in rehearsal in New York for a television special to be presented live and in color on NBC on October 18, only ten days before the world premiere of his second independent film. For two intense weeks, Otto commuted daily from Manhattan to the Kaufman Studios in Queens to rehearse *Tonite at 8:30,* a trio of one-acts ("Red Peppers," "Still Life," and "Fumed Oak") by Noël Coward. Early on, it was apparent that he was in trouble. "He didn't know anything about live television," recalled actor Larkin Ford (then known as Wil West), who had had extensive experience in the then new medium. "We all felt Otto looked down at the medium, and he made the mistake of trying to transfer film technique to what we were doing. He set camera and lights as for a movie, and he was so concerned about the camera—he didn't seem to be aware that he'd be in front of a monitor pushing buttons—that there was no time for us actors."

The stellar company included Trevor Howard, Gig Young, Ilka Chase (with whom, years before, Otto had had a fling), and Gloria Vanderbilt, but the only performer Preminger seemed to pay any heed to was Ginger Rogers. "Ginger was the star and she was very nervous about the show," as Ford recalled. "She knew she needed direction and she demanded it. Otto did work closely with her, and she really listened to him. For the rest of us, he'd bark directions from a distance. His approach was so different from that of Arthur Penn, with whom I had worked on live television. Penn knew a lot about acting and understood actors and he would get up very close to each of us."[41]

At the beginning of the third week of rehearsals, as Preminger continued to be preoccupied with technical details (and, no doubt, with Dorothy and *Carmen Jones*), there had still been no complete run-through. "He had no sense of what was needed to play this kind of material. Otto didn't 'get' Noël Coward," Larkin Ford felt.

Rehearsing Ginger Rogers and Gig Young in *Tonite at 8:30* for NBC, the director's misbegotten foray into live television.

As tensions began to build, I became the chosen one on the set. Whatever I did, he grumbled. I don't think he had cast me just to humiliate me, but I was miscast and he was responsible for miscasting me. Gig Young was miscast too, but Gig couldn't have cared less; he just sailed through and said the pay was good. Trevor Howard, who thought Otto's direction was nothing, was bored, and tiny Gloria Vanderbilt just smiled all the time. Otto called himself a liberal, but a true liberal doesn't treat people the way he did; I have a feeling he would have voted for George Bush.[42]

With a live performance in less than a week and three essentially undirected playlets in shambles, something had to give. Something did. On October 15, three days before the show was scheduled to air, NBC producer Fred Coe walked onto the set to talk to Preminger. The next day, Otto wasn't there, and Coe, noted for his diplomacy, announced that " 'Mr. Preminger will not be with us. I will be with you through the presentation.'

Otto was never seen again," Ford said. "He had been fired offstage. We *did* feel sorry for him, a man of that stature to be summarily dismissed for incompetence. But he *was* incompetent. Otto had great confidence in himself and it must have been disturbing to him when he discovered that he hadn't been prepared."[43] When the show aired, however, Otto Preminger received credit as producer and director, and in taped segments, shifty-eyed and noticeably ill at ease, he introduced each of the one-acts. *Tonite at 8:30* is a classic example of primitive early television. The sets are wobbly; the actors' timing is always a beat or two off; the pacing is sluggish. Technical glitches—a microphone covers Gig Young's face for a moment; a door sticks on one of Ginger Rogers's exits—add to the blurred focus. In later years Preminger would appear regularly as a talk show guest, but he never again directed for television.

The reception of *Carmen Jones* at the end of the month, however, more than compensated for Otto's disappointing television debut. He was elated by Dorothy's reviews and basked in his role as a star maker. On February 12, 1955, as Preminger had assured her she would be, Dorothy was nominated as best actress by the Academy of Motion Picture Arts and Sciences, the first black woman ever to be recognized in this category. Otto repeatedly cautioned Dorothy, however, that Hollywood was not ready to give her the best actress Oscar and that there was no chance she would be making a triumphant walk to the stage of the Pantages Theatre on Oscar night. And indeed, when the awards were handed out on March 30, the best actress Oscar was given to Grace Kelly for *The Country Girl.* (Not until nearly forty years later, when Halle Berry was honored for *Monster's Ball,* would a black woman win a best actress Oscar.)

As she continued a punishing schedule of public and nightclub appearances, Dorothy signed a contract with Darryl Zanuck to make one picture a year for a three-year period. Despite his own hectic schedule, Preminger began to direct Dorothy's cabaret act. In ironic contrast to how he had presented her in *Carmen Jones,* Otto desexualized Dorothy's nightclub performance. As Earl Mills observed, "Dorothy thought of herself as a patrician lady of elegance and wanted to be a lady, a nun, onstage."[44] Otto bought her a black, loose-fitting, floor-length gown and worked with her in selecting a less jazz-based repertoire. But like live television, the nightclub was not Preminger's métier, and when Dorothy opened her Preminger-inspired act at a Miami Beach hotel, it was, according to Earl Mills, "an abysmal failure. She soon went back to the old Dorothy Dandridge. Otto's hand was constantly in evidence in her professional life. Had he been just her lover it would have been better but he wanted to control every facet of her life."[45]

Although she would sometimes complain when Otto would arrive, unannounced, at one of her openings—his take-charge personality could enflame her anxiety—by and large she was a compliant pupil. Otto represented a cultivated world she longed to be part of. He taught her about art and literature as well as about fine furniture and fine dining. He helped her to buy a new home (which, he said, befit her new status as an international star) and to furnish it in exquisite taste. And at this point, Dorothy hoped that being the dutiful Galatea to Preminger's bombastic Pygmalion would lead to marriage.

In late February Dorothy and her director attended the film's premieres in London and Berlin (in both cities the film would play for more than a year in exclusive first-run engagements). There was no Paris opening, however, because a technicality in French copyright laws prevented the film from being shown in France. Nonetheless, in an out-of-competition screening *Carmen Jones* was selected to open the Cannes Film Festival in May. To be present, Dorothy had to negotiate for a week's leave of absence from her engagement at the Empire Room of the Waldorf-Astoria in New York. On May 7, she and Otto departed for France, where on their arrival at the Nice airport they were met by a cordon of international journalists and photographers. They posed for pictures for over an hour before they were ushered through the throngs to a long, cream-colored Cadillac, in which they were driven to the Carlton Hotel in Cannes. The night of the screening, dressed in a white gown and white fur stole, Dorothy arrived on the arm of her director. Gallantly, Preminger moved aside to allow his star to face the flashbulbs on her own. She struck the pose of a haughty, radiant diva who looked as if she had conquered the world; and that night, when the film was received with a thunderous ovation, she had. Perhaps because they were in a foreign country, and perhaps feeling protected by the fact that they were honored guests of the world's most prestigious film festival, the director and his star were seen together in public throughout their brief stay. Not only on official occasions but also at private luncheons and dinners and for drinks on the Carlton terrace, they were an item: Otto and Dorothy. And anyone with eyes could have spotted the fact that they were crazy about each other. More than gratitude was contained in the star's rapt gaze at her director.

For Preminger, the international acclaim at Cannes was the beginning of an illustrious decade at the top of the Hollywood hierarchy. For Dorothy, however, it was the beginning of the end. Soon after returning from Cannes, Dorothy agreed to appear in a supporting role as an Asian in the film of Rodgers and Hammerstein's musical play, *The King and I*. Otto, however, urged her to turn down the offer, assuring Dorothy that if she accepted the role she would be relegated ever after to the category of a supporting player.

Preminger directing Gary Cooper in *The Court-Martial of Billy Mitchell*, the only dull court-room drama in the filmmaker's career.

Acting on her mentor's advice, she withdrew. "Preminger, usually adroitly pragmatic and perceptive, was in this instance blind to movieland realities," as Donald Bogle pointed out.[46] And as Dorothy herself was to reflect, "My decline may have dated from that decision. Otto was sincere. He had never believed in playing bit parts as an actor himself, and he passed on his convictions to me. Though he was honest, his advice could have been in some part my undoing. I would have received seventy-five thousand dollars for playing Tuptim, and I would have been in a picture seen by millions. [And] it would not have been the role of a Negro."[47] (Rita Moreno, also non-Asian, got the part.)

At the time that he was immersed in supervising Dorothy's life and career and had already begun planning his next independent project, *The Man with the Golden Arm,* Preminger accepted an assignment from producer Milton Sperling to direct *The Court-Martial of Billy Mitchell.* Otto admired the defiant protagonist, Brigadier General Billy Mitchell, assistant chief of the Army Air Service, who provoked his own court-martial in the 1920s in order to expose the indifference of his military commanders to developing a strong air force. And he was enticed by the fact that the film's lengthy third act is set in his favorite dramatic location, a courtroom. It's possible to see why Preminger was tempted by the material, as well as by the chance to work with the film's star, Gary Cooper. But he should have passed.

Otto didn't like the original script, by Emmet Lavery (whose play *The First Legion* had been his farewell production in Vienna), and at his insistence Milton Sperling hired the speedy Ben Hecht, who in less than a week rewrote to Preminger's specifications. (When the film received an Academy Award nomination for best screenplay, Emmet Lavery and Milton Sperling were credited as the cowriters.) Throughout the shooting, which took place in the summer of 1955 from June 18 to August 13, Otto fulminated against Sperling's indecisiveness. But he enjoyed working with Gary Cooper, always courteous, reliable, and understated. Sandy Gardner, frequently on the set, recalled that Otto was "very gentle with Cooper, and very solicitous about the star's lighting and makeup. Cooper was playing a character who was younger than himself, and I saw Otto change the lighting so Gary's dewlaps would not be visible."[48]

Preminger and Cooper, however, made the curious choice of turning Billy Mitchell, a firebrand, into a weary figure who seems to embrace defeat. The night before he is to testify, the character is ill with malaria and the next day in the courtroom he seems physically as well as intellectually depleted. Preminger reinforces the downbeat atmosphere by pinning the haunted-looking Cooper against a brick wall in isolating one-shots. The most energetic character is Mitchell's nemesis, the chief prosecuting attorney, played by Rod Steiger with a full cut of ham, the kind Preminger usually trimmed to the bone. Although the film's strangely icy, dispirited portrait of a mutinous character typifies Preminger's resistance to conventional Hollywood heroism, the script isn't strong enough to support a revisionist approach.

EIGHT

"Chicago"

Finished by the end of August 1955 with his obligations on *The Court-Martial of Billy Mitchell,* Preminger turned with relief to filming *The Man with the Golden Arm,* Nelson Algren's novel about a drug addict in a Chicago slum that won the first National Book Award in 1950. Otto already had a long involvement with the novel, which Ingo had recommended to him in 1951. "He wasn't interested at first," as Ingo recalled.

> But I kept pushing because Otto, even before he decided to film *The Moon Is Blue,* was looking for a way to violate the Production Code and here was a story that would do that because there was a clause in the Code prohibiting verbal references to, or the depiction of, drug-taking. I was Otto's agent at the time, and he listened to me, but only after we had many violent arguments. It was almost against Otto's will that I put a group together that made a deal where Otto would have the first option to do the picture.[1]

Ingo's group of investors bought the rights from the estate of John Garfield, who had died in 1952. When he had learned of the Code's prohibitions, however, Garfield in 1951 had abandoned his plans to turn the novel into a star vehicle for himself. Otto, after finishing *Carmen Jones* and all the while prodded by his brother, began to get enthused about the project for the very reason that Garfield had dropped it. He realized that in tackling a prohibited subject for his third outing as an independent filmmaker he would again be offering moviegoers the kind of material that the major studios were afraid of and that could not be seen at home on television.

Before Otto had become involved, Ingo had hired one of his clients, Lewis Meltzer (Otto had directed Meltzer's play *Yankee Fable* in 1940), to write a screenplay. "He was not very talented," Ingo said, "and his adaptation wasn't good, but Meltzer felt, and I felt too, that something could be done with it. Once Otto came on board, he threw Meltzer out."[2] In the late summer of 1954, as he was supervising postproduction on *Carmen Jones,* Otto had brought Nelson Algren to Hollywood from Chicago to talk about the film and possibly to collaborate on the script. Between the director and the novelist a complete lack of rapport was immediately apparent. Preminger arranged for Algren to stay in a cottage at the Beverly Hills Hotel, but when he called to schedule a meeting he discovered that the novelist had checked out. Later in the day Algren telephoned to inform Preminger that the hotel had been too "fancy" and that he had relocated to a dump in Skid Row, "a disreputable, broken-down, flea-ridden hotel full of pimps, addicts, and drunks," according to Preminger. After a few days of working with Algren, Otto discovered that the novelist "couldn't write dialogue or visualize scenes."[3]

Algren, however, had a quite different recollection of their meeting. "I never gave him a script," he contended.

> When I went out to Hollywood working for Otto was the farthest thing from my mind. My two days with Otto were a farce. He picked me up in his Caddy and drove me to his office. A Japanese electrician was stringing lights. . . . Otto sat at his desk and a makeup man began working on him [in preparation for a television appearance], stopping only while Otto was using the telephone. A man who looked like a PR man came in puffing a pipe and made Otto furious: "Take pipe *out!*" he commanded. . . . I began helping the electrician string the lights while the makeup man kept working between telephone calls. I was pleased to be in a place where so many people were keeping busy while accomplishing absolutely nothing. Suddenly I smelled smoke; it was coming from the PR man who had stuffed the pipe in his lapel pocket. "Fool!" Otto shouted, "you're on fire!" Later that morning, after the PR man's fire had been put out, the makeup man and the electrician had left, and the telephone had stopped ringing, Otto approached me, stopped

beyond hand-shaking distance and said, clicking his heels: "I am happy to have met such an interesting man."[4]

To Nelson Algren, who lived in a lower-depths area in Chicago, Preminger's world of Hollywood protocol seemed to consist of fatuous, self-aggrandizing gestures: sound and fury signifying "absolutely nothing." "Otto has always enjoyed special privilege," Algren scoffed. "When his family was trapped by the invasion of Austria, a Viennese chief of police obtained a plane for them to escape. The family arrived in New York with only temporary visas. Tallulah Bankhead spoke to her father, then Speaker of the House. A special bill was passed making the Premingers American citizens. So much for the Holocaust," he reported, inaccurate on almost all counts. "[My] book dealt with life at the bottom," Algren observed. "Otto has never, not for so much as a single day, had any experience except that of life at the top."[5]

Algren made a hasty departure, convinced that a director who only knew "life at the top" had no chance of making an authentic film about human wreckage in an urban underbelly. A few weeks later, on September 14, 1954, Preminger signed an agreement with television writer Robert Alan Aurthur, paying him $2,500. On December 23 Aurthur signed a formal contract at a higher salary—and then he was gone, replaced by Walter Newman, who on February 11, 1955, signed a contract for $70,000. To help Newman, Preminger, curiously enough, rehired Lewis Meltzer, Ingo's "untalented" client who had written the original adaptation. Newman and Meltzer are credited as the film's coauthors. As Preminger and his battalion of writers discovered, it was hard work cobbling a workable screenplay out of Algren's novel.

"At once a philosopher of despair and a comedian of the lower depths, [Algren] lets us in on the condition of the lost," writes literary historian David Castronovo in *Beyond the Gray Flannel Man: Books from the 1950s That Made American Culture*. "He's our poet of hopelessness, which is to say the most unusual of American poets."[6] For its poetry as well as its despair, Algren's novel is doubly damned as a prospect for successful Hollywood transplantation. The man with the golden arm is Frankie Majcinek (Machine), a vet who got hooked on heroin during his stint in the Army. He's an ace card dealer (his golden arm) trapped in a loveless marriage to Zosch, a woman whose legs became paralyzed in a car accident caused by his drunkenness. Glimpsing possible redemption in a romance with Molly, a neighbor, and a career as a jazz drummer, Frankie thinks he can kick his habit. But in Algren's fetid underworld, a one-way ticket to oblivion is the only destination for Frankie. After he kills his drug dealer in a rage, Frankie becomes a fugitive who haunts alleys and rooming houses. With the arm that has dealt cards and received needles filled with heroin, Frankie hangs himself; his crippled wife descends into madness; and Molly slides into a life of prostitution.

Algren's authorial voice, alternately luminous and bleak, a self-infatuated blend of hard-boiled lyricism, charnel-house imagery, and compassion, guides the reader through an underworld of deadbeats, misfits, petty criminals, and drunks. As his characters hurtle toward death or damnation Algren periodically pauses to offer philosophical asides or to explore the inner monologues of minor characters. Atmosphere, not narrative momentum, is Algren's concern, and the heart of the novel—the author's wise presence, the sprung-rhythm music of his voice—is not translatable to film. "There was no delivery from the dead end of lost chance," the novel's narrator muses, with almost biblical cadence, as he observes Frankie looking out of a jailhouse window.

> No escape from the blue steel bars of guilt. Somewhere far above a steel moon shone, with equal grandeur, upon boulevard, alley, and park; flophouse and penthouse, apartment-hotel and tenement. Shone with that sort of wintry light that makes every city chimney, standing out against it in the cold, seem a sort of altar against a driving sky. Beyond the bars light and shadow played ceaselessly, as it played beneath so many long-set moons, for so many that had lain here before Frankie: the carefree and the careful ones, the crippled and the maimed, the foolhardy phonies and the bitter rebels; each to go his separate way, under his own private moon. Against a driving sky.[7]

Preminger's intention was to wrestle a standard sensation melodrama out of Algren's literary web. He and his writers give Frankie's drug addiction far more prominence than it has in the novel, where in fact it was an afterthought, an addition encouraged by the novelist's agent. And they twist the story in order to conjure a spurious Hollywood ending in which Molly helps Frankie to kick his habit. Only Zosch is unredeemed. Unlike the character in the novel, she only pretends to be a cripple, as a way of binding her husband to her, and it is she rather than Frankie who kills the drug dealer. As Frankie and Molly face the future, Zosch jumps to her death.

Preminger's careerlong disclaimer about adaptation was never more pertinent than here: "When a producer buys the rights to a book or a play he owns it," Preminger declared. "The property rights are transferred, as in any sale. The writer gives up his control, as the word 'sell' implies. When I prepare a story for filming it is being filtered through my brain, my emotions, my talent such as I have. . . . I have no obligation, nor do I try, to be 'faithful' to the book."[8] Understandably, Algren, the poet of the lower depths, felt Preminger, the man who lived "only" at the top, had "done violence" to his book. As Preminger admitted, when he read the final draft the novelist was "furious."[9]

As Newman and Meltzer were finishing the script over the spring and summer of 1955, Otto began to line up his cast. For Frankie Machine, he wanted either Frank Sinatra (who, in fact, is cited twice in Algren's novel) or Marlon Brando. Sinatra accepted the role before Brando's agent even had time to respond. (Although there would have been explosions between the Method-trained Brando and the anti-Method Preminger, America's greatest film actor would surely have given an electrifying performance.) On June 14, for $100,000, Sinatra signed a contract with Carlyle Productions. For Molly, Preminger wanted Kim Novak, a newcomer under contract to Harry Cohn, the profane czar of Columbia Pictures, where Preminger now had his Hollywood office. "Harry and I had a love-hate relationship," Otto recalled. "In order to disarm him I always recited his favorite four-letter words the minute I saw him."[10] Cohn was reluctant to release Novak, who with her recent starring role in *Picnic* was about to replace Rita Hayworth as the first lady of the lot. Playing hard to get, Cohn asked for, and Preminger agreed to, $100,000 for Novak's services. As Frankie's forlorn wife, Preminger cast Eleanor Parker, who, on loan-out from MGM, received the highest salary, $125,000.

For good reason Preminger was apprehensive about working with Sinatra, an obscene man with proven Mafia connections and a well-documented history of violent outbursts. Spoiled rotten by his ever present entourage, Sinatra was accustomed to having the world around him move to his own measure—or else. Alternately sullen and convivial, the actor hated to rehearse and when shooting began never wanted to do more than one take. "I was warned about Sinatra, and I had my misgivings," Preminger said.

> I was told he was difficult. I could see that he was; that he was a highly temperamental man, very touchy and very, very moody. He has a chip on his shoulder all the time. Also, unlike most stars, he doesn't really get along with little people. He can be small in little things. Perhaps this comes from his youth, a feeling he shouldn't be soft by being nice to small people. He's full of contradictions. He

With Frank Sinatra, on the set of *The Man with the Golden Arm*. The two notoriously temperamental men got along.

treats women rather badly. If he thinks a person is untalented he can be unbearable. And you always have a feeling he may be about to blow up."[11]

When Sinatra early on exploded at an electrician and then urged Preminger to replace the man, Otto made it clear that he alone did the hiring and firing on his films. "I explained that he was engaged only as an actor. I 'handled' him," Preminger said, and claimed that for the remainder of filming Sinatra became "as congenial as Gary Cooper. He proved to be tractable and full of humility; he always got to work on time and always knew his lines."[12]

Sinatra, himself on guard about Preminger—"I had heard about him"—also developed "handling" strategies. "I would tease him tremendously and he really loved it because nobody wanted to get involved with him because they were afraid he would chew you up. I had a lot of fun with Otto about his wonderful Vienna or Berlin accent, whichever one it was. I would ape him and he would say, 'Vy, vy you talk, I don't talk that vay, vy are you speaking that vay with me?' And I said because that's the way you talk. He said, 'I don't talk that vay.' "[13] Costar Darren McGavin (playing the drug dealer) noticed how "when things got extra bad, Sinatra would use a German dialect on Preminger. It broke the tension every time. It was Sinatra's way of fighting for us."[14] The relationship between the director and his star grew so cozy that they had nicknames for each other. Sinatra called Preminger by his middle name, Ludwig, and unaccountably Preminger called Sinatra "Anatol." "I don't know where he got the name but that was what he called me. 'Anatol!' he would say. 'Ve are ready for you on the set!' "[15]

It would have been out of character for Preminger to pick on a big male star like Sinatra—"little people" and fragile women were his usual targets. But under the circumstances there was no reason for the director to go after Sinatra, who respected Otto for his intellect ("Otto was so smart in every possible way") and was working hard to prove himself in a demanding part. "When I read the script, I thought this is a great piece of work and it's going to be tough to do," Sinatra recalled.

> I got permission to watch a kid who was in the dryout position in a padded cell. I advise anybody never to go look at that. I left with tears streaming down my face. The little guy must have weighed about ninety pounds, they were drying him out and he was trying to knock the walls down. I watched through a peephole, even though it was against the law. That's how I got some of my moves during the withdrawal scenes. I saw how he felt and what he did. The poor kid was out of his head. I couldn't handle it, I walked away, I couldn't control myself. To see the actual thing was scary, but it helped me when we started shooting. I knew what I wanted to do.[16]

Preminger's stepson, invited to the set during the drug withdrawal scenes, observed that "Frank was doing *some* work. Otto didn't have much to say, and I could see that Frank was quite grateful to be let alone. When Otto was admiring, as he was of the work Sinatra was doing, he was very solicitous; and he let Frank do what he wanted to. Frank, like Cooper in *The Court-Martial of Billy Mitchell*, was really playing himself; with people who had no personalities or were not known, Otto's approach would be different."[17]

Overseeing his studio-created Chicago slum in *The Man with the Golden Arm*.

Remarkably, both Sinatra and Preminger were patient with Kim Novak, so unsure of her abilities that she needed as many as thirty or forty takes before she was able to deliver her lines with even minimal competence. "She was a warm girl with a great, great wish to please people and make a success," Preminger observed. "What I didn't know at the time was that her earlier movies had been dubbed afterwards because she could never get the lines right. I didn't want to dub. Because she was so nervous Sinatra went through all the takes she needed, just like a pro. She just had no self-confidence, none at all. She'd been treated like a nincompoop, but she's really quite shrewd. And I knew she was right for the part. She has a sadness inside, just the quality I wanted, and I knew it could come through if we made her feel comfortable."[18]

The director, however, was not patient with Darren McGavin, playing the demonic drug dealer—Mephistopheles on Division Street. "I felt he was fighting himself, getting in his own way, and I treated him pretty rough," Preminger admitted. "Don't you shout at me!" McGavin called out in a voice even more bellowing than his director's when Preminger began to scream at him in front of the cast and crew. Knowing he had a captive audience, and savoring the dead silence that had overtaken the set, Preminger paused before saying in a small voice, "Very well, Mr. McGavin, you're a bad actor on stage, a bad actor in front of the camera. Can you hear me, Mr. McGavin? Shall we proceed?" "I almost chased him up the boom," McGavin said. "He's of the German school, which thinks 'I have to destroy you before I can create you.' He can be cruel and sadistic; he was to me. But in spite of all this nonsense I have a tremendous liking for him. Besides, look at the results."[19]

Preminger's original intention had been to shoot the entire film on location in Chicago, but to keep costs down he decided instead to build "Chicago" on a sound stage. Artistically the wrong choice (the studio sets give the film a cramped, artificial look), it was financially prudent, allowing the producer to remain well within his trim $1,135,000 budget. Preminger began shooting on September 15 and, despite the numerous retakes required for Novak's scenes, finished a few days ahead of his projected November 1 wrap date.

The weekend after the end of shooting, Sinatra treated Otto, Mary, and Sandy to a weekend in Las Vegas at the Sands Hotel. "Sinatra picked up the tab for everything, and it was first-class all the way," Sandy recalled.

> Otto was used to being in that role, paying for everything for everybody in a very generous way. But that weekend he was a guest who knew how to accept Frank's hospitality. That ability to receive graciously is not always a quality that someone like Otto, so used to giving and to the power that comes with being in the giving position, would necessarily have. But Otto had it. He was grateful to Sinatra for the hard work he had done, and Sinatra was grateful to Otto for giving him the chance to play a great part and for seeing him through it.[20]

When he returned from Las Vegas, Otto began working with Saul Bass on the ad campaign. "Making a commitment to one central idea that would

tell audiences what the film is about, we wanted to develop a seductive, provocative image that would cause a large number of people to say, 'Hey, I'm interested in seeing that film,' " Bass recalled. "Our idea for the film was a crooked arm [that signals this is] the story of a dope addict; we thought of that arm as a metaphor for the distorted life of the addict." Bass recalled that a number of film executives assured them their campaign was "absolutely, outrageously incorrect. They told us we would be committing suicide if we opened with that image of a crooked arm." Once the ad was sent out, Preminger began to receive complaints from exhibitors, some of whom threatened to replace the ad with photos of Frank Sinatra and Kim Novak. Bass overheard Otto's response to one disgruntled caller:

> "We have thought about all these matters, we have considered your point of view, and we have rejected it. These are the ads, and if you change anything I will pull the picture." There was a long silence at the other end of the line, then, "O.K., Mr. Preminger." That conversation revealed Otto's strength, his belief, and his commitment: I would have jumped off the roof for Otto. The truth of the matter is that those qualities that made him difficult also made him a man

that you could count on: I would have trusted my life with him, and I know he would always have saved me, no matter what."[21]

Once they had their logo, Preminger and Bass decided to use it for the film's title sequence. "As we began to think about it, it made a lot of sense because the very qualities that made it work as a metaphor for a film in an ad campaign certainly made it work as a mood setter, a metaphor for what was to come in the film. In a sense, we also wound up reinventing the title sequence." Bass's idea, a series of lines cutting across the screen in a staccato rhythm which ultimately coalesce into the image of the distorted arm, caused furious rows with his boss. " 'The lines must move,' I told Otto. 'Wrong, they must be static,' he said. 'Must move,' I insisted. 'Must be static,' he repeated. This escalated. We started to scream. He began to pound the desk and his head turned purple. Then he started pounding the wall behind his desk. I walked out. 'No way I am gonna do it that way,' I yelled before slamming the door."[22] On the way back to his office, Bass, cooling down, began to consider the merits of Otto's thinking. As soon as he entered his office, Otto was on the line saying that perhaps Bass had been right all along: yes, the lines should move. With equal fervor, the two warriors now reversed their former convictions. In the title sequence, as if they are responding to Elmer Bernstein's pulsating jazz score, the lines move.

Weeks before the film's scheduled premiere on December 14, 1955, Preminger launched the ad campaign, personally selected the first-run theaters where the film would open in New York and Los Angeles, and geared up for the censorship battle he fully expected to confront. As he hoped it would, the Production Code Administration office objected to the film's basic subject matter and refused its Seal of Approval. For Preminger, there was no possibility of compromise or negotiation—and there was also little to fear. His earlier battles had seriously punctured the Code's authority, and because of the consent decree Otto had no trouble getting playdates. The staid Loew's chain, by now officially divorced from MGM, booked the film without the Seal. "And this time," as Preminger boasted, "United Artists stood behind me. They went so far as to resign from the Association of Motion Picture Producers and [then] distributed the picture."[23]

Still, in his many public appearances to promote the film, Preminger remained in battle mode, presenting himself and his film as under attack. Once again, as with the fracas over *The Moon Is Blue,* Preminger enlarged the playing field, transforming Joe Breen's attempts at censoring a single film into a discussion that touched on freedom of speech, the responsibilities and privileges of the artist, and the state of the nation. As Mike Beck, the United Artists East Coast press agent, noted, "Otto is most bold when attacked. He called the Code people dolts, idiots, imposers on freedom."[24] "I am not a rebel," Preminger said, defending himself against Breen's charges. "My only instrument of censorship is my own taste—which I think is good. To be successful a film must have a moral, as mine most certainly does. Only a small section of the public will buy sensation for sensation's sake. I don't feel that I made a picture that in any way could induce people to take narcotics. On the contrary, I feel that if anything this picture is a warning against the consequences of taking narcotics."[25]

When censor boards in Baltimore, Atlanta, and Milwaukee refused to show the film in an uncut version, Preminger promised that "there will be no compromise with the forces of censorship. I will bring every legal force to bear, going to the United States Supreme Court if necessary to permit my film to be shown in its complete form."[26] When the Maryland Board of Censors demanded a two-minute cut in the scene in which Frankie Machine gets ready to inject heroin, Preminger and United Artists took their case to the state court of appeals. In March 1956 the appellate court reversed the decision of the censorship board, claiming that the film did not advocate the use of heroin. "[My successful case] established freedom of expression for motion pictures," Otto contended.[27]

Preminger was to savor three other legal triumphs in his battles over *The Man with the Golden Arm*. Before the film opened, the screenwriters' union protested Otto's billing, "a film by Otto Preminger," and lost its case. (Otto was establishing his bid for admission to the pantheon of auteur directors several years before the French auteur theory had gained a secure foothold in America.) On June 14, 1961, six years after the film had opened, Geoffrey M. Shurlock issued the film a Production Code Seal of Approval. And on December 28, 1966, when Otto sold *The Man with the Golden Arm* to ABC, he exacted two landmark concessions: the film would be shown without deletions and Preminger himself would select places for commercial breaks.

Preminger's skillful pre-opening campaign ensured notoriety for his film before a single ticket had been sold. As Bass recalled, "By the time the film had its world premiere in New York the basic symbol had been so widely disseminated that the marquee of the Victoria Theatre on Broadway carried only the arm: there was no need for any writing whatever."[28] The buzz was so mighty that not even a negative notice from Bosley Crowther in the *New York Times* on December 15—"There is nothing very surprising or exciting here," he declared—could hurt business. The film earned a very healthy $4,350,000 in rentals.

Nonetheless, there is no mistaking that as the impresario of Nelson

Algren's lower-depths Chicago, Otto Preminger was miscast. The novel is an insider's account, written in a feverish hipster's prose that approximates the inner monologues of characters steeped in chaos and despair. The film is distinctly an outsider's view, a tourist's glance at the urban dispossessed. Where Algren is loose, anarchic, overheated, Preminger for the most part remains within his characteristic zone of aloofness. Where Algren is fearless and unruly, Preminger is measured, cautious, tame. As Preminger in one of their misbegotten meetings told Algren, "Write a screen treatment for me about the suffering of drug addicts, but not too much suffering; what we want is something creative that everybody wants to see."[29]

Preminger's detachment is apparent in the opening tracking shot, which follows Frankie Machine as he gets off a bus and walks down the street toward his neighborhood bar. In a series of smooth movements that Preminger worked out (too) carefully with his cinematographer, Sam Leavitt, the camera presents an urban streetscape groomed to represent a "sordid" environment—"Chicago" rather than Chicago.

In his December 20 review in the *Nation,* Robert Hatch accused Preminger of replacing Algren's "respect" for his characters with "contempt." The charge is too severe. But Preminger's distance, from which he displays for mainstream audiences a simulacrum of a strange new world, a museum of the life of slum dwellers, works against the temper of the material. There is no pulse in the film's eerily underpopulated, too clean street scenes. Pedestrians glimpsed through windows and doors look like extras. And the stiff-jointed scenes set in the bar, a home away from home for Algren's down-and-outs, contain no trace of the carnivalesque energy, the roiling give-and-take of the urban inferno Algren creates in his novel.

But even disregarding Algren's searing novel altogether and judging the film on its own terms, as mainstream, middlebrow entertainment, *The Man with the Golden Arm,* "a film by Otto Preminger," lacks the fluency of the director's most assured work. To Nelson Algren, the film's sternest critic, "the scenes, like those picture postcards we once viewed in the corner drug store, at 10-for-a-penny, by turning the crank of a kinescope machine, drop one by one before your eyes with mechanical precision."[30]

Nonetheless, the film has its moments. The famous title sequence, with Saul Bass's moving lines playing against the rhythms of Elmer Bernstein's percussive main theme, achieves a dynamic force that nothing in the film quite matches. Although Preminger overuses it, Elmer Bernstein's landmark score (deservedly Oscar-nominated), at the time as original and daring as Saul Bass's title sequence, approximates the meter of Nelson Algren's jazzlike prose. In the rhythms of Bernstein's music are echoes of the novel's delirium.

(For romantic scenes and for scenes of Frankie's redemption, Bernstein also writes effective "straight" music.) Working with and often screaming at Sam Leavitt, Preminger creates some stark black-and-white images. During the card games that Frankie deals, an overhanging light casts minatory shadows onto the intent players. In a few scenes set at the smoke-laden Safari Club, a strip joint, dancers in deep focus perform joyless gyrations. The staircase and hallways in Frankie's tenement, and the drab apartment that he and his wife cohabit, seem engrained with sorrow.

Preminger doles out the few scenes of drug-taking and withdrawal like the X-rated set pieces the audience has been primed to expect and gives them an illicit frisson. It's as if Preminger is saying to his 1955 viewers, "You're really not supposed to be seeing this." Whereas almost any contemporary director would shoot the big scenes with visual overkill—rapid cutting, subjective renderings of the character's frenzy—Preminger retains his composure, departing only slightly from his usual objectivity. He shoots all the drug scenes in a single, uncompromising take and with minimal visual punctuation, relying mostly on Sinatra and on Bernstein's jazz scoring to crank up the volume. The first time Frankie injects heroin, Preminger moves the camera in for an extreme close-up on the actor's face, reverting to a rare use of visual italics as compensation for not showing the needle entering the character's arm (an impermissible image in the mid-1950s). In the first and still powerful withdrawal scene, Preminger starts with a discomfiting high-angle shot before moving the camera in closer to watch Frankie's twitches and spasms.

Unlike the film's airless, studio-built "Chicago," Frank Sinatra, with his coarse-grained speech, his hard eyes, and his slumped posture, comes across as the real thing. He never pushes for an effect. Simply, without any actorly fuss, he conveys his character's differing attitudes to the two women in his life, his pity for the wife he no longer loves, his conflicted attraction to Molly. With a wounded look in his eyes and body language that signals his character's agony, he rises fully to the long-take demands of the drug-taking and withdrawal set pieces that Preminger has given him. Sinatra is equally persuasive when Frankie, wearing a crooked bow tie, his hands shaking and his face covered in sweat, bombs in an audition as a drummer for a jazz band. Finally, though, Sinatra, who indeed earned his Academy Award nomination for best actor, does not have the technique or the depth to offer what Marlon Brando would have, a sense of the inner life of the character and of the tormented past that drove him to his addiction. But that kind of revelation is not what Preminger had in mind.

In contrast to their bedraggled-looking costar, Eleanor Parker and Kim

Novak seem like visiting celebrities with hair and makeup just so. Some of the acting in Parker's voice can perhaps be defended on the grounds that she is playing a character who is faking her life, pretending to be a cripple when she is not and "performing" misery in order to hold on to her distracted husband. Even if she is often strained, a result of her simply being and sounding too cultivated for the character, her performance is courageous nonetheless.

Kim Novak, too, never quite looks and moves as if she lives in the world of the film. She doesn't fully inhabit her character's apartment or the burlesque house where she is a "hostess." And when Preminger pauses at one point to watch the character walk home from work in a spangled, tight-fitting dress, Kim Novak looks unmistakably like a movie star. She doesn't have the fire for her two big scenes, convincing Frankie to quit drugs, and then, after locking him in her closet, frantically pacing back and forth; and Preminger, typically, does not try to cover for her with cinematic embellishments. He shoots both scenes without a single cut. But in many of her moments with Frankie, Novak is touching, and rather than seeming like a nervous Hollywood beauty trying her best, she evokes Algren's sad-eyed young woman facing a dead-end life. Preminger has helped the actress to endow these scenes with her own warmth and insecurity—the qualities that caused two notoriously impatient men, her director and costar, to subdue their tempers and go to bat for her. Throughout, Novak focuses on Frankie Machine a gaze filled with solicitude, hurt, and love. And in the last shot, her eyes glued to her man as she walks a step behind him, she gives Frankie a worried look which, just before the camera moves in for a sly medium shot on a sign that says "No Right Turn," helps to qualify the "happy" ending that Preminger and his scriptwriters whipped up. Novak's stare of intense concern signals the possibility that Frankie's cure may not be for good after all.

Like *The Moon Is Blue, The Man with the Golden Arm* is historically if not artistically a film to remember. As Nelson Algren conceded, "Inasmuch as the film Preminger made from my book broke the censorship on the drug traffic, it was worth making."[31] Although the controversy that both films created in the 1950s is understandable now only by placing them within a historical context in which taboo words and subjects had an aura of black magic, the films have had different legacies. *The Moon Is Blue* is regarded as a historical footnote, while *The Man with the Golden Arm* has enjoyed a lingering reputation as a major artistic achievement. Accurately enough described in 1955 as "daring" and "hard-hitting," a half century on it seems hollow at the core, a stodgy, at times crudely drawn period piece that nonetheless manages to attain a creepy power. As Otto Preminger's only overrated film, however, it holds a unique place in the canon.

NINE

Miss Iowa

For his first three independent projects, Preminger tackled controversial material. For his fourth, he went out on a different kind of limb.

At the top of an application form distributed to theaters, drama schools, high schools, and colleges in the spring of 1956 appeared the following statement:

> Otto Preminger (producer-director of *Laura, The Moon Is Blue, Carmen Jones, The Man with the Golden Arm*) is convinced that there is somewhere in the world an unknown young actress who can be an exciting Joan of Arc. By means of a competition conducted with the cooperation of motion picture theatres throughout the world, he intends to find a young actress who will play this role. Mr. Preminger will visit 15 cities, starting in September [1956], to audition selected candidates who have fulfilled the requirements listed below. For these auditions, contestants must be prepared to play Scene I of [George Bernard] Shaw's *Saint Joan* and Scene VI, the latter starting with Joan's speech, "Perpetual imprisonment! Am I not then to be set free?" The most promising candidates will be selected for screen tests, and the 5 best tests will be shown on a national television show. Mr. Preminger will select the winner and cast her in *Saint Joan*.

The statement concluded with a warning: "Mr. Preminger's decisions shall be final."

Four requirements were listed. The candidates had to be between the ages of sixteen and twenty-two; had to have a complete command of the English language; had to submit a photo; and had to complete the entry blank "shown below" and mail it before midnight August 23, 1956, to Otto Preminger, Hollywood 51, California. At the bottom of the entry blank the contestant was asked to check which city "[she] can most conveniently reach for an audition if selected: Atlanta, Boston, Chicago, Cleveland, Dallas, Denver, Detroit, Los Angeles, Montreal, New York, St. Louis, San Francisco, Seattle, Toronto, Washington." Preminger, appearing in a trailer shown in theaters throughout the United States and Canada, explained the terms of the search. "I have no specific image or character in mind," he stated. "I only know there are certain qualities necessary to portray this part: a great deal of sincerity, honesty, an almost fanatic devotion, and naturally, also talent."[1]

It may have had the trappings of a show business hustle ("My worldwide search met with equally worldwide skepticism," Otto noted wryly),[2] but his quest was genuine. He had not already cast the role, and no secret favorites were waiting in the wings. Preminger's search—the filmmaker was hoping it would become as celebrated as David O. Selznick's for an actress to play Scarlett O'Hara in *Gone with the Wind*—also expressed his belief that Joan, only seventeen when she was burned at the stake, should be enacted by a fresh unknown of approximately the same age. "In the theater the audience accepts an older actress in the role," he said, noting that the part was "originally played by Sybil Thorndike when she was forty-one." "The greatest stage actresses, however, developed a certain style and nothing that is very stylized has ever succeeded in movies. The movies are looking for a 'being.' The camera is more discerning, it comes closer and so we have to be more authentic. Also the film going public is less sophisticated. They don't forgive."[3]

He didn't realize it at the time, and no one told him, but Preminger's plan contained a probably fatal flaw. Whereas many naturally talented, unknown seventeen-year-olds could play a seventeen-year-old as conceived by Hollywood screenwriters, how many could persuasively embody the exceptional teenager Shaw had written, a young woman of extraordinary, perhaps even supernatural, gifts? Communing with the voices of Michael and Margaret that come to her through the bells in the church of her native Domrémy, this divinely inspired teenager possessed powers that would alter the course of history. Moreover, the illiterate young woman is both a poet

With a group of unknown young women hoping to play Saint Joan, in September 1956.

and dialectician who speaks in the long, rolling sentences of a Shavian orator. Surely the odds of finding, anywhere in the world, an inexperienced, unprofessional teenager blessed with the technical, intellectual, emotional, and spiritual capacity to portray Shaw's great heroine—one of the most demanding roles in world theater—were close to zero. Probably only a miracle, of the kind that the messianic heroine herself would be capable of, could have delivered such a person.

But in the spring and summer of 1956, as he began to publicize his search for Joan, Otto was optimistic. And so were the over 18,000 applicants who mailed in their entry forms by the August 23 deadline. Preminger and his staff narrowed the field to around three thousand young women, each of whom the producer was planning personally to audition on a thirty-seven-day tour budgeted at $150,000, during which he would fly over 30,000 miles visiting nineteen cities in the United States, Canada, and Europe. His marathon began in London at the end of August.

Before he held the first of 250 auditions scheduled in London, where the film was to be shot starting in January 1957, Preminger set up an office at 144 Piccadilly in a suite in a mansion that belonged to producer Alexander Korda. To head his London base of operations Otto hired an English-woman, Rita Moriarty, who had worked in New York for the producer Alexander Cohen. "I specialize in difficult people," Moriarty recalled. "I'm interested in them to see if I can handle them. I had been warned that Preminger was dreadful to work for—he really had a terrible reputation. When I met him—he was at the Dorchester Hotel in Cecil Beaton's suite—I liked him without being mad about him. We got along well but not that wonderfully well. I had to fight for my salary. But I knew I was valuable to him because he needed a British anchor in his office, and since I had worked in England and Otto hadn't I had the upper hand." As Moriarty began to help Preminger hire his crew, she tried to point out that his criteria were wrong. "Foolishly, Otto was impressed by people who had the right address and who knew the Queen. But that's not what you need for a crew. You need cockneys who work hard. He hired too many effete ones. Otto wasn't knowledgeable about the British, but I also saw that it was larger than that: he just didn't understand people. He was interested in them, but he didn't understand them."[4]

During the London auditions, held in the ballroom of a great house on Park Lane, Rita Moriarty sat on one side of Preminger while on the other was Lionel Larner, his twenty-two-year-old London casting director who pre-interviewed all the candidates. As Larner recalled, "The auditioners were to read a single speech, 'Give me that writing.' One girl came in and said, 'I'm not going to read because I am going to play Saint Joan, my voices told me.' 'You misunderstood your voices,' Preminger answered." After London, Larner traveled with Preminger to coordinate auditions in Edinburgh; their bond strengthened when Larner made Otto laugh. " 'You are the only member of my crew who is not married,' Otto said to me. 'Will you let me pick a wife for you? After all, I am the man who is going to select Saint Joan.' 'Let me see her performance first,' I said. He was tickled. Otto loved wit."[5]

After Edinburgh Preminger held auditions in Manchester, Dublin, Glasgow, Copenhagen, and Stockholm. Returning to America, he auditioned 268 candidates in New York. By the time he reached Los Angeles, he realized that there were far fewer potential Joans than he had expected. "I thought I could find at least 50. But I won't test that many. I began to realize if looking for an unknown were so easy, a star would be easier to find."[6]

For the American auditions Sandy Gardner accompanied Preminger. "It was exhausting, and very fast," Sandy recalled. "Some of the ones Otto looked at had sent in nude shots in which they were spread out on leopard skins. They didn't understand the nature of the part. The girls were given a single long speech and it was my job to escort each girl into the ballroom of a hotel, where the auditions were usually held. The girls would get a cue from me when to begin."[7]

Midway through his American tour, at the Sherman Hotel in Chicago on September 15, 1956, Preminger thought he might have found his Joan. "Something clicked," he recalled, when Jean Seberg, a seventeen-year-old from Marshalltown, Iowa, entered the audition room. (Like all the others, Jean's interview was filmed.) When an off-screen Preminger asked, "Do you want to be an actress?" Jean, with an affecting clarity and directness, answered: "Very badly." "Why haven't you worn a cross?" Preminger inquired. "My family is too poor to afford one," Jean replied, bowing her head. But after Preminger responded with a doubtful "Really?" she giggled. "Because I knew all the other girls would be wearing them," she admitted. Surprised by her statement, Preminger laughed.[8] When Jean performed the audition scene, he was impressed by her delivery, free of the theatrical curlicues he had no patience for. The young woman's charm and sincerity touched him, and he liked her smile, her all-American vigor, and the confident way she carried herself. He was certain Jean would be among the finalists he would test in New York in mid-October.

"I saw Jean's audition in Chicago," Sandy said. "Up to that point, Otto had really been impressed by only one other actress, Kelli Blaine, whom we had seen earlier in New York. Kelli was tough, with a gap between her front teeth like David Letterman. She was not beautiful, but she looked the part: she was *right* for the part. Still, in Chicago, I put my vote in for Jean, who was damn good too. But Otto didn't think my opinion was worth much."[9]

Preminger called Jean's startled parents to ask them to allow their daughter to come to New York two weeks before the scheduled screen test so that he could work with her. At his first meeting with Jean at the Ambassador Hotel in New York, Otto started to worry. Had someone been coaching his discovery? She no longer seemed to be as spontaneous as she had been in Chicago. Disappointed, he began to bark at the frightened novice. "His anger bore a double edge," as Jean's biographer, David Richards, observed. "On the one hand, he genuinely appreciated her untutored freshness, a quality he was determined to preserve on film, and he was distressed to see it endangered. On the other hand, his ego was at stake. The actress he chose for Saint Joan would be his creation, and his alone. Meddling would be forbidden."[10] Preminger's evident disapproval stung Jean, who was certain she no longer had any chance of getting the role.

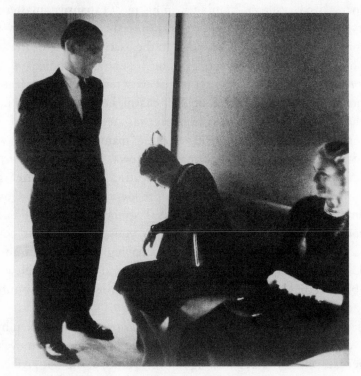

Jean Seberg waiting with a production assistant and an unidentified
woman to hear if she has been chosen to play Saint Joan.

After auditioning over three thousand candidates, Otto in the end made
only three screen tests: Jean's, Kelli Blaine's, and one of a woman from
Stockholm, Doreen Denning. For the test he asked Jean if she'd be willing to
have her long hair cut short—a sign that despite his disappointment in her
during rehearsals she remained the front-runner. Jean, of course, complied.
The androgynous short haircut highlighted her fine bone structure, her
clear, sensitive eyes, and a tremulous sex appeal waiting to be released. As he
prepared Jean for the test, Preminger's temper flared as he asked her to
repeat scenes many times until he got exactly the gestures and intonations
he wanted. "What's the matter? Don't you have the guts to go on?" he yelled
when he had driven Jean to the breaking point. "I'll rehearse until you drop
dead," Jean answered.[11] He was testing her limits, a usual Preminger strategy,
and he was impressed by the young woman's stamina. "Kelli Blaine was even
stronger than Jean," Otto's stepson observed, "but I think Otto chose Jean
because in the end he felt he could manipulate her more easily."[12]

On Friday, October 19, Otto informed Jean Seberg that she was his

Saint Joan. Two days later Preminger, in his most expansive, master show-man style and beaming like a new father, introduced his discovery to the press corps he had summoned at noon to the executive suite of the United Artists offices in New York. That night, he presented his choice on *The Ed Sullivan Show,* where, before an estimated sixty million viewers, Jean reen-acted her audition scene. Her beauty, her charm, her vivacity could not dis-guise the irreducible fact that Jean Seberg was an amateur. Indeed, in her entry form she had listed as her entire résumé "many local plays and winner at the State University of Iowa, Iowa City, Iowa, for an exerpt [*sic*] from Shaw's *Saint Joan.*" (Attached to Jean's application had been a letter of sup-port from a local booster, J. W. Fisher, president of the Fisher Governor Company, manufacturers of gas regulators, diaphragm control valves, liquid level controllers, and pump governors. "A young lady of our commu-nity . . . is within the age requirements, having graduated from High School. This summer she is playing summer stock at Cape May, New Jersey. She is blonde, and most attractive. Her voice carries the proper authority and she has talent.")[13]

A few days after her appearance on *Ed Sullivan,* Jean was taken by lim-ousine to Boston, where she underwent a secret operation to remove moles from her face and throat. Returning to Marshalltown, she was greeted with a welcome befitting a world leader. She remained at home until November 13, her eighteenth birthday, when she left Marshalltown to begin her jour-ney to London. On her arrival Preminger sequestered her in a suite at the Dorchester Hotel, where he hoped, in a few short weeks, to transform Jean of Iowa into Joan of Arc. In preparation for the first read-through with the entire cast, scheduled for December 14, Preminger arranged for Jean to be given elocution lessons designed to transform her flat Midwestern twang into a more refined mid-Atlantic diction and to be tutored in French (which, as preparation for performing Shaw, seemed rather beside the point). In nearby Rotten Row Jean was taught how to ride a horse, to wear armor, and to draw a sword.

While Jean was studying, Preminger lined up the rest of his cast. (The only actor he had signed before Jean was Richard Widmark, who was to play the Dauphin.) Lionel Larner "rushed around seeing all the plays. I kept files and lists and then brought in the cream of the London theater to see Otto," Larner recalled.

> He had an idea that English actors would play the English charac-ters, and Irish actors would play French characters. The actors would come to see him dressed in Turnball and Asser shirts, and

Otto thought they were all gay. "You don't understand, Mr. Pre-minger, they have to be properly dressed at the Dorchester," I told him. I began to ask actors to "look ordinary." Preminger would say to important actors, "You're not right," and I told him he couldn't dismiss them like that, he had to spend more time with each of them.

Preminger "wanted to go with strength," Larner said, "but he didn't seem to realize that Jean would be dwarfed by playing opposite British knights like John Gielgud. We all felt that she wouldn't be able to stand up to the top-drawer actors he was signing up. When he showed me Jean's Chicago audition and asked my opinion, I told him Jean's American accent seemed wrong, but I quickly added, 'I have to bow my head to your superior knowledge of these things.' "

Larner saw Jean regularly as she was preparing for the first read-through with the cast. "Jean grew up very fast. When she first came over, she wore a shapeless dress, then there was an amazing transformation. With her hair cut and her moles removed, she was incandescently beautiful, and she became an instant celebrity. And when she appeared for the press in a black Givenchy dress, no one else in the world looked like her. Otto bought her jewelry and took her dining with the Oliviers. Her ego was such that she thought the Oliviers were dining with her." Inevitably there were rumors that Preminger was romantically involved with his discovery. "Nonsense," Larner said. "She was a schoolgirl to him. He liked young people—and he really believed in giving young people a break. He wanted to use the newest, freshest actor, and he believed in Jean's freshness. There was no affair: period."[14]

On the first read-through, held at Alexander Korda's office, Preminger had a set-to with Paul Scofield, cast as Brother Martin. Scofield walked out. With Larner's assistance Preminger quickly replaced him with Kenneth Haigh, who had been acclaimed for his recent performance in *Look Back in Anger.* After the fracas with Scofield, the three-week rehearsal period that followed was, for Preminger, the most pleasurable part of the project. He was thrilled to be working on one of the great plays he had memorized in his youth.

The script that he and his cast were reading, however, was an edited ver-sion of Shaw's long play, which had a running time of three hours. After over two years of negotiating with Shaw's estate, Otto and his scenarist Gra-ham Greene had been given an extraordinary concession: they could change up to 25 percent of Shaw's dialogue. In the event they altered only 5 percent, but to reduce the play to a manageable 110 minutes they had had to make cuts and changes. They had trimmed lengthy set speeches, removed much of Shaw's political discourse, expanded the action to include a coronation scene and preparations for battle, and decided to open the film with a portion of Shaw's epilogue. Purists and die-hard Shavians, as Otto was aware, would cry foul, but for the filmmaker, and never more so than in the three-week read-through with his cast, the play remained the thing. Despite the changes he and Greene had made, it was Preminger's intention to honor, not to mutilate, the work of a playwright he revered.

While Otto was in London with his cast, at Shepperton Studios twenty full sets were being constructed. When the sets were ready after December 20, Preminger relocated the company to Shepperton for full-dress rehearsals. On January 8, 1957, at 8:30 a.m., he began shooting. In addition to the camera that was shooting *Saint Joan,* a second unit was on the spot filming a short promotional, "The Making of a Movie." The international press corps Preminger had assembled watched the double filming.

Recorded for the promotional film, Jean's first take of the scene in which Joan, encased in armor, makes her entrance at the Dauphin's court, reveals her terror. Jean doesn't seem to have any point of view about her character; her voice is constricted with tension; her gestures are tentative and inescapably contemporary. Poor Jean Seberg looks as if she would rather be in Marshalltown than where she was, on exhibit before the critical, expectant gaze of the international press and two cameras. Under the circumstances that Preminger had set up with an almost perverse disregard for the well-being of his young discovery, how could Jean have felt other than crushed? "It's my belief that Otto wanted Jean to feel and actually to be overwhelmed," Lionel Larner observed. "That was how he saw the part: that Joan was enclosed by representatives of the powerful institutions of church and state. That was why he cast powerful actors opposite her: it conformed to his idea of a birdlike Joan of Arc. Of course such an interpretation could not work out."[15]

Preminger could not and would not admit it, but he must have sensed from the start that Jean was out of her league. A director with a different temperament might have admitted he had made a mistake and replaced Jean with a more experienced performer. But Otto was not capable of such a course of action, and besides he still believed in Jean and was convinced that, despite the odds, he could force his vision of the character onto her. For his sake, to vindicate his choice of her and to justify the hullabaloo he had created in his worldwide search, Jean Seberg *had* to succeed. As Rita Moriarty claimed, "Otto was conceited enough to think he could extract a

Preminger rehearses the trial scene in *Saint Joan* with Felix Aylmer, Anton Walbrook, Jean Seberg, and Kenneth Haigh.

performance from her."[16] To the increasing dismay of onlookers, however, he seemed incapable of creating an environment in which Jean might be able to flourish.

As he became more frustrated, Otto would frequently demonstrate how he wanted Jean to play a scene. In "The Making of a Movie," there's an eerie moment when Otto enacts, with precisely the kind of theatrical artifice his casting of Jean was meant to defy, how he wants the character to crack up at the end of a tense scene. "If Jean didn't get it right away, he would give her traffic directions, 'Go from here to there, and keep in line with the camera,' " Rita Moriarty recalled.[17] Larner observed that in the cathedral scene, when Preminger couldn't get Jean to cry, he bellowed, "You are ruining my picture!"[18] "You're not thinking the part!" was a line he often uttered in one of his rants. But he didn't seem to realize that his mistreatment was preventing Jean from doing any thinking at all. "What she was supposed to be thinking was increasingly mysterious to her," as David Richards noted. "Forced to repeat some takes ten or twenty times, she felt the spontaneity draining from her. Her face froze and her body stiffened."[19] As Richards commented, Preminger "had not discovered an actress; he had engaged a puppet. If the character was distraught, Jean could be rendered distraught."[20]

Cast and crew were all sympathetic to Jean. "You couldn't not like her," Kenneth Haigh said, surely speaking for all.[21] Nonetheless, though some of the most respected actors in the British theater of the time witnessed Preminger's mishandling of Jean, no one, not even John Gielgud, who had great sympathy for her, had the nerve to stand up to the director. "Having chosen her but then decided it was a mistake, Preminger was utterly horrible to her on the set," Gielgud observed. "She didn't know anything about phrasing or pacing or climax—all the things the part needed—but she was desperately eager to learn and also desperately insecure about everything." When Gielgud at the end of shooting presented Jean with a cup and saucer that had belonged to his great-aunt, the legendary actress Ellen Terry, Jean "simply broke down in tears," Gielgud recalled.[22]

Despite the circumstances, Jean Seberg never cracked on the set. "Otto had cast her because of a strength he had seen in her, and during the filming he could not break her," Lionel Larner said.[23] Rita Moriarty agreed. "The steel that got her the part prevented her from crying. She was a tough cookie, and I must say I was impressed by Jean's self-control. That was what Otto had liked about her at first, and I believe it's that quality that through it all held his respect for her. Otto admired those who would not fall apart when he yelled. Jean was firm, stoic, and she would *not* let him get her down."[24] Away from the set, though, Jean's stalwart façade crumbled, according to production photographer Bob Willoughby, who befriended her. "Often at the end of the day's shooting, she would be sobbing hysterically. Jean would be broken."[25]

His outbursts unsettled everyone except Otto, who recovered from his tirades in a matter of seconds, ready to carry on as if nothing had happened. He may have had hourly tantrums, but as the shooting progressed he was not displeased. His master cinematographer, Georges Périnal, and Roger Furse, his equally accomplished set designer, were giving him what he had asked for. His classically trained company was performing in a style adjusted to films rather than the stage. And he saw in the rushes plentiful evidence of Jean's naturalness and strength—the qualities for which he had hired her. "The dailies looked excellent," he recalled.[26]

Preminger's intemperance with Jean did not mean he disliked her; quite the contrary. As much as everyone else, he cared for her personally, and he never ceased feeling responsible for her. He gave her lavish presents, and many times after hours at the Dorchester he reverted to a calm, fatherly demeanor. On one drive back to the hotel from Shepperton, about midway through shooting, he informed her that he was going to cast her in the leading role in his next film, *Bonjour Tristesse,* an adaptation of Françoise Sagan's recent best-selling novel about *la dolce vita* on the French Riviera. Jean's "gratitude was immense," as David Richards reported.[27]

Near the end of shooting, Jean was involved in a near catastrophe that epitomized how she felt about working with Preminger. "I'm burning!" Jean screamed as smoke and flames from two of seven gas cylinders enveloped her during the filming of the Maid being burned at the stake. Lining up the shot on a crane high overhead, Preminger was horrified as crew members quickly released Jean from her chains while studio firemen poured water onto the flames. Singed but unhurt, Jean offered to redo the shot but Otto sent her back to the Dorchester in a limousine and arranged for a doctor and nurse to be on hand. Jean never remounted the pyre. Although Preminger was accused, preposterously, of having arranged the mishap as a publicity gimmick, after it had occurred he certainly didn't block newspapers and magazines from reporting the incident. A journalist and photographer from *Life* had been on the set, and Otto was pleased when the event was given a big spread in the magazine. "We got it all on film. The camera took 400 extra feet. The crowd reaction was fantastic. I'll probably use some of it," Preminger boasted, seemingly unaware of how callous he sounded.[28]

Jean's last day at Shepperton was March 15. Soon after, weary yet relieved, Jean returned to Marshalltown, which had never looked smaller or more provincial to her. She knew at once she could never again live at "home" and realized as well that the kind of conventional lives her high school friends were pursuing would never be available to her. Is it possible that during her monthlong stay in Marshalltown it occurred to Jean (and to her family as well) that having been chosen by Otto Preminger might not have been the luckiest moment of her life?

In mid-April Otto called her to New York for publicity. At the beginning of May he brought her to Paris, where, on May 12, as the crowning touch to the drumroll of publicity that had enveloped the project first to last, Preminger presented the world premiere of his film at the Paris Opéra.

The unrivaled splendor of the Palais Garnier and the assemblage of celebrities from show business, politics, fashion, and international business who paid a thousand dollars a seat to benefit the Polio Foundation transformed the premiere of *Saint Joan* into an event that surpassed any Hollywood opening. Appearing on the arm of her director, Jean was radiant in an aqua Givenchy evening dress that Preminger had presented to her as a gift. Although test screenings of the film in New York in April had evoked tepid reactions and tonight she would be facing the judgment of an international

Preparing Jean Seberg for the burning scene in *Saint Joan*. (Below)
A few minutes later, a mechanical malfunction engulfed the actress
in flames that almost killed her.

tribunal, for the furiously clicking cameras Jean projected the poise of an acclaimed star. On this gala occasion she looked far less like Saint Joan than like a cosmopolitan young woman who embodied a new style, Gallic chic garnished with an all-American twist.

The applause at the end of the screening was lukewarm. But at the reception at Maxim's later in the evening, Preminger, with a resplendent smile, personally greeted every single guest and behaved as if the premiere had been a triumph. The French critics, by and large, dismissed the film as a betrayal of a national heroine, and business on the Champs-Élysées was lackluster. Although he realized that the film would be likely to receive the same cool reception when it opened in America at the end of June, he proceeded to promote it with flair. He booked Jean on a grueling twenty-seven-day tour that included press conferences, photo sessions, radio and television interviews, and appearances at special promotions. The star of *Saint Joan* appeared frequently at downtown department stores and greeted the public on the steps of numerous city halls. Just before the American premiere, however, Preminger whisked Jean to London for the opening at the Odeon Leicester Square. The British reaction was also dispiriting, with critics complaining that Preminger and Graham Greene had not been sufficiently reverential toward Shaw.

From London Otto sent Jean to recuperate on the French Riviera and to begin to prepare for *Bonjour Tristesse*. When *Saint Joan* had its American premiere at the Orpheum Theater in her hometown on June 24, Jean was in Nice studying French, swimming, lingering over coffee in outdoor cafés, and acquiring a French boyfriend. Distracted by the easy life, and with the burdens of her instant celebrity lifted, Jean was all but immunized against the American reviews, which ranged from barely respectful to scorching. "Too often Jean Seberg looks as though she'd be more comfortable on a soda fountain stool," Paul Beckley huffed in the *New York Herald Tribune* on June 27. "Skimpy," "sketchy," "not well-articulated," and "a series of dissertations on an important theme" were typical complaints, though many reviews acknowledged that both the director and his star took command during the climactic trial sequence. Business was dismal, and after its first-run engagements—Preminger himself booked the film on a then-thriving art-house circuit; in Los Angeles, he opened *Saint Joan* at the Four Star, the upscale venue where *The Moon Is Blue* had premiered—the film never received a wide general release. A year after it opened, the worldwide grosses were less than $400,000, making *Saint Joan* Preminger's first financial failure as an independent filmmaker. "What good are successes if you can't have a failure once in a while?" he quipped, affecting a cavalier indifference he could not truly have felt.[29] Preminger's attempt to promote *Saint Joan* with the kind of showmanship befitting a Hollywood blockbuster seems, in retrospect, strangely but also endearingly naive, the most touching merger of idealism and commerce in the filmmaker's career. How could he ever have imagined that his reasonably faithful adaptation of a dense, talky Shavian masterwork could ever have achieved popular acceptance?

Both at the time and ever after, Preminger defended Jean. "I think this girl has great talent, great poise," he said in an interview in the *New York Times* on January 12, 1958, "and it would be unfair to blame her for the picture. Maybe it was just as much my fault. Maybe it was an error to try to make a movie out of Shaw." "I made the mistake of taking a young, inexperienced girl and wanted her to be Saint Joan, which, of course, she wasn't," he told Jean's biographer. "I didn't help her to understand and act the part. Indeed, I deliberately prevented her, because I was determined that she should be completely unspoiled. I think the instinct was right, but now I would work with her for perhaps two years until she understood the part right through. Well, that was a big mistake, and I have nobody to blame but myself."[30] In his autobiography, Preminger offered his final assessment: "Many people blamed Jean Seberg and her inexperience [for the failure of the film]. That is unfair. I alone am to blame."[31]

Some of Preminger's comments about *Saint Joan* after the fact revealed it wasn't only Jean Seberg who had been overmatched by George Bernard Shaw. "I misunderstood something fundamental about Shaw's play," Preminger said. "It is not a dramatization of the legend of Joan of Arc which is filled with emotion and religious passion. It is a deep but cool intellectual examination of the role religion plays in the history of man."[32] *Saint Joan,* to be sure, is a play of ideas, but it is not, as Preminger claimed, a "cool intellectual" exercise stripped of emotion. To the contrary, if it is interpreted properly—that is, according to the playwright's intentions—turbulent emotions are released *through* the characters' engagement with ideas. As Preminger didn't fully grasp, the playwright's great characters are great talkers for whom the play of language—discourse, debate, ratiocination—is deeply emotional, and sometimes, as it is with Joan, tinged with eroticism.

Although Preminger and Seberg were not equal to Shaw, their film does not deserve its outcast reputation. Even if the most zealous revisionist critic could not possibly rehabilitate the film as an overlooked masterpiece, it is far from being a disgrace. Enriched by Georges Périnal's ravishing yet realistic black-and-white cinematography; Mischa Spoliansky's distinguished score, a contemporary interpretation of medieval motifs with a plangent central theme; and Saul Bass's elegant title sequence, in which ringing bells are transformed into a truncated torso of Joan wielding a sword, Preminger's condensed, *Reader's Digest* version of Shaw's play is a flawed, courageous American art film of its era.

Yes, Jean Seberg lacks the technical and emotional resources to embody, in all its theatrical majesty, the variegated character Shaw conceived. Hers is an unfinished performance, a sampling. In many fundamental ways, however, she gave her director exactly the Maid he had in mind: a vulnerable figure thwarted by manipulative representatives of church and state whom she cannot understand; a religious naïf whose girlishness is graced with a budding sensuality. The qualities in Shaw's conception that Preminger himself did not seem fully to believe in—Joan's genius as a military leader and as a public orator, the assertiveness that enabled an illiterate teenager to alter the destiny of France—are the ones either missing or deficiently represented.

Under Preminger's guidance, Seberg gives a performance carefully crafted for the camera rather than the proscenium. Rather than a mannish stage diva galloping through the part on her high horse trilling lines with technical bravura, Jean is a deeply feminine young woman who approaches Shaw in a fresh, unaffected way. Her Maid of Orléans, as Shaw intended, is decidedly not unsexed. When she smiles at the sympathetic Brother Martin or teases the childlike Dauphin, she is distinctly fetching—a charming warrior-saint. With lingering traces of her Midwestern roots, Jean speaks in a light, splintery voice which takes on a lyrical lilt in all the soft moments, as for instance when Joan talks of her saints who tell her what to do, or when she recalls her country home. But her voice and body language do not project the "born boss" Shaw describes in his preface. When in the early scenes she must make demands of a gruff soldier or convince the court of the truth of her voices, she lacks the authority that a genuine born boss like her director would be able to summon as if by divine right.

Preminger presents Jean cautiously. "Here is the chosen one; what do you think?" he seems to be saying to the audience as he photographs Jean primarily in neutral long takes, not for a moment trying to protect her or to amplify her work with editing, lighting, or camera movement. He presents Jean's big scene at the end of the trial, for instance, in a single uninterrupted take. He does provide a lovely entrance for his discovery, however. In the opening scene Joan appears first in shadow, standing by the sleeping Dauphin like a spectral figure emerging from his dream. After a beat, she steps into the light.

Finally, the ordeal of Jean Seberg is an indelible part of her performance. In the conclusion of the trial sequence, in which Joan is plunged into uncertainty, first recanting and then ultimately denying her recantation, Jean, no doubt drawing on her own terror and giving everything she has to give, performs with enormous commitment, her body and voice trembling. The moment is thrilling and it is possible, after all, to see why Preminger cast Jean Seberg, and what he saw in her.

As a producer, Preminger came on like a carnival barker, bristling with bluster and braggadocio, but as a director of Shaw he proceeds in his usual subdued way. He is a scrupulous, perhaps even intimidated, Shavian caretaker who honors the word more than the image. But he is of course showman enough to provide periodic visual grace notes—brief respites from the wordplay. He offers a striking opening image of the Dauphin's castle reflected in a lake, painterly pastoral shots of Joan on her journey to see the Dauphin, and occasional high-angle shots of Joan cowering in her cell. With Reinhardt-like authority he stages the one fully articulated action sequence in the film, the burning at the stake, shot on the largest sound stage in Europe with a cast of 1,500 screaming, pummeling witnesses seized by an almost sexual frenzy at the prospect of Joan's imminent death. His handling of the coronation and of the siege of Orléans, however, is curiously perfunctory. He shoots the coronation less for pageantry than for physical comedy, with the Dauphin struggling with his massive robes. And a long shot of Joan leading the siege of Orléans is an elaborate visual appetizer for a battle sequence that does not take place.

Sometimes, Preminger is self-effacing to a fault. In the play there is a rousing moment at the end of scene two, when Joan has been charged with leading the army against the English invaders. "Suddenly flashing out her sword as she divines that her moment has come," as Shaw writes, Joan cries out in triumph, "Who is for God and his maid? Who is for Orléans with me?" The character's ecstasy demands a response from the medium, a bit of cinematic bravura—a burst of triumphal music, perhaps, a heroic camera movement, or a dramatic shift in lighting. Refusing to permit the film to do any "acting" of its own, Preminger keeps the camera at a neutral distance from Joan. His static shot of the Maid as she tentatively raises her sword and Seberg's shaky whispering of lines that ought to ring with the weight of destiny defuse Shaw's theatrical thunder.

In the trial scenes, however, Preminger's conservatism yields many dividends. He ordered a week of rehearsals for the sequence, which he then shot over an intense two-week period. Fifty actors appear in the scenes, all without makeup and many wearing bald wigs. Quite unlike Carl Dreyer's montage editing in *The Trial of Joan of Arc,* which separates Joan in isolating one-shots, Preminger in dispassionate, eye-level compositions often keeps the Maid and her prosecutors within the same spatial frame. Avoiding disfiguring low angles and providing only a few close-ups of Joan, he presents the trial objectively in a series of deep-focus long shots. The visual balance underscores the equality of both sides in the Shavian debate ("there are no villains in the piece," as Shaw warned in his preface) and puts the emphasis in the right place—on Shaw's dialogue.

Saint Joan, the most honorable failure in Preminger's career, lost money and damaged the prestige he had accumulated as an independent filmmaker with three hits in a row. Would he and Jean Seberg bring each other better fortune on their next venture?

When midway through *Saint Joan* Preminger informed Jean that she was to star in *Bonjour Tristesse,* the project had already had a complicated history. In 1954, before publication and with no awareness of the success her little story was to achieve, Sagan had sold the rights to a French producer, Ray Ventura, for ten thousand dollars. A year later, early in 1955, when the book was selling briskly in twelve countries, had appeared on the *New York Times* best-seller lists for an astonishing thirty-eight weeks, and had sold over 1,300,000 copies in paperback, Preminger bought the rights from Ventura for a sum ten times what Ventura had paid the author. Otto's initial plan was to extract a double dividend from his catch—before turning it into a film, he would first present *Bonjour Tristesse* as a play. On August 5, 1955, he signed S. N. Behrman (whose favorite subject was the manners of the out-of-sight rich) to adapt the novel into both a play and a screenplay. Preminger announced that he would produce and direct *Bonjour Tristesse* on Broadway during the 1955–56 season and then shoot Behrman's screenplay on location in the summer of 1956. No further word about the play ever appeared, but in the late winter and early spring of 1956, as he was preparing his search for Saint Joan, Preminger worked with Behrman on a screenplay. On April 6, the two sailed to France on the *Liberté.* From April 23 to May 10 Preminger served on the jury at the Cannes Film Festival and then joined Behrman in Antibes to continue to work on the script that he expected to shoot in July and August. As it happened, Otto didn't shoot *Bonjour Tristesse* until the summer of 1957, and the screenplay was not by Behrman but another man of the theater, Arthur Laurents, the author of two successful plays and several screenplays, including *Rope* (directed by Alfred Hitchcock) and *Anastasia.*

Preminger was drawn to Sagan's story of Cécile, an amoral young woman with an incestuous attachment to her father who indirectly causes the death of a rival for her father's love. He admired Sagan's casual attitude toward the rituals of the sweet life on the Riviera as well as her seductive evocations of landscape and weather. Arthur Laurents, however, did not share Preminger's enthusiasm. "When I read Sagan's book in French, I thought it was a hot fudge sundae that might well become a best seller, but I also thought it was a trick, and indeed it turned out to be her fifteen minutes," Laurents recalled. "When I met her, I thought she was cultivating an attitude. She was pretending to be jaded, which she was too young to be. She was of the moment—it was chic to be depraved at that moment—and at the time she was taken seriously. A lesbian who lived a very fast life, she was quite unattractive, and that always helps to be taken seriously."[33]

Thinking little of the author or her novel ("I couldn't have cared less about that story"), Laurents nonetheless accepted Otto's offer to write a screenplay. "This was before I had written the libretto for *West Side Story* and I needed the money. I was recommended by Anatol Litvak, a friend of Otto's for whom I had written *Anastasia,* but I think the real reason Otto hired me was because he knew I had lived in Paris in the early 1950s and had known all these degenerate people Sagan writes about." Laurents was surprised, but also relieved, that as he wrote he had little contact with Preminger. "He really just left me on my own, with one basic instruction, that we are to be removed from the characters, who don't have passionate emotions. Otto thought that kind of distance was 'high style.' From beginning to end he was terribly nice to me, and I found him amusing, cultured, and not too much of a director. He was never an ogre to me, but I've been called an ogre too, and I'm not." Laurents wrote the script quickly—"it took two minutes"—and Preminger approved it without asking for any significant changes. He invited Laurents to be on the set throughout filming. "I declined. The only set I was on often was *Rope,* because Hitchcock needed a lot of dialogue in the background. Much later, I got asked to *leave* the set of *The Turning Point.*"

Laurents was indifferent not only because he felt no commitment to the story or characters but also because he disagreed with Preminger's casting. "Why had Otto cast English actors like David Niven and Deborah Kerr to play French characters? And then, in the midst of this chic atmosphere, there is Jean Seberg—Miss Iowa." Laurents had met Jean in Preminger's suite at the Plaza Athénée when Otto had hired him.

She was lovely, but I felt she was "performing" as an innocent young American girl. When I suggested she order profiteroles for dessert, she said, "I'm so young I break out." I was told that Otto liked to watch her take a bath. He turned on her when he found out she was sleeping with a French lawyer [François Moreuil, twenty-three, whom she was to marry on September 5, 1958]. He had thought she was a virgin, and he felt betrayed. He wanted to think of her as *his* virgin. European men don't understand American women. Jean was posing, acting American innocence, and Otto had fallen hook, line, and sinker for this cornfield approach. He was besotted. An intelligent, cultured man, Otto had fallen for a hooker, Gypsy Rose Lee, and now for a "virgin," and they are flip sides of the same coin. After I turned in the script, I saw *Saint Joan* and I immediately cabled Otto: "Jean will sink me, you, and the picture." Preminger's response was that Jean will be a "triumph." I bet Otto five dollars that she wouldn't be.[34]

Believing in Jean and confident that, unlike *Saint Joan*, *Bonjour Tristesse* had the ingredients to become a commercial as well as critical success, Preminger set up production offices in Paris and Cannes in early June 1957, almost two months before he was to begin shooting. One of his first staff appointments was Hope Bryce, a former model who was personally acquainted with many prominent designers and had once roomed with another model, Otto's wife Mary. "I was hired as costume coordinator and given complete charge of the wardrobe department and the budget," Hope recalled. "I worked with Givenchy on wardrobe and designed three of the dresses." Over the summer, the elegant, reserved young woman, separated from her first husband, and Otto, by now long estranged from Mary and no longer seeing Dorothy Dandridge, "unexpectedly fell in love," as Hope said. Although she had met Otto casually, when she and her first husband had socialized with Otto and Mary, she had had "no idea" that they would have a future. But as Hope, living in a garret at the top of the Plaza Athénée, spent time after hours with Otto, who was staying in "a magnificent apartment on the Île Saint-Louis filled with Vuillard paintings," she became "enthralled" by the filmmaker's energy and erudition. Although it might seem that Otto also satisfied a desire for the kind of strong male figure she had not had growing up—her father had died before her birth and she had been raised by her mother—Hope "never for one moment thought of Otto as a father figure."

That summer, Hope had ample opportunity to observe Preminger's "contradictions" and his "tantrums," which neither intimidated her nor dampened her affection. "Otto was certainly variegated," she said. When the French crew struck because they wanted wine at lunch, "we all thought Otto would explode. But no, when he knew he was expected to explode, he wouldn't. He agreed to the request, and the French went back to work. No one liked to see Otto go into a rage, and cast and crew wondered who was going to be 'it' today," she recalled.[35] Hope herself, despite her closeness to the director, was not immune. "She sometimes got the same kind of rollicking as we all did," said British production manager Martin Schute, who was to work for the director on three other films and to become "an expert in Otto Preminger-ship." "If Hope saw some danger flying in the air, she would tip me off because she knew I could cure it."[36]

As on *Saint Joan,* the coiled relationship between Preminger and Jean Seberg became the inevitable focus of the shoot. "When Otto's assistant, Max Slater, ran lines with Jean, often you could see she wasn't thinking about what the character was saying," Hope Bryce observed.

> Her eyes would look blank, and when Otto saw that vacant look, he'd start to scream, telling her she had to concentrate. He would only get angry when he felt she wasn't trying hard enough. He saw the performance was in Jean, but he had to work hard to get it out of her. When Otto would yell, Jean's chin would jut out and she'd start to cry, but I felt that she seemed able to act *only* when she got mad or was upset. I didn't think Otto really intimidated her, though, and certainly Jean never talked back. But I did notice that the other actors were upset to see Jean upset.[37]

Deborah Kerr, playing Anne, Cécile's prim rival who disapproves of *la dolce vita,* was dismayed.

> I couldn't stand it, when he was absolutely ranting and raving at poor little Jean Seberg. I said, "Please, Otto, do you have to shout at the poor little girl like that? *She* seems to be taking it all right but *I'm* not. I cannot work with this kind of atmosphere. I'm terribly sorry, but I just can't." The battering she received finished me, but it didn't her. I used to be a bit frightened for Otto. I thought he was going to have a heart attack, with his eyes popping and his face purple. But the next minute, it was gone. Completely gone. And this man who could be such a bully on the set, and who could destroy people, would then be a charming, witty companion at dinner who knew the best wines and caviar.[38]

It wasn't easy for Kerr to stand up to Otto ("She was very shy," Hope said), but the actress felt she had to. Like everyone else, Preminger had great respect for Kerr and after she berated him he backed off, for the moment.

Geoffrey Horne, cast as Cécile's boyfriend Philippe, "felt sorry" for Jean because Otto "yelled at her so much she was a basket case. But she did get through it somehow." The actor remembered Seberg speaking up only once, when she got momentarily confused in a scene on a rowboat and called, "Cut!" which is not an actor's prerogative, and was certainly a hanging offense on a Preminger set.

> Otto went berserk; he seemed to get pleasure in going nuts, and it was *not* an act. I never saw him be affectionate with Jean. He was not really a father figure for her, and though there were rumors, which I did not believe, he certainly was not her lover either. I would have known if he had been her lover. He was an Old Testament God figure who was never inappropriate with the beautiful women who were on the set. He had some notion that Jean and I would become a couple, and that that would make the movie sexier. I was a naughty boy then and Jean and I flirted a bit, but Jean had a French boyfriend.[39]

Everyone admired Jean's seeming ability to survive Otto's explosions, but there was mixed reaction about her work. According to Deborah Kerr, Jean was "amazing in the role."[40] But Martin Schute felt that Jean "wasn't particularly talented, and that was part of the problem. Otto wanted so much for Jean to be a star, which would validate his having chosen her for *Saint Joan*. But she was really a child at the time, more into her French boyfriend and reading press clippings about herself while Otto reckoned she should be concentrating entirely on her work."[41] Geoffrey Horne felt Jean's acting was akin to her personality: "immature."

> I liked her, we all did, but there was something a little fraudulent about her, a conflict between the American girl she was and the European girl she was trying to be. She would walk into the makeup room in panties to show she was liberated, but it was fake. She was trying so hard to be sophisticated. She always had a mask, a disguise, which kept you from seeing her troubles and pain. But you could see it in her body and in her acting: she was stiff and awkward. There was no ease about her. She was pretty in close-ups, but not when she moved.[42]

Horne also received his share of the Preminger "treatment." Trained by Lee Strasberg, Horne (who for decades has taught at the Strasberg Institute in New York) clashed with Preminger over interpretation. "I thought my role was a character part," Horne said.

I knew I looked like a leading man—my looks got me lucky so young—but I felt like a character actor. I was good in neurotic parts, as unhappy, troubled, sensitive boys, which is how I saw Philippe. But Otto didn't want that. He told me to stand there and do the part. "Be what you were the day I met you, and gave you the role," he said. I had been very confident that day, because I had just returned from filming my part in *The Bridge on the River Kwai*. But I had a problem playing the kind of straight part he wanted, and Otto didn't make me feel confident, the way Elia Kazan did at the Actors Studio when he would put his arm around me and make me feel I could do anything. David Lean [the director of *The Bridge on the River Kwai*] too had made me feel good, but Otto didn't do that. He didn't really seem to have any sense about actors as people. I don't remember him directing for acting at all. "Stand here, move there," he'd bark.[43]

With his two stars, David Niven and Deborah Kerr, Preminger observed a hands-off policy. "Otto didn't have to say *anything* to Deborah Kerr: she was wonderful in the role, and she was generous, beautiful, and sexy, too," as Horne said.[44] Preminger also didn't have to say much to Niven; as Raymond, Cécile's sybaritic father, he was playing the same kind of role he had performed so deftly in *The Moon Is Blue*. Preminger and Niven were buddies who fraternized after working hours in Paris and on the Riviera. But one time Preminger blasted the actor in an incident that became famous, although nobody seems to remember it in exactly the same way. Niven's biographer, Sheridan Morley, set the scene on the Champs-Élysées, with Preminger berating the star for tardiness (Niven had been misinformed about the schedule) in a voice that could be heard "across several boulevards." Niven managed to defuse the tirade by telling Preminger that he had "a terrible handicap. Whenever anyone shouts at me I forget all my lines."[45] Deborah Kerr recalled the blowup as taking place in the Bois de Boulogne, with Niven flummoxing his director by whispering, in a voice that could barely be heard, "Otto, don't shout." "David had his typical quizzical look—he had such a humorous face—and we all roared with laughter, including Otto, who just couldn't hear what Niven was saying."[46] Martin Schute, who also set the scene in the Bois de Boulogne, recalled that the actor shouted back with a matching volume. "Eventually the terrific roar calmed down, and when it had, Otto turned to me and said, 'It will be good for the newspapers.' Otto *never* held any grudges."[47] Geoffrey Horne claimed the fracas took place in Cannes. "Niven had gone to Nice to gamble, because there had been a change in the schedule he hadn't been told of.

When he showed up, late, with Otto looking purple, David said to him, 'Otto, where the hell have you been?' It was so funny and charming, and Otto laughed along with the rest of us."[48]

Niven charmed Preminger and the cast, but was unpopular with the crew. "He was really a terrible mean bugger," Martin Schute recalled. "He was impossible on the set and was often rude and nasty to his wife, Fjordis. 'I don't want your dirty wine in my glass,' he said to her once at dinner. He wanted to walk away with his wardrobe, but I charged him and he argued like hell."[49] Rita Moriarty, still in charge of Otto's London office, recalled that "David always tried to be one of the boys with the crew, but it struck me as phony." Her reservations about the actor may have been colored by an unnerving incident. "Though married, David, like Otto, was one for the ladies," Moriarty said.

> He had let Otto talk him into a "date" in London, where David was given Otto's London chauffeur. David tipped the driver heavily, and then nobody knew where he was when it was time for him to return to France for shooting. Otto, frantic, called from Cannes to tell me I had to find him; but the chauffeur was getting well paid not to say where David was. I said I didn't know, and then I spoke up and told Otto he had had no right to let David go off like that during a shoot. Otto knew he was wrong and perhaps as a result he started screaming at me over the phone. I could hear him pounding his desk, pounding it furiously for minutes on end. He was stammering with rage. I yelled right back at him.[50]

Despite the flare-ups, *Bonjour Tristesse* was a lucky shoot. The locations—Paris, Cannes, Le Levandou, Antibes—were heaven-sent. The weather for the entire filming, which lasted from late July to early October, was delicious. As always with Otto, the accommodations were strictly first class, as were the food and drink. At night, the day's contretemps completely forgotten (by Otto if not always by those he had berated), Preminger was a world-class host, welcoming to all. And yet, despite the apparent extravagance, Preminger as always remained within the budget he had set. "*Bonjour Tristesse* was not a small movie," Martin Schute recalled. "It was a major production of a best seller—at the time, Sagan was the sun, the moon, and the stars—and I had told Otto before filming that his projected budget of one and a half million was much too low. We had a terrific row. But I was naive, because Otto could do what others couldn't. He brought the film in exactly as he had budgeted it—not a penny more."[51]

Having survived another round with Preminger, Jean Seberg after five months in France returned to Marshalltown in mid-October accompanied by her French fiancé, François Moreuil. More than ever she felt like an outsider, and her high school friends as well as her family regarded her with suspicion: was she, they wondered, a young woman who knew too much? She had had an extraordinary year of great good fortune mixed with brutalizing disappointment; under enormous pressure, she had persevered. But when she returned to Marshalltown, she was unemployed. Preminger had not mentioned any upcoming project and she had nothing to look forward to except the opening in January of her new film, for which she might have wondered if she would receive another barrage of withering notices. At nineteen, was she already played out? François tried to lift her spirits as she made plans to move to New York to take acting lessons.

Preminger opened *Bonjour Tristesse* on January 15, 1958, without any of the fanfare he had lavished on his earlier independent productions. In a rare miscalculation, he booked the film into the inappropriately mammoth Capitol Theatre on Broadway, a movie palace with a huge, wide screen and over four thousand seats. "The theater could easily have seated the entire cast of *Ben Hur,*" as Arthur Laurents recalled. ("I met Otto at '21' right after I had seen the film at the Moorish palace and I asked for my five dollars, because I didn't think Jean was any better in *Bonjour Tristesse* than she had been in *Saint Joan*. Otto laughed, but I don't remember whether or not he paid me.")[52] Geoffrey Horne also saw the film at the Capitol. "During a matinee opening week there were twenty-five people and acres of empty seats. I was on my way to a class with Lee Strasberg which was held above the theater."[53]

For both Preminger and Jean Seberg the reviews were unsparing. In the *New York Herald Tribune* William Zinsser wrote that "Mlle. Sagan's book is uniquely French, rueful and passionate, it is jaded in its view of sex, if not downright arch. But as directed by Otto Preminger it is as self-conscious as a game of charades played in an English country home. In the pivotal role, Jean Seberg is about as far from a French nymph as milk is from Pernod." In the *New York Times* Bosley Crowther wrote, "As a literary effort, it was somewhat astonishing but thin. The same must be said for the movie that Otto Preminger has made from it—with the astonishment excited for the most part by the ineptness with which it has been done." In his notice in the *Saturday Review,* Arthur Knight concluded that Preminger "apparently has not succeeded in convincing Miss Seberg that she is an actress." The *New Yorker'*s suggestion for her was "a good solid, and possibly therapeutic, paddling."[54]

Critical redemption arrived in March 1958, when, paradoxically, the film that American reviewers dismissed because it lacked a Gallic touch opened in France to a rapturous response. French critics saluted Preminger for his atmospheric handling of sun-baked settings and his treatment of characters with too much money and leisure time. Georges Périnal's Cinema-Scope lensing was hailed for its plein-air magnificence. And this time most Parisian critics were intoxicated by Jean Seberg. Christened "the new divine of the cinema," she appeared on the March cover of *Cahiers du cinéma*. Inside, in the most important review of her career, the young cinephile François Truffaut wrote about her performance and her screen presence with the kind of rhapsody that seems to be the exclusive province of besotted French critics. His ecstasy based on a misconception (he called the film "a love poem to [Jean Seberg] orchestrated by her fiancé"), Truffaut concluded that only a lover would be able "to obtain such perfection." "This kind of sex appeal hasn't been seen on the screen. It is designed, controlled to the nth degree by her director. When Jean Seberg is on the screen, which is all the time, you can't look at anything else."

Ironically, then, if Preminger on native grounds was dismissed as an impostor, to the French the Austrian-American director's approach to French material seemed revelatory. Not distracted by (and looking beyond) the assorted accents of the cast, Parisian critics credited Preminger with wise insights about the national psyche. Nearly three decades after its release, the film continued to exert the same hold, as an article by Jean-François Rauget in 1986 in *Cahiers du cinéma* revealed. "The genius of Preminger completely bursts with the discovery of a musicality in the movements of the bodies and the characters' consciousness. The film is some sort of abstract painting where the mixture of black and white with vivid colors, of a rocky and liquid nature with the psychological insignificance of the characters, brings forth a particular sensuality which Godard will remember for *Le mépris*."

If, on the one hand, *Bonjour Tristesse* is indeed far sturdier than the original American reception suggests, and, on the other, not quite the incandescent achievement that many Gallic cinephiles have claimed it to be, it definitely casts a spell. In spite or perhaps precisely because of her flaws, if you love Jean Seberg, then you must also love the film. Her performance, like Preminger's direction, is by turns problematic and sublime. In a strange way Jean's fragility as an actress—her constricted movements, her masked expression, her untrained yet distinctive voice, shivery and enchanting—mirrors Preminger's own inconsistency, his sometimes imperfect mastery of his own gifts. Seberg's stiffness on-screen echoes the occasionally stilted quality of Preminger's direction. No wonder he could not give up on her.

Seberg's near-delirious unevenness is displayed right at the beginning. On a dance floor in an underground Paris club her body language is self-conscious. Then, in a following shot, scrutinizing herself in a mirror as her eyes fill with tears of self-condemnation, she eloquently limns the despair of an already jaded young woman trapped in *la ronde*. Ultimately her performance as a remote beauty with a capacity for casual destructiveness is bewitching.

A good part of the film's visual enchantment derives from Preminger's recurrent use of dissolves between black-and-white and color. For scenes set in Paris in the present, with a melancholy Cécile brooding about her responsibility for the death of her father's fiancée as she moves aimlessly from one social event to the next, Preminger and Périnal use a slightly grainy black-and-white. For contrast, they shoot Cécile's memories of last summer on the Riviera in sumptuous color. "I suggested the dissolves, which provided fluidity, but it was Otto who added the brilliant touch of setting off black-and-white against color," Arthur Laurents recalled.[55] In the first dissolve to the past, as color gradually saturates the black-and-white image, the effect is stunning—the cinematic equivalent of a coup de théâtre. Much of the action takes place in a villa (the home of Pierre Lazareff, a publisher) perched spectacularly on a hilltop in Le Levandou overlooking the Mediterranean. As rendered by Georges Périnal's cinematography, the landscape—a pine forest next to the villa, the turquoise sea, rust-colored rocks along the shore—shimmers in a sparkling light.

Can a viewer drawn to the color and the bejeweled settings overlook the fact that Preminger's three leads are not remotely French? Yes, since in all other ways David Niven and Deborah Kerr are ideally cast, while Seberg is a case unto herself. Skeptical viewers can perhaps regard Niven and Kerr as English vacationers on the Riviera and Seberg, who sometimes sounds as if she is translating her lines from another language, as a cosmopolitan young woman who has traveled widely with her father. With his usual aplomb, Niven plays a confirmed roué. Seberg mirrors Niven's insouciant tone—it's clear that their entente, often visually underlined by the matching outfits they wear, could not possibly include anyone else. As embodied by Deborah Kerr, brittle, genteel Anne is an outsider who could never understand or accept the rules of their game.

Once again, Preminger takes a dispassionate view of neurotic, well-to-do characters. Nonetheless, while the film recalls the pattern set by *Laura,* it also anticipates Fellini's *La Dolce Vita* (1960) and Antonioni's *L'Avventura*

Anne (Deborah Kerr) looks uneasily at Cécile (Jean Seberg), the worldly young woman who will defeat her, in *Bonjour Tristesse*.

(1961), which also explore the alienation of the European upper bourgeoisie. The Italian films are far more ambitious than *Bonjour Tristesse,* but it was Preminger who first sensed the subject's potential.

The director's preference for wide-angle group shots gilds his chronicle of the easy life with a friezelike formality. It's significant that when Cécile begins to feel threatened by Anne, Preminger places Cécile outside the group, hovering uncomfortably at the edge of the frame or isolated in a frame of her own. Because Preminger uses close-ups rarely, they carry a particular charge. In an early scene in a Parisian nightclub he cuts between close-ups of Cécile dancing absently with a new beau and a singer, the world-weary Juliette Greco, performing the title song; the editing enforces a comparison between Cécile, confronting her *tristesse,* and the melancholy torch singer. For the climactic moment in which Cécile has contrived to have Anne overhear Raymond flirting with a former paramour, Preminger keeps the camera tight on Anne with no countershot to "the lovers." "I've always liked scenes where there's no dialogue—they're often, in film, more powerful," recalled Deborah Kerr. "When Anne overhears the off-screen conversation, she has this awful realization that Raymond is unfaithful, and you see its impact without my saying anything. I thought it was terrific that my character's big moment is conveyed without dialogue—just that close-up."[56]

The film ends on a close-up of Jean (shot on the last day of filming, October 9, 1957, at Shepperton Studios, where the actress's career had been launched with worldwide fanfare in January) that is a tour de force. Preminger wanted Seberg to be impassive, stripped of any readable expression, as she removes her makeup looking into a mirror. It is one of the beguiling paradoxes of this uneven, captivating film that, frozen-faced, her eyes filling with tears as Cécile faces a hollow future, Jean Seberg is intensely expressive. A cool, stylish beauty with ultra-chic, trendsetting short hair and wearing a smart black Givenchy cocktail dress, Jean Seberg in the last shot she was to make with her mentor looks like the real thing, a movie star who can also act.

In August 1958, eight months after *Bonjour Tristesse* bombed in America, François Moreuil persuaded Preminger to sell his contract with Jean to Columbia. "We simply had to get her out from under Otto's thumb," Moreuil, a lawyer, maintained.[57] Preminger, however, reserved the right to use Jean in one film a year. "Otto did not think at the time, or later, that Jean had been that bad in *Saint Joan,*" as Hope recalled, "and he certainly would have used her again if he had had a part for her. But as it turned out he didn't."

Witnesses have testified to Preminger's hard treatment of the unprepared young woman he had plucked from obscurity. He was, indeed, a demanding, impatient, and often wrathful mentor whose bullying tactics demolished her confidence. But no matter how many times he fulminated against her laziness and lack of focus, he also refused to give up on her. And on October 9, 1957, when she worked for him for the last time, she was a far stronger actress than she had been on January 7, when, in an apparent daze, she had shot the scene of Joan entering the court of the Dauphin. Otto Preminger made Jean Seberg famous, and perhaps only Jean could have told if her trial by fire had been worth it.

Without Preminger's belief that she could portray Sagan's character,

Seberg's improbable second career in European films would not have happened. Jean-Luc Godard, admiring the aura, "the sense of being" that Preminger had created for Jean in *Bonjour Tristesse,* cast her in *Breathless,* where her wonderfully relaxed performance as an American Circe who loves and betrays a French hood transformed her from a Hollywood has-been into a leading figure of the French New Wave. Preminger must be given full credit for delivering "Jean Seberg" to Jean-Luc Godard, but he cannot be held accountable for her later despair, her descent into drugs and radical black politics, and, at forty, looking preternaturally aged, her suicide.

"Otto was really thrilled by Jean's success in *Breathless,*" as Hope recalled. "He thought she was terrific in the film, and he was as proud of her as if she had been his daughter."[58] And after the film turned her into an international star, Preminger, vindicated at last, boasted, "I was right about Jean Seberg after all, wasn't I?"[59]

TEN

Censored!

In the first six months of 1958, after the successive failures of *Saint Joan* and *Bonjour Tristesse*, Otto Preminger's career as a pioneering independent filmmaker seemed to have stalled. Rather than a bullish producer who had won landmark victories for free speech, he was now perceived, in an industry with a notoriously short memory, as a European egghead who turned out stillborn art-house pictures.

Adding to the bad news was *This Is Goggle*, a play he put into rehearsal at the same time that *Bonjour Tristesse* was beginning its first-run engagements. "I recommended the novel to Otto," Sandy Gardner said. "It was a charming book, filled with local color, about an eccentric New York kid. Otto, who loved New York, was drawn to the New York atmosphere as well as to the story's father-son relationship, told from the point of view of the son."[1] The material did indeed stir Otto's paternal instincts—throughout his long estrangement from Mary he had continued to maintain a fatherly attitude toward Sandy; he wanted to claim his paternity of Erik; and at fifty-three, he might have wanted another son (or daughter) as well.

To play Goggle's parents Preminger hired two solid actors, James Daly and Kim Hunter, the original Stella in *A Streetcar Named Desire*. And for Goggle he chose an appealing child actor, London-born Michael Ray, making his stage debut after impressive film credits including leading roles in *The Divided Heart, The Brave One,* and *The Tin Star.* "I think Otto knew early on that the show wasn't going to work or that he wouldn't be able to make it work," Kim Hunter recalled.

> The focus of the show was the boy, Goggle, but I thought Otto wasn't saying the right things to the young actor—he wasn't saying what the boy needed to hear to help him play the part. I knew Otto's rep, of course, but I wasn't intimidated—I never am—and I told him how I thought he should approach the boy. He not only didn't scream, he was delighted to know, to get it right. (When Jim and I called him on his reputation for being a bastard, he replied, "I'm only that when people aren't doing what they're supposed to.")[2]

Preminger was also even-tempered with his scenic designer, Boris Aronson. "Boris and Otto got along royally," as Lisa (Mrs. Boris) Aronson recalled. "Boris didn't like to design realistically; he always wanted to try something stylized or off-center, and Otto went right along with him on that. But they didn't trust the simplicity of the material, and so they tried to make it visually interesting. They made the mistake of dressing it up, and the show was overdesigned and overdirected. Otto did not delude himself. He knew it wasn't working."[3]

Preminger did not seem "concentrated," according to Kim Hunter. "He was focused on his next film, on Jean Seberg, on whatever, but certainly not on us. He didn't talk about motivation or psychology. He was present, but he didn't offer much of anything. All in all, it was a strange experience that does not appear in my bio."[4]

Preminger had good reason to be distracted. "In early January, as he was starting to rehearse, Otto asked me to go to the Playhouse Theatre with him," Sandy recalled. "He was going to be negotiating for the lease of the theater, where *Goggle* was scheduled to open. [After tryouts in Princeton and Washington, D.C., the play was to open on Broadway on February 17, 1958; in the event, *This Is Goggle* opened at the McCarter Theatre in Princeton on January 23 and shuttered there on February 1.] He became very fatherly to me, and when he put his arm around me I realized that something was up. He said my mother would be suing for divorce."[5] Mr. and Mrs. Otto Preminger, alienated from each other for many years, had lived apart since April 20, 1957. By early 1958, Preminger was regularly seeing Hope Bryce, and Mary had for some time been involved with Michael Rennie. "It's my belief that the trouble really started when my mother started spending a lot of time with Rennie," Sandy speculated. "Like my mother, he was a painter and they had a lot in common. For Otto it was a status thing:

he felt that Rennie was only a contract player while he was a producer-director. He felt it was inappropriate for my mother to see Rennie, but she didn't think so. She was quite independent, and Otto did not appreciate that."[6]

Preminger had tried to negotiate a divorce settlement with Mary the preceding November, urging her, for the sake of peace, to accept the financial terms he was prepared to offer. But Mary was not inclined to. She wanted a lot more than Otto was willing to part with, and to get what she felt she was owed she was ready for a long, down-and-dirty battle. She wanted a healthy chunk of Otto's yearly income, which she estimated at $200,000, and she was demanding equitable division of all community property, which, under California law, she was entitled to share with her husband on a fifty-fifty basis. When she failed to receive financial satisfaction, she went public. In newspaper interviews she accused Otto of making "threatening phone calls," of removing "valuable art objects and financial records to New York to preclude enforcement of court orders," and of intimacy with three women, two London models and Hope Bryce, her former friend and roommate.[7]

On February 15, Otto "confided" to gossip columnist Louella Parsons that while it had been his intention to settle everything on a friendly basis, after Mary had drawn Hope into the proceedings he was now promising "a fight to the finish."[8] In an interview in the *Los Angeles Times* on March 6, he claimed that Mary had deserted *him* on October 23, 1956. He also denied the adultery charges and accused Mary of having been intimate with Michael Rennie for the past three years, providing evidence given to him by a private detective he had hired of trysts at the Malibu house that Mary was claiming as community property, two hotels, an apartment in New York, and one in Miami. He asked that all community property be awarded solely to him. To Mary's request of $3,000 a month, he made a counteroffer of $500; and rebutting Mary's claim that he earned $200,000 a year, he said the most money he had ever made in a year had been $93,000. He dismissed Mary's claim that she had a financial interest in *The Moon Is Blue*, while admitting that she had "some interest" in *The Court-Martial of Billy Mitchell* and *Bonjour Tristesse*, "which was not earning enough to cover production costs."[9]

The battle dragged on for months, with Mary repeatedly presenting an image of her estranged husband intended to cause him acute embarrassment. "His temper was so bad that he would beat his head on the floor and throw himself about the room," she said. "When he went into a rage, he would pound the wall and the furniture and he'd throw books and brushes at me, yelling and using bad language. He did not try to control himself in private or public. He stayed out nights and was constantly dating other women."[10] One of the women with whom Mary accused Otto of committing adultery was a former stripper in a Parisian boîte who sold her story of an alleged encounter with the director to two scandal sheets, *Confidential* and *Whisper.* Despite the escalating ugliness, Otto at the last moment withdrew his cross-complaint about Mary's affair with Michael Rennie, and he did not appear in court on March 10, 1958, when the divorce was granted. Mary was awarded a default decree and alimony of $171,000 to be distributed over a ten-year period, even if the former Mrs. Preminger were to remarry. In addition, Mary was awarded the house at 19300 Pacific Coast Highway, valued at $50,000; a New York apartment; and a 1955 Cadillac.

"It had been such a bitter and prolonged divorce—and so unnerving," Sandy recalled.

> Detectives were sent to the beach to watch the house. And I was forced to testify against Otto; I didn't want to, and my mom didn't want me to, but the attorney wanted me to. It was disturbing, even though Mary had been divorced before and I guess in some way I was used to it. It turned out the economic rewards of the marriage didn't amount to much. Otto's power managed to buy off our attorney, Arthur Crowley, called "the attorney to the stars," who sided with Otto and didn't do a good job for my mother. But that's the way the business worked: that was part of the corruption of Hollywood. My mother and I remained at 19300 Pacific Coast Highway for twenty-four years. Otto had put down $3,000 at my mother's request and we sold it for $400,000. The new owner remodeled and a year later sold it for one and a half million. The house is still standing, but I haven't been back since 1985.[11]

To Sandy Gardner, far more significant than the "economic rewards" of his mother's marriage was Otto's abrupt disappearance from his life. After the divorce he never saw Otto, for whom he had warm feelings he had thought were reciprocal, or any of the Preminger family again. "I used to wonder: did Otto have to divorce me too? During the divorce my mother spoke negatively about Otto; she resented the fact that he didn't take her work seriously and that he was to be the only one in the family with a career. But in later years she would speak about how much she admired him and how much she had learned from him. She still loved him."[12] (Mary was to remain single until her death, at eighty, on August 29, 1998.)

"The Premingers had drawn together against us, and I'm sure harsh things were said at the time of the divorce and later," Sandy surmised.[13] Indeed they were. In a most ungentlemanly fashion, Otto in his memoir dismissed Mary in a few bare sentences. "I married Mary Gardner on the fourth of December, 1951. We were divorced in 1958. A forgettable marriage."[14] "I didn't like Mary Gardner, and the less said the better," Ingo Preminger stated, allowing no space for further discussion.[15] "Until he found Hope, it was hard to judge Otto's taste in women," Eve Preminger said. "Mary was tall and thin, vapid, boring, and dumb. She had a two-year-old mind. Horrible things had gone on between them and long after their breakup she told me how sexy and romantic Otto was in *Stalag 17*. It was absurd. She was an absence: she wasn't even pretty."[16]

Preminger as always looked ahead, and while in rehearsal for the ill-fated *This Is Goggle* he bought the screen rights to two novels, *Mardios Beach* by Oakley Hall, about the romantic escapades of a married man, and *The Wounds of Hunger* by Luis Spota, about bullfighting (an unlikely Preminger subject). He announced that the former title would go into production in the spring; and the latter was to be shot in the late summer in Mexico in both English and Spanish versions. Otto, however, dropped both projects when, with a great deal of cunning, he nabbed the screen rights to three red-hot properties. First up was *Les voies du salut* (*The Ways of Salvation*), a new novel by Pierre Boulle, author of *The Bridge on the River Kwai*. In mid-April, before the novel had been published in France and before it even had an American title, Preminger flew to Paris to work out the terms of the sale. He guaranteed a payment of $150,000 for the novel (the American title was to be the not-so-enticing *The Other Side of the Coin*). Otto was drawn to the novel's exotic setting, a rubber plantation in Malaysia, and its political framework—the nineteen-year-old heroine is a devout Communist. But his primary motive was to grab the book before Sam Spiegel, who had made a fortune with his film of *The Bridge on the River Kwai,* was able to. Acting on "an important tip," the equivalent of insider trading in the literary market-place, Preminger made the trip to Paris "in strictest secrecy," as Willi Frischauer reported. Spiegel "did not relish being pipped at the post, and his friendship with Preminger came to an end. Spiegel would not talk to his old friend, who took the rebuff badly."[17]

While he was in Paris Otto also scrambled to obtain the screen rights to a current best seller, *Anatomy of a Murder,* a courtroom drama based on a true story by a Michigan Supreme Court justice, John Voelker, writing under the pen name of Robert Traver. The property already had a tangled history. In August 1957, six months before the book was to be published, and as Otto was on the Riviera filming *Bonjour Tristesse*, his New York story editor Tom Ryan had read the galleys and recognized at once that the material was a perfect fit for his boss. He sent an enthusiastic report to Preminger in Cannes, urging him to buy the book. But Preminger was preoccupied trying to scream a performance out of Jean Seberg, and both the stage and screen rights were snapped up by others. As expected, the novel had a sensational sale. While he was in Paris in April 1958 outfoxing Spiegel, however, Otto read in a trade paper that the movie rights to *Anatomy of a Murder* might still be on the market; this time he acted with the speed of lightning. But after he announced his purchase of the property, three other producers, claiming title to the stage rights, threatened lawsuits. Undaunted, Otto began to plan his film as soon as he returned from Paris. In late spring he visited John Voelker in the Upper Peninsula of Michigan, the rugged landscape where the novel was set, and decided to shoot the entire film on location.

At the same time he also laid plans for filming the Boulle novel. On May 10, with his production manager Martin Schute and his screenwriter, A. E. Hotchner, he departed for Kuala Lumpur to visit a plantation similar to the one that was the setting of the novel. "Leo Jaffe, head of Columbia [the film's distributor], who had warned me about Otto, and who used to sit in fear of him, said, 'Go with our blessing,' " Schute recalled. "But Otto was a wonderful traveling companion, even when he realized that Kuala Lumpur, which had none of the high style he seemed to require, was not exactly to his liking."[18] When one of the planters Preminger spoke to began talking about snakes, Preminger's face, as Frischauer reported, "grew paler and paler. Finally he confessed: 'I've had one phobia since childhood— snakes!' "[19] Returned from the scouting expedition, Preminger was less interested in *The Other Side of the Coin*. He was disappointed at the direction Hotchner's script was taking and concerned about weather conditions at the time when he was planning to begin shooting, in February 1959. Otto canceled the project "for technical difficulties," which may have been true enough. But the underlying reason may have been because, in addition to *Anatomy*, he acquired another property that potentially was even more of a blockbuster than *The Other Side of the Coin*.

On May 25, 1958, soon after he had returned from the Far East, he announced that he had purchased the screen rights to *Exodus*, a novel by Leon Uris about the birth of Israel to be published by Doubleday on September 18. Visiting Ingo in Los Angeles in April, Otto had noticed a manuscript of monumental length on his brother's desk. He was interested immediately when Ingo told him the subject, and that night, although Ingo warned him that MGM held the rights, Otto began to read Uris's book. "I read until five o'clock the next morning," he remembered. "I could not put the book down. Before I was halfway through I knew I had to make the movie."[20] As soon as he returned to New York, Preminger launched a campaign to win the rights from MGM, and he was in a good position to do so. Several years earlier, in an unusual arrangement, Ingo, who had been Uris's agent at the time, had persuaded Dore Schary, then head of production at MGM, to take an option on his client's proposal, at that point no more than a rough outline. Further, Ingo had convinced Schary to underwrite some of the author's research expenses. "Since Uris was a dedicated Jew I suggested he go to Israel for research," Ingo recalled. "I went to MGM for financing, and in exchange we gave them an option to acquire the rights for $75,000. Uris went to Israel and wrote the book, which I brought in manuscript to MGM."[21] But by the end of the more than three years it had taken Uris for research and writing, Schary was no longer at the studio, and, as Otto was pleased to find out, Schary's successors were not enthusiastic about Uris's partisan and politically controversial novel. "If you make it the Arab countries will close all MGM theaters and ban all MGM films," Preminger warned the company president, Joseph Vogel. "You can't afford an Arab boycott but I can. Since I am an independent producer, they can't hurt me too much."[22] Vogel hesitated, but Otto's argument must have sounded a warning note, since within a week he and Ingo were asked to make an offer. Otto maintained that he and his brother paid MGM the amount MGM had paid Uris: $75,000, a terrific deal, because the author's price would certainly have risen steeply after September 1958 when the book zoomed to the top of best-seller lists.

Preminger was elated. Leon Uris most definitely was not. "Ingo was working for me as my agent at the time, and I woke up one morning to find out that Otto now had the rights," Uris recalled over forty years later.[23] "Ingo stole the property from Metro and gave it to Otto, and I got a royal fucking from the Preminger brothers, who were a couple of Viennese thieves. I have never spoken about it, and I have a fifty-year reputation to consider, so I'm ambivalent about saying anything at all. But it was a monstrous experience. Otto was a terrorist—he's Arafat, a Nazi, Saddam Hussein—who never knew the difference between lying and not lying."

Ingo offered a differing account of the transactions. "MGM turned the book down because of the Arab issue and because they felt it was too unfriendly to England. Then, *after* discussing it with Uris, who said fine, I went to Otto. We all made money. Without me, the picture wouldn't have been made."[24]

Armed with the rights, Preminger went to his former colleague Arthur

Krim at United Artists. Krim, who was keen on the project because his wife Matilda was a research scientist at the Weizmann Institute of Science in Rehovot, Israel, offered Preminger about $3.5 million in backing. The sum was low, but Preminger knew he could stay within the budget.

His battles to secure the rights to *Exodus* and *Anatomy of a Murder* over, Otto in July 1958 chose the relatively unknown Wendell Mayes to adapt the Traver novel and in his usual way began working with the writer on a daily basis. At this point, in what was already the busiest time of his career, Otto received an offer from Samuel Goldwyn to direct a film of George Gershwin and DuBose Heyward's 1935 black folk opera, *Porgy and Bess.* Although Otto was eager to get *Anatomy* before the cameras as quickly as possible—the book was still selling and he was certain his film would end his recent string of failures—he felt he could not decline Goldwyn's offer. For years he had himself wanted to make a film of *Porgy and Bess.* But along with many other Hollywood troubadours, including Hal Wallis, Arthur Freed, Joseph L. Mankiewicz, Anatol Litvak, Dore Schary, Louis B. Mayer, and Harry Cohn (who had had the mad notion of casting Al Jolson, Rita Hayworth, and Fred Astaire in blackface), Preminger had haggled unsuccessfully for the rights. George Gershwin's brother Ira, who had worked with DuBose Heyward on the lyrics, had firmly rejected all overtures for twenty-five years because he "feared [the work would be] debased in Hollywood hands."[25] But when Goldwyn agreed to his stiff terms—$650,000 as a down payment against 10 percent of the film's gross earnings—Ira was finally persuaded. However, he and his wife Leonore (known as Lee) would never have sold their prized property for any amount of money unless they had had faith in the buyer. And for good reason they trusted Samuel Goldwyn. On May 8, 1957, Goldwyn, who had been lobbying Ira for years, had proudly announced that at long last he had finally succeeded where many others had failed: he had acquired the screen rights to *Porgy and Bess,* his favorite show. In the same press release he had also stated that the film would be his farewell, the climax to a long career as a producer that had included, among many other movies, *Wuthering Heights* (1939), *The Little Foxes* (1941), and *The Best Years of Our Lives* (1946).

In light of the fact that *Porgy and Bess* surely had no greater chance than *Saint Joan* for commercial success, Samuel Goldwyn's persistence and that of many other prominent Hollywood entrepreneurs is astonishing. The original Broadway production, performed with all of Gershwin's passages of recitative, closed after a disappointing 124 performances. A 1942 revival, stripped of recitative, fared better, as did an international tour. But in financial terms the piece had a far from robust track record. Based on a 1925 novel and a 1927 play, both written by DuBose Heyward, *Porgy and Bess* is set in a teeming black ghetto, Catfish Row, in the white author's hometown of Charleston, South Carolina. The title characters are, respectively, a crippled beggar and a drug-taking prostitute. The supporting characters are superstitious, hard-drinking, drug-addled, lusty, and violent ghetto dwellers. *Porgy and Bess,* in short, presents a view of black life open to the charge of racist stereotyping. And as if that were not discouragement enough, Gershwin's groundbreaking work has engendered a still extant debate about whether its primary musical allegiance is to the opera house or to the commercial musical theater. But overriding all concerns, as it had for Goldwyn and the other Hollywood figures who wanted to turn it into a film, was the fact that George Gershwin's score, which closes the distance between elitist and popular musical idioms as it mixes elements of jazz, blues, spirituals, gospel, American folk music, European opera, Tin Pan Alley, and musical comedy, is arguably the greatest ever composed for the American lyric stage.

Once he had secured the rights to the prized property, Goldwyn, as always, proceeded to approach the best possible collaborators. But he received many rejections. To write the screenplay, his first choice (a sign that he intended to be sensitive to racial issues) had been Langston Hughes, the black poet who was one of the leading figures of the Harlem Renaissance. Hughes spurned the offer, as did a succession of playwrights including Sidney Kingsley, Clifford Odets, and Paul Osborn. Finally, N. Richard Nash, most noted as the author of *The Rainmaker,* had accepted, and by the end of 1957 had turned in an overlong screenplay. To direct, Goldwyn had asked, and was turned down by, Elia Kazan, Frank Capra, and King Vidor. Although Goldwyn had had reservations, he had signed Rouben Mamoulian, the director of the original play, *Porgy,* as well as the 1935 Broadway opera.

Adhering to his long-established belief in star casting, Goldwyn had pursued the best-known black actors of the time, regardless of whether they could sing the roles. (As in *Carmen Jones,* the stars' singing voices were dubbed.) Again, he encountered resistance. Harry Belafonte, his first choice for Porgy, rejected the offer because he felt the material was racially demeaning. Reluctantly, and only because Goldwyn cornered him into it, Sidney Poitier agreed to play the role. (Goldwyn, still capable of formidable wheeling and dealing, pulled strings so that in order to play a part the actor wanted in *The Defiant Ones* as an escaped prisoner chained to a white man, Poitier was obliged first to appear as Porgy.) Committed at the time to playing only affirmative characters, Poitier disdained the role of a crippled beggar as well as the depiction of Negro life in Catfish Row.

Between shots of *Porgy and Bess:* Dorothy Dandridge, Sidney Poitier, and Brock Peters.

Goldwyn's first and only choice to play Bess was Otto's Carmen, Dorothy Dandridge, who said yes but was unenthusiastic. Although Otto and Dorothy had not been seeing each other romantically for over a year, they were still in touch, and when Otto heard Dorothy had been offered the role he urged her to take it. "Do it. It'll make you as big a star as you were when you did Carmen," he told her.[26] For other roles, Goldwyn raided the cast of *Carmen Jones,* all of whom in 1950s Hollywood had found few other opportunities. Brock Peters, Diahann Carroll, and Pearl Bailey signed, but each had a list of objections. Bailey resented the script's use of heavy dialect and threatened she wouldn't appear if the women had to wear bandannas. Only one actor, Sammy Davis Jr., a card-carrying member of Frank Sinatra's Rat Pack and a smug, brash, hard-drinking nightclub crooner with an oppressively energetic performing style, was eager to appear in the film. Davis was desperate to play Sportin' Life, a drug-dealing low-life—Satan in Catfish Row—who has two show-stopping Broadway-style numbers, and he arranged to audition for Goldwyn at a party at Judy Garland's house. Lee Gershwin saw him perform at the party and was horrified by Davis's vulgarity. Famous for speaking her mind, Lee cornered Goldwyn. "Swear on your life you'll never use him," she pleaded with the producer. "Him? That monkey?" Goldwyn sneered.[27] Davis was aware that Goldwyn wanted Cab Calloway, and he got Sinatra and his Mafia entourage to put pressure on Goldwyn. After Calloway turned him down, Goldwyn relented. "Mr. Davis, you are Sportin' Life," he informed the actor. "The part is yours. Now will you get all these guys off my back?"[28]

For the sets Goldwyn hired Oliver Smith, an acclaimed theatrical designer. For costumes he turned to Irene Sharaff, whose background was also primarily theatrical. André Previn, with extensive experience scoring films for MGM, was given the crucial job of musical director. During the lengthy preproduction period Goldwyn and Rouben Mamoulian, opposites in almost every way, had many collisions. Mamoulian was articulate; the malaprop-prone Goldwyn was tongue-tied. As N. Richard Nash observed, Mamoulian "got into the habit of scoffing at everything Sam had to say."[29] To their temperamental difference was added an artistic disagreement. Goldwyn wanted the film to look and sound as much as possible like the original Broadway production, whereas the director had no interest in re-creating his original staging. It was his intention to transform a stage work into a fluid, realistic film that he wanted to shoot on location in and around Charleston.

After months of elaborate planning Goldwyn announced that full-cast rehearsals would begin on July 3 at 9 a.m. on the cavernous Stage 8 of his studio. At six that morning, a phone call to his house informed the producer that a fire had destroyed the Catfish Row set and all the costumes. That afternoon, a remarkably composed Goldwyn gathered together the entire cast and crew to assure them that the set would be rebuilt and the production would resume. Unsubstantiated rumors circulated that the NAACP, presumably in protest against the film's treatment of black characters, had started the fire. Although the fact that the fire had occurred in the early morning when the studio was empty seemed to point to arson rather than accident, the cause of the fire has never been determined.

During the hiatus (Goldwyn anticipated it would be about six weeks), Mamoulian continued to press for an opened-up, plein-air version of *Porgy and Bess*. Goldwyn's huffy response was to order Nash to reduce the number of settings in his screenplay. At the end of July, paying him his entire salary of $75,000, Goldwyn fired his director. Adding insult to injury, the next day at twice the sum he hired Otto Preminger. "I was Otto's agent for *Porgy and Bess* and carried out the mechanics of the deal," said Ingo.[30] Although he worked out a highly lucrative salary for his brother, Ingo in his talks with Goldwyn couldn't reach a figure on Otto's profit participation. Ingo pushed for 50 percent, Preminger's standard terms; Goldwyn offered 10 percent. When negotiations were at an impasse, with Goldwyn refusing to raise his offer, Otto backed off, telling Ingo to allow Goldwyn to decide on the participation after the film was completed. "Goldwyn was surprised and promised to be fair," Otto said.[31]

In mid-August Otto relocated to Los Angeles for preproduction and rehearsals. From the moment he arrived he was under fire. Mamoulian, no doubt recalling that Preminger had replaced him on *Laura,* took his case to the Directors' Guild, charging Goldwyn with firing him for "frivolous, spiteful or dictatorial reasons not pertinent to the director's skill or obligation." The Guild determined that until the matter was settled Preminger "may not enter into a contract with Samuel Goldwyn."[32] At first, there was a great deal of sympathy for Mamoulian and very little for Otto. But Mamoulian made a fatal error. He produced a bit actor, Leigh Whipper, who announced he was withdrawing because of his opposition to Preminger, "a man who has no respect for my people."[33] As performers who had worked with Otto on *Carmen Jones* testified, the charge of racism against Preminger was absurd and completely unsustainable. After Mamoulian's agent, Irving Lazar, admitted that his client "had grossly misrepresented the facts in the case,"[34] the aggrieved director had no choice but to end his campaign.

Goldwyn, relieved to be rid of Mamoulian, treated his new director with deference. But once Preminger began to voice some of the same concerns Mamoulian had, the producer's attitude changed. Like Mamoulian, Otto, as he had with *Carmen Jones,* wanted to transform a stage-bound opera into a realistic story with music to be shot entirely on location. "I think this sort of film calls for the smell of reality," he stated.[35] While Goldwyn was decreeing a reverential approach to Gershwin, with the score to be presented as preserved-in-amber musical treasures, Preminger was asking for orchestrations favoring jazz over symphonic arrangements and intending to embed the songs within the action rather than framing them as separable show-stopping numbers.

Once he realized that Goldwyn was determined to have the entire film shot in his own studio, Otto began to raise objections to the theatrical-looking sets by Oliver Smith and the too-fancy costumes by Irene Sharaff. "Look," he scolded the producer, "you've got a two-dollar whore in a two-thousand-dollar dress."[36] Producer and director, equally stubborn, had daily run-ins, and Otto's bellicose voice reverberated throughout the lot.

Although he seemed to be losing the war to a formidable adversary who also happened to be footing the bill, Preminger, in a series of underground moves, tried to puncture the producer's "make it beautiful" demands. Behind Goldwyn's back, Otto ordered some of the crew, after hours, to repaint the sets and to mangle the costumes. Preminger was adamant on one point, however, making it a condition of his employment: he insisted on the right to shoot a picnic scene on location (on Venice Island near Stockton, California). No doubt eager to get the project under way at last, Goldwyn assented.

Locked in daily skirmishes with his boss, most nights Otto met with Wendell Mayes to work on the screenplay of *Anatomy of a Murder*. Goldwyn, too, was busy on other fronts. At seventy-seven, the elder statesman among Hollywood producers could not understand the fury that his beloved *Porgy and Bess* was causing in the black community. The way he saw it, Gershwin's glorious music ennobled the characters and the setting. He was puzzled and hurt when an anonymous article in a local black newspaper attacked him after he held a press conference in which he attempted to address the concerns of the Negro community. "Mr. Goldwyn smiled in gentle reproof that we should feel we knew more about being colored than he does, or that we would feel that a colored writer, like John O. Killens or Langston Hughes, could come anywhere near preparing a workable script for a Samuel Goldwyn picture. Directly after earlier blasts at Goldwyn for his plans to make this piece of ante-bellum gingerbread," the article continued, "the producer gave a thousand dollars to the local NAACP drive. Rather like blood-money, wouldn't you think?" "The only thing left to go wrong on this picture," Goldwyn said, "is for me to go to jail."[37]

When he heard that Preminger was replacing Mamoulian, Brock Peters was "thunderstruck." The actor recalled:

> I was insecure about playing Crown, a hunk who has Bess in his sexual grip, because I didn't think I was physically right for it. But Mamoulian had helped me and I was gaining in confidence. With Otto directing, I was sure I would be fired—I thought he would remember me as the young buck who had tried to jump at him on *Carmen*. And when I saw Woody Strode on the lot—Woody was stunning-looking, strapping, an ideal choice to play Crown—I knew I was finished. I dreaded going to the first day of rehearsal with Otto. "Now I get it," I thought. But instead, in a completely friendly tone, Otto said, "Hello, Brock, how are you?" Boy, was I relieved![38]

At the prospect of working with her erstwhile lover, Dorothy Dandridge was plainly horrified. She still had powerful feelings—attraction coiled with repulsion—for Otto. On the one hand she remained intensely grateful for all that he had done for her and taught her; on the other, she was bitter about how the affair had ended. Her manager, Earl Mills, claimed that Dorothy had become pregnant and Otto had urged her to have an abortion. "In my biography of Dorothy I left it ambiguous about the abortion and Otto's paternity, but because Mills was so specific with me I am convinced it was true," Donald Bogle said. "Regardless, however, considering their affair was over, and that Dorothy had liked working with Mamoulian, Otto's coming on the film was bad news for her. Very bad news."[39]

"No one could be more fully forewarned than I was about [Otto] and by him," Dorothy recalled.

> He told me why he was tough on a set, and tough with others, and tough in all his dealings. "Don't show kindness," he said. "People will construe that as weakness, and they'll take advantage of you." "Don't show kindness": what a key to Hollywood success. It never occurred to me that one day he would be as tough about me. . . . In a way I felt a certain compassion for him. Out of his own hurt, whatever it was, he had fashioned his own drives. Otto was ugly. Truly ugly. Many of those little men who run Hollywood are ugly. . . . I think now that Otto never loved and never was loved. . . . He could have been afraid of it. Love would weaken his essential conviction about toughness as the way, the truth, and the life.[40]

Otto's feelings for Dorothy were much less complicated than hers for him. He had ended the relationship not because he had ceased caring for her but because he knew he would not be able to marry her, as Dorothy repeatedly requested. Dorothy's being black was not an issue for a man with Otto's willful temperament—to prove a point, he might almost have married her *because* she was black. The obstacle was Dorothy's tormented psyche. Professionally Otto clearly was drawn to working with wounded beauties, but for his wives he chose women who were far more secure and self-possessed and who, unlike Dorothy, or Jean Seberg or Maggie McNamara, were not remotely suicidal. Even if Otto had been in turmoil about Dorothy, however, he had a far greater capacity than she did for separating his private life from his professional obligations.

For the first week of the three full weeks of rehearsals that he requested,

Otto, tactful with everyone, seemed to treat Dorothy with special consideration. He could see she was having trouble with the role—she was blurry and hesitant—but he had confidence in her. When after two weeks Dorothy didn't seem to be making any progress, his "famous temper was directed as fully upon me as I had been spared it in *Carmen Jones*," as Dandridge reported. "Now I was the idiot. . . . I was doing this wrong, that wrong. . . . He lit into me. 'You were rotten in [*The Decks Ran Red*, a minor film released while *Porgy and Bess* was in rehearsals],' he stormed for all to hear. The old romance was now as cold as iced cucumbers."[41]

Dorothy, lacking the self-assurance or the stamina to fight back, crumbled. And as on *Carmen Jones*, she often spent her time away from the camera isolated in her dressing room. Then, her coplayers had viewed her retreats as aloofness; now they saw her disappearances as the behavior of a victim wounded in battle and retiring to gather strength enough to withstand the next attack. "Dorothy was the most vulnerable member of the cast," Sidney Poitier observed. "Preminger smelled this, and she became sacrifice number one. Her defense mechanism was that of the prey, and the predator had selected her, staked her out, marked her for the kill, then struck without warning."[42] Finally, at a point when Dorothy had two days off, a group of actors led by Nichelle Nichols, a member of the ensemble, confronted Preminger. "The actors ate him alive," Nichols recalled. "He knew he had a mutiny on his hands. . . . We told him to treat [Dorothy] differently. . . . She was our queen, and it demeaned *us* to see this man attempt to destroy her every day. Everyone knew they had had a relationship. After the meeting, he was more respectful of us. He was a little more respectful of Dorothy. At least, she was able to get through [the filming] in a more respectful way."[43] Brock Peters maintained, however, that Preminger "never found a really kind way to talk to Dorothy."[44]

In addition to her fear of the director, Dandridge had difficulty performing intimate scenes with her dark-skinned costars. When Preminger asked her to stroke Poitier's head, she hesitated. Some of the cast felt that Dorothy, whose attraction to white men was well known, was reluctant to touch a black man. Others believed she was simply being sensitive to her costar's dignity. However, a few days before shooting the scene in which Crown rapes Bess, Dorothy called Preminger to ask him to replace Brock Peters. "I can't stand that man. When he puts his hands on me I can't bear it. And—and—and he's so black!" Preminger interpreted her statement as "the tragedy of Dorothy Dandridge. She was divorced from a black man who had fathered her retarded child. From then on she avoided black men."[45]

As he was lining up the shots for the rape scene, Preminger took Peters aside to tell him that Dorothy was having trouble with him. "Otto told me that Dorothy didn't think I was 'right' and he implied that my skin color was the problem," Peters recalled.

> He assured me, though, that I was doing well in the role and that I was to disregard any outburst from Dorothy. We completed the scene without incident, and both at the time and even now so many years later, I questioned Otto's intention. Was that Otto's way of getting what he needed from me in the scene? Did he really think Dorothy would explode at me? I don't know. I've never figured it out. I guess it could have been a color issue. Dorothy *never* mentioned being black, and on *Ed Sullivan* she said she was Cherokee. Although I didn't know the reason, when we were on *Carmen Jones* Dorothy had been distinctly unfriendly to me, but on *Porgy and Bess* her attitude seemed to soften. And after we filmed the rape scene, on location in Stockton, we shared a plane ride to Los Angeles during which we talked personally and I felt I began to know her for the first time. I saw how lonely and insecure she was. A lot of the things in her life, certainly including her color, affected her negatively, and I have to say that her suicide was not a mystery to me.[46]

Unlike Dandridge, Sidney Poitier had no trace of the victim in his bearing. Early on, when Preminger exploded at him, the actor walked off the set and would not return until Preminger apologized. Otto said he was sorry, and realizing he could not raise his voice to Poitier, never again did. "Otto *could* control himself," as Brock Peters observed. Poitier achieved another victory when, without discussing it with the director, he refused to speak in the exaggerated, ungrammatical dialect that N. Richard Nash had written, following the style of the original novel and libretto. "We all used Sidney's intelligent performance as our model," Brock Peters said. "He set the example for how we spoke—no 'dems,' 'dese,' 'dose.' We were determined not to demean ourselves and language was one way to keep it straight up, to avoid caricature. Otto never tried to correct us, or to force us to go back to the dialect; I suspect he wasn't attuned to hearing dialects anyway."[47]

While his relations with his two stars remained prickly, Otto enjoyed working with the other principals. He had noisy run-ins with Sammy Davis Jr., fully able to defend himself. "I felt Sammy and Otto had fun yelling at each other," Peters noted. "I think it was a way for both to let off steam. Sammy seemed to be having fun with the part, and with life."[48] "Otto loved Pearl Bailey to pieces, and so did I," as Hope Bryce recalled. "We thought she was Mother Earth."[49] But as she had been on *Carmen Jones,* Bailey was decidedly unpopular with the cast. As Brock Peters affirmed, "Pearl was two-faced and we all saw that she was competitive with Dorothy. For good reason Dorothy disliked Pearl, and distrusted her."[50]

Embroiled with his actors during the day and working most nights with Wendell Mayes on the script of *Anatomy of a Murder,* Preminger was also busy blocking interference from Samuel Goldwyn. "He didn't contribute one useful thought or word of advice throughout the entire production," Otto maintained. "He only knew always to buy the best. He bought William Wyler, he bought the best writers and actors . . . for the cheapest money. . . . He had an awful way of testing people, a cold-blooded, very egotistical man, always afraid of people."[51] Otto surmised that "much of Goldwyn's curious behavior was due to the fact that he didn't understand the technical side of filmmaking." For instance, *Porgy and Bess* was being shot in 70 mm film and Goldwyn became perturbed when Preminger told him it was not going to be shot in 35 mm as well. "I tried to explain: pictures shot in 70 mm are printed down in the lab to 35 mm. You don't have to shoot two versions. He couldn't grasp it."[52]

Goldwyn may have been ignorant about how films were made, but watching the dailies he noticed that most of Otto's shots were boom and master shots; that there were no close-ups; and that entire scenes played out with no editing at all. Deliberately, Otto was including no extra footage or coverage for Goldwyn to tamper with. "In his sly way," as the Goldwyn biographer Arthur Marx noted, Preminger was "cutting the picture as he shot it—right in the camera."[53] When Goldwyn challenged him, Preminger erupted, declaring that he was the director and would shoot the film as he saw fit. He issued a warning: if Goldwyn did not stop interfering, he would walk off the film. Goldwyn tolerated Preminger's high-handed treatment, as Otto expected he would, because the producer could not take the chance of dismissing a second director. "His reputation as a fair employer really would be in ruins if Preminger walked off," as Arthur Marx wrote. "And so Sam swallowed his pride and remained holed up in his office, barely speaking to Preminger when he bumped into him on the lot."[54]

When principal photography was completed on December 16, 1958, Goldwyn, Preminger, and the cast were immensely relieved. At the wrap party Goldwyn was a serene host, smiling benevolently and praising Preminger as a brilliant director. Sly fox Sam, however, may have claimed the last laugh. Before the film was to be released, Ingo inquired about the profit participation for Otto that had remained unsettled at the time the contract had been signed. When Ingo reminded Goldwyn that they had left the amount up to him, Goldwyn snapped, "You left the participation up to me? So there is no participation."[55]

The response to the film after the screening for executives at Columbia (the releasing studio) was far from enthusiastic. "One of the top people at Columbia came up to Otto after the screening to express concern about the downbeat ending," Hope Bryce recalled. " 'Can't you have Porgy get up and walk at the end?' he asked. Otto thought that was so typical of the Hollywood mentality."[56] But Goldwyn, undeterred, and every bit the showman that Preminger was, went ahead with his original plan of presenting his farewell production in hard-ticket, two-a-day screenings at a handful of opulent movie palaces. Offering his beloved *Porgy and Bess* in a dignified atmosphere, Goldwyn wanted audiences to behave as if they were going to the legitimate theater or the opera house, with gentlemen in coat and tie, and for the ladies dresses rather than slacks.

Samuel Goldwyn opened the film on June 25, 1959, at the Warner Theatre on Broadway, the house where *The Jazz Singer* had premiered in 1927 and where Cinerama was first presented in 1952. On July 5, *Porgy and Bess* opened in Los Angeles at the resplendent Carthay Circle Theater, the site of many Golden Age premieres, including the one in 1939 for *Gone with the Wind*. (*Around the World in 80 Days* had only recently concluded a run at the theater of two and a half years, the longest exclusive engagement in the history of American film exhibition. The Carthay Circle was so refined that its doors remained closed when there wasn't a film deemed important enough to be shown on its expansive, curved screen.)

"A stunning, exciting, and moving film," wrote Bosley Crowther, not usually a Preminger enthusiast, in the *New York Times*. "It bids fair to be as much a classic on the screen as it is on the stage." No other reviewer concurred, and on virtually every aspect of the film reaction was mixed. Some reviewers hailed Preminger's direction as immaculate; others accused it of being stage-bound. Sidney Poitier was both admired and criticized for his dignified Porgy; Dorothy Dandridge both applauded and derided for her ladylike Bess. Oliver Smith's sets, the removal of dialect, the stylized color and lighting, the Todd-AO wide screen, the six-track stereo sound—each was either saluted or roundly condemned. It seemed as if no two reviewers had seen the same film. Almost every critic liked something about the film, but none approved of everything. Even George Gershwin was not immune. According to an anonymous scribe in the July 20 *London Observer*, "the work fails—this is heresy—because George Gershwin's music is not inventive enough or robust enough to support a full-length opera." When it opened in Atlanta, *Porgy and Bess* angered some black viewers, and a still mystified Goldwyn decided to pull his film, incurring the accusation that he was censoring his own picture. "For a film that is neither controversial nor inflammatory the studio's action [of canceling the Atlanta run] looks like excessive timidity or excellent press agentry," the *Atlanta Journal* huffed on August 11.

Following reserved-seat long runs in major cities, *Porgy and Bess* was shown only briefly in general release. In the end the film earned back only half its sizable $7 million cost. After a few television screenings in the 1970s, it became unavailable, and at this writing, as it has been for nearly four decades, the Goldwyn-Preminger *Porgy and Bess* is "forbidden," in effect a censored property. Only a few prints survive (most in private collections) and none is in prime condition. *Porgy and Bess* as it was exhibited in its original road-show version in lush color, six-track magnetic stereo, and Todd-AO, apparently exists no longer. It is indeed an indefensible fate that the troubled film has suffered, and an ironic one, too, in view of the fact that a work by Otto Preminger, a filmmaker who fought landmark battles against censorship, has in this instance been the object of the ultimate censorship of invisibility. Opposition of the Gershwin estate, rumored to have been displeased with the dubbing and with the treatment of the score; fear of militant black reprisals; a mysterious clause in Samuel Goldwyn's will—each has been circulated as an explanation for the film's disappearance.

Perhaps because he wanted to keep costs down, perhaps because, at the time, he did not have an eye on posterity, Goldwyn bought only a fifteen-year lease of the rights. After that, the film could not be shown without the permission of the authors or their estates; and if they granted permission, the estates would have to be handsomely compensated. In 1972, when his father's lease expired, Samuel Goldwyn Jr. tried to obtain permission from the Gershwin and Heyward estates to rerelease the film and was turned down. Shamefully, the Gershwin estate over the years has continued to veto requests to make the film available again. Surely, whatever their objections, the estate has a moral responsibility to ensure that viewers have the opportunity to come to their own conclusions about this still contested work. As Donald Bogle noted,

> There has been a curiosity among blacks to see a film that, through its absence, has now acquired a legendary status. But you have to let the black community know it is seeing a 1959 film and that the images are dated. You can't dismiss the concerns of black audiences, you can't tell a black audience, "Don't be upset." But you can ask, what else can we see here? The black audience does not want to see

a "hero" like Porgy, but of course they would respond to the music, even if they could not fully involve themselves in the story. If they see it in a great print, the black audience might well appreciate the film in terms of its visuals and performances. But blacks, like everyone else, haven't had the opportunity to see it in decades.[57]

Both Rouben Mamoulian and Otto Preminger wanted to turn Heyward and Gershwin's folk opera into a realistic film about a Southern black ghetto, but were forcibly prevented from doing so by Samuel Goldwyn. The directors were wrong and the producer they regarded as a simpleton was right. In his original novel, as well as his play and opera, DuBose Heyward's express intention was to present a highly stylized evocation of Negro life. With its rolling cadences in both dialogue and descriptive passages, Heyward's novel indeed "sings," precisely the quality that had attracted George Gershwin, who shaped his musical idioms to cues he received from the novelist. The literal approach that first Mamoulian and then Preminger wished to pursue would have disfigured the material, destroying its lyricism and only emphasizing its racial stereotyping. Catfish Row is a separate realm, a "dream" of a black ghetto of the past not to be confused with the real world of 1912, the period in which the novel takes place, nor with the realities of black life at the time of the film's release. Appropriately, therefore, Oliver Smith's not quite realistic settings and cinematographer Leon Shamroy's painterly use of color and light underscore the fact that Catfish Row is a place for musical expression rather than a site for social protest or grievance. (Shamroy was nominated for an Academy Award.) When the characters slide from speaking to singing there isn't the rupture there would have been if the story had been set in a realistic environment, a ghetto rendered with documentarylike authenticity.

Preminger, to be sure, had initially resisted Goldwyn's aim of confining the action to a studio-built Catfish Row. But once he had won the right to shoot the opening scene ("Summertime," exquisitely rendered in yellow tones) and the picnic scene on location, he played by Goldwyn's rules, designing *Porgy and Bess* as exactly the kind of stately pageant the producer wanted. Preminger's measured staging—his preference for long takes and camera movement over editing—enfolds Gershwin's music in ceremonial elegance. And the director's style, dignified and clean, complements the decision of the actors to speak well.

To viewers who demand visual realism, the film's limbolike world may look theatrical, but Preminger's approach is decidedly not filmed theater. His group shots and deep-focus compositions fused to the horizontal dimension of the Todd-AO wide screen, Preminger in supple and unobtrusive ways employs the language of film to enhance the language of music. (A nice touch that reveals the filmmaker's understanding of the role of music in the life of Catfish Row is its complete absence, including underscoring, on the few occasions when white outsiders invade the ghetto. In Catfish Row white men don't, and can't, sing.) Throughout, as in *Carmen Jones,* Preminger stages songs not to stop the show but to underline their narrative relevance. His direction of "Bess, You Is My Woman Now," for instance, supports the dramatic reason for the number, which expresses the title characters' growing feelings for each other. At the beginning of the song, through intercutting Porgy and Bess occupy their own separate frames; but as their soaring voices celebrate their love, Preminger shoots them within the same frame. As if out of respect for their swelling emotion, the camera, in mid-shot range, remains stationary while, seen in deep focus through the open window of Porgy's cottage, Catfish Row residents pass by. Preminger's mise-en-scène draws contrasts within the same visual field between the private, intimate space of the new lovers and the public world outside.

Private as opposed to public space is again meaningfully counterpointed in Preminger's staging of a lament, "My Man's Gone Now," sung by Serena after Crown has killed her husband in a crap game. Placed in deep focus, mourners in stylized postures turn away from the widow, as if to allow her privacy in her time of sorrow. Yet the fact that the mourners occupy the same frame as Serena reinforces the motif sustained throughout of Catfish Row as a close-knit community that protects itself against outsiders like Crown and Sportin' Life as well as white folks who don't belong there.

To offset what is ideologically if not musically the show's most problematic number, Porgy's anthem, "I Got Plenty o' Nothin'," in which a black cripple celebrates his joy in not-having, Preminger begins the song with Porgy framed in his window—the character is on display "performing" a song. Once he has to some extent protected the song by setting it in a frame within the frame, Preminger then pays tribute to the rhythm and melody of the number by expanding the space in which it is performed. He moves Porgy from the shadowed interior of his cottage to the open square outside, bathed in a golden early morning light. His handling of space in Porgy's aria, "Where's My Bess?" is also resonant. Preminger places Porgy on the bottom right of the frame, at the opposite side of the vast wide screen from his neighbors. The empty space between the isolated cripple and the ensemble seems to augur the loss that is to engulf the character when he discovers that Bess has left him.

Throughout, the camera responds to the needs of the music. In a beau-

Porgy (Sidney Poitier) and Bess (Dorothy Dandridge) isolated in a deep-focus, wide-angle shot on the vast Catfish Row set designed by Oliver Smith.

tifully choreographed long take, the camera stays on a woman selling straw-berries as she makes a circle around the Catfish Row set while singing a glo-rious melodic fragment. As she exits a hawker of she-crabs enters, promoting his wares in another melodious outburst as the camera follows his movement. Preminger's unifying long take provides a visual counter-point to the way the two song fragments flow together. The camera sweeps alongside the citizens of Catfish Row, dressed up for a picnic, as they sing "I Can't Sit Down." Freer and more mobile than any previous camera move-ment, the lateral tracking shot here underscores the characters' excitement about an excursion to the outside world. (Preminger's insistence on filming the picnic sequence on location makes thematic sense—the picnic is an out-ing, an escape from the ghetto.) The camera is also released during "It Ain't Necessarily So," the subversive sermon that Sportin' Life performs during the picnic. High-angle moving shots and a swooping crane shot are cine-matic salutes to the character's swaggering, vaudevillian turn.

Preminger is strict. His film contains not a single close-up, even in moments such as a climactic fight to the death between Porgy and Crown where a variety of visual punctuation might be expected. The director departs from his austere regime in only a few places, as when he presents the fight that erupts during a crap game with a blast of cinema rhetoric. In an ominous low-angle shot, the silhouetted figures of the combatants, Crown and Robbins, strain against each other in the foreground as in deep focus the inhabitants of Catfish Row open their shutters to observe the struggle. A vertiginous high-angle shot that italicizes the moment when Crown strikes Robbins a fatal blow is followed by an extreme long shot of the observers closing their shutters in unison. In passages in earlier films such as *The Man with the Golden Arm* and *Saint Joan,* Preminger's reserve undermines tension, but not here: his unyielding procession of medium and long shots provides the right frame for a fable, an opera, taking place in a limbo world.

By the director's design, cues for passion come not from the grammar of filmmaking but from the performers. And in this "expurgated" *Porgy and Bess,* star iconography is crucial, a way of binding the audience to the characters. Protecting the image he had been building throughout the 1950s, Poitier plays Porgy with an ineffable dignity. We never see the character begging, and far from being illiterate or primitive, Poitier's beautifully spoken character is unmistakably intelligent. In a hotter version the actor's containment—Porgy is a character, after all, nearly driven mad by his feelings for Bess—might have been damaging. But Poitier's restraint matches the cool elegance of Preminger's direction. Nonetheless, the actor apparently has "not yet completely forgiven [himself for having taken on the role]."[58]

Dorothy Dandridge's Bess is also a victory of star acting. She may be less Heyward's original hard-living, hard-luck, good-time gal, "a whore in a two-dollar dress," than she is "Dorothy Dandridge," a woman of regal carriage. Still, the actress vividly suggests her character's contradictory nature, the painful split between Bess's love for Porgy and her lust for Crown. Without the aid of a single close-up, Dandridge conveys a sense of Bess's tortured inner self, the strain of a life addicted to sex and drugs. Typical of the challenges Preminger handed her is the way she must react, in an uncut long shot, to Sportin' Life's temptation song, "There's a Boat That's Soon Leaving for New York." In the course of the song, as Sportin' Life tries to bend Bess to his will, Dandridge manages to delineate her character's gradual shift from resistance—she stiffens when the tempter first slinks toward her—to capitulation.

Both professionally and personally, Dandridge's courageous and undervalued performance was the end of the line. At the New York premiere, accompanied by her new husband Jack Dennison, a white Las Vegas restaurateur and huckster whose financial misdealing was to lead her to bankruptcy, she looked wan, played out. Missing was the sparkle she had had at the opening of *Carmen Jones* only five years earlier. Then, radiant with possibility, she might have believed she could win against the odds to become

Crown (Brock Peters) in a scene from *Porgy and Bess.*

America's first black leading lady. But the disappointments in the interven-
ing years had made her confront the reality that despite her beauty and her
talent she would be unlikely to break the color barrier. After *Porgy and Bess*
she would have nothing but defeats: starring roles in a few poverty row productions and nightclub bookings at ever less prestigious hotels. At her professional nadir, she would be the lounge act in a Las Vegas hotel where
Nancy Wilson was the showroom headliner. On September 9, 1965,
Dorothy Dandridge committed suicide.

In the Broadway-style roles scored for nonoperatic singers, Pearl Bailey
and Sammy Davis Jr. also project strong star personas. Bailey may have been
a nuisance on the set, heartily disliked by most of the company, but as
Maria, a character who embodies the communal spirit that draws together
the citizens of the ghetto against troublemaking outsiders, she suffuses the
film with a warm, droll, earthy presence. Sammy Davis Jr. plays Sportin'
Life, drug dealer and cynic, in perhaps the only way he could, as a hoofer
determined to wow the audience. Dressed in skintight pants, he glides in
and out of scenes with slithering dancelike movements. As a tempter he's
reptilian rather than charming, but his Las Vegas–style showmanship is elec-

tric. He attacks with ebullience Sportin' Life's two great pop numbers, "It Ain't Necessarily So" and "There's a Boat That's Leaving Soon for New York," potent reminders of Gershwin's roots in Broadway razzmatazz. Brock Peters, who didn't have a star presence to project, enacts Crown as a figure of primal force. In Preminger's mise-en-scène the character is linked to the dark forest into which he drags Bess and the thunderstorm from which he emerges to create havoc in Catfish Row.

André Previn's orchestrations pay tribute to George Gershwin's dual allegiances to "high" and "low," elitist and popular, musical idioms, and the singing throughout (Poitier is dubbed by Robert McFerrin, Dandridge by Adele Addison) has an emotional vibrancy that plays productively against Preminger's formal approach. Considering its era, and the circumstances under which it was produced, neither musically nor dramatically is the film a definitive version of the folk opera. It is unlikely, however, that any single production of this deeply problematic piece can ever claim the final word. Black viewers and aficionados of opera and of musical theater will almost inevitably find elements of any interpretation to be objectionable or only partially realized. The Goldwyn-Preminger *Porgy and Bess* is nonetheless one of the most misunderstood, underrated, and unfairly treated works in the history of American film. It deserves, indeed demands, to be seen again in its original road-show version. Made near the end of the studio era, *Porgy and Bess* is a lustrous "studio" film of a kind we are not likely to see again. "It is a work of great historical value," Brock Peters said. "It represented a special assemblage of talent, and students of film are unfairly being deprived of seeing it. It is a work of art and I am proud to have been a part of it."[59]

Working for hire and juggling the concerns of Goldwyn, Ira and Lee Gershwin, and his racially sensitive cast, Preminger placed his own signature on the final product. First to last, *Porgy and Bess* is an Otto Preminger film, one of his most commanding performances and an overlooked American masterpiece.

ELEVEN

On Trial

"I knew Otto was having a lot of problems on the set of *Porgy and Bess*," Wendell Mayes said,

> but when he would meet me nearly every night to discuss the work I had done that day [on the script of *Anatomy of a Murder*] he would be completely focused, and completely calm. When he was with me, the difficulties with *Porgy* were forgotten, and the only thing in the world that mattered was our script. Off the set, Otto was not into his act, and remember, Otto was an actor first, an actor second, an actor third, and fourth and fifth, and remained so all his life. He was a man of rather astonishing contradictions and despite the fact that he was an enormously sophisticated European gentleman he was not a cynic, as you might expect—in my experience, the Europeans of Otto's nature and status in life were cynical. Not Otto, who had the optimism of a child. He believed that everything was going to go right.

Mayes observed that Preminger responded to the script as a director rather than a writer. "The only thing Otto ever had to say as we went through the script was, 'Wendell, I don't know how to shoot this scene,' and then he would explain to me why he didn't know how to shoot it. And I would make the necessary changes. He was very considerate, and never changed a word, or even a comma, without my consent."[1] Mayes finished the script in mid-December at almost the same time Preminger completed shooting *Porgy and Bess.*

In January 1959, with his art director Boris Leven, Otto made a second scouting expedition to the Upper Peninsula of Michigan that confirmed his earlier resolve to shoot the entire film, including all the interiors, on location in the actual settings where the murder and subsequent trial had taken place. Leven backed him up, remarking that "the peculiar provincial individuality of the area could not be recreated on a studio set." "It's not only the *look* of the place that I want to get on the screen," Preminger said. "I want the actors to *feel* it, to absorb a sense of what it's like to live here—to smell it. This is a story that requires reality. I'm going to bring the whole cast and crew up here and install them in Ishpeming [Michigan]. We'll live through it together and that will help to make the film more 'real' than any single thing I could do."[2]

Returning from Michigan, Otto scheduled a March 23 starting date and then, commuting regularly between his New York office on West Fifty-fifth Street and his office at Columbia in Hollywood, he began to assemble his cast. For Paul Biegler, the lawyer who takes on the job of defending Frederick Manion, a second lieutenant accused of killing a bartender who had allegedly raped Manion's wife, Preminger wanted, and got, James Stewart. For Laura Manion, the officer's seductive wife, who may or may not have been raped, Preminger, impressed by her performance in the recent film *A Face in the Crowd,* sought newcomer Lee Remick. When he interviewed her, the actress was in the eighth month of a pregnancy; but since she would have given birth by the time shooting was to begin, Preminger handed her a script and led her to believe he would cast her in the role. However, before she had finished the script he called to tell her he had signed Lana Turner and asked if she would be interested in playing a supporting role. "I did a very brave thing, or perhaps a foolish thing," Lee Remick recalled. "I said, 'No, thank you, I really would not.' "[3] Hope Bryce, hired as costume coordinator, began to have a problem with Lana Turner.

> Otto told me he wanted everything in the film to be realistic, and so I suggested to Lana, who would be playing a character who lives in a trailer park, that she should wear slacks, capri pants, or Western pants. I made an appointment for us to have a fitting at a Western shop on Rodeo Drive. At the time she was only two blocks away, and yet she didn't show up. This happened twice. Lana's agent, Paul

Kohner, informed us that she wanted her clothes made by Jean Louis, who usually designed her wardrobe. But you can't custom-make junky clothes. When Otto went with her to Westmore about wigs, she exasperated him. "This woman is going to drive me crazy," he told me. He began to think that Lana wasn't right for the part, that maybe she was really too old for the part.[4]

"I told Paul Kohner that Lana was to play a second lieutenant's wife and that the outfit Hope had selected was therefore correct," Preminger recounted. "Besides, I and nobody else determines what the actors wear in my films."[5] When Kohner informed him that his client wouldn't agree, Preminger said she could cancel the contract. "Kohner thought I was bluffing. But I never am."[6] Lana Turner had a different account of her collision with Otto. "I went for my fittings," she insisted. "It was a very nice shop, but one of the costumes didn't look good on me. Later, Otto called and immediately started to abuse me. He yelled, 'I'll show you this isn't Universal-International or MGM. This is my independent picture. You'll do and wear exactly what I say.' He kept on and on. I couldn't stop him. Finally I hung up on him. I wouldn't quit any film over something as trivial as a costume. But I've been in this business too long to take that kind of shouting from anybody."[7] Otto's rebuttal: "No one is indispensable."

Otto quickly hired Lee Remick. "Lee was much more fun to work with than Lana," Hope said. "We bought Lee's costumes at the kind of places where her character, who would buy cheap, sleazy clothes, would actually shop. We bought off the rack and we went to Beck's to buy clear plastic shoes."[8]

For Lieutenant Frederick Manion, the officer charged with murder, Preminger chose Ben Gazzara, a stage actor he had admired playing a sadistic cadet in a Southern military academy in *End as a Man.* When he called him into his New York office, Preminger wanted George C. Scott, another stage actor whose work he had noted, to play a bartender, but having read the script before the interview Scott had decided he wanted the larger, showier role of the prosecuting attorney. "Wow, there was this dazzling joker who comes in, the attorney from Lansing, with the name of Dancer: how could you lose? It was a terrific part. I went to see Otto, who was very imposing, very intimidating, and when he asked me if I wanted to play the bartender part I said no. 'Why not?' 'Because I want to play this other part.' He looked hard at me and after a few seconds said, 'Oh, okay.' Just like that!"[9]

As the presiding judge—a role he was having trouble casting—Preminger's director of publicity Nat Rudich suggested Joseph N. Welch, the

Boston lawyer whose question to Senator Joseph McCarthy during the Army-McCarthy hearings—"Have you, at last, sir, no sense of decency?"— had marked the beginning of the witch-hunting senator's downfall and been etched into the conscience of the nation. Welch agreed to look at the script; and when he came down from Boston to meet with the director, admitting to having read only his own part, Preminger knew he had found his actor. On March 4, three weeks before the start of filming, Otto introduced Welch to the press at a luncheon at Romanoff's in Beverly Hills. "I'm using a new 68-year-old face," he announced, his blue eyes twinkling. In high impresario mode, Preminger also announced that he planned to complete the film in eight weeks and that he had already booked a preview screening in San Francisco on June 17.[10] Confident he could maintain his schedule, he promised that the film would have its world premiere on July 1 at the Warner Beverly Theatre on Wilshire Boulevard, only a few blocks from Romanoff's.

For the start of shooting in the Upper Peninsula, Preminger planned a flamboyant entrance: cast and crew arrived on a train of their own at 6:30 on a blustery March evening. Despite the thirty-five degrees below zero temperature, most of the population of Ishpeming and Marquette, the two towns where the film was to be made, showed up to welcome them. "We all arrived looking so glamorous and they were very poor in Ishpeming," Rita Moriarty, Otto's executive assistant, remembered. "During the shooting of *Bonjour Tristesse* on the Riviera, I had grumbled about having to stay in London, and I told Otto that on the next one I wanted to be on the set. My 'reward' was Ishpeming! I'd never been to a small American town before." Preminger booked everyone into a colonial-style hotel where the entire company shared meals in the dining room. And as he had hoped it would, a family feeling developed. Thrown together in an isolated small town, cast and crew established a communal spirit that would not have been possible in the studio. "We all used to go to the local dancing place, but not Otto; people would not have been relaxed if he had," Rita Moriarty said. "Otto hung out with Welch and with Voelker, the author of the novel."[11] James Stewart recalled that Duke Ellington, the film's composer, "played for us in the dining room at night, until ten, eleven, which was great fun for us. But then Otto heard about it and he said to Duke, 'Now these kids have to get up in the morning to act and I don't want them to stay up until midnight.' So 'the kids' weren't allowed in the dining room after dinner. It was a natural thing for Preminger to do: we *were* staying up too late."[12]

Otto encouraged family members to stay for the entire shoot. To provide company for her husband, he hired Mrs. Welch to play a juror. Lee

On location in Ishpeming, Michigan, for the filming of *Anatomy of a Murder.* Left to right: Agnes (Mrs. Joseph) Welch, Otto, Lee Remick, and Joseph N. Welch.

Remick came with her husband and baby. Duke Ellington brought his common-law wife, Evie, along with jazz legend Billy Strayhorn. George C. Scott's wife, Colleen Dewhurst, was with him the entire time. Eve Arden, cast as James Stewart's secretary, was with her husband, Brooks West, appearing in the film as a straight-arrow prosecuting attorney. And, as often on his films—a sign of his interest in young people—Otto had an intern, "an enthusiastic fellow from Hong Kong; Otto got a kick out of him," as Rita Moriarty recalled.[13]

Preminger asked Duke Ellington to remain on location for the entire shoot. "Usually a composer is hired when the film is over and he writes the score in a few weeks," Preminger noted. "But I hire a composer before I begin shooting."[14] Preminger expected Ellington to compose on the spot, after he had absorbed the atmosphere. "Otto told me to look after Duke, who was the only black man in the area," Rita Moriarty said. "Otto liked him enormously—we all did—and felt protective. Fortunately, there were no incidents."

After the trouble-filled sets on *Saint Joan, Bonjour Tristesse,* and *Porgy and Bess,* the location filming of *Anatomy of a Murder* in the barren Upper Peninsula of Michigan was virtually problem-free, the luckiest shoot in Preminger's career. "Otto seemed to get along with everyone," Rita Moriarty observed. "He felt sure of himself in Ishpeming, whereas he hadn't been sure of himself in London on *Saint Joan.* He loved location shooting, and *Anatomy* was *all* location." Potential problems never materialized. "George Scott was already a complete alcoholic when Otto hired him, and he and his wife, Colleen Dewhurst, also an extreme alcoholic, were drunk every night during the shoot," Rita Moriarty said. "But Scott was never drunk on the set. Off the set James Stewart was awfully vague, really not there at all, but word-perfect on the job. Stewart had great respect for Otto."[15]

In casting Ben Gazzara, Lee Remick, and George C. Scott, Preminger, as he often did, was taking a chance on newcomers, all of whom had challenging roles. Not once did he raise his voice, and rather than monitoring every gesture and intonation, as he had with Jean Seberg and Dorothy Dandridge, he kept his distance.

"He was not a hands-on director with actors," Gazzara observed.

He was detached, diffident. His focus was not on his actors but on the exigencies of setting up the shots, and he had a very good eye. He talked much more to Sam Leavitt [the film's cinematographer] than to any of us. He cast well; he had hired us because he thought we fulfilled his idea of the roles and he expected us to bring him everything. In the few moments we had together on-screen Lee and I worked out our relationship and motivations between ourselves— we supplied the subtext of resentment and suspicion between the characters. With Otto, it was a job: be on time and know your lines. I was used to a different approach because I was trained in the Method and had worked with Elia Kazan on Broadway in *Cat on a Hot Tin Roof.* With Gadg [Kazan], who always knew how to help an actor who was having trouble, you felt you had a friend. He put his arm around you and walked you off to the side. You were showered with that warm Anatolian smile; with Otto, it was Germanic formality and no sense of a collaborative effort. He did not know how to talk to an actor in the actor's own language, in the language of the actor's craft, and I expect that's why he got so frustrated when an actor wasn't giving him what he wanted. I had the feeling he didn't like actors. But I certainly didn't dislike him; I just didn't get to know him.[16]

"When Otto thought it was working, which I think is how he felt about all of us in our roles, he knew well enough to stay quiet," George C. Scott said. "He left me almost entirely alone, in fact he almost didn't say anything to me at all. I was kind of wondering: am I doing this right? The occasional eruption was with the technical people, not with the actors."[17]

In this charmed shoot Preminger did not once attack the most vulnerable player, Kathryn Grant, cast in the pivotal role of the young woman who turns out to be the daughter of the murdered man. "She had a singsong delivery that was driving Otto wild," Hope Bryce recalled. "She's really not an actress, and as a person she was blank. She didn't mix with the company and dined every night with a priest."[18] "I had heard Mr. Preminger was fearsome, but he wasn't," Kathryn Grant (Mrs. Bing Crosby) said. "I never saw him in that forbidding way. I just did my lines and he didn't say anything." Grant had a method of her own for reducing her fear of Preminger,

the most important producer-director I ever knew, a person with a great vision. Alice Faye, a friend of Bing's who had worked with Otto [on *Fallen Angel*] and had had no trouble, gave me some encouragement before we started. "He has bad breath," she told me, "and you can't be afraid of someone with terrible breath." Now I don't know if he did—I never got close enough to find out—but once I had it in my mind I realized that he was just a person and I was no longer afraid. Mr. Preminger always treated me professionally. When I was in his office before filming, I informed him I was three months pregnant and he said nothing required of me would interfere with the pregnancy. He said the pregnancy might even have advantages: my breasts would be bigger! Maybe that's why he was always nice to me.[19]

In handling Joseph Welch, Preminger remembered a rehearsal at the Theater in der Josefstadt in which Max Reinhardt had asked an amateur actor to move on a line. "Oh, if you want that you must get yourself a real actor," the clever amateur had replied. "I was very careful while directing Joseph Welch never to make him move and talk at the same time," Preminger noted.[20]

To avoid the inclement weather when production started at the end of March, Preminger had arranged beforehand to shoot all the interiors first. He began with the trial scenes, shot in sequence. The procedure benefited the actors, allowing for the kind of continuity rarely obtained in filming, and it also saved money—Otto didn't have to pay actors to hang around when they weren't needed. Toward the end of the shoot, however, the bubble of contentment surrounding the project almost burst because of a legal

The courtroom in *Anatomy of a Murder*. Preminger shot the trial in sequence in the Marquette County Court House, the site of the actual trial on which the film is based.

battle begun in July 1958 between Preminger's Carlyle Productions and Ray Stark's Seven Arts. Each had claimed priority in having bought the screen rights to the novel. In October 1958 Stark had announced that he and a partner, Eliot Hyman, would also produce a stage version to be adapted by John van Druten (who died in December after having completed his dramatization). The following May, Stark, maintaining he had a signed agreement between van Druten and John Voelker "provid[ing] for a sale and transfer of all motion picture rights to me," said he was "surprised by Preminger's plans since he approached me some time ago with the proposition to join me in the production of this film, which proposition I subsequently rejected."[21] For a moment, with Stark threatening to block Otto from releasing his film, it looked as if Preminger's about-to-be victory would be snatched from him at the eleventh hour. Preminger pursued the matter in court and prevailed, the judge deciding that the right to produce a film of Voelker's novel was his and his alone.

Although Otto put up an unflappable front, Ray Stark's legal maneuverings gave him momentary pause. The prospect of a looming censorship hassle, however, delighted him. For the fourth time he would be playing a congenial role as a free-speech advocate, and once again he welcomed a row because he knew it would be good for business. The issue, as with *The Moon Is Blue,* was over language deemed "offensive" by a number of local censorship boards. The offending words were "rape" (uttered in *Anatomy of a Murder* more frequently than in any previous American film), "seduce," "contraceptive," "penetration," and "panties" (the outcome of the trial hinges on a woman's ripped undergarment). (Among the offended was James Stewart's father, who berated his son for a scene in which he held up the panties. "My father said I shouldn't have done it, and he warned his friends to stay away from the film," the actor recalled.)[22] Several dozen local boards made threats, but in the event only the one in Chicago took action. In the middle of the Detroit premiere, Nat Rudich, Otto's assistant, rushed into the theater to inform him that the board was demanding five cuts before they would allow the film to open. Otto flew to Chicago the next day to confront the city's Catholic chief of police, who said he would ignore four of the objections but would not budge in demanding the removal of "contraceptive" because he didn't want his eighteen-year-old daughter to hear it. "If I had an eighteen-year-old daughter, sir, I would teach her that word and explain to her carefully all about it," Otto replied.[23] The next morning a district court judge ordered the film shown without any cuts. "The film had no difficulty anywhere else," as Otto reported, perhaps a little disappointed.[24]

Although he did not publicize it, according to Wendell Mayes Preminger did in fact agree to make one cut demanded by the Production Code Administration office. "He called me, as he always did when he wanted to make a change, to say we had to change the word 'penetration' to 'violation,' " Mayes remembered. "He said, 'That's the only thing I gave on.' That wasn't much, though, and for its time the film really was quite daring in the way sex was discussed. Probably only Otto Preminger would have gotten away with it."[25] (Preminger was to have two other battles over attempts to

James Stewart and Duke Ellington, seated together on a piano bench, for a scene in *Anatomy of a Murder.* Preminger refused to delete the scene for South African exhibitors.

mutilate his film. Shortly after the opening he received a call from a film agent in South Africa wanting to excise a scene in which James Stewart sits on a piano bench with Duke Ellington. "It's only 15 seconds and not too important," the agent claimed. "Well, it's important to me," Preminger responded. "My movie isn't a South African film, it's an American one. You either run the picture as it is, or you don't run it at all." The agent continued to call for six years, and each time received the same answer.[26] In 1965, when Otto saw a television screening of the film with thirteen interruptions for twenty-nine commercials, he took the matter to court, claiming that his contractual right of first cut also applied to television. "It is not my film anymore; it is a misrepresentation of my film, a fraud committed against the public," Preminger argued in a press conference on December 2, 1965. On January 19, 1966, however, Justice Arthur G. Klein of the New York State Supreme Court ruled against Preminger, determining "final cut" does not apply to television showings.)

Preminger was guest of honor at a state-sponsored banquet when *Anatomy of a Murder* was named "Michigan product of the year." The sixty-five-foot-long backdrop with the Saul Bass logo was designed by the film's art director, Boris Leven.

On June 5, only twenty-one days after shooting was completed, Preminger, as he had said he would, presented *Anatomy of a Murder* at a preview screening in San Francisco. The enthusiastic response was echoed the following month when the film opened in selected theaters on July 1 to the most positive notices of Preminger's career. "Hews magnificently to a line of dramatic but reasonable behavior and proper procedure in a court" (the *New York Times,* July 2); "nigh flawless" (*Saturday Review,* July 10); "a beautifully drawn battle, full of neat little triumphs on each side" (the *Nation,* July 11); "forceful, enthralling" (the *Los Angeles Times,* July 2).

Opening within days after the premiere of *Porgy and Bess, Anatomy of a Murder* reversed Preminger's recent lackluster track record. As the director of two major films, Preminger was again at the top. He saturated newspapers, television, and radio, trumpeting his own film, but he also complied with Goldwyn's requests to promote *Porgy and Bess.* The differences he had had with Goldwyn were forgotten as he spoke to reporters about the "honor" of directing the great producer's final film. In some of the public appearances he made for Goldwyn, Otto appeared with Dorothy, looking a little shaky but trying still to project the aura of a Hollywood diva. When he was in Beverly Hills, Otto enjoyed driving back and forth between the two theaters, the Warner Beverly and the Carthay Circle, where the films were playing to full houses. After some screenings of *Anatomy of a Murder,* exiting audiences were delighted to find Otto holding court in the lobby of the Warner Beverly, genuinely interested in finding out what they thought of the verdict that the jury in the film had arrived at.

The summer of 1959 was the high-water mark of Preminger's career, and the filmmaker luxuriated in the attention and the praise. He was proud of the work he had done for Goldwyn under difficult circumstances and of his accomplishment with *Anatomy of a Murder.* He had not needed the critics to tell him that in that movie everything works: the story, the acting, the location settings, Sam Leavitt's black-and-white cinematography, Duke Ellington's jazz score. To be sure, this cool film about a hot subject is a triumphant display of all the filmmaker's strengths: his objectivity, his visual fluency, his resistance to sentimentality, his attraction to ambivalence in characterization and theme, his control of every element of the mise-en-scène.

Like his later epics on institutions (the Catholic church in *The Cardinal,* the federal government in *Advise and Consent,* the Navy in *In Harm's Way*), at heart *Anatomy of a Murder* is about procedure. With patient detail the film documents the way lawyers assemble a defense case and the means, the rules and regulations, by which a trial is conducted and courtroom decorum is maintained. Although the film's immediate focus, the trial of a man accused of killing a bartender in a small town, may seem narrow, ultimately *Anatomy of a Murder* engages large issues about law and the process of trial by jury. The film asks the audience to consider how the American system defines and determines guilt and innocence, to what extent the law can be manipulated to protect or punish the accused and to uphold or obscure the truth. In order to arrive at their own conclusions, spectators, like the jurors in the film, are placed in the position of assessing the conflicting testimony of equivocal witnesses. In its respect for due process and its love of the courtroom as a privileged site of dramatic conflict, this is a lawyer's film—a tribute to American jurisprudence tendered by a doctor of law from the University of Vienna.

Like the film itself, its protagonist, defense attorney Paul Biegler, regards the law as flexible, imperfect, fascinating, and ultimately indestructible. A die-hard pragmatist, capable of seeing *around* any legal issue, Biegler takes on Lieutenant Manion as a client simply because the case and its cast of

George C. Scott, playing the prosecuting attorney, questions the arrogant defendant (Ben Gazzara). Joseph N. Welch is the judge.

characters interest him. He doesn't like Manion and is far from convinced of his innocence—all he knows for sure is that Manion shot the bartender, Barney Quill. Yet Biegler is enticed by the legal issues the case raises. The point he pursues with academic rigor is whether or not the lieutenant killed the bartender when he was in a state of mind that under the provisions of the law might make him appear to be innocent to a jury. Biegler isn't Perry Mason, alight with moral fervor and determined to see justice vindicated—that kind of hero held little interest for Preminger, who, as here, is typically drawn to the compromises and contradictions that govern human behavior. Biegler is a regular guy with no romantic attachments. Off the job he likes to play jazz and to fish, and to his work as a lawyer he brings a logical temperament as well as a knack for improvising—precisely the traits that make him good at devising strategies for catching fish and riffing at the piano.

Self-contained offstage, Biegler in the courtroom knows how to turn up the volume. He's crafty. On demand he can become boisterous or sarcastic. And beneath his masquerade as a seemingly ingratiating country bumpkin he can cut the legal mustard second to none. One of the film's wisest observations, to be sure, is that since trials are a kind of performance art, cases are likely to be won by the most able actor. And as the film's starring attraction,

James Stewart, as the story needs him to be, is indeed the best actor on view. In the courtroom scenes, engaging in a sly dialogue with the upstanding protagonists he had played earlier in his career, he reveals "James Stewart," idealized all-American, as a performance, an actor's mask. Stewart lets us see him put on and take off the persona that made him a star. In a film like *Mr. Smith Goes to Washington* (1939), Stewart is unshakably sincere; here, his sincerity is qualified, even questioned. (The film's portrait of lawyers as actors anticipates by some four decades the appalling public spectacle of Johnny Cochran "performing" racial outrage to the primarily black jury that acquitted O. J. Simpson, Cochran's obviously guilty-beyond-a-reasonable-doubt client, in a murder case that had nothing to do with race.)

As the niftily named prosecuting attorney, Claude Dancer, George C. Scott also struts like a seasoned player, an agile "dancer" indeed. Light on his feet, Dancer moves and thinks quickly. In a delicious scene, as he takes the measure of the forever hot-to-trot Laura Manion during cross-examination, he moves in toward her to caress her with his voice, lowering it to a seductive purr. From time to time, clearly amused by his own theatrics, Dancer smiles surreptitiously to himself.

The defendant, Lieutenant Manion, also puts on a show, one with an unexpected script. Refusing to enact the cliché-ridden role of a man who bristles with indignation because he has been accused of a crime he did not commit, Manion, cocky and insolent—he smokes cigarettes through a holder—makes no attempt to perform innocence for Biegler. He seems so indifferent toward his wife that entering a plea of temporary insanity—the only way that Biegler believes he can win acquittal for his client—becomes problematic. How would such an icily self-contained man have been capable of a crime of passion? And yet, as Biegler observes, the tightly wound lieutenant is jealous of his wife's flirtations, has a hair-trigger temper, and might well have snapped just before killing Quill. Indeed, Manion loses his temper twice. First, in jail, he lashes out at another prisoner, and then in the courtroom he screams out when the con testifies falsely against him. Enticingly veiled, Ben Gazzara plays Manion as an unknowable character, a man knotted by inner tensions. "Of course the guy was guilty, but as an actor you play the opposite," Ben Gazzara said. "I thought of him as innocent, a wonderful person. As an actor, you take the side of the character."

Laura, Manion's far too seductive wife, is another ambivalent character who often seems, like the lieutenant, to be behaving inappropriately. Worried that her sultriness will antagonize the jury, Biegler forces Laura to dress in a prim suit, to wear glasses, and to put her hair up—whenever she appears in the courtroom, she too is acting. Since Lee Remick has such a likable presence, viewers may be predisposed to accept her character's testimony despite her masquerade. Sexually provocative, favoring every man but her husband with smiles and wiggles—her husband may be the only man she is afraid of—Laura seems more likely to have been a consenting partner in an illicit rendezvous than a victim of rape. Yet she claims Barney Quill took her against her will. She also claims Quill gave her a black eye, and the dark glasses she wears add another barrier to reading the character clearly. But it also seems reasonable that her husband could have struck her in a moment of rage. In a charged private moment during the trial Manion repels Laura's attempt to light his cigarette, and the two exchange a poisonous look that evokes a dark history, an aura of something unspoken between them that we will never find out about. Deciphering the motives of this untrustworthy couple who nonetheless may be telling the truth provides the primary interpretive challenge for the jurors on-screen and in the audience.

Mary Pilant, the murdered man's daughter, is also hard to read. Like the Manions, Mary doesn't appear to be responding to circumstances in the expected way. Her father has been murdered, yet she seems oddly detached, as if she is no more than an employee at the hotel that Barney owned (which in fact is the character's status in the novel). Preminger's decision to make Mary Barney's daughter (a fact that Barney had concealed) adds another dark possibility to the story's proliferating ambiguities. At the trial, when Mary produces Laura's panties, which her father had hurled down the laundry chute at the hotel, she may be offering proof of his guilt or perhaps hinting at some secret ceremony the two of them might have shared. Like the other central characters in the crime, Mary Pilant is equivocal, not quite "right." Preminger shrewdly uses Kathryn Grant's glassy-eyed, matte, starlet-in-a-B-movie performance to encourage the viewer's suspicion that Mary, too, is a character with secrets.

In contrast, Biegler's two assistants, his soused partner Parnell (Arthur O'Connell), who redeems himself by helping Biegler to win the case, and his devoted, down-to-earth secretary, Maida (Eve Arden), who works even when her boss is behind in paying her salary, have nothing to hide. Parnell's love of the law permeates the film. For this failed lawyer working on the case is therapeutic. When he finds a precedent that might exculpate their client—in Michigan, if a defendant can be shown to have committed a crime under an irresistible impulse, there is reasonable doubt about his guilt—he reacts like a scientist confronted with a momentous discovery. The scene near the end, of Biegler, Parnell, and Maida awaiting the verdict, is surely among the most deftly drawn pieces of local-color realism in the

Defense attorneys (James Stewart and Arthur O'Connell) and their secretary (Eve Arden) await the verdict in *Anatomy of a Murder*. Performed by three great actors, the scene represents the finest work of Preminger's career.

history of American filmmaking. Paul doodles on the piano; Parnell praises trial by jury as a system that most of the time almost miraculously seems to work; Maida, pouring coffee, hopes for a new typewriter on which all the keys work.

Preminger's avoidance throughout of psychological and visual cliché culminates in the choices he makes at the end of the trial. He eliminates summations and stages the verdict in an unorthodox way. As the not-guilty verdict is announced, Lieutenant Manion (Laura, oddly yet somehow fittingly, isn't even in the courtroom) is seen in long shot in an all-inclusive wide-angle composition. (Biegler does not stand up with his client.) In order to encourage the audience to consider larger issues about the law and the jury system, Preminger ingeniously withholds the conventional reaction shot close-ups that would reveal how Manion and his legal team are responding to the verdict. On strictly legal grounds—if in fact he did kill Barney Quill under an irresistible impulse, the law is not obligated to distinguish right from wrong—Manion may not be guilty beyond a reasonable doubt. But, as the filmmaker hoped, many viewers do not agree with the jury's decision. To Preminger, lawyer and proud American, an occasional miscarriage of justice is the price to be paid for the system of trial by jury that is unavoidably imperfect but that most of the time arrives at the right decision. From Preminger's and the film's point of view, the refusal to rush to judgment, implicit in the injunction to assign guilt *beyond* a reasonable doubt, is a necessary prophylactic, salutary and even noble. Preminger's own deep respect for American jurisprudence is reflected in the character who is the highest representative of the law in the film, the presiding judge, played with unassailable courtliness, urbanity, and rectitude by Joseph N. Welch.

(In the fall of 1962, when Preminger accepted an invitation from the Union of Soviet Picture Makers in Moscow, he asked if he could bring a copy of *Anatomy of a Murder* because he wanted to see how Russian audiences would respond. He was interested to discover that they had no problem with the sexual content but were puzzled, or angry, that Manion had won acquittal since "obviously" he was a mean man who had *not* killed under "an irresistible impulse." "The evidence was not conclusive," Preminger explained, trying to outline the American system of justice. "And in our country a man is presumed to be innocent until he is proved guilty beyond a shadow of a doubt."[27] As Hope recalled, "Russian students didn't understand why it was necessary to have the trial; they felt the character should just have been beheaded."[28])

Preminger's refusal to satisfy audience expectation—almost any other director would have provided a close-up on Lieutenant Manion during or right after the verdict—sets up the film's ironic coda. Manion, released from prison, disappears, claiming an "irresistible impulse" to leave town without paying his lawyers. In the last shot of this sentiment-free movie, Preminger provides a rare close-up as the camera moves in to examine Laura's floozie shoes, which in her hasty departure she has tossed into a garbage can. Leaving behind her shoes, has Laura also perhaps abandoned her life as a good-time gal?

Although he moves in for an occasional close-up, especially in the trial scenes, and in the wry final shot, Preminger typically places the camera in the position of an observant spectator who knows the value of discretion and of maintaining a certain distance. Like the law, the objective camera refuses to come to quick decisions about the characters. And from the comparative safety and anonymity afforded by medium-to-long group shots, viewers are allowed to arrive at their own conclusions. Preminger relies more on editing than he usually does, but he uses few one-shots. Characters are almost always seen in relation to other characters within the same frame. One-shots, for the most part, appear only in early scenes when Biegler questions Manion and Laura—isolating the two characters in frames of their own underlines the lawyer's doubts about them, his feeling of separation from them.

Preminger handles the location settings with restraint. Sam Leavitt's sparing shots of a wintry landscape avoid being picturesque. Interiors—the courtroom, a roadside bar, a hospital, Biegler's house and office, Barney's hotel—look used. Everything seems true, from the battered fridge and floral wallpaper in Biegler's house to the worn-out typewriter Maida complains about. Yet the reality isn't paraded for its own sake, and the film never becomes a museum exhibit of an Upper Peninsula community as seen by outsiders.

Preminger uses Duke Ellington's score with the same tact. "Most musicians are overzealous: instead of rendering the ambiance, the general feeling of the scene, they put the scene into music and try to write a symphony," Preminger observed. "The ensemble is then false, because you have two scenes, one played by the actors, the other played by the music. The score should not be a go-between in telling the story, it should only underline it."[29] And indeed, following Preminger's orders, Ellington's terse score enriches the action without ever intruding on or dominating it. In a smart move, reserving music for "offstage," Preminger does not use any underscoring in the courtroom scenes. Jazz expresses Biegler's cool way of thinking as he assembles his case; underlines Laura's sexuality, Manion's disdain, Parnell's drinking. It is heard in a roadside bar, in a hotel restaurant, and in a few driving scenes. The film ends on a wailing trombone shrieking at the spectacle of Laura's shoes in a garbage can.

It's unlikely that there has ever been a more lucid, more unexpected, and more entertaining movie about the law. After a succession of critical and box-office failures that might well have unnerved a less self-assured personality, Preminger rebounded to deliver the most poised work of his career. *Anatomy of a Murder,* a film that sets the viewer thinking because it challenges complacency and refuses to come up with easy or pious answers, is one of the great American movies. The film grossed over four million dollars in the United States and earned over a million in foreign engagements. Preminger, who had profit participation, earned over half a million, a substantial sum at the time. The film earned Academy Award nominations for James Stewart for best actor; Arthur O'Connell and George C. Scott for best supporting actor; Louis Loeffler for best film editing; and Wendell Mayes for best adapted screenplay. The film was nominated for best picture (Preminger's only nomination in this category) but, unaccountably, Preminger was not nominated for best director.

TWELVE

In the Promised Land

In May and June 1959, as he was preparing for the openings of *Anatomy of a Murder* and conferring with Sam Goldwyn about promotional appearances on behalf of *Porgy and Bess,* Preminger began working full time on *Exodus.* On no other film were his stamina and his stubbornness more essential: in order to shoot a story of the founding of Israel entirely on location, he would require the cooperation of a country that had much more on its mind than participating in the making of a Hollywood super-spectacle.

Otto's initial plan was for Leon Uris to adapt his novel into a screenplay. But any kind of collaboration between the volatile author and the equally hotheaded director was destined to fail. Otto was pro-Israel, but he did not share Uris's hard-core Zionist stance, and in his film he was determined to modify the novelist's anti-British and anti-Arab bias. Another obstacle was Uris's clunky dialogue, lacking cinematic swiftness as well as a convincing illusion of characters speaking to each other. Preminger claimed that he "labored [with Uris] through almost a third" of a first draft before removing him.[1] Uris, however, maintained that he "never wrote a line. I was taken off the picture before I wrote one single line of a screenplay, because of a personality clash—a moral clash. Otto wanted to soften my treatment of the British and Arab characters, an approach I could not condone or tolerate. I sensed trouble the moment I met Otto, a man hated by everybody. I did not write one line, and there isn't a line of dialogue from the novel in the film. After he removed me, I never spoke to Preminger again."[2]

"Uris *did* write part of a script," Hope insisted.

But he didn't want to change a word. He didn't understand, or didn't want to understand, that films are a different medium from novels. Whatever he wrote was unusable, totally bad. How do you tell him? Otto respected Uris as a historian and for the terrific amount of research he had done—he *loved* the story Uris told; that's why he wanted to make the film. When he told him he would have to replace him, Leon was enraged and he never stopped hating Otto and me. A few weeks after the film was released we were invited to a state dinner at the White House, where, in the receiving line, guests were lined up alphabetically; Uris was close to Preminger. Otto went over to him and said, "Hello, Leon, how are you?" and Uris turned his back, refusing to speak.[3]

After jettisoning Uris in early May, Preminger quickly hired Albert Maltz, a blacklisted writer living in Mexico. Maltz had been working on the script for several weeks when Preminger, accompanied by Hope, visited him in mid-June. Preminger saw evidence of massive research but was disheartened to find that Maltz had not yet written a single line. If he was to keep to his schedule—he planned to begin shooting in Israel in March 1960—he felt he had no option but to fire Maltz. At this point Ingo suggested one of his clients, Dalton Trumbo, another blacklisted writer who for years had been working under pseudonyms and who was known for being speedy and reliable. From Otto's point of view, Trumbo had another asset: he was not Jewish, and Preminger was hoping that he would tell the story of the founding of the Jewish state with more objectivity than Uris. Once hired, Trumbo worked quickly.

Encouraged by the progress Trumbo was making, Otto began to lay the groundwork for filming in Israel. To help him gain the permissions he would need, and also to give him entrée to the highest echelons of Israeli politicians, he made a call to an old friend, Meyer Weisgal, the head of the Weizmann Institute of Science, whom Otto had first met in Salzburg in 1924. Weisgal had a lifelong genius for ingratiating himself with great figures. In the 1930s, as Max Reinhardt was forced to leave Austria, Weisgal became one of the impresario's principal backers; and in the 1940s he was an intimate of Chaim Weizmann, who was to become the first president of Israel. Weisgal agreed to making Israel available to Preminger not out of friendship (or at least not solely out of friendship) but because Otto "promised [him] the Israeli royalties from *Exodus* and income from all world

In Rehovot, Israel, on one of his initial scouting expeditions for *Exodus,* with Meyer Weisgal, his Israeli liaison, and Prime Minister and Mrs. David Ben-Gurion.

premieres for the Institute. It meant approximately one million dollars for scientific and a wide variety of cultural and artistic purposes."⁴ Weisgal also agreed to appear in the film in a wordless cameo as David Ben-Gurion, whom he resembled.

In July, immediately following his promotional appearances for *Anatomy of a Murder* and *Porgy and Bess,* Preminger traveled to Israel to meet with Weisgal and to survey possible locations. The trip did not begin promisingly, however, as the Pan Am jet on which Otto was flying to London with Hope was forced to crash-land. As the best-known passenger, his picture was on the front pages of many newspapers. "Look at those photos; they were obviously prepared for my obituary," Otto quipped. "There was no time for philosophy during the landing. I never had the feeling something bad would happen, because I am an optimist. I had confidence."⁵

At Rehovot, where the Weizmann Institute is located, Meyer Weisgal gave a reception for Preminger and introduced him to politicians, the mayors of Jerusalem and Haifa, army and police officers, and the heads of Israeli trade unions. "Meyer had vim and vigor," as Hope recalled. "He was a great fund-raiser and he was good with people. He knew every prominent person in Israel. He got us everything we needed, and he even got us the Israeli Army, who were always on twenty-minute alert. He told us Ben-Gurion wanted to meet us. Otto went off alone with Meyer to see the prime minister, but when they got there Mrs. Ben-Gurion called me and said, 'Come over, I'm sending a car for you.' The Ben-Gurions lived in a modest cottage and they were so completely natural, as was Golda Meir."[6]

"In those days the government machinery for helping a producer make a film in Israel was not what I would call ideal," Meyer Weisgal observed. "We operated in a wilderness. I was in effect the liaison between Mr. Preminger and the government. They didn't speak exactly the same language, and I am not referring to Hebrew. Preminger is very demanding, and usually in the right; but his manner of asking sends a shudder down the spine of government officials and bureaucrats who are prone to think that the sun rises and sets with them. The shouting continued for a considerable time until everything was set—or until we thought that everything was set."[7]

During this visit, in addition to securing full government cooperation, Preminger also made the decision to film in color. "Originally, I had felt the book lent itself more to black and white. Then, after seeing the country, I definitely made up my mind to shoot in color. I want to show Israel, the real 'star' of *Exodus,* with as much realism and authenticity as possible. I think I can do this best in color, while still retaining the documentary feeling I want to give the film."[8]

Soon after returning from Israel, Otto in forty-four intense days in September and October worked on the script with Dalton Trumbo. Although based in New York, Preminger relocated to Los Angeles, where he moved into a cottage on the grounds of the Beverly Hills Hotel. Every morning he would arise at six to be driven to Trumbo's house forty-five minutes away in Pasadena. As Trumbo handed him pages Preminger would edit, then Trumbo would work on revisions. With short breaks for food and drink the two would work straight through until six or seven. Throughout their collaboration there was not a single tremor. "Otto had incredible faith in the work Trumbo had written," noted Martin Schute, once again serving as Otto's general manager.[9] And Trumbo appreciated Preminger's editing skills. "I'm verbose and sentimental, Otto has a sharpshooter's eye for verbosity and knows how to assassinate sentimentality," the writer observed, adding that Otto was "most helpful in construction. He knew how to keep the story moving and how to balance all its elements."[10] After their almost biblical labor of "forty days and forty nights," Preminger felt the script was finished. During production he would not change a word.

Although faithful to the narrative outline of the novel, Trumbo's screenplay achieves a Preminger-like balance. "I think that my picture is much closer to the truth, and to the historic facts, than is the book," Preminger said.

It also avoids propaganda. I am trying to give both sides and I realize events are apt to look contrived: a good person here, who is balanced by a bad one over there. I didn't let myself be swayed by either side, and I felt that it was the right balance. The book by Uris has a pox against all the enemies of the Jews in it and that is difficult to defend. I found in many talks with Israelis who lived through the time of the British mandate that their feelings toward the British are now very friendly. I learned that there is almost a unanimous consent that any other nation would have been much rougher on Israel. Uris would never be able to acknowledge that. I don't believe that there are any real villains. If somebody is a villain I try to find out why. I don't necessarily excuse him, but I try to understand him.[11]

On November 10, 1959, Preminger flew to London, where he set up base at the Dorchester Hotel. "His [hotel suite] was like a railway station as he began to get his cast and crew together," Willi Frischauer reported. "An unending procession of friends, agents, actors, technicians came to pay their respects or apply for jobs."[12] On November 16, accompanied by Martin Schute, his production manager Eva Monley (who had been recommended by Schute), his first assistant director Gerry O'Hara, and his art director Richard Day, Preminger returned to Israel to scout locations and to solidify technical support for shooting, now firmly scheduled to begin on March 28.

"Papa, which is what I called Otto, was quite sure I couldn't handle Israel," Eva Monley recalled. "After all I was only a girl, and girls didn't have a break in those days. And too, I was a very quiet little person." Though quiet, Monley already had a formidable vita: born in Kenya, she specialized in African locations and had worked on *The African Queen, The Snows of Kilimanjaro, White Witch Doctor,* and *Mogambo,* and her job following *Exodus* was as location manager for *Lawrence of Arabia.*

I was scared of him and to his face always called him "Mr. Preminger." I was well brought up so I never yelled back when he would get excited—because I was a girl I took the shit when anything went wrong. There was no favoritism with Otto Preminger: we all stayed at the same deluxe hotel throughout our stay. I went to the first meeting with representatives of the Israeli government—we had to make our plans months in advance of the actual shooting—and after the meeting Otto said that we have to respect our hosts. Saturday will be our day off.

I scouted locations with Richard Day. Otto depended on my

location notes, the daily report I wrote. I always had to be ahead on these so they'd be ready whenever he asked. Otto and Day decided that we would have to build Gan Dafna [a kibbutz bordering an Arab community where much of the action is set] and it was my job to make it possible to build it. Moshe Dayan assigned his son to work with me on it. When Papa came to the location we had selected for Gan Dafna he snapped, "This is not what I wanted: I wanted purple clover not white clover. Change it!" We replanted the clover and a set painter touched it up with purple.

Then Papa sent me to Italy and Greece to find a ship to appear as the *Exodus* [which carries European refugees from British-controlled Cyprus to Haifa]. I found a lovely ship in Greece, and I came back with photographs. Of course Papa would make the final decision. He made *all* the decisions. And unlike John Huston, with whom I had just worked in French West Africa and the Belgian Congo on *The Roots of Heaven,* Otto *never* changed his mind.

From the first, I could read the signals of when he was about to blow—his body language was very revealing. And from this first trip he knew I knew how to read him. I just sensed that Otto was a human being: when he shook your hand, he shook your hand. I was so proud when at the end of our trip he told me I was smart enough to be Jewish![13]

After their visit, Martin Schute wasn't quite as happy as Eva Monley.

I could tell that Israel was going to be a very difficult country to shoot in because of the temperament of the people. Otto invited me to sit in on his meetings with the Irgun [radical anti-British resistance fighters] and, being wicked, told them I was English. The Irgun were not best pleased with how they were to be treated in the film. They made threats, and they meant business: they did *not* approve of Otto's approach and they told us they would block us. But they couldn't scare Otto, a shrewd political mover who had the crucial assistance of Meyer Weisgal, also shrewd as hell.

Meyer was chairman of the *Exodus* company and I was its director, and we both helped to facilitate things. So much Israeli law was based on English law, which I was familiar with, and Meyer had the contacts. He ran the Israeli 10,000 Club, made up of Americans who had donated ten thousand dollars or more for Israel. (Meyer was also a great procurer, who brought in tins of ham for Ben-

Gurion to have for breakfast.) During our visit Otto decided on a fourteen-week shoot, whereas an average schedule for a picture like *Exodus* would be twenty to twenty-five weeks. But Otto knew he could do it in less time. Otto was a *great* producer—but he didn't have the patience to be a great director.[14]

On December 9, 1959, a week after returning from Israel, Preminger held the first of many press conferences about his blockbuster. On this occasion, he treated each announcement as a bulletin of historic significance. He informed the press that he would be setting up unit headquarters in Haifa and would be ready to begin shooting, in a superwide-screen process, either 70 mm Panavision or MGM Camera 65, on March 28, 1960. As he had on his recent Michigan safari with *Anatomy of a Murder,* he said he planned to watch the rushes and to edit as he was shooting—a lab in Hollywood would process the footage and return it to him on location within six days. "Ecstatic" about the locations he had just scouted, he boasted that *Exodus* would be the first American picture to be shot entirely in Israel, and he pledged to welcome on a daily basis a delegation from Israel's nascent film industry. He also pointed out that a major section of the story, a prison break, would be filmed where the event actually happened, in the former Acre prison, now an insane asylum.[15]

Over the next several months, as Gan Dafna was being built in Israel, Preminger regularly kept the press informed about his progress and his casting. On January 20, he made international headlines when he announced that he would be giving screen credit to the blacklisted Dalton Trumbo. His gesture, which in effect would break the blacklist, was greeted by some commentators as another of Preminger's courageous stands against intolerance and the forces of censorship. Skeptics, however, decried it as yet another example of what they regarded as the filmmaker's compulsive publicity mongering. As often with Preminger, it's likely that it was both—a principled stand as well as an example of promotional savvy. The commercial instincts that influenced the filmmaker's decision might have qualified the "purity" of his gesture but did not alter its fundamental moral sincerity: Preminger regarded the blacklist as un-American, an infringement on his own and Trumbo's constitutionally guaranteed freedom of choice. "My decision to hire Dalton Trumbo was realistic and practical, and not political," Preminger declared. "I will not participate in the blacklist because it is immoral and an illegal extension of due process of law, just like lynching. It is not my job to inquire into the politics of the persons I sign."[16] In a television interview on January 26, Preminger, maintaining that it had been his intention all along to give screen credit to Trumbo (who had offered to do the job under an assumed name) stressed that he was "violently opposed to Communism. I also believe you never punish a man for what he thinks—you only punish him for what he does. I have complete confidence that if Dalton Trumbo were engaged in activities that endangered the United States, our government would take care of him. It's the FBI's job, not mine, to weed out subversives." A strong objection from the American Legion in February prolonged the debate while also, of course, furnishing the impresario with more preproduction buzz. "I must confess I don't even know what the American Legion does," Preminger said in an interview in the *New York Herald Tribune* on February 2, 1960. "But it certainly has no right to tell other people what to do. Seriously speaking, the Legion should praise me for putting the name on the screen. Without credit for everyone to see, there is suspicion. It is a risk [that Trumbo's name will hurt the box office] but there are certain risks one must take to keep self-respect."

"We're glad to learn that the major studios intend to keep the blacklist rather than follow the Preminger lead," said an editorial in the *New York Daily News* on February 5. "There is no lynching spirit in the Hollywood blacklist. Rather the idea is to deny aid to those whose chief ambition is to lynch liberty. No law compels Mr. Preminger to go along with the blacklist. But neither does any law require patriotic Americans to go and see the Preminger-Trumbo movie." Following Preminger's lead, Kirk Douglas, producing and starring in *Spartacus,* for which Trumbo had written the screenplay, announced that he too would be giving the writer screen credit. "Kirk Douglas didn't announce that Trumbo had written *Spartacus* until September, many months *after* Otto had declared his intention," Hope recalled. "It was Otto who broke the blacklist, yet after Otto died the Writers Guild gave an award to Kirk Douglas for being the first to break it. Dalton's widow, Cleo, was furious and wrote to the Guild to say it was Otto who should be getting the award; but the Guild never answered. Cleo and her family did not attend, and Kirk Douglas, a living celebrity, got the award. After he received the award I met Kirk at several parties, but he refused to speak to me."[17]

In Haifa on March 25, three days before the start of shooting, Preminger provided another column item for the international press he had assembled to cover the production: he married his costume coordinator, Hope Bryce, twenty-two years his junior. In Israel interfaith marriage (Hope is Episcopalian) is a virtual impossibility—to everyone, that is, except Otto Preminger. To facilitate the marriage, Otto once again called on Meyer Weisgal. "[Preminger] corralled . . . a trio consisting of Abba Khousky, the Mayor of

Otto and Hope, blissful newlyweds on the set of *Exodus*.

Haifa, Khousky's secretary Milka [who would appear in the film, briefly, as Golda Meir], and me, as coordinators," Weisgal recollected. "We had to convince the rabbinate of the urgency of the marriage without revealing too many unnecessary details about Hope's ancestry."[18]

> We weren't planning on getting married in Israel [Hope said]. We thought at first we could get married in the American embassy, because there we'd be on American soil. Then we thought we'd marry when the film moved to Cyprus in early July. But Meyer and the mayor of Haifa said that was nonsense. Meyer called the rabbis together and I went to a "trial," with Meyer as my witness. The tribunal, glum and grumpy, asked Meyer in Yiddish if I was Jewish. I had had to memorize the Jewish names of my mother and aunt, who weren't Jewish—I hope they understood! Meyer had coached me all afternoon how to say the names. I "passed," but the tribunal knew if they refused us, funding would be taken away from them. During the wedding ceremony in our hotel room, Meyer began to whisper to me, and the rabbi said, "No coaching." A chuppah was set up in our hotel room and according to tradition Otto stomped on the glass.[19]

Included in the small wedding party were Ingo and Kate, who had flown in from Los Angeles, Eva Monley, and Martin Schute. "I'd never been to a Jewish wedding before," Eva Monley said. "It was quite beautiful—very simple."[20] "I held the canopy at the wedding," Schute recalled. "For the occasion, Hope was made Jewish. 'I'm so glad you've come, Martin; we Anglicans must stick together,' she told me."[21] ("Otto and I had been married for twelve years when Meyer 'exposed' us in his autobiography," Hope said. "When Otto heard the rabbi in Israel might deny our marriage, he asked his friend, the [New York State] attorney general Louis Lefkowitz, to marry us in his office. And so we were married a second time, and this time I did not have to pretend to be Jewish.")

The newlyweds had no time for a honeymoon. "Early Monday morning we were both needed on the set for the first day of filming," said Hope, who from here on would serve as costume coordinator on every one of her husband's films but one. "Right after the ceremony I went to my office, set up in the basement of our Haifa hotel, to meet with my crew. I had more people working under me than I would have on any other film—I felt like a general in charge of an army."[22]

As the commanding officer of a superproduction, Preminger exerted a godfatherlike authority. He expected everything to be done when and exactly as he wanted, as Schute recalled:

My job as general manager of the whole company was to keep the machine rolling at colossal speed, and to do what the boss wanted. "Get that ship out of the ocean; take it away, Martin," he told me when he wanted to clear Haifa Bay for a shot. Through the contacts we had made I was able to send the SS *Jerusalem* out to sea until Otto got the shot he wanted. There were so many problems at every turn. Israel didn't have the equipment we needed—we were shooting on 65 mm negative, in Panavision 65—and we had to fly in all equipment from Italy. The klieg lights were shipped in from Rome. In addition to some Israeli assistants—we used as many as we could, but Israel at the time had no film business to speak of—there were five nationalities in the crew: Greek, American, Turkish, Italian, and English, many of whom had worked with Otto at Shepperton on *Saint Joan.* We had the army working for us. They helped us in "moving the troops," transporting cast and crew around the country. But when there were air raid warnings, everything stopped and there would be no movement of any kind. Because Otto didn't like the food in Israel—there was lots of boiled duck, kosher, and it was awful—we brought in our own caterers. The extras on the *Exodus* were Israelis, and the consumption of ham rolls by the Israelis was staggering.

Schute's biggest challenge was in moving the entire company from Jerusalem to Cyprus. (Although the scenes set on Cyprus open the film, they were the last to be shot.) "We finished all the Israeli scenes at lunchtime on a Friday," Schute said,

and Otto told me, "Let's start in Cyprus at 9 a.m. on Monday." It was my job to make it happen—and it was a huge job. First of all, I couldn't start flying the cast and crew until after sundown on Saturday. We had a crew of about 120, the ship, twenty army trucks in English colors, camera equipment, twelve electrical generators, thirty lamps. I slept on Friday night and then not again until Monday night. Eva Monley was putting people into hotel rooms on Cyprus. I arrived on Cyprus from Israel on the last plane out, 2 a.m. Monday morning, and we were ready to shoot at 9 a.m. that morning, exactly as Otto had ordered. I received no thanks: I was doing my job. That's what I was there for.[23]

"Otto expected Martin and me to do the impossible," Eva Monley remembered.

We were to do as he said, and to find a solution even when there didn't seem to be any options. You couldn't say no to Otto, you didn't dare tell him that what he was asking couldn't be done. You *had* to find a way. Because Otto insisted that the composer, Ernest Gold, had to be on hand for the entire shooting (Otto told me, "Gold will live the film with me and write music as we go along"), it became my job to see that Gold's grand piano was shipped to the location. Then I had to see that the piano moved with us whenever we moved. It was not easy, and I knew that if there had been so much as a single chip in that precious instrument, my head would roll.[24]

Throughout the shooting in Israel, Otto, whose lifelong policy was not to turn anyone away from his office, received a stream of complaining visitors. Representatives of the moderate Haganah party and the extremist Irgun objected to the way they had heard they were to be depicted. Irgun spokesmen demanded that Preminger give them sole credit for having masterminded the Acre prison break that was to be the big action set piece in the film's second part. "Menachem Begin, who had been with the Irgun, felt the script was giving the group short shrift," Hope recalled. "When Otto asked how he had gotten a copy of the script, Begin answered, 'I wasn't in the Irgun for nothing.' "[25] A delegation of Sabras (native-born Israelis) decried the character of Ari Ben Canaan, the film's hero, insisting that Israel had been founded through collective action rather than the Hollywood-style heroics of a single political adventurer. Israeli Arabs asked Preminger not to have Arabs attack the children's village of Gan Dafna. "You do not want to rewrite the script, you want to rewrite history," Preminger countered.[26]

He handled every Israeli complaint with aplomb. With a number of his actors, however, he was not as deft. He got off to a bad start with his star, Paul Newman, playing the heroic Sabra Ari Ben Canaan. "On the first day of shooting Paul arrived on the set with five typed pages filled with suggestions for improving the script and his dialogue," Hope said. With a tight smile Preminger informed Newman that he had approved Trumbo's script and would not change one word of it. For a scene in which he was to stand behind two other actors, eavesdropping on their conversation, Newman asked his director what he should be thinking. "To Otto this seemed like an exercise for the Actors Studio," Hope said. "Otto had no patience or respect for the Method, which was so different from the Max Reinhardt tradition he had been trained in, and he told Paul, 'Oh, for God's sake, just stand there.'

"Newman, a cold man, was remote from the minute he walked on the set, and he remained icy throughout the shooting," Hope said. "On the plane from Cyprus to New York after the filming was over he told Otto, 'I could have directed the picture better than you.' "[27]

"After a certain point in the filming, Paul would not take direction from Otto," as Jill Haworth, making her film debut at fourteen, recalled. "They had an arrangement: if Otto had something to say, he was to say it to Paul privately, away from the rest of us."[28] Ironically, when they were filming a scene when Preminger should have had "something to say" to Newman, he didn't think he needed to. "Otto didn't seem to realize that Newman was not doing a good job delivering Ari's big speech in the final scene," Martin Schute recalled. "Otto shot the scene in his favorite method, in a long take, because he wanted to let the camera just watch what Newman was doing. Newman, however, was doing a poor job with it, but Otto shot that speech in a way that we couldn't cut—he hadn't covered the shooting, so there was nothing to cut away to. And that was a mistake because in the film New-man's inadequate performance of that final speech takes the speed out of the picture."

Eva Marie Saint, playing what in many ways was the pivotal role, a Gen-tile nurse who falls for Ari and gradually becomes converted to the Zionist cause, was also unhappy with Preminger. Like her costar, Saint was Method-trained and a member in good standing of the Actors Studio. "Eva Marie didn't like Otto," Martin Schute recalled. "She felt he was directing traffic rather than helping her to explore her character's motivation."[29] "Eva Marie went to sleep every night crying," according to costar Michael Wager.[30] "I don't like to say anything bad about anyone—I've been in the business too long," Eva Marie Saint said. "I'll just say that Otto yelled a lot, but not at the stars. He was a very good filmmaker, nonetheless."[31]

Like both Paul Newman and Eva Marie Saint, Michael Wager, playing a prominent resistance fighter, was also a member of the Actors Studio and therefore, from Preminger's point of view, a potential adversary. Wager, who is Meyer Weisgal's son, was accustomed to a bellowing patriarch. "My father and Otto were of the same ilk," he observed. "After my opening night on Broadway in *A Streetcar Named Desire* [Wager appeared as the newspaper boy], my father came backstage and said, 'For this they pay you?' Not nice. It was no fun being Meyer Weisgal's son. But I never heard yelling from him of the kind we got from Otto, who was very Hapsburg." Wager received the Preminger treatment on a scene in which his character is reunited with his fiancée. " 'Don't you know how to kiss a girl?' Otto yelled. He made us do the scene twenty times. It was humiliating. Mike Wallace was there the day we shot the scene, and maybe Otto felt he had to prove something. The first assistant director walked off the set. It was the worst thing to scream at me." And in this instance counterproductive: in the film Wager's embrace is passion-free.

"The next day I confronted Otto in our hotel and criticized him for yelling at me. With that seductive quality he shared with Elia Kazan, he said, '*I* yell at you? You're a charming young man. Why would I do that?' " Unlike Wager, George Maharis, playing a member of the Irgun, responded in kind to a Preminger tirade. "We were in a small room, Paul, George, and I," as Wager recalled, "when Otto started in on George, who yelled back at full volume. Otto said, 'I wish you had such emotion in your acting.' That shut George up. Otto had a huge talent as a filmmaker, but not as a director of actors. 'Just do it,' he'd say."[32]

Preminger's skirmishes with Newman and Saint were as nothing com-pared to the full-force explosion that occurred during a scene shot in the plaza of the Russian Compound in Jerusalem, where, to a crowd of 40,000 extras, Lee J. Cobb (also Actors Studio), playing Ari's father, Barak Ben Canaan, was to announce the United Nations vote to partition Palestine. To attract extras, Eva Monley had come up with the idea of holding a lottery with cash prizes of 20,000 Israeli pounds and six free trips to the film's opening in New York, and the night of the shooting her ploy drew more than one-fourth of Jerusalem's 160,000 inhabitants. The scene was scheduled to be shot at 5 p.m., and Preminger assured Meyer Weisgal, who was to appear briefly as Ben-Gurion, that he would be needed only for "five or ten minutes." But as Preminger demanded take after take, "ten minutes" stretched into twelve hours. After Preminger had asked for at least a dozen retakes, Cobb, who had the only spoken lines in the scene, and Preminger, perched on a crane at the opposite side of the square, started screaming at each other. Eyewitnesses agreed about the intensity of the outburst—it was Vesuvian— but disagreed about what had provoked it.

Hope Preminger: "Lee had had three or four weeks off, and the night of the shooting he did not know his lines. Otto didn't want to cut the speech— he wanted to film it in one take, to give it a sustaining power. Lee said,

Barak Ben Canaan (Lee J. Cobb) announcing the birth of a nation to a crowd of 40,000 extras in *Exodus*. A disagreement with Cobb ignited one of Preminger's most incendiary flare-ups.

'Otto, you can always piece it together.' To Otto, those were fighting words. There was no excuse for Lee to have to ad-lib his lines—and of course Otto was the least likely director to accept any ad-libs. It gave him an opportunity to explode. And explode he certainly did."[33]

Eva Monley: "Cobb didn't know his lines and the confrontation became two stubborn men bumping heads."[34]

Martin Schute: "Cobb knew the lines but he didn't say them the way Otto wanted him to. Cobb, a Method actor, wanted to perform the scene *his* way, and when Otto started yelling, Cobb yelled back. They screamed at each other at long range. Another problem was that we didn't have enough lights for a long shot of the whole crowd. We couldn't shoot the whole square and the figures on the balcony all in one great long shot, which is what Otto wanted. I had thirty lights but I needed more. Otto was frustrated because he couldn't get the all-inclusive wide shot he wanted."[35]

Lee J. Cobb: "To pinprick this idiocy, it wasn't a question of any 14 lines. I *knew* those lines, for God's sake! Otto Preminger forced thousands of extras to stand in the square—these were local people, some quite elderly—and it got to be 3 a.m. I suggested something should be done. Unpredictably, like a madman, Preminger flared up. So I gave him a piece of my mind."[36]

An anonymous crew member: "The shocking thing is evidently Otto is spreading his version, and I think he's probably convinced himself it's true. The lottery cost him only 30,000 [Israeli pounds] to get the extras, whereas if he had paid regular rates it would have been 100,000 or more. Drawing for prizes was supposed to be at midnight, but Otto kept stalling around, from 8 to 3. The crowd was standing there hour after hour, and old women were fainting—it was just awful. Of course Cobb knew his lines—and it was two pages, not 14 lines. Otto kept doing it over and over, first from one angle, then another. Finally, at 3, he was satisfied and then he decided he wanted one more shot. It was then Cobb told him off. He really let him have it—told him he was inhuman, had no consideration or a shred of decency."[37]

During the blowup, Meyer Weisgal tried to intervene but Preminger silenced him. After Preminger came down from the crane, he and Weisgal were driven to the King David Hotel. "That son of a bitch, I pay him $95,000 and he doesn't even know his lines," Weisgal recalled Preminger saying.[38] Otto fired Cobb, a moot point as all the actor's scenes had been shot, and canceled Cobb's room at the King David. "It was mean," Michael Wager said. "Everyone thought his behavior to Cobb was unforgivable."[39] "Before Cobb left Israel, every member of the company shook his hand and thanked him for having the guts to do what no one else had," reported the irate crew member who, six years after the fact, requested anonymity.[40] Preminger and Cobb never spoke again. "Lee is excellent in the film," Hope Preminger conceded.[41]

In a characteristic turnabout, Preminger was especially kind to his two youngest actors, Sal Mineo, giving the performance of a lifetime as Dov Landau, a Holocaust survivor determined to join the Irgun, and Jill Haworth, doing superbly as Karen, a Danish refugee. Haworth had been the last actor to be cast. "Otto and I went to drama schools in England, and in Cologne, Germany, auditioning a great many youngsters for the role, all of them about fourteen," Hope said. "I think Otto felt a little as if he was auditioning again for *Saint Joan*. When we tested a young English girl, Jill Haworth, we thought she had an extraordinary instinct for how to play the role."[42] "I was in a children's theater school, taking day classes," as Jill Haworth recalled.

Mr. Preminger saw my photo in the school book and wanted to see me. I auditioned along with five other English girls, three times. Then Otto asked me to make a screen test. The next day I went with my mother and a lawyer to see Preminger in his suite at the Dorchester, and two weeks later I was in Israel.

I learned acting from Preminger on the set of *Exodus*. I felt rescued by him, and he had such patience with me, such insight. I have seen photos taken on the set of him pointing at me, and it looks threatening; but it wasn't. People would say, "It's your turn today," and I got paranoid. But it was *never* my turn. Yes, he was an exacting taskmaster: didn't he have a right to be? But some of it was tongue-in-cheek—he was parodying himself in *Stalag 17*. I heard rumors that his feelings for me were incestuous: nonsense. He was fatherly; he tried to educate me; he looked after me every moment. I had to be in bed by nine every night and on the set at nine the next morning. He made sure I had a chaperone at all times. He fired the first one because she was always in a bar. After the first two weeks my mother came over to act as my chaperone. I didn't even know how to kiss for the kissing scenes—Preminger, along with Hope and Sal, helped me there. I overheard Ursula Andress calling her husband John Derek [cast as Taha, Ari's Arab friend] a faggot, and I had to ask Preminger what that meant. A driver once took me to the wrong place, and Hasidic Jews stoned me: it would never have happened if Preminger had been there. He was wonderful to Sal, too, and Sal loved him; he knew Preminger was helping him to give a really strong performance. When I got close to Sal, however, Otto advised me against it.[43]

Despite (or maybe because of) the tensions on the set, which Preminger seemed both to provoke and to thrive on, he finished ahead of schedule. "Amazingly, we came in under Otto's projection of fourteen weeks, which was already a good six to ten weeks under what I thought the film needed," Martin Schute said. "Midway through the thirteenth week we wrapped. Otto had managed to shoot all three hours and forty minutes of *Exodus* in a little over thirteen weeks." Part of why the machinery spun along with such precision was the arrangement Preminger, with Schute's assistance, had made for screening the rushes. "Our transport manager, an Israeli just out of the Marine Corps, had the job of seeing that the film we shot in Israel was on a plane to Los Angeles and then flown back to Israel the following day," Schute said.

Three days after the footage had been shot we saw our rushes on 35 mm in a big theater in Tel Aviv. With Otto supervising, we cut as we went along—and two weeks after the end of shooting we had a rough cut. This was all the more remarkable because Otto had no technical sense about sound or the camera. To say the least, he was very unmechanically minded—he gave me his pocket calculator because he couldn't work it, he had stubby fingers. He could say why he didn't like something, but not how to cure it. But he hired the best technical support, and we never had a second-rate anybody. Noteworthy, too, is that Otto did not go *one penny* over his original four-million-dollar budget.[44]

Throughout filming Preminger conducted a carefully worked out promotional campaign. The scores of local and international journalists he invited to each day of shooting ensured extensive coverage in newspapers throughout the world. And at four strategic points during the production— on the first day; midway through, when the company moved from Haifa to Jerusalem; near the end, when cast and crew traveled from Jerusalem to Cyprus; and on the final day—Otto placed large ads in newspapers in New York, Los Angeles, Chicago, and Miami, the cities where the film would open hard-ticket engagements in December. Each ad included a mail order form. As a result, before *Exodus* opened on December 19 it had racked up over one million dollars in advance sales, a record at the time. "*Exodus*

looms as a Klondike entry," reported *Variety* on December 7, 1960. "Preminger stands to pocket one of the largest amounts ever earned by an independent. He will receive 75% of the profits in addition to a fat producer's fee
as against 25% for United Artists. Uris will receive a small percentage of Preminger's 75%. Despite his reputation for being difficult Preminger can command the top deals in the industry because he gives fewer headaches to
studios than other independents."

As an executive working on foreign soil, "remaking Israel to his own
design," as Willi Frischauer observed,[45] Preminger was in top form: both
unstoppable and irresistible. He got what he wanted, even if that meant
clearing an entire harbor; cordoning off rural roads and busy streets in Haifa
and Jerusalem; taking over the entire premises of the former Acre prison.
And throughout the production daily bullets from his own press office
about the making of the film entertained thousands of Israelis. Perhaps
inevitably, the film's critical reception did not match the hullabaloo Preminger had generated throughout its making. Archer Winsten's equivocal
review in the *New York Post* on December 16 was indicative: "Distinctly better than the book, but it still falls short of distinction," he wrote. "It has
weight, appearance, and a good sense of story and publicity. What it lacks is
a sensitivity to people, motives, emotions. . . . Otto Preminger may not
achieve the finest cinematic quality—in fact some might assert he never
does—but you have to hand him the prize for knowing a hot subject, cutting it down to the sensational core and exploiting that to the last full measure." In the *New York Herald Tribune* Paul Beckley commented that "the
very bigness of Preminger's theme makes his film an important one and well
worth seeing—its defects by no means offset the excellences."

In many ways the film condenses, distorts, and simplifies history: it
offers a contrived ledger of ideological checks and balances, with one compassionate British officer, for instance, played off against a British bigot; it
virtually erases any Arab perspective; it makes a naive though well-
intentioned effort to invoke a spirit of brotherhood between Jews and
Arabs; and, as in the novel, the teeming historical background is often, perhaps unavoidably, more compelling than the leading characters. Nevertheless *Exodus* does not fail its great subject. Working on a vast canvas
Preminger rises to the challenge, employing a more varied stylistic range
than on any other film.

Throughout, there are magisterial tracking shots that follow the principal characters. The camera moves with Kitty as she walks through the
refugee camp in Cyprus and among the refugees huddling in groups on
board the *Exodus,* and it tracks Dov Landau marching through uphill streets

Freedom fighters Ari (Paul Newman) and Reuben (Paul Stevens) in Jerusalem, in one of Preminger's wide-angle Panavision shots for *Exodus*.

in Jerusalem as he tries to locate the secret headquarters of the Irgun. Without relying on a single close-up, in these sweeping wide-angle shots Preminger trusts the audience to notice details.

But in this story pitted with conflict, the filmmaker relies on other kinds of syntax besides his customarily dispassionate long shots and long takes. In the film's single most stirring passage, as Ari's uncle Akiva Ben Canaan (David Opatashu), an Irgun leader, conducts an interrogation of Dov Landau, Preminger abandons his usual detachment, creating through cutting and camera placement a greater identification with Dov than he allows with any other character. As Akiva, methodically preparing and then drinking tea, presses the young man to reveal the truth of how he survived in a concentration camp (by allowing himself to be used "like a woman"), Preminger and his cinematographer Sam Leavitt darken the edges of the wide screen and move the camera in for tighter shots of Dov. With lighting and editing enhancing the performances, the scene attains a shattering impact. Preminger's uncharacteristic use of close-ups in the scene in which Barak Ben Canaan visits his brother Akiva in prison achieves equal force. The brothers, political opponents who have not spoken in years, regard each other across prison bars in a silence eloquent with choked love.

Preminger goes for broke in three action set pieces. His handling of Dov

Landau's hair's-breadth escape from British soldiers come to arrest Akiva and his posse for blowing up a wing of the King David Hotel is a masterpiece of wide-screen mise-en-scène. Photographed in wide-angle deep-focus shots, Dov scrambles down stairs, climbs over walls, creeps along side streets, and hides out in a church, the Ethiopian Cathedral in Jerusalem, as a ceremony is in progress. Preminger and his favorite editor, Louis Loeffler, choreograph the film's major action sequence, the escape of political prisoners from Acre prison, as a vast relay race in which each participant enacts a small, perfectly timed role. Although he didn't have the equipment to light a high-angle shot that would have included within the same frame 40,000 Israelis congregated in a square and Barak Ben Canaan on a balcony announcing partition, the sequence nonetheless has the size it needs. The milling crowd is among the most wired in film history, a result of the excitement of waiting for the lottery, the tension brought on by numerous retakes, and the announcement Preminger made to the throng that Adolf Eichmann had just been caught.

In other scenes where the audience might have expected to be overwhelmed, Preminger understates. For Akiva Ben Canaan's death scene, for instance, the director's every choice refutes cliché. Instead of filming Akiva's death in shadowy close-ups overlaid with musical accompaniment, Preminger places it in the back of a car in bright sunlight as American jazz crackles on the car radio. Richly ambivalent, his direction here is shot through with visual and aural surprise. Also skirting expectation is the sequence that concludes Act I, in which the *Exodus* is given permission to leave Cyprus for Palestine. Choosing not to play the moment for pathos or as an ultimate victory—the release of the ship, after all, is only a prelude to the rest of the story—Preminger and Leavitt film the departure in a terse single take that intentionally does not rise to a swelling climax. Preminger concludes the film on a similarly restrained note. There's no sweep or triumph in the final shot of many Israeli soldiers scrambling onto trucks that will carry them into battle. Honoring history, the film ends not with a period or a flourish, but in a state of suspension, as in a grim lineup the trucks rumble off to a war that over six decades later is far from terminated. Preminger's sobering mise-en-scène underlines the fact that a nation may have been created but its struggle for survival has only just begun.

In the film, as in the novel, the two leading characters are unequal to the electrified history against which their conventional romance is played out. Leon Uris's protagonist, Ari Ben Canaan, is a swashbuckling superhero who confronts and overcomes great obstacles. He orchestrates the exodus of six hundred Jewish refugees from Cyprus to Palestine in Act I and the release of political detainees from Acre prison in Act II. The character is conceived as a Hollywood stereotype, and Paul Newman, who makes his entrance from the sea bare-chested and flashing his deep blue eyes, looks as if he stepped off the jacket of a romance novel. Even in the scenes in which Ari masquerades as a British officer and as an Arab, Newman looks, sounds, and moves like an American movie star. Nonetheless, Newman's stern, tight-lipped performance—sentiment is a luxury a character like Ari has no time for—melds with Preminger's tone, which emphasizes history rather than histrionics. Newman evokes the hard-driving quality of a Sabra engaged in a life-or-death struggle to secure a Jewish homeland. However, the character's aria at the end, as he presides over the joint burials of a Jew, Karen, and an Arab, Ari's childhood friend Taha, and anticipates the long fight ahead, demands an oratorical weight Newman was unable, or unwilling, to provide. His tone is too casual, his diction too sloppy. Trumbo's writing for this climactic moment, both blessing and prophecy, is far from incandescent, but it rises to a lyrical pitch Newman's inner-directed style does not begin to accommodate. Newman fails the film at this moment, but Preminger's friezelike composition, with the principal actors lined up above the graves as a stationary camera observes them from a distance, attains a formal beauty that honors the significance of the scene.

Israel, the "star" of *Exodus,* a landscape of harsh, demanding beauty. Eva Marie Saint and Paul Newman, backs to the camera, are at the left; Preminger, in hat, surveys the scene at right.

As in the novel, Preminger and Trumbo place Kitty Fremont's conversion, from anti-Semitic outsider to committed Zionist, as the narrative fulcrum, a device that contains a perhaps unconscious racism (equivalent to telling a story about apartheid in *Cry Freedom* by focusing on the travails of a white family). But the strategy of presenting Zionist struggle primarily from the viewpoint of an outsider affords Preminger a ready-made alibi for his detachment. Kitty is a character it would be easy to resent, but Eva Marie Saint plays her subtly and with an edge that chafes against the Hollywood-style clichés of her character's romance with Ari.

Also transcending sentimentality is the way Preminger presents Israel, the film's true protagonist, as a country of harsh beauty, a land as fierce as the pioneers who dedicate their lives to possessing it. In *Exodus,* the deserts, valleys, mountains, and seas of Israel have a wild, challenging, untamed grandeur worth fighting for. "Otto was proud to be Jewish," Hope said, "and he was proud of the country of Israel. He appreciated the pioneer spirit—with everybody so focused on making this little country work."[46] It is that rugged spirit that his levelheaded yet ultimately moving pageant pays tribute to. And despite Preminger's attempts to be fair to all the players in 1948 Palestine, despite his and Trumbo's efforts to transform Leon Uris's partisan screed into a narrative with a more politically balanced perspective, *Exodus,* finally, is imbued with Zionist fervor. In the end, this powerful, important, and underappreciated film expresses the commitment of a Jewish director to a Jewish homeland.

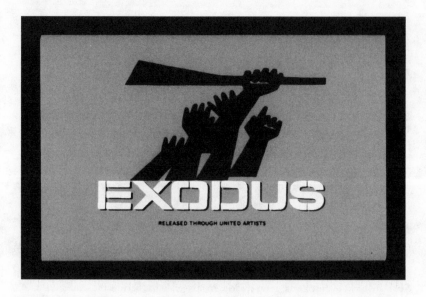

THIRTEEN

Playing Washington

On October 3, 1960, Otto was showing *Exodus* to United Artists executives in New York when his assistant Nat Rudich rushed into the screening room to tell him to go to Doctors' Hospital, where Hope, who had gone into labor on October 2, had just given birth to twins, Mark, four and a half pounds, and Victoria, four pounds. "We hadn't expected the babies quite so soon, but we have known for three months we were to have twins," Preminger told Louella Parsons.[1] Since his apartment at 40 East Sixty-eighth Street was inadequate for his enlarged family, Otto rented two suites at the Sherry Netherland Hotel. "Otto and I had our own suite, and the twins had a suite with an English nanny we had already hired," Hope said. "The kids were born very early—Mark was in an incubator for five weeks, Vicky for six. Thank God they are healthy grown-ups. We knew we needed a house, and only a little while after the kids were born we bought one, at 129 East Sixty-fourth Street, for $128,000. Nat Rudich had lined it up for us. We gutted it and had Saul Bass design a *very* modern house, which is what Otto wanted. We moved in on January 1, 1961, although it wasn't quite finished. Otto said it was like a play out of town: if you don't bring it in, it will never open."[2]

Realizing that as a new father he would have to settle down in New York for a while, Preminger decided to return to the theater. He chose a play about the theater, a breezy comedy by Ira Levin called *Critic's Choice* that

Otto delighted in playing with his infant twins, Mark and Victoria.

was typical of the kind of ephemera that dotted Otto's inglorious Broadway résumé. "Inspired" by the careers of drama critic Walter Kerr and his wife Jean, a playwright, the show is about a drama critic facing the dilemma of having to review a bad new play by his wife. Unlike Jean Kerr, who had a modest talent for concocting lightweight fare like *Mary, Mary,* the character in the play is ungifted. After her show opens to disastrous notices, she returns to being a wife and mother, admitting (in prefeminist 1960) that her disapproving husband had been right all along.

"It's not much of a play," as Howard Taubman noted in his review in the *New York Times* on December 15, "but drama critics will always be grateful to Mr. Preminger who, as the producer, has spent money lavishly to let George Jenkins create a resplendent, many-chambered home worthy of a drama critic." Henry Fonda, who starred as the title character, was "a huge draw," Hope recalled. "Otto adored him: Fonda was off book at the first rehearsal, and his performance never varied." As the persistent wife Preminger originally had cast Gena Rowlands, but fired her early on when he realized she was wrong for the part. (How could he ever have thought Rowlands, with her coarse, slurred voice, hardened face, and glum manner, would be at home in a smart Manhattan drawing room?) He replaced her with Georgeann Johnson, a charmer with a touch of class. "Otto thought the play was quite funny at the time, but it's clear that the show was only for its time and that time has passed," Hope said.[3] This bit of retrograde trivia ran for 189 performances, with Preminger reaping additional profits when he sold the rights to Warner Bros. In 1963 the studio released a strictly dead-on-arrival film directed by Don Weis and starring a miscast Bob Hope and a clueless Lucille Ball.

Critic's Choice opened on December 14, 1960, at the Barrymore Theatre. Two days later *Exodus* began its reserved-seat engagement around the corner at the Warner Theatre on Broadway. "I can run back and forth when I get nervous," Preminger joked.[4]

While Otto had certainly earned some time off to spend with his newborn twins, taking it easy was not his style. And so in the first few months of 1961, with his play and film doing strong business and no new project at the ready, he began to oversee renovations on his new town house. He treated the project, having the four floors of his residence redesigned to his exacting specifications, as though it was his latest superproduction. "Otto fought desperately with the architect and the contractors," Hope remembered. "If I made pictures the way these contractors work, my movies would cost $50 million apiece," he grumbled.[5]

Otto wanted a residence from which any trace of his parents' Old World Biedermeier taste was to be proscribed. "Our modern house was certainly a reaction to the Ringstrasse ornateness Otto had grown up in and felt inundated by in Vienna, which has a corner on the market for gilt, red plush walls, and ormolu," Hope said.[6] It was Otto's intention that each room was to be decorated completely in black and white, relieved only by an occasional accent of gray. Accessories were to be limited to silver and crystal. He wanted white walls and gray rugs as a neutral background for his collection of colorful paintings by Picasso, Chagall, Dufy, Modigliani, Klee, Braque, Matisse, and Degas. To hang over the sofa in the high-ceilinged living room he purchased a twelve-foot-long Miró. For the small rock garden he purchased a huge (fifty feet by twenty-two) bronze by Henry Moore called *Hungry Women* and commissioned the artist to construct a special base that

The screening room in Preminger's Manhattan town house. With a flick of a remote control buzzer, a screen would descend from the ceiling and cover the window and television cabinet.

at the slightest touch of a finger would cause the statue to rotate. He hired Abe Feder, a theatrical lighting specialist, to install lights to illuminate *Hungry Women* at night.

Marble being Preminger's material of choice, he ordered gray marble tables of different shapes and sizes for every room. For the staircase he had marble banisters installed. Since Preminger's favorite piece of furniture was the basic Charles Eames swivel-based desk chair, he placed Eames chairs in every room, along with furniture by other modernist masters such as Eero Saarinen, Arne Jacobsen, and Hans Wegner. When Otto found fault with the fact that the chair seats were twenty-nine inches from the floor, he called the designer to complain and requested that the chairs be one inch higher. Eames, considering this a valid suggestion, asked his manufacturer Herman Miller to include the new height among the firm's regular offerings.[7]

Otto ordered remote control devices and push buttons for every room. His prize button was the wireless remote buzzer system installed in the dining room. "If you can put on a television set by remote control, I figured you could use the same type of device to summon the maid from the kitchen," Preminger reasoned. "Turn on the twins," he would say, and he'd push a button in any room in the house and hear them gurgling in the nursery.[8]

Hope, who loved antiques but in time came to appreciate her husband's taste, argued for "frolicsome" wallpaper in the nursery. "Otto wanted white walls and a couple of Picassos, and he thought that anything else might 'warp' the twins' aesthetic development," she recalled. "But I really wanted the nursery to have a dash of bright colors and fun, and we compromised on white walls and a couple of Bemelmanses."[9] Preminger's only other concession to color was his and Hope's bathroom, a sanctum of luxury dominated by two bathtubs in blue marble placed end to end. At opposite ends of the room stood two blue-tiled washbasins.

For each of the three upper floors, Otto had the contractors transform closets into kitchenette units. "It makes life so much easier," Preminger claimed.[10] But, as Hope pointed out, "Otto couldn't cook at all. He couldn't even boil water without scorching the pan. Once he made grilled cheese sandwiches by putting the cheese in the toaster without any bread and he caused a fire. He caused another fire when he tried to grill cheese directly on the stove. He hadn't a clue."

Like his films, Otto's domestic mise-en-scène—cool, severe, conceived down to the last detail according to the owner's demands—was not for everyone. "People who hate modern gasped when they saw what Otto had designed," Hope admitted. "It looked like the house of a celebrity: that was what Otto wanted to convey."[11] Preminger modern struck Helen Lawrenson, a visiting journalist, as akin to "one of those austerely elegant new banks."[12]

"Cozy" and "intimate" were not the master's intentions, and yet in the kind of paradoxical turn that was the essence of Otto, the house with an oddly uninviting décor was always filled with guests. "I often felt I was running a hotel," Hope said.

> Otto was always interested in people, and by no means only people in show business. For dinner, in addition to movie stars, he would invite lawyers, judges, politicians, academics, and people he might

have just met on the street. Despite his reputation for yelling, Otto really was the most accessible of famous persons: if you greeted him on the street with a "Hello, Mr. Preminger," he would stop to talk and might even invite you to dinner that night. One night he had invited Sophia Loren and someone he'd met on the street, a Jesuit priest from the University of Nevada who made enormous sculptures. Often I'd find out too late that there would be extra people for dinner. We had a live-in couple and a nanny but even so it was quite a job running the house.[13]

Although they were not there very often, living almost around the corner at 48 East Sixty-third Street in a pink house with a white trim façade were Gypsy Rose Lee and Erik. Gypsy's décor, Victoriana run amok, would certainly have drawn disapproval from Otto. But Otto's commitment to black-and-white minimalism was equally overwrought. For the brief time they were neighbors there was no contact between the former lovers or between father and son. In April 1963, Gypsy sold her house for $115,000 and relocated to a hilltop in Beverly Hills.

By the end of February 1961, as renovations on 129 East Sixty-fourth Street were nearing completion, Preminger was eager to return to his day job. He began working with Wendell Mayes on the screenplay of another best seller, *Advise and Consent,* by Allen Drury. A story of a U.S. president's nomination for secretary of state, the novel contains enough ingredients, including a sexual scandal in the Senate and political skulduggery that reaches into the Oval Office, to qualify it as another controversial Preminger undertaking. In late March and April the director made several trips to scout locations in Washington, where he expected to shoot the entire picture beginning in September, and to curry favor with senators in order to gain permission to go where no filmmaker had ever gone before—inside the Senate chamber itself.

In May, satisfied with the progress Mayes was making, he took time off to go to the Cannes Film Festival, where *Exodus* was screened out of competition. Leading a party that included cast members Sal Mineo, Jill Haworth, and Peter Lawford, Preminger arranged a flashy entrance. He chartered a Caravelle jet to fly one hundred French theatrical and political figures from Paris to Cannes. At the Carlton Hotel he hosted a sumptuous lunch for the press, in effect treating the *Exodus* screening as the film's European bow. After Cannes he traveled with his three actors to London for a May 9 opening at the Astoria, a theater he had helped to remodel for the film's reserved-seat engagement. He and his entourage then moved on to Paris, where

Mr. and Mrs. Otto Preminger and the two young stars of *Exodus,* Jill Haworth and Sal Mineo, at the Cannes Film Festival screening, May 1961.

Exodus opened on May 17 at two mammoth theaters on the Champs-Élysées. The next day *Exodus* bowed in Tel Aviv, with all receipts going to the Weitzmann Institute, as Preminger had promised. At the end of the month Otto returned to London to respond to critical blasts. At a luncheon he hosted, he chastised his guests for reviewing the politics of the novel rather than those of the film; called some of the notices "malicious"; and expressed resentment that several British critics had made a point of mentioning that both he and Leon Uris were Jewish. "We are first of all Americans, and *Exodus* is an American picture," he announced.[14]

When he returned to New York in June, in long daily meetings with Wendell Mayes he completed the script of *Advise and Consent.* As on *Anatomy of a Murder,* Preminger and Mayes were working on a good yarn, an insider's exposé of Washington power plays. But they had their work cut out for them. Their first task was to trim Drury's prolix novel. Their second, as Preminger, a lifelong Democrat, stated, was "to correct Drury's conservative Republican bias. It is our intention to disguise the political affiliations of the characters."[15] Otto wanted to detach the film from Drury's Cold War agenda, which presents appeasement toward Communist Russia as a poten-

Burgess Meredith (seated, second from the left), a fearful witness, denounces the president's nominee for secretary of state (Henry Fonda, standing) as a former Communist. Preminger called Meredith's performance "one of the greatest" he had ever seen.

tially mortal threat to the nation. But he was going to retain the novelist's view of politics as the art of the possible, a set of maneuvers requiring compromise, subterfuge, and diplomacy on a grand scale. The question Drury's omniscient narrator poses in the last line of the novel, "whether history still had a place for a nation so strongly composed of great ideals and uneasy compromise as [America]," epitomized the equivocal realist tone Preminger was hoping to capture.

"The Senate itself—our remarkable system of checks and balances— will be the hero," Preminger said.[16] And indeed, as the script was evolving, no single character, neither the president nor his nominee nor any individual senator, dominated the action. Nonetheless, Preminger assembled an all-star cast of mostly elder Hollywood statesmen with a well-bred air. (In the Camelot era, wasn't it reasonable for politicians to be played by charismatic film stars?) As the controversial left-of-center nominee with a possibly Communist past: Henry Fonda. As the defiant president: Franchot Tone. As the august majority leader of the Senate: Walter Pidgeon. As a Southern demagogue enraged by the specter of appeasement: Charles Laughton. As

the self-effacing vice-president: Lew Ayres. As a witness against the nominee: Burgess Meredith. As a Washington hostess: Gene Tierney, making a
comeback after years of mental illness.

For the role of a playboy senator, Preminger's first and only choice was
Peter Lawford, who as everyone at the time was aware was President
Kennedy's brother-in-law. Lawford was right for the part, but Preminger
knew the casting would ensure publicity and he was hoping the actor might
help in obtaining permission to shoot some scenes in the Oval Office and in
the president's living quarters. "One phone call from Peter to Jack was all it
took to smooth the way," as Lawford's biographer, James Spada, reported.
"The President—still such a movie buff that he would call Peter to discuss
the British box-office receipts of *Ocean's 11*—thought it would be fun to
have a movie crew around for a few days, and he granted Preminger permission to film in the White House."[17]

To play a black senator from Georgia, Preminger hired Dr. Martin
Luther King Jr. "I sought Dr. King for the role and he accepted simply
because his appearance will make a positive statement for this country here
and abroad," Preminger said. "It should indicate that it is possible for a
Negro to be elected to the United States Senate at any time, now or in the
future."[18] Casting Dr. King, as Otto fully expected, generated an avalanche
of publicity, but the civil rights leader reconsidered and withdrew.

Two roles were hard to cast: Senator Brigham Anderson, head of the
subcommittee charged with investigating the president's controversial nominee, who is blackmailed because of a wartime homosexual relationship; and
Fred Van Ackerman, a hyper-eager, power-hungry senator who master-
minds the blackmail plot. "I understand that several stars had turned down
the role of Brigham Anderson because of the homosexual element," recalled
Don Murray, who accepted the part.

> Otto asked me if playing a homosexual would bother me—remem-
> ber, this was a very different time. Homosexual characters barely
> existed; happily, forty years later attitudes have changed. I told Otto
> that in *Bus Stop* I had played a cowboy: does that make me a cow-
> boy? I did hesitate, however, but not because of the gay angle; I hes-
> itated because of Otto's reputation. I'd worked successfully with
> another director, Henry Hathaway, who had the same reputation,
> and I'd learned how to handle a bully. I figured that people who
> were bullies acted that way because they are basically insecure about
> addressing people in a normal way. I decided from the first meeting
> with Preminger that I would be assertive, very direct, and very defi-

nite because if you show people like that any kind of weakness, they attack; they're like sharks when they smell blood.[19]

"Frank Sinatra wanted to play Van Ackerman, but Otto wanted an unknown," recalled George Grizzard, who at the time Otto cast him had been in four plays on Broadway and only one film, *From the Terrace*.

When I went in to see Otto, I hadn't read the book: you can't act the book. But I had read the script and next to Charles Laughton's, Van Ackerman was the best part in the film. You didn't have to audition for Otto, which I liked. I was simply brought in to talk to him; he saw something in me that he wanted for the role, and he cast me. I went in not afraid of Otto, mostly because I had enjoyed hearing about a conversation he'd had with Charlton Heston, who wanted to play Laughton's part. When Otto told Heston he wasn't right for it, Heston said, "Have you seen me in a beard?" "How else have I seen you?" Otto had replied.[20]

Many times in advance of his September 5 starting date, Preminger traveled to the capital, where, as skillfully as he had in Israel, he cultivated a cadre of local movers and shakers who became liaisons, scouts, and advisers. But despite his influential lobbyists and his own perseverance, Otto was not allowed to shoot in the Senate chamber; he would have to re-create the Senate on a sound stage at Columbia Pictures. He was, however, granted an extraordinary privilege—his art director, Lyle Wheeler, and his set decorator, Eli Benneche, were admitted into the Senate to take extensive photographic documentation; once the photos had served their purpose, all of them had to be destroyed.

Preminger's primary inside man in Washington was Paul Green, a former journalist who ran Hollywood-on-the-Potomac. "Preminger was the most striking person I have ever met," Green recollected. "He dripped personality, and he had the most marvelous accent. He was masterful, dominant, yet everybody seemed to like him. I certainly liked him instantly. I never witnessed one of his rages—he was always polite. And Nat Rudich, his assistant who handled the press, was also a very nice guy." Green, who was on the Senate staff working for Estes Kefauver, a Tennessee Democrat, knew his way around Washington and had Hollywood connections besides. "Estes was a rascal," Green said. "He had a keen interest in movies and in starlets and he couldn't wait for the film people to come to town; he wanted to meet all of them. I had no trouble getting clearances for the film crew's

Otto on the set of the Senate, a replica of the actual chamber in Washington, D.C., constructed for *Advise and Consent* at Columbia Pictures in Hollywood.

cumbersome equipment, which cluttered Senate hallways and meeting rooms for days on end. I arranged it so that Preminger could film anywhere inside and outside any building or room on Capitol Hill except for the Senate chamber itself."[21]

In what was probably the most persuasive public relations performance of his career, the filmmaker turned Washington into an Otto Preminger set as he courted politicians and the press throughout the five weeks of location work. "He really presold the film by having the world press there throughout the Washington shooting," George Grizzard observed. "Every Sunday night he would hold a banquet for the press and he expected all of the actors to be present. You had to have a note from your mother to miss that."[22] For a scene in which the president addresses the Washington press corps the extras were the real thing. A Washington hostess, Mrs. E. Fontaine Brown, lent Preminger her estate for a dinner party scene, populated by 360 eager socialites who, arrayed in their finery, arrived at seven and did not depart until after two in the morning. "Prince Otto made all but 80 wait in a garage without food or drink for four hours. No one could leave until 1 a.m.," Richard Gehman reported in the *New York Journal American* on September 27. Partygoers were treated to some mild Otto barbs. "You did not smoke in the previous take," Preminger bellowed, ordering one guest to put out a cigarette. "Get out!" he snapped when one partygoer moved in the wrong direction. "I'm from *Look*," the banished man protested. " '*You* look!' Preminger retorted, visibly pleased with his own joke," as Willi Frischauer commented.[23]

Throughout the shoot, as *Time* reported, Preminger himself, "Hollywood's aging (54) *enfant terrible* . . . thundering like an Erich von Stroheim Prussian officer, was really the show."[24] Journalist Donald Zec, on location for the *New York Daily Mirror*, noted that "the balding, brilliant filmmaker . . . known as Otto the Terrible and Otto the Ogre, has captured the capital, and the mesmerized neighbors have surrendered without a fight."[25] Speaking at a National Press Club luncheon, Preminger "got a standing ovation usually reserved for potentates from lands other than Hollywood, and took it in his usual snide," *Time* punned. In a much publicized turn of events, the overscheduled Preminger twice declined a lunch invitation from President and Mrs. Kennedy. "I see where Otto Preminger has snubbed two invitations from Kennedy on the excuse he was too busy. HE was too busy?" clucked gossip doyenne Louella Parsons. "This is the man who rants and raves and seems to have Washington bowing in humble submission. What gives?"[26]

When it finally took place, the twice-deferred gathering was a triumph. "Preminger and the president were very knowledgeable about each other's work," Don Murray noted. "Otto was so interested in politics and so well informed he could have been the politician; the good-looking president could have been the man who was in show business."[27] During the lunch Preminger believed that he would be shooting some scenes in the Oval Office as well as in the president's private quarters. But later that day, through his press secretary Pierre Salinger, the president informed him that Mrs. Kennedy objected to the shooting and that, reluctantly, he would have to withdraw permission.

As Otto himself quipped, "This is the first time a movie about the democratic process has been made by an absolute dictator."[28] Ultimately, his persona would destroy him and mar his legacy; but in Washington in 1961, his reputation was buoyed by the enormous box-office success of *Exodus,* and his "Prussian" image was fused to the then widespread belief that he was a "brilliant filmmaker." Once again Otto had good timing. "It was a wonderful moment to be in Washington," as George Grizzard commented. "This was Camelot, after all, when all the bright young things were there to build a new world."[29]

The five weeks the *Advise and Consent* company spent in Washington proceeded under a particularly lucky charm. The troupers from Hollywood and the Washington politicos and socialites, mesmerized by each other's glamour, enjoyed a kind of social interaction rare at the time. "I would have thought Washington would have been more blasé," Preminger noted wryly.[30] The goodwill filtered onto the set, where Preminger was working with an ensemble of virtually untouchable and gentlemanly professionals. Don Murray, who had the most difficult part, set the tone. "Don was the sweetest man in the world," Grizzard said.[31] "Fortunately, we had no Marilyn Monroes on the set," recalled Murray, who had worked with Monroe in *Bus Stop*.[32]

"Everyone was waiting for Otto and Charles Laughton to have a fight, but it never happened, and I knew it wouldn't," Hope recalled. "Before we

Preminger with Charles Laughton, struggling with a Southern accent, on location in Washington for *Advise and Consent*.

started shooting Otto had invited Laughton to dinner and when he arrived the first thing he said to me was, 'My dear, your husband is purest mush.' From that moment he was one of my favorites."[33]

The famously self-critical Laughton, who unlike most of his costars made acting look like hard work, was no problem except to himself. Overwrought about developing a Southern accent, he asked Paul Green to take him to see the Senate in operation. "He wanted to listen to some of the debate on the floor and to familiarize himself with a variety of Southern accents," Green recalled. "Several speakers were Southern, including John Stennis and Olin Johnston, both with broad regional accents. Laughton kept his eye and ear on the floor, often leaning over to hear better. He was very intent."[34] "As a Southerner, I knew the accent Laughton worked out was phony," Grizzard said. "He was wonderful in the long shots but up close he was hambone: classy hambone."

In a troubled production Gene Tierney, visibly nervous about making a comeback, might have been a flash point, but not here. "Gene was frightened," as George Grizzard recalled. " 'Do you think Otto is going to yell at me today?' she would ask me. But no, Otto didn't yell at her."[35] "Otto was very gentle with Gene," Don Murray said. "He could have been cruel, but he wasn't. She was very subdued and didn't express much joy of living. There was something missing in Gene: she lacked a spark."[36]

A completely friction-free set would have been anomalous and no doubt uncomfortable for Preminger, who thrived on starting fights and testing other people's limits. Inevitably, on the set of a director whose creativity was fueled by abrasion, a few fuss-ups occurred. Otto periodically screamed at his sometimes slow-moving cinematographer, Sam Leavitt. "For one of my big speeches Otto said I was being too theatrical," Grizzard recollected.

Under my breath I muttered, "That's where I come from, maybe I should go back." "What makes you think you belong in the theater, Mr. Grizzard? I've seen you, you're not so good," he said in front of everyone, and then he added, "He's done one play and some summer stock and he thinks he's John Barrymore." Peter Lawford gave me a big wink, and somehow I got through it. I haven't yet recovered from Otto yelling at me in front of everybody, but I liked him anyway. Otto Preminger was a pain in the neck, but he was a lot of things—a lot of good things—besides being someone who yelled. At the time I knew nothing about filmmaking and I learned a lot from him. "Don't make it so big, I have to come in for a close-up," he told me. Otto taught me how to bring it down for the camera.[37]

"Otto had trouble with Inga Swenson [in the demanding role of the wife of the senator with a homosexual past] and Inga had trouble with Otto," Hope said. "She was a very nice girl, but she was afraid of Otto. The house where her character lived was a real house that was in the traffic pattern of Dulles Airport and because of that the sound was a big problem in some of her shots. Things had to be done quickly to get shots before the sound of the planes interrupted us. It was a hot set, and crowded, and Inga would get flustered and then Otto would start shouting."[38] Lew Ayres, disturbed by Preminger's treatment of Inga Swenson as well as of Sam Leavitt, spoke "gently to Otto about his behavior," Don Murray said. "Otto did not get upset—nobody could get upset with Ayres, who was the most beautiful person; it was an honor to be in the same room with him. But I don't remember that Otto's attitude toward Inga or Sam changed much either."[39]

After finishing the Washington scenes in mid-October, Otto moved the production to Columbia, where replicas of the Senate chamber and the Oval Office had been built. He was finished shooting by early November and by early December he had completed final editing and scoring. In order to qualify for Academy Award consideration, he planned to open the film just before Christmas at the Warner Beverly Theatre in Beverly Hills. But a contractual stipulation—his film could not open if a first-class production of the play of *Advise and Consent* was running either on Broadway or on the road—thwarted him. An adaptation by Loring Mandel, directed by Franklin Schaffner, had opened on Broadway on March 17, 1960, and had closed on May 20, 1961; but under a new management, in October 1961, the play had gone out on tour starring Chester Morris from the original cast and Farley Granger. The road producer, Martin Tahse, along with the original Broadway producers, Loring Mandel and Allen Drury, sued Otto to block the film from opening. Otto's defense was that the tour was not first-class. As a theatrical expert he called Hal Prince, then at the start of a career as producer and director that would earn him a record twenty-one Tony Awards (and counting). "I regret to say that I never met Preminger," Prince recalled. "I would certainly have liked to. I was flattered that he had called me to testify in the case—it was the only time I have ever been called upon in a trial as a theatrical expert. I hope I helped him; I was told that my testimony did."[40] Although Prince did say that the touring production did not fully satisfy his understanding of "first-class," the judge nonetheless ruled that Otto could not release *Advise and Consent* until June 1962. The plaintiff, however, said that Otto could release the film in December for "substantial cash payment." "Exorbitant," Preminger responded.[41] He canceled the Beverly Hills booking and rescheduled a June 1962 opening.

The dispute was good if unwanted publicity, and in terms of promotion the delay actually worked to Otto's advantage. In advance of its postponed American premiere, Preminger was invited to screen the film, out of competition, as the opening event at the Cannes Film Festival on May 8. To Preminger's utter delight an irate Senator Stephen Young from Ohio introduced a bill to prevent the film's release outside the United States on the grounds that "it would do irreparable harm to the prestige of America abroad." Preminger was determined to show the film abroad even in the unlikely event that Senator Young could get his crackpot bill passed, and so he brought a negative with him to France. When he returned, he announced that "in Europe they like it. The film showed how free our democracy could be. They were surprised I didn't have to get government approval."[42]

After returning from France, the filmmaker corralled fifty-eight senators into sponsoring benefit premieres of *Advise and Consent* in their home states. Before the premieres, however, a group of dissenting senators attacked the film as "un-American." Their action, of course, gave the film a jolt of notoriety Preminger always felt was good for business while also handing him another opportunity to advocate freedom of speech. "There were complaints that making a film about misbehaving politicians constituted a sinister attempt to overthrow the government," Preminger stated. "I was convinced that just the opposite was true. The fact that we could make the picture in Washington with the cooperation of the government . . . proved that our system was sound and strong. This country's tolerance of free expression is its greatest asset. I believed that the picture would show the world that liberty isn't an empty word in America."[43]

"Preminger had all Washington at his feet when filming; now he has a good part of Washington at his throat," proclaimed a feature article in *Life* on July 6, 1962, about the divided reactions of senators. "Is the film a ringing tribute to democracy? Or is it an unpatriotic exposé bound to backfire abroad?" the article queried. "Overseas, this could be used as a strong propaganda weapon against us," railed Senator Henry Dworshak, a Republican from Idaho. "I fear the film will do harm abroad by painting an evil picture of America," joined in Senator Ralph Yarborough, a Democrat from Texas. "A splendid picture. We are grateful to Mr. Preminger for having made it," opined Everett Dirksen, Republican from Illinois. Senator Kenneth Keating, a Republican from New York, was quoted as having told the filmmaker: "Henceforth practicing Senators shall look to you for extra tips on how a Senator should walk, dress, and posture with his hands. Terrific." Senator Karl Mundt, a Republican from South Dakota, had the cleverest comment:

"The movie is fictionalized entertainment with a touch of reality, while the United States Senate is a lot of reality with a touch of entertainment." The final tally in *Life*'s straw poll: twelve senators against, thirteen in favor. Preminger was granted the last word: "This movie is pro-U.S. Its fallible human beings share a common goal—making democracy work."

Hedda Hopper, gossip columnist and a political reactionary, launched a campaign to prevent the film's export. "How many members of Congress made asses of themselves by endorsing the film before they saw it?" she asked. "This film could present a highly damaging picture of the so-called American image," she warned her readers.[44] The Catholic Legion of Decency urged "extreme caution in viewing of this film."

Tagged as another "controversial" Otto Preminger project, *Advise and Consent* received mixed notices. "A striking job of turning a delicate and complicated story into a single dramatic strand, and considering the sensitive subject matter, Preminger has built his film with the skill of a born diplomat," observed Paul Beckley in the *New York Herald Tribune* on June 6, 1962. Bosley Crowther in the *New York Times* groused, "This country is . . . able to survive cinema fictions as slickly meretricious as this one." Surprisingly, the most vituperative review appeared in the left-leaning *Village Voice*. Preminger has "held our government up for a basically shameless and dirty caricature," Richard Nason wrote in his June 9 review, calling the film "a degrading cartoon. The implication is that the appointment of a Secretary of State could hang crucially and directly upon an early aberration [a homosexual affair] of a United States Senator. The film substitutes a perverse fancy for the hard mechanics of political machinery." Nason cataloged "the subtle means by which Preminger selected the novel's events out of context and arranged them according to a pornographic bias" and concluded that "we must be mad to tolerate this picture of ourselves for distribution all over the world." An incendiary article in *Human Events* attacked Preminger personally for "publicly welcom[ing] back those who had Red connections" and accused him of "toss[ing] away the central message of the novel . . . [that] there is an aura of appeasement and lack of patriotism within the American Republic which could lead to its downfall. . . . Preminger turns everything upside down and appeasement comes out smelling like a rose."

Preminger defended himself against charges of having committed treason by claiming that it had not been his intention "to make a political drama or to take a political stance. We have tried to eliminate any stand the book might have taken to the Right or Left."[45] Reviewers who flayed the film for not being political enough and for removing the novel's partisan sting failed to appreciate Preminger's purpose, examining the American political process of checks and balances. If in *Anatomy of a Murder* the law itself is the ultimate protagonist, so in *Advise and Consent* the Senate, its hierarchies of power, the means it uses to function and to maintain itself, is the film's principal character. Politicians are on temporary passport, coming and going, whereas the Senate chamber, like the political system it represents, is ultimately beyond the reach of individuals or of time itself. And in the moving last shot, the Senate, emptied of its fractious inhabitants and commanding the attention of the camera in a high-angle shot, endures, inviolate.

Preminger's fundamental belief in the Senate as an institution able to correct itself is reflected in the changes he and Wendell Mayes made to Allen Drury's original ending. In the novel the Senate rejects the president's leftist candidate; in the film, the ailing president dies during the vote—a narrative contrivance needed in order for Preminger to conclude the film on his own terms rather than Drury's. The new president refuses to break the tie, announcing that he will name his own nominee. And therefore the bargaining and deal making, the rituals of the Washington merry-go-round that ensure the survival of the American government, will begin all over again. As *Anatomy of a Murder* depicts Preminger's endorsement of due process and trial by jury, *Advise and Consent* dramatizes the filmmaker's faith in the validity of another process. Preminger's unfinished ending underlines the point that more important than the outcome of the voting is the method by which the voting was conducted. Downplaying Drury's anti-Communist paranoia and minimizing Cold War references, Preminger and Mayes lift the story out of its own era, and as a result five decades later their portrait of how the Senate operates remains substantially undated.

The filmmaker's admiration for the institution and its procedures is revealed in the film's ceremonial aura—Preminger presents the Senate's rituals in the high, dignified tone of a state occasion—and in his casting. Except for Charles Laughton's disheveled Southerner, the politicians are fastidiously groomed, and one and all are well spoken. The film's depiction of the Senate as a body of articulate patricians may well be its single dated component. Walter Pidgeon, Lew Ayres, Henry Fonda, Don Murray, Peter Lawford, and Franchot Tone project grace and wisdom, regardless of their characters' political affiliations.

In not choosing political sides Preminger protects the characters from rigid designations of "good" or "bad," "Republican" or "Democrat." Instead, typically refusing to rush to judgment about any of the characters, even the disruptive figures played by Charles Laughton and George Grizzard, he presents his Washingtonians as complicated men of affairs. Neither morally spotless heroes on the one hand nor melodramatic villains on the other, they act out of sometimes contradictory and ambivalent motives. Thus, the film's president, unlike Drury's, is not soft on Moscow, nor is he complicit in Van Ackerman's blackmail scheme, but he is also a stubborn, savvy politico not above trying to put the squeeze on Brigham Anderson to approve his nominee. The president's candidate for secretary of state may lie under oath about his Communist past but he is an American patriot who has no plan, unlike his counterpart in the novel, to hand over his country to Communist adversaries. Van Ackerman is not the Machiavellian henchman Drury depicts but an overambitious junior senator who gets carried away. "He truly believes the nominee is the right man for the job," as George Grizzard pointed out, "and to ensure the nomination he concocts the blackmail scheme. Otto wanted me to play the character not as if he were the villain of the piece, but as the character would have seen himself, that he was right to do what he did and that what he did was for the good of the country."[46]

Preminger also refuses to make glib moral assessments about the senators' private lives. In 1962 politicians were presumed to lead immaculate lives beyond the reach of desire, or if they did not, they were fully expected to be able to conduct their extracurricular indulgences in secret. In fusing sex to politics Preminger (despite the fact that he was both realistic and prescient) violated the era's codes of decorum, and some Washingtonians cried foul at the way the film entwines the two subjects. That Bob Munson (the regal Walter Pidgeon), Senate majority leader, is having an affair with a Washington hostess (Gene Tierney) in no way undermines the filmmaker's evident respect for the character. And Preminger makes a point of presenting Senator Lafe Smith (Peter Lawford), a compulsive womanizer, as being capable of compassion and independent judgment—in the end he votes according to his conscience rather than party allegiance. Placed at a distance from the political machinations, wives and children are often seen in deep focus, glimpsed through doorways and windows. But Preminger does not jump to facile conclusions about how politicians neglect their families; rather, his dispassionate observation allows viewers to arrive at their own judgments.

In introducing homosexuality, an all but unspeakable topic at the time, Preminger aroused further animosity. "Typical of the film's keyhole approach is a scene in a homosexual dive, found nowhere in the novel," a disapproving journalist, Peter Bunzel, noted.[47] "Some people think my handling of the homosexual subplot was sensationalism," Preminger said. "But I wanted to *show* something, not talk about it. The film never mentions

'homosexuality.' But I went beyond the book and followed the character to
New York and to a gay bar to show not only that he was horrified by this life,
but also attracted to it, that he hadn't really put his past completely behind
him."[48] When Senator Brigham Anderson hunts down his former lover in a
dark subterranean bar populated with Quentin Crisp types ogling a few
muscular studs, he is indeed horrified, and no wonder: saturated with an
illicit aura, the place seems to be an incubation chamber for guilt and
despair. Anderson flees in panic and on a plane trip back to Washington
decides to commit suicide.

For Preminger to have presented a humane, life-affirming view of gay
life would most likely have been a cultural impossibility in 1962; it would
also have been false to the character of Brigham Anderson, a conservative
from Salt Lake City tormented by his sexual ambivalence. While the film
makes no attempt to provide other than a fleeting, outsider's view of a contemporary homosexual underground, in taking his camera for the first time
in a mainstream American film into a gay bar, Preminger yet again smashed
a Hollywood taboo. (Can we really afford to be smug about the film's presumably dated depiction of homosexuality? For someone with a background as conservative as Anderson's, might not homosexual feelings still

Opening the closet: Don Murray as a senator tormented by sexual ambivalence enters the first
gay bar ever depicted in a mainstream American film.

The New York opening of *Advise and Consent*. The Saul Bass logo of a raised Capitol dome promised to lift the lid off Washington.

cause discomfort, or fear of exposure? And isn't it still possible that the revelation of homosexuality could destroy a political career, or for that matter a Hollywood one, too, especially for a closeted man or woman?) For a television screening in 1965, CBS wanted to cut the scene that, as Bob Lardine reported in the *New York Sunday News* on July 25, 1965, "takes place in a noisy bar that caters to perverts." Preminger refused and forfeited the $250,000 CBS was offering. "It's utter nonsense that the scene would shock. It played all over the world. No one was shocked," Preminger stated.

Nowhere else in his work has Preminger's preference for long takes, camera choreography, and carefully composed group shots been used with greater refinement or thematic purpose. The film's visual fluency, which confers on governmental procedures a sense of order and integration, rests primarily on two motifs: most of the time, characters who have something to say to each other appear in the same frame; and the camera moves whenever the characters do. When the camera glides across the Senate floor, encompassing senators on both sides of the aisle in one unbroken take, an ideological point, the interconnections that the system depends on, is being underscored. Preminger reserves one-shots and close-ups for isolated moments—when the blackmail threats begin to drive a wedge between Senator Anderson and his increasingly suspicious wife, for instance, or when Anderson, his repressed sexual past having returned to haunt him, scrutinizes himself in a mirror. Like Washington's sturdy system of checks and balances, the film itself is a smoothly working mechanism that interweaves multiple characters and plot lines.

Beautifully filmed and acted, and thematically both far-reaching and timelessly contemporary, *Advise and Consent*, made by a maestro at the height of his command of the language of film, may well be the most intelligent American film about American politics. As Geoffrey O'Brien wrote, it is "Hollywood's most underrated movie classic" and "the only American film to address seriously the mechanics of democratic government. The movie stands at the end of an era, in terms both of politics and filmmaking. Against all odds, Preminger, here at the peak of his directorial abilities, succeeded in making a film of novelistic density, in which the real star is the political structure within which the individual characters go to their separate ends."[49]

FOURTEEN

The Prodigal

"When Otto hired me as a reader in December 1961 he had just cut *Advise and Consent* and was readying the publicity campaign," recalled Mike Macdonald, the son of the critic Dwight Macdonald.

> Saul Bass did many variations on the Capitol dome going up, which was the film's logo, and was to be used on everything, including envelopes and stationery: no detail was too small for Otto. For the previous three years Otto had had a Midas touch for potboilers when he had grabbed the film rights to *Anatomy of a Murder, Exodus,* and *Advise and Consent* before they became the leading fiction best sellers for 1958, 1959, and 1960, respectively. That was quite a record. But when I was there no production clock was ticking, and beyond a rusty option on *The Cardinal,* a 1950 best seller, his property pipeline was empty.[1]

When Macdonald signed on, Preminger's office was located in the penthouse at 39 West Fifty-fifth Street, next door to La Caravelle, a traditional French restaurant that along with "21" was the director's favorite New York meeting place. Macdonald remembered "a creaky old elevator" that opened onto a surprisingly dingy and mildewed hallway. But then you entered Preminger's throne room, quite attractive and modern, lit by recessed ceiling lights and hung with colorful oils by Miró and Picasso. Otto's famous ovoid head was nicely set off by his diplomat's uniform: conservative suits custom-tailored by Alexander Shields, whose cologne he also wore. As Otto held court sitting behind a long Brancusian slab of beige-veined marble in a black leather boardroom chair, he might have been a late Roman emperor, a tough old mercenary elevated to the purple by admiring comrades in arms.

Macdonald noticed that the centerpiece of Otto's desk, and of his working life, was a "then exotic white speakerphone" on which Preminger conducted a massive volume of calls to and from agents, producers, and actors.

Macdonald was "third down the line" after Nat Rudich, Preminger's general factotum, and Bill Barnes, who headed the story department.

Nat dressed like Otto, very conservatively and tastefully, usually in a blue serge suit, a navy blue silk tie, and a spread collar. He wore the same cologne as Otto—they both smelled very nice, like freshly talcumed babies' bottoms. They both had black raincoats, though, a sinister touch. Nat was obsequious—Uriah Heep. He was yelled at more than anyone else but he always translated Otto's tantrums into something positive. Barnes, a closeted but fairly obvious homosexual, wore Brooks Brothers tweeds and button-down shirts. He was an intelligent, pleasant, somewhat anxious young Southerner who acted as if nothing short of genius ever passed Otto's lips, and when the whip was cracked he'd go into gear. It was Barnes's job to take agents to lunch, to follow *Publishers Weekly*, and really to keep the boss current with the industry.

It was a laissez-faire atmosphere, and I was never told what or how to read. It was my job to read all the unsolicited manuscripts, whereas Bill read the choice properties. I did the dirty work, wrote long synopses with recommendations, all of which Otto turned down. When I recommended Joseph Conrad's *Heart of Darkness*, Otto replied that "great novels don't make great movies." I also recommended *Fail Safe*, but Otto laughed when the agent wanted $750,000. But he turned down *Who's Afraid of Virginia Woolf?*, a mistake. And my mistake was to bypass *To Sir with Love*—it was a good idea for a film, and a good setup for Otto.[2]

As Macdonald recalled, Preminger "was after Nat Rudich for every lightbulb, but neither Nat nor Bill ever once raised their voices. Not once, no matter the provocation. Barnes would roll his eyes theatrically, and that's all that had to be 'said.' The feeling was to let Otto blow off steam." What Macdonald remembered with pleasure forty years later were the twice-weekly invitations for drinks with the boss. (No food was ever served.) Held from 4:30 to 6, these gatherings were a mixture of business and relaxation during which Otto "did almost all the talking, and he was a great talker. But it must be said that he listened too. When I raved about Antonioni's *L'Avventura,* he said it was a box-office flop. When I responded that 'there are more important things,' he was amused. At these meetings he never talked politics, although he was very interested in the subject and certainly well informed." Mostly the boss recounted stories from Old Vienna; discussed current plays and movies; took calls on the speakerphone; and made calls to Hope at home. "Otto was a very solicitous husband and father, and there were hourly bulletins on the twins' health." Sometimes, for the enjoyment of his staff, Otto put on a show during speakerphone calls.

> One afternoon, Spyros Skouras calling from Los Angeles went on at understandable length about Richard Burton, Elizabeth Taylor, and the rising, unprecedented *Cleopatra* bills in Rome which would soon end his reign at Fox. Suddenly, Skouras paused. "Otto, you don't have that speaker thing on, do you?" he inquired plaintively. As we suppressed giggles, Preminger wrinkled his formidable pink forehead in dismay. "Spyros, please," he purred, as his ice-blue eyes swept merrily over Bill, Nat, and me. "Vat do you take me for, eh?"[3]

When he was in town, Ingo, who had "good Viennese manners, an ebullient quality, and was kind of handsome in his own way," as Macdonald observed, would appear during the cocktail hour. "Swinging his arms, Ingo took up the room; Otto wasn't as physically imposing. They didn't look like brothers." Sometimes some of Preminger's cronies from Vienna, including Gottfried Reinhardt, the son of Max, and Max Slater, on Otto's payroll, would show up. "There were never any actors," Macdonald noted. "When I dropped by for a visit in 1964, however, I was surprised to see Jane Fonda with her husband, Roger Vadim. Otherwise, the only movie star I ever saw in the office was Preminger himself." The front office receptionist, Pam Elliot, was never invited to the cocktail hour. "No women ever were," Macdonald said. "This did not mean that women were demeaned: quite the opposite. I never heard a coarse word from Preminger, who was at all times extremely proper. But this was a man's world, especially in those days. Otto was a true gentleman of that old school."

For the first few months of Macdonald's tenure most of Preminger's time was spent preparing for the opening of *Advise and Consent*. Otto supervised the advertising campaign, as he always did, and personally selected all the first-run theaters. He also hosted numerous press screenings and arranged extensive public appearances for himself and some of his actors. A new father at fifty-five, he devoted considerable time to his private life. In February 1962 he began preparations for moving his office from Fifty-fifth Street to a suite in the Columbia Pictures building at 711 Fifth Avenue. For many weeks prior to the move, scheduled for mid-April, he shuttled back and forth between the old and new offices, conferring with (or more often, screaming at) architects and designers. "After the official move, the setup became more formal," Macdonald remembered. " 'Drinks' became *a* drink, and invitations were no longer twice weekly. In the new office the feeling just wasn't the same. Our old sociable nest was gone, and I found it dispiriting."

Preminger's suite at 711 covered half the top floor of the Columbia building. In minuscule metal letters designed by Saul Bass, "Otto Preminger" appeared on an intimidating black door, which opened into a suite consisting of a massive reception area; an office for the story department; Nat Rudich's office; and, behind a second forbidding black door, Otto's office, more than twice the size of his office on Fifty-fifth Street. "It was a daunting layout that reminded me of another lifeless interior, the tasteful, dull offices of the Museum of Modern Art [designed by Preminger's East Sixty-fourth Street neighbor, Edward Durrel Stone], where I'd recently been a summer student intern," Macdonald recalled. With black leather Charles Eames swivel chairs, paintings by Picasso, Kandinsky, Sam Francis, and Diego Rivera on the severe white walls, and marble tables, the 711 suite also, of course, resembled Preminger's town house. "Seven-eleven was a bit of a cliché," according to Macdonald, "but it was the natural setting for the last of the old-time, fierce-tempered moviemakers." The suite, emanating the authority of the bald man with twinkling blue eyes who presided over a marble desk the size of a Ping-Pong table, seemed to issue a warning: "Timid souls, beware."

When *Advise and Consent* opened in June, Otto was "so hands-on," according to Macdonald, that he had Bill Barnes constantly on the phone, tracking the grosses at the Sutton Theater on East Fifty-seventh Street. "The grosses were disappointing, but Otto was optimistic nonetheless."

In late July Preminger received an extraordinary job offer. After firing

Spyros Skouras, unable to stem runaway costs on *Cleopatra* in Rome, the board of directors of Twentieth Century-Fox asked Otto to take over as the president of the company. Preminger enjoyed the vindication of being asked to lead a studio from which, twenty-five years earlier, Darryl Zanuck had expelled him, but not for a moment was he tempted to take the job. His answer was a swift and final no. Otto would have been a first-rate CEO, his eye fixed firmly on the bottom line, but he relished his independence, and besides, he wanted to make his own films rather than supervise the films of others. After Otto's brushoff, Zanuck, semiretired, stepped in, attempting to salvage the ailing studio he had cofounded nearly three decades earlier. "Otto may have had the last laugh," Mike Macdonald speculated.

> He felt he didn't need the sausage factory anymore, and as he told me, "Let Zanuck sort out the Fox basket of crabs." Otto was at a point where he felt he could wait and wait and wait for the right property to come along. I couldn't—and quit two weeks after he said no to Fox. In his modest way, Otto Preminger was after art, while I wasn't after money but experience. So I took a big pay cut from the $250 a week that Otto paid me—about $1,250 in today's terms—to $65 a week to work as David Susskind's assistant on *All the Way Home*.[4]

In late July, Preminger finally decided that "the right property" would indeed be *The Cardinal,* based on Henry Morton Robinson's best-selling 1950 novel which, since its publication, had had worldwide sales of over 25 million. Columbia Pictures, the original rights holders, had abandoned the property because of the opposition of New York's notorious Cardinal Spellman. Spellman was convinced the title character, a priest who becomes an important cardinal of the Roman Catholic church, was modeled after him, and, as Otto noted, he "attacked the book with all his ferocious energy." "He was particularly incensed because the fictional Cardinal had a sister who became pregnant, although she was not married. He maintained that this was an insult to his own sister, despite the fact that she was happily married and nothing of the kind had happened in her life."[5] While Spellman's denunciations had succeeded in deterring Leo Jaffe, the president, and Abe Schneder, the chairman, of Columbia, to Otto the prospect of public battles with Spellman was music (or money) to his ears. Preminger was hoping that clashes with the intemperate, reactionary prelate would stir up interest in the project.

First, however, he had to derive a workable script out of Robinson's sprawling chronicle. It took a record six months for Otto to develop a narrative through-line for Robinson's protagonist Stephen Fermoyle, who in order to embrace a life of devotion must overcome pride, doubt, and temptation. In August Otto began working with Robert Dozier on a first draft, but after three months he was not satisfied. On a scouting expedition to Rome in late October he hired Gore Vidal "to polish the script and to add his own brand of acid wit to what Dozier had written," as Hope recalled.[6] Otto also hired Ring Lardner Jr., who was working on the script of a comedy called *The Genius* that Otto was expecting to film. "I don't know whether Otto realized that both Gore and I were atheists," Lardner said. "Another thing we had in common, and which we jointly communicated to Otto, was our verdict that he had fallen into the habit of buying the movie rights to some of the worst-written best sellers on the market."[7]

Robert Dozier receives sole screen credit, but Preminger maintained that "almost all of it was rewritten by Gore Vidal. The Screen Writers Guild handed down a strange and arbitrary ruling, insisting that Dozier and Vidal share in the billing equally and alphabetically, although their contributions were far from equal. Vidal preferred to withdraw his name rather than be a party to such an unfair arrangement."[8] It is likely, however, that the script contains far more Preminger than Vidal or Dozier or Lardner. "Now, I don't want to take anything away from the writer, but if you really ask whose thoughts are mainly represented, or whose personality is represented in the picture, I must claim this, for better or for worse. I feel that I am not an illustrator of books. I feel I have the right to re-create them, with the help of a writer."[9] With an episode set in Vienna, the city of Otto's youth, at the time of the Anschluss in 1938 that has no counterpart in the novel, and the manner in which it examines and ratifies the intricate ways in which the Catholic church governs itself, the script does indeed reveal the imprint of the director.

Throughout the fall, Otto took brief sabbaticals from working on the screenplay to scout locations in the four places where the story is set: Boston, Rome, Vienna, and the American South. At each site, many months before he was to begin filming in February 1963, he hired a cadre of production assistants.

As Preminger got closer to the start of shooting, Cardinal Spellman began to renew his attacks on the novel and now on the filmmaker. "He sent letters to every bishop in the United States asking them not to cooperate with me," Preminger recalled.[10] Spellman, the ranking American cardinal, tried to obstruct Preminger in every way that he could, but Otto managed to circumvent him. When Otto, thanks to Spellman, could not find any priest willing to serve as a technical adviser, he hired a man named Donald Hayne, who had left the priesthood to become an adviser to Cecil B. DeMille on *The Ten Commandments*. "Donald Hayne, a lovely man, was the unsung hero of the film who knew everybody in Rome and got us immediate access to the Vatican," Hope recalled.[11] When, again because of Spellman, Preminger was unable to find a church in Boston willing to host a film crew, Nat Rudich located a church in Stamford, Connecticut, his hometown. (Boston's Cardinal Cushing was friendly to the project and to Preminger personally, but because of Spellman's animosity he felt he could not offer a church anywhere within his jurisdiction.) When the bishop who had jurisdiction over the church in Stamford insisted it was he and not Cardinal Spellman who had the authority to make the final decision in the matter, Otto was delighted. The claim confirmed one of the themes he hoped to express in the film, "that there [is] considerable freedom of action within the Church."[12]

Outside America, beyond the reach of Spellman's influence, Preminger received the same kind of extraordinary cooperation he had enjoyed in Israel and Washington. The pope permitted filming in his summer residence and in a Baroque church in Rome. In Vienna, Cardinal Franz König granted permission to shoot in St. Stephen's and in the cardinal's palace.

At the end of January and early February, as Otto and his production designer Lyle Wheeler were finalizing the Boston area locations, Eva Monley was in Vienna hiring a local crew and arranging housing, meals, and transportation. She also had to supervise the building of sets for a scene in which Nazis on the loose loot the cardinal's palace. "I had to do all the legal permissions," Monley remembered. "Otto would not shoot anywhere unless he had clearance. I would line up a number of possible locations for each setting that we needed, and then Otto made the final selections. Everything had to be done *now,* it had to work, and it had to be for real—Otto hated studios."[13]

Filming began at the church in Stamford on February 14, 1963. By the end of the first day's shooting Preminger had dismissed and then rehired his leading man, Tom Tryon. The actor recalled his baptism under fire:

> It was 40 miles away from my hometown of Hartford, and all of my family were there. Friends had come from miles around and we were out in the middle of the street when, at eleven that morning, Otto fired me. He fired me because poor dear Cecil Kellaway, with whom I had a long tracking shot, kept going up on his lines. Well, he didn't hit Cecil, he hit me. After I said, "Otto, I know my lines,"

he told me I was through. I went down to the basement of the church where we were shooting and changed my clothes. The assistant director came down, and asked why I wasn't on the set. I said I'd been fired and I was leaving. I wish to hell I had. Then Preminger came down in a rage. "What do you think you're doing?" "Well, you fired me, Otto, and I'm going." "Don't be silly," he said, as if it had all been a joke. Well, it wasn't a joke. I had to go back up to start filming again. The first day wasn't over yet, I had started to shake, and for the entire filming I never stopped.[14]

Throughout the long shoot, which was to last until June as the production moved from Boston to Vienna to Rome to Hollywood, Preminger and Tryon were trapped in a torturous duet from which there seemed no way out. "For me in the morning to go on that set was like getting into the tumbrel and going to the scaffold," Tryon said. "At noon, after the lunch break, it was like going to my own funeral. Day after day after day."[15]

Before production started, however, the director and the actor had gotten off to a promising start. "In Tom's screen test—and Tom tested better than the other candidates, including Robert Redford and Warren Beatty—Otto had seen a quality that he felt was right for the part," Hope said.[16] Tryon, too, had been pleased with the test, during which he had found the director to be "quietly helpful. He pulled things out of me; he made suggestions; he never raised his voice." When a number of people had warned Tryon that he would regret taking the role, his response had been, "No, you don't understand. I have a rapport with Otto and we're going to get on just fine."

His range was limited—he projected a stalwart, tight-lipped masculinity—but Tryon, commandingly handsome and six foot six, with intense dark eyes and a deep voice, had the kind of natural, understated quality that Preminger was always drawn to. In hiring the self-effacing, relatively untried actor, Otto was once again casting himself in the role of a would-be starmaker.

But once production started, he became frustrated when Tryon was not giving him the performance that he had already mapped out in his mind as carefully as he had all the camera movements and shot compositions. He began to heckle and humiliate the actor in public displays of bad temper. For the entire cast and crew, these episodes became the inevitable focus of the shoot. However, the witnesses, who in a sense became on-the-spot psychologists, drew their own, differing conclusions about the contretemps.

"Otto gave Tom a bad time on every shot," recalled Bill Hayes, who was playing Stephen Fermoyle's brother and who kept a diary during his three weeks on the production. "He never took him aside, but always insulted him in public. 'No, Tom, you don't understand,' he'd tell him, in a loud voice. I believe Otto thought Tom was so placid he had to be needled: I disagree. I saw Tom as a bright and highly skilled actor who might have been brought to just as great histrionic heights by positive means rather than negative."[17]

"In a funny way, I felt Tom invited the treatment he got," said Carol Lynley, cast in a double role as Stephen's sister Mona and as Mona's daughter Regina.

> When Otto would shout, Tom just rolled over and became like a small boy being whipped. He would get the shakes. In one scene, a cup and saucer had to be taped to his hands. He couldn't control the shakes and he had tics, so Otto couldn't shoot him from certain angles. I asked Tom why he didn't tell Otto to knock it off—Otto could not have fired him. I sometimes wondered if Tom somehow thought of Otto as a demented father. Tom was a lovely man, and gorgeous, but he was not a natural actor. He had enormous charm offstage, but on camera he became wooden. I began to feel that Otto realized he had made a mistake—he should have gone with Robert Redford—and began to try to force a performance out of him that Tom wasn't capable of giving.[18]

"I felt terrible for Tom, who was such a nice man; we all did," recalled Jill Haworth, Preminger's young discovery from *Exodus,* appearing in *The Cardinal* as a saintly nurse. "Tom was plain scared; and after a while Tom's fear began to terrify me. Tom ended up blaming Preminger for everything. If I'd been a star I would have gone to Otto to say, 'Listen, leave him alone and let him perform.' But I was in no position to do that."[19]

"When I first met Tryon on the set in Rome, I noticed his knees were shaking," recalled Ossie Davis, cast as a black priest from Georgia who comes to the Vatican asking for help against the Ku Klux Klan.

> I said to Tom, "I'm going to tell Mr. Preminger you are not well." With an alarmed tone Tom said, "No, please, no." I saw that for Tom it was a form of torture being in Otto's presence and his discomfort was exponentially increased because he was simply unable to confront Otto, who reacted fiercely when he saw any sign of weakness. He really could not abide it when people were intimidated by him—

he got upset when he saw others were upset by him! The more he pushed Tom, the more the performance was not happening. There was a raving monster side to Otto that I thought, had I been more closely associated with him, I could have tamed. I always believed he would listen to me.[20]

Preminger's impatience with Tryon spilled over into his treatment of other actors, and the filmmaker had more explosions on *The Cardinal* than on any other film. As Bill Hayes noted in his diary, Tryon was by no means the only "President of the Club," the name Hayes gave to anyone who was the recipient of a public dressing-down. "I had that honor, too," Hayes admitted. " 'You look perfect for the part, why don't you just say the words and not add anything to them?' he yelled at me once. He made Cameron Prud'homme [playing Stephen's father] so nervous that he kept forgetting his lines and after a while he couldn't say anything." (In postproduction Carroll O'Connor dubbed Prud'homme's voice.) John Saxon, cast as the Jewish fiancé of Stephen's rebellious sister, also served as "President of the Club." "I have an ear for accents, and I worked hard developing a subtle Yiddish lilt for my character," Saxon remembered. "I had rehearsed with Max Slater, Preminger's dialect coach, who thought the accent was appropriate. But after I played my first scene, Preminger called out, 'Who do you know who talks like that?' To myself I thought that he did, but I didn't say it. I had rehearsed it for three weeks and I couldn't start without the accent, but Preminger said, and I will never forget it, 'Kill the Jew!' He threatened to fire me if I didn't eliminate the accent on the spot."[21]

Perhaps as a form of self-protection, Hayes and Saxon became astute students of their director's behavior. "Because he knew the script cold and wanted to hear the words spoken as he heard them in his mind, he needed to hear specific words read in a most specific way," Bill Hayes observed.

Now if an actor happened to coincide with Otto in the conception of a character saying those words in that scene, then Otto's beaming smile would shine brighter than the lights on the set. If, however, the actor's idea happened to differ from Otto's idea, the opposite occurred. A grimace of pain would destroy his personality, his voice would take on an edge of growing hostility. Hitler in a tantrum could not have conveyed a more frightening demeanor than Preminger as he set out to demean or castigate a wrongly motivated actor. It was *his* chess game, after all, and all the players were his pawns.[22]

"I could see that Otto was tremendously intelligent," John Saxon said, "but the moment he hired you he began to act as if you were going to ruin his movie. Yet, in the way that he created difficulties *he* was ruining his own movie. All of us, except John Huston [playing Stephen's spiritual adviser], the only one he never tangled with, were under suspicion of sabotage. But I began to feel that it was his alter ego that was committing the sabotage. He had a fear that we were going to disappoint him, but there was something in himself he didn't quite tolerate."[23]

As always with the variegated director, however, yelling was by no means his only means of communicating with his actors ("Otto daily ran the gamut from sunny warm spring to thunderous stormy winter," as Hayes wrote). And fear or anger were by no means the only responses of the actors to Preminger. "I survived because I wasn't afraid of him, and he knew it," Carol Lynley said. "Otto really did not have a mean bone in his body, but he liked to play his reputation as a legendary ogre—when I said nice things about him in an interview he told me I was ruining his reputation—and I think he paid a price for that." Everyone noticed that Preminger treated Maggie McNamara, his *Moon Is Blue* star, who had fallen into professional obscurity and had suffered through several breakdowns, with great kindness. To give her a job, he had cast her in a small role as Stephen's spinsterish, anti-Semitic sister. "He told me we must be *very* careful with her," Carol Lynley said. "He treated her like gold."[24]

"Amazingly, Otto understood my part as a black man would, without any condescension or patronization," Ossie Davis noted.

There is a tendency among some whites, embarrassed by racism, to become more passionate on the subject than blacks, to become blacker than you. Otto was never that. On matters of race, he was direct and clear and compassionate. Over the years I often thought about why Otto didn't go after me the way he attacked others. I think it was because he was always looking for a spark in whomever he met, some fire, and as a performer and as a person I satisfied his need for that spark. The rapport between us was cemented in my first shot, a close-up in which I was reacting to Stephen Fermoyle's elevation to bishop. I gave Otto a luminous reaction, the quality he wanted from Tom but had to get from me. Now, Otto hadn't spoken to me about that look, but to me it was the actor appreciating what the moment was about. I'm not a religious man but it was not too difficult to reach into my own memory, and I responded, as my character, a deeply religious man, would have. I think Otto truly appreciated those moments when some of us treated the craft with the respect and the mastery he demanded.[25]

Preminger also did not "go after" John Huston and Raf Vallone, because, as Carol Lynley observed, "He knew they'd yell right back and match him in volume." Huston, who was making his acting debut, conducted himself like a hired hand with good manners. Under the circumstances, however, he was far too polite. Because of his stature, more than anyone else on the set he was in a position to defend Tom Tryon against Preminger's tirades, but to his discredit he said and did nothing—unlike Raf Vallone, who behaved with compassion. When Tryon forgot his lines during lengthy walking scenes, Vallone (playing Stephen's mentor in Rome) would cue him, and several times with a few quiet words to Preminger he even managed to stifle an explosion.

When the production was about to relocate from Boston to Vienna in early March, Preminger, anxious about returning to the city where he had grown up, began to let up a little on Tryon. A preview of problems he would face in Vienna occurred during the end of the Boston shoot when he received a wire from a spokesman for St. Stephen's canceling permission for filming because it was Lent. "Otto attributed this attempted blockade to the far-reaching power of Cardinal Spellman," Bill Hayes wrote in his diary. "He fired back a cable which said he had a contract that gave him the right to film in Vienna, Lent or no Lent, and that if the Church representatives there tried to prevent him on any occasion from shooting his film he was prepared to sue the Catholic Church for many millions of dollars. Contract in hand, Otto shot in Vienna according to his prepared schedule."

Preminger had inserted the Viennese episode into *The Cardinal* in order to chastise his former countrymen for having welcomed Hitler's takeover in 1938, but his attitude toward Vienna was ambivalent. Along with animosity—"Otto hated going back," Hope said[26]—he approached the city with nostalgia as well as admiration for its architectural and cultural riches.

"At the time of Preminger's arrival in 1963, Vienna had finally recovered from the war but still had no night life to speak of," claimed Wolfgang Odelga, a Vienna native Otto hired as his transportation manager. "Otto and his film crew brought some color and spark and a touch of Hollywood glamour to Vienna, and the city gave him a royal reception." Otto and Hope occupied the grand suite at the Hotel Imperial, which overeager publicists claimed to be the one Hitler had commandeered when he swept into the city with his hordes in 1938. But the hotel had been rebuilt since the war, and along with everything else the Hitler suite had been demolished.

Nonetheless, with its high ceilings, imperial furnishings, and sweeping views of the Ringstrasse, the suite looked like fit quarters indeed for a conqueror. "Each day we all stood in front of the hotel until Otto came down—everybody had to stand by and wait for him, and then we drove off to the location," Odelga recollected. "Every morning a black Chrysler was waiting for him. Otto wanted the biggest car, but it had to be an *American* car. He didn't want a Mercedes: that was out of the question! He was a terror in a *reasonable* way."[27] "There was no doubt that Otto Preminger was the star," Wolfgang's wife Hilde, who was the Viennese location manager, pointed out. "He had the biggest suite by far, while poor Tom Tryon had just a normal room."

"Preminger was the only producer-director I have worked with who insisted that all his cast and crew must be put up in the best hotels," Hilde said.

So, following his orders, we booked everyone into the Imperial or across the street at the somewhat less expensive [but still first-class] Bristol. Otto set up a suite of offices right in the Imperial, which was highly unusual. He was the only director I've ever worked with who, two months in advance, said, "I want my characters here, my camera there, the catering over there," and once he was here, he changed nothing. He insisted there was to be a legal paper for each location. We paid for police when we blocked off streets and removed cars. I respected him for his efficiency, and though he could be rude—from Otto Preminger you cannot learn: you must already know—he was fair to people who did their jobs.[28]

Soon after Preminger's arrival, Viennese journalists began to grumble about how the city was to be portrayed—as a stronghold of Nazis-in-waiting eager for the return of the native, the Führer himself. They also expressed concern about Preminger's allegedly unflattering treatment of Vienna's Cardinal Innitzer, who had tried to befriend Hitler, and the filmmaker's plans to stage a Nazi march that would erupt into a riot in the streets around St. Stephen's.

In "casting" Vienna as a city steeped in Nazi brutality, Preminger, to be sure, was exercising his genius for provocation, and when reports of complaints filtered into his makeshift office at the Imperial he did what he certainly had intended to do from the moment he had arrived: he called a press conference. At the Imperial Hotel on March 20, 1963, he defended "the right of the press to point out anything about himself and his pictures, but

Many Viennese were upset by Preminger's presentation in *The Cardinal* of the city's Cardinal Innitzer (Josef Meinrad) as a Nazi collaborator.

at the same time he denounced prejudgment; assured the press that the film's treatment of Cardinal Innitzer would be historically accurate; and answered objections to his casting of the notably worldly actor, Curt Jurgens, in the role of the notably ascetic Cardinal. Preminger made it clear," according to Willi Frischauer, "that in matters of casting and interpretation, he would not be dictated to."[29] "This response to Jurgens as the Cardinal is nonsense," Preminger argued. "We would never be able to cast murderers, or saints. If a man behaved like a cardinal he would *be* a cardinal not an actor."[30] In the event, when Jurgens proved unavailable—he refused to leave a hit play in Paris—Preminger quickly recast the role with a leading Viennese actor, Josef Meinrad, who barely knew English and had to memorize his lines phonetically.

Viennese officials insulted by Preminger's intention to tar the city with its Nazi past put up a number of obstacles. Otto could not persuade St. Stephen's officials to allow him to fly a swastika from one of the church's spires. The education minister, a Dr. Drimmel, would not permit him to shoot a scene in the National Library. In spurning Otto, the education minister voiced a widespread local sentiment: "At long last the grass has grown over the evils of 1938, and now there comes this camel and gobbles it up!"[31]

Otto's belief that anti-Semitism continued to thrive in Austria was borne out during the shooting. As Martin Schute recalled, "For a scene with the Hitler Youth crowd, the second assistant director put a note on the bottom of the call sheet to bring your own swastika armband, and a number of people did."[32] "We had to get police permission to sing the 'Horst Wessel' song," Hope said, "because after the war it had been outlawed. Our second assistant director had been a brownshirt and some of the elderly members of the crew leaped to their feet when they heard the song."[33]

"Although Otto remained wary of the Viennese, he also enjoyed and appreciated the attention and the great respect they gave him," Martin Schute noted. "He liked Viennese formality, which is how he had been raised. He was amused to be addressed as Herr Doktor Preminger and he expected us to smile at it. Otto complained to me about the Viennese, but we had a lot of cooperation, and really it was so much easier than in Israel with *Exodus,* where we had been up against the Israelis.

"Otto grumbled a lot, but he really did have a soft spot for the place and even for some of the people," Schute observed. "This was where he had grown up, and he spoke warmly to us about his childhood memories. He boasted about his father's prominence and about his own apprenticeship with Max Reinhardt. When he was shown his father's table at the Café Landtmann, where we shot two scenes, he was very moved."[34] "Otto took such pride in showing me the Theater in der Josefstadt, where he had had his first big success as a young man," as Hope recalled, "and his eyes filled with tears when he showed me the plaque on the lobby wall where his name is listed along with all those who have been at the head of the theater. At the theater he met some actors he had worked with so many years before and he was so touched. He also loved showing me the National Library, where he had so often played hooky from school."[35]

Joining the cast in Vienna was Viennese-born Romy Schneider, high-strung and arrogant and in despair over the end of her affair with Alain Delon. (Schneider was another Preminger star who was to commit suicide.) "She was a toughie," Eva Monley said, "and her presence added to a set that was already loaded with tension."[36] In a recent interview the actress had been quoted as referring to her fellow Viennese as *teppen* (Viennese slang for "idiots"), and when Otto introduced her at a press conference he ordered the journalist who had included her insult in his interview to apologize to her. When he refused to do that, Schneider began to shriek, "Get lost! Get out of my sight or I'll kill you!" Working herself into a fit, she spat at the journalist and raised her hand to strike him when Otto forcibly restrained her. Schneider, cursing in English and German, stormed out of the room as Otto, always able to summon an almost preternatural calm in such moments, carried on as if nothing had happened.[37]

"Romy really was an awful person," Martin Schute said, "but she did make two people happy. Leon Shamroy, the bull who growled at everybody else, went nutty over her beauty, and I have to admit that she was good with Tom."[38] As Tryon recalled, filming a ball scene with Schneider was the only

With Romy Schneider visiting the Theater in der Josefstadt in Vienna during the making of *The Cardinal.* The theater was unchanged from the time thirty years earlier when Preminger had been its artistic director.

time during the production that he actually enjoyed himself. "I was in fish and soup and Romy was in a beautiful Donald Brooks gown. Otto called us over to the camera and said, 'Now in this scene I want you should . . .' and he looked at us and smiled. 'You know what to do,' he said. So we went and we danced and we talked and we had a great time. It was terrific. And you can see the difference in the scene—it was the only moment in the film where I look relaxed."[39]

Over Easter, the production moved from Vienna to Rome. "Otto, as always, expected the impossible," Martin Schute said.

"What do you mean the customs aren't open on Good Friday?" he asked when I told him. "Open them!" He wanted the film ready to go at exactly the time he wanted it—no matter what. In Rome, we shot outside the Vatican, and in a church in Fiuggi, about fifty miles outside Rome. Everything was laid out smoothly because of a Vatican lawyer who played one cardinal off against another, a well-known legal practice, and was indispensable to us. Dino De Laurentiis was also very helpful to us in Rome.[40]

As Otto was pleased to report, the Vatican "cooperated fully in spite of opposition from the New York branch of the Church. The Vatican officials made no attempt to control the script—nor did they ask for an advance copy, which I would never have given no matter what. So you see there is more freedom and autonomy in the Church than you might think."[41]

During the Rome setups Tom Tryon was absent for ten days. "Dressing room gossipers explained Tom's vacation as a rest cure from Otto's relentless denunciations," Bill Hayes wrote in his diary. When he returned, Tom was noticeably fatigued. As Hayes recorded, "At the end of the final day of shooting, when I got into a car with Tom to be driven back to the Grand Hotel, over an hour away, Tom opened his trusty briefcase, extracted some little paper cups and then a fifth of Cutty Sark. He drank several ounces, smiled benignly, drank several more ounces, and went directly to sleep. Max Slater and the driver and I had to carry Tom up to his room."

After Rome, Otto moved the production to the last stop, the Columbia lot in Hollywood, where the scenes originally to be shot on location in Georgia were filmed. For this section Tryon had to face a grueling physical ordeal as his character is stripped and beaten by the Ku Klux Klan. The exhausted actor, no doubt feeling he as well as Stephen Fermoyle was undergoing a kind of purgatory, forced himself to endure the scene without complaining, and Preminger was easy on him.

Tom Tryon in the title role of *The Cardinal*. During the shooting, Tryon himself felt he was being crucified by Preminger.

When the nearly four-month shoot finally wrapped on May 10, Tom Tryon was profoundly relieved. But he was also disappointed in himself and furious with his director:

> I never did anything in my life I regretted more. Otto Preminger never allowed me to characterize the part. I had to play that boring priest just straight out, like he was Jack Armstrong. It was a badly written part, because the guy never acted, he was acted upon: he was a Boy Scout with a collar. Preminger wouldn't let me wear glasses; he wouldn't let me find little things to do. So what contribution could I make as an actor? If I had felt the performance he was getting out of me was valid, that would have been one thing; but I stank, and I knew it. I don't think Preminger is a good moviemaker. His great claim to fame, *Laura,* is an invalid claim because that is not a Preminger film; it was mounted by Mamoulian [*sic*]. And yes, *Anatomy of a Murder* holds up, although it's a cold film. But I think

the rest of his films have been disastrous going all the way back to Betty Grable movies [*sic*] and *A Royal Scandal:* that is a royal bore. He has no sense of humor, and it shows in his work. It's all plodding; there is no rhythm, no sense of change, nothing symphonic or musical. Dreary, boring, like endless, endless rain.

In my heart I forgave Otto for every cruelty and unkindness he ever performed against me. I just ended up feeling sorry for the man. It was a tough school, but I learned because I never again let anybody ride roughshod over me. No one. Ever. The last image I have of him was from a taxi coming down Park Avenue. We stopped at a light and here came this figure trudging across the street. I thought, Holy God, that's Otto Preminger. I remember looking at him and I thought, "Tom, that's the man who destroyed your life."[42]

"Otto did not treat Tom well," Hope conceded.

Jean Seberg, whom he also did not treat well, was a lot tougher than Tom, however, who was like a whipped puppy. Tom was fine in the simple scenes, but when his character had to think complexly he had trouble, and Otto would get impatient because he felt Tom had more to give. Poor Tom was very hurt, I know that; and in later years he had vicious things to say about Otto. I think of all the people Otto yelled at, Tom was the one who was the angriest and who held on to his anger the longest. He was so bitter about the experience, and I don't think he ever got over it. Tom Tryon was a very nice man—he and I always got on beautifully—and to this day I'm very sorry he felt the way he did about Otto.[43]

After Preminger completed editing *The Cardinal* at Shepperton Studios during Ascot week, he called a press conference to defend himself against accusations that he had become the ringleader of "runaway productions" that were taking jobs away from Americans. "Building sets in Hollywood would have been vastly more costly," Preminger admitted, but denied that he was robbing American workers of jobs. "At each location during the filming of *The Cardinal* we had a hard core of 38 Hollywood technicians," he said, adding that he supplemented the basic crew with indigenous labor as needed.[44]

In September, as a favor to a friend, Alexander Paal, who had worked as a still photographer on *Exodus,* Preminger performed a short role as a butler in a virtually unseen comedy called *Millie Goes to Budapest,* starring Peter Sellers and directed by James Hill. Preminger's only salary was an all-expense-paid trip to Budapest, a city he loved. On his return he began pre-production on *The Genius,* a comic novel by Patrick Dennis about an egocentric movie director who terrorizes underlings. Preminger had bought the rights a year earlier, in September 1962; in February 1963, just as he was beginning to film *The Cardinal,* he had hired Ring Lardner Jr. to write the screenplay. Because Lardner, like Dalton Trumbo, had been blacklisted, Otto's choice once again enflamed the American Legion, who "demand[ed] to know why he couldn't find a 'patriotic writer' for the job," as Lardner recalled. "Just as it was their right to boycott the movie when it was released, Otto replied, so it was his right to pick a screenwriter."[45]

Otto planned to shoot on location in Mexico in December, where the "genius" with a swollen ego is shooting a film, but by the end of October he abandoned the project. Perhaps after the state-of-siege atmosphere on *The Cardinal* the prospect of directing a movie about a temperamental director no longer seemed amusing.

Throughout the fall Preminger worked on the publicity campaign for the mid-December opening of *The Cardinal.* He asked for reactions from prominent Catholic churchmen, and in the September 14 issue of *The Pilot,* a diocesan paper, Cardinal Cushing gave the film a ringing endorsement. His praise may have been sincere, but it may also have been prompted by Preminger's promise that if the cardinal liked the film the American premiere in Boston would be arranged as a benefit for the Cardinal Cushing Charity Fund. On November 7, Otto returned to Rome, where in a ceremony as impressive as any in his film he was awarded the Grand Cross of Merit by the Vatican Order of the Holy Sepulchre of Jerusalem. Before an audience of five thousand prelates gathered for the Ecumenical Council, Preminger, looking appropriately somber, was escorted by seven footmen in white uniforms trimmed with gold buttons into the chamber of the order. Another footman carried a silver tray on which rested the red-and-white Maltese Grand Cross that a 250-pound marchese dressed in a floor-length white cloak pinned on Otto, "thus conferring the highest honor of an order that bestows favors on those who buy their way in," a reporter for *Show Business* claimed on November 8, puncturing the pomp. "In Otto's case he had promised to split the proceeds of the Roman premiere of the movie." ("Otto did *not* pay for the honor, which was the highest that could be given to a non-Catholic," Hope said.)[46] About the ceremony, Otto commented that "the Church likes show business. Historically, it has always *been* in show business."[47]

On Friday and Saturday during his visit Preminger screened his film for the cardinals of the Roman Curia of the church and the bishops attending the Ecumenical Council. "Because there is no theater at the Vatican, we screened it at the College of Cardinals, where everyone sat on wooden benches," Hope said. "I was the only woman present. The audience loved it—they did not feel the film was at all anti-Catholic." Mr. and Mrs. Preminger were granted a private audience with Pope Paul VI, "a very cold man, but very learned," Hope noted.[48]

As he had for *Saint Joan*, Preminger arranged a world premiere in Paris at the Palais Garnier. "The opening in Paris—indescribable," Josef Meinrad recalled. "The French premier was there, and members of the French government along with distinguished actors from the Comédie Française. It was everything you could ask for."[49] "It was the only picture ever sponsored by de Gaulle, and that was because he was Catholic," Hope pointed out. "Jean Seberg sat in the box with us, looking so poised, and more beautiful than ever. Otto and I were delighted to see her and she seemed happy to see us, or at least she didn't seem to be mad at Otto any longer; I certainly hope she wasn't. We both liked Jean and wished for her nothing but the best."[50] "The music was piped in from the organ at Notre-Dame," as Tom Tryon remembered. "*Tout Paris* was in the orchestra and we were seated in the horseshoe."

After the premiere—*The Cardinal* was more warmly received than *Saint Joan* had been—Otto hosted what Tryon described as "an incredibly lavish party" at Maxim's. "There were huge floral arrangements on every table and expensive champagne flowed freely and in great quantities. Otto, in his element, was in top form, with a jovial greeting for everyone. Jean Seberg, whom I had never met before, grabbed me and we commiserated with each other at the bar. Our cases, after all, were very similar: we were landsmen who had undergone a similar experience with Otto Preminger."[51]

As he had with *Exodus*, Preminger opened *The Cardinal* in reserved-seat, two-performances-a-day, advanced-price engagements in a handful of deluxe first-run theaters. Reviews were mixed, although Tom Tryon earned some praise of a kind he did not expect or feel that he deserved. "Tryon, who has had a mediocre career in the movies, suddenly looms up," wrote Kate Cameron in the *New York Daily News* on December 13, 1963. "He gives a sensitive characterization and comports himself with humility as the young man and as he grows older, with the dignity of an old churchman." "The story of a man, rather than a priest, played with true humility by Tom Tryon, is pictorially exquisite, intelligently cast, and painstakingly, if not thrillingly directed," Irene Thirer wrote in the *New York Post*. Bosley

Crowther, however, felt that "the young man is no more than a callow cliché, a stick around which several fictions of a melodramatic nature are dropped. As colorless as is the hero, however, that colorful is the film." In the *New York Herald Tribune,* Judith Crist, a confirmed Preminger adversary, grumbled that the picture is "a mélange of meandering melodrama, mouthed pieties, and pretentious irrelevance. . . . For all its pomp and circumstance, *The Cardinal* serves only to demonstrate the length (175 minutes) to which cynicism can go." The most sustained diatribe was issued by *Esquire* critic Dwight Macdonald, a personal friend who enjoyed Otto's company but not his movies. "How could such a bright fellow make such corny drivel?" he inquired, dismissing *The Cardinal* as "100% insincere kitsch." Preminger, he concluded, was "a great showman" with "a genius for publicity" who was without an equal for seeming to deal "with large 'controversial' themes in a 'bold' way without making the tactical mistake of doing so."[52]

The Cardinal, to be sure, is middlebrow, and to the uninitiated it might seem to be interchangeable with impersonal, expensively produced reserved-seat epics of the period. To the sympathetic Preminger viewer, however—to all those who "get" Preminger—*The Cardinal* reveals the non-transferable touch of its stubborn impresario. No one but Otto Preminger could have produced and directed this square, ponderous, magnificent film.

To appreciate the showman's achievement in *The Cardinal* it's necessary first to take a close look at his leading man, who in all the ways that count is exactly the right actor for a Preminger epic. Stephen Fermoyle is not the monochromatic character that Tryon complained about, but neither is the evolving drama of Stephen's faith overcoming his doubt Preminger's primary concern. The filmmaker's focus, rather, is to present, in a pageantlike way, the social and political issues—abortion, fake miracles, interfaith marriage, racism, fascism, power struggles within the church—against which the character's spiritual history is enacted. As in *Exodus,* Preminger is engaged more by the narrative's panoramic backgrounds than by the travails of its leading character. Tryon's smooth minimalism helps Preminger to make the kind of objective epic that is his forte, whereas a "brilliant" or overinventive actor playing Stephen would have interfered with the filmmaker's intention.

Preminger does not secure his command over the project at the expense of his star, however. Tryon's modest, thoughtful presence—reviewers who cited the actor's humility were correct—anchors the film. He is adept in all the external elements of the role, no small matter. He moves with dignity, speaks in a resonant voice, and wears the costumes and vestments of

Catholic ritual with ease. If you were Catholic, you would want this man to be your priest and you would be justified in having faith in him. Tryon also delivers in the moments where he is called on to suggest a sense of Stephen's inner life. The story is presented as a series of flashbacks, and periodic close-ups in which Tryon stares raptly into off-screen space are effective segues into the past. Tryon plays with genuine power the climactic scene just before intermission in which Stephen announces his decision to leave the priesthood. Preminger's artful mise-en-scène—shadowy lighting, Stephen's placement against a wall on which hangs a painting of Christ on the cross—helps, but Tryon palpably conveys the drama of his character's spiritual struggle. In romantic scenes with Annemarie (Romy Schneider), a Viennese student who falls for Stephen, Tryon suggests the emotional scars that will prevent Stephen from ever being a fully committed lover. Looking at himself in a mirror after having been out with Annemarie, Tryon with a lovely simplicity reveals Stephen's confusion about his increasing worldliness. Preminger thought Tryon was not reacting in the scene in which the character faces the choice of which life to save, his unmarried sister's or that of the child she is carrying. But Tryon's understated response is apt—overwrought emoting would have been false to the character as well as the film.

In the final scene, set in a Roman monastery on the eve of Stephen's becoming a cardinal, Tryon had to deliver a long speech on the urgency of

Tom Tryon in *The Cardinal,* a convincing man of the cloth.

fighting all totalitarian systems. There was no possible margin for error, since Preminger wanted to shoot the speech in a single uninterrupted take in which Tryon was to remain virtually motionless, while to his right, like a figure frozen in time and listening to his words with total stillness, stands his mother (Dorothy Gish). Intent on getting the tableau exactly as he had envisioned it, Preminger was prepared to keep his cast and crew working through the night. After dozens of takes, Otto remained vibrant, while his actor, on the verge of a complete emotional and physical breakdown and having difficulty remembering his lines, was becoming increasingly weary. Finally, around 2 a.m., a take satisfied Preminger. For a similar kind of aria that ends *Exodus,* Paul Newman let down his director and the film, while Tom Tryon prevails, delivering Stephen's oration with a gravitas that matches the precision of the mise-en-scène. After the speech, as he makes a slow processional through the monastery, Tryon, smiling softly, holds his hand to his heart in a gesture of modesty. In its subdued masculinity and grace, his comportment suits the moment of his character's ascension and also fully reveals the actor's own charm.

Because Preminger does not allow Stephen's spiritual odyssey to overtake a subject of more pressing interest to him, power relations within the church, *The Cardinal* is not a religious film, nor strictly speaking is it even a film about religion. By and large Preminger's prelates are as cunning as the solons in the American Senate in *Advise and Consent.* And in their readiness

In *The Cardinal*, Preminger presents a tourist's view of Vienna as a wonderland of Baroque architecture. Stephen Fermoyle (Tom Tryon), who has left the priesthood for the time being to pursue a worldly life, bicycles on the grounds of Schoenbrunn Palace and visits a church with his student (Romy Schneider).

to debate as well as in their rhetorical skills, they often sound like the dueling lawyers in *Anatomy of a Murder*. As contrast to the priestly "players," Preminger includes two (beautifully acted) characters whose holiness remains untouched by worldly considerations. Burgess Meredith's Father Ned Halley, a failure in any worldly sense, is a true man of God, and his assistant (Jill Haworth) is a saint in the making whose dedication to a life of service causes Stephen to examine his own imperfect spirituality.

Introducing topics for further discussion, Preminger wants *The Cardinal* to be thoughtful as well as thought-provoking. But in the end it is no more a Shavian drama of ideas than it is a work of Catholic piety. The film has a moral center—of course it is against Nazis and the Ku Klux Klan—but it's hard to tell where it lands on more controversial issues such as abortion. On potentially divisive topics, Preminger, ever aware of himself as a purveyor of popular entertainment, treads cautiously. Typical of the film's approach to "difficult" subject matter is its vacillating treatment of Cardinal Innitzer, who at first is blind to the evils of fascism, but then undergoes a rapid, unconvincing change of heart. Despite his avowed animus toward Viennese collaboration with the Nazis, Preminger seems to be pulling his punches here. "In a dramatic medium, you show all sides," he said, as if providing an alibi for his evasiveness.[53]

Presenting the rituals of religion as a form of show business, the filmmaker's ultimate commitment—and why not—is to visual spectacle. *The Cardinal* is an album of painterly compositions arranged by Preminger and his cinematographer Leon Shamroy that has the aura (if not the substance) of an elaborate Christian pageant. Jerome Moross's lush score, slow-moving, exalted, and containing echoes throughout of liturgical music, helps to sustain the ceremonial mood, as does the processional leitmotif, familiar from *Exodus* and *Advise and Consent,* of characters opening and closing massive doors and entering and exiting a series of monumental public spaces. Preminger's attraction to the picturesque is especially apparent in his treatment of Vienna, presented as a tourist's paradise. Stephen goes for a boat ride on the Danube; has coffee at the elegant Café Landtmann; and bikes through the gardens of Schoenbrunn Palace, with a view of the Gloriette in the distance. Photographed from the perspective of an outsider entranced by the city's superficial charm, Vienna, made up to look its best, becomes "Vienna," a royal city of strudel, Baroque architecture, and fancy-dress balls. In *The Cardinal,* even where it shouldn't be, the pictorial is Preminger's essential métier.

The director's attraction here to surface rather than depth, to spectacle as opposed to substance, is underscored in the places where the film literally comes to a stop for performances. When Stephen enters a vaudeville theater looking for his sister, who has become a dancer, he and the film take the time to watch musical theater star Bobby Morse (under contract to Preminger) and the Adora-Belles perform an entire musical number, "They Haven't Got the Girls in the U.S.A." The song has only a tangential connection to the story and Morse performs it with a Broadway flair that outclasses the setting, but only a sourpuss would complain. When Nazi brownshirts surround St. Stephen's, Preminger converts dark history into entertainment. Churchgoers ordered by the hastily reformed Cardinal Innitzer to stand up to the Nazi menace begin to sing the Hallelujah chorus, and their resistance is staged as a performance with the singers perfectly placed on a ladder with the lead singer (Wilma Lipp, a well-known opera star) standing at the top.

As an ideologue Preminger may be a once-over-lightly generalist, but as the firmly in-command master of ceremonies of a particular kind of spacious and stately film spectacle, he is without an equal. On the cusp of being passé in 1963, Preminger's brand of showmanship can now be fully savored as nostalgia. Judged on its own, albeit shallow terms, this quirky, straight-faced, visually majestic, reserved-seat epic is one of the triumphs of Otto Preminger's career.

FIFTEEN

Location/Location

After launching *The Cardinal* in its road-show engagements, Otto was sitting pretty. In February the film received six Academy Award nominations, including a Best Director nod to Preminger. In March he signed a lucrative three-picture deal with Paramount, his terms a solid 15 percent plus participation in the profits. In addition, two films remained on his agreement with Columbia, and he had a commitment with United Artists for two distribution deals. With solid ties to three major studios, Preminger enjoyed a virtually unrivaled vote of confidence from industry financiers and distributors. He was an independent producer who had managed to insulate himself against the convulsions of the poststudio era. And despite his preeminence and the royalist trappings of his bearing and his office, anyone could make an appointment to see him or could reach him by phone. His voice rising and falling in rivulets of alternating frolic and ferocity, Otto not only answered all his calls, he just as readily made them. Many are those with visions of Hollywood glory who can attest to the memorable occasion when they answered their phones to hear a friendly, booming voice announcing, "This is Otto Preminger calling."

Throughout the spring Preminger worked with Wendell Mayes trying to extract a scenario from *In Harm's Way*, a long, episodic novel by James Bassett, a syndicated columnist for the *New York Times* who had been Nixon's campaign manager for the 1956 and 1960 elections and during

World War II had been a press aide to Admiral William F. Halsey. Once again, as in *Exodus,* Preminger chose a story that unfolds against a seething historical canvas—*In Harm's Way* is set in Hawaii in 1941 just before and immediately following the Japanese attack on Pearl Harbor. And once again, as in *The Cardinal,* he was interested in exploring the inner workings of a monolithic institution, in this instance the United States Navy.

"Nobody but Otto would have dealt with the Navy as he did," claimed Mayes, who accompanied Preminger to a meeting at the Pentagon with eight Navy admirals. As Mayes observed, the filmmaker presented himself not as a supplicant needing favors but as a potentate accustomed to issuing demands.

> Otto said he needed a destroyer and he needed a cruiser, and he wanted them out at sea. But the Admirals we met with wouldn't cooperate until we agreed to make changes in the script. [Given Preminger's firm policy of keeping his scripts under wraps, it's unlikely any of the admirals had actually read or seen a script; their concerns were probably based on material in the novel.] Because they were worried about recruiting, they didn't want certain things told to the public, for example that the officers of the Navy are human beings with human failings. They definitely didn't want the leading man to have an affair without being married. Otto, of course, was prepared for this. He said he would not make a single change, and he added, "If you won't give me what I want, I am prepared to hire the Brazilian Navy. They will give me a cruiser that was built in the United States, a destroyer built in the United States, and I won't need you. And all they are asking is $500,000." Well, there was dead silence around the table. "Mr. Preminger, let us think about this," the Admiral in charge said. The next day he called to say, "Mr. Preminger, we will give you what you want." Now Otto was not bluffing; he really was going to hire the Brazilian Navy.[1]

Because Preminger, of course, wanted to shoot on location, in the actual places where the events had taken place, he and Lyle Wheeler, his veteran production designer, along with the trusted Eva Monley, made several trips to Hawaii in advance of his June 24 starting date. Over three months in advance of shooting, Eva Monley set up a command post in a new wing of the Ilikai Hotel in Honolulu that included a production office, an art department, a costume department, and makeup facilities. On Otto's orders she booked everyone who would be working on the film into the best rooms in the hotel. Monley also lined up two real Navy ships, the USS *St. Paul* and the USS *Philip,* and commandeered three Matson Line ships as well as a fleet of air freighters that would bring personnel, supplies, and equipment to the location.

Although there were to be only two brief battle scenes—the attack that begins the film, and at the end a battle between American and Japanese ships at Leyte Gulf, the first major sea clash of World War II—both required extensive preparation. In setting up the shots for the Japanese attack, Preminger had to guarantee that he would not disrupt Navy routine or cost taxpayers any money, and following shooting he would have to return all Navy facilities to their former state as quickly as possible. As Preminger quipped, "The Japanese had it easier because, unlike me, they didn't care about American taxpayers."[2] Preparations for the Leyte Gulf encounter required over two months of research and a special effects crew to build ships. This was not to be a battle fought by actual ships, but rather a fiberglass flotilla scaled three-quarter inch to the foot. Preminger insisted nonetheless that all external details, down to the last rivet, were to be authentic. When completed, the fleet was trucked 2,500 miles to a shallow bay on the Gulf of Mexico where a crew of forty spent one month and one million dollars to film a battle that was to take only five minutes of the film's 165-minute running time.

As Mayes was finishing the script and Monley was preparing Honolulu for the arrival of the crew, "Admiral Preminger," as the filmmaker was called by naval officers who recognized the logistical problems of getting Hawaii camera-ready, rounded up his cast. "The script wasn't finished, but I got all my first choices by simply showing them the book and on my say-so," he boasted.[3] The three leads—John Wayne, Kirk Douglas, and Patricia Neal—were newcomers to the Preminger fold, but among the large supporting cast were such veterans as Burgess Meredith, Franchot Tone, Henry Fonda, and Jill Haworth. Preminger offered a part to Dana Andrews, who had been struggling with alcoholism for years and unable to work. "Otto, who hated scenery chewers, always appreciated Dana's underplaying, and in the Fox days had also liked him very much personally," Hope recalled. "He had only a short part for Dana, but was delighted that he accepted, and when Dana showed up in Hawaii looking fit and healthy Otto was so pleased." Amazingly, Preminger also hired Tom Tryon for a major supporting role. "Otto had Tom under contract," as Hope pointed out, "and if Tom had refused the role he would have been in breach of contract. No matter what he might have felt, Tom behaved beautifully.

"Everyone, including Otto, liked Tom, and everyone was rooting for him," Hope said. "Tom and I were very friendly and I tried hard to put him at his ease. But he was nervous on the set and had trouble getting his lines out. Tom had a certain formality, and also a certain weakness. When you got any kind of emotion on his face it was because he was about ready to cry."[4] "Tom went out of his way to avoid any contact off the set with Preminger," Jill Haworth remembered. "But a problem developed. After Tom had been in Hawaii for nearly two months he had a great tan; then when he wasn't needed, he went away for a few weeks—he certainly wasn't going to be around Preminger any longer than he had to be. But when he returned he no longer had his tan and was white as a sheet. Preminger, a stickler for continuity, was upset but he did *not* explode."[5]

Tryon was spared, but Paula Prentiss, cast as his wife, was not. "Paula was a wonderful actress, light and airy, and she had a lot of pizzazz," Tryon commented. "When we were shooting in San Francisco, in what was our characters' apartment, Otto started in on her and I thought, 'Oh, Jesus, Otto, don't.' It was only the second or third day of shooting and he was zinging it to her for no reason. Paula took it as long as she could and then she blew. And I mean she blew and Otto sidled over to me, as if for protection."[6] A second eruption occurred during a scene in which Prentiss is told that her character's husband is missing in action. Added pressure was on the actress because Preminger wanted to shoot the scene in one take rather than cut to a close-up reaction shot. "Paula got so flustered she couldn't remember her lines," Hope said. "At one point, she yelled 'Cut!' which is not the actor's choice. An actor should never say that to any director, least of all Otto! Paula also had a propensity to ad-lib—also not a good idea when Otto is your director. Many, many takes were required and Paula, who was very conscientious and eager to get the scene right, would stamp her foot. She didn't realize until after the scene was over that she'd broken her ankle."[7] Unable to walk, she was taken to a hospital. Rumors circulated on the set that an enraged Preminger had kicked the actress, but Preminger's attacks were never physical.

"Paula and Tom would huddle together yakking about how terrible Otto was," co-star Patrick O'Neal recalled. "It got to be a big bore. I told them, 'If your life means anything to you, you'll stand up to him once and find out he's a human being.' Everybody who says they hate Otto Preminger hate him because they won't fight back. There are two groups of actors. One needs to be browbeaten—and Preminger can smell them a mile off. He knows if you're frightened and *he* can't cope with it. The other group—I'm one—fight back and Otto respects me for it."[8]

Preminger had no problems at all with his two leads, John Wayne and Patricia Neal. Because Wayne was ideally cast as an officer who disobeys orders during the Pearl Harbor attack and must fight his way back to a position of authority, there was no need to get in his way. "John Wayne and Otto agreed not to discuss politics," Hope pointed out. "They had completely opposite views, and as Otto said, they were both too old to change and wouldn't succeed in converting each other, so why bother? They played chess instead, and they were both good: very competitive."[9]

With Neal as with Wayne, Otto was strictly hands off.

Look, I was right for the part of the nurse [an earth mother cut from solid rock] and Otto didn't have to tell me much. I had had instructions from a real nurse and besides, I have good instincts. For actors, Otto was not the best. But he did one thing for us that really helped: there were no sets, everything was real, and that made a difference in how the actors felt.

His screaming bothered me, but I didn't dare say anything: I was only an actress, after all. But he never screamed at me, because after winning the Oscar for *Hud* in 1963 I had become a star, and Otto was always great to stars. He was also *the* most generous producer I ever worked for, and he was divine to my family and me. I was pregnant at the time we went to Honolulu, and he put up Roald [Dahl, Neal's husband] and me and our three children and two nurses at a fabulous hotel. We were beautifully cared for, and all at Otto's expense. He would call regularly to find out if everything was all right.

(Preminger's kindness toward Neal, whom he had dated briefly in Hollywood in the early 1950s, continued after the film was completed. In March 1965, after the actress suffered a series of massive strokes, Preminger wanted to start a fund that would support her for the rest of her life. "Thank God I didn't need the fund, but I remember his concern. I appreciated it then, and I appreciate it now.")[10]

As in his other location shoots, Preminger believed it was part of his job to charm the locals. He persuaded a Honolulu paper to assign a journalist to write a daily feature on the making of the film, and during the eleven weeks of shooting Hawaiians were regaled with anecdotes of the production. "We went to lots of parties," Eva Monley said, "and Otto hosted lots of galas." And, as *Variety* reported on August 26, 1964, "Hawaii filming got international publicity via Preminger's timeworn but ever-effective technique of flying in selected journalists and columnists from Europe as well as the U.S. mainland to watch various phases of shooting."

Preminger completed principal photography on September 3, eleven days ahead of schedule and well under his original budget of $5.5 million. A few weeks before the film's premiere on April 6, 1965, he held press conferences and hosted luncheons and dinners for American and foreign journalists. This time, nobody was up in arms; no group had been offended. "The only thing I was asked to delete was the word 'screw,' and I told them I thought it preferable to another word that the navy officer would probably use. They let it remain," Preminger reported.[11] To his surprise, Japanese exhibitors voiced no objections, and he signed contracts for *In Harm's Way* to open in Japan in August.

The film received mixed reviews. "Strikingly dramatic," enthused Kate Cameron in the *New York Daily News*. "The kind of movie that probably hasn't been made since Pearl Harbor," Judith Crist, guns blazing as always in Otto's direction, wrote in the *New York Herald Tribune*. In the *New York Post*, Archer Winsten cited two performances for "absolute economy of means coupled with beautiful projection of feeling, those of Paula Prentiss and Tom Tryon as the young couple who survive a great deal of suspense."

For the film's out-of-competition screening as the opening event of the Cannes Film Festival on May 12, Preminger orchestrated a hootenanny. He gathered one hundred critics in London and booked them on a chartered plane to Nice, where he had them taken on a private bus with a specially installed bar to the Carlton Hotel. At the hotel, both before and after the screening he served them caviar and champagne of the finest quality. For the after-screening soirée he flew in Diahann Carroll from Los Angeles to entertain the troops. The cost of this Otto special was $25,000, a staggering sum at the time. "You can't force a critic to like a film, but you can try to create the conditions that might make him well disposed," wrote Leonard Moseley of the *London Daily Express*, one of Preminger's hundred guests. Despite (or perhaps because of?) Preminger's hospitality, for the most part the reviews, and later the European box office, were lukewarm.

"It is not really a war picture," Preminger claimed in his press conferences at Cannes. And in the same sense that *The Cardinal* is not a religious film and *Advise and Consent* is not a political film, the statement is accurate. Measured by battle scenes, which after all are the set pieces by which the genre defines itself, the film comes up short. The inciting incident, the attack on Pearl Harbor, is more or less presented in one long, packed master shot, and viewers expecting a traditional action scene must wait over two hours. But there, too, war film fans are likely to be disappointed, as the climactic naval battle is shot in a perfunctory way and by today's standards the special effects are crude.

In *In Harm's Way,* Preminger presents the attack on Pearl Harbor in one long, roving, deep-focus shot.

Hardly unexpectedly, battle scenes hold little interest for Preminger. More surprising, however, is his apparent indifference to the political and historical significance of Pearl Harbor. The film offers so little context or point of view about the attack or about World War II that the story could be taking place in almost any war. The Japanese are an absent presence, glimpsed only once, in long shot, to the accompaniment of "Oriental" music. Of the European theater of the war or of the Nazis there is no mention at all. Preminger's focus is on military process: how the Navy conducts its business, enforces its rules, punishes offenders, and rewards heroes. As a result, the real catalyst in the film is not the attack on Pearl Harbor but the response to the attack of Captain Rockwell Torrey (John Wayne), the sturdily named hero. Because the captain (the "Rock") disregards orders by leading what turns out to be an unsuccessful sea attack against the invaders, he is demoted to a desk job. In this melodrama of male redemption, in which Preminger's concern is with how Torrey regains his place within the

Patricia Neal as the earth-mother nurse tending to the wounded hero (John Wayne) in the last shot of *In Harm's Way*.

naval hierarchy, the "enemy" isn't the Japanese so much as it is Torrey's adversaries in the military who try to block his comeback.

Like Stephen Fermoyle in *The Cardinal*, Rockwell Torrey learns how to curb a streak of defiance in order to be able to function within the system; and like the priest, by the end rock-solid Torrey becomes an ideal company man. A sincere (if far from hip) tribute to the Navy and to military preparedness, *In Harm's Way* is the work of a filmmaker who first to last was an American patriot. "War does not necessarily make animals out of men," Preminger claimed in a pre-opening interview. "They can also make great friends and by having to defend themselves become gallant and courageous and inventive. When attacked you do not become hysterical and give up. The film tells how a handful of Americans reacted to attack without the necessary weapons but with courage and decisive action. People don't become bad in war, they become stronger, more resourceful, braver. I don't say that in the picture, I try to show it."[12]

As in *The Cardinal*, scenes of arrival and departure display the director's Viennese attraction to the trappings of protocol. But throughout there are curious dry spots, scenes of groups of men in anonymous rooms examining maps and discussing military strategy. Clearly, battleships and Quonset huts don't have the same allure for Preminger as the marmoreal Senate in *Advise and Consent* or the palatial rooms in which the officers of the Catholic church conduct their affairs in *The Cardinal.* His occasionally flaccid direction is contrasted by Saul Bass's dynamic end titles set against crashing waves, which, along with Jerry Goldsmith's stirring exit music, prefigure the battles the American armed forces will have to wage before victory over the Axis enemy can be claimed.

The least commanding work of Preminger's epic phase, *In Harm's Way* is also the warmest. The director presents the relationships between John Wayne and Patricia Neal, and between Wayne and Brandon de Wilde as his estranged son (was Otto thinking again of his own "estranged" son, Erik?), without his customary detachment. Significantly, he ends with a close-up rather than his usual long shot—of the nurse giving Torrey, who has been wounded in action, a benevolent, protective smile. *In Harm's Way* "reads" like an engrossing, plot-heavy work of popular fiction, a lending library favorite.

Throughout the filming Otto huddled almost nightly in his suite at the Ilikai Hotel with John and Penelope Mortimer, who were writing the screenplay for his next production, *Bunny Lake Is Missing,* a small suspense story that had already had the longest gestation period of any Preminger project. On the recommendation of his niece Eve, who thought the novel by Merriam Modell (writing under the pen name of Evelyn Piper) had the makings of a good thriller, Otto had bought the rights in 1958 for $75,000. On November 10 of that year he had signed a contract with Walter Newman, who had written the screenplay for *The Man with the Golden Arm,* for $1,500 a week. Dissatisfied with Newman's treatment, on May 11, 1959, he hired Charles Beaumont at $1,000 a week. Again Otto was displeased. In October 1959 he signed a contract with Ira Levin, "who shall proceed to London and commence, on August 30, 1960, two weeks of conferences with Otto Preminger with respect to the rewrite of the first draft." Levin received $60,000 for his work: $15,000 on signing, $30,000 on submission of a first draft, and $15,000 on submission of a rewrite. During this period Preminger produced Levin's mediocre play, *Critic's Choice,* on Broadway, but he and the writer parted company over *Bunny Lake Is Missing.* On January 4, 1961, Preminger signed his *Exodus* writer Dalton Trumbo, also for $60,000. No luck again. Not giving up, on April 13, 1964, for $5,000 he signed a newly successful playwright, Arthur Kopit, to deliver a treatment. If Otto felt the treatment warranted a first draft, Kopit would receive $7,500 in advance followed by another $7,500 for a finished first draft and $7,500 for a final draft. If he was still standing, on completion of all services Kopit would receive

$2,500. Kopit survived, but his work did not. Finally, conferring with the Mortimers in Honolulu in July and August 1964, Preminger felt he was on the right track.

What was the problem? The novel has an intriguing premise: a neurotic mother, Blanche, visiting New York, where she does not know anyone, claims that her daughter has gone missing. Because Blanche appears so unstable there is doubt about whether the child exists. If Bunny does exist, as her increasingly hysterical mother insists, then where is she? If she has been kidnapped, who is responsible? Evelyn Piper fills the novel with eccentric suspects, but in working out whodunit she gets entangled with plot twists and unconvincing villains—it turns out that a spinster teacher at the school where Bunny has just been enrolled, working in cahoots with Blanche's own mother, has kidnapped Bunny. "When I worked on the original story, I found that the villain, the old woman who stole the child, was uninteresting," Preminger said. "It's a completely arbitrary solution; and it doesn't make much sense. Then we created a rich heiress who manufactured this whole thing because she had no children and wanted a child. This also turned out to be terribly phony. I finally came to the conclusion that it would have to be someone very close [to the mother] from the beginning."[13]

It was Penelope Mortimer who suggested a new villain, Blanche's mad brother Stephen (the character does not appear in the novel), determined to eliminate Bunny because he views her as a rival for his sister's love. Otto's initial gratitude toward Penelope darkened into crankiness. Penelope, "a strange, mixed-up lady altogether," according to Martin Schute, "had written a good treatment, but her final draft wasn't working. When Otto started berating her, there were a lot of sour looks. And then when Otto ordered John to substantially rewrite Penelope's draft, she was not best pleased, to say the least," Schute said.[14]

Otto chose London for the city the hapless American family visits because, as Hope maintained, he felt "very comfortable there. By that time he had edited five or six pictures at Shepperton, and he had lots of friends in London from the old days in Vienna. And both of us liked the British style."[15] As he was also preparing promotion and publicity for the American and European openings of *In Harm's Way,* Preminger set up a production office for *Bunny Lake* in the top floor suite of the Carlton Tower Hotel in February 1965. With Hope, the twins, and a nanny, he moved into a suite at the Dorchester.

Working with Martin Schute as his associate producer and liaison, Otto hired a crew that was entirely British except for Hope and Eva Monley. ("Because of me, Otto crossed wires with unions in England," Monley said. "At the union office he said he wouldn't leave until they issued me a union card. Well—I got my card. Otto was incredibly loyal to me, even if he never told me I was doing a good job.") With Monley and Schute, who both knew London well, and his production designer Don Ashton, Preminger searched for eerie locations. "We found a doll hospital in Soho," Monley recalled. "And the house where the finale takes place we found in Hampstead Heath; it belonged to the estate of Daphne Du Maurier and had just the creepiness Otto wanted. We also found a hospital in Hammersmith that was plenty weird-looking. It had lots of empty wards, which we took over for filming."[16] As Martin Schute remembered, "For one scene, set against a row of Soho strip clubs with pictures of naked women out front, I was told that we needed a copyright fee only if the camera was moved. So I had to tell Otto to be sure to keep the camera still, so the women would not appear to be bumping and grinding. He listened, as he always did to anything legal."[17]

Otto's casting was lucky. For the American visitors, he signed Carol Lynley and Keir Dullea, who looked so much alike they could actually have been brother and sister. "When we checked our genealogies Keir and I found that we are distantly related," Carol Lynley said. "We share some relatives from Waterville, Ireland. Otto told me that Columbia had wanted him to cast Jane Fonda and Ryan O'Neal, but he said he wanted Keir and me. Then they came back and said they wanted him to use Ann-Margret. He refused again. And again he said he wanted Keir and me. This time, Columbia agreed."[18]

"Otto had offered me the part that Brandon de Wilde played in *In Harm's Way,* but I had turned it down," Keir Dullea remembered. "I had just done a war film, *The Thin Red Line,* and, to be honest, I didn't want to work with John Wayne. This time I accepted. I was in awe at the prospect of working with Otto Preminger, who was world-famous."[19]

For the subsidiary role of a stiff-upper-lip inspector, the kind of part that a journeyman British actor like John Williams could have walked through, Preminger, on February 20, 1965, for a fee of $200,000 and a six-week shooting commitment to start on April 21, signed Laurence Olivier, the premier actor of the English-speaking world. To play delicious British eccentrics he cast Noël Coward, Martita Hunt, and Finlay Currie.

With young American actors in the leading roles surrounded by a galaxy of theater-trained British veterans, the setup recalled *Saint Joan.* And indeed, Keir Dullea responded to Preminger much as Jean Seberg had, with a mixture of fear and loathing.

> I had heard all the rumors about Preminger, but I felt he wouldn't do that to me. I was wrong, oh so wrong. I began to feel that the

character he played in *Stalag 17* was Otto on a good day. Our relationship started on a wrong note. When we were walking in London toward the Dorchester before shooting started I was ill at ease and to make conversation I told a story about the Duke of Wellington whose house is a museum that we were passing by. "That is the most fascinating story I ever heard," he said in a sarcastic tone that told me it wasn't. Once shooting began he just started in on me, and going to work I felt like the Al Capp character with a black cloud over his head.

I was playing a crazy character and the director was driving me crazy. Worse than the screaming, far worse, was the sarcasm. When, from sheer nerves, I would go up on lines, he would say, "Well, Mr. Dullea, you were such a promising actor; now you can't remember lines. What's the matter with you?" Slight at first, the sarcasm would build and build. He had a real sadistic streak that went beyond being a "technique" for working with actors. He enjoyed inflicting horrendous humiliation in front of an audience. (I couldn't help noticing that when we did the looping at the end, he was very nice to Carol and me because he had no one to show off for then.) About halfway through the shoot, I began to wonder, Who do you have to fuck to get off this picture?

Dullea remained silent for three-quarters of the shooting. "I was so cowed I felt beaten before the day would begin, praying he wouldn't do it every day. I never cried; I swallowed it." When Irvin Kershner, who had directed Dullea in his first film, *The Hoodlum Priest,* and had remained a close friend, visited the set, the actor unburdened himself. Kershner gave him advice that proved instrumental. " 'You will never out-Preminger Preminger,' he told me. 'You have to find a way that's typically you that will take him by surprise.' " Soon thereafter, when Preminger began to scream at him, Dullea sat down and, in a voice so small and squashed it could hardly be heard, said he didn't feel well. "What are you saying? I can't hear you," Preminger bellowed.

His attention was so much on me that he forgot his "act." "You scare the shit out of me," I said. "You scare the shit out of every actor." I really went bananas. "Keir, we don't want to scare you," he said with great composure. "Take a half hour and we'll begin again." He was incapable of an apology, but he never got at me again. Not once. I shouldn't have had to do that.

There seemed to be a pattern. Otto went after a certain kind of sensitive, good-looking young leading man: Tryon, John Saxon, me. But as always with Otto there were contradictions, because he didn't go after Sal Mineo on *Exodus*.

Dullea was convinced that Preminger prevented him from being as strong as he might have been. "Nobody ever gave the performance of his career in a Preminger film," Dullea claimed.

No actor ever peaked with him. How could you? Everybody was watching his back. If part of you is busy protecting yourself, you're not in the role entirely: you can't be. Because I was so tense my voice is in a higher register than it is in any other film. If I had felt secure I would have given a more dimensional performance. I would have made the character more normal-seeming at the beginning, before he turns. The subtlety that I felt I was able to give to my work in *2001*, because Stanley Kubrick created a safe atmosphere where actors were not afraid to be foolish or wrong, was missing on Otto's set. I don't hate him; it's too long ago. But the experience was the most unpleasant I ever had.[20]

("Otto thought Keir was terrific in the role and that no one at the time could have been better," Hope recalled.[21] Dullea's response: "Why didn't he ever tell me?"[22])

Unlike her costar Carol Lynley survived the filming with good memories. "Otto never got to me the way he got to Keir," she said.

But unlike Tom Tryon, Keir was able to handle the pressure. He never fell apart. I liked the way Otto worked; he always allowed plenty of time for rehearsals, and I loved his shooting in long takes, which helps actors to get a rhythm going.

Otto did yell at me once or twice, however, and I finally got to fight with him. The worst time was during a scene in the school where I go up the stairs looking for Bunny and kids are coming down. He started in on me and in front of two hundred kids I yelled back. It was a terrific shouting match. An explosion! It was wonderful!

Patricia Bosworth, one of the many journalists Preminger had invited to the set, caught Lynley on a bad day. "Preminger begins to give Carol line readings, he tries to show her how a particular word should be stressed. Finally,

Otto coaches Laurence Olivier, the world's leading actor at the time, on the set of *Bunny Lake Is Missing*.

in exasperation, he rushes over to show Carol Lynley the way he thinks the character should be played. He continues his savage criticism of Carol until she is sobbing uncontrollably. When she is completely hysterical, he shoots the close-up. 'I don't think Lee Strasberg would approve,' Olivier said."[23]

"I could handle Otto's explosions, but I was petrified of working with Laurence Olivier," Lynley recalled.

> He told us to call him Larry, and he made a point of talking about his wife and kids, but still I was so intimidated that I stiffened up in all the early scenes. Otto said I was terrible and that he was going to replace me with Barbara Bouchet—with Otto you had to do it full out the first time and then he would either edit or leave you alone. When I told him the reason was that I was in awe of Olivier, he said, "We are going to break for lunch, and you have one hour to get over it." The way I got over it was I transferred my own fear into the character's fear about having lost her daughter.[24]

Keir Dullea noticed that Preminger didn't carry on as much with him and Carol Lynley whenever they had scenes with Olivier. "Olivier did not defend Carol and me publicly," Dullea recalled, "but I know that he went to Otto privately and asked him not to yell at the 'children.' 'I'm too old to change,' Otto responded." To help out "the children," or perhaps because of his own nerves (at the time Olivier was struggling with the fear that he would dry up whenever he was onstage) he ran lines frequently with the young actors behind Otto's back. "Otto didn't have to 'direct' Olivier, who had figured out his role beautifully before he had ever come onto the set," Dullea noted. "But he wouldn't have yelled at the big names anyway, and to that extent he was both a coward and a hypocrite. He was deferential to all the British actors except Martita Hunt, whom he treated horrendously. When she complained about her wig, he screamed, 'Don't talk to me about your wig. You're an ugly old hag anyway! You want to be in my film? Do it my way!' "[25]

Preminger shot *Bunny Lake* entirely on location in London from April 21 to June 19. Because he did not want to shoot day for night, midway through he scheduled eighteen grueling nights of filming, when he and his team worked from eleven to about four or five in the morning. Despite the added tension of the night shooting, he not only kept ahead of his schedule, he also met each day with the playwright Horton Foote, who was writing the script of *Hurry Sundown,* an epic set in the American South, which Otto was planning to film on location the following summer. His indispensable assistants, Martin Schute and Eva Monley, helped to keep Otto on schedule. For Monley, the shoot was problem-free and she would go on to work for "Papa" on two more films. But for Schute, who liked and understood Otto and who with his wife Pat remained a good friend of the Preminger family, *Bunny Lake* was the end of the line professionally. "I had to quit after the film, when Otto accused me of taking money on the side," Schute recalled. "My brother ran a car hire and Otto said I pocketed the 50 percent commission, which wasn't the case."[26]

Bunny Lake Is Missing was well received in Europe, especially in London, where critics enjoyed the film's distillation of local atmosphere into a mise-en-scène of mounting terror. When the film opened in the United States on October 3, 1965, however, it was dismissed. "Nothing outside of a new script could save this phony film from going . . . straight down the drain," Bosley Crowther grumbled. Frances Herridge in the *New York Post* concurred, writing that Preminger "has come up with some stunning scenes . . . but without a strong screenplay to go with them they seem technique for the sake of technique."

"We all had such high hopes—I thought I might even be Oscar-nominated," Carol Lynley said.

But the film was not a success in America. Maybe it was the subject. I was told that people with children didn't want to see it and people who didn't have children didn't care. Maybe it was because it was one of the last films shot in black-and-white. I also felt the critics reviewed Otto the Terrible more than the movie. There was block voting then, and when I asked Mike Frankovich, the president of Columbia Pictures, why they weren't pushing the film, he told me they were going with *The Collector*. Columbia just sat on the film. I was heartsick.[27]

A number of reviewers objected to the last-act revelation that it was Stephen who kidnapped Bunny. But planting clues of Stephen's guilt from the beginning, Preminger and the Mortimers justify their denouement. In the opening tracking shot, for instance, Stephen walking across a garden stops to pick up a white teddy bear, his seemingly casual gesture drawing a link between him and Bunny. Keir Dullea, as he must, portrays the character with a tantalizing duality—on the surface Stephen seems a devoted family man, a pleasant-looking all-American. But dark undercurrents, sudden blasts of prickliness and rage, periodically disturb his Boy Scout veneer. Also

An odd couple, a sister (Carol Lynley) and brother (Keir Dullea) who behave like husband and wife, in *Bunny Lake Is Missing*.

unsettling is the illicit aura of the brother-sister relationship. High-strung and often mistaken by the British characters for husband and wife, Stephen and Ann seem to be harboring a secret. In a scene simmering with incestuous overtones, Stephen, lounging in a bathtub, and Ann, seated on the rim of the tub, take turns smoking a cigarette.

Even if the viewer can't buy the way the story ends, *Bunny Lake Is Missing* can and indeed demands to be savored as a collection of scintillating set pieces. In Preminger's calibrated mise-en-scène, seemingly neutral locations—the Little People's School, where Ann enrolls her daughter; a pub; the bare apartment Ann moves into—acquire threatening undertones. And as the increasingly distraught mother searches for her daughter, every setting begins to rumble with menace. Decorated with African masks, whips, skulls, and chains, the dwelling of her lubricious landlord (Noël Coward, whooping it up) becomes a Sadean den. Stephen attacks Ann and thereby reveals his villainy in a doll hospital, lit only with candles that turn the characters' faces into minatory masks. Its only apparent resident a nurse glimpsed in deep focus through an inside window, the hospital where Stephen takes Ann after he knocks her out has high-ceilinged corridors crawling with ill will and only an off-screen cough breaks the creepy silence. Escaping through the hospital's basement, Ann runs past engines and pistons whirring, chugging, and pumping, and a lab with caged rats overseen by a robotic janitor.

Relying uncharacteristically on canted angles, fractured editing, disfiguring close-ups, and shock cuts from silence to sound and from light to shadow, Preminger and his cinematographer Denys Coop transform the house in which Ann at the end plays a potentially deadly game of cat-and-mouse with her now unhinged brother into a trap-laden lair. The giddy, whipped-up style—a rare display of the director indulging himself in rococo virtuosity—is an artful subterfuge, a means of attempting to paper over some gaps in narrative logic. Preminger may resort to montage editing for the finale, but in the body of the film he does not abandon his usual repertoire of long takes and camera movement. As both Dullea and Lynley recalled, Preminger "spent hours and hours" conferring with Denys Coop and camera operator Gerry Fisher, lining up shots. And throughout, the tracking, swiveling, pivoting, craning, pirouetting camera enhances the atmosphere of intimidation that engulfs the worried mother, a stranger in a strange land.

In the unlikely event that neither the story nor Preminger's direction—the flashiest in his career—persuades the viewer, resistance is guaranteed to crumble at each appearance of Laurence Olivier, who plays with incomparable deftness the methodical, urbane Inspector Newhouse, an amateur philosopher and a skillful phrasemaker who presides over the mystery of whether Bunny Lake is missing. For the eighteen days of night shooting that Otto scheduled, Olivier would arrive after having performed Othello onstage at the National Theatre, where, altering his gait, voice, demeanor, and skin color, the actor did a great deal of great acting. Working into the wee hours with Preminger on *Bunny Lake,* however, he hardly seems to be acting at all. His lean performance is arguably his finest on film, the work of a master craftsman who has refined the elements of his trade to an irreducible minimum.

Preminger managed to define "a certain social theme here: if [like Ann, who has had a child out of wedlock] you do not conform to the rules of society, the law does not protect you. That is an important part of the film."[28] But he conceded, after all, that *Bunny Lake Is Missing* is "a small story." Indeed, with none of the narrative scope or middlebrow seriousness that marked his recent epic cycle, the film is no more, and no less, than a well-crafted entertainment, a shimmering postnoir film noir and the last fully assured work of Otto Preminger's career.

SIXTEEN

In Klan Country

If *Bunny Lake Is Missing* is "a small story," *Hurry Sundown*, which Preminger worked on with Horton Foote as he was shooting in London, is just the opposite, an adaptation of a monumentally lengthy novel (1,064 pages) by Katya and Bert Gilden set in Georgia in 1946. Preminger had high hopes for the project. He had acquired the novel about eight months before its January 1965 publication. "I read it in a manuscript that Ingo showed to me," Otto recalled. "It was very long, longer even than the published version, which is also very long, and I was fascinated by the people, and by the whole implication of the South in 1946 after World War II which, in my opinion, was the starting point of the civil rights movement."[1] Fully expecting the novel to become a best seller, Preminger had paid $100,000 for the rights and participated eagerly in all the prepublication fanfare organized by Doubleday, the book's publisher. On November 17, 1964, he had called a press conference where, with much ado, he revealed his plans to film the Gildens' "great" novel. He also announced that his film would be a four-and-a-half-hour hard-ticket attraction that he would open in December 1966 in a handful of movie palaces at what was then the highest price scale in the history of American film exhibition. Otto promised he would charge twenty-five dollars for the best orchestra seats for the Friday and Saturday night performances, at which he was requesting that gentlemen wear black tie. (None of Preminger's grandiose plans materialized.) "The novel has already been #2 on the best-seller lists for about 8 weeks," he said in the *Los Angeles Times* on March 30, 1965, continuing to beat the drums. "Some critics say it is another *Gone with the Wind.* I certainly hope the picture is!" Despite Preminger's and Doubleday's persistent promotion, *Hurry Sundown* sold a respectable but not blockbuster 300,000 copies.

Preminger chose Horton Foote because he admired the writer's adaptation of another Southern novel, Harper Lee's *To Kill a Mockingbird.* Otto thought the Texan, whose plays about his home state are suffused with local color, would feel a kinship with the novel's Southern setting and theme, but he didn't seem to appreciate that Foote's quiet style is far removed from the overripe manner of the Gildens, a married couple making their literary debut. "When Otto sent me the book I didn't like it at all," Foote recalled.

> The authors had done their research all right, but they were not Southerners and nothing was authentic. There was no genuine Southern flavor at all. It was embarrassing. But I was younger then, and egotistical, and I thought I could do something with it. Otto brought my wife and children and me over to London and put us up in a house in Hyde Park where for three months we all lived high on the hog at Otto's expense.
>
> He was busy filming, but even so I saw him every day. He would make suggestions that I would obediently follow, and he seemed to like what I was doing. He was sharp as a tack. He laughed a lot with me—I guess I was the court jester. He wasn't working on *Bunny Lake* every minute, and when he wasn't he was a wonderful raconteur. And he was very sweet to my children. "Now keep them in line," he'd say. Working every day with that far-fetched story [about the determination of two sharecroppers, a white man and a black man who have been lifelong friends, to prevent the sale of their adjoining land to corporate developers], I felt I was wrestling with unbeatable material. When I turned in a draft after three months I thought it was good, or at least as good as could be. After reading it—Otto had enormous confidence in his opinion—he said that we had different visions of the material. He wanted more melodrama and ultratheatricality than I gave him. I thought Otto was a wonderful filmmaker, but it wasn't always my style—his story sense was different from mine. He could have insisted I go on working, but he didn't. He paid me generously, exactly what he said he was going to. Then he hired Tom Ryan, who had worked for him and the next year had a success adapting Carson McCullers's *Heart Is a*

Lonely Hunter. Later Otto called and asked if he could put my name on the script. I was touched, actually, and I felt I owed it to him. I ask now, however, not to have it on my résumé. I never saw the final script or the film, and I don't know how much of my work is there. Not much, I suspect.[2]

At the time Otto hired him, in the summer of 1965, Tom Ryan was in fact his chief reader. "He weighed about three hundred pounds, and when we shared an office at Columbia, he smoked me out," Hope said. "He was talented and very bright—he was a walking encyclopedia and he retained every fact. Otto appreciated his skills in casting and as a reader. But Tom was bitter about his life: he was an unhappy homosexual who tried several times to commit suicide."[3] In August and September, as he was preparing for the opening of *Bunny Lake,* Preminger worked closely with Ryan, who was on his staff and in the office every day. He was pleased with Ryan's approach—Ryan was giving him the "ultratheatricality," the Hollywood melodrama take on the material that he wanted. Over the fall, as he oversaw openings of *Bunny Lake,* Preminger began to assemble the large cast. To play the sharecroppers who resist selling their land, he chose two newcomers with stage experience, Robert Hooks and John Phillip Law. And in addition to court favorites Burgess Meredith, Doro Merande, and Diahann Carroll, he signed Michael Caine, Jane Fonda, Madeleine Sherwood, George Kennedy, Rex Ingram, and—to his infinite regret—Faye Dunaway. Because, of course, he wanted to shoot the entire film on location, in Georgia where the Gildens had set the novel, he made several trips in November and December to line up settings. Although he knew the weather would be fierce, he was planning to shoot the film in the dripping humidity of June, July, and August.

In the midst of preproduction on *Hurry Sundown* he received unwanted headlines for an incident that took place at "21" on January 7, 1966. Seated next to the Premingers, who were dining with columnist Louis Sobol and his wife, were the agent Irving "Swifty" Lazar and his wife Mary. According to Lazar, Otto was determined to provoke an argument over a deal that had gone sour. Two years earlier, as Lazar recalled, Otto had wanted, prepublication, to buy the rights from him to Truman Capote's *In Cold Blood* and have Frank Sinatra star. "I'd given him some hope, but had carefully avoided saying anything binding. Which was just as well—when the book was finished, Truman decided we should sell it to Richard Brooks without inviting other bids. Left out in the cold Otto was miffed."[4] That night at "21," according to Lazar's recollection, Otto said that Sinatra was enraged and was planning to beat up the agent. To verify his claim Preminger demanded a phone so he could call Sinatra in Las Vegas at the Sands Hotel. "You're making it impossible for us to remain here, Otto," Lazar said. When he and his wife got up to leave, Lazar claimed that Preminger began to insult Mary. "You pitiable creature, I feel sorry for any woman who has to go home and go to bed with that crook," Otto allegedly said to Mary Lazar. According to her husband, at that point Mrs. Lazar called Otto "a dirty old man" and slapped him. When Preminger rose up from his chair and raised his hand against Mary, Lazar reached for a glass and whacked Otto in the head with it. "Blood was streaming down Otto's face as Mary and I beat a retreat," Lazar contended.[5] "I regret very much that it happened," Lazar confided to columnist Earl Wilson. "For people who are not hoodlums these things are always regrettable. But I was provoked."[6]

Otto denied that he had insulted Mrs. Lazar or that she had slapped him. "His wife did not take part in this at all," he told Earl Wilson.[7] "The argument had nothing to do with *In Cold Blood*," as Hope recollected. "It was about Sinatra and Las Vegas: Swifty told us that he had just come from Sinatra's opening in Vegas, but Otto knew that couldn't be true; the opening wasn't until later. When he said so, Swifty, a strange little man—I don't know that he liked anyone—got annoyed. He stood, with a glass of scotch in his hand, and hit Otto. Hardly any words had been exchanged. The manager rushed Otto into the men's room and called the ambulance. I called the police. Otto was conscious, but dazed." Pictures of Otto exiting the restaurant with a puzzled expression and with his head bleeding profusely—he looked like the subject of a photo by Weegee, the chronicler of New York's lower depths—were splashed across the next morning's newspapers.

"The police wrapped his head in a towel and took Otto to New York Hospital, where a plastic surgeon had to remove pieces of glass from Otto's scalp," Hope said. "The operation required fifty-one stitches and Otto was in bed for the next three days. When the police asked Otto if he wanted to charge Swifty, Otto called our good friend Louis Nizer, who said yes, to go ahead."[8]

In court on January 28, the combatants glared frostily at each other as Lazar pleaded not guilty. "The incident was not Otto's fault, but because he always played the heavy he took the rap for it," Hope said. Whatever the cause, the argument certainly reinforced Otto's image as an ogre, a man you love to hate, and reflected poorly on him as well as Lazar. Both men behaved disgracefully, like petulant children. (A year later, on January 18, 1967, Lazar pleaded guilty to misdemeanor charges of hitting Preminger, the original felony charge having been reduced months earlier, and was given a suspended sentence. "Otto was not litigious and decided not to sue," Hope said. Years later, Lazar became a patient of Otto's son Mark, at the time a cardiology intern. "When Mark asked me if he should become involved in the test I told him, 'Of course,' " Hope said. "Mark told me that Swifty had asked him if he was a fellow who holds a grudge. He certainly is not, any more than Otto was. Mark conducted the test and happily, Swifty survived.")[9]

The fracas with Lazar put Otto a few weeks behind on preproduction for *Hurry Sundown,* but by the beginning of February he was back on track. In late March, about eight weeks before his long-scheduled June 1 starting date in Georgia, he had to change location because of a union dispute. When Preminger announced that because of the severe heat he would need to shoot at night and in the early morning starting at 6 a.m., the New York union (which had jurisdiction over the Georgia union) balked. They refused to alter a rigid 8:30 a.m. start time and demanded double time after 4 p.m. Preminger, who paid his crew above scale, claimed the costs of meeting the New York union demands would have been prohibitive. He had budgeted the film at a trim $3,785,000, compared to the $5,440,000 he had allotted the year before for *In Harm's Way,* and he was resolved to remain within that sum.

Otto's production designer, Gene Callahan, a native of Baton Rouge, Louisiana, suggested his home state as a possibility. Otto was persuaded, especially when he found out that Louisiana unions were under the jurisdiction of the Chicago union, more liberal than the one in New York. Still hoping to meet his June 1 starting date, Preminger in early April dispatched Callahan, along with Eva Monley, once again his production manager, to line up locations. When they brought him down to Louisiana in late April to examine the sites they had selected, he was satisfied. "Otto trusted Gene on this because Gene was from the Deep South," as Monley pointed out.[10] Nonetheless, Preminger wanted to "enhance" the locations. To fit the needs of the story and, as Willi Frischauer wrote, "to lend verisimilitude to a big flood scene, Preminger hired a large local work force to build a big dam and a reservoir holding seventeen and a half million gallons of water. Cornfields were planted and sharecroppers' cabins erected."[11]

What Gene Callahan did not seem to realize, or what he had omitted mentioning to Preminger, was that they would be filming a story of an interracial friendship in the heart of Ku Klux Klan territory. "It's like going to the Vatican to make a movie about Martin Luther, or going to a synagogue to make a film about putting down the Jews," a local observer pointed out.[12] Eva Monley booked office space for Otto and rooms for the more than one hundred members of the cast and crew at the Bellemont

Motor Hotel, which over the entrance prominently displayed a Confederate flag. Trouble started at once. "It was evident from the first day of shooting that many of the local people didn't want us there because we had a mixed cast," Eva Monley said. "One day, on the wall of a set, there was a message from the KKK: 'Eva Monley, go home.' To protect me, I was made honorary sheriff. Going to and from the set I changed cars every day."[13] Some of the extras and local crew were members of the local Klan, sent to spy and to cause disturbances wherever they could. Tires on company trucks were slashed. One morning at 3 a.m. a burning cross appeared on the set. The day after black and white members of the cast swam together in one of the motel's two pools, local Klansmen made an abortive attempt to blow it up. "We had dared to pollute their sacred waters by allowing our mixed company to swim in it together," noted Robert Hooks, who kept a diary of the production. When the manager informed Preminger that "no mixed bathing" was allowed on the premises, the filmmaker promised to remove his entire company from the motel and to default on the payment of the bill unless one pool were set aside for integrated swimming. "During the time that the pool was barred to mixed bathing, my kids said they wouldn't go without their friends, the children of Diahann Carroll and Robert Hooks, who had come along with their parents at Otto's insistence," Hope said.[14] The pool was integrated, but, as Hooks wrote, the Klan "labeled us 'that nigger pitcher' and they were determined to get us out of there, one way or another." After armed state troopers were brought in to guard the wing of the motel where the cast and crew were housed, many of the actors began to feel as if they were under house arrest, their discomfort spiked by the paralyzing heat and humidity during summer on the bayou.

"It was beginning to dawn on us just what kind of place we had landed in," Hooks noted.

The lesson was learned in somewhat different ways by different members of the cast. When Michael Caine was walking in downtown Baton Rouge with his friend [the journalist] David Lewin, a paunchy cop recognized him, which was not unusual, although his response was not what Michael was used to hearing from his fans. The sheriff looked him up and down and said he didn't want him [or any of the actors in the film] in his town and he'd "bettah get his nigga-lovin' ass the hell outah heah." Michael was speechless. He hadn't really believed what it was like in the American South in those days. But he did now.[15]

When Caine, along with Jane Fonda, Diahann Carroll, Rex Ingram, and Hooks drove into New Orleans one night, they were refused entrance at Brennan's, a famous restaurant. "Michael could barely control his anger," as Hooks recalled. "He asked the man if he knew who we were. The man did, but it made no difference. 'What do you *mean* it doesn't make any difference?' Jane jumped in. She was ready to draw blood. The man said finally with a trace of irritation in his deep Southern drawl, 'Say, don't chall unnastan'? We don' 'low no niggers in hyah. Thass it.' Movie stars or not, in New Orleans in 1966, if you were black or hung out with blacks, Southern hospitality suddenly became Southern hostility."[16]

On the way back to the Bellemont from a location one evening, as a line of cars and trucks was moving through a heavily wooded area, the twilight silence was abruptly shattered by a volley of gunshots. "We were being shot at by people we didn't know, couldn't see, and couldn't defend ourselves against," Hooks reported. "We were in a war in our own country." The barrage lasted less than a minute before the Klansmen departed into the steaming wilderness. "Several windshields were blasted out and the sides of the

110° in the shade: A lunch break, with linen tablecloths, silverware, and good china, during shooting for *Hurry Sundown,* filmed on location in the summertime heat in Baton Rouge, Louisiana.

cars were riddled with bullet holes, but by some great good fortune, no one had been hit or hurt," Hooks wrote. "The shooters had made their point. All of us were convinced that we were surrounded by some of the dumbest and meanest people on the face of the earth, to say nothing of being the most cowardly."[17]

Madeleine Sherwood, playing a small-town bigot, received numerous telephone death threats. "Perhaps they were after me because I had been down south with the civil rights movement," Sherwood reflected. "I'd spent time in jail and when I received a sentence of six months' hard labor, I was the first white woman to be defended by a black lawyer. One night at the motel, after the seventh or eighth call, I was really scared, and I phoned Otto, who was a caring person and was concerned about all of us. 'Come outside to the pool,' he said. I met him there. He took my wrist in his hand and he raised both our hands and cried out, 'Shoot!' I was trembling. But thanks to Otto I never got another death threat."[18]

"When I had to go shopping locally with Diahann Carroll to get a hat for her character, our driver said that I was to sit up front and Diahann had to sit in the back," Hope remembered. "The governor [John McKeithen], a Democrat, kept asking us and some of the white stars to a dinner but didn't invite any of the black actors. Otto didn't accept the invitation."[19] Preminger retaliated by inviting the governor and his wife to attend a dinner he was hosting for visiting French journalists; the starstruck governor readily accepted, but was surprised to discover that Preminger pointedly had invited none of the film's actors, white or black.

"Otto behaved beautifully through it all," Eva Monley observed. "He refused to negotiate and continued to demand equal treatment for everyone in his cast and crew."[20] And despite the intimidation from local hoodlums and the heat, the director, as John Phillip Law enthused, was

the best host on a movie set ever. There we were in the middle of nowhere, threatened by the Klan, and every day under tents in the boiling sun we sat down to tables set with thick tablecloths, fine silver and china. There were no box lunches with Otto, but the finest food, as fine as you would get in the best restaurants in New York or Paris. And Otto would ask—and he really wanted to know—if our hotel rooms were okay. Nowadays you are just flown in and out; with Otto there was a real communal feeling. He kept his eye on his actors off the set, and in fact he might have saved my life. I was having a fling with a local girl who had a boyfriend who was a nut from Vietnam. When I took her home he jumped out of the bushes with a knife. He told me later he bought a pistol to kill me with, but then said he wanted to give it to me as a gift, and that I should meet him face to face in the lobby. Otto arranged with the local police to have him put in jail "until you guys leave town," as the cops told me. Filming with Otto in Louisiana for three months was my golden age.[21]

Perhaps because of the us-versus-them atmosphere that overtook the location shooting, Preminger got on remarkably well with most of his actors. Michael Caine, with shrewd instincts about how to handle Otto, told him on the first day of shooting that he

knew of his reputation and that he should know that I was a very shy little flower, and if anybody ever shouted at me I would burst into tears and go into my dressing room and not come out for the rest of the day. He stared at me for a long moment and I waited to be bawled out immediately, as he was not used to being spoken to like this. Certainly he did seem a little taken aback. Finally, however, he smiled and said, "I would never shout at Alfie." That was the key to the long friendship I subsequently enjoyed with this unpopular man.[22]

I used to have a go at him when he shouted at the other actors, however. "You're scaring everybody. You're getting everybody tense." "I'm not, Alfie, I wouldn't do this. They're not afraid of me." "They are all scared." "Of me?" He was truly amazed that anyone was scared of him. He was a very abrasive man but his heart was in the right place at all times. Very much so. He was schizophrenic, because he could be two people. My favorite moment of observing Preminger—and I always watched him very closely—was in a hospital scene with Jane. It was a very, very hot day. And with the extra heat added by all the lights [that were needed to shoot the scene], the sprinkler system in the hospital was ignited. Otto went purple, his voice wouldn't come, his eyes started to pop out of his head, and my God did he start to scream. And then, as we were getting drenched, we both started to laugh. I'd never heard Otto laugh out loud before. But he just started to laugh. A big, full, wonderful laugh—oh, it was gigantic and gorgeous, that laugh—because he realized the situation and his response were so ridiculous.[23]

"In the rushes Otto saw how good Jane was; he felt she was holding the film together," Hope said. "Her politics weren't at all apparent at the time and it wouldn't have mattered to Otto anyway. She did her job, attended to her kids, and despite the fact that the Fondas had a reputation for being so icy she was friendly and warm to everyone." "Jane was *extremely* disciplined, which of course Otto appreciated," John Phillip Law said. "I lived with her and Roger Vadim [Fonda's husband] while we were shooting *Barbarella,* and she ran the house, took ballet before being on the set, and was professional all the way. Jane was just as pleased as Otto about her work in *Hurry Sundown,* which she thought was her best until *Klute.*

"Otto yelled at me quite a lot, but I could just feel that he liked me, and so I was able to shuffle off things he would say to intimidate me," Law said.

> You had to know how to take him. He cast you because you were the archetype of what he wanted, but if you frustrated him by acting too much he'd start in on you. He didn't approve of the Method, and one time when I was doing push-ups, which was my preparation for an emotional scene, he said, "This is not a gymnasium, Mr. Law, I pay you to act, not to exercise." Even though asking him to do another take was like getting dispensation from the pope, I felt secure with him in a way I hadn't with Elia Kazan, who had just directed me in the leading role in *The Changeling* at Lincoln Center. I felt Kazan resented good-looking guys, but Otto didn't—he was above it all. For a love scene with Faye Dunaway, who was playing my wife, he said, "Roll over, you have a nice-looking backside."[24]

Madeleine Sherwood, devoted to Lee Strasberg and an Actors Studio member, had exactly the kind of training Preminger had no patience for. But he hired her anyway because he had admired Sherwood's vivid performances as Southern-fried crackpots in both the stage and film versions of *Cat on a Hot Tin Roof* and *Sweet Bird of Youth* and thought she was right for the role. "I developed a good character and Otto thought so too. I asked for props: a box of chocolates, curlers for my hair; Otto laughed and thought they were fine. His focus was the shot, and he was totally absorbed with the technical side, with lighting and placement, and he did not impose any kind of direction on me, or on Burgess Meredith who played my husband. I didn't like German people then; I recalled World War II, as people of my age did. But I really and truly liked Otto—I *enjoyed* him."[25]

"Something just clicked between Otto and me," Robert Hooks said.

Preminger showing John Phillip Law how to kiss Faye Dunaway. Throughout the filming of *Hurry Sundown,* Preminger and Dunaway were bitter antagonists.

"We had one incident when I got my hair cut too short, but I just liked and admired Otto. I lost my father when I was young and Otto in a sense became my father."[26]

The goodwill stopped here. If, as some of his colleagues attested, Otto could not function creatively in a conflict-free zone, if he needed somebody to be "it" on each production, in Faye Dunaway, neither then nor later a likely candidate for Ms. Congeniality, he was handed a gift from the gods. From the start Preminger and Dunaway looked each other over and did not like what they saw. As Hope said, "Otto *never* hated actors—he was simply not a hater. But he hated Faye Dunaway. Otto thought she was the toughest cookie he'd ever met, and she thought Otto was an idiot."[27] Indeed she did. "Otto was one of those directors you can't listen to because he doesn't know anything at all about the process of acting," she maintained. Dunaway, a Southerner playing a character who she felt resembled her own mother, was certain she knew best. "I didn't think [Otto] was ever right. Later I was to work for Roman Polanski . . . who was just as autocratic and dictatorial in many ways as Otto, but he was a good filmmaker. And Otto wasn't."[28]

Dunaway claimed that Preminger screamed at her only once, when she challenged him after he "went crazy and began yelling at Freddy [Jones]," a hairdresser who, she felt, seemed "defenseless." "Otto turned on me like a mad dog and went at me. . . . I think it's the only time I've really looked full in the face at somebody who's gone into that complete state of rage. . . . For the duration of the film, Otto never raised his voice to me again, though there was no attempt to smooth things over either," Dunaway recalled. "There was only that one time, but that's all I needed. Once I've been crossed, I'm not very conciliatory."[29]

About that there is no doubt; but a number of witnesses contradicted Dunaway's self-serving account of her feud with Preminger, maintaining that the screaming never stopped. "Faye was the whipping boy on the set, and she and Otto fought the whole way through," Michael Caine said.[30] "Everybody could see the anger between them, and it was not pretty," Madeleine Sherwood corroborated.[31] John Phillip Law suggested that the ill will began with "the love scene Faye and I had worked so hard on. As I was bending down, Otto said, 'Stop, you don't know how to kiss a girl. You don't bend over, you bring her up to you.' Then he banged our heads together. It gave her a fat lip. Faye, a tough gal, was not too pleased."[32]

For the only time in his career, Preminger's "whipping boy" did not have the sympathy of the cast and crew, because Faye Dunaway, hard-bitten, competitive, and self-centered, managed to alienate everyone. "Ms. Dunaway did *not* defend the hairdresser, as she claimed: quite the opposite, she insisted on getting him fired," as Hope recalled.

> But that was only one of her many misdemeanors. She took over an air-conditioned trailer and banished dear Diahann Carroll who was to have shared the trailer with her. She made Diahann learn her lines outside the trailer, in the heat. She was insolent to the crew. She was incredibly slovenly about her personal appearance. She wasn't even nice to John Law, when everybody else loved him—he is a wonderful man, so friendly, and he was terrific with our twins. Ms. Dunaway was even rude to them. She tried to have an affair with Michael Caine, because he was the biggest star on the set.[33]

(When the shooting ended, the actress took her employer to court to win her release from the five-picture contract she had signed with him. "I could not imagine doing another five films with this man," she said. The

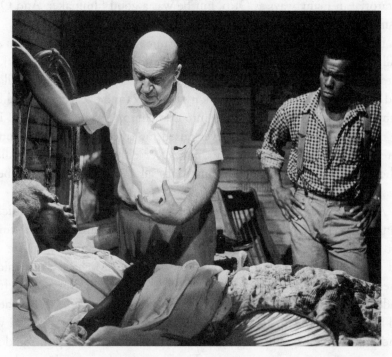

"How do you know how a black woman would feel and act, white man?" Beah
Richards said to Preminger as Robert Hooks looked on during a rehearsal for a
key scene in *Hurry Sundown*.

case dragged on until March 1968, when an out-of-court settlement was
reached. "It cost me a lot of money to not work for Otto again," Dunaway
admitted. "I paid him, I paid his attorneys, I paid my attorneys. I regret paying him. . . . I thought he was awful to work with. . . . Otto never had
another big hit," she noted, gracious as ever.)[34]

In his single contretemps with a black performer Otto played a losing
hand. As Robert Hooks reported, Beah Richards,

> much to everyone's surprise . . . effectively stood up to Otto. It hap-
> pened the day she and I [Richards was playing Hooks's mother]
> were shooting the scene where she dies. It was a beautiful, sensitive
> scene, and she was putting her whole heart and soul into it. Her
> performance was brilliant. It even made members of the crew cry.
> But for some reason Otto didn't like it, which no one but him ever
> understood. He kept asking her to do it over and over, and we
> would, much to Beah's irritation. Each time she would do it with
> the same depth of feeling as she had done before and each time he

was not satisfied. Finally, he rode her about it once too often. Beah looked up at him with an expression I was glad was not directed at me, and said, "How do you know what a black woman in this situation would feel and act? What do you know about it, white man?" There was absolute dead silence on the set. . . . We all waited with baited breath for the explosion. Otto didn't say anything at first. Finally he said, "Let's try it once again, please." And we did. And it was just as gripping as before. When it was over, Otto just sat there for a moment, then sighed and turned to his cameraman and said, "Print it. Let's move on." And we did.[35]

The heat, the Klan, and Faye Dunaway took their toll, and during the three-month shoot Preminger had a number of blowups. He fired a script girl and a secretary. As John Phillip Law recalled, "On the way to work one day Otto said to a cop, 'You're fired!' 'I don't work for you, sir,' the cop responded. 'You're fired anyway!' Otto steamed."[36] Mystifyingly, he also dismissed Gene Callahan, the production designer who had found the location and negotiated all the construction contracts. "I was notified by an assistant while I was in the hospital recovering from an operation," Callahan said. "That's the way Otto does business. I still don't know why he fired me."[37] Preminger also fired his screenwriter, Tom Ryan. "Before we started shooting Otto had hired a few brushup writers who usually don't want credit," Hope said. "As we were shooting Tom kept muddling around with the script and would bring in suggestions, which is not a good idea with Otto, who did not make or welcome script revisions once he began shooting. But Otto really blew up at Tom because when Rex Reed (Tom and he were good friends) came to the location to write a piece for the *New York Times*, Tom gossiped about the cast to Rex. Otto got very cross. 'You don't do this,' he said. (After Otto fired him, we never heard from Tom again.)"[38] Rex Reed's article, "Like They Could Cut Your Heart Out," which appeared in the *New York Times* on August 12, 1966, was certainly unflattering—Reed characterizes Otto as an autocrat who seems to be losing his grip. But it is no worse and perhaps even a little milder than other pieces over the years that had contributed to the filmmaker's reputation. Nonetheless, it cut to the quick. "When the article appeared it was full of the grossest misstatements and described me as a ruthless tyrant," Preminger, uncharacteristically, complained, as if he were hearing something new about himself. He objected particularly to a quote from Michael Caine: "He's only happy when everybody else is miserable. Still, if you can keep his paranoia from beating you down, you can learn a lot from this guy." In his autobiography

Preminger took pains to point out that after the article appeared Caine wrote a disclaimer to the *New York Times* explaining that he had not known what "paranoid" meant and that after looking it up, "I can assure you, paranoid Otto is not." Preminger also resented Reed's claim that "in a moment of uncontrolled fury" he had fired his cameraman, Loyal Griggs. "The truth was that [Griggs] had to quit because of a back injury and kept on working in spite of pains until his replacement [Milton Krasner] arrived from California. I was not troubled by [Reed's] lies," Preminger protested, unconvincingly, "but Griggs, through his lawyer, demanded and received a retraction from the *New York Times*."[39]

Preminger did not succeed in winning over the Deep South in the way he had conquered Israel, Washington, the Vatican, and Hawaii on his other recent shoots. His sense of racial fair play could make no real dent in the racism that had infected the Louisiana bayou for generations. His victory was in finishing on schedule with all of his cast and crew still alive. At the end of filming he addressed the Louisiana legislature. "I spoke of the right we enjoy to disagree without fear," he said afterward.[40] "Governor George Wallace [of Alabama], who at the time was not allowing buses to unload black children at white schools, spoke first," Hope recalled, "and then Otto spoke. 'I am a naturalized American citizen and only in America could such two diametrically opposed speakers share the same podium,' he said, and he got a standing ovation."[41]

In September 1966, as he was editing *Hurry Sundown*, Preminger, to please his six-year-old twins, accepted the role of arch-villain Mr. Freeze, who thrived in temperatures under fifty degrees below zero in the television series *Batman*. (Formerly the part had been played by George Sanders, whom Preminger had directed at Fox in *Forever Amber* and *The Fan*.) Dressed in a jumpsuit, with purple lips, curled bright red eyebrows, and his head and face painted blue, Otto cheerfully parodied his image. After devoting a full day to makeup tests, for one week he reported to work daily at 6:15 a.m. and remained on the set until seven in the evening, when he was driven to the editing rooms of MGM to continue cutting *Hurry Sundown*. His one request, quickly granted, was a private phone on which, when he was not needed on the *Batman* set, he would confer with his two veteran editors, Lou Loeffler and James Wells. For the entire week Preminger earned an A for conduct. "It is much easier being an actor than a director," he said. "You just take orders. They tell you where to stand and what to say. You become a child again. It's play."[42]

Although Preminger and his editors managed to trim the Gildens' 1,064-page novel into a comparatively meager 146 minutes, many reviewers, along with a host of other gripes, complained of *Hurry Sundown*'s excessive length. "Sheer pulp fiction . . . an offense to intelligence," Bosley Crowther wrote in the *New York Times* on March 24, 1967. More tolerantly (and accurately), *Variety* saluted Preminger for "a hard-hitting and handsomely produced film about racial conflict in Georgia circa 1945. Told with a depth and frankness possible only today, the story develops its theme in a welcome, straightforward way that is neither propaganda nor exploitation." As Madeleine Sherwood correctly claimed, "Otto was trying to deal with racial issues in a way that at the time nobody else was. The film was dismissed out of hand in 1967, but now it should be regarded as an important piece of history. Yes, it's too long, it goes all over the place, there are too many stories— but really, it's a wonderful bad movie."[43]

And so it is. Despite the charges that can be leveled at *Hurry Sundown*—that it is a simplistic view of the Deep South by a team of outsiders; that it is contrived, meandering, overplotted—it is another example of Preminger tackling previously off-limits subject matter. This time, though, he didn't get any credit for taboo smashing. And other, more modern-seeming films on race relations such as *In the Heat of the Night* and *To Sir with Love* (which were released after *Hurry Sundown*) earned praise while Preminger's epic was branded with an ill fame it doesn't merit.

As a white liberal's utopian view of racial integration, *Hurry Sundown* is ideologically, if not artistically, immaculate. The film treats the Negro characters with notable respect. Neither saints nor holy victims, on the one hand, nor militants bristling with rage and rhetoric, on the other, the characters, in a way that was rare at the time, transcend stereotype. And Preminger places them carefully within the period of the story, 1946, rather than imposing a 1966 perspective on them. Neither Reeve (Robert Hooks) nor his girlfriend (played by Diahann Carroll), who has been educated in the North, is played as a contemporary 1960s firebrand. Rather, it is Reeve's mother Rose (Beah Richards, magnificent) who, in her deathbed epiphany, expresses the kind of anger that will lead to the civil rights movement. "I was wrong," she announces to her son. "I was a white folks' nigger [who] help[ed] them to do it [to me]. I grieve for this sorry thing that has been my life."

In his usual fashion Preminger attempts to be fair to "the other side" as well. Some of the white characters, like the racist Judge Purcell and his shrewish, social-climbing wife Eula (Burgess Meredith and Madeleine Sherwood) are beyond reclamation. But the central characters representing white privilege (played by Jane Fonda and Michael Caine) are not. Fonda reveals her character's growing awareness of the tainted legacy she will ultimately reject. And Caine discovers in his grasping capitalist a vein of regret.

There are many familiar Preminger touches: beautifully orchestrated

There are empty seats in the room but blacks have to stand in the back, a social point made unobtrusively by Preminger in this long shot in *Hurry Sundown*. (The witnesses: Jane Fonda, Michael Caine, and Robert Hooks.)

tracking shots that follow the characters walking through scenic locations; objective, frontally staged group shots that reveal connections among the characters; meaningful deep-focus compositions, as in a scene in a court-room in which blacks are made to stand against the rear wall despite there being many empty seats. A heroic, high-angle helicopter shot at the begin-ning introduces the land that the white and black sharecroppers will fight for with a determination recalling the pioneers in *Exodus*. But there are some shortcomings here. Preminger undermines the sweep of some of his tracking shots with nervous cutting. More crucially, the South that the film depicts resembles a studio-era confection, a constructed world from which the warp and woof of reality have been more or less excluded. Despite the fact that all the exteriors were shot on location, the settings are curiously antiseptic. Poverty and architectural decrepitude have been carefully excised, and notwithstanding the enervating heat the characters always look suspiciously fresh. Interiors, many shot at MGM, are also too manicured, adding to the film's "made-in-Hollywood" aura.

It's tempting to speculate that as a story of race relations in America, with a vivid cast of local racists, visiting movie stars both nice and monstrous, and a good-hearted, temper-prone director, a film about the making of *Hurry Sundown* might have been more pertinent. Business was respectable—rentals were just over $4 million as against a budget of just under $3.8 million—but hardly encouraging. In spite of its fresh subject for the time, *Hurry Sundown* is stodgy, its earnest tone and multistranded narrative throwbacks to a kind of moviemaking that seemed almost fatally out of step with the new Hollywood struggling to reflect the counterculture emerging in the late 1960s.

As he was well aware, Preminger was no longer an industry trendsetter. Concerned about making a place for himself at a time of great change both within and outside the film business, on his next project he attempted to banish "Otto Preminger."

SEVENTEEN

Father and Son

At sixty-one in 1966, Preminger, becoming bored with newspaper and magazine articles that branded him with such labels as "Peck's Bad Boy, the aging crown prince of Hollywood," and "the last of the bad-tempered, old-style Hollywood patriarchs," was eager to revamp his image. To do that, he was on the lookout for material that had a more contemporary kick than either *In Harm's Way* or *Hurry Sundown,* his two epics set in the 1940s. When he read *Too Far to Walk,* a novel by John Hersey about rebellious college students experimenting with drugs, he thought he had found it. He grabbed the screen rights prepublication, began to work on a script with unknown young writers, and experimented with LSD. "Timothy Leary gave it to me after a small dinner party in my home," he recalled. "While Hope was out of the room, Leary and two of his friends brought out some LSD pills and swallowed them."[1] In his altered state, aware that "everything that happened was imaginary," he saw Hope shrink to "the size of a small doll" and he noticed "every bone" in the spine of the back of a nude woman in the Degas painting that hung in his bedroom. He also sensed that he lost track of time. Hope disapproved, reminding her husband that he hadn't taken heroin to prepare for *The Man with the Golden Arm.*[2]

Working with inexperienced young people, Otto couldn't seem to get a decent script, but indirectly the project yielded a huge dividend. One day early in January 1967 a young man named Chuck Wein, whom Preminger called his "technical adviser" on Hersey's hard-to-crack novel, casually informed him that Erik had known for over a year that Otto was his father. At that point, as Otto remembered, he called Gypsy to point out that "there was no reason anymore for Erik and me not to meet." When Otto, preparing for the American and European launch of *Hurry Sundown*, found out that Erik was in the Army, stationed in Augsburg, Germany, he wrote to ask if they could meet in Paris in February, when he would be hosting the European premiere of his film. "Erik replied promptly that he would be happy to meet me," as Preminger recalled.[3]

Erik with his mother, Gypsy Rose Lee, on the set of *Screaming Mimi* in 1958.

"I had found out about Otto in a strange way," Erik recalled. "It happened when I had asked Bill [Alexander] Kirkland (to whom my mother was married at the time and the person she had always told me was my father) for money for a car, and he refused. He told my psychiatrist to tell me that he wasn't my father and he didn't want to give me any financial help." When Erik confronted his mother, she insisted at first that Kirkland was his father, but after Erik kept questioning her she finally admitted the truth. However, she made Erik promise that he would not get in touch with Otto. "She had made this decision to have me and to raise me on her own, even though Otto had always made it clear to her that he was interested in being my father," Erik said. "Gypsy was interested in having a child, but not a relationship. Neither Gypsy nor Otto, as I was to discover, left a lot of room for discussion: their basic philosophy was 'I'm going to do it my way.' "4

For both father and son, the timing seemed right. As the doting father of six-year-old twins, Preminger was a confirmed family man who welcomed having another son, while at twenty-two Erik belonged to the generation that the aging filmmaker was hoping to connect with in his work. For Erik, who had been through a few difficult years before joining the Army—he'd dropped out of college, experimented with drugs, held a smattering of unchallenging jobs—Otto represented professional salvation. As Erik recalled, "From my point of view at the time, Gypsy's decision seemed a good one: I had the advantage of meeting Otto when he could offer me work."

Nonetheless, the meeting, scheduled for February 15, 1967, at the Hôtel Plaza Athénée in Paris, was anxiety-provoking for both Otto and Erik, as well as for Hope. "When Otto and I had first started dating, he never admitted to having had affairs—he was a gentleman, and never talked," Hope said.

He never talked to me about his relationship with Dorothy Dandridge, for instance: not a word, at any time. I figured this was all in the past and had nothing to do with me, and I didn't ask. Before we married, however, he did tell me about Gypsy, that it had been a one-night stand, and that he was the father of Gypsy's son. I have to admit I was surprised, because I wouldn't have thought Gypsy would have been Otto's type. He told me that he had offered to support the boy, but Gypsy had refused and made him take an oath not to reveal who he was to Erik, or to tell anyone. Otto said he told me in case the matter ever came up. But after that one time, he didn't mention Erik again. As we were waiting at the hotel for Erik to arrive, Otto was very nervous, and I suggested that perhaps the two of them should go out for a walk and to dinner on their own, without me.[5]

When Erik arrived at the Plaza Athénée, he expected to go to the room his father had reserved for him. But the concierge informed him that Mr. Preminger had been calling the desk every few minutes to find out if his son had shown up yet and left instructions that the minute he did he was to go directly to his father's suite. His nerves jangling, Erik knocked on the door of the Premingers' suite. "For a brief moment, time seemed frozen, and the tableau remains vivid in my memory today and probably forever," Erik recalled. In the middle of the baroque magnificence of the suite, with elaborate floral arrangements on every table and a room-service cart stocked to overflowing, "Otto was standing . . . wearing a dark blue suit. He appeared to have been pacing and caught midstride. I had recently seen a small photograph of him in *Time* magazine, so I was prepared for a heavy-set, bald man. No photograph, however, could capture the strength of his presence. He emanated power."[6]

"The minute Erik came into our hotel room he was very sweet and I could see that Otto liked him instantly," Hope said. Following his wife's suggestion, Otto asked Erik to go for a walk. When Erik, embarrassed by his "disreputable" raincoat, said that despite the chilly weather he would prefer not to wear it, Otto said, "If my son doesn't wear a coat, then neither do I." Quite accurately, Erik regarded the statement as "a declaration of love and acceptance, and I felt the warmth of it even through my self-conscious reserve."[7] Indeed, as Erik would come to recognize, "With family Otto was like a marshmallow, and was capable of great love in a primal way. This love superseded everything."[8]

During their walk, which lasted for several hours, Otto was "gallant" about Gypsy and also candid, as Erik recollected. "He told me he had asked Gypsy to put his paternity in her will, so I could turn to him if she died before him; I never saw her will, so I don't know if she did as he asked." When Otto asked Erik if he wanted to work with him on making films, Erik was elated.

Joining Erik at the hotel later in the evening was his fiancée Barbara Ann Van Natten, a stewardess with American Airlines whom he had met through mutual friends at the American Exchange in Munich. "Erik was exceedingly polite, well mannered, and well traveled—and in those days, when Europeans didn't bathe, he smelled good," Barbara said.

He had bangs (he had to keep his hair short because he was in the Army) and he looked collegiate. He had lived in New York and I thought he was a real New Yorker, youthful but sophisticated. He cared about books, he was bright and well educated. Before I had met him I was told he was Gypsy's son, but I'm not starstruck and I didn't care about that. It was his duffel bag and his bangs I couldn't resist. When he told me he was also Otto Preminger's son—actually, he made it seem a little iffy—I believed him. I had seen *Stalag 17* and the resemblance was unmistakable. But from the first I could see that he wanted people to like *him,* not his parents. After all, he wasn't Otto or Gypsy. He didn't even know his father at that time and he and his mother were at odds.[9]

After Erik had invited her to join him in Paris, "Otto himself called me," as Barbara remembered.

He made all our reservations. We had a lovely room, with crushed violets everywhere and a vase filled with spectacular long-stemmed roses that Otto had sent. The first night, when Erik and his father had walked around on their own, Erik was overwhelmed when he returned to our room, but he seemed to like his father a great deal. The next morning we went to the Premingers' suite for breakfast. Then Otto took us to Maxim's for lunch. Otto was exceedingly charming and slightly formal: a courtly European man of good breeding. Erik was a little withdrawn, and I was a little intimidated too: by the restaurant rather than Otto and Hope. With Otto, of course, we were ushered to the best seats. There were immense amounts of silverware, at least fifteen utensils. I decided I would order just what Hope did; and that meant no sauces, no oil, no garlic, no dessert. Erik and I were both so nervous we couldn't eat anyway.[10]

("Otto and I both adored Barbara when he brought her to our suite," Hope said. "She was just as sweet as Erik, and beautiful and smart as well.") A few nights later Otto took Erik and Barbara to dinner, "a royalty kind of place," as it seemed to Barbara, where Otto's other guests were Jane Fonda and Roger Vadim. "Otto said to the headwaiter, 'You decide for all of us; we want the best you have.' When we were served truffles, I didn't know what to do. How would an American eat this? I wondered. It's not so easy to cut a truffle. Seeing my difficulty, Vadim, who told me truffles are an aphrodisiac, helped me out. It was all like a fairy tale." Preminger invited the young people to join him and Hope in London, where he would be opening *Hurry Sundown*. He put them up in a suite at the Dorchester. "I took it as my due," Barbara explained. "I was very young, and foolish, and I thought, 'Of course, this is going to be my life.' We saw *Hurry Sundown* at the London premiere and we were under a lot of pressure to like it. Erik even convinced himself that he did like the movie. But I thought it was awful, so clunky. Neither of us knew what to say to Otto about the film. The next night Otto got us the best seats in the house at Covent Garden to see Nureyev and Fonteyn in *Swan Lake*."[11]

On March 18, 1967, shortly after returning to Augsburg, Erik and Barbara were married. Preminger, who had to return to New York to prepare for the opening of *Hurry Sundown* on March 23, was not present, but as a gift he gave them ten thousand dollars, "an enormous amount in those days," as Barbara acknowledged. The only witnesses at the wedding were the mutual friends who had introduced the bride and groom. "It was a religious ceremony in the church on the Army base, and although Otto was Jewish he had no objections," Barbara maintained. "Otto had no religion; he told me he hadn't been in temple for three generations. He prided himself on his modernity, on trying to be with it, which he wasn't always able to achieve."[12]

Otto told Erik that he would begin working for him, at his office at Paramount in Hollywood, in September 1967, after he had completed his military service. "Thanks to Otto, who had no patience for anything bureaucratic and who wanted me to get out of the service right away, I was released ninety days early, in July," Erik said. "I got out on July 5. Barbara and I flew to Los Angeles and went to my mother's house. I was to start working for Otto Monday morning at nine."[13] "Gypsy called at nine, asking to speak to Otto, who was in the shower," Hope recollected. " 'Tell Otto that Erik is exhausted and will be in the office a little later,' she said. I told her I would give Otto the message. That was the only time I ever spoke to Gypsy."[14]

When Erik began working for his father, Otto was still trying to wrestle a screenplay out of *Too Far to Walk*. "Otto felt the development of the script was the most important part of making a movie, and he wanted me to sit in on all his sessions with the writers," Erik recalled.

In addition to spending hours on script sessions, I had responsibilities in the office. Learning on the fly, and having to meet my father's expectations, I was under tremendous strain. At the time I was not introduced as his son because Gypsy had a television program that catered to ladies and she felt her audience would be offended by the announcement that I was Otto's son. She made us promise to keep

With his son Erik in 1971, on the set of *Such Good Friends.*

it to ourselves. When we were not at work, my father could not have been more generous and loving—his role model for parenting was to be giving, because he had been truly spoiled by his own parents. When I would travel with Otto, he liked to take long walks and if even for a moment I would stop to look at something in a store window it would arrive twenty minutes later at our hotel. He was that way to all his children. But at work he was not interested in being a father; he was interested in being a mentor and he felt a teacher's job was not to cut any slack. I got equal treatment with everyone else.[15]

Erik worked beside Nat Rudich, Preminger's longtime general facto-tum. "Otto had two assistants, basically, Nat and me," Erik pointed out. "Nat was the business person, and in time I became Otto's casting director. Nat was decent, sweet, and patient, and yes, he got yelled at; but he loved my father, loved him as a human being truly and completely. And Otto loved Nat in return, in full measure. When Nat died [in December 1975] Otto was shattered; he was destroyed. Nat, and all the rest of us who loved my father, made allowances for Otto's tantrums. Afterward, he was oblivi-ous to the fact that the other person was bleeding, because for him it had meant nothing."

As Erik shuttled back and forth between his father's two offices, at Paramount in Hollywood and in the Columbia Pictures Building at 711 Fifth Avenue in New York, he became adept in reading his father's personality and moods. It didn't take him long to conclude that he could not envision his father and his mother as a couple.

> I can't even see them appearing in public together. Gypsy and Otto could not have been together for more than twenty minutes without an argument erupting. My mother's attraction to Otto was very Shavian: it was strictly about genes, and her sense that Otto was decent and honorable. They shared an independence of spirit that was quite remarkable, and they were both extremely intelligent. Otto had been formally educated; my mother was entirely self-educated. Gypsy was not a bully, though, and Otto was. My parents were two blessings—I consider myself one of the luckiest people—but, my God, they were both so difficult.

In addition to adjusting to a demanding new job, Erik also had to face the responsibility of being a father himself, when (in January 1968) Barbara gave birth to their son, Chris.

"When I started working for him my father was facing a deadline," Erik recalled.

> He was going to have to deliver a picture to Paramount, with whom he had a unique contract: Paramount had to do a lot, Otto only had to deliver. But he was still having trouble with the Hersey book. Despite the contemporary setting, the story really was an allegory, a retelling of Mephistopheles, and Otto was a realist who didn't really respond to nonrealistic material: that's why his best film was *Anatomy of a Murder.* His first plan was to get rid of the allegory, which left him with a story that seemed to be on quicksand. *Too Far to Walk* just wasn't coming together, and he was worried about what his next project was going to be.[16]

"Otto hired me as something like the seventeenth writer on *Too Far to Walk* after he had read a screenplay of mine about hippies in San Francisco called *Skidoo,*" Doran William Cannon recalled.

> My agent, who had worked for Otto as a secretary, had sent him the screenplay as a writing sample. He liked it and summoned me to New York, putting me up royally at the Plaza Hotel, to work with

him on the screenplay. When I told him why I thought *Too Far to Walk* wasn't working—I had read all the versions, and each one was worse than the last—Otto responded by saying, "I want short scenes, like in your marvelous *Skidoo*." "Why not make *Skidoo*?" I said. "I think I will," he responded, and just like that he called his agent and put the deal together.[17]

"Otto latched onto *Skidoo* for many reasons," Erik said. "He had done research on the drug scene for *Too Far to Walk;* he had some sense of where he was, sociologically, on *Skidoo,* and that sense was important to him. And he liked the antiestablishment thrust of Bill's script; in reality, Otto never had much respect for the establishment, and he appreciated the absurdity of conservatism. He also felt it was a story he could make quickly."[18]

Cannon's screenplay was about a retired mobster, Tony Banks, forced by a Mafia chieftain called "God" to make one final hit—in Alcatraz he is to kill Packard, a gangster planning to cooperate with a Senate crime-investigating committee. But after he has an accidental acid trip, Banks has a jailhouse epiphany, deciding once and for all that he will forsake violence. In the finale, he joins his wife and daughter, who have fallen in with hippies, on a love-in on "God's" yacht. "Otto loved my concept of pitting hippies against the Mafia, which I represented as the establishment, which may have been the way the Mafia thought of itself," Cannon said.

> To Otto I represented youth and freshness and the counterculture, and when we started he thought I was the most talented writer in the world.
>
> But frankly, I knew from the beginning that working with Otto would go from good to worse. He really did want me to do well, but his story sense flew in the face of mine. At the time, as in my screenplay for *Brewster McCloud,* I wanted to use movies to change the world. I thought *Skidoo* delivered an important message of peace and love at a time when America was engaged in the war in Vietnam. But Otto was trying to deal with his own demons, as well as with the sheer improbability of his directing a movie like this.[19]

Tension developed between Preminger and Cannon about how the Mafia figures were to be depicted. The author wanted them to be treated realistically; Preminger was itching to turn them into cartoons. "Otto wanted to magnify the silliness rather than the truth of the Mafia," Cannon recalled. "I told Otto from the start that if he directed *Skidoo* the way he had directed *In Harm's Way,* it would be funny. But he thought the broader you played comedy the funnier it could be. There wasn't a chance of his understanding that if you played it straight, it would be funnier."

When Preminger asked him to write a violent scene early in the film Cannon balked.

> My story was about the powers of nonviolence, and I refused to write violent things. Otto's sense was that these are gangsters, this is Hollywood, this is what people want. To have a violent scene so early in the film would destroy the comedy, but Otto's sense of comedy was perverse. I was out, and to rewrite me he brought in Mel Brooks, a nice madcap choice. "I am not going to hire this man," Otto told me later. "Between you and him I would go crazy." Instead, with my blessing, he hired Elliott Baker, the author of *A Fine Madness,* to do the rewrite. When Elliott showed me what he had written, I said, "You are doing just what he wants."[20]

When the rewritten script was completed to his satisfaction by the end of 1967, Preminger, with help from Erik, who had sat in on most of the writing sessions and was now in charge of casting, quickly assembled a one-of-a-kind all-star ensemble. As Tony Banks, the reluctant hit man: television icon Jackie Gleason. As Tony's ditzy wife Flo: Broadway's original Dolly Gallagher Levi in *Hello, Dolly!*: Carol Channing. As the jailhouse stool pigeon: Mickey Rooney. As "God": Groucho Marx, in what was to be his last film. As an up-and-coming mafioso: former teen idol Frankie Avalon. As senior mafiosi: Old Hollywood stalwarts Cesar Romero and George Raft. As hippies: John Phillip Law, Otto's young leading man from *Hurry Sundown,* and John's brother Tom, a real hippie. As various figures of authority: Burgess Meredith (a prison warden), Peter Lawford (a senator), Doro Merande (a prissy mayor eager to get the hippies out of town).

To play the pivotal role of "the Professor," a draft-dodging drug guru and technical wizard who orchestrates his and Tony's escape from Alcatraz by getting the entire prison high on LSD-spiked soup, Preminger cast a movie newcomer, stage actor Austin Pendleton, who was a friend of Bill Cannon's. When Preminger was in San Francisco in late February scouting locations, he summoned Pendleton for an interview. "I was to meet him at his hotel and to ride out with him to a location he would be using in the film," Pendleton recollected.

> He was "auditioning" me as a favor to Bill. This happened right in the middle of an incredibly turbulent time when opposition to the war in Vietnam was escalating; Eugene McCarthy had done well in

the New Hampshire primary; Johnson was to withdraw; and Martin Luther King was to be assassinated. We talked politics, about which Preminger had such a good grasp. At the end of the drive, during which we had not exchanged one word about *Skidoo,* he asked his driver to take me to the airport where I was to catch a plane to Los Angeles. I thought he had decided I was out. But just before we parted, he said, "I like talking to you; you don't need to do the test because the part is yours."

I liked Preminger's movies, even the ones people didn't like, and he was enchanting on that drive, simply and completely enchanting. But I felt *Skidoo* would be a disaster—I had a terrible sense there would be a head-on collision between Otto and the material—and I turned him down. He said fine, but Bill was after me, and with a little more money offered in a second round of negotiations—they get interested when you say no—I had to accept. A couple of weeks later, I went out to Hollywood with a heavy heart.

I had just finished a tour of *Little Foxes* with Beah Richards, who laughed when I told her I'd be working with Otto. "He's a monster," she said, but she liked him anyway. She told me that she had complained to him that from a black person's point of view a scene in *Hurry Sundown* made no sense. "I wrote the scene," Otto told her, clearly offended. "But you've never been black," Beah said. "How would you know?" Otto shot back. At that moment Beah said she decided that she would just enjoy him.[21]

Shooting his first scene standing naked in a prison shower with Otto yelling at him, Pendleton wished he were back on the stage. Fearing that if he stayed this first film was certain to be his last, he placed desperate calls to his agent, Deborah Coleman, asking to be released.

"I can't get you out of this, they've got you on film," Deborah said. So I had to keep on. One day soon after, Otto came up to me and said, "I am so pleased with what you are doing I am expanding your part." I was very upset. And then, the next day, when I didn't hit my marks during camera blocking, he exploded. "You are an amateur, you don't know how to behave in front of a camera," he screamed. "Yes, I know I am, Mr. Preminger. Can you help me?" And at that, he melted, he just melted, and for the rest of the film he coached me while the crew was setting up the lights. Explaining what the scenes were about and how I should play them, he directed me more than he did anyone else; Otto Preminger gave me a course in film acting, and I began to see why Jane Fonda had told me that *Hurry Sundown* was her best work. Otto kept saying the camera liked honesty; well, I was a scared actor playing a scared character, and the camera recorded my fear. I thought the camera was going to reveal how insecure I was—it did. And that's why the performance worked.[22]

Pendleton felt that Preminger devoted so much time to him because he didn't know how to direct anybody else.

Otto didn't understand comedy, or the sudden left turns of the script—he kept trying to make it clear, in a way it didn't want to be. He didn't know what to say to the comic actors like Gleason and Channing and Groucho. I was not playing a clown, but the kind of role that could have been in other Otto Preminger films, and so I was the only one in the film to whom he could give the kind of direction he knew how to give.

Between Preminger and Jackie Gleason there was no point of contact. "There was no yelling," as Austin Pendleton observed, "there was just no communication at all. Gleason wasn't hostile, he was depressed—the pilot light was out, and Otto sensed it. Gleason never wanted to rehearse. He couldn't even do camera blocking, which with Otto was always complicated. He had no humor offstage and he was a prima donna who made his wardrobe man kneel down to tie his shoes."[23] "There was a kind of wall between us," Preminger conceded. "While I could not argue about what he was doing—it was all *correct*—there is such a difference between us, in the texture of our characters (he would probably say he is very happy about the difference). There is a different attitude toward life, toward our profession, toward man, toward woman, toward friendship, toward love, toward war, toward peace, toward politics—toward everything."[24]

"Preminger and Gleason were afraid of each other," Bill Cannon felt. Preminger, however wasn't afraid of the other legendary comic actor on the set, and several times he went after Groucho. "I had wanted Otto to play 'God,' but he wouldn't and so I suggested Groucho Marx," Bill Cannon said. "Otto's reaction had been negative. 'He's too old.' But he hired him anyway. When Groucho showed up on the set, he asked Otto, 'Are you drunk?' But Otto at that point was always in complete control of his faculties. Otto didn't like the comment, and when he couldn't get anything out of Groucho

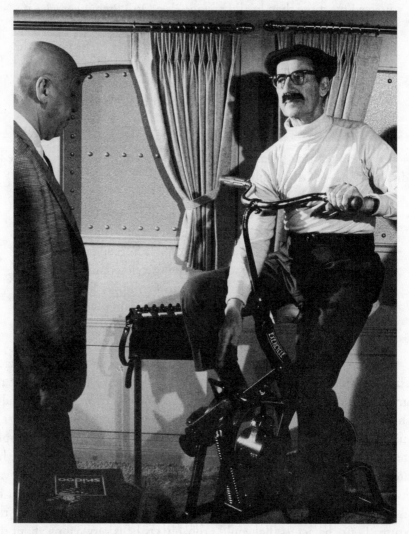

The lack of rapport between Preminger and Groucho Marx is apparent on the set of *Skidoo*.

as an actor he yelled at him, many times."[25] As Hope said, "There were many tense moments with Groucho, who was gross, uncouth, extremely unpleasant to everyone, and like Jackie Gleason did not have a funny bone in his body. A more humor-free person you could not imagine."[26]

Unlike her costars, Carol Channing worked hard to please the boss. "Preminger was a wonderful producer, but I didn't like working with him," Channing recalled.

He enjoyed beating me up in front of the company—and I just made a dishrag of myself. My son says I have a sign: "Take me, I'm a masochist." I was wrong. I should have said, "Mr. Preminger, I'm leaving. You get someone else." But it's my nature not to walk. Because he was extremely able in his field I kept blaming myself, thinking I was just not able to give him what he wanted. How sweet he could be to other people; he wanted to show me how sweet he was to his wife and children, and I felt there was something sadistic about it, toward me. He adored Hope, there was no doubt of that, and she was adorable: kind and gentle and nice to everyone on the set, just the opposite of him. I thought I would try to kill him with kindness, but it didn't work. For me it was like having a nightmare in which you open your mouth and no sound emerges. I never saw the film, and I never will.

Channing's refuge was Erik, "kind and good and I loved him. When I was upset Erik would be so caring, so sensitive about my feelings. I thought he was trying to make up for how Preminger was behaving."[27] "In Hollywood there are two categories of people," Erik said. "There are those who don't remember you, and those who are human beings. Carol Channing, bless her, is in the latter category. She was delightful to work with, and whenever she sees me, it's 'Hi, Erik,' accompanied by her big welcoming sunburst of a smile."[28]

"I don't think Otto knew what to tell me about playing a hippie," John Phillip Law said.

On *Hurry Sundown* he knew exactly what he wanted; on *Skidoo,* where he actually yelled much less, he was not less interested but he was less focused. We all knew it was a mishmash of styles: social satire/musical/slapstick/melodrama/family story. But the cast did not bitch and moan and stand around making judgments; we all tried to make it work. And that communal spirit, which existed more back then than it does now, came from the top: Jackie Gleason and Carol Channing were both very conscientious and were trying to make some sense of it. We all hoped that Otto had a concept.[29]

Whether he did or not, Otto kept to his original schedule—shooting began on March 18 and wrapped two months later, on May 17—and delivered *Skidoo* to Paramount on time. At the wrap party at the Factory, a hip

Los Angeles disco, Preminger in a Nehru suit smiled effulgently all evening. "It was an incredible party," as Bill Cannon remembered. "Preminger wanted so hard to be a thoroughly modern Millie, and laughing and greeting the guests—he was delightful with Sidney Poitier, I recall—you'd have thought he'd just finished a film for all time."[30]

"I was at Otto's house when he screened *Skidoo* for Paramount executives, including Robert Evans," recalled Peter Bogdanovich. "There wasn't one laugh or titter the entire film. When it was over Otto acted like he'd just shown them *Laura.* He behaved with such aplomb, such grace and charm. Evans didn't like Preminger's deal with Paramount, and he certainly didn't like *Skidoo.* But since Preminger always came in under budget nobody at Paramount could bother him."[31]

Otto arranged for the world premiere to be held in Miami as a fundraiser for the not-yet-built Miami Arts Center. At a press luncheon prior to the screening he touted *Skidoo* for its cutting-edge subject matter. Then with four cast members he was driven to the premiere in the first car of a long motorcade that made its way along the Miami Expressway. "It was all so beautifully orchestrated," as Austin Pendleton recalled. "Otto had whipped up a feeling of a big, important premiere—you'd have thought it was the Atlanta opening of *Gone with the Wind.* But twenty minutes after the film started there began an ever gathering parade of rich people exiting. I knew then that we were in trouble. At the party afterward the atmosphere was strained, but Otto was smooth as silk where other directors would have been rattled."[32]

When *Skidoo* opened in Los Angeles on December 18, 1968 (to qualify for Academy Award consideration!), and in New York on March 5, 1969, it received scathing reviews. "*Skidoo* is something only for Preminger-watchers or for people whose minds need pressing by a heavy object," Vincent Canby wrote in the *New York Times,* setting the tone for the film's reception. "The movie has the form of comedy, but its almost complete lack of humor, its retarded contemporaneousness . . . its sometimes beautiful and expensive-looking San Francisco locations; and its indomitable denial that disaster is at hand (apparent from almost the opening sequence)—all give the film an almost undeniable Preminger stamp." Although he wouldn't admit it in public, Preminger, as Hope claimed, "knew the film didn't work. He really hated it, as I do still. I wish people would just forget about it."

As the impresario of a tune-in, turn-on, drop-out hippie extravaganza, of course Otto Preminger, a sixty-three-year-old fuddy-duddy, was almost sublimely ill suited. "My God yes, Otto was the wrong director for it," Bill Cannon said, "but probably nobody but Otto could have gotten it green-lighted. Nobody working within the studio system could or, likely, would have done it, whereas Otto, an independent, with his unique contract with Paramount, actually made the film."[33] As John Phillip Law commented, the filmmaker had "the courage to jump into something new. That he made the film at all represents an extraordinary combination of chutzpah and ego."[34]

Preminger didn't have the touch, or the life experience, to capture the San Francisco hippie scene in its late-1960s heyday. An early shot in a packed hippie caravan indicates his outsider's viewpoint. The too composed setup—a sedentary camera stares at the hippies as they sing, paint their bodies, embrace each other—places the audience in the director's chair looking at a group of exotic others with a cautious, removed interest. Preminger enjoys the hippies—he makes no judgment about their drug taking or their free love—but he is not capable of either understanding or revealing them. As if sensing this himself, his focus shifts repeatedly from the young people to the old-timers. And instead of the with-it comedy about the contemporary zeitgeist that Preminger hoped to make in order to renovate his image, at heart *Skidoo* is a not hip, not funny story about post-middle-age male anxiety.

Tony Banks obsesses about whether he is really the father of his daughter, and in his acid trip phallic guns float and bend, "God's" head appears at the top of a gigantic screw, and protruding eyes stare at him accusingly. "God's" paramour is a tall black woman who cheats on him with two virile young men, a hippie and a mobster, and in order to prevent the old man from watching her trysts she drapes the hidden cameras that "God" has installed in each room on his yacht.

The fear of loss of potency and mastery that runs through the film is announced in the odd opening, in which Tony and Flo, with remote control devices, switch television channels. Their battle for control of representation, for gaining dominance over the image—Flo wants to watch a Senate crime commission investigating mobsters; Tony looks at ads for deodorant and toothpaste, another example of his insecure self-image—anticipates the director's struggles throughout the film to contain an alien subject.

Despite Preminger's attempts to gain the upper hand, Bill Cannon's loopy, anarchic story keeps slipping out of his control. The result is a fascinating train wreck, deeply fractured, schizophrenic through and through, as Otto, an inveterate realist, tries without success to ground the mayhem on terra firma. He boasted that, except for one set, the electronics-laden apartment of the hot-blooded young mafioso played by Frankie Avalon, he shot on location. "I feel that wherever possible, even in a comedy like this, it gives a feeling of reality to work in real places rather than in studio built sets."[35] But *Skidoo,* a pop-art cartoon, needs fantasy and whimsy rather than "a feeling of reality."

Nonetheless, Preminger occasionally nabs the "sharp left turns" in the script, as for example in his smart use of Day-Glo colors for the hippie scenes as against the virtual absence of color in the prison scenes. However, for the three big production numbers—Tony's life-changing acid trip, a phantasmagoric garbage can ballet, and Carol Channing's performance of the title song—Preminger can't disguise the fact that, creatively, he is skating on perilously thin ice. In each case, his editing decisions are the wrong ones. For the acid trip and the ballet, which could have been delirious showstoppers, his cutting is flaccid and halfhearted when it should spin with a manic staccato flair. And, maddeningly, he breaks up Channing's eleven o'clock number into fragments when he should have shot it in a single take, standing back to observe the musical theater veteran dressed in a sailor suit out of Gilbert and Sullivan perform "Skidoo" in a joyful style that could melt any but the most unforgiving viewer.

However, despite the fact that its raft of old-time stars pulls the film into the orbit of Hollywood past rather than anchoring it in a late-1960s summer of love; despite Preminger's transformation of a supposed comedy about hippies into an almost laugh-free examination of his own "demons"; despite the fact that neither Jackie Gleason, a good straight actor who gives an inappropriately strong dramatic performance, nor Groucho Marx, no actor at all, has a single funny line or piece of business, this infamous, endearing flop ends up revealing more about the hippie sensibility than any other film of its time. Preminger's goodwill toward all the characters, the mobsters as well as the hippies, and his neutrality about free love and drugs capture a sense of the film's cultural moment. Indeed, *Skidoo* may have the most permissive attitude toward LSD of any film in Hollywood history, and in the love-in at the end (filmed on John Wayne's yacht!) several taboos are smashed. "God's" black mistress marries a young white mobster in a service officiated by saturnine George Raft holding a book called *The Death of God.* And "God," wearing what looks like an Indian wedding veil, "marries" the Professor, their union consecrated as they share a tote on a boat.

At the end Preminger himself interrupts the hippie bacchanal to bestow his blessing. "Stop! We are not through yet," he announces in a voice brimming with bonhomie and good cheer. "Before you skidoo we'd like to introduce our cast and crew." And then the credits are performed to music and lyrics composed by Harry Nilsson. "Reading the credits at the end was in my original screenplay," Bill Cannon said. "But the idea of hiring Harry

Carol Channing performs the title song in the finale to *Skidoo*, Preminger's strangest movie.

Nilsson was Otto's. I was skeptical, but I feel now that Nilsson was a fabulous choice."[36]

In 1968, everyone, including the filmmaker, regarded *Skidoo* as a mistake. Over the years, however, the film has acquired a considerable underground reputation, and some of those who worked on it have softened their original opinions. "There was definitely a sweet side to Otto, and that side is displayed in the film, which is very sweet-natured," Bill Cannon said. "I had no love for the movie in 1968, but now I like it much better and I can see why growing numbers of people are fascinated by it. I'm grateful for the cult appreciation, and I have enjoyed being both maverick (in 1968) and icon (over thirty years later)."[37] "It wasn't the greatest career move on my part," John Phillip Law reminisced. "I did *Skidoo* instead of *Midnight Cowboy,* but I've grown to like the film, and I'm proud to be in something that has developed a big cult reputation."[38] At the time Erik thought the film "was just horrible, but when I gave a talk at one of the annual screenings of the film held at the Roxy Theater in San Francisco, at least I could see what Otto had been trying to do. However, isn't being a cult favorite a sign you did it wrong?"[39]

A writer named Christian Divine (his real name, even more improbable when he discloses that he is Jewish) was hooked when he first saw the film, on acid, at the Crest Theater in Sacramento in 1990 on his twenty-third birthday. At this writing he is working on a book about *Skidoo*:

> Before I saw it, I'd heard about how bad it was; I'd been told it was one of the worst films ever made, and I had always wanted to see it. But that's hard to do because it just isn't available. Seeing it was mind-blowing. I saw it again the next day because I had to be sure I'd seen what I thought I saw. It's so bad it's good—it's great. It's straight camp that represents an awful union between Old and New Hollywood: Billy Wilder's *Kiss Me Stupid*, which was Wilder's *Skidoo*, is in the same category. Preminger in *Skidoo* is on a weird page no one else was on. His direction is misguided; the lighting is atrocious; the film is edited with a butcher knife and yet despite the fact that because of his Teutonic nature Preminger can't fit into the hippie ethos—he just doesn't get it—the film has a good spirit, a likable, quite captivating naïveté. It's a psychedelic Rorschach blot. The minute you think it can't get any weirder, it does. In the late 1960s, the studios did not know what was happening in the real world. With filmmakers breaking free of the Hollywood codes, the rug was being pulled out from under the studios. The big roadshow movies were bombing. In his own way with this film Preminger helped to break through the massive repression and hypocrisy that was strangling Old Hollywood at this transitional period. I knew in 2000 I needed to find out what it was like on the set: Otto Preminger directing Jackie Gleason in an acid trip; Otto Preminger directing Groucho Marx smoking a joint. My title: *The Unmaking of "Skidoo": A Psychedelic Movie Misfire.*[40]

During the summer of 1968, as he was working on postproduction of his hippie comedy, Preminger turned to another project he hoped would alter his old fogy persona. *Tell Me That You Love Me, Junie Moon*, based on a novel by Marjorie Kellogg, is a story about three young misfits struggling with physical disabilities who meet in a hospital and form a surrogate family. On *Skidoo*, Erik had been more or less a bystander—*Skidoo* had been his apprenticeship—but this time Otto wanted his son to take a more active part. He gave Erik, billed as Erik Kirkland, a title, executive assistant to the producer, and had him attend all the meetings with Marjorie Kellogg, who was adapting her novel. "Otto had minor disagreements with Marjorie, but in my presence I never heard him raise his voice. Nobody could yell at Marjorie because she exuded acceptance, calm, and love," Erik said.[41]

"When I started working with Otto, he gave me a little office of my own, down from his office at Paramount, where he was finishing *Skidoo*," Kellogg said.

> One morning he began to get very abusive, as if it were in his blood, which I think it was, and I simply started packing to leave. He came down the hall like a lamb. There was never another cross word during the almost four months we worked together. *Junie Moon*, a simple story that avoided becoming maudlin, was very different from the kind of big epics he had been working on and I saw that he was trying to respect the understated quality of my writing. But the fact that this was a very small, personal story was the aspect that was difficult for him—he had been used to directing the Israeli army, but this had to be done in an intimate way.[42]

With the endorsement of Erik and Marjorie, Preminger selected newcomers for the two male leads. For Warren, a gay paraplegic, he cast Robert Moore, who wasn't an actor at all but a director with two current stage hits, *Promises, Promises,* a Broadway musical, and *The Boys in the Band,* an off-Broadway play with an all-gay cast of characters. For Arthur, an epileptic, he chose another movie tyro, Ken Howard, whom he had seen on Broadway playing Thomas Jefferson in the musical *1776.* As the title character, whose face has been badly burned, he cast Liza Minnelli, who had been seen in only one film, *Charlie Bubbles,* in 1967.

On June 10, 1969, two weeks before shooting, Preminger began to rehearse with his cast as if they were preparing for a play. "The gratifying thing is that the three actors became friends, very much like the characters in the book," Preminger observed.[43] Erik agreed that "the spirit of the company was very good—that translated into everyone working very hard. There really developed a huge feeling of camaraderie: the three leads bonded, and Otto was patient because he saw they were trying to do their best."[44] Adding to the bonhomie was James Coco, cast as a fishmonger who befriends the outcasts. "He was warm and cuddly, and enormously funny—he was one of the great loves of my life," Hope said.[45]

On June 22, Liza's mother Judy Garland died in London; it was left to Liza to make the arrangements for the funeral. As always in this kind of crisis, Preminger behaved with compassion. He offered to suspend rehearsals, but Liza asked only that they be held at her apartment so she could handle calls and be spared from reporters. "Liza was a mensch," Erik observed. "Throughout rehearsals she never showed the slightest hint of temperament, and once we started shooting she never once asked for a single favor."[46] At one point during shooting, as Ken Howard recalled, "Liza's lips started to tremble and you could see this emotion about her mother start to take over. Otto said, 'Are you all right?' and he stopped what we were doing. 'You tell me when you can began again,' he said."[47] When filming began in San Diego, Minnelli had a kidney-stone attack, and when Otto found out that she would have to be taken to the hospital that night, at 1 a.m., he insisted on going with her.

Working happily on the film with an inexperienced screenwriter and a trio of movie novices, Preminger also hired a first-time editor, a young black man named Harry Howard. "I played tennis at a club in Grand Central, The Tennis Club, and a lady in the waiting room asked me what I did," Howard recalled.

> When I said I was a film editor, she said that her husband was looking for an editor. When she said her husband was Otto Preminger, I was impressed. She said she could get me an interview, but I mentioned that I had only edited thirty-second television commercials. "Otto's given people a shot before," she said.
>
> When I went to his office at 711 Fifth Avenue he was shaving his head with an electric razor. "Please come in," he told me as he continued to shave. We talked, and after looking at my résumé he said it was not possible for someone with my credentials to work on an Otto Preminger film. I told him I was an editor and I could cut anything. I left, thinking that was it. Two weeks later I got a call to come up to the office. "I'm going to take a chance here," he said. "I have a good feeling about you. Can you start in two weeks?"
>
> He hired me to help Henry Berman, the editor of record of *Junie Moon*. The film was being cut in New York, but Henry, who was so old he had cut *Gunga Din* in 1939, didn't want to stay in New York that long. I was there every day for about two months and I learned a lot. Otto was very good with Henry; he wasn't telling him everything, and giving him a lot of leeway. When Henry left I finished up.
>
> Otto gave me my first shot, then he hired me to edit his next film, *Such Good Friends*, and I went on to have a big career because I had a credit on a Preminger film. It meant a lot. Otto was like a teacher to me—I think he felt like he was training me, and he

seemed to enjoy that. He hired me when he could have hired a blue-eyed white guy, and I'm very grateful. Later I heard rumors about Otto being a racist. Otto Preminger was not remotely a racist—my God, not even close![48]

At the time Preminger was finishing postproduction on *Junie Moon* in the fall of 1969, Gypsy was diagnosed with lung cancer. Whenever Erik asked to be released from his responsibilities on the film and at the office so he could spend time with his mother, Otto readily assented. Although their relationship had often been fraught, Erik, with Otto's blessings, now became close with his mother. During the last months of her life Erik traveled back and forth from New York to Los Angeles more than a dozen times. On one of Erik's last visits she inquired for the first time about his relationship with Otto. "He's been great through all this," Erik told her. "He gives me all the time I need to visit you, and he always finds an excuse so the studio pays the way." "I sensed he was a good man, in spite of his reputation," Gypsy said. "That's one of the reasons I picked him. That and his mind. I could have had a child by Mike [Todd] any time, but Mike had a mean streak that I didn't want my child to inherit."[49] Gypsy died, at fifty-six, on April 26, 1970.

The following month, Erik joined his father, his stepmother, and the cast of *Tell Me That You Love Me, Junie Moon* for the film's world premiere as the in-competition opening attraction of the Cannes Film Festival. "Otto had been part of Cannes for so many years he could have shown a home movie there," Hope said. *MASH,* the first film produced by Ingo, was also in competition. "Ingo's film got wonderful reviews, and we didn't," Hope pointed out.[50] Indeed, Ingo's debut production was awarded the Grand Prize, while Otto's film went home empty-handed. "I never saw anything as warm as Otto's reaction to my father's success with *MASH,*" Eve Preminger said. "Otto wasn't doing so well at that time, and I'm not sure he even liked the movie—it wasn't his sort of thing. He was so proud of Ingo nonetheless. There were no ambivalent feelings whatsoever."[51]

The atmosphere on the set of *Junie Moon* may have been the most amicable in Preminger's career, but the film is a failure on every level. On the page Marjorie Kellogg's cool, unadorned style defuses her story's sentimental premise, whereas on film a more charged approach—the hue and cry of temperamental actors who have been encouraged to let it rip—is needed. All the performers, however, are hollow, and two are downright atrocious: Robert Moore, fey and preening; and Kay Thompson as the rich owner of the house the outcasts rent, a dragon lady who lives in a castle, is chauffeur-driven in a leopard-striped limousine, and seems to have dropped in from another film. Preminger's insecurity with the material is reflected in the film's technical incompetence. Pointlessly disorienting zoom shots frequently replace the director's signature tracking camera and the sound is often tinny and sometimes out of sync. Even the title sequence—Pete Seeger warbling a song of manufactured sentiment—and Saul Bass's uninspired logo, a drawing of entwined hands and arms, come up empty.

Scorched by the reception in Cannes and expecting the worst, Paramount opened the film in the summer of 1970 (on July 17 in New York; on August 19 in Los Angeles), a slot usually reserved at that time for bottom feeders, and Otto did not promote the movie with his usual fanfare. Notices were downbeat, business lackluster. "The film is so cool and ordinary that it almost made me nostalgic for *Skidoo,* which was epically bad but the obvious work of a brazenly gifted director," Vincent Canby wrote in his *New York Times* review. To be sure, for all its missteps *Skidoo* exuded the kind of temperament that has been bleached out of *Junie Moon.* "The film doesn't work," Hope said. But more than that, coming on the heels of *Skidoo, Tell Me That You Love Me, Junie Moon,* a film awash in the kind of sloppy sentimentality Otto had always avoided and the only film in his entire career without a single redeeming feature, seemed confirmation that the once masterful director had lost his way.

After working with his father on two unsuccessful pictures, Erik was disappointed, for himself as well as for Otto. But both father and son remained eager to please each other. When Otto, in the spring of 1970, acquired the screen rights to *Such Good Friends,* a new novel by Lois Gould about a group of prosperous, not-so-nice New Yorkers, he made sure that Erik was by his side throughout preproduction and filming. "Because Marjorie Kellogg had been such a calm collaborator adapting her own novel, Otto decided to hire the author of *Such Good Friends* to write the screenplay," Erik said. "But Lois did not have Marjorie's detachment or her easy manner, and once again Otto discovered that someone who can write a book cannot write a screenplay."[52]

Preminger dismissed Lois Gould, and asked Elaine May, a good choice to write about a group of Manhattan neurotics, to take over, but May was busy with other projects and declined. His next hire was Joan Micklin Silver, who had had a recent success writing and directing *Hester Street,* which shared with *Such Good Friends* a social setting, New York Jewish, but little else. Silver was gone in less than two weeks. Next up, he hired a male, David Slavitt, to write what Preminger called "a woman's story." Slavitt's tenure was three weeks. Over the summer of 1970, when he was in Los Angeles to prepare for the opening of *Junie Moon,* Preminger worked with Mr. and Mrs. John Gregory Dunne (Mrs. Dunne, Joan Didion, certainly had the edge Preminger was looking for). The Dunnes lasted longer than the previous writers, but when the Premingers relocated to New York come September, the script wasn't finished and the Dunnes were. At this low point Erik suggested a television and short-story writer named David Shaber: another no-go. The problem was finding the right tone for Gould's comedy of urban bad manners. Its narrative premise is challenging: a wife discovers her husband's infidelity with her best friend as well as with many others when he is hospitalized in order to remove a benign mole; through medical malpractice Richard becomes progressively sicker and expires. The story blends black comedy and social satire with a dose of old-fashioned woman's-film sentimentality, a recipe that none of the treatments had captured to Preminger's satisfaction.

With *Such Good Friends* stalled, Otto on November 29, 1970, acquired the screen rights to *Genesis 1948: The First Arab-Israeli War,* by Don Kurzman, which in both setting and scope promised to be an *Exodus II.* "We'll show both the conflict on the battlefield and in the political arenas in Washington, Moscow, the United Nations, and the Mid-East," Preminger said in a press conference, and then in vintage mode expressed the hope that the film "will offend neither Arabs nor Jews."[53] In January 1971, with *Such Good Friends* still on hold, he made a location-scouting visit to Israel, where he told the local press that he expected to return in October for further reconnaissance and to begin shooting in the spring of 1972. He announced that a completed film would be ready in time for the twenty-fifth anniversary of the birth of Israel in 1973. "There are few countries I like better than Israel, and there is no country which believes more optimistically in the future," he said.[54]

Genesis 1948 was a promising project for the filmmaker and a chance to redeem himself after the failure of his two pictures about young people, but it was never made. In February 1971, almost a year after he had first offered her the assignment of adapting Lois Gould's novel, Preminger returned to Elaine May, who this time accepted. "They worked well together," said Erik, who attended all the writing sessions.[55] Erik became friendly with May, who would hire him for a future project. After an intensive ten-week sprint Preminger at last felt he had a script he could work with and he began to prepare for filming on location in New York over the summer. (For reasons of her own Elaine May asked for a pseudonymous credit as "Esther Dale.")

As he was working on the script, Otto solidified his relationship with Erik. At a press conference on February 17 at the Dorchester Hotel in Lon-

don he announced that Erik was his son, and for the first time spoke publicly about his relationship with Gypsy. One month later, on March 11 in the
office of Surrogate Judge S. Samuel DiFalco in lower Manhattan, Otto formally adopted Erik, who changed his last name from Kirkland to Preminger. In addition to Erik and Otto, also present for the occasion were
Erik's wife Barbara; Hope and the twins, Mark and Vicky, now ten; and Eve
Preminger, acting as Otto's attorney. Erik and Barbara's three-year-old son,
Chris, was at home, at 75 Central Park West. Afterward, father and son
embraced as they talked with reporters. "I consider finding Erik one of the
best things that has happened to me in my life," Otto said.[56]

For at least one member of the family group, however, the smiles were
forced. Less than a month after the adoption, Barbara left Erik, taking Chris
with her; and on June 8, 1971, she sued Erik for divorce on grounds of "cruel
and inhumane treatment." "It had been a terrible marriage, and it was a bitter divorce," Barbara said.

> At first Erik had stayed in touch with the wonderful person I fell in
> love with, but then he changed. Once he became a young prince—
> well, he couldn't have a child and wife and still be a prince. I think
> working for Otto twelve to fourteen hours a day seven days a week
> was a real hardship. Erik wanted so much to measure up to his
> father's expectations, but he was unable to pull it off very well. He
> became so nervous his leg shook, and he bit the cuticles off his fin-
> gers. I thought he should just quit, and I'm afraid I wasn't sympa-
> thetic or supportive.
>
> Erik was very good with actors, and when he was offered a job
> as a theatrical agent, away from Otto, I said he should take it. But
> when he said he would stay with Otto, I felt crushed. We couldn't
> have had a good marriage under those conditions. If we'd been
> older and stronger, maybe, but we were both very young and nei-
> ther of us had the skills at that time to get through it. Although we
> were poised on the surface, we were both misfits—I had also come
> from a broken home—and that's part of what had attracted us to
> each other.[57]

Throughout the marriage Barbara had been very conscious of the negative impact both his parents had on her husband. "Erik pretended not to
care about his mother being a stripper, but I felt it did bother him. (Gypsy
was really quite puritanical; it was all right for her to do things, but nobody
else.) Erik kept a lot of his past with her under wraps, but he was always

angry with her because she was cheap, the opposite of Otto. Both Otto and Gypsy loved Erik, there was never a moment's doubt of that, but Erik also always got the short end of the stick with his mother, and in the end, with Otto too." Although she tried hard not to be, Barbara herself also felt stifled by Erik's world-famous parents.

Gypsy wanted us to stay in her house, but I couldn't breathe there. She had a loud, very old-time theatrical voice, and she spoke with exaggerated vowels. She was very smart, and Otto must have found her challenging. But she was also brusque and outgoing, just the opposite of Hope, who was reserved and could be a little cool. Gypsy could be very funny but I was afraid of her, and I always tried to avoid her. I was tongue-tied around her, always, and around Otto, too, nice as he was. I never felt that way with Hope.

When I became pregnant, Gypsy was the only one who had been happy. Otto said it was the worst thing. "You're starting a career; a baby will tie you down," he told Erik. I was very upset when Otto accused me of interfering with Erik's career; I didn't think I was. Otto and Hope, whom we saw all the time, made an effort to accept us and they were both very nice to our son. I felt Otto liked me, and he stood up for me against Erik a few times. Otto yelled at me only once, for five minutes, when I wouldn't agree to going with him and Erik to the Toronto Film Festival because my best friend was coming to New York. "You are standing in his way to success," Otto stormed in an almost childlike voice. Erik wasn't there, but when I told him later, he turned white and got furious. Otto called later to apologize. No human being should get away with how Otto behaved in a tantrum. He had been spoiled as a boy, when he should have had his hide tanned.

One day, about six or seven months after his mother had died, Erik said he wanted a divorce, and he was totally right. We were living on delusion. We went to couples therapy for four months but it didn't work. From Erik's point of view I must have been unbearable. He was emotionally needy but pretended not to be, and I wasn't mature or strong or wise enough. We were both too selfish. Also, Erik may have found someone else, he may have been dabbling. After the divorce and during procedures I didn't see Otto or Hope for six or seven months. Then Hope called and suggested we meet for lunch. I complained that Erik wasn't sending money, and Hope told Otto. But I didn't hear anything. Ingo's wife Kate was the warmest and most human of the Premingers, and she wanted Chris to be part of the family. Chris and I were the paupers—a lot of the time we had no money. Chris, who started working when he was ten, as a result now has a great work ethic. But the family, which is so close and protective, cut us off. I've had no contact with Hope, or with any Preminger except Erik—we talk once in a while about Chris, and why he hasn't sent money.[58]

Throughout the summer of 1971, as he was going through divorce proceedings, Erik was by his father's side during the making of *Such Good Friends,* a story about a failed marriage. Otto scheduled three weeks of rehearsals beginning in mid-June and ten weeks of shooting to start on July 7. Planning to make the entire film in the city where he lived, Otto thought the production would be a snap. But once he cast Dyan Cannon in the leading role of Julie Messinger, the prospect of a hassle-free shoot was blown sky high. "Dyan Cannon and Faye Dunaway—these two were in a class by themselves," Hope recalled.

But in the final analysis first prize must go to Dyan, the most temperamental actor Otto ever worked with. She was rude to the other actors and high and mighty to the crew. She would yell "Cut!" She was late. Because she always knew best, you couldn't tell her anything. At night Otto and I would long for Deborah Kerr, a real star who was lovely to everyone; but as Otto said, "There is only one Deborah Kerr." I know very well that over the years Otto had offended a number of actors, but except for Faye and Dyan (Tom Tryon, I think, is in a separate category), I always felt they eventually forgave him. But with Dyan, even more than with Faye, I felt that she truly despised Otto, and I am sure that over thirty years later she reviles his memory. I am certain she feels exactly the same way about me. She and I simply did not get along. She badmouthed Otto everywhere: in the makeup room, in front of the other actors, on the set, when we were shooting in the middle of the Guggenheim Museum. She told everyone Otto couldn't direct his way out of a paper bag, couldn't direct his niece to the bathroom. I finally blew my stack, which I should not have done, and told her not to talk about Otto like that while I was around. Dyan has a good comic flair, but the career never quite happened because the word about her got out: we weren't the only ones who felt this way.[59]

The animosity between the director and his leading lady transformed the sweltering summertime shoot into a prolonged war of nerves. Costars and staff lined up, for or against Otto or Dyan Cannon, who, quite unlike Faye Dunaway, had staunch defenders. Firmly in Otto's corner, in addition to Hope, was the blunt, no-nonsense assistant director, Charlie Okun, who had survived a far more harrowing production, Michael Cimino's misfire, *Heaven's Gate.* "Dyan was a pain in the ass," Okun said.

> She had an attitude a mile wide, and she was a nutcase who'd only eat grapes. She hated Otto, truly hated him, and because my job as a.d. was to bring her to the set she hated me too. For a scene to be shot at Elizabeth Arden, there was a terrific argument over wardrobe, with Dyan crying and Otto screaming, "I am not dressing *you,* I am dressing the character!" Dyan left the set and refused to return. I had to go back to her four times. "I know he's an s.o.b., but I'm only doing my job, don't take it out on me," I said. When I finally got her to come onto the set her face was puffy and red from crying. This happened many, many times.
>
> As a.d., my job is to protect the director 150 percent, and I wanted to protect Otto because I had great respect for him. (That's why I would never call him "Otto.") I don't interfere creatively—I never wanted to be a director, and I wouldn't dream of talking to actors. I break down the script, for logistics, but I don't make any artistic judgments. That was Otto's department, and he was always emphatic. Arrogance was a part of his persona—there were no conferences, ever—and that style didn't work for Dyan, to say the least.[60]

"Dyan was not easy to work with," recalled Nina Foch, cast as Julie's fashionable mother.

> I tried to make friends with her but it didn't work. We had nothing in common. She was all over the place, and Otto didn't know what to do with that kind of "let's be free," marijuana-smoking world. She deserved to be talked to, because she really was acting up, but she should not have been yelled at. Otto, who was the most charming man when he wasn't yelling, used yelling where he never should have. It was wrong—it was appalling. He didn't understand that if you yell at people, then they cannot work. My father was a Danish conductor, so I knew what these "important" European gentlemen

could be like: they thought they could break you down and then build you up again. What you want from the people you hire is what they can uniquely bring, and it takes courage to allow them to use their own stuff. I don't know if Otto understood that. Now Otto didn't yell the whole time, not even at Dyan; they had their peaceful moments and even a few laughs. But he was wrong to have yelled at her at all.[61]

Erik had an equivocal response to the stand-off between his father and Dyan Cannon, a sign perhaps of a growing alienation between him and his stepmother. "Hope selected the wardrobe, which Dyan didn't like," he recalled. "When Hope went to complain to Otto that Dyan was being difficult, from that moment on Dyan was dead meat. Otto's loyalties to Hope were beyond question, and after that the relations between Otto and Dyan were not redeemable. The war raged with such ferocity because Dyan gave as good as she got. She was much stronger than a lot of people when confronting Otto; she would not be bullied."[62]

Costars Rita Gam and Ken Howard were firmly on Dyan's side. "Why should he have hated her so much?" wondered Gam, cast as one of the dying husband's many ex-lovers.

> There was no reason. Dyan is a fine actress, and we could all see that she was giving a lovely performance. Yet Otto tortured her. He just had a case against poor Dyan, who was desperately unhappy, always crying and just miserable. He drove her to Valium. He beat a performance into her, and the result is there on film for everyone to see: she is magnificent. But surely this isn't the way to do it. As a director Otto was like a throwback to the silent era; I felt he should be carrying a whip and wearing puttees. In one shot in a hospital scene where nine of us are waiting for news of Richard's death, he screamed at each of us individually. Once, when I wasn't on my mark—and I was just a fraction off—he screamed with such intensity you would have thought I had committed murder.[63]

During rehearsals for a scene in which Julie rages at Richard (Laurence Luckinbill), near death in his hospital bed, Dyan Cannon, with tears streaming down her face, suddenly laughed. It was a brilliant choice, appropriate for the character and the moment. But because it wasn't in the script, Preminger, as Ken Howard observed, "just lost it. He just devastated her because of that laugh, which is wonderful and sort of crazy, sexy and funny and part of Dyan's own temperament."[64]

"Otto did not destroy Dyan in the end," Erik pointed out. "He couldn't destroy Dyan, she was too strong. But he *did* destroy Jennifer O'Neill," playing Richard's current mistress and Julie's supposed best friend.[65] "He was cruel," Jennifer O'Neill remembered. "He was terrible to me and of course to Dyan Cannon. He loved to intimidate and once he got started you couldn't stop him. It was like he was on drugs or drink: he wasn't, but that's how it felt or seemed. He would go for the jugular. He had made good films before, but not this one, which was very bad. He could be nice, however, and I liked and appreciated that side. When he heard my daughter was sick, he insisted I go home and take care of her."[66]

Away from the set and working with his editor, Harry Howard, Preminger was becalmed.

> He never told me about any fights on the set, and I didn't want to get into it anyway: the actors were not my friends. But as we were editing, he gave Dyan credit. He said she was doing a very good job, and he said that at the end, too. I don't know that all his yelling was anger; it could have been passion. You had to understand that. I would make rough edits of the previous day's shooting, and then each night I'd go with Otto to his town house and we'd look at the dailies. He had a good sense of how to play the dramatics on-screen. In a rough cut of a scene I had between Dyan Cannon and Ken Howard, I was cutting between them; he said I missed the point of the scene. "The drama is on her, stop cutting to him." That was informative to me.[67]

Bad feelings continued to fester after the shoot was over in early September. "Dyan refused to attend Otto's wrap party and threw her own party," the unit publicist Bud Rosenthal remembered. "I was the only one from the production side she invited."[68] When the star asked to have a private screening of the finished film, Preminger refused. "She can come to the preview just like the others," he told columnist Earl Wilson. Ungallantly, he "confided" to Wilson that Dyan "wouldn't work in the nude—maybe she doesn't like her body. But I respect that wish."[69]

"I have absolutely no words for Preminger," Cannon fumed, after canceling a coast-to-coast promotional tour. "I will come up with a word for him one day. It hasn't been invented yet." As the film opened across the country early in 1972, the actress did not let up. "How can a director who has no feeling make a movie about a feeling woman?" she asked. "The discord and mayhem on his set sent me reeling. I would never make another film rather than work with Preminger again."[70] "Imagine how good her performance will be in her next film if her performance in this one was so brilliant with a bad director," Preminger countered. "Anyway, I didn't hire her to praise me; I hired her to give a good performance. And she did."[71]

Alight with crack timing and a buzzing subtext, Dyan Cannon's performance is far more than good. It's exquisite, ironically enough (along with Dorothy Dandridge's in *Carmen Jones*) the finest work by an actress in any Otto Preminger film. Cannon received the best reviews of her career—nothing but raves. Her character's first line, "Oh, why did they abolish slavery?" spoken in exasperation when her black maid doesn't answer the doorbell lickety-split, is enough to send the character to p.c. detention camp; and a later complaint, "Those people in ghettos think they have problems?" compounds her guilt. Yet, as she learns of her husband's multiple infidelities ("Oh, Richard, you screwed us all"), Cannon earns sympathy

Dyan Cannon wearing the costume that launched a major battle with Preminger on the set of *Such Good Friends*.

for her character, an anxious, neglected wife who uses sarcasm as a way of covering her wounds. In the crucial scene in which a friend tells her over lunch that her husband has been having an affair for over a year, Cannon takes a pause that rumbles with Julie's anguish. Finding her voice, she says, "Oh, my goodness, the eggs will get cold," and manages to infuse the seemingly off-hand remark with a sense of the nearly mortal wound Julie has just received. It is an inspired moment brimming with an intuition and spontaneity that her battles with Preminger did not subdue.

Many of the eruptions between the star and her director were about wardrobe, in many instances the epitome of early-1970s bad taste. Julie wears some eyesores, including a too-short, too-bright yellow skirt and a baby-doll powder-blue dress. The biggest blowup occurred when Cannon refused to wear a fishnet, see-through blouse. "Julie wouldn't be caught dead in that hideous blouse," Cannon protested. Preminger won the battle, but it's likely that the actress knew better than her director what a pampered Manhattan matron of means would and would not wear.

While Preminger is interested in Lois Gould's characters, as he is in all his characters, he does not regard them with his usual evenhandedness, and his disapproval is reflected in the way the characters dress and the rooms they live in. The family doctor (James Coco), for instance, another "good friend," has an even more garish wardrobe than Julie does: loud pink shirts with mismatching ties and a jacket of bilious red. And, like Julie's, his taste in interior décor—walls covered with floor-to-ceiling frosted glass mirrors, gaudy lamps that seem poised to attack, a zebra-striped phone—would surely please Victoria Gotti. The déclassé taste—Bronx baroque run amok—expresses Preminger's overstated comment on the doctor's vulgarity.

Two scenes continue a macabre fascination with the decay of the flesh that Preminger injected into *Skidoo*. At a rooftop party to celebrate the publication of a children's book written by Richard, the ever-hot-to-trot Julie, always spurned by her husband, has a fantasy flash in which she sees a famous author (played by Burgess Meredith) dancing in the nude. The scene, which turns the flabby physique of the far-from-young Burgess Meredith into a spectacle to laugh at, casts doubts about Preminger's point of view and his control of the material. "Burgess wanted to do that scene," as Hope recalled. "Otto would never have forced him to do it, and besides nobody could have coerced Burgess, who was very stubborn, into doing anything he didn't want to. But it was a very bad scene and should not have been in the film."[72] A later scene, when the sartorially challenged doctor jabbers on the phone as Julie is on her knees before him performing fellatio, cruelly and for no thematic purpose exposes James Coco's overweight torso.

Countering these missteps, however, are many scenes organized with a formal rigor securely in the Preminger mode. Throughout, group shots of the "friends," gathered to celebrate Richard's book, or later commingling at the hospital, at first to donate blood and then on a death watch, are potent. In long takes from a detached perspective, Preminger presents a visual field packed with information—the intersecting betrayals and grievances among the characters that viewers are allowed to discover for themselves.

Directing a comedy of Manhattan manners of a kind that Woody Allen was to claim as his own in a series of ensemble films beginning with *Annie Hall* in 1977, Preminger for the third time was clearly not on native grounds. His precarious direction teeters between comedy-of-manners satire and melodrama, between irony and playing it straight. To Otto, a secular European Jew, Elaine May's brand of American Jewish comedy must have seemed a foreign idiom. Her material needed an insider's touch and an insider's affection that Preminger simply did not have.

For *Such Good Friends* he received some of the worst reviews of his career. "In what world do movie directors live that they ask us to feel sorry for a well-heeled young married woman in a well-staffed house who is hard put to answer a doorbell or get to a party on time?" asked Pauline Kael in her review in the December 23 *New Yorker.* "The screenplay by Elaine May (under a pseudonym, which is no excuse) is full of that bitchiness which in movies is passed off as Manhattan chic. You're supposed to enjoy it while feeling how depraved it is. The rancid fake smart atmosphere suggests that Otto Preminger is eager to do porno pictures but wants the prestige of a modern-woman's sensibility picture. He might as well go all the way; he has become too crude to do anything else." An even more scathing notice came from Otto's nemesis, Rex Reed, writing in the *New York Daily News* on December 22, 1971. "I would like to keep thousands of sane people away from this vile and rotten piece of junk by describing in detail the unprecedented vulgarity and filth that goes on in it," he declaimed. "But this is both a family newspaper and a season of good cheer. Just take my word for it. *Such Good Friends* is the worst movie of 1971. To make it . . . Paramount must have a death wish. To release it during Christmas week is an insult to world peace."

"Nobody sets out to make a bad film," Hope said. "I wanted all of Otto's films to be good, but they weren't. *Such Good Friends* seems worse to me now than it did back then, but still it's a lot better than *Skidoo* or *Tell Me That You Love Me, Junie Moon.* Otto and I were disappointed in all the late films."[73]

"I knew from watching the rushes of *Skidoo* and the two following films that they would be disasters," Erik said.

Looking back, I feel it was around the time that I started working with him that Otto started dealing with the Alzheimer's disease that was to claim his mind. One day [on *Skidoo*] in front of the cast he treated Hope appallingly. I was stunned. He was anything but your typical husband, but he loved Hope as much as he could love anyone. I thought then that he was losing his grip. The disease begins ten to twelve years before symptoms are manifested. At first, its victims cover up and use their routines to keep going, as Otto did. But a spark is missing, and an inability to think outside the box.[74]

"That Otto had Alzheimer's is Erik's diagnosis," Hope said. "No doctor ever said so."[75]

EIGHTEEN

Endgames

In February 1972, two months after *Such Good Friends* opened to blasé business, Paramount did not renew Preminger's "ironclad" contract. Otto had to vacate his office with its oversized marble desk, its Eames chairs, and its expensive modern art; but he continued to behave in a kingly fashion. Near the end of February, he and Hope flew to London to prepare for the European premiere of *Such Good Friends.* As in his heyday, with his usual ebullience he greeted the press in a suite at the Dorchester. After returning to New York to oversee further American openings of the film, the Premingers flew to Paris where, at the Plaza Athénée, Otto worked on the campaign for the Paris premiere, behaving all the while as if he were selling a huge hit.

After Paris, Otto and Hope went to Monte Carlo. "Otto loved gambling in the casino, dining at the Hôtel de Paris, and seeing opera and ballet at the magnificent theater," Hope recalled. "He allowed himself to lose five thousand dollars a year and stopped when he reached that point. It was on this visit that Otto decided he would build a house on the Riviera, and he bought a piece of property that I believe was the last lot on Cap Ferrat that had a sweeping ocean view. It was close to Monte Carlo, and at night the lights were unbelievably beautiful. We could see all the way to Italy.

"We didn't need a second house or a house abroad," Hope said,

because we did our traveling when we were on location, and whenever we had to be in Los Angeles, usually over summers, we always

Preminger's house in Cap Ferrat.

rented houses. But Otto had talked about owning a house on the French Riviera—a lot of Middle European people in his parents' generation had used Cannes as a winter resort, and since he had been a boy he had had a vision of a place in the south of France. He loved the Mediterranean, and we stayed often at the Hôtel du Cap d'Antibes. When he bought the Cap Ferrat property, though, Otto had no idea how much trouble was in store. It took over two years to get the house built—we bought the property in the winter of 1972 and the house wasn't finished until the summer of 1974. Otto wanted to build in a simple modern style, all white marble, which did not fit in and upset the neighbors, who had houses in traditional styles. But Otto didn't care. He had screaming fights with the architect, an M. Cauchon, a protégé of the man who had designed Brasília, and with the contractors, who were taking forever. When Otto had a last, huge fight with M. Cauchon, I took over all the negotiations.[1]

For Preminger, aside from the spectacular location, the setting had a certain political significance. Part of the allure of Cap Ferrat was that it was not in Austria, where Ingo and Kate had a longtime vacation home in Bad Ischl. " 'Why don't you have a house in a good place, like the south of

France?' I heard my father ask Ingo more than once," Vicky Preminger recalled. "The two brothers, who had an intense love-hate relationship, would fight all the time over this. My father hated Austria and felt people there were still Nazis, while Ingo felt a connection to Austria."[2] "My father never forgave my uncle for having a house in Austria, which, to Otto, was an awful thing," Mark Preminger said. "Ingo, however, perceived himself as being Austrian, but my father, on the other hand, never forgot that on *The Cardinal* his sound technicians stood up at attention during a Nazi children's march. Whenever Ingo would speak to him in German, my father would answer in English. My father never spoke German—not a word."[3]

"Our white-marble house looked like the Museum of Modern Art sitting on a cliff," Vicky said.

> Inside, too, with Eames chairs in Matisse blue and abstract paintings, it was *severely* modern. All the neighbors were up in arms. One, a Viennese dowager, very grand, was constantly suing us. Her house, in a traditional Mediterranean style, was filled with knickknacks and clutter, the kind of décor my father couldn't tolerate. I remember once going with him to her house, when she was complaining about something or other. "Have you ever seen anything so ugly?" she asked haughtily, pointing to our house. My father paused and looked all around her house before answering, "Yes!" She was incensed.[4]

"My father really loved the house and the location, and it was an idea of his that eventually he would retire in the south of France," as Mark recalled.[5] But Hope knew, "early on," that Otto would never be able to retire in Cap Ferrat or anywhere else.

> He was just not a country person—he would have died of boredom if we'd ever had a house in Westchester or the Hamptons, and I saw that he got quickly bored in Cap Ferrat too. He certainly always enjoyed gambling in Monte Carlo; he liked the ocean; and as in New York he had his favorite dining places—we both loved the Colombe d'Or and the Château de la Chèvre d'Or. But he'd get fidgety. "I'm driving to Nice to window-shop," he'd say, and he'd come back laden with presents for all of us. One time he bought boxes of ashtrays at Christofle.

Because Otto was "a terrible driver," Hope was worried whenever he'd drive on the tortuous and often narrow lanes of the Grand Corniche.[6] As Vicky observed, "Behind the wheel of a car he had no idea what he was doing, and that was especially true when he was in the south of France."[7]

As he supervised construction of the house, Preminger faced an uncertain period in his professional life. His schedule was becoming far less hectic than it had ever been, and the interval between films was longer than at any earlier time. Nonetheless, Preminger regularly announced new projects. At the top of his list, announced while he was shooting *Such Good Friends* in the summer of 1971, was *Open Question,* which was to be his first made-for-television movie. "It's about a couple, like the Rosenbergs, accused of passing atomic secrets to the enemy," Preminger told two dozen journalists he had invited to his office at 711 on July 29. "I'll be the narrator—or reporter—interviewing the participants in the trial. I will appear as myself, as a reporter and a commentator on the trial and on public opinions about the trial. You might say I will be a sort of Greek chorus. I got my friend Louis Nizer to write the script. We want the show to capture the fears of the United States in the early 1950s, the McCarthy era. The 'message' will be against capital punishment."[8] Despite repeated attempts, by other writers besides Louis Nizer, the structure failed to jell; shortly after he returned from Monte Carlo in March 1972, Preminger terminated the project.

Soon after, he announced that he would produce and direct *The Man with the Golden Arm* as a Broadway musical. At a time when the musical theater was expanding its subject matter, a dark show about drug addiction featuring a moody, jazz-based score might have worked. To succeed, however, it would have required a director like Hal Prince or Bob Fosse who was more familiar with musical theater tradition than Preminger and not afraid to defy it. After a flurry of announcements about the musical—silence.

Otto's next realized project would not come until the fall of 1973, when he would produce and direct a play, *Full Circle,* on Broadway, and his next film would not begin shooting until May 1974. But Preminger carried on as if he had just opened *Exodus.* He continued to supervise construction of his house in Cap Ferrat and to run his office at 711 with the panache he had always had. Also conforming to business as usual were the contrasting responses he evoked from his employees.

"I began working for Otto, as his executive assistant, when *Such Good Friends* started preproduction in the late spring of 1971, and I stayed for two years, until the time he was starting to produce *Full Circle,*" Leslie Jay said.

The office staff at that period consisted of Bud Rosenthal, story editor and casting director; Nat Rudich; Blanche Berger, Otto's accountant; Erik; and me. And Otto always had an intern. One was Tony Gittelson, a smart, nice New York kid; another was Ken Kaufman. Both were friends of Bud. Erik had his own office, and after *Friends* wrapped he was there all the time. It was Nat who told me how to handle Otto—I felt it was Nat's job to make it up to every-one Otto had insulted, or who hated him. I was never scared of Otto; at Columbia I had worked for Bud Rosenthal, who had a tough reputation and who had been difficult, and I had had no problem with him. Erik was also not afraid of his father, though of course he was aware of his father's wrath. Although I never heard him, I can't imagine Otto didn't yell at Erik, and at Hope and the twins, too; he *must* have, it was built into him. When I started, Erik was working on a screenplay and then he left to work with Elaine May on *Heartbreak Kid.* He *had* to get away from Otto, but then he returned.

My goal was not to be yelled at. Every morning at 8:30 I checked Otto's desk. He was extremely orderly and he hated dirty blotters, so I changed the blotter daily. When we would send out press material and letters, never more than a page, they had to be lined up just so—he was a stickler for the pages lining up *exactly.* He also dressed meticulously, always with a jacket and tie. Otto was a true gentleman; there was never *any* suggestion of a casting couch. He had tons of phone calls and appointments every day. Every Israeli who came to New York came to see him; his office was their first stop. And he always had lunch out. Eve Preminger came by a lot, and so did Ingo. Hope and the twins came to the office, too. I sat at a white desk with, in those days, a typewriter. I typed script changes on *Friends* and went with Otto regularly to see dailies at Paramount. We looked at different shots and Otto would discuss which ones worked. In one shot Dyan's bra was showing, and Otto asked me if I saw it; I did. We heard in the office how difficult she was on the set, and a few times Otto asked me to have flowers sent to her.

After he was finished shooting *Such Good Friends,* he was in the office every day from nine to six. He always put in a full workday. Nat said he was more difficult when he didn't have a project, but after *Friends* opened he never mentioned that the film wasn't a suc-cess and he never took it out on me. If he took it out on anyone it was probably Nat. After *Friends* he worked on the Nizer project, *Open Question.* He was very tough on the writers. Philip Friedman worked on it first, then Lionel Chetwyn. Otto hated everything Lionel wrote—he ripped it apart and yelled at him. I did feel that his Alzheimer's was starting; he wouldn't remember me on the street, and Nat would have to remind him who I was.

During her time at 711, Leslie Jay discovered a lump in her breast. "Otto was very upset and insisted I go to Hope's gynecologist. When it was found to be malignant, Otto was very concerned. After my operation I went back to work pretty fast, but Otto wanted me to take as much time as needed, and more. You know, finally it doesn't really matter how much he screamed, or what people said about him: Otto had a heart. There is simply no doubt about it: Otto had a heart."[9]

When Leslie Jay left in the spring of 1973, Arlene Leuzzi replaced her.

I was there about a year, from the time of *Full Circle* until he began preproduction on *Rosebud* in the spring of 1974. I was hired as his administrative assistant–secretary, although I did not do secretarial stuff. Then I became a reader, along with three aspiring young people, who also did errands and were unpaid. Nat was still there—so nice, and he was *not* a doormat, as I know people claimed. I heard him yell back. "Otto, you're off base," he would say. There was a mutual respect between Nat and Otto, a rapport. Nat understood him. After a blowup he'd tell us not to be upset. The accountant, Blanche Berger, was a very mean old lady who lived her entire life through Otto and thought he walked on water; she always called him "Otto Preminger," and he treated her in a very kindly way. Blanche was terrified of Hope, however, and I felt there was a competition between them for Otto's affection. Blanche would do things to force Otto to be mad at other people—she didn't want him to like other people as much as he liked her. She watched every penny. You would have to justify getting more paper clips, but the pettiness came from her, not from Otto.

Erik, always there in his own office, was terrific: talented, motivated, and so kind I wondered how he had Otto's genes. I loved Erik: everybody in the office did. He and Otto, I felt, were "overly" father and son, trying so hard to *be* father and son but they weren't there yet. They frequently said to each other, "I love you." It was *very* endearing, and you couldn't help but be touched. I never once heard Otto yell at Erik. In fact, when Erik was there Otto was noticeably calmer. A number of times with Erik I saw him struggle to keep his temper in check: his head would turn red but he wouldn't blow up.

When I first started, Otto was pleasant. He told jokes, he acknowledged appreciation, and I liked him. I liked him a lot. But I knew from day one that I simply did not have the subservient temperament he needed. In time I began to feel that working for him was a daily wearing down. Every once in a while he'd throw you a bone but it had a second piece to it. The reader-interns, Ted Gershuny and Ken Kaufman, were in awe of him and would sit straight up when he walked in. They were aspiring Otto Premingers and I was not. Otto used a lot of medication, bottles and bottles of uppers and downers, Dexedrine and Valium. They were in huge prescription bottles in his name that we would steal handfuls of pills from. I felt that the drugs created the mood swings; within a few hours' time there would be enormous changes in his personality that I couldn't cope with. For example, Otto ordered the same lunch every day, from the Carnegie Deli; I served it to him on china with cloth napkins, on a tray I rolled in. Once, when the cole slaw was on the same plate as the sandwich, he screamed, "You are *not* to put the cole slaw on the same plate." He took the china plate and hurled it into the garbage. "Now, order it again!"

"Today is your last day," Blanche told me one day when Otto was out of town scouting for *Rosebud* in Tehran. He had never said good-bye. It was sad that after I had been there for a year he couldn't tell me that I would be gone. I had never been treated that way by anyone. After I was fired, Erik called me to work for him, which I did part time. I told him, "I can't believe your father would have let Blanche fire me." "My father is a complicated man," he said.

After having worked for him, I thought less of Otto's talents as a filmmaker. I could never bring myself to see *Rosebud* and I can't even watch *Laura* without gritting my teeth.[10]

Still with no film project in development, in the fall of 1973 Preminger decided to return to the theater. He would produce and direct *Full Circle*, the only play by the Austrian novelist Erich Maria Remarque, which the writer's widow, the actress Paulette Goddard, had sent to him. The play's setting, Berlin at the end of World War II as the Red Army is entering the city, and its ironic story about a German anti-Nazi who becomes a victim of Communism, enticed Otto at once. To help him prepare an English-language edition he enlisted playwright and screenwriter Peter Stone, who in 1956 had worked with Remarque on the original German version, called *The Last Station*. "Erich had asked me in 1956 to do the next draft in English," Stone recalled, but he didn't like what I did and withdrew it. After Erich died, Paulette was looking for any shred of income from him, and she sent the play—the German version, which is the only one she had—to Otto because he had been a friend of Erich's. When Otto came to me he said, "There's a catch: Paulette insists it be by Erich and adapted by you." I didn't care. As we worked on the script, Otto, who had a good story sense, was bearable. When he felt it was ready to go, he got the cast he wanted: Bibi Andersson, a big catch, a terrific actress and a member of Ingmar Bergman's repertory company, and Mr. Spock, Leonard Nimoy. He also got the best designer, Robin Wagner, and his coproducer was Roger Stevens, who ran the Kennedy Center in Washington, which as a result was where we played our out-of-town tryout.

Once rehearsals started, Stone no longer found Preminger to be "bearable." "He pushed everyone to their limits until they said, 'Stop!' At that point, he would stop, because that's as far as he knew he could go," Stone said. "Roger Stevens was angry because Preminger refused to make a single change in the script, and then Stevens got mad at me, too, when I couldn't convince Otto to allow any changes during rehearsals and out of town."[11] "There were also some big blowups with Leonard Nimoy," as the play's associate producer Bud Rosenthal remembered, "but unlike those with Dyan Cannon, they were not irreparable. On the last day of rehearsals in New York, however, before we left for Washington where the show was scheduled to run for a month [*Full Circle* opened in Washington on October 6, 1973], we got a call in the office telling us that Leonard was leaving. I spoke to both of them, and Leonard agreed to stay. In Washington, both Otto and Leonard, who was very active in Democratic politics and had a steady stream of visitors backstage, were in their element and that helped."[12]

Preminger also had problems with his leading lady. "Bibi was confused by Preminger's direction," Peter Stone said, "and she had the benefit of some after-hours coaching from another director, Milos Forman, with whom she was living at the Watergate Hotel. Forman was not working at the time and in bed with back spasms, and he would redirect Bibi. Then at 3 or 4 a.m. she would call her mentor, Ingmar Bergman, in Sweden. She was in thrall to Bergman, as all his actors were. Otto never knew about the outside direction his star was getting."

Adding to his trouble was the widow Remarque, "a dragon lady nobody liked," according to Stone. "Paulette was a Jewish girl who had married Chaplin and who had had a strange and difficult life. She was very complicated, and was looking out for herself only."[13] As Arlene Leuzzi remembered,

"Otto's phone never stopped ringing, and he always took his calls (he loved to talk on the phone, which he used as a way of entertaining his staff), but my instructions were that if Paulette Goddard called he was *not* in. Otto was not a gossip; he never talked about colleagues, and he never said anything derogatory about anyone—except Paulette. I suspect, though, that he did call her back at times."[14] "Paulette watched every rehearsal and wanted to direct the actors," Hope said. "Otto lost his temper once—'take your script and shove it!' he told her—and she went off in a huff to Switzerland, where she had lived with Remarque. But she was there for the opening dressed in a full-length white lynx coat. She wanted to hold on to her glamour and feared it was leaving her; Otto had compassion for that, but he found her impossible to work with."[15]

The show opened at the ANTA Theatre on November 12, 1973, to a mixed response. Richard Watts in the *New York Post* hailed Preminger's "skillful direction." In *Women's Wear Daily* Martin Gottfried called it "a disgrace to professional theatre." *Full Circle* closed after twenty-one performances. Rather than evoking an aura of postwar Berlin, Preminger's stiff-jointed production seemed airless—"it was a melodrama that didn't shed light on anything," according to Peter Stone.

> It could have been good, but what we ended up with wasn't. One of the critics said it was like a B-movie thriller from the 1940s, and that wasn't far off. It would have made a better movie, something like *Decision Before Dawn.* And at times Otto seemed to be directing it as if it were a movie, almost with a viewfinder. Otto wanted so much to get back to the theater, but at this point he wasn't a good theater director. We thought he was just forgetful and exhausted, but the truth was that he was entering into senility and wasn't connecting. Otto had an amazing lack of interest in the public opinion about his work. He liked the show, he believed in it, and the indifferent reception really didn't seem to phase him. He also didn't care about his personal reputation. He was creating a legend—but you can't invent too far from your own nature.[16]

While he was in Washington with *Full Circle,* Preminger, on October 7, bought the rights to *Rosebud,* a French best seller by Paul Bonnecarrère (for the English-language edition, Joan Hemingway, Ernest's granddaughter, had a coauthor credit). The story of a kidnapping by Palestinian terrorists featuring an international cast of characters, a sprawling episodic structure, and a dusting of political timeliness, *Rosebud* was a return, for Preminger, to familiar territory. Divorced from Paramount, Otto approached his *Exodus* partners at United Artists, who agreed to back him but did so without much enthusiasm.

From the beginning Otto intended the project as a gift to Erik, who would write the screenplay. "We're going to work differently on this," Preminger told Bud Rosenthal, who in the fall of 1973 had replaced the loyal but understandably weary Nat Rudich and who would receive associate producer credit on the film. "Otto was going to be involved so closely with Erik, that he didn't want me to participate on a daily basis," Bud Rosenthal said. "Otto was being very protective of Erik. He loved his son, and it was my sense that he had some feelings of guilt. I wasn't the enemy, and Otto wasn't treating me that way; rather, he wanted me to be able to maintain objectivity and distance. So after he and Erik had written about fifty pages, he brought them to me and it took me three days to make notes."[17]

"When I read the book I saw it as an interesting way of looking at the Arab/Israeli conflict," Erik recalled. "As in the book, I wanted to show the point of view of both sides, as well as to present the power of the media at a moment of international crisis." A schism developed early on, however, between Erik's conception of the story and his father's. "Otto felt that the audience had to care about the five girls who were kidnapped by the Arabs, and Hope felt you had to *love* the girls. But I didn't think that was important at all."[18] With Erik on one side against his father and stepmother on the other, the making of *Rosebud* turned into a tense family drama, and in a way the completed film could be regarded as the most expensive home movie ever made.

After he first entered his father's life, Erik had been quite friendly with Hope. "When he met Hope in Paris, he really liked her," Barbara Preminger said. "And I felt those feelings were returned. The twins were quite fond of him too, and Erik spent time with them—he made a point of spending time with them."[19] "At first we all appreciated Erik enormously," Hope said. "But after a while he began to ignore the kids. Still, I tried very hard to like him— Otto had such a strong sense of family that I felt I *had* to like him, for Otto's sake." By the time that Erik began to write the *Rosebud* screenplay, however, Hope's feelings for her stepson had darkened considerably.

> Otto felt so sorry that he hadn't known Erik as he was growing up that he tried to devote special time to him—Saturday was Erik's day with Otto—and of course that was fine; that's what Otto should have done for his son. But when Erik was given the *Rosebud* opportunity—Otto risked his career to give Erik this chance because

United Artists was not happy with this picture from the start—I felt Erik behaved badly. He would go out at night, and Otto couldn't get pages out of him. Erik would sit in our living room and talk about what he was *going* to do. I began to feel that Erik didn't care enough that Otto was doing so much for him.[20]

"I didn't feel at this time that Erik was a good influence on my father," Mark recalled. "He separated him from other people, and he'd supply my father with alcohol, and at this point in his life my father had begun to drink heavily."[21]

It was apparent to Tony Gittelson, at eighteen the youngest of the interns in Preminger's office at the time *Rosebud* was being written, that Otto had made

a mistake, as a father. Erik, who was a gracious man—we all liked him very much—was not ready to write such a big screenplay, and his father shouldn't have asked him to do it. It was an enormous act of love: here was Otto Preminger placing what was likely to be his last big movie in his son's hands. He was trying very hard to be a father to Erik, we all saw that; when he would kiss Erik on the cheek, it was very touching. But the work wasn't coming out right. In the big bullpen in New York, when we were proofing script pages, we were laughing: frankly, it was lousy. Erik later said, sweetly, "I heard you guys laughing."[22]

The setup could not have been easy for Erik, who had to contend with his own uncertainty about his writing skills, a growing estrangement from Hope and the twins, and most troubling of all, his father's disapproval, sometimes expressed in thundering rage. As Erik recalled, "One day when I was in my office meditating—anything to survive—Otto burst in carrying new pages I had just given him, screaming, his head and face a bright red. He disliked them, as he had disliked everything I had written. I walked out. Later that day he gave me expensive cologne, his way of apologizing."[23]

Before he approved a final draft, and with a number of characters still undeveloped, including the master terrorist who orchestrates the kidnapping as well as the kidnap victims themselves, Otto scheduled shooting to begin in the south of France in early June. Periodically from February to May, often with Erik and his favorite production manager Eva Monley, he racked up a record number of reconnaissance expeditions to the four countries in which the story takes place. "I did the surveys with Otto in Corsica,

France, and Germany, but I didn't go to Israel," Monley recalled. "Frankly, I thought I was going to go completely crackers because Otto just kept hounding me. He kept thinking I was the girl I had been in 1959, but I had learned a lot since then and somehow he didn't seem to trust me. We couldn't see eye to eye, and I knew I had to quit. Martin [Schute] said I couldn't quit until I replaced myself. I handed over a good guy, Wolfgang Glattes. 'Did you have to give me a German?' Otto asked."[24]

"Eva Monley was a nervous wreck at the time she asked me to take up her job," Glattes recalled.

> Actually, Graham Cottle was to be production manager, but Eva said that Otto desperately needed an assistant director, and that I was the one for it. I went to see Otto in Paris, where he was at the Plaza Athénée. He invited me to go out walking with him and it was as if God had returned to France and was holding court. In Paris, everyone knew him on the street—people would call out to him and he would always respond in a friendly way. I accepted the job because I could see that Otto had a good sense of humor and a good heart, and I never changed my initial opinion, not for a minute. We opened production offices in Nice and Juan-les-Pins, and preproduction stretched out over four months. During that time I went with Otto to Berlin, Hamburg, Tel Aviv, Haifa, Paris, the south of France. We went to every location two or three times. "Each time you get a different viewpoint about how to set up the shots," he told me.

Calm, affable, and in bearing and demeanor clearly no pushover, Glattes seemed to know from the first how to handle his boss, and as they traveled together, Preminger to an unusual degree came to depend on him.

Along with finding locations, Preminger's other primary concern was in casting the *Rosebud,* the pleasure yacht from which the five young women are abducted. The *Rosebud* was as hard to cast as the ship in *Exodus* had been. A number of deals fell through before a suitable boat became available, for a limited amount of time only. "We had to start at the end of May, a little earlier than Otto had planned, because that's when the boat, a major expense, would be available to us," Wolfgang Glattes said. "We were locked into a certain time frame because of that boat."[25]

Otto invited three interns to join the production. Tony Gittelson, who had been at 711 in the summer of 1973, was "thrilled" when Preminger asked him to come along on the *Rosebud* shoot. " 'Pay your own way over, and I can find you a hotel room,' he told me. At eighteen, I would be traveling around Europe with a famous director—and in fact with this on my résumé I got into Harvard. Otto even made me dialogue coach on the film; as it developed the dialogue was one of the big problems!"[26] Preminger also asked Ken Kaufman, another 711 veteran. As Kaufman pointed out, "Otto always had observers—it was the European system. 'I can give them graduate school,' he boasted. He was proud that he was great with young people, and he loved them, or so he claimed."[27] The third student in the Preminger "graduate school" was Ted Gershuny, who was planning to write a book about the making of the film. "Otto, who never did anything privately, gave Ted Gershuny total access," Kaufman said. "That was typical of Otto," Bud Rosenthal agreed. "He was fearless, and he didn't feel vulnerable. Despite all the signs right from the beginning, he really didn't know that it was a troubled project. I asked Ted to keep me out of the book because I knew it was going to be a rough road."[28]

"Otto was not so generous to these young men," Glattes said. "There was no salary or per diem, and they worked sixteen hours a day." But working with Otto Preminger in exotic locations in the summer of 1974 provided the interns with the experience of a lifetime. (The three interns and Glattes struck up a friendship that endures to the present.)

During four months of frequent scouting trips, Preminger, always with Glattes at his side, had lined up locations in Corsica, Paris, Berlin, Hamburg, Juan-les-Pins, Haifa, Tel Aviv, and the Israeli desert. He had also found his *Rosebud* yacht along with another hard-to-nail prop, a flight simulator on which one of the hostages is taken, blindfolded, by her abductors. He had his production team, including his three interns, in place. And because he had landed Robert Mitchum for the leading role, an international spy who leads the hunt for the kidnappers, the financing from United Artists was ensured. What he still did not have when he began filming in Juan-les-Pins on May 19, 1974, was a completed script.

"It was the only time in his career that Otto started shooting without a finished script," Hope recalled, "and it was the only time Otto was worried about a picture while it was being made."[29] "From the first morning, as he was setting up shots of the five women arriving at the yacht, Otto wanted me to remain within three meters of him at all times," Glattes recalled. "I saw I was to be a kind of security blanket. No other director I ever worked for was like this. I couldn't direct the extras because I had to be right next to Otto. I had to be there to answer every question."[30]

Preminger knew at once that the dialogue for the young women wasn't working. It was stilted, the actresses seemed to have no idea how to approach their ill-defined characters, and Preminger seemed to have no idea how to help them. He continued shooting, but decided he needed a writer to help Erik punch up the dialogue. He called Marjorie Kellogg, "a good friend of Erik's from *Junie Moon,* and from Otto's point of view she wouldn't have been threatening," Bud Rosenthal said. "But Marjorie also wasn't right for the project. It needed a writer who could give it the cynical bite the novel had, someone who would have been congenial to Otto's iconoclastic approach."[31]

"Otto called me and said his son was in trouble with the script, and though I didn't want to go, I flew to Nice to help Erik get through without losing face," Marjorie Kellogg said.

> Playing Mama, I worked with Erik twelve to fifteen hours a day and he began to learn how to write a screenplay. Sometimes we were writing on the set, a half a scene ahead. In some scenes we started five minutes ahead of shooting. I was there for about four weeks, in the south of France, just enough time to get it finished. I had a good relationship with Erik, but his relationship with Otto at that point was not too hot, and I didn't want to get in the middle of it. I didn't understand the relationship between them: I felt Erik had always been Otto's whipping boy and that he didn't have the strength to handle his father. He was always getting put down by his father and to me he seemed squashed. I didn't want to stay around longer than I needed to.[32]

"Often at seven at night we would get script changes, and Tony and I and Erik's girlfriend Brigitte would stay up all night Xeroxing," Ken Kaufman said. "It was incredibly intense and it went on for months."[33]

Even with substantial rewriting, the opening scenes of the chattering young women arriving at the yacht refused to ignite. The irresolvable problem was that after having conducted extensive interviews and working closely with a top French casting director, Margot Capellier, Preminger and Erik had selected five young actresses who were not convincing playing characters from prominent wealthy families who attended one of the finest European finishing schools. "All five of them were tough-looking and so scruffy in appearance that they would have been thrown out of Le Rosey in Switzerland," Hope said. "Actually, they would never have been accepted in the first place."[34] And as actresses one was worse than the other, although everyone agreed that the prize went to Kim Cattrall, cast as the American hostage, daughter of a senator. Three decades later Cattrall became famous playing an urban nymphomaniac on television in *Sex and the City,* but in her first film, as Ken Kaufman recalled, "She was just awful. At that time she had no talent, not a whit of talent. She was only seventeen, so green and raw. The two other finalists for the role had been Connie Selleca and Kim Basinger; Otto didn't think either one could act, but both were drop-dead gorgeous. Kim Cattrall not only couldn't act, she was also, at seventeen, not sexy. But if she had any chance at all to be good, Otto robbed her of it the first day of shooting."[35] As Erik recalled, "In one shot Kim had to lean out of a window on the yacht and say some bad dialogue that I had written. I rewrote it, and asked Otto if she could try it the new way. He said, 'No, she can do it the original way.' Why did he do this to the poor girl? It was painful. After making Kim do the shot over and over, Otto said to her, 'Darling, you remind me of Marilyn Monroe, not in looks, of course, but in lack of talent.' I'm amazed Kim stayed in the business."[36]

No matter what he did, whether he shouted or whispered, threatened or cajoled, Preminger could get nothing from any of the young women. "The girls were frightened of him, the big Hollywood director," Wolfgang Glattes said. "They just froze up with him. He could not get through to them, and it was *his* deficiency." The second day he fired one French actress, who was

The five hostages (from left, Brigitte Ariel, Isabelle Huppert, Debra Berger, Kim Cattrall, Lalla Ward) in *Rosebud,* watched over by their Palestinian captor (Josef Shiloah). In casting the hostages, Preminger, with almost perverse perfection, batted zero.

an anorexic, and replaced her with another one, Brigitte Ariel, who was almost equally scrawny and had blackened teeth. All the women were terrified of doing a harshly lighted nude scene. "Of course they didn't want to do the scene," Glattes said. "But on the day we shot it they didn't rebel. You didn't rebel with Otto."[37] Of the five hapless women, Isabelle Huppert was the one most able to hold her ground against Preminger. But speaking up did her no good; her performance is as empty of talent and charm as that of the others.

Preminger's other casting was also ill-starred. As a high-powered Israeli agent, Preminger chose Cliff Gorman, an actor who had had a great success in the stage and film versions of *The Boys in the Band* and onstage as the self-destructive comedian Lenny Bruce in *Lenny.* "Cliff came prepared, ready to work, trying to do an Israeli accent," as Tony Gittelson observed. "But he was a meteor that had burnt out. And Otto, who never bullied him as he did the girls, just couldn't shape a performance out of him."[38] Although nabbing former New York City mayor John Lindsay to play a senator had generated almost as much publicity as his almost casting of Dr. Martin Luther King Jr. in *Advise and Consent,* Preminger "couldn't extract even the barest semblance of acting from Lindsay," Wolfgang Glattes said. "He was very nice to the mayor, very nice indeed, but as we all saw on the set he just could not get any sign of life out of Lindsay."[39] ("I tracked Lindsay down in Majorca, and he agreed to do it, although his first asking price was unrealistically high," as Bud Rosenthal recalled. "Otto was adamant that the casting had to be a front-page story in the *New York Times.* It was, but not without some heavy-duty arm-twisting on my part. I thought if I was unable to persuade Abe Weiler at the *Times* I might lose my job.")[40]

Preminger's biggest problem, however, was with his leading man. "Robert Mitchum loved Otto, and the two of them used to whore around in the old days, in London in the early 1950s on press junkets," Ken Kaufman said. "But when he arrived in Corsica, where his first scenes were to be shot, Mitchum was drunk, and he stayed that way."[41] "He was also on drugs," Glattes claimed.[42] "The problem," according to Erik, "was in bringing Mitchum in a few weeks before he was needed. That was pure stupidity on Otto's part. Mitchum had no problem at all with dictatorial directors and remembered Otto with great fondness (their blowup during *Angel Face* was long since forgotten), but with nothing to do and just hanging around he started to drink more and more heavily, and that was the end of the story."[43]

"Mitchum was reeling in every scene, and slurring his words," Hope said. "When Otto brought in the press, Mitchum stood up and said, 'I'm only doing this crap because I need the money.' He was not long for us after that."[44] According to Tony Gittelson, on the day of reckoning Preminger took the actor aside and told him in a quiet, level voice, " 'Bob, we can't go on like this.' Mitchum, blind drunk that morning, said to Otto, 'Shake my hand.' And then Mitchum, who really didn't give a shit, left the set." Always calm in such a moment, Preminger "stood there for thirty seconds," as Gittelson remembered, "and then said, 'Let's move to the chapel scene.' Then he knocked off and went back to the office. Otto didn't brood, he didn't look back, but put his mind to what he knew he had to do: find another star quick."[45] ("The next day Mitchum ripped a phone off the wall," Ken Kaufman recalled. "Otto, furious now, told me to get the police. But I hid in the bathroom; I knew not to call the police, because I knew Otto's anger would pass.")[46]

"We got Peter O'Toole down to Corsica within forty-eight hours," Bud Rosenthal said.[47] Like Mitchum, however, O'Toole had a history of acute alcoholism, and as a result of his illness had only one lung and one kidney. As a replacement for an alcoholic, he was indeed a peculiar choice, but somehow a fitting one for this bedeviled project. O'Toole showed up, as Gittelson noted, "looking totally dissipated, at death's door."[48] "Otto knew he was going from one drunk to another," Glattes said, "but he and O'Toole respected each other—from a distance."[49] Like Mitchum, the new star was indifferent to his role and to the film. "This gig was merely a payday for O'Toole, and he couldn't have cared less," Kaufman said.[50]

"Peter did not drink on the picture," Hope claimed.[51] Nonetheless, the health of the ravaged-looking actor was fragile and when the production moved to Paris he had a serious ulcer attack and had to be rushed to the American Hospital. Otto had no choice but to suspend shooting, and for the next two weeks, as Glattes remembered, "the crew loved relaxing in Paris on a per diem."[52] As his crew dallied, Otto went off to Israel with Erik to check once again on the locations he had lined up.

When Preminger resumed in Paris, O'Toole received a letter informing him he would be the target of a bomb. "We were filming in an apartment on top of the Tour d'Argent, and we evacuated the building after the threat," Glattes said. "Later that day we found out that the letter was a joke, an ugly joke, perpetrated by [the critic] Kenneth Tynan. O'Toole went bananas. He went and beat up Tynan."[53] "O'Toole, a nasty man nobody liked, was also a coward," Ken Kaufman said. "His henchman held Tynan as O'Toole hit him hard, over and over again. He could have killed him. He certainly wanted to."[54]

Preminger, O'Toole, Erik, the interns, and a skeleton crew then went to

Berlin and Hamburg for a few days. After returning for some pick-up shots in Paris, Preminger was to relocate the entire production to Israel. Ten days before the Israeli shoot was scheduled to begin, however, Otto and Erik still did not yet have a "villain," the chief terrorist who had planned the kidnapping. "We'd been dealing with the heavy since Otto had bought the book," Erik said.

> We both felt casting the mastermind as a German, as in the novel, was a mistake: Germans shouldn't be the villains in this story. We kept looking for who else could be the bad guy. Roy Clark, a writer Peter O'Toole brought in to make his part sound more British (Peter claimed the dialogue we had written for Mitchum didn't sound right for a Brit), suggested we use an Arabist, who would conform to the long tradition of Arab-infatuated Brits like T. E. Lawrence. Otto and I liked the idea. We decided to call the character "Sloat," and Roy Clark wrote a scene for Sloat that was completely brilliant. It made the character complex enough to be sympathetic—it explained the character's political and psychological motivations. But Otto would not allow it. He didn't want *any* sympathy for the character. He screamed at me across the room in a Paris restaurant that United Artists would rather burn the film than release it with that scene.[55]

Erik had a great deal of trouble writing the scene that his father wanted. "Otto could not get that scene out of Erik," Hope said. "When Erik said he had writer's block, Vicky said you have to be a writer to be blocked; Erik was not pleased—by this point they were not friends. Vicky, at fourteen, wrote the scene and Otto accepted it."[56]

There was a mutiny as the company was about to leave for Israel. "The crew wanted to know if there would be sufficient security in Israel," as Tony Gittelson remembered. " 'If you don't want to go, you can go home,' Otto said. It was not said with any anger or rancor at all. He was firm. He did not, however, say he would get the Israeli Army to protect us."[57] "When we got to Israel, I thought Otto went a little crazy," Glattes said.

> One day he fired two drivers. Then we did night shooting near an Arab border, and we had thirty or forty Israeli soldiers guarding us. Otto insisted that this was the only area where we could shoot: once he had locked into an area that was it. Yet there was nothing special about the area. He decided he wanted to shoot Sloat's scenes in a

cave—like Osama bin Laden, the character lived in and issued his orders from caves. The scenes didn't make sense, yet Otto didn't seem aware of this. Richard Attenborough, whom we brought in quickly to play Sloat, was doing the role out of friendship to Otto; he knew the scenes were ridiculous. Yet he took his notes from Otto without a word of protest.[58]

(As the batty Arabist, Attenborough gives a sly performance that, under the circumstances, is also remarkably inventive.)

"Otto wanted to film the scene in which Israeli soldiers enter Sloat's cave and capture him in salt mines, where you couldn't use any explosives," Erik said. "The scene of Sloat's capture required action, and cutting between Sloat and the soldiers; but because we were shooting in the salt mines we couldn't have any action and Otto shot the scene in one take. When preview audiences guffawed at the absurdity of the rescue scene—soldiers in deep focus scale down the walls of the cave unseen by Sloat, facing front as he genuflects in prayer—Otto refused to reshoot."[59]

After nearly four months of filming in far-flung locations in Juan-les-Pins, Paris, Corsica, Berlin, Hamburg, Tel Aviv, Haifa, and the Israeli desert, the production finally ended, on September 6, 1974, in the place where it began, in Juan-les-Pins, with reshoots of scenes in which Robert Mitchum had appeared. The wrap party was held at the Hôtel du Cap d'Antibes. "Erik sat in the corner crying his eyes out," Ken Kaufman said. "I was a basket case," Erik admitted.

> I broke down for eight hours, and the day after the wrap party I left. I just couldn't stay around for the editing. It was one of the hardest periods of my life. I loved Otto a lot and desperately wanted his approval. At the beginning, when I saw the problems about the script, I had said to him, "You love me; I love you, but we have different points of view about this. You deserve a script that suits you." He said that was nonsense. "This is our chance to make a movie together." It came totally with love from him, and it still makes me feel so sad. I'm not totally responsible; a number of people played a role in this abomination. The script for *Rosebud* is one of the worst scripts to make it past the wastebasket, and if you like it, you must be crazy.[60]

When Wolfgang Glattes said good-bye to him at the wrap party, Preminger looked chagrined. " 'Wolf, you can't leave me in the middle.' So I went with him to London on postproduction for about five weeks. I was holding his hand, really. He had gotten used to me. I stayed with him at the Dorchester, and the two of us—Hope was busy with the children—went for caviar lunches every day. He looked at the film over and over and he liked it. Otto had been a great director, but not on *Rosebud;* you can see the decline. Maybe his Alzheimer's was already starting," Glattes speculated.[61]

Tony Gittelson did not agree that Preminger was losing his grip.

> Otto ran the set with supreme authority. The problem was that he was saddled with a bad script. He never once betrayed any hesitation or doubt, and he always knew exactly what his next shot would be. His shadow was on everything. He was both respected and feared, and your day centered on not having Otto blow up at you. He was still a force of nature, and he knew it. And he did everything—from signing checks to climbing huge scaffolds. With complete command he managed a lot of petrified actors and Peter sloshing his way through. During the making of that movie Otto Preminger was sharp as a tack: he was *not* a director in decline.[62]

Throughout four months of strenuous preproduction and nearly four months of a peripatetic, plague-ridden shoot, the filmmaker at sixty-nine had maintained a killing pace as for the first time in his career he worried about the possibility that he would fail to remain within the shooting schedule and the budget (a remarkably tight $2,476,000 for below-the-line costs). Regularly he put in fourteen-to-sixteen-hour days struggling with a never-quite-finished script, a number of temporarily brain-dead actors, and a sometimes defiant crew. At the end of the day, after all the on-the-spot rewrites, the recasting and delays, the illness of his leading man, and complicated location shooting in four countries, he brought the film in under budget and only one day late. On September 25, 1974, *Variety* dubbed him "the indomitable Otto, never more in evidence than on *Rosebud.*"

His talent as a promoter also intact, Preminger in pre-opening interviews pointed up all the film's newsworthy elements. He talked frankly about firing Robert Mitchum and about Peter O'Toole's poor health. He expressed a sly-fox "astonishment" at all the fuss being made of John Lindsay's cameo appearance; and when asked if he had told the former mayor that he should be an actor rather than a politician, Preminger quipped, "I don't ever give this advice. But the difference is not so big."[63] He admitted that although "he qualified on many counts for the Arab blacklist, there have been no threats up to now, but don't give anyone ideas."[64] In disavowing *Rosebud*'s connection to the Patty Hearst kidnapping, he cannily under-lined its similarities. And in all the interviews he complimented Erik and predicted a bright future for his son. "He has legs. He can stand on his own talents as a writer, and even as director or producer," Otto boasted to Dorothy Manners in the *Los Angeles Herald Examiner* on March 23. "Elaine May thinks highly of him. Right now he is in California working on a pro-ject of his own, *The Return of Moriarty*." When Manners asked if he planned to turn over any of his future projects to Erik to direct or produce, Pre-minger answered, "I direct and produce ALL my films, Dorothy. You should know that."

The film opened (in New York on March 24, 1975, and in Los Angeles on April 30) to a clobbering reception both critically and commercially. In her *New Yorker* review on April 7 Penelope Gilliatt wrote, "It would have taken Hitchcock, perhaps . . . to divert our attention from the film's missing moral comprehension of the story. The enormous ethical questions raised are tempestuously ignored in the tantrums of narrative minutiae." "Absolutely nothing in the film itself evokes even remotely the fire, the pas-sion, fanaticism and commitment of the political forces which at this very moment [early 1975] could precipitate another global war," A. D. Murphy wrote in his *Variety* review on March 26. In the March 30 *Village Voice* Pre-minger advocate Andrew Sarris noted with evident disappointment that the filmmaker's "treatment of Arab terrorist plot material is by turns disconcert-ingly casual and coldly ambiguous."

Juggling three interconnected plot lines—the kidnapping, the media's handling of the kidnapping, and the search-and-rescue operation coordi-nated by intelligence officers in several countries—Preminger does not exert the same grip as in earlier films with a similarly serpentine format. Transi-tions are occasionally ragged, and at times it isn't clear where the action is taking place, whether in Paris or Berlin, Corsica or Israel. And because of the last-minute tinkering (unprecedented in Preminger's career), some plot details—how the location of the kidnappers and their hostages is discov-ered, how the hostages are rescued, how Sloat is captured—are almost deliri-ously far-fetched. But even with its gaps, Otto and Erik have constructed a narrative engine that hums along with workmanlike proficiency. Obviously flawed and assailable on many grounds, *Rosebud* is nonetheless a high-wire balancing act without a single dull moment. And throughout, sweeping camera movements remind the viewer of who is in charge. One dazzling setup is a moving shot that follows a car swerving along the Grand Cor-niche, the blue Mediterranean sparkling in the distance. The shot, which has no thematic relevance—one of the five young women is traveling with her mother to meet her friends aboard the *Rosebud*—is included for its own sake, as proof that the *metteur-en-scène* was still a master of his trade.

The real problem—and the reason why, in addition to its evident faults of scripting, performance, and direction, *Rosebud* remains beyond critical rehabilitation—is that the kidnappers are identified as Palestinian terrorists, and therefore the film raises significant issues that it radically shortchanges. It's as if the burden of assembling the vast narrative distracted Preminger from paying much attention to the pressing ideological concerns *behind* the plot. Far too little time is devoted to considering the political convictions that motivated the kidnapping. And yet, to rise above the charge of exploitation or to transcend the category it tumbles into, that of an ephemeral political thriller, the film needed to place the origins and ramifications of a terrorist act in a much more probing context. Still it must be noted that no one else at the time was willing to take on the subjects of the Israeli-Palestinian conflict or the international threat posed by Arab and Islamist terrorism. And in some of its details the film is prescient. Sloat issuing his mad utterances from secret desert caverns eerily anticipates Osama bin Laden. And the blunt, powerful ending, in which another terrorist group hijacks a plane in retaliation for the capture of the kidnappers, makes the appallingly timely point that terrorism may be uncontainable.

"After *Rosebud*, it was very hard with Otto," Erik said.

> I didn't stay on for the editing, I just couldn't. I bought a book, *The Return of Moriarty*, to adapt into a screenplay, and I worked on it out of my home. I would see Otto, but it wasn't easy. When *Rosebud* opened in Los Angeles, I was in New York; when it opened in New York, I was in Los Angeles. The film's failure affected our personal relations. I think my father blamed me in part for the way it turned out, and I blamed him. We were both right. It might have been smarter not to have made the film, but I can't say now, so many years later, that I wished I had done something else.[65]

(In 1980, five years after the film had come and gone in ignominy, Ted Gershuny published an account of its making called *Soon to Be a Major Motion Picture: The Anatomy of an All-Star, Big-Budget, Multimillion-Dollar Disaster.* "To one man I owe the existence of this book," Gershuny stated in his acknowledgments. "I watched him as closely as possible for almost a year. Whatever emotion I saw in him, I never saw fear. I wish to thank Otto Preminger. Who hid nothing." Gershuny's prevailing theme is that from the beginning the project was on a collision course with artistic and financial disaster and that everyone, including the bemused director, whom Gershuny presents as often addled and only fitfully in command, knew it. "Ted's book should be a mandatory text in every film production class," Erik said. "The book tells the truth. Hope, who is absolutely loyal to Otto, and who has never said a critical thing about Otto's filmmaking, felt the book was a terrible betrayal. But everybody knew that the book was being written as we shot."[66] "Gershuny was not on our team, he was on Erik's team," Hope responded. "The book's chaotic form reflects the chaos of the content. But Otto was not as indecisive or as disorganized as Gershuny makes him out to be here. *Rosebud* is not a good film, and I felt then and continue to feel now that Otto ruined his reputation by doing the film for Erik. Certainly, as the book presents it, this is *not* the way a film should be made; I would argue, however, that this was *not* the way *Rosebud* was made. The book is misleading."[67])

"Would you like to work for me?" Preminger asked Ken Kaufman after *Rosebud* wrapped. "You'll stay with me in London and go back to New York with me." Although he knew that he had caught Preminger "beyond the tail end of his career—by 1975, he was just hanging on, grasping at straws," Kaufman accepted the offer. He knew he had the essential requirement of working for Otto: he understood him. "Otto had fired me during filming in Paris, with thousands of Parisians watching. 'What are you doing?' he had said, when he saw me standing around; he thought I should be busy every second. 'Go home, I never want to see you again.' But I knew he didn't want me to go home, he just wanted to make a point."

After returning from London with Preminger, Kaufman quickly settled into an office routine.

> Otto would call first thing every morning. "What's going on?" You could *not* say "Nothing." You had to come up with something just to get him thinking. He walked to work every day from East Sixty-fourth (and he never passed a beggar without giving money). There were a lot of visitors and hangers-on, and many, many calls. He spent a lot of time each day on the speakerphone. Lunches would be at "21," Giovanni's, Romeo Salta, or La Côte Basque. At most, he'd drink one glass of wine at lunch. In the afternoon I sat around with him, and we often talked about the news of the day. He would bring out brandy, and when he started to drink he would get red in the face and start to sweat. My job, I saw quickly, was to keep him on an even keel, to get his mind going and to keep him happy so he

wouldn't get into a horrible mood. A lot of the job was hand-holding, and he appreciated it. Otto was so charming and persuasive, and so wearing. Working for him was 24/7.[68]

Preminger at seventy, with no thought of retiring, continued to pursue and announce projects as he always had. He glanced through publishers' galleys and kept up with current events, sifting them for kernels of a movie scenario. "Read this book, and write a synopsis," he'd tell Kaufman frequently. "After I'd write a synopsis, he would attack it." The most significant project to be developed during Kaufman's tenure, and the one that got closest to getting produced, was a two-hour television movie based on the life and landmark legal decisions of Supreme Court Justice Hugo L. Black. "This will be the first dramatic treatment of the high court," Preminger announced in *Variety* on June 19, 1975, only three months after he had overseen the domestic and international openings of *Rosebud.* "Justice Black fascinated me because he started out as an archconservative and became one of the most liberal and noteworthy justices in the annals of the court."

To prepare a script he hired Howard Koch, the cowriter of *Casablanca.* When he was dissatisfied with Koch's work, he hired Max Lerner to rewrite. "There was no doubt in Otto's mind that he would make this movie," Kaufman observed. " 'We must shoot in the Supreme Court,' he said. 'You're not allowed to do that,' I told him. 'That's ridiculous! Get me Chief Justice Berger on the phone.' Within thirty seconds Berger was on the phone. 'Mr. Berger, I would like to come to see you,' Otto said, with the greatest charm. Max Lerner, Otto, and I took a shuttle to a 9:30 Monday morning meeting where we were told, decisively, 'You can't shoot here.' I think Otto wanted to prove to me he could get to Berger."[69]

Perhaps frustrated by not being able to film the story "where it happened," Preminger abandoned the project. In February 1976 he hired Eleanor Perry to write a screenplay of a Graham Greene novel, *A Burnt-Out Case.* In June he announced that Ring Lardner Jr. would adapt *Blood on Wheels,* the story of Dr. Norman Bethune, a Canadian surgeon who became Mao Tse-tung's best friend. In September he acquired the rights to *The Story of My Life,* by Moshe Dayan, and three months later with his screenwriter J. P. Miller he traveled to Israel for a ten-day scouting expedition and to meet with General Dayan, who was to be technical adviser on the film. The visitors also met with a number of prominent government officials, attended the Knesset, and appeared at lunches and dinners where they were the guests of honor. It may have seemed like old times, but the film was never made.

One project started during the post-*Rosebud* era that did come to fruition was one Preminger was not really committed to: writing a memoir. "Otto knew he wasn't a writer and he really did not want to do the book," as Hope recalled.[70] And as Mark observed, "My father left no papers because he didn't write; he didn't take notes, he didn't write memos or letters. He talked, in person and on the phone. And so he did not 'write' his autobiography: he taped it, and he had a lot of trouble with it."[71] "I would sit there on Saturday mornings as Otto dictated the book to June Callwood, a Canadian writer who did not want to have her name on the book," Kaufman said. "I couldn't help noticing that he was always the hero of all the stories he told June."[72] With a jacket designed by Saul Bass—on the front is a photo of the back of Otto's famous bald, ovoid head; on the back is a photo of Otto, face front, smiling pleasantly, his knowing, incisive, bemused blue eyes lighting up for the camera—Doubleday published *Preminger: An Autobiography* in April 1977. "Otto's book is unreadable," Ingo claimed. Reviews were more tolerant, but lukewarm. "He is clearly a resourceful and clever man, even if he is the first to say so," Christopher Lehmann-Haupt wrote in the *New York Times* on April 26, 1977. "Preminger shows no interest in the art or technique of filmmaking except to insist and demonstrate that he has always been in total charge of his productions," Kenneth Turan wrote in *American Film* in May 1977. "No one can accuse Mr. Preminger of being dull in this account of his progress up every ladder that has ever been set before him," he added.

The book is indeed egocentric (isn't that to be expected of an autobiography?) and insistently self-congratulatory. As a memoirist Preminger is defensive, disorganized, sketchy, sometimes fast and loose with facts and chronology, and far from candid—there is no mention of his affair with Dorothy Dandridge, for instance. Yet throughout, in clever turns of phrase and many astute asides about the temperament of co-workers and the craft of filmmaking, there are generous samplings of Preminger's wit and perspicacity.

By the summer of 1977, Ken Kaufman felt it was long past the time for him to move on. "I'd sit in the office on Saturdays as Otto read a book," Kaufman said.

> It got oppressive. I began to feel I shouldn't be there because it wasn't doing anything for my career. Otto had started appearing on cable access shows instead of Mike Douglas, and he couldn't seem to tell the difference. I thought he was beginning to make a fool of himself. And at the end of my tenure, he was starting to lose his memory, and to dodder. Momentarily, he would have no memory,

then this would be followed by moments of great lucidity. *I* was his memory. He had me around to remind him. He was out of touch with the modern era, and didn't know it, and I was beginning to feel I was out of touch too. He had no clue, no clue at all, that time had passed him by; he never acted as if "I'm a declining director off my game." And nobody, certainly not Hope, who never had one critical thing to say about Otto or his work, would tell him.

When Kaufman began to date one of the interns at 711, Otto was displeased.

He had a strict rule: no fooling around in the office. The first year Pam and I kept our relationship a secret, but after Otto found out that we were living together, it was never the same. Pam got another job, and then we were married. Otto sensed independence in me that he didn't like. He really did take great pleasure in discovering young people and in promoting them; but then he felt he had ownership rights. He was totally demanding, petulant, and childlike—and *nobody* ever called him on his cruelty. I don't think he could get away with it now. I *had* to move on. I had to think of my own career.

(Kaufman is a successful television producer.)

Nearly thirty years after he had been a Preminger employee, Ken Kaufman in a voice choked with feeling said, "I loved Otto, and I hated him."[73]

In 1978, as he continued in press releases to tout his projects on Moshe Dayan and Dr. Norman Bethune, Preminger signed with a lecture bureau that billed him as "America's greatest director." "With the same candor that has characterized his life, Otto Preminger—director, actor, producer, writer—exposes himself along with an impressive line-up of show business people in his unique lecture series," the catalog announced. "Preminger reveals the funny, outrageous, and often exasperating moments of his career, and his association with the eccentric, the gracious, the wealthy, the egomaniacal. . . . This program is a unique chance to talk with Otto Preminger. It's not just a lecture—it's a dialogue between Preminger and the audience. If you ask the right questions you could hear some pretty shocking answers. He makes no bones about naming enemies or exalting his friends."

About the same time Otto also began to teach at the Loft Theatre School, run by Elaine Gold, in Greenwich Village. "Joe [José] Ferrer, who was teaching for us, got us to Otto," Gold recalled.

He taught acting and some directing—scene study. He was with us for three years, until he got ill. He got a hundred dollars a week, the same as Joe. "If Joe is getting it, why shouldn't I?" he asked. He was a good teacher, and he could spot talent right away. He was not articulate in making comments, though, and toward the end there would be long pauses. Although names would elude him, he never rambled on. He made short shrift of the people he felt didn't work hard, but the students liked him. He was always courtly with the women. We picked him up at his town house to drive him down to the classes, and he was always *exactly* on time, and always beautifully dressed—sharp and crisp. I thought of myself as the chauffeur, and I always felt Otto turned our old Chevy into a Dusenberg. One day he brought along with him another European gentleman in a vest—"My brother Ingo." When I asked Ingo what he did, he said, "I'm a producer." Otto laughed. "A producer he calls himself: he produced one lousy film." Otto wasn't joking.

He always introduced me as "Ellen"—it was never Elaine— "Gold, who runs the best acting school in the country, but she's too fat." He always made me laugh. Although he called me by my first name, his very bearing demanded "Mr. Preminger." I'm surprised I didn't say "Dr." He seemed to like what we were doing, and frankly I was surprised when he didn't leave any money to the Loft.[74]

As he kept busy teaching and on the lecture circuit, against all the odds Preminger was able to put through a deal for another film. Early in 1978, prepublication, he acquired the rights to a novel by Graham Greene called *The Human Factor,* an ironic wrong-man story with an interracial romance that seems to have been made to order for an Otto Preminger film. After a leak is discovered in the African section of the British Secret Service, an agent named Davis is targeted and then eliminated. But it is Davis's partner Castle, a burnt-out bloke with no political convictions, who has been passing secrets to the Russians because a Communist had helped him and his new black wife escape from Kenya.

Preminger asked Greene, who had adapted *Saint Joan* for him in 1956, to write the screenplay, but the novelist was not well at the time, and claiming "he was too close to the material," turned him down.[75] The director then hired a leading British playwright, Tom Stoppard, who quickly wrote a script that Preminger just as quickly accepted. When for the first time in his career Otto was not able to find backing from a major studio, through business contacts in London he reached a group of Saudi Arabian financiers who promised to deliver his projected budget of $7.5 million. On that expectation Otto assembled a cast of British players including John Gielgud, Nicol Williamson, Derek Jacobi, Robert Morley, Ann Todd, and his good friend Richard Attenborough; hired a British crew; and began to search for locations in London and Kenya.

"When Otto came over to London for preproduction in the spring of 1979, I knew his executive producer and asked to be introduced," Val Robins said.

> Otto hired me to help out the production manager, who it turned out wasn't suited to him. He fired her, and I became the production manager as well as the associate producer. From the beginning the project was fraught with problems, and for me it was an initiation by fire. Otto was frustrated and disappointed that after all his years in the business no one was supporting him and that he had had to find outside financing. But he knew he would complete the film no matter what. All the cast and crew realized that this might be the last Otto Preminger film, and we felt, watching him work, that we were looking at a brilliant filmmaker even then. He knew exactly what he wanted. He cut as he went along, and he rarely made a lot of takes, and then only because an actor had fluffed his lines. He was precise, quick, and punctual, and he was *not,* as some have claimed, suffering from Alzheimer's. But he did keep to his reputation for firing people: we went through first assistant directors as if they were going out of style, and I was fired twice, but fortunately rehired three times.

During the first six weeks of shooting in London, from the end of May to early July, Preminger's main challenge was monitoring his temperamental star, Nicol Williamson, who according to Robins had been "fired from his previous film and was uninsurable."[76] "Nicol was surly to everyone but Otto, whom he respected," Hope said.

> But he was rude and nasty to me. After the first wardrobe people quit, Otto hired me, and Nicol, who thought he was God's gift— "Is my stomach flat enough?" he'd ask, looking into a mirror— expected me to hand-wash all his Turnbull and Asser shirts. He warned me that his shirts were not to have a single wrinkle, and he would not leave his hotel room until I sent his shoes to be cleaned in the hotel barbershop. "I will not do this until I am properly taken

care of," he said. He was a mean drunk who beat up all his former   ,
wives, but he did not drink on the job.[77]

As Val Robins recalled,

Near the end of the London shoot the money Otto was expecting
had not come through yet—Otto sold a painting in order to pay the
company—and at a company meeting Nicol said it was all my fault
they didn't have financing. The cast and crew had to find somebody
to blame, and I was it. I accepted that role. "You're not to blame
Otto Preminger," I told them. Nicol told Otto that they must continue; he couldn't afford a disaster because he had been fired from
his previous film. A few days later, over an incident involving petty
cash, Nicol actually struck me. I said nothing to Otto, who would
have been horrified.

Preminger also had trouble with the model Iman, making her acting
debut as Castle's wife. "Iman really wanted the part, and she offered to do it
for nothing when she saw Otto in New York," Val Robins said. "Somehow
Otto, who liked her personally, believed he could get a performance out of
her."[78] "Nicol will be very good with the girl," Preminger told a reporter
during the London shoot. "She is very black. He is very white. Both are very
tall. It is my choice, my intuition. It's the only way I can work."[79] But on the
set Iman's East African speech patterns, and her evident struggles with saying her lines fluently, began to irritate him, and he started in. Iman shouted
back, however. "Otto knew as we were shooting that Iman was giving a terrible performance—she couldn't even speak the language," Val Robins said.
"And from her point of view, Iman believes Otto ruined her chances for an
acting career."

Richard Attenborough, playing (beautifully) an uptight security officer
who investigates the leak, proved a terrific trouper, as he had been on *Rosebud*. "He did the role as a favor to Otto," Robins recalled, "and though he
was about to direct *Gandhi* and making our film was not one of his happiest
experiences, he was a delight, so calm and even at all times. Otto was
tremendously grateful to him."

After Robins flew the company to Nairobi, she discovered there was no
money. "I would never have flown a crew to Africa if the accountant hadn't
told me it was all right," Robins said.

The crew—there were about forty-five, including our caterers—
told me the checks were bouncing. I asked them to consider contin-

uing to work, but they decided not to. They struck. They were paid their per diems, and they became tourists. To pay his crew Otto sold another painting. In a way the delay was good because we had sent Nicol Williamson to Africa early to get a tan, and he burned his lips so we couldn't have started on time anyway. Once we were ready to start, we finished in Nairobi in five days. But we did owe money.

The Nairobi Hotel, where the *Human Factor* company had been in residence from July 18 to August 9, sued Preminger for paying $21,783 in worthless checks and for walking out on the remaining $10,021. "It was horrific to Otto that not everyone was paid until some time afterward," Robins said.[80]

News of Preminger's financial difficulties generated publicity of a kind the filmmaker had never had to deal with before. Privately mortified but in public continuing to play Otto the indomitable, on August 22 he called a press conference in London, held not at the Dorchester but at the far less imposing Sheraton Park Tower in Knightsbridge. Otto revealed the identities of the three Saudi financiers who had failed to fulfill the contract they had signed with him on March 20 to ante up $7.5 million. To keep the production going he said he had begun to finance the film himself, and at the time of the conference claimed to have spent $2.5 million of his own money. Preminger estimated that he would be able to reduce the total production cost to "about $5.5 million."

When *The Human Factor* wrapped two days later, Preminger's financial problems were far from over. The next day an article in the *Hollywood Reporter* asserted that "in a desperate bid to cover the costs of his trouble-torn production, Preminger was negotiating the sale of several paintings, including a Picasso, to pay off cast and crew. But Equity has served a writ for $180,000 on Preminger's Wheel Productions Company for cast salaries, and a second $100,000 for fees for Attenborough and others. An irate driver for the crew claims he is owed over $5,000 and has started his own legal action." In all, as the trade paper claimed, twenty actors had sued for money owed. Preminger's "problems," as the *Reporter* speculated, "must put his next production, *Blood on Wheels,* due to be filmed in Canada and China next year, in some jeopardy."

In Los Angeles in mid-December to publicize the film's opening for Academy Award consideration, Otto tried to strike a philosophical pose. "It's the first time I've ever made a film without a studio, and I ended up spending my own money, but I can't complain," he said. "I had complete autonomy to make the movie, and now MGM is distributing it through United Artists in the U.S. and Canada, Rank is releasing in England, and there are other distributors in other parts the world."[81]

"I sold my beautiful home in the South of France, and two of my beautiful Matisses," Preminger announced ruefully a few weeks later. "I think the movie will make money, then I'll buy my two Matisses back, and two more besides," he said.[82] By early 1980, when *The Human Factor* was released across the country, Otto was able to pay off most of his creditors, and he set up a special bank account from which all proceeds from the film would be used to honor the remaining creditors. But his financial problems with the film were to linger for several years. The modest profits were not sufficient to pay off all the creditors, and the expected sale to television never happened. In a British court, on January 28, 1984, the remaining creditors sued him. The case was finally settled three days later when the parties reached "a private settlement."[83]

Otto Preminger's final film had a warm reception from most critics. "The film must be accounted a triumph for the director," Arthur Schlesinger wrote in the March 29 *Saturday Review*. "It is his finest in twenty years, unfolding with emphatic pace and force at the same time, with the controlled understatement that makes every gesture and inflection so much more telling." "One of the best Preminger films in years," agreed Vincent Canby in the *New York Times* on February 8. "It is so good in so many ways that I think it's possible to say that . . . its weaknesses are more those of Mr. Greene than of Mr. Preminger and Mr. Stoppard." "A lucidly impressive return to form for the 73-year-old director," noted David Ansen in the February 11 *Newsweek*. "It's not really a thriller at all, but an understated, uncompromising dissection of an event: an anatomy of the murder of a soul." Only a poison-pen review from Rex Reed broke the chorus of praise. "Under Preminger's decrepit direction, it turns out to be not only the dullest espionage movie ever made, but the dullest movie ever made—period," he wrote in the February 8 *New York Daily News*. "*The Human Factor* is Preminger's first film in five years. With any luck, it will be his last." ("My father never questioned himself or his abilities, but despite what he said he did have a fragile ego about critics, and in particular he thought Rex Reed was unfair," Mark recalled.)[84]

While Preminger's ordeal in completing the film had been widely reported, the mostly affirmative reviews were by no means a sympathy vote. By any measure his handling of *The Human Factor* demonstrates a serene command of the medium. The formality that had been an element of Preminger's style from the beginning—his work had never exuded a youthful, jaunty spirit—attains, in this valedictory project, the assurance of an old master, an elder statesman certain of his gifts who has no need of showing off. Preminger's approach was never more lean, even, in a sense, more "barren," than here. Long passages of dialogue, as in Castle's climactic confession scene in which he tells his wife he has been a double agent, are played in long takes in front of a detached, unmoving camera. As it pursues its own cool and rigorous course, *The Human Factor* is a kind of zero degree cinema, almost avant-garde in its austerity.

Reversing his procedure on *Rosebud*, where character is sacrificed for narrative momentum, Preminger approaches Graham Greene's spy story primarily as a character study, "an anatomy of the murder of a soul," in David Ansen's fine phrase. The settings reflect the blank façade with which Castle confronts the world. The modest house that Castle and his family live in reveals nothing about the inhabitants. The Secret Service pursues its masked endeavors in anonymous, brightly lighted offices. Castle and a few colleagues attend a cheerless strip club where they watch the show with glazed expressions. In the finale Castle is relocated to a shabby apartment in Moscow. Some reviewers cited the set—"Moscow" is a painted backdrop glimpsed through a smudged window—as evidence of Preminger's financial crisis. But the film doesn't need to take us to Moscow. It isn't the place that matters but the irony of Castle's discovery once he is in Moscow that the agency had all along had a mole in Russia and so he had been releasing

Maurice Castle (Nicol Williamson), a burnt-out case, and a Russian agent (Boris Isarov), in a decrepit apartment in "Moscow" in the last scene of Preminger's final film, *The Human Factor*.

information to the Russians that they already had. In the last shot, as abrupt as the ending of *Rosebud,* Castle's phone connection to his wife in London is terminated, presumably forever.

As he must, Nicol Williamson carries the film, and without any of the surface tics of "great acting" that Preminger had no patience for. His pinched manner of speaking, his collapsed body language and hangdog expression suggest a character burdened by wounds he cannot reveal: Castle is a defeated man with something to hide. Most reviewers as well as Preminger thought Iman's performance was amateurish. But no, the director's instinctive sense that she could play the role proved to be correct. Iman is indeed a cold fish, but a hot-blooded actress would have broken the frame; Iman's minimalism—she suggests just enough feeling to convey her character's plight—is to the point. Also to the point is top-billed John Gielgud in a cameo as an intelligence agency higher-up with a sublimely opaque expression.

If *Rosebud* was Otto's gift to Erik, *The Human Factor* was his gift to himself. No wonder he sacrificed so much to ensure the film's completion. For his own sense of honor he had no choice but to finish the film, to prove that he could.

NINETEEN

After the Fall

On July 22, 1980, as he was crossing Fifth Avenue at Fifty-fifth Street in lunch-hour traffic, Preminger was struck down by a taxicab. "He had been hit from the back and was thrown onto the hood of the cab," recalled Lewis Chambers, an agent with an office at 663 Fifth Avenue who witnessed the incident.

> The fact that he was able to get up at all was through sheer force of will. When his body hit the pavement, the impact was ferocious. Outwardly he only suffered a tiny cut on the back of the head, and he wasn't bleeding. But when he was lying on his back on the street I was sure he was dead. His eyes rolled back; his right hand was shaking. It was beastly hot, and I thought this man will be dead any second. From a distance I didn't know who it was, but when I knelt down I recognized Otto Preminger and I felt obligated to stay. He got up, with my assistance and that of someone else, who knew him, and we pleaded with him to stay for medical attention, or to wait for the ambulance that had been called. "Why did you do this to me?" he asked the taxi driver. "Who stole my necktie?" he asked when he discovered it was missing. He walked off with the other gentleman. I later found out that they went to have lunch at La Car-avelle. A few days later Louis Nizer's office called to ask if I'd be will-

ing to testify; I was, because Preminger had not been responsible; he had not run into the traffic. A week or so later the Nizer office called back to say that the taxi insurance company had settled.[1]

"After he was struck by the taxi, Otto was still able to walk to and from the office," Hope said. "But he was getting frail. I had sensed that on location in Africa for *The Human Factor,* when I noticed that he had trouble getting up a small hill. We found out later that year he had Parkinson's, which caused him to dodder. One night during the winter after the accident he got lost coming home from the office and turned up freezing cold in the snow. I was terrified. We went to doctors, but they couldn't find anything."[2]

Refusing to announce retirement, Preminger continued to go to his office at 711 on a daily basis, and still continued, periodically, to issue press releases about future plans. "I was hired to do Otto's next picture," Val Robins said,

> and waiting for that to fall into place I decided to make myself useful. At first we were busy doing promotion and tours for *The Human Factor,* and then, when no other film was forthcoming, and it became clear that there would be no other film, I thought a legacy can't be allowed to die. I helped Otto to amalgamate his six or seven different companies into Otto Preminger Films, one entity, with Hope as president, and Otto appointed me to keep it going. I knew I wanted to make a documentary about him. [*Anatomy of a Director,* Robins's documentary, was released in 1990.] I worked with Otto for the last five years of his life, and he became like a father to me. Yes, he was a difficult man, but a unique human being, and I loved him.[3]

Val Robins ran Otto Preminger Films from 1986 until the summer of 2005; since then, Otto's daughter Victoria has been president and treasurer. Hope is chairman, and Mark is vice-president and secretary.

In November 1980, as an in-house project at the Loft Theatre, where he would continue to teach through 1981, Preminger directed one last play, *The Killer Thing,* a drama by William Packard about a supposed mass murderer who hides out in the tarpaper shack of a hermit. "I had twenty or thirty scripts every week," Elaine Gold recalled. "I'd read a few pages at the beginning and at the end to judge whether it was fit to send to any of my directors. This one, by a poet and Harvard graduate, scared me, and I sent it to my three directors, Joe Ferrer, Joe Stein, and Otto. If anybody had the nerve to do it, it would have been Otto. He liked it right away, and put it together so fast. He saw it as a major motion picture. I thought it was twenty years ahead of its time."[4]

John Martello, who played the hermit and is now the executive director of the Players Club in New York, recalled,

> Otto cast me on the spot, by instinct. He was exactly the opposite of a Method director, and in some ways it was refreshing. He had a unique way of rehearsing—only what had been memorized. "You will go home and learn some lines," he told us. When all the lines had been memorized, he said we were ready to open. When he started to scream at me in an early rehearsal, I don't know why but I started to laugh. And then he started to laugh, and we got along just fine after that. He walked very slowly, and at each rehearsal he would make an entrance walking to a thronelike chair. The second he was seated he expected us to begin rehearsing. If there was any real direction it was about movement and placement—he directed us as if we were making a film. His comments were about blocking, not about acting values or theme or character. He talked about the future, about his Hugo Black project in particular. And he thought our project would lead to a major Broadway production and then a film. At the time I thought the reason Ingo came around was because of plans Otto had for the film. He told me that for the film he wanted James Cagney for my part: he was thinking in those terms. He still had a sense of who he was, very much so: he was Otto Preminger. I never got any feeling that he was near the end. I got to work with a legend, and I'll always be grateful for that.[5]

Directing *The Killer Thing* at the Loft on Twelfth Street and University Place in Greenwich Village was Preminger's last job. "After the play Otto was so frustrated about not being able to get another deal together," Hope recalled.

> He became increasingly frail. Doctors told me the bash on his head in the taxi accident had given him a concussion, and with the Parkinson's his hands started shaking more and he began to lose strength in his legs. From about the end of 1981 on, he didn't look well and he got more and more distant. He would stare into space. Gradually he began to lose his ambition to get a deal—I think he knew he couldn't do it. Doctors didn't think any antidepressant

would help. But for the last six years of his life we thought a miracle would happen. I so wanted him to have a rage attack, an "Otto attack," as we called it. I kept wishing, "If only he would yell at somebody, at anybody, at the kids, at me." I didn't care who it was, but he didn't. Instead, he just sat there, and in the last four or five years there were no rages at all. His long-term memory was good; sometimes he thought he was in Vienna at the Josefstadt Theater giving notes to his actors. But his short-term memory got weaker and weaker. He knew the people who were around him every day, but sometimes he'd call Mark "Ingo" and then say, "I mean Mark."

But he did begin to lose his memory, and his conversation became very simple. I know people said he had Alzheimer's, but our doctors never made the diagnosis of Alzheimer's. I would admit it if they had. People also said he was an alcoholic, and he wasn't. He enjoyed drinking, but he was never a falling-down drunk. As he got older, he did not drink more, but he wasn't able to hold it as well. Erik kept pouring liquor when he was with him, maybe he felt it was easier to talk to him that way.

As Otto grew ever more feeble, Hope investigated a nursing home on Manhattan's Upper East Side, but decided she would "never be able to send" her husband there or "to any nursing home." "Otto didn't want nurses in the house because he still wanted independence, and he wouldn't eat anything I hadn't cooked," Hope said. Throughout her husband's long decline, Hope would leave Otto's side only infrequently, to meet a friend for lunch, perhaps, or to get her hair done, or to sit in the back of the St. Thomas Church on Fifth Avenue. "I was raised Episcopalian, but didn't go to church when I was married to Otto, who believed in God but not in the ritual. He knew it brought me great peace, though. I needed my religion to get through Otto's dying, and after his death I went back to the church."[6]

"As my father began his gradual deterioration, my mother became his caretaker," Mark recalled. "During the last four years, when he really couldn't be left alone, she almost never left the house, except once in a while when Louise, our housekeeper, was there. It was a role reversal: now she was taking care of him, and she made that transition so gracefully. She never once complained, or resented it. During those last four difficult years her devotion went above and beyond."[7]

Hope was disappointed that "only a few stalwarts came to visit. Erik came only infrequently. I felt Otto was somewhat forgotten when he was no longer in the limelight. There weren't many calls; of the Hollywood group,

Burgess Meredith was the most loyal. Otto wasn't aware of what was happening, and that was a blessing. He didn't like to discuss human weakness, his own or anyone else's, but he would have been so hurt."[8]

Those who paid visits to Otto Preminger on East Sixty-fourth Street in his last years found a man radically diminished by illness. Traces of "Otto the Terrible," the fearsome independent filmmaker who had rowed with censors, studio czars, actors, and crew, grew ever fainter as the great lion was transformed into a lamb, becalmed, detached, and finally absent. "Hope was a friend of mine and when I heard Otto was ill I went to see him," Patricia Neal recalled. "When he came down the stairs, Hope said to him, 'You remember Pat Neal, don't you?' But he barely did. He was concerned with his hearing aids. 'Hope, I'm having trouble with these,' he said; and the hearing aids got more attention than I did. It saddened me to see him this way, but I could tell on this visit something I already knew: Hope loved him, really and truly."[9]

Peter Bogdanovich had several encounters with Preminger during the final years.

> In the summer of 1980, when I knew he was having trouble getting a picture, I met Otto at "21," where I was having dinner with Frank Sinatra, Audrey Hepburn, and Ben Gazzara. Otto came over to our table to say hello, but I sensed he felt awkward, as if he somehow wasn't sure he had permission to be there. He was not his usual blustery self. Frank was nice to him, but not all that interested in talking to him. Otto seemed a little foggy or distracted. A few years later I visited him on East Sixty-fourth at a time when I wasn't in great shape myself. He was wearing slippers and a ratty cardigan, and he shuffled. He hardly remembered anything about pictures, but he kept smiling and I did feel he was happy to see me. He seemed so much smaller, and the house looked rundown. When he walked me to the door I had the thought I wouldn't see him again.[10]

Moments of the old Otto would sometimes reappear, however, as in Eva Monley's last visit with him.

> Otto and I hadn't ended well, when I left on *Rosebud.* Because Hope had asked me, I became involved, briefly, with the African locations for *The Human Factor.* I had to go to meetings with people who were owed money, and I couldn't deal with it—something was

wrong. When I visited him at home a year or two later, he was lying in bed and really seemed quite ill. But when I walked into his room, he called out my name in a loud voice, and the way he said "Eva!" I could tell that he liked me. And I could also tell that beneath all that bluster Otto was a softie.[11]

"The last two years Otto started having little ministrokes and he would fall," Hope said. "And then the last year he was in a wheelchair. Toward the end I had a big burly woman from Jamaica who could pick Otto up from the floor when he fell. And then we found out he had colon cancer, which wasn't painful and we hadn't known about it. The specialist we went to told us he wouldn't live more than two years, but he died three weeks later."[12]

Otto Preminger died, at eighty-one, on April 23, 1986. In a twenty-page will signed on November 17, 1983, and in force at the time of his death, Otto left the vast majority of his estate—the amount was listed as "more than $500,000," a category indicating that the estate could have been worth much more than that—to his widow. Hope received one-half of the estate outright, while the remaining half, after the payment of debts, was put in trust for her. At the time of his death Preminger's three children received no money, and they will receive none until Hope's demise, at which point the remainder of the trust is to be divided equally among Erik, Mark, and Victoria. When Erik protested the will, the already festering ill feelings between him and the rest of the family resulted in a rupture, and other than legal communications he has had no contact with any other Preminger since his father's death.

Despite the peculiar terms of his will, Otto Preminger was a family man through and through, deeply devoted to all the members of his family, who, in turn, retain loving memories of him. To do that, each of them has had to come to terms with his "Otto attacks." "Otto had tantrums, and nobody could deny it," Hope said.

But he was not a cruel man, he really wasn't. He was an impatient man who couldn't bear it when he felt people hadn't tried. But when he would start to scream, the crew would see me wince, which happened more than I care to remember. *He* enjoyed getting it off his chest, but he didn't realize the effect his tantrums had on others; he just wasn't tuned in to what the screaming could do to people. I wonder if he had seen a tape of himself turning red how he would have reacted. I used to wish, for everybody's sake, that Otto wouldn't scream—it would have been so much easier if he hadn't.

But without the rages he would not have been Otto. I was seldom "it," but I was sometimes, and when I was he yelled at me just as loudly as he yelled at others. On *The Cardinal* I quit three times, and got rehired each time, and I was "it" a few times on *Skidoo* as well. He didn't give it much thought that he had enemies, and he always professed not to care if he got bad reviews. Otto enjoyed playing up the persona he had created, a persona that could not have worked in this era. But he paid a price for it during his lifetime, and as I am well aware, and it hurts me, he has continued to pay a price for it since his death.

At home he did *not* rage, and he was not tyrannical. He was a loving husband and father. He was my best friend and I was crazy about him. I was very fortunate to have had this life with Otto.[13]

"Yes, my father yelled, especially at airports, rarely at us," Vicky Preminger said.

And then, after he screamed, the anger disappeared and he never held a grudge. I'm not one of these bitter children of a famous parent. I had a wonderful childhood. My father was a doting parent, really a pushover, who spoiled my brother and me terribly, and yet we had a totally normal childhood. And today, my brother and I are stable, normal people. My father gave us our sense of self, which is the sense that he had. He was very secure and never cared what other people thought of him.

Although we are twins, my brother doesn't look like me at all. You'd never know we are related. We get along, but we're totally opposite. Mark has my mother's temperament—they're both pacifists. People say I'm like my father. I'm good at managing my time, and I have his coloring.

My father had great energy. He would get up at 4 a.m. because he was so interested in what he was reading, and he'd tell me with such excitement about a book he was reading that he thought would make a good film. He had terrific optimism, and until he got very ill in the last two or three years of his life he always believed he was going to get the next project made. He lived in the moment—he would never chat about the past, about Vienna or Max Reinhardt or about my grandparents. And he could handle the future. And how he loved to eat: at "21," at La Caravelle, every Sunday night with Louis Nizer at Trader Vic's in the Plaza Hotel. What pleasure a tin of caviar would give him. I'm proud to be the daughter of Otto Preminger.[14]

"He was a different person at home than his public reputation, but we did see some of the temper at times," Mark said.

With my sister he had a more volatile relationship than with me. He did not approve of our riding horses and would blow up at that. He couldn't control the excessiveness of his explosions, and as he got older he had even a little less control. It was not really upsetting to see it, however, because we accepted the flare-ups as part of who he was. Sometimes he played up to "Otto the Ogre." I think he sometimes enjoyed the effect his explosions had. Sometimes the blowups were self-serving, and for a purpose. As an example: I remember once when I drove up from college [Johns Hopkins], I went directly to his office to visit him, and when I got there I was told he was at lunch at La Caravelle. I went to the restaurant just to say hello, but he told me to pull up a chair and to join him and his guests. The maître d', however, came over to say I wasn't dressed properly. My father would have none of that. He raised his voice, the maître d' backed off, and I stayed for lunch. My father would always defend his family: there I was, I would have lunch with him, and that was that.

He was a terrific father whose love for us kids was unequivocal. He didn't push us, but gave us pure emotional support. If you came home with a bad grade he was accepting. My sister, who is much brighter than I am, had two majors at Smith. She went to law school and is now a very successful lawyer. I was always very goal-oriented, as Otto was, and I knew at eight I wanted to be a doctor. From the start my father supported me completely—he never pushed me to take after him. He had a very secure ego and he didn't see what I did as in any way a reflection of him. At home he never boasted, or told stories to make himself seem bigger, and he never reflected on the past. I hadn't been aware of any of the incidents I read about in his autobiography.

He wasn't like the fathers of any of my friends—he wasn't interested in baseball, or in an "American way of life." But he loved the fact that he *was* an American and not an Austrian. He admired the American legal system and was enamored of its procedures. He truly believed in the Constitution, and in the country's founding principles.

If people, who see what they want to, want to see the ogre and the bully, then they will. He was a controversial figure, as all of us were well aware, and he lived his life the way he wanted to. There is nothing not to be proud of.[15]

Although he did not have the same experience as the twins of having grown up with Otto as his father, Erik agreed that offstage, "Otto Preminger" was banished. Arriving late, Erik claimed "a unique relationship" with Otto. "I worked alongside him, unlike Mark and Vicky, and that was important because that work was his life. He was fulfilled by it. Of course he expressed interest in what the kids were doing, but it wasn't the same interest as he had for his work. But there is no question about it: he loved each of us. We were his family, and to him family really counted. And in the final reckoning, it was more important than anything else."[16]

At this writing, more than twenty years after Preminger's death, Hope lives in New York, where for many years she has served on the boards of numerous charitable organizations and is an active member of her church. Mark, who lives with his wife Michelle, a doctor, and their two children, Evan and Kimberly, in New Jersey, is a noted cardiologist. Victoria, who lives in Los Angeles, is a lawyer, an active horsewoman, and president of Otto Preminger Films. Remarried, Erik lives in Northern California. "I have a life with no glamour but great comfort," he said. "I'm not writing, but doing consulting and entrepreneurial work. When I was in the Army I showed great aptitude with computers, and I have opened my own editing studios."[17]

Otto Preminger's historical importance as a producer who defied the Production Code Administration and broke the blacklist and as a pioneer independent filmmaker who set a business model that continues to be followed is secure. Opinion about his artistic legacy, however, remains divided. Obituaries, setting a precedent that more or less endures to the present, routinely cited his personality more than his films and placed his achievements as a producer above his directing. "He had become nearly as famous for his curmudgeonry as for his art," the notice in the *Los Angeles Times* on April 24, 1986, attested. Alvin Krebs in the April 24 *New York Times* noted that "Preminger's tempestuous personality often obscured the fact that he was one of the most competent independent producer-directors of his time." As David Ansen commented in *Newsweek* on May 5, 1986, "Preminger was canny enough to realize that his public image as a Prussian autocrat would help more than hinder him in the carnival world of Holly-

Setting up shots for *Advise and Consent* (above) and *In Harm's Way.*

wood." But Ansen acknowledged that Otto "made much more than head-lines; he created a climate in which Hollywood could join the adult world, and he conjured a handful of movies that will always be watched with grat-itude and pleasure." Roger Ebert in the April 24 *Chicago Sun-Times* wrote, "The line on Otto Preminger was that he was the greatest producer and the worst director in Hollywood history. Both statements contained a measure of truth."

"Almost all the obituaries failed to conceal an attitude of cool detach-ment bordering on contempt," Andrew Sarris wrote in the *Village Voice* on May 27, 1986.

> In New York, Otto Preminger was never even remotely a culture hero. He was despised most by the people with whom he was socially and politically most in rapport. . . . He was never given any credit for moral sincerity. *Laura* was for Preminger what *Citizen Kane* was for Orson Welles, an ego buster for people who like to revel in the decline and fall of just about everyone but themselves. For a long time he was the only major director I knew socially. He was aware that I was one of his few local defenders. I always liked Preminger, but I'm not sure that I would ever have wanted to work for him. He was far more intelligent than most people thought, and much of his mock-Teutonic bombast was for show, but there was still something insidiously domineering in his personality that made me a bit uncomfortable. I have underestimated his career considerably. Since *Laura,* the only film he has made that seems utterly beyond revisionist redemption is *Rosebud.* So many of the films have become such esteemed cult favorites here and abroad that a massive revaluation seems in order on both the thematic and stylistic fronts. . . . He cared very deeply for his characters by not judging them. And in the end he was one of those rare directors who made a dramatic difference on the screen.

Over twenty years after his death, "Otto Preminger" may still be better remembered than any of his films. He has appeared as a character (played by John Savident) in *Jean Seberg,* a failed 1983 musical (music by Marvin Ham-lisch, lyrics by Christopher Adler, book by Julian Barry) that opened at the National Theatre in London on November 15; and in a mediocre 1999 tele-vision movie, *Introducing Dorothy Dandridge,* starring Halle Berry, in which he was played by Klaus Maria Brandauer.

Preminger's critical standing, at least in America, where the prevailing

opinion is to regard him as a director of topical or "scandalous" films of merely ephemeral interest who late in his career supplied redundant evidence of a loss of power, is far lower than it should be. On the whole, both during his lifetime and ever since, French critics have been more perceptive in recognizing Preminger's authoritative signature. A master of long takes (who regarded every cut as an interruption), and of complexly composed long shots and sinuous camera movement, Preminger was an exacting stylist who imposed on himself the same prohibitions against overstatement that he wielded against actors intent on doing too much acting.

One of the engaging paradoxes of Preminger's career is that he was a famously hotheaded man who at his best made beautifully restrained films.

In his work, Preminger sought and often enough attained a measure of control that he could not, or did not want to, attain over his temper. Objectivity, detachment, lucidity, *mésure,* evenhandedness—these qualities, which provide the stylistic as well as thematic underpinning to many of his strongest films, are decidedly not the characteristics those scorched by an outrageous tirade would have assigned to the man himself. At his most assured, in *Laura, Angel Face, Carmen Jones, Anatomy of a Murder, Porgy and Bess, Exodus, Advise and Consent, The Cardinal, Bunny Lake Is Missing,* and, remarkably enough, *The Human Factor,* he was a supremely fluent *metteur-en-scène* who made thoughtful, challenging films on a broad range of subjects that continue to matter.

Otto Preminger, perhaps a victim still of the intimidating, domineering, Prussian persona he created and may have played all too well, remains one of the most underrated of the masters of American filmmaking. All of his films, the clinkers as well as the triumphs, the ones that now look like back numbers as well as the ones that, in retrospect, seem to have been remarkably ahead of their time, deserve the same kind of fair-minded appraisal with which the director himself regarded his characters.

"Otto, who believed in the intelligence of the audience and made truly sophisticated movies, has been consistently underappreciated while his fellow Austrian Billy Wilder has been deified," Peter Bogdanovich said.

> Wilder needed yes-men, but Otto was too self-sufficient, and too arrogant, I suppose, to need anybody. He seemed not at all to be bothered by the opinions of others, and he certainly seemed able to slough off bad reviews. People believed the cold image, which wasn't really the man, who was in fact warm and paternal and encouraging. He made three certified masterpieces—*Laura, Anatomy of a Murder, Advise and Consent*—which rank among the best of all American pictures, and *Exodus* holds up as the best of all the big-budget, all-star epics.[18]

As Preminger's longtime friend, the legendary New York agent Robert Lantz, said, "Otto was larger than life. He was extreme in almost every way: colorful, large of spirit, loyal, and generous. When crossed he could be a rambunctious Hun. He regretted Vienna, as I regret and reject my native city of Berlin. These days, when almost everybody is so boring, how I miss him. He played 'Otto Preminger' with such vigor and vim, such outsized energy. Perhaps above all—and it is by no means common to those who are rich and successful—he knew the art of living."[19]

Notes

PROLOGUE   AN ENCOUNTER

1   Ingo Preminger, interview by author, June 12 and August 21, 2001.

I   A RING FROM THE EMPEROR

1   Otto Preminger, *Preminger: An Autobiography* (New York: Doubleday, 1977), p. 24.
2   Ingo Preminger, interview by author.
3   Preminger, *Preminger,* p. 24.
4   Ingo Preminger, interview by author.
5   Ibid.
6   Ibid.
7   Eve Preminger, interview by author, January 2, 2002.
8   Preminger, *Preminger,* p. 24.
9   Ingo Preminger, interview by author.
10 Preminger quoted in Gerald Pratley, *The Cinema of Otto Preminger* (New York: Barnes, 1971), p. 34.
11 Ingo Preminger, interview by author.
12 Eve Preminger, interview by author.
13 James Preminger, interview by author, November 23, 2002.
14 Kathy Preminger, interview by author, November 11, 2002.
15 Ingo Preminger, interview by author.
16 Ibid.
17 James Preminger, interview by author.
18 Ingo Preminger, interview by author.
19 Preminger, *Preminger,* p. 25.
20 Ingo Preminger, interview by author.

21 Preminger, *Preminger*, p. 25.

22 Ingo Preminger, interview by author.

23 Ibid.

24 Paul Hofmann, *The Viennese: Splendor, Twilight and Exile* (New York: Doubleday, 1988), p. 105.

25 Ingo Preminger, interview by author.

26 Ibid.

27 Willi Frischauer, *Behind the Scenes of Otto Preminger* (New York: William Morrow, 1974), p. 29.

28 Ibid.

29 Ingo Preminger, interview by author.

30 Hofmann, *The Viennese*, p. 1.

31 Ibid.

32 Ibid., p. 5.

33 Hitler quoted in Hofmann, *The Viennese*, p. 143.

34 Ibid., p. 163.

35 Ingo Preminger, interview by author.

36 Ibid.

37 Unsourced newspaper clipping, 1936, Academy of Motion Picture Arts and Sciences, Margaret Herrick Library, Beverly Hills, California.

38 Preminger quoted in Pratley, *Cinema*, p. 29.

39 Hofmann, *The Viennese*, p. 169.

40 Preminger, *Preminger*, p. 26.

41 Ingo Preminger, interview by author.

42 Eve Preminger, interview by author.

43 Preminger, *Preminger*, p. 34.

44 Ibid., p. 30.

45 Ibid., p. 31.

46 Ibid., p. 33.

47 Ingo Preminger, interview by author.

48 Frischauer, *Behind the Scenes*, p. 42.

49 Preminger quoted in Pratley, *Cinema*, p. 31.

50 Preminger, *Preminger*, p. 34.

51 Paula Laurence, interview by author, July 11, 2002.

52 Preminger, *Preminger*, p. 34.

53 Frischauer, *Behind the Scenes*, p. 43.

54 Ibid., p. 44.

55 Ingo Preminger, interview by author.

56 Preminger quoted in Pratley, *Cinema*, p. 41.

57 Preminger quoted in ibid., p. 46.

58 Preminger quoted in ibid., p. 40.

59 Ingo Preminger, interview by author.

60 Marion Mill Preminger, *All I Want Is Everything* (New York: MacFaden, 1957), p. 110.

61 Eve Preminger, interview by author.

62 Preminger, *Preminger*, p. 44.

63 Kathy Preminger, interview by author.

64 Marion Mill Preminger, *Everything,* pp. 112–13.

65 Ibid., p. 114.

66 Ibid., p. 141.

67 Eve Preminger, interview by author.

68 Preminger, *Preminger,* p. 36.

69 Ibid., p. 37.

70 Ibid., p. 39.

71 Ingo Preminger, interview by author.

72 Preminger, *Preminger,* p. 38.

73 Ibid.

74 Ibid., p. 41.

75 Ingo Preminger, interview by author.

76 Luise Rainer quoted in Frischauer, *Behind the Scenes,* p. 56.

77 Ingo Preminger, interview by author.

78 Cecil Beaton, *Beaton in the Sixties* (New York: Knopf, 2004), p. 168.

79 Preminger, *Preminger,* p. 2.

80 Ingo Preminger, interview by author.

81 Ibid.

82 Preminger, *Preminger,* p. 44.

83 Marion Mill Preminger, *Everything,* p. 154.

84 Hofmann, *The Viennese,* p. 199.

85 Preminger, *Preminger,* p. 44.

86 Ibid., p. 43.

2   RISE AND FALL

1   Preminger, *Preminger,* p. 3.

2   Preminger quoted in Earl Wilson, *Los Angeles Mirror,* March 25, 1961.

3   Preminger quoted in "Vienna's Dr. Preminger as a Broadway Director," *New York Post,* December 14, 1935.

4   Preminger quoted in Pratley, *Cinema,* pp. 42–43.

5   Unsourced newspaper clipping, January 1936, Academy of Motion Picture Arts and Sciences, Margaret Herrick Library.

6   Celeste Holm, interview by author, June 26, 2002.

7   Ruth Warrick, interview by author, May 20, 1999; May 25, 2001; and June 9, 2002.

8   Preminger, *Preminger,* p. 15.

9   Ibid.

10 *Variety,* November 9, 1936.

11 Preminger, *Preminger,* p. 16.

12 Ibid., p. 17.

13 Ibid., p. 48.

14 *Variety,* October 1, 1937.

15 *Los Angeles Examiner,* August 12, 1942.

16 Preminger quoted in Pratley, *Cinema,* p. 48.

17 Preminger, *Preminger,* p. 20.

18 Ibid., p. 21.

19 Preminger quoted in Pratley, *Cinema,* p. 50.

20 Luise Rainer quoted in Frischauer, *Behind the Scenes,* p. 73.

21 Preminger, *Preminger,* p. 48.

22 Ingo Preminger, interview by author.

23 Ibid.

24 Ibid.

25 Ibid.

26 Preminger, *Preminger,* p. 49.

27 Marguerite Courtney, *Laurette* (New York: Atheneum, 1968), p. 378.

28 Ibid., p. 379.

29 Preminger quoted in ibid.

30 Ibid., p. 381.

31 Preminger, *Preminger,* p. 52.

32 Ibid., p. 55.

33 Trumball Barton, interview by author, November 18, 1998.

34 Elaine Barrymore, interview by author, July 7, 2001.

35 Preminger, *Preminger,* p. 56.

36 Elaine Barrymore, interview by author.

37 Ibid.

38 Preminger, *Preminger,* p. 56.

39 Elaine Barrymore, interview by author.

40 Ibid.

41 Ibid.

42 Preminger, *Preminger,* p. 57.

43 Ibid., p. 58.

44 Ibid.

45 Elaine Barrymore, interview by author.

46 Ibid.

47 Ibid.

48 Trumball Barton, interview by author.

49 Ibid.

50 Preminger, *Preminger,* p. 62.

51 Ibid.

52 Trumball Barton, interview by author.

53 Preminger, *Preminger,* p. 62.

54 Trumball Barton, interview by author.

55 Louis Nizer, interview by Val Robins, July 1990, typescript in files of Otto Preminger Films, Inc.

56 Preminger quoted in *Los Angeles Examiner,* May 20, 1942.

57 Paul Kohner letter, April 15, 1942, in Academy of Motion Picture Arts and Sciences, Margaret Herrick Library.

3 SEIZING THE DAY

1   Preminger quoted in Pratley, *Cinema,* p. 53.
2   Preminger quoted in ibid.
3   Preminger quoted in ibid.
4   Preminger, *Preminger,* p. 80.
5   Marion Mill Preminger, *Everything,* p. 173.
6   Ibid., p. 166.
7   Ibid., pp. 185–88.
8   Preminger, *Preminger,* p. 44.
9   Preminger quoted in *Los Angeles Times,* July 12, 1943.
10 Otto Preminger and Peter Bogdanovich, "The Making of *Laura,*" *On Film* 1, no. 1 (1970), p. 48.
11 Vera Caspary, "My *Laura* and Otto's," *Saturday Review,* June 26, 1971.
12 Vera Caspary, quoted in Preminger and Bogdanovich, "The Making of *Laura,*" p. 49.
13 Caspary, "My *Laura* and Otto's."
14 Ibid.
15 Darryl F. Zanuck quoted in George F. Custen, *Twentieth Century's Fox: Darryl F. Zanuck and the Culture of Hollywood* (New York: Basic Books, 1997), p. 66, from Stephen M. Silverman, *The Fox That Got Away: The Last Days of the Zanuck Dynasty at Twentieth Century-Fox* (Secaucus, N.J.: Lyle Stuart, 1988), p. 75.
16 Preminger, *Preminger,* p. 72.
17 Preminger quoted in Pratley, *Cinema,* p. 70.
18 Frischauer, *Behind the Scenes,* p. 113.
19 Preminger, *Preminger,* p. 84.
20 Byrnie Foy quoted in Preminger and Bogdanovich, "The Making of *Laura,*" p. 49.
21 Preminger and Bogdanovich, "The Making of *Laura,*" p. 49.
22 Darryl F. Zanuck quoted in Custen, *Twentieth Century's Fox,* p. 291.
23 Darryl F. Zanuck quoted in ibid., p. 290.
24 Lewis Milestone quoted in Preminger and Bogdanovich, "The Making of *Laura,*" p. 49; ibid., p. 50.
25 Ibid., p. 50.
26 Rufus LeMaire quoted in ibid.
27 Ibid., p. 51.
28 Darryl F. Zanuck quoted in ibid., p. 62.
29 Ibid., p. 51.
30 Gene Tierney, *Self-Portrait* (New York: Wyden Books, 1978), p. 114.
31 Vincent Price, interview by Val Robins, July 1989, typescript in files of Otto Preminger Films, Inc.
32 Preminger and Bogdanovich, "The Making of *Laura,*" p. 51.
33 Vincent Price, interview by Val Robins.
34 Ibid.
35 Tierney, *Self-Portrait,* p. 113.
36 Ibid., p. 116.

37 David Raksin, interview by author, July 29, 2002.

38 Darryl F. Zanuck and Walter Winchell quoted in Preminger and Bogdanovich, "The Making of *Laura*," p. 52.

39 Ibid., p. 52.

40 Caspary, "My *Laura* and Otto's."

41 Frischauer, *Behind the Scenes*, p. 91.

42 Arthur Laurents, interview by author, February 25, 2002.

43 Ibid.

44 Preminger, *Preminger*, p. 95.

45 Ibid.

46 Ibid.

47 Ibid., p. 96.

4 ON THE JOB (I)

1 Frischauer, *Behind the Scenes*, p. 114.

2 Nicola Lubitsch, interview by author, June 11, 2003.

3 Phoebe Ephron quoted in Scott Eyman, *Ernst Lubitsch: Laughter in Paradise* (New York: Simon and Schuster, 1993), p. 324.

4 Nicola Lubitsch, interview by author.

5 Preminger, *Preminger*, p. 89.

6 Eyman, *Lubitsch*, p. 335.

7 Preminger, *Preminger*, p. 89.

8 Ibid., p. 85.

9 Ibid., p. 86.

10 Vincent Price, interview by Val Robins.

11 Preminger quoted in Pratley, *Cinema*, p. 70.

12 David Raksin, interview by author.

13 Preminger, *Preminger*, pp. 99–100.

14 Preminger quoted in Fox press release, April 1945, Academy of Motion Picture Arts and Sciences, Margaret Herrick Library.

15 Ibid.

16 Ibid.

17 David Raksin, interview by author.

18 Celeste Holm, interview by author.

19 David Raksin quoted in Ronald L. Davis, *Hollywood Beauty: Linda Darnell and the American Dream* (Norman: University of Oklahoma Press, 1991), p. 89.

20 David Raksin, interview by author.

21 Preminger quoted in Pratley, *Cinema*, p. 74.

22 Preminger quoted in *Los Angeles Times*, June 26, 1955.

23 Preminger quoted in Pratley, *Cinema*, p. 75.

24 Preminger quoted in Mel Gussow, *Don't Say Yes Until I Finish Talking: A Biography of Darryl F. Zanuck* (New York: Doubleday, 1971), p. 148.

25 Preminger, *Preminger*, p. 81.

26 Ibid.

27 Ibid., p. 104.

28 Preminger quoted in Pratley, *Cinema*, p. 63.

29 Preminger, *Preminger*, p. 104.

30 Ibid.

31 Ring Lardner Jr., *I'd Hate Myself in the Morning* (New York: Thunder's Mouth/ Nation Books, 2000), p. 107.

32 Philip Dunne quoted in Davis, *Hollywood Beauty*, p. 97.

33 Philip Dunne quoted in ibid., p. 98.

34 Lardner, *I'd Hate Myself*, pp. 116–17.

35 Preminger, *Preminger*, p. 105.

36 Linda Darnell quoted in Davis, *Hollywood Beauty*, p. 98.

37 Linda Darnell's sister quoted in ibid., p. 100.

38 Ibid., p. 110.

39 Cornel Wilde quoted in ibid., p. 100.

40 Leon Shamroy quoted in ibid., p. 101.

41 David Raksin, interview by author.

42 Preminger, *Preminger*, p. 105.

43 Ibid.

44 Ibid., p. 106.

45 Preminger quoted in *New York Times*, February 17, 1957.

46 David Raksin, interview by author.

47 Preminger, *Preminger*, p. 105.

5   ON THE JOB (2)

1   Ruth Warrick, interview by author.

2   Ibid.

3   Ibid.

4   Ibid.

5   Preminger, *Preminger*, p. 100.

6   Eve Preminger, interview by author.

7   David Raksin, interview by author.

8   *Variety*, November 29, 1947.

9   Ingo Preminger, interview by author.

10 Eve Preminger, interview by author.

11 Ibid.

12 Ingo Preminger, interview by author.

13 Eve Preminger, interview by author.

14 Ingo Preminger, interview by author.

15 James Preminger, interview by author.

16 Ingo Preminger, interview by author.

17 Nicola Lubitsch, interview by author.

18 Tom McGee, *The Girl with the Million Dollar Legs* (Vestal, N.Y.: Vestal, 1995), p. 146.

19 Douglas Fairbanks Jr. quoted in Eyman, *Lubitsch,* p. 356.

20 Ibid., p. 359.

21 Preminger quoted in Pratley, *Cinema,* p. 72.

22 Vera Fairbanks, interview by author, June 12, 2002.

23 Preminger quoted in Eyman, *Lubitsch,* p. 365.

24 Douglas Fairbanks Jr., interview by author, October 4, 1998.

25 McGee, *Girl,* p. 148.

26 Ibid., p. 149.

27 Vera Fairbanks, interview by author.

28 Nicola Lubitsch, interview by author.

29 Preminger quoted in Pratley, *Cinema,* p. 72.

30 Virginia McDowall, interview by author, August 8, 2002.

31 Preminger quoted in Pratley, *Cinema,* p. 91.

32 Virginia McDowall, interview by author.

33 Joseph L. Mankiewicz, interview by Val Robins, July 1990, typescript in files of Otto Preminger Films, Inc.

34 José Ferrer, interview by Val Robins, July 1989, typescript in files of Otto Preminger Films, Inc.

35 Ibid.

36 David Raksin, interview by author.

37 Marion Mill Preminger, *Everything,* p. 224.

38 Marion Mill Preminger quoted in *Los Angeles Herald Tribune,* April 21, 1958.

39 Preminger, *Preminger,* p. 81.

40 Preminger quoted in Pratley, *Cinema,* p. 65.

41 Marion Mill Preminger quoted in *Los Angeles Herald Tribune,* April 21, 1958.

42 *Los Angeles Times,* October 1, 1953.

43 *Library Journal,* October 15, 1957.

44 *McCall's,* March 1965.

45 Preminger, *Preminger,* p. 82.

46 Frischauer, *Behind the Scenes,* p. 65.

47 Preminger, *Preminger,* p. 82.

48 Ibid., p. 106.

49 Ibid.

50 Ibid., p. 121.

51 Howell Gilbert, interview by author, June 6, 2003.

52 Biff McGuire, interview by author, July 15, 2002.

53 *New York Herald Tribune,* January 19, 1951.

6 THE DECLARATION OF INDEPENDENCE

1 Diana Herbert, interview by author, January 20, 2003.

2 Preminger, *Preminger,* p. 107.

3 Diana Herbert, interview by author.

4   Barry Nelson, interview by author, June 16, 2002.

5   Biff McGuire, interview by author.

6   Paula Laurence, interview by author.

7   Diana Douglas Darrid, *In the Wings* (New York: Barricade Books, 1999), p. 181.

8   Ibid., p. 183.

9   Preminger, *Preminger,* p. 131.

10 Kathy Preminger, interview by author.

11 Preminger, *Preminger,* p. 132.

12 Kathy Preminger, interview by author.

13 James Preminger, interview by author.

14 Preminger quoted in Charlotte Chandler, *Nobody's Perfect: Billy Wilder, A Personal Biography* (New York: Simon and Schuster, 2002), p. 168.

15 Billy Wilder quoted in ibid.

16 Preminger quoted in ibid.

17 Preminger quoted in ibid.

18 Preminger, *Preminger,* p. 124.

19 Peter Harry Brown and Pat H. Broeske, *Howard Hughes: The Untold Story* (New York: Dutton, 1996), p. 241.

20 Jean Simmons, interview by author, August 31, 2003.

21 Brown and Broeske, *Hughes,* p. 241.

22 Preminger, *Preminger,* p. 124.

23 Preminger and Oscar Millard quoted in Frischauer, *Behind the Scenes,* p. 118.

24 Preminger, *Preminger,* p. 124.

25 Jean Simmons, interview by author.

26 Robert Mitchum quoted in Lee Server, *Robert Mitchum: "Baby, I Don't Care"* (New York: St. Martin's, 2001), p. 239.

27 Jean Simmons, interview by author.

28 Mona Freeman, interview by author, August 16, 2002.

29 Server, *Mitchum,* p. 239.

30 Joseph Breen quoted in Leonard J. Leff and Jerold L. Simmons, *The Dame in the Kimono: Hollywood, Censorship, and the Production Code from the 1920s to the 1960s* (New York: Grove Weidenfeld, 1990), p. 191.

31 David Niven, *The Moon's a Balloon* (New York: Putnam, 1971), p. 324.

32 Jack Vizzard, *See No Evil: Life Inside a Hollywood Censor* (New York: Simon and Schuster, 1970), p. 157.

33 Leff and Simmons, *Kimono,* p. 192.

34 Geoffrey Shurlock quoted in ibid., p. 193.

35 Ibid.

36 Ibid., p. 194.

37 Niven, *Balloon,* p. 324.

38 Biff McGuire, interview by author.

39 Ibid.

40 Johanna Matz, interview by Val Robins, August 1989, typescript in files of Otto Preminger Films, Inc.

41 Joseph Breen quoted in Leff and Simmons, *Kimono,* p. 194.

42 Preminger quoted in ibid., p. 195.

43 Lawyer for Production Code Administration office quoted in ibid., p. 196.

44 Nicholas Schenck quoted in ibid.

45 Preminger, *Preminger,* p. 109.

46 Saul Bass, interview by Val Robins, July 1989, typescript in files of Otto Preminger Films, Inc.

47 Ibid.

48 Preminger quoted in Leff and Simmons, *Kimono,* p. 198.

49 Preminger quoted in *Los Angeles Times,* June 1, 1953.

50 Preminger, *Preminger,* p. 109.

51 Judge Herman Moser quoted in Vizzard, *See No Evil,* p. 157.

52 Leff and Simmons, *Kimono,* p. 203.

53 Jack Vizzard quoted in ibid., p. 155.

54 Diana Herbert, interview by author.

55 Gilbert Gardner, interview by author, August 2 and 3, 2003.

56 Ibid.

57 Preminger, *Preminger,* p. 127.

58 Stanley Rubin, interview by author, January 22, 2003.

59 Ibid.

60 Preminger, *Preminger,* p. 128.

61 Ibid.

62 Paul Helmick quoted in Server, *Mitchum,* p. 249.

63 Stanley Rubin, interview by author.

64 Barbara Leaming, *Marilyn Monroe* (New York: Crown, 1998), p. 92.

65 Paul Helmick quoted in Server, *Mitchum,* p. 249.

66 Preminger, *Preminger,* p. 128.

67 Stanley Rubin, interview by author.

68 Preminger, *Preminger,* p. 129.

69 Stanley Rubin, interview by author.

70 Ibid.

71 Preminger, *Preminger,* p. 132.

72 Preminger quoted in Pratley, *Cinema,* p. 109.

7 LIGHTNING STRIKES TWICE

1 Oscar Hammerstein II, liner notes for *Carmen Jones Original Cast Album,* Decca Records, 1943.

2 Preminger, *Preminger,* p. 133.

3 Ibid.

4 Ibid., p. 134.

5 Joseph Breen quoted in Donald Bogle, *Dorothy Dandridge* (New York: Amistad, 1997), p. 266.

6 Preminger quoted in Pratley, *Cinema,* p. 110.

7   Preminger memo quoted in Bogle, *Dandridge,* p. 268.

8   Diahann Carroll, *Diahann!* (Boston: Little, Brown, 1986), p. 50.

9   Ibid., p. 52.

10   Brock Peters, interview by author, August 27, 2002.

11   Preminger quoted in Earl Mills, *Dorothy Dandridge: A Portrait in Black* (Los Angeles: Holloway House, 1970), p. 172.

12   Preminger quoted in ibid.

13   Preminger quoted in Dorothy Dandridge and Earl Conrad, *Everything and Nothing: The Dorothy Dandridge Story* (New York: Abelard-Schuman, 1970), p. 156.

14   Dorothy Dandridge quoted in Mills, *Dandridge,* p. 172.

15   Dorothy Dandridge quoted in ibid., p. 173.

16   Dandridge and Conrad, *Everything and Nothing,* p. 157.

17   Mills, *Dandridge,* p. 173.

18   Dandridge and Conrad, *Everything and Nothing,* p. 158.

19   Olga James, interview by author, September 11, 2003.

20   Dandridge and Conrad, *Everything and Nothing,* p. 158.

21   Phoebe Brand, interview by author, April 13, 2002.

22   Dandridge and Conrad, *Everything and Nothing,* p. 158.

23   Ibid.

24   Donald Bogle, interview by author, June 25, 2003.

25   Frischauer, *Behind the Scenes,* p. 135.

26   Dandridge and Conrad, *Everything and Nothing,* p. 160.

27   Donald Bogle, interview by author.

28   Dandridge and Conrad, *Everything and Nothing,* p. 162.

29   Gilbert Gardner, interview by author.

30   Olga James, interview by author.

31   Brock Peters, interview by author.

32   Olga James, interview by author.

33   Brock Peters, interview by author.

34   Olga James, interview by author.

35   Brock Peters, interview by author.

36   Olga James, interview by author.

37   Donald Bogle, interview by author.

38   Bogle, *Dandridge,* p. 303.

39   Reviews quoted in ibid., p. 206.

40   Donald Bogle, interview by author.

41   Larkin Ford, interview by author, May 31, 2003.

42   Ibid.

43   Ibid.

44   Mills, *Dandridge,* p. 194.

45   Ibid., p. 192.

46   Bogle, *Dandridge,* p. 333.

47   Dandridge and Conrad, *Everything and Nothing,* p. 173.

48   Gilbert Gardner, interview by author.

8   "CHICAGO"

1   Ingo Preminger, interview by author.
2   Ibid.
3   Preminger, *Preminger,* p. 111.
4   Nelson Algren, *Los Angeles Times,* May 15, 1977.
5   Ibid.
6   David Castronovo, *Beyond the Gray Flannel Man: Books from the 1950s That Made American Culture* (New York: Continuum, 2005), p. 98.
7   Nelson Algren, *The Man with the Golden Arm* (New York: Doubleday, 1949), pp. 184–85.
8   Preminger, *Preminger,* p. 111.
9   Ibid.
10 Preminger, *Preminger,* p. 112.
11 Preminger quoted in Evelyn Herbert, "The Man Who Changed the Moral Code," *Pageant,* September 1956.
12 Preminger quoted in *New York Journal American,* May 27, 1962.
13 Frank Sinatra, interview by Val Robins, August 1989, typescript in files of Otto Preminger Films, Inc.
14 Darren McGavin quoted in *Pageant,* September 1956.
15 Frank Sinatra, interview by Val Robins.
16 Ibid.
17 Gilbert Gardner, interview by author.
18 Preminger quoted in *Washington Post,* August 12, 1980.
19 Preminger and McGavin quoted in *Pageant,* September 1956.
20 Gilbert Gardner, interview by author.
21 Saul Bass, interview by Val Robins.
22 Ibid.
23 Preminger, *Preminger,* p. 136.
24 Mike Beck quoted in *Pageant,* September 1956.
25 Preminger quoted in Pratley, *Cinema,* p. 112.
26 Preminger quoted in *New York Post,* January 29, 1956.
27 Preminger, *Preminger,* p. 114.
28 Saul Bass, interview by Val Robins.
29 Preminger quoted by Nelson Algren, *Los Angeles Times,* May 15, 1977.
30 Nelson Algren, ". . . But Most of All I Remember Otto," *Chicago Sun Times,* May 21, 1972.
31 Algren, *Los Angeles Times,* May 15, 1977.

9   MISS IOWA

1   Preminger in trailer quoted in Pratley, *Cinema,* p. 118.
2   Otto Preminger, "The Making of *Saint Joan.*"
3   Preminger on CBC, September 9, 1956, quoted in Pratley, *Cinema,* p. 119.

4 Rita Moriarty, interview by author, December 14, 2001.

5 Lionel Larner, interview by author, February 20, 2002.

6 Preminger quoted in *New York Morning-Telegraph,* October 3, 1956.

7 Gilbert Gardner, interview by author.

8 Preminger and Jean Seberg quoted in David Richards, *Played Out: The Jean Seberg Story* (New York: Random House, 1981), p. 74.

9 Gilbert Gardner, interview by author.

10 Richards, *Played Out,* p. 35.

11 Ibid., p. 36.

12 Gilbert Gardner, interview by author.

13 Letter in files of Otto Preminger Films, Inc.

14 Lionel Larner, interview by author.

15 Ibid.

16 Rita Moriarty, interview by author.

17 Ibid.

18 Lionel Larner, interview by author.

19 Richards, *Played Out,* p. 49.

20 Ibid., p. 43.

21 Ibid., p. 49.

22 John Gielgud quoted in Sheridan Morley, *John Gielgud* (New York: Simon and Schuster, 2002), p. 312.

23 Lionel Larner, interview by author.

24 Rita Moriarty, interview by author.

25 Bob Willoughby quoted in Richards, *Played Out,* p. 48.

26 Preminger, *Preminger,* p. 153.

27 Richards, *Played Out,* p. 52.

28 Preminger quoted in ibid., p. 51.

29 Preminger quoted in ibid., p. 58.

30 Preminger quoted in ibid., p. 43.

31 Preminger, *Preminger,* p. 153.

32 Ibid.

33 Arthur Laurents, interview by author.

34 Ibid.

35 Hope Preminger, interview by author, June 2, July 5 and 12, September 14, and December 11, 2001; February 8, March 11, April 5, May 2, and November 15 and 16, 2002; February 20, 2003; and June 3 and 4, 2004.

36 Martin Schute, interview by author, July 16, 2001.

37 Hope Preminger, interview by author.

38 Deborah Kerr, interview by Val Robins, August 1989, typescript in files of Otto Preminger Films, Inc.

39 Geoffrey Horne, interview by author, December 4 and 18, 2001.

40 Deborah Kerr, interview by Val Robins.

41 Martin Schute, interview by author.

42 Geoffrey Horne, interview by author.

43 Ibid.

44 Ibid.

45 Sheridan Morley, *The Other Side of the Moon: A Biography of David Niven* (New York: Harper and Row, 1985), p. 202.

46 Deborah Kerr, interview by Val Robins.

47 Martin Schute, interview by author.

48 Geoffrey Horne, interview by author.

49 Martin Schute, interview by author.

50 Rita Moriarty, interview by author.

51 Martin Schute, interview by author.

52 Arthur Laurents, interview by author.

53 Geoffrey Horne, interview by author.

54 Excerpts from reviews in *Saturday Review* and *New Yorker* quoted in Richards, *Played Out*, p. 70.

55 Arthur Laurents, interview by author.

56 Deborah Kerr, interview by Val Robins.

57 François Moreuil quoted in Richards, *Played Out*, p. 74.

58 Hope Preminger, interview by author.

59 Preminger quoted in *Los Angeles Times*, June 10, 1960.

10   CENSORED!

1   Gilbert Gardner, interview by author.

2   Kim Hunter, interview by author, November 10, 2001.

3   Lisa Aronson, interview by author, June 15, 2005.

4   Kim Hunter, interview by author.

5   Gilbert Gardner, interview by author.

6   Ibid.

7   Mrs. Otto Preminger (Mary Gardner) quoted in *Los Angeles Times*, January 6, 1957.

8   Quoted in *Los Angeles Herald Examiner*, February 15, 1957.

9   Quoted in *Los Angeles Times*, March 6, 1958.

10 Mrs. Otto Preminger (Mary Gardner) quoted in *Los Angeles Times*, February 26, 1958.

11 Gilbert Gardner, interview by author.

12 Ibid.

13 Ibid.

14 Preminger, *Preminger*, p. 121.

15 Ingo Preminger, interview by author.

16 Eve Preminger, interview by author.

17 Willi Frischauer, *Behind the Scenes*, p. 167.

18 Martin Schute, interview by author.

19 Willi Frischauer, *Behind the Scenes*, p. 169.

20 Preminger quoted in Tom Ryan, *Otto Preminger Films Exodus: A Report* (New York: Random House, 1960), n.p.

21 Ingo Preminger, interview by author.

22 Preminger, *Preminger,* p. 166.

23 Leon Uris, interview by author, June 19, 2002.

24 Ingo Preminger, interview by author.

25 Hollis Alpert, *The Life and Times of Porgy and Bess: The Story of an American Classic* (New York: Knopf, 1990), p. 259.

26 Preminger, *Preminger,* p. 188.

27 Lee Gershwin and Samuel Goldwyn quoted in A. Scott Berg, *Goldwyn* (New York: Knopf, 1989), p. 479.

28 Samuel Goldwyn quoted in Alpert, *Porgy and Bess,* p. 261.

29 N. Richard Nash quoted in Carol Easton, *The Search for Goldwyn* (New York: William Morrow, 1975), p. 277.

30 Ingo Preminger, interview by author.

31 Preminger, *Preminger,* p. 136.

32 Rouben Mamoulian quoted in Berg, *Goldwyn,* p. 485.

33 Leigh Whipper quoted in ibid., p. 485.

34 Irving Lazar quoted in ibid., p. 485.

35 Preminger quoted in *Movie,* London, No. 4, November 1962.

36 Preminger quoted in Berg, *Goldwyn,* p. 486.

37 Anonymous article in black newspaper and Samuel Goldwyn quoted in Easton, *Search,* p. 280.

38 Brock Peters, interview by author.

39 Donald Bogle, interview by author.

40 Dandridge and Conrad, *Everything and Nothing,* p. 167.

41 Ibid., p. 190.

42 Sidney Poitier quoted in Bogle, *Dandridge,* p. 413.

43 Nichelle Nichols quoted in Bogle, *Dandridge,* p. 420.

44 Brock Peters, interview by author.

45 Preminger, *Preminger,* p. 138.

46 Brock Peters, interview by author.

47 Ibid.

48 Ibid.

49 Hope Preminger, interview by author.

50 Brock Peters, interview by author.

51 Preminger quoted in Pratley, *Cinema,* p. 125.

52 Preminger, *Preminger,* p. 137.

53 Arthur Marx, *Goldwyn: A Biography of the Man Behind the Myth* (New York: Norton, 1976), p. 350.

54 Ibid.

55 Samuel Goldwyn quoted in Berg, *Goldwyn,* p. 485.

56 Hope Preminger, interview by author.

57 Donald Bogle, interview by author.

58 William Hoffman, *Sidney* (New York: William Morrow, 1971), quoted in Easton, *Search,* p. 276.

59 Brock Peters, interview by author.

11 ON TRIAL

1 Wendell Mayes, interview by Val Robins, July 1989, typescript in files of Otto Preminger Films, Inc.

2 Boris Leven and Preminger quoted in Richard Griffith, *Anatomy of a Motion Picture* (New York: St. Martin's, 1959), n.p.

3 Lee Remick quoted in Frischauer, *Behind the Scenes,* p. 171.

4 Hope Preminger, interview by author.

5 Preminger, *Preminger,* p. 155.

6 Preminger quoted in Pratley, *Cinema,* p. 129.

7 Lana Turner quoted in *Los Angeles Herald Tribune,* March 1, 1959.

8 Hope Preminger, interview by author.

9 George C. Scott, interview by Val Robins, August 1989, typescript in files of Otto Preminger Films, Inc.

10 Preminger quoted in *Los Angeles Times,* March 4, 1959.

11 Rita Moriarty, interview by author.

12 James Stewart, interview by Val Robins, August 1990, typescript in files of Otto Preminger Films, Inc.

13 Rita Moriarty, interview by author.

14 Preminger quoted in *Los Angeles Times,* March 2, 1959.

15 Rita Moriarty, interview by author.

16 Ben Gazzara, interview by author, May 21, 2002.

17 George C. Scott, interview by Val Robins.

18 Hope Preminger, interview by author.

19 Kathryn Grant, interview by author, August 29, 2002.

20 Preminger, *Preminger,* p. 155.

21 Ray Stark quoted in *New York Times,* May 5, 1959.

22 James Stewart, interview by Val Robins.

23 Preminger, *Preminger,* p. 157.

24 Ibid., p. 158.

25 Wendell Mayes, interview by Val Robins.

26 Agent and Preminger quoted in *New York Sunday News,* July 25, 1965.

27 Preminger quoted in Frischauer, *Behind the Scenes,* p. 177.

28 Hope Preminger, interview by author.

29 Preminger quoted in unsourced newspaper clipping, Academy of Motion Picture Arts and Sciences, Margaret Herrick Library.

12 IN THE PROMISED LAND

1 Preminger, *Preminger,* p. 166.

2 Leon Uris, interview by author.

3 Hope Preminger, interview by author.

4 Meyer Weisgal, *Meyer Weisgal . . . So Far: An Autobiography* (New York: Random House, 1971), p. 314.

5   Preminger quoted in *New York Post,* July 13, 1959.

6   Hope Preminger, interview by author.

7   Weisgal, *Meyer Weisgal,* p. 314.

8   Preminger quoted in Ryan, *Otto Preminger Films Exodus,* n.p.

9   Martin Schute, interview by author.

10 Dalton Trumbo quoted in *New York Post,* November 29, 1961.

11 Preminger on CBC, February 24, 1961, quoted in Pratley, *Cinema,* p. 135.

12 Frischauer, *Behind the Scenes,* p. 182.

13 Eva Monley, interview by author, July 17, 2001.

14 Martin Schute, interview by author.

15 Preminger press conference reported in *New York Times,* December 9, 1959.

16 Preminger quoted in *Variety,* January 20, 1960.

17 Hope Preminger, interview by author.

18 Weisgal, *Meyer Weisgal,* p. 314.

19 Hope Preminger, interview by author.

20 Eva Monley, interview by author.

21 Martin Schute, interview by author.

22 Hope Preminger, interview by author.

23 Martin Schute, interview by author.

24 Eva Monley, interview by author.

25 Hope Preminger, interview by author.

26 Preminger quoted in Burt Glenn, "Preminger in Israel," *Esquire,* March 1961.

27 Hope Preminger, interview by author.

28 Jill Haworth, interview by author, June 4, 2003.

29 Martin Schute, interview by author.

30 Michael Wager, interview by author, September 13, 2001.

31 Eva Marie Saint, interview by author, February 5, 2002.

32 Michael Wager, interview by author.

33 Hope Preminger, interview by author, June 2, 2001.

34 Eva Monley, interview by author.

35 Martin Schute, interview by author.

36 Lee J. Cobb quoted in Helen Lawrenson, "Is It True What They Say about Otto?" *McCall's,* March 1965.

37 Anonymous crew member quoted in ibid.

38 Weisgal, *Meyer Weisgal,* p. 316.

39 Michael Wager, interview by author.

40 Anonymous crew member quoted in Lawrenson, "Is It True?"

41 Hope Preminger, interview by author.

42 Ibid.

43 Jill Haworth, interview by author.

44 Martin Schute, interview by author.

45 Frischauer, *Behind the Scenes,* p. 185.

46 Hope Preminger, interview by author.

13 PLAYING WASHINGTON

1 Preminger quoted in *Los Angeles Examiner,* October 4, 1960.

2 Hope Preminger, interview by author.

3 Hope Preminger, interview by author.

4 Preminger quoted in *New York Herald Tribune,* December 11, 1960.

5 Preminger quoted in *New York World-Telegram,* February 16, 1960.

6 Hope Preminger, interview by author.

7 Details of town house from Rita Reif, "Otto Preminger: Life in a Push-Button World," *New York Times,* August 11, 1967.

8 Preminger quoted in Earl Wilson, *Los Angeles Mirror,* March 25, 1961.

9 Hope Preminger, interview by author.

10 Preminger quoted in *New York Herald Tribune,* November 3, 1963.

11 Hope Preminger, interview by author.

12 Lawrenson, "Is It True?"

13 Hope Preminger, interview by author.

14 Preminger quoted in *New York Times,* May 28, 1961.

15 Preminger quoted in *New York World-Telegram and Sun,* February 16, 1961.

16 Preminger quoted in ibid., February 6, 1961.

17 James Spada, *Peter Lawford: The Man Who Kept the Secrets* (New York: Bantam Books, 1991), p. 278.

18 Preminger quoted in Frischauer, *Behind the Scenes,* p. 201.

19 Don Murray, interview by author, August 20, 2002.

20 George Grizzard, interview by author, October 1, 2002.

21 Paul Green, interview by author, May 13, 2002.

22 George Grizzard, interview by author.

23 Preminger quoted in Frischauer, *Behind the Scenes,* p. 203.

24 *Time,* September 29, 1961.

25 *New York Daily Mirror,* September 29, 1961.

26 Louella Parsons, *Los Angeles Times,* October 3, 1961.

27 Don Murray, interview by author.

28 Preminger quoted in *Time,* September 29, 1961.

29 George Grizzard, interview by author.

30 Preminger quoted in *New York Times,* October 13, 1961.

31 George Grizzard, interview by author.

32 Don Murray, interview by author.

33 Hope Preminger, interview by author.

34 Paul Green, interview by author.

35 George Grizzard, interview by author.

36 Don Murray, interview by author.

37 George Grizzard, interview by author.

38 Hope Preminger, interview by author.

39 Don Murray, interview by author.

40 Harold Prince, interview by author, June 20, 2003.

41 Preminger quoted in *New York Times,* November 30, 1961.

42 Preminger quoted in *New York Post,* June 4, 1962.

43 Preminger, *Preminger,* p. 159.

44 *Los Angeles Times,* June 1, 1962.

45 Preminger quoted in *New York Times,* June 2, 1962.

46 George Grizzard, interview by author.

47 Peter Bunzel, "Controversy over *Advise and Consent," Spotlight,* June 1962.

48 Preminger quoted in *New York Herald Tribune,* June 3, 1962.

49 Geoffrey O'Brien, *American Heritage,* May–June 1998.

14   THE PRODIGAL

1 Mike Macdonald, interview by author, May 15, 2001.

2 Ibid.

3 Ibid.

4 Ibid.

5 Preminger, *Preminger,* p. 177.

6 Hope Preminger, interview by author.

7 Lardner, *I'd Hate Myself,* p. 155.

8 Preminger, *Preminger,* p. 178.

9 Preminger quoted in Pratley, *Cinema,* p. 144.

10 Preminger, *Preminger,* p. 177.

11 Hope Preminger, interview by author.

12 Preminger, *Preminger,* p. 180.

13 Eva Monley, interview by author.

14 Tom Tryon, interview by Val Robins, July 1989, typescript in files of Otto Preminger Films, Inc.

15 Ibid.

16 Hope Preminger, interview by author.

17 Bill Hayes, interview by author, June 17, 2002.

18 Carol Lynley, interview by author, August 23, 2001.

19 Jill Haworth, interview by author.

20 Ossie Davis, interview by author, January 15, 2003.

21 John Saxon, interview by author, August 9, 2002.

22 Bill Hayes, diary, March 1963.

23 John Saxon, interview by author.

24 Carol Lynley, interview by author.

25 Ossie Davis, interview by author.

26 Hope Preminger, interview by author.

27 Wolfgang Odelga, interview by author, July 21, 2001.

28 Hilde Odelga, interview by author, July 21, 2001.

29 Frischauer, *Behind the Scenes,* p. 208.

30 Preminger quoted in *New York Herald Tribune,* March 23, 1963.

31 Dr. Drimmel quoted in Frischauer, *Behind the Scenes,* p. 209.

32 Martin Schute, interview by author.

33 Hope Preminger, interview by author.

34 Martin Schute, interview by author.

35 Hope Preminger, interview by author.

36 Eva Monley, interview by author.

37 *Variety,* March 23, 1963.

38 Martin Schute, interview by author.

39 Tom Tryon, interview by Val Robins.

40 Martin Schute, interview by author.

41 Preminger quoted in *New York Post,* September 12, 1963.

42 Tom Tryon, interview by Val Robins.

43 Hope Preminger, interview by author.

44 Preminger quoted in *New York Times,* August 25, 1963.

45 Lardner, *I'd Hate Myself,* p. 154.

46 Hope Preminger, interview by author.

47 Preminger quoted in *Los Angeles Times,* November 8, 1963.

48 Hope Preminger, interview by author.

49 Josef Meinrad, interview by Val Robins, August 1990, typescript in files of Otto Preminger Films, Inc.

50 Hope Preminger, interview by author.

51 Tom Tryon, interview by Val Robins.

52 Dwight Macdonald, *Esquire,* March 1963.

53 Preminger quoted in *Films and Filming,* November 1963.

15   LOCATION/LOCATION

1   Wendell Mayes, interview by Val Robins.

2   Preminger quoted in *Los Angeles Times,* July 25, 1964.

3   Preminger quoted in ibid.

4   Hope Preminger, interview by author.

5   Jill Haworth, interview by author.

6   Tom Tryon, interview by Val Robins.

7   Hope Preminger, interview by author.

8   Patrick O'Neal quoted in *New York Herald Tribune,* October 17, 1965.

9   Hope Preminger, interview by author.

10 Patricia Neal, interview by author, May 19, 2001.

11 Preminger quoted in *Film Daily,* March 31, 1965.

12 Preminger quoted in *New York Post,* March 29, 1965.

13 Preminger quoted in *New York Times,* June 6, 1965.

14 Martin Schute, interview by author.

15 Hope Preminger, interview by author.

16 Eva Monley, interview by author.

17 Martin Schute, interview by author.

18 Carol Lynley, interview by author.

19 Keir Dullea, interview by author, June 26, 2003.

20 Ibid.

21 Hope Preminger, interview by author.

22 Keir Dullea, interview by author.

23 Patricia Bosworth, "Preminger Technique," *New York Herald Tribune,* October 17, 1965.

24 Carol Lynley, interview by author.

25 Keir Dullea, interview by author.

26 Martin Schute, interview by author.

27 Carol Lynley, interview by author.

28 Preminger quoted in Pratley, *Cinema,* p. 152.

16   IN KLAN COUNTRY

1 Preminger quoted in Pratley, *Cinema,* p. 155.

2 Horton Foote, interview by author, September 25, 2002.

3 Hope Preminger, interview by author.

4 Irving Lazar, *Swifty: My Life and Good Times* (New York: Simon and Schuster, 1995), p. 187.

5 Ibid., p. 189.

6 Irving Lazar quoted in *New York Post,* January 10, 1966.

7 Preminger quoted in *New York Post,* January 10, 1966.

8 Hope Preminger, interview by author.

9 Ibid.

10 Eva Monley, interview by author.

11 Frischauer, *Behind the Scenes,* p. 223.

12 Anonymous local observer quoted in Rex Reed, "Like They Could Cut Your Heart Out," *New York Times,* August 12, 1966.

13 Eva Monley, interview by author.

14 Hope Preminger, interview by author.

15 Robert Hooks, interview by author, June 22, 2002.

16 Ibid.

17 Ibid.

18 Madeleine Sherwood, interview by author, October 18, 2002.

19 Hope Preminger, interview by author.

20 Eva Monley, interview by author.

21 John Phillip Law, interview by author, January 22 and September 9, 2002.

22 Michael Caine, *What's It All About?* (New York: Turtle Bay Books, 1992), p. 262.

23 Michael Caine, interview by Val Robins, August 1990, typescript in files of Otto Preminger Films, Inc.

24 John Phillip Law, interview by author.

25 Madeleine Sherwood, interview by author.

26 Robert Hooks, interview by author.

27 Hope Preminger, interview by author.

28 Faye Dunaway, *Looking for Gatsby* (New York: Simon and Schuster, 1995), p. 113.

29 Ibid., pp. 113–14.

30 Michael Caine, interview by Val Robins.

31 Madeleine Sherwood, interview by author.

32 John Phillip Law, interview by author.

33 Hope Preminger, interview by author.

34 Dunaway, *Gatsby*, p. 114.

35 Robert Hooks, diary.

36 John Phillip Law, interview by author.

37 Gene Callahan quoted in Rex Reed, "Like They Could Cut Your Heart Out."

38 Hope Preminger, interview by author.

39 Preminger, *Preminger*, p. 174.

40 Preminger quoted in *Los Angeles Times*, October 12, 1966.

41 Hope Preminger, interview by author.

42 Preminger quoted in *Newsday*, October 6, 1966.

43 Madeleine Sherwood, interview by author.

17   FATHER AND SON

1 Preminger, *Preminger*, p. 96.

2 Preminger quoted in *Los Angeles Times*, October 10, 1966.

3 Preminger, *Preminger*, p. 97.

4 Erik Lee Preminger, interview by author, December 22, 2002.

5 Hope Preminger, interview by author.

6 Erik Lee Preminger, *Gypsy and Me* (Boston: Little, Brown, 1984), p. 256–57.

7 Ibid., p. 258.

8 Erik Lee Preminger, interview by author.

9 Barbara Preminger, interview by author, October 17, 2002.

10 Ibid.

11 Ibid.

12 Ibid.

13 Erik Lee Preminger, interview by author.

14 Hope Preminger, interview by author.

15 Erik Lee Preminger, interview by author.

16 Ibid.

17 Doran William Cannon, interview by author, June 21, 2002.

18 Erik Lee Preminger, interview by author.

19 Doran William Cannon, interview by author.

20 Ibid.

21 Austin Pendleton, interview by author, December 18, 2002.

22 Ibid.

23 Ibid.

24 Preminger quoted in Pratley, *Cinema*, p. 164.

25 Doran William Cannon, interview by author.

26 Hope Preminger, interview by author.

27 Carol Channing, interview by author, June 6, 2003.

28 Erik Lee Preminger, interview by author.

29 John Phillip Law, interview by author.

30 Doran William Cannon, interview by author.

31 Peter Bogdanovich, interview by author, June 13, 2002.

32 Austin Pendleton, interview by author.

33 Doran William Cannon, interview by author.

34 John Phillip Law, interview by author.

35 Preminger quoted in Pratley, *Cinema,* p. 165.

36 Doran William Cannon, interview by author.

37 Ibid.

38 John Phillip Law, interview by author.

39 Erik Lee Preminger, interview by author.

40 Christian Divine, interview by author, August 12, 2002.

41 Erik Lee Preminger, interview by author.

42 Marjorie Kellogg, interview by author, February 8, 2002.

43 Preminger quoted in Pratley, *Cinema,* p. 167.

44 Erik Lee Preminger, interview by author.

45 Hope Preminger, interview by author.

46 Erik Lee Preminger, interview by author.

47 Ken Howard, interview by Val Robins, August 1990, typescript in files of Otto Preminger Films, Inc.

48 Harry Howard, interview by author, February 14, 2002.

49 Erik Preminger, *Gypsy,* p. 265.

50 Hope Preminger, interview by author.

51 Eve Preminger, interview by author.

52 Erik Lee Preminger, interview by author.

53 Preminger quoted in *New York Times,* November 29, 1970.

54 Preminger quoted in *Variety,* January 13, 1971.

55 Erik Lee Preminger, interview by author.

56 Preminger, *Preminger,* p. 98.

57 Barbara Preminger, interview by author.

58 Ibid.

59 Hope Preminger, interview by author.

60 Charlie Okun, interview by author, January 24, 2003.

61 Nina Foch, interview by author, April 15, 2002.

62 Erik Lee Preminger, interview by author.

63 Rita Gam, interview by author, June 20, 2002.

64 Ken Howard, interview by Val Robins, August 1990, typescript in files of Otto Preminger Films, Inc.

65 Erik Lee Preminger, interview by author.

66 Jennifer O'Neill, interview by author, January 18, 2003.

67 Harry Howard, interview by author.

68 Bud Rosenthal, interview by author, February 3, 2003.

69 Earl Wilson, *New York Post,* December 11, 1971.

70 Dyan Cannon quoted in *Los Angeles Times,* January 2, 1972.

71 Preminger quoted in Frischauer, *Behind the Scenes,* p. 246.

72 Hope Preminger, interview by author.

73 Ibid.

74 Erik Lee Preminger, interview by author.

75 Hope Preminger, interview by author.

18   ENDGAMES

1   Hope Preminger, interview by author.

2   Victoria Preminger, interview by author, June 10, 2001.

3   Mark Preminger, interview by author, February 24, 2002.

4   Victoria Preminger, interview by author.

5   Mark Preminger, interview by author.

6   Hope Preminger, interview by author.

7   Victoria Preminger, interview by author.

8   Preminger quoted in *New York Times,* July 11, 1973.

9   Leslie Jay, interview by author, December 13, 2002.

10 Arlene Leuzzi, interview by author, April 19, 2002.

11 Peter Stone, interview by author, June 26, 2002.

12 Bud Rosenthal, interview by author.

13 Peter Stone, interview by author.

14 Arlene Leuzzi, interview by author.

15 Hope Preminger, interview by author.

16 Peter Stone, interview by author.

17 Bud Rosenthal, interview by author.

18 Erik Lee Preminger, interview by author.

19 Barbara Preminger, interview by author.

20 Hope Preminger, interview by author.

21 Mark Preminger, interview by author.

22 Tony Gittelson, interview by author, February 26, 2003.

23 Erik Lee Preminger, interview by author.

24 Eva Monley, interview by author.

25 Wolfgang Glattes, interview by author, January 17, 2003.

26 Tony Gittelson, interview by author.

27 Ken Kaufman, interview by author, January 23, 2003.

28 Bud Rosenthal, interview by author.

29 Hope Preminger, interview by author.

30 Wolfgang Glattes, interview by author.

31 Bud Rosenthal, interview by author.

32 Marjorie Kellogg, interview by author.

33 Ken Kaufman, interview by author.

34 Hope Preminger, interview by author.

35 Ken Kaufman, interview by author.

36   Erik Lee Preminger, interview by author.

37   Wolfgang Glattes, interview by author.

38   Tony Gittelson, interview by author.

39   Wolfgang Glattes, interview by author.

40   Bud Rosenthal, interview by author.

41   Ken Kaufman, interview by author.

42   Wolfgang Glattes, interview by author.

43   Erik Lee Preminger, interview by author.

44   Hope Preminger, interview by author.

45   Tony Gittelson, interview by author.

46   Ken Kaufman, interview by author.

47   Bud Rosenthal, interview by author.

48   Tony Gittelson, interview by author.

49   Wolfgang Glattes, interview by author.

50   Ken Kaufman, interview by author.

51   Hope Preminger, interview by author.

52   Wolfgang Glattes, interview by author.

53   Ibid.

54   Ken Kaufman, interview by author.

55   Erik Lee Preminger, interview by author.

56   Hope Preminger, interview by author.

57   Tony Gittelson, interview by author.

58   Wolfgang Glattes, interview by author.

59   Erik Lee Preminger, interview by author.

60   Ibid.

61   Wolfgang Glattes, interview by author.

62   Tony Gittelson, interview by author.

63   Preminger quoted in Earl Wilson, *New York Post,* October 19, 1974.

64   Preminger quoted in *Bergen Daily Record,* March 9, 1975.

65   Erik Lee Preminger, interview by author.

66   Ibid.

67   Hope Preminger, interview by author.

68   Ken Kaufman, interview by author.

69   Ibid.

70   Hope Preminger, interview by author.

71   Mark Preminger, interview by author.

72   Ken Kaufman, interview by author.

73   Ibid.

74   Elaine Gold, interview by author, June 26, 2001.

75   *Washington Post,* March 10, 1980.

76   Val Robins, interview by author, May 3, 2001.

77   Hope Preminger, interview by author.

78   Val Robins, interview by author.

79   Preminger quoted in *Los Angeles Times,* June 24, 1979.

80   Val Robins, interview by author.

81   Preminger quoted in *Los Angeles Herald Examiner,* December 17, 1979.
82   Preminger quoted in *Los Angeles Times,* January 21, 1980.
83   *Screen International,* February 4, 1984.
84   Mark Preminger, interview by author.

19   AFTER THE FALL

1   Lewis Chambers, interview by author, July 24, 2002.
2   Hope Preminger, interview by author.
3   Val Robins, interview by author.
4   Elaine Gold, interview by author.
5   John Martello, interview by author, July 3, 2001.
6   Hope Preminger, interview by author.
7   Mark Preminger, interview by author.
8   Hope Preminger, interview by author.
9   Patricia Neal, interview by author.
10   Peter Bogdanovich, interview by author.
11   Eva Monley, interview by author.
12   Hope Preminger, interview by author.
13   Ibid.
14   Victoria Preminger, interview by author.
15   Mark Preminger, interview by author.
16   Erik Lee Preminger, interview by author.
17   Ibid.
18   Peter Bogdanovich, interview by author.
19   Robert Lantz, interview by author, July 15, 2002.

Bibliography

Algren, Nelson. ". . . But Most of All I Remember Otto." *Chicago Sun Times,* May 21, 1972.

———. *The Man with the Golden Arm.* New York: Doubleday, 1949.

———. "Otto Preminger: Man with the Golden Prerogative." *Los Angeles Times,* May 15, 1977.

Alpert, Hollis. *The Life and Times of Porgy and Bess: The Story of an American Classic.* New York: Knopf, 1990.

Andersen, Christopher. *Citizen Jane.* New York: Henry Holt, 1990.

Arden, Eve. *Three Faces of Eve.* New York: St. Martin's, 1985.

Balfour, Michael. *The Kaiser and His Times.* Boston: Houghton Mifflin, 1964.

Barea, Ilsa. *Vienna.* New York: Knopf, 1966.

Bassett, James. *In Harm's Way.* Cleveland: World, 1962.

Beaton, Cecil. *Beaton in the Sixties.* New York: Knopf, 2004.

Belton, John. *Cinema Stylists.* Metuchen, N.J.: Scarecrow, 1983.

Berg, A. Scott. *Goldwyn.* New York: Knopf, 1989.

Berle, Milton, with Haskel Frankel. *An Autobiography.* New York: Delacorte, 1974.

Blaetz, Robin. *Visions of the Maid: Joan of Arc in American Film and Culture.* Charlottesville: University Press of Virginia, 2001.

Bogdanovich, Peter. *Who the Devil Made It: Conversations with Directors.* New York: Knopf, 1997.

Bogle, Donald. *Brown Sugar: Eighty Years of America's Black Female Superstars.* New York: Da Capo, 1990.

———. *Dorothy Dandridge: A Biography.* New York: Amistad, 1997.

———. *Toms, Coons, Mulattoes, Mammies, and Bucks: An Interpretive History of Blacks in American Films.* Third edition. New York: Continuum, 1994.

Bonnecarrère, Paul, and Joan Hemingway. *Rosebud.* Paris: Fayard, 1973.

Brown, Peter Harry, and Pat H. Broeske. *Howard Hughes: The Untold Story.* New York: Dutton, 1996.

Caine, Michael. *What's It All About?* New York: Turtle Bay Books, 1992.

Callow, Simon. *Charles Laughton: A Difficult Actor.* London: Methuen, 1987.

Carroll, Diahann. *Diahann!* Boston: Little, Brown, 1986.

Caspary, Vera. *Laura.* Boston: Houghton Mifflin, 1943.

Castronovo, David. *Beyond the Gray Flannel Man: Books from the 1950s That Made American Culture.* New York: Continuum, 2004.

Chandler, Charlotte. *Nobody's Perfect: Billy Wilder, A Personal Biography.* New York: Simon and Schuster, 2002.

Clare, George. *Last Waltz in Vienna.* New York: Holt, Rinehart and Winston, 1980.

Cook, Bruce. *Dalton Trumbo.* New York: Scribner, 1977.

Courtney, Marguerite. *Laurette.* New York: Atheneum, 1968.

Crankshaw, Edward. *The Fall of the House of Hapsburg.* New York: Viking, 1963.

Custen, George F. *Twentieth Century's Fox: Darryl F. Zanuck and the Culture of Hollywood.* New York: Basic Books, 1997.

Dandridge, Dorothy, and Earl Conrad. *Everything and Nothing: The Dorothy Dandridge Story.* New York: Abelard-Schuman, 1970.

Darrid, Diana Douglas. *In the Wings.* New York: Barricade Books, 1999.

Davis, Ronald L. *Hollywood Beauty: Linda Darnell and the American Dream.* Norman: University of Oklahoma Press, 1991.

Davis, Sammy, Jr., with Jane and Burt Boyar. *Yes I Can: The Story of Sammy Davis, Jr.* New York: Farrar, Straus and Giroux, 1965.

Dewey, Donald. *James Stewart.* Atlanta: Turner Publishing, 1996.

Douglas, Kirk. *The Ragman's Son.* New York: Simon and Schuster, 1988.

Drosnin, Michael. *Citizen Hughes.* New York: Holt, Rinehart and Winston, 1985.

Drury, Allen. *Advise and Consent.* New York: Doubleday, 1960.

Dunaway, Faye. *Looking for Gatsby.* New York: Simon and Schuster, 1995.

Easton, Carol. *The Search for Goldwyn.* New York: William Morrow, 1975.

Eksteins, Modris. *Rites of Spring: The Great War and the Birth of the Modern Age.* Boston: Houghton Mifflin, 1989.

Endore, Guy. *Methinks the Lady.* New York: Duell, Sloan and Pearce, 1945.

Eyman, Scott. *Ernst Lubitsch: Laughter in Paradise.* New York: Simon and Schuster, 1993.

Fairbanks, Douglas, Jr. *The Salad Days.* New York: Doubleday, 1998.

Farkas, Andrew, ed. *Lawrence Tibbett, Singing Actor.* Portland, Oreg.: Amadeus, 1989.

Fishgall, Gary. *Pieces of Times: The Life of James Stewart.* New York: Scribner, 1997.

Fonda, Henry, with Howard Teichmann. *My Life.* New York: New American Library, 1981.

Fonda, Jane. *My Life So Far.* New York: Random House, 2005.

Fowler, Gene. *Good Night, Sweet Prince: The Life and Times of John Barrymore.* New York: Buccaneer Books, 1976.

Freiman, Ray. *The Samuel Goldwyn Motion Picture Production of Porgy and Bess.* New York: Random House, 1959.

Friedrich, Otto. *City of Nets: A Portrait of Hollywood in the 1940s.* New York: Harper and Row, 1986.

Frischauer, Willi. *Behind the Scenes of Otto Preminger.* New York: William Morrow, 1974.

Gay, Peter. *Schnitzler's Century: The Making of Middle-Class Culture 1815–1914.* New York: Norton, 2002.

Geist, Kenneth L. *Pictures Will Talk: The Life and Times of Joseph L. Mankiewicz.* New York: Scribner, 1978.

Gershuny, Theodore. *Soon to Be a Major Motion Picture: The Anatomy of an All-Star, Big-Budget, Multimillion-Dollar Disaster.* New York: Holt, Rinehart and Winston, 1980.

Gilden, K. B. [Katya and Bert]. *Hurry Sundown.* New York: Doubleday, 1964.

Goudsouzian, Aram. *Sidney Poitier: Man, Actor, Icon.* Chapel Hill: University of North Carolina Press, 2004.

Gould, Lois. *Such Good Friends.* New York: Random House, 1970.

Greene, Graham. *The Human Factor.* London: Bodley Head, 1978.

Griffith, Richard. *Anatomy of a Motion Picture.* New York: St. Martin's, 1959.

Grob, Norbert, Rolf Aurich, and Wolfgang Jacobsen. *Otto Preminger.* Berlin: Jovis, 1999.

Gussow, Mel. *Don't Say Yes Until I Finish Talking: A Biography of Darryl F. Zanuck.* New York: Doubleday, 1971.

Hall, William. *Raising Caine.* Englewood, N.J.: Prentice-Hall, 1982.

Hammerstein, Oscar, II. *Carmen Jones.* New York: Knopf, 1945.

Harris, Marlys J. *The Zanucks of Hollywood: The Dark Legacy of an American Dynasty.* New York: Crown, 1989.

Heilbut, Anthony. *Exiled in Paradise: German Refugee Artists and Intellectuals in America from the 1930s to the Present.* Boston: Beacon, 1984.

Henry, William A., III. *The Great One: The Life and Legend of Jackie Gleason.* New York: Doubleday, 1992.

Herbert, F. Hugh. *The Moon Is Blue.* New York: Random House, 1950.

Heyward, Dorothy, and DuBose Heyward. *Porgy: A Play in Four Acts.* New York: Doubleday, Doran, 1928.

Heyward, DuBose. *Porgy.* New York: George H. Doran, 1925.

Higham, Charles. *Charles Laughton.* New York: Doubleday, 1976.

Hill, Holly. *Playing Joan: Actresses on the Challenge of Shaw's Saint Joan.* New York: Theatre Communication Group, 1987.

Hirsch, Foster. *The Dark Side of the Screen: Film Noir.* New York: Da Capo, 1983.

———. *Laurence Olivier on Screen.* New York: Da Capo, 1984.

Hoare, Philip. *Noël Coward.* New York: Simon and Schuster, 1995.

Hofmann, Paul. *The Viennese: Splendor, Twilight and Exile.* New York: Doubleday, 1988.

Holden, Anthony. *Laurence Olivier.* New York: Atheneum, 1988.

Holland, Marty. *Fallen Angel.* New York: Dutton, 1945.

Huston, John. *An Open Book.* New York: Knopf, 1980.

Idell, Albert E. *Centennial Summer.* New York: Henry Holt, 1943.

Israel, Lee. *Miss Tallulah Bankhead.* New York: Putnam, 1972.

Jablonski, Edward. *Gershwin: A Biography.* New York: Doubleday, 1987.

Janeway, Elizabeth. *Daisy Kenyon.* New York: Doubleday, Doran, 1945.

Janik, Allan, and Stephen Toulmin. *Wittgenstein's Vienna.* New York: Simon and Schuster, 1973.

Johnston, William M. *The Austrian Mind.* Berkeley: University of California Press, 1972.

Jones, J. Sydney. *Hitler in Vienna 1907–1913: Clues to the Future.* New York: Cooper Square, 2002.

Jungk, Peter Stephan. *Franz Werfel: A Life in Prague, Vienna, and Hollywood.* New York: Grove Weidenfeld, 1990.

Kaminsky, Stuart M. *Coop: The Life and Legend of Gary Cooper.* New York: St. Martin's, 1980.

Kellogg, Marjorie. *Tell Me That You Love Me, Junie Moon.* New York: Farrar, Straus and Giroux, 1968.

Kimball, Robert, and Alfred Simon. *The Gershwins.* New York: Atheneum, 1973.

Krebs, Albin. "Otto Preminger, 80, Dies." *New York Times,* April 24, 1986.

Lardner, Ring, Jr. *I'd Hate Myself in the Morning.* New York: Thunder's Mouth/Nation Books, 2000.

Lawrenson, Helen. "Is It True What They Say About Otto?" *McCall's,* March 1965.

Lazar, Irving. *Swifty: My Life and Good Times.* New York: Simon and Schuster, 1995.

Leaming, Barbara. *Marilyn Monroe.* New York: Crown, 1998.

Lee, Gypsy Rose. *Gypsy: Memoirs of America's Most Celebrated Stripper.* New York: Harper and Row, 1957.

Leff, Leonard J., and Jerold L. Simmons. *The Dame in the Kimono: Hollywood, Censorship, and the Production Code from the 1920s to the 1960s.* New York: Grove Weidenfeld, 1990.

Lobenthal, Joel. *Tallulah! The Life and Times of a Leading Lady.* New York: Regan Books, 2004.

Lourcelles, Jacques. *Otto Preminger.* Paris: Éditions Seghers, 1965.

Luce, Clare Boothe. *Margin for Error.* New York: Random House, 1946.

MacAdams, William. *Ben Hecht: The Man Behind the Legend.* New York: Scribner, 1991.

Macdonald, Dwight. *Dwight Macdonald on Movies.* Englewood Cliffs, N.J.: Prentice-Hall, 1969.

Malden, Karl. *When Do I Start?* New York: Simon and Schuster, 1997.

Marx, Arthur. *Goldwyn: A Biography of the Man Behind the Myth.* New York: Norton, 1976.

McGee, Tom. *The Girl with the Million Dollar Legs.* Vestal, N.Y.: Vestal, 1995.

McGilligan, Patrick. *Fritz Lang: The Nature of the Beast.* New York: St. Martin's, 1997.

McGuinness, Richard. "River of No Return." *Film Comment* 8, no. 3 (September–October 1972).

Meredith, Burgess. *So Far, So Good.* Boston: Little, Brown, 1994.

Meyers, Jeffrey. *Gary Cooper: American Hero.* New York: William Morrow, 1998.

Mills, Earl. *Dorothy Dandridge: A Portrait in Black.* Los Angeles: Holloway House, 1970.

Milne, Tom. *Mamoulian.* Bloomington: Indiana University Press, 1969.

Morley, Sheridan. *John Gielgud.* New York: Simon and Schuster, 2002.

———. *The Other Side of the Moon: A Biography of David Niven.* New York: Harper and Row, 1985.

———. *A Talent to Amuse: A Biography of Noël Coward.* Boston: Little, Brown, 1969.

Morrison, Michael A. *John Barrymore: Shakespearean Actor.* New York: Cambridge University Press, 1997.

Morton, Frederic. *A Nervous Splendor: Vienna 1888/1889.* Boston: Little, Brown, 1979.

———. *Thunder at Twilight: Vienna 1913/1914.* New York: Scribner, 1989.

Mosley, Leonard. *Zanuck: The Rise and Fall of Hollywood's Last Tycoon.* Boston: Little, Brown, 1984.

Nadel, Ira. *Tom Stoppard: A Life.* New York: Palgrave Macmillan, 2002.

Neale, Stephen. *Genre.* London: BFI, 1980.

Niven, David. *Bring on the Empty Horses.* New York: Putnam, 1975.

———. *The Moon's a Balloon.* New York: Putnam, 1971.

Oumano, Elena. *Paul Newman.* New York: St. Martin's, 1989.

Paul, William. *Ernst Lubitsch's American Comedy.* New York: Columbia University Press, 1983.

Piper, Evelyn [Merriam Modell]. *Bunny Lake Is Missing.* New York: Harper and Row, 1957.

Poitier, Sidney. *This Life.* New York: Knopf, 1980.

Pratley, Gerald. *The Cinema of Otto Preminger.* New York: Barnes, 1971.

Preminger, Erik Lee. *Gypsy and Me: At Home and on the Road with Gypsy Rose Lee.* Boston: Little, Brown, 1984.

Preminger, Marion Mill. *All I Want Is Everything.* New York: MacFaden, 1957.

———. *The Sands of Tamanrasset.* New York: Hawthorn Books, 1961.

Preminger, Otto. "*The Cardinal* and I." *Films and Filming* 10, no. 2 (November 1963).

———. Interview. In *Max Reinhardt 1873–1973: A Centennial Festschrift of Memorial Essays and Interviews.* Binghamton, N.Y.: Max Reinhardt Archive, 1973.

———. "Keeping Out of Harm's Way." *Films and Filming* 11, no. 9 (June 1965).

———. *Preminger: An Autobiography.* New York: Doubleday, 1977.

———, as told to Peter Bogdanovich. "The Making of *Laura.*" *On Film* 1, no. 1 (1970).

Price, Victoria. *Vincent Price: A Daughter's Biography.* New York: St. Martin's, 1999.

Pulzer, Peter G. J. *The Rise of Political Anti-Semitism in Germany and Austria.* New York: Columbia University Press, 1964.

Rainer, Peter. "The Man We Loved to Hate." *Los Angeles Herald Examiner,* April 24, 1986.

Reed, Rex. "They Could Cut Your Heart Out." *New York Times,* August 21, 1966.

Reinhardt, Gottfried. *The Genius: A Memoir of Max Reinhardt by His Son.* New York: Knopf, 1979.

Richards, David. *Played Out: The Jean Seberg Story.* New York: Random House, 1981.

Robinson, Henry Morton. *The Cardinal.* New York: Simon and Schuster, 1950.

Ross, Lillian. "Profiles: Anatomy of a Commercial Interruption: A Film: 70mm UltraPanavision Technicolor: Filmed Entirely on Location: Starring Otto Preminger." *New Yorker* 41, no. 53 (February 19, 1966).

Ryan, Tom. *Otto Preminger Films Exodus: A Report.* New York: Random House, 1960.

Sagan, Françoise. *Bonjour Tristesse.* New York: Random House, 1955.

Santer, Michael. *The Worst Movies of All Time. Or: What Were They Thinking?* Secaucus, N.J.: Citadel, 1996.

Sarris, Andrew. *Directors and Directions 1929–1968.* New York: Dutton, 1968.

———. "Preminger's Two Periods: Studio and Solo." *Film Comment* 3, no. 3 (Summer 1965).

———. "Two Cheers for the Film-Flam-Man." *Village Voice* 31, no. 21 (May 27, 1986).

Schorske, Carl. *Fin-de-Siècle Vienna: Politics and Culture.* New York: Vintage, 1981.

Server, Lee. *Robert Mitchum: "Baby, I Don't Care."* New York: St. Martin's, 2001.

Shadegg, Stephen. *Clare Boothe Luce.* New York: Simon and Schuster, 1970.

Shaw, George Bernard. *Saint Joan: A Chronicle Play in Six Scenes and an Epilogue* (1924). New York: Penguin, 1946.

Shepard, Donald, and Robert Slatzer with Dave Grayson. *Duke: The Life and Times of John Wayne.* New York: Doubleday, 1985.

Sikov, Ed. *On Sunset Boulevard: The Life and Times of Billy Wilder.* New York: Hyperion, 1998.

Silverman, Stephen M. *The Fox That Got Away: The Last Days of the Zanuck Dynasty at Twentieth Century-Fox.* Secaucus, N.J.: Lyle Stuart, 1988.

Solomon, Aubrey. *Twentieth Century-Fox: A Corporate and Financial History.* Metuchen, N.J.: Scarecrow, 1989.

Spada, James. *Peter Lawford: The Man Who Kept the Secrets.* New York: Bantam Books, 1991.

Spiel, Hilde. *Vienna's Golden Autumn 1866–1938.* London: Weidenfeld and Nicolson, 1987.

Spoto, Donald. *Marilyn Monroe.* New York: HarperCollins, 1993.

Thomas, Bob. *King Cohn.* New York: Putnam, 1967.

Tierney, Gene, with Mickey Herskowitz. *Self-Portrait.* New York: Wyden Books, 1978.

Todd, Michael, Jr., and Susan McCarthy Todd. *A Valuable Property: The Life Story of Michael Todd.* New York: Arbor House, 1983.

Traver, Robert [John Voelker]. *Anatomy of a Murder.* New York: St. Martin's, 1968.

Trumbo, Dalton. *Additional Dialogue.* New York: Evans, 1970.

Uris, Leon. *Exodus.* New York: Doubleday, 1958.

Vanderbeets, Richard. *George Sanders: An Exhausted Life.* New York: Madison Books, 1990.

Vergo, Peter. *Art in Vienna, 1898–1918.* New York: Phaidon, 1975.

Vizzard, Jack. *See No Evil: Life Inside a Hollywood Censor.* New York: Simon and Schuster, 1970.

Weisgal, Meyer. *Meyer Weisgal . . . So Far: An Autobiography.* New York: Random House, 1971.

Wilde, Oscar. *Lady Windermere's Fan: A Play about a Good Woman.* London: Methuen, 1893.

Winsor, Kathleen. *Forever Amber.* New York: Macmillan, 1944.

Zierold, Norman J. *The Moguls.* New York: Coward-McCann, 1969.

Zolotow, Maurice. *Billy Wilder in Hollywood.* New York: Limelight, 1987.

Directed by Otto Preminger

PLAYS IN VIENNA AT THE THEATER IN DER JOSEFSTADT

1931 *Voruntersuchung* (*Preliminary Inquiry*), by Max Alsberg and Otto Ernst Hesse
  Reporter (*The Front Page*), by Ben Hecht and Charles MacArthur
1933 *Die Liebe des Jungen Nosty* (*The Love of Young Nosty*), by Koloman von Mikszath
  Makart, by Duschinski
1934 *Mehr Als Liebe* (*More Than Love*), by L. Bus Fekete
  Christiano Zwischen Himmel und Hölle (*Christiano Between Heaven and Hell*),
    by Hans Jaray
  Die Princessin auf der Leiter (*The Princess on the Ladder*), by Louis Verneuil
  Sensationsprozess (*Libel!*), by Edward Wooll
  Einen Jux Will er Sich Machen (*He's Going to Have Fun*), by Johannes Nepomuk
    Nestroy
  Menschen in Weiss (*Men in White*), by Sidney Kingsley
1935 *Adrienne Ambrosat*, by Georg Kaiser
  Eine Frau Luegt (*A Woman Lies*), by Von Ladislaus (László) Fodor
  Der König mit dem Regenschirm (*The King with the Umbrella*), by Ralph Benatzky
  Kleines Bezirksgericht (*The Little District Court*), by Otto Bielen
  Die Erste Legion (*The First Legion*), by Emmett Lavery

ON BROADWAY

1935 *Libel!*, by Edward Wooll
1938 *Outward Bound*, by Sutton Vane
1939 *Margin for Error*, by Clare Boothe Luce
1940 *My Dear Children*, by Catherine Turney and Jerry Horwin
  Beverly Hills, by Lynn Starling and Howard J. Green
  Cue for Passion, by Edward Chodorov and H. S. Kraft

1941   *The More the Merrier,* by Frank Gabrielson and Irvin Pincus
        In Time to Come, by John Huston and Howard Koch
1951   *Four Twelves Are 48,* by Joseph Kesselring
        The Moon Is Blue, by F. Hugh Herbert
        A Modern Primitive, by Herman Wouk (closed in Hartford, Conn.)
1953   *The Trial,* an opera by Gottfried von Einem (for the New York City Opera)
1958   *This Is Goggle,* by B. Plagemann (closed in Princeton, N.J.)
1960   *Critic's Choice,* by Ira Levin
1973   *Full Circle,* by Erich Maria Remarque, adapted by Peter Stone

FILMS

1931   *Die Grosse Liebe* (*The Great Love*). Screenplay: Siegfried Bernfeld, Arthur Berger,
        based on a true story. Camera: Hans Theyer. Music: Walter Landauer, Frank Fox.
        Cast: Hansi Niese (The Mother), Attila Hörbiger (Franz), Hugo Thimig (Chief
        of Police), Maria Waldner (Frau Huber). Released by Allianz Film, Vienna,
        E.M.L.K. Weissman Tonfilm.
1936   *Under Your Spell.* Screenplay: Frances Hyland, Saul Elkins, based on stories by
        Bernice Mason, Sy Bartlett. Camera: Sidney Wagner. Editor: Fred Allen. Music
        and lyrics: Arthur Schwartz, Howard Dietz. Cast: Lawrence Tibbett (Anthony
        Allen), Gregory Ratoff (Petroff), Wendy Barrie (Cynthia Drexel), Arthur
        Treacher (Botts). Associate Producer: John Stone. Released by Twentieth Cen-
        tury-Fox.
1937   *Danger—Love at Work.* Screenplay: James Edward Grant, Ben Markson, based on a
        story by James Edward Grant. Camera: Virgil Miller. Art director: Duncan
        Cramer. Music: David Butolph. Cast: Ann Sothern (Toni Pemberton), Jack
        Haley (Henry Mac Morrow), Edward Everett Horton (Howard Rogers), Mary
        Boland (Alice Pemberton), John Carradine (Herbert Pemberton). Associate
        Producer: Harold Wilson. Released by Twentieth Century-Fox.
1943   *Margin for Error.* Screenplay: Lillie Hayward, based on the play by Clare Boothe
        Luce. Camera: Edward Cronjager. Art directors: Richard Day, Lewis Creber.
        Editor: Louis Loeffler. Cast: Joan Bennett (Sophie Baumer), Milton Berle (Moe
        Finkelstein), Otto Preminger (Karl Baumer), Carl Esmond (Baron Max von
        Alvenstor). Producer: Ralph Dietrich. Released by Twentieth Century-Fox.
1944   *In the Meantime, Darling.* Screenplay: Arthur Kober, Michael Uris. Camera: Joe
        MacDonald. Editor: Louis Loeffler. Music: David Buttolph. Cast: Jeanne Crain
        (Maggie Preston), Frank Latimore (Lt. Daniel Ferguson), Mary Nash (Mrs.
        Preston), Eugene Pallette (H. B. Preston), Jane Randolph (Jerry Armstrong),
        Cara Williams (Mrs. Sayre). Producer: Otto Preminger. Released by Twentieth
        Century-Fox.
        Laura. Screenplay: Jay Dratler, Samuel Hoffenstein, Betty Reinhardt, based on the
        novel by Vera Caspary. Camera: Joseph La Shelle. Art directors: Lyle R. Wheeler,
        Leland Fuller. Editor: Louis Loeffler. Music: David Raksin. Cast: Gene Tierney
        (Laura), Dana Andrews (Mark McPherson), Clifton Webb (Waldo Lydecker),

Vincent Price (Shelby Carpenter), Judith Anderson (Anne Treadwell). Producer: Otto Preminger. Released by Twentieth Century-Fox.

1945   *A Royal Scandal.* Screenplay: Edwin Justus Mayer, adapted by Bruno Frank from the play *Czarina,* by Lajos Biro and Melchior Lengyel. Camera: Arthur Miller. Art directors: Lyle R. Wheeler, Mark Lee Kirk. Editor: Dorothy Spencer. Music: Alfred Newman. Cast: Tallulah Bankhead (Catherine II), Charles Coburn (Chancellor Nicolai Ilyitch), William Eythe (Lt. Alexis Chernoff), Vincent Price (Marquis de Fleury), Sig Ruman (General Ronsky), Mischa Auer (Captain Sukov), Anne Baxter (Countess Anna Jaschikoff), Eva Gabor (Countess Demidow). Producer: Ernst Lubitsch. Released by Twentieth Century-Fox.

Fallen Angel. Screenplay: Harry Kleiner, based on the novel by Marty Holland. Camera: Joseph La Shelle. Art directors: Lyle R. Wheeler, Leland Fuller. Editor: Harry Reynolds. Music: David Raksin. Cast: Dana Andrews (Eric Stanton), Alice Faye (June Mills), Linda Darnell (Stella), Charles Bickford (Mark Judd), Anne Revere (Clara Mills). Producer: Otto Preminger. Released by Twentieth Century-Fox.

1946   *Centennial Summer.* Screenplay: Michael Kanin, based on the novel by Albert E. Idell. Camera: Ernest Palmer. Art directors: Lyle R. Wheeler, Leland Fuller. Editor: Harry Reynolds. Music: Jerome Kern. Lyrics: Oscar Hammerstein II ("All Through the Day"), Leo Robin ("In Love in Vain," "Up with the Lark," "The Railroad Song," "Centennial Reprise," "The Light Romance," "Concerto Piece," "Happy Anniversary," "Free America"), E. Y. Harburg ("Cinderella Sue"). Cast: Linda Darnell (Edith Rogers), Jeanne Crain (Julia Rogers), Cornel Wilde (Philippe Lascelles), William Eythe (Benjamin Franklin Phelps), Walter Brennan (Jesse Rogers), Constance Bennett (Zenia Lascelles), Dorothy Gish (Harriet Rogers), Barbara Whiting (Susanna Rogers), Avon Long. Producer: Otto Preminger. Released by Twentieth Century-Fox.

1947   *Forever Amber.* Screenplay: Philip Dunne, Ring Lardner Jr., adapted by Jerome Cady from the novel by Kathleen Winsor. Camera: Leon Shamroy. Art director: Lyle R. Wheeler. Editor: Louis Loeffler. Music: David Raksin. Cast: Linda Darnell (Amber), Cornel Wilde (Bruce Carlton), Richard Greene (Lord Almsbury), George Sanders (Charles II), Richard Haydn (Lord Radcliffe), Jessica Tandy (Nan Britton), Anne Revere (Mother Red Cap), Natalie Draper (Countess of Castelmaine), Alma Kruger (Lady Redmond), Robert Coote (Sir Thomas Dudley). Producer: William Perlberg. Released by Twentieth Century-Fox.

Daisy Kenyon. Screenplay by David Hertz, based on the novel by Elizabeth Janeway. Camera: Leon Shamroy. Art directors: Lyle R. Wheeler, George Davis. Editor: Louis Loeffler. Music: David Raksin. Cast: Joan Crawford (Daisy Kenyon), Dana Andrews (Dan O'Mara), Henry Fonda (Peter Lapham), Ruth Warrick (Lucille O'Mara), Peggy Ann Garner (Rosamund O'Mara), Connie Marshall (Mariette O'Mara), Martha Stewart (Mary Angelus). Producer: Otto Preminger. Released by Twentieth Century-Fox.

1948   *That Lady in Ermine.* Screenplay: Samson Raphaelson, based on an operetta by Rudolph Schanzer and E. Welisch. Camera: Leon Shamroy. Art directors: Lyle R. Wheeler, J. Russell Spencer. Editor: Dorothy Spencer. Music and lyrics: Leo

Robin and Frederick Hollander. Choreography: Hermes Pan. Cast: Douglas
Fairbanks Jr. (Col. Ladislas Karolyi Teglasch and the Duke), Betty Grable
(Angelina and Francesca), Cesar Romero (Mario), Reginald Gardiner (Alberto).
Producer: Ernst Lubitsch. Released by Twentieth Century-Fox.

1949   *The Fan*. Screenplay: Walter Reisch, Dorothy Parker, Ross Evans, based on the play
Lady Windermere's Fan, by Oscar Wilde. Camera: Joseph La Shelle. Art directors:
Lyle R. Wheeler, Leland Fuller. Editor: Louis Loeffler. Music: Daniele Amfithe-
atrof. Cast: Jeanne Crain (Lady Windermere), Madeleine Carroll (Mrs. Erlynne),
George Sanders (Lord Darlington), Richard Green (Lord Windermere), Martita
Hunt (Duchess of Berwick), Virginia McDowall (Lady Agatha). Producer: Otto
Preminger. Released by Twentieth Century-Fox.

Whirlpool. Screenplay: Ben Hecht (under the pseudonym Lester Bartow), Andrew
Solt, based on the novel by Guy Endore. Camera: Arthur Miller. Art directors:
Lyle R. Wheeler, Leland Fuller. Editor: Louis Loeffler. Music: David Raksin.
Cast: Gene Tierney (Ann Sutton), Richard Conte (Dr. William Sutton), José
Ferrer (David Korvo), Charles Bickford (Lt. Colton), Barbara O'Neill (Theresa
Randolph), Constance Collier (Tina Cosgrove). Producer: Otto Preminger.
Released by Twentieth Century-Fox.

1950   *Where the Sidewalk Ends*. Screenplay: Rex Conner, based on an adaptation by Victor
Trivas, Frank P. Rosenberg, and Robert E. Kent of a novel by William L. Stuart.
Camera: Joseph La Shelle. Art directors: Lyle R. Wheeler, J. Russell Spencer.
Editor: Louis Loeffler. Music: Cyril Mockridge. Cast: Dana Andrews (Mark
Dixon), Gene Tierney (Morgan Taylor), Gary Merrill (Scalise), Bert Freed (Paul
Klein), Tom Tully (Jiggs Taylor), Karl Malden (Lt. Bill Thomas), Craig Stevens
(Ken Payne), Oleg Cassini (Mayer). Producer: Otto Preminger. Released by
Twentieth Century-Fox.

The Thirteenth Letter. Screenplay: Howard Koch, based on the script by Louis
Chavance for *Le Corbeau* (H. G. Clouzot, 1943). Camera: Joseph La Shelle. Art
directors: Lyle R. Wheeler, Maurice Ransford. Editor: Louis Loeffler. Music: Alex
North. Cast: Linda Darnell (Denise Tourneur), Charles Boyer (Dr. Paul Laurent),
Michael Rennie (Dr. Pearson), Constance Smith (Cora Laurent), Françoise Rosay
(Mrs. Simms), Judith Evelyn (Sister Marie). Producer: Otto Preminger. Released
by Twentieth Century-Fox.

1952   *Angel Face*. Screenplay: Frank Nugent and Oscar Millard, based on a story by
Chester Erskine. Camera: Harry Stradling. Art directors: Albert S. D'Agostino,
Carroll Clark. Editor: Frederick Knudtson. Music: Dimitri Tiomkin. Cast: Jean
Simmons (Diane Tremayne), Robert Mitchum (Frank Jessup), Mona Freeman
(Mary Wilton), Herbert Marshall (Charles Tremayne), Leon Ames (Fred Barrett),
Barbara O'Neil (Catherine Tremayne), Kenneth Tobey (Bill Crompton), Jim
Backus (Judson). Producer: Howard Hughes. Released by RKO.

1953   *The Moon Is Blue*. Screenplay: F. Hugh Herbert, based on his play. Camera: Ernest
Laszlo. Production designer: Nicolai Remisoff. Titles: Saul Bass. Editors: Louis
Loeffler, Otto Ludwig [Preminger]. Music: Herschel Burke Gilbert. Lyrics: Sylvia
Fine. Cast: Maggie McNamara (Patty O'Neill), William Holden (Don Gresham),
David Niven (David Slater), Dawn Addams (Cynthia Slater), Gregory Ratoff

(taxi driver). Producers: Otto Preminger and F. Hugh Herbert. Released by
United Artists. A German version, *Die Jungfrau auf dem Dach,* was filmed at the
same time with the same technicians and the following cast: Hardy Krüger (Don
Gresham), Johanna Matz (Patty O'Neill), Johannes Heesters (David Slater),
Gregory Ratoff (dubbed by Otto Preminger).

1954 *River of No Return.* Screenplay: Frank Fenton, based on a story by Louis Lantz.
Camera: Joseph La Shelle. Art directors: Lyle Wheeler, Addison Hehr. Editor:
Louis Loeffler. Music: Cyril Mockridge. Lyrics: Ken Darby. Choreography: Jack
Cole. Cast: Robert Mitchum (Matt Calder), Marilyn Monroe (Kay Weston),
Rory Calhoun (Harry Weston), Tommy Rettig (Mark Calder), Murvyn Vye
(Dave Colby), Jarma Lewis. Producer: Stanley Rubin. Released by Twentieth
Century-Fox.

Carmen Jones. Screenplay: Harry Kleiner, based on the musical by Oscar Hammer-
stein II, adapted from the opera by Bizet, Meilhac, and Halévy, based on the
novel by Prosper Mérimée. Camera: Sam Leavitt and Albert Myers. Art director:
Edward L. Hou. Titles: Saul Bass. Editor: Louis Loeffler. Music: Herschel Burke
Gilbert, based on the music of Georges Bizet. Choreography: Herbert Ross. Cast:
Dorothy Dandridge (Carmen Jones), Harry Belafonte (Joe), Olga James (Cindy
Lou), Pearl Bailey (Frankie), Diahann Carroll (Myrt), Joe Adams (Husky Miller),
Brock Peters (Sgt. Brown). Producer: Otto Preminger, for Carlyle Productions.
Released by Twentieth Century-Fox.

1955 *The Man with the Golden Arm.* Screenplay: Walter Newman, Lewis Meltzer, based
on the novel by Nelson Algren. Camera: Sam Leavitt. Art director: Joe Wright.
Titles: Saul Bass. Editor: Louis Loeffler. Music: Elmer Bernstein. Cast: Frank
Sinatra (Frankie Machine), Kim Novak (Molly), Eleanor Parker (Zosch), Arnold
Stang (Sparrow), Darren McGavin (Louis), Robert Strauss (Schwiefka), Doro
Merande (Vi). Producer: Otto Preminger, for Carlyle Productions. Released by
United Artists.

The Court-Martial of Billy Mitchell. Screenplay: Milton Sperling and Emmet Lavery,
based on a true story by General William Mitchell. Camera: Sam Leavitt. Art
director: Malcolm Bert. Music: Dimitri Tiomkin. Cast: Gary Cooper (Brig. Gen.
William Mitchell), Charles Bickford (Gen. James Guthrie), Rod Steiger (Maj.
Allen Gullion), Ralph Bellamy (Congressman Frank Reid), Elizabeth Mont-
gomery (Margaret Lansdowne), Darren McGavin (Russ Peters), Jack Lord
(Zachary Lansdowne). Producer: Milton Sperling, for United States Productions.
Released by Warner Bros.

1957 *Saint Joan.* Screenplay: Graham Greene, based on the play by George Bernard Shaw.
Camera: Georges Périnal. Production designer: Roger Furse. Titles: Saul Bass.
Editor: Helga Cranston. Music: Mischa Spoliansky. Cast: Jean Seberg (Joan),
Richard Widmark (Charles, the Dauphin), Richard Todd (Dunois), Anton
Walbrook (Cauchon, Bishop of Beauvais), John Gielgud (Earl of Warwick), Felix
Aylmer (The Inquisitor), Harry Andrews (John de Stogumber), Barry Jones (de
Courcelles), Finlay Currie (Archbishop of Rheims), Kenneth Haigh (Brother
Martin), Bernard Miles (The Executioner). Producer: Otto Preminger, for
Preminger Productions. Released by United Artists.

1958 *Bonjour Tristesse.* Screenplay: Arthur Laurents, based on the novel by Françoise Sagan. Camera: Georges Périnal. Production designer: Roger Furse. Titles: Saul Bass. Editor: Helga Cranston. Music: Georges Auric. Costume coordinator: Hope Bryce. Cast: Jean Seberg (Cécile), Deborah Kerr (Anne), David Niven (Raymond), Mylène Demongeot (Elsa Mackenbourg), Geoffrey Horne (Philippe), Juliette Greco (nightclub singer), Walter Chiari (Pablo), Martita Hunt (Philippe's mother), Roland Culver (Mr. Lombard). Producer: Otto Preminger, for Wheel Films. Released by Columbia.

1959 *Porgy and Bess.* Screenplay: N. Richard Nash, based on the musical by George Gershwin, from the novel *Porgy* by DuBose Heyward and the play *Porgy* by Dorothy and DuBose Heyward. Camera: Leon Shamroy. Production designer: Oliver Smith. Editor: Daniel Mandell. Music: George Gershwin. Musical director: André Previn. Choreography: Hermes Pan. Cast: Sidney Poitier (Porgy), Dorothy Dandridge (Bess), Sammy Davis Jr. (Sportin' Life), Pearl Bailey (Maria), Brock Peters (Crown), Diahann Carroll (Clara), Ruth Attaway (Serena), Clarence Muse (Peter), Joel Fluellen (Robbins), Ivan Dixon (Jim). Producer: Samuel Goldwyn. Released by Columbia.

Anatomy of a Murder. Screenplay: Wendell Mayes, based on the novel by Robert Traver. Camera: Sam Leavitt. Production designer: Boris Leven. Titles: Saul Bass. Editor: Louis Loeffler. Music: Duke Ellington. Costume supervision: Hope Bryce. Cast: James Stewart (Paul Biegler), Lee Remick (Laura Manion), Ben Gazzara (Lt. Frederick Manion), Joseph N. Welch (Judge Weaver), Kathryn Grant (Mary Pilant), Arthur O'Connell (Parnell McArthy), Eve Arden (Maida Rutledge), George C. Scott (Claude Dancer), Brooks West (Mitch Lodwick), Orson Bean (Dr. Smith), Murray Hamilton (Alphonse Paquette), Duke Ellington (Pie-Eye), Mrs. Welch (a juror). Producer: Otto Preminger, for Carlyle Productions. Released by Columbia.

1960 *Exodus.* Screenplay: Dalton Trumbo, based on the novel by Leon Uris. Camera: Sam Leavitt. Art directors: Richard Day, Bill Hutchinson. Titles: Saul Bass. Editor: Louis Loeffler. Music: Ernest Gold. Costume supervisor: Hope Bryce. Cast: Paul Newman (Ari Ben Canaan), Eva Marie Saint (Kitty Fremont), Ralph Richardson (General Sutherland), Jill Haworth (Karen), Peter Lawford (Major Caldwell), Lee J. Cobb (Barak Ben Canaan), Sal Mineo (Dov Landau), John Derek (Taha), Hugh Griffith (Mandria), David Opatashu (Akiva), Gregory Ratoff (Lakavitch), Felix Aylmer (Dr. Lieberman), Marius Goring (Von Storch), Alexandra Stewart (Jordana), Michael Wager (David), George Maharis (Yaov). Producer: Otto Preminger, for Carlyle/Alpha Productions. Released by United Artists.

1962 *Advise and Consent.* Screenplay: Wendell Mayes, based on the novel by Allen Drury. Camera: Sam Leavitt. Art director: Lyle R. Wheeler. Titles: Saul Bass. Editor: Louis Loeffler. Music: Jerry Fielding. Costume supervisor: Hope Bryce. Cast: Henry Fonda (Robert Leffingwell), Charles Laughton (Senator Seabright Cooley), Don Murray (Senator Brigham Anderson), Walter Pidgeon (Senator Bob Munson), Peter Lawford (Senator Lafe Smith), Gene Tierney (Dolly Harrison), Franchot Tone (The President), Lew Ayres (The Vice-President), Burgess Meredith (Herbert Gelman), Eddie Hodges (Johnnie Leffingwell), Paul Ford (Senator

Stanley Danta), George Grizzard (Senator Fred Van Ackerman), Inga Swenson (Ellen Anderson), Betty White (Senator Bessie Adams). Producer: Otto Preminger, for Alpha-Alpina Productions. Released by Columbia.

1963 *The Cardinal.* Screenplay: Robert Dozier, based on the novel by Henry Morton Robinson. Camera: Leon Shamroy. Production designer: Lyle Wheeler. Titles: Saul Bass. Editor: Louis Loeffler. Music: Jerome Moross. Costume coordinator: Hope Bryce. Cast: Tom Tryon (Stephen Fermoyle), Carol Lynley (Mona Fermoyle and Regina Fermoyle), Dorothy Gish (Celia), Maggie McNamara (Florrie), Bill Hayes (Frank), Cameron Prud'homme (Din), Cecil Kellaway (Monsignor Monaghan), John Saxon (Benny Rampell), John Huston (Cardinal Glennon), Robert Morse (Bobby and his Adora-Belles), Burgess Meredith (Father Ned Halley), Jill Haworth (Lalage Menton), Raf Vallone (Cardinal Quarenghi), Tullio Carminati (Cardinal Giacobbi), Ossie Davis (Father Gillis), Chill Wills (Monsignor Whittle), Doro Merande (woman picket), Patrick O'Neal (Cecil Turner), Murray Hamilton (Lafe), Romy Schneider (Annemarie), Josef Meinrad (Cardinal Innitzer), Wilma Lipp (soloist). Producer: Otto Preminger, for Gamma Productions. Released by Columbia.

1965 *In Harm's Way.* Screenplay: Wendell Mayes, based on the novel by James Bassett. Camera: Loyal Griggs. Production designer: Lyle Wheeler. Titles: Saul Bass. Editors: George Tomasini, Hugh S. Fowler. Music: Jerry Goldsmith. Costume coordinator: Hope Bryce. Cast: John Wayne (Capt. Rockwell Torrey), Kirk Douglas (Cdr. Paul Eddington), Patricia Neal (Lt. Maggie Haynes), Jill Haworth (Ens. Annalee Dorne), Tom Tryon (Lt. [jg] William McConnel), Paula Prentiss (Bev McConnel), Brandon de Wilde (Ens. Jeremiah Torrey), Dana Andrews (Adm. Broderick), Burgess Meredith (Cdr. Powell), Franchot Tone (CINCPAC I Admiral), Patrick O'Neal (Cdr. Neal Owynn), Carroll O'Connor (Lt. Cdr. Burke), James Mitchum (Ens. Griggs), George Kennedy (Col. Gregory), Bruce Cabot (Quartermaster Quoddy), Barbara Bouchet (Liz Eddington), Hugh O'Brian (Major Mark Wilson), Henry Fonda (CINCPAC II Admiral). Producer: Otto Preminger, for Sigma Productions. Released by Paramount.

1965 *Bunny Lake Is Missing.* Screenplay: John and Penelope Mortimer, based on the novel by Evelyn Piper. Camera: Denys Coop. Production designer: Don Ashton. Titles: Saul Bass. Editor: Peter Thornton. Music: Paul Glass. Costume coordinator: Hope Bryce. Cast: Laurence Olivier (Newhouse), Keir Dullea (Stephen Lake), Carol Lynley (Ann Lake), Martita Hunt (Ada Ford), Noël Coward (Wilson), Anna Massey (Elvira), Finlay Currie (Dollmaker), Clive Revill (Andrews), the Zombies (themselves). Producer: Otto Preminger, for Wheel Productions. Released by Columbia.

1967 *Hurry Sundown.* Screenplay: Thomas C. Ryan, Horton Foote, based on the novel by K. B. Gilden. Camera: Milton Krasner, Loyal Griggs. Production designer: Gene Callahan. Titles: Saul Bass. Editors: Louis Loeffler, James D. Wells. Music: Hugo Montenegro. Costume supervisor: Hope Bryce. Cast: Michael Caine (Henry Warren), Jane Fonda (Julie Ann Warren), John Phillip Law (Rad McDowell), Faye Dunaway (Lou McDowell), Diahann Carroll (Vivian Thurlow), Robert

Hooks (Reeve Scott), Burgess Meredith (Judge Purcell), Jim Backus (Carter Sillens), Beah Richards (Rose Scott), Madeleine Sherwood (Eula Purcell), Doro Merande (Ada Hemmings), George Kennedy (Sheriff Coombs), Rex Ingram (Professor Thurlow), Donna Danton (Sukie Purcell). Producer: Otto Preminger, for Sigma Productions. Released by Paramount.

1968   *Skidoo.* Screenplay: Doran William Cannon. Camera: Leon Shamroy. Art director: Robert E. Smith. Editor: George Rohrs. Music and lyrics: Harry Nilsson. Costume coordinator: Hope Bryce. Cast: Jackie Gleason (Tony Banks), Carol Channing (Flo Banks), Groucho Marx ("God"), Frankie Avalon (Angie), Frank Gorshin (The Man), John Phillip Law (Stash), Austin Pendleton (The Professor), Arnold Stang (Harry), Doro Merande (Mayor), Mickey Rooney ("Blue Chips" Packard), Peter Lawford (The Senator), Burgess Meredith (The Warden), George Raft (Captain Garbaldo), Cesar Romero (Hechy), Alexandra Hay (Darlene Banks), Luna (the mistress of "God"), Tom Law (Geronimo), William Cannon (convict). Producer: Otto Preminger, for Sigma Productions. Released by Paramount.

1970   *Tell Me That You Love Me, Junie Moon.* Screenplay: Marjorie Kellogg, based on her novel. Camera: Boris Kaufman. Editors: Henry Berman, Dean O. Ball. Music: Philip Springer. Music and lyrics for "Old Devil Time": Pete Seeger. Costume coordinator: Hope Bryce. Cast: Liza Minnelli (Junie Moon), Ken Howard (Arthur), Robert Moore (Warren), James Coco (Mario), Kay Thompson (Gregory), Fred Williamson (beach boy), Ben Piazza (Jesse), Emily Yancy (Solana), Leonard Frey (Guiles), Anne Revere (Miss Farber), Pete Seeger (sings "Old Devil Time"). Producer: Otto Preminger, for Sigma Productions. Released by Paramount.

1971   *Such Good Friends.* Screenplay: Esther Dale [Elaine May], based on the novel by Lois Gould. Camera: Gayne Rescher. Art director: Rouben Ter-Arutunian. Editor: Harry Howard. Music: Thomas Z. Shepard. Costume supervisor: Hope Bryce Preminger. Cast: Dyan Cannon (Julie Messinger), James Coco (Dr. Timmy Spector), Jennifer O'Neill (Miranda Graham), Ken Howard (Cal Whitting), Rita Gam (Doria Perkins), Nancy Guild (Molly Hastings), Nina Foch (Mrs. Wallman), Laurence Luckinbill (Richard Messinger), Louise Lasser (Marcy Berns), Burgess Meredith (Kalman), Sam Levene (Onkel Eddie), William Redfield (Barney Halstead), Doris Roberts (Mrs. Gold), Lawrence Tierney (Wachter), Joseph Papp and his Shakespeare Theater in the Park. Producer: Otto Preminger, for Sigma Productions. Released by Paramount.

1975   *Rosebud.* Screenplay: Erik Lee Preminger, based on the novel by Joan Hemingway and Paul Bonnecarrère; additional dialogue by Marjorie Kellogg, Roy Clark. Camera: Denys Coop. Art director: Michael Seymour. Titles: Saul Bass. Editors: Peter Thornton, Thom Nobble. Music: Laurent Petitgirard. Cast: Peter O'Toole (Larry Martin), Richard Attenborough (Sloat), Cliff Gorman (Hamlekh), Claude Dauphin (Fargeau), John V. Lindsay (Senator Donovan), Peter Lawford (Lord Carter), Raf Vallone (George Nikolaos), Adrienne Corri (Lady Carter), Amidou (Kirkbane), Brigitte Ariel (Sabine Fargeau), Isabelle Huppert (Hélène Nikolaos), Lalla Ward (Margaret Carter), Kim Cattrall (Joyce Donovan), Debra Berger

(Gertrude Freyer), Ted Gershuny (Saul). Producer: Otto Preminger. Released by United Artists.

1979   *The Human Factor.* Screenplay: Tom Stoppard, based on the novel by Graham Greene. Camera: Mike Molloy. Art director: Ken Ryan. Titles: Saul Bass. Editor: Richard Trevor. Music: Richard Logan, Gary Logan. Costume coordinator: Hope Bryce. Cast: Nicol Williamson (Maurice Castle), Richard Attenborough (Colonel Daintry), John Gielgud (Brigadier Tomlinson), Joop Doderer (Cornelius Muller), Derek Jacobi (Arthur Davis), Robert Morley (Dr. Percival), Ann Todd (Castle's mother), Iman (Sarah Castle), Richard Vernon (Sir John Hargreaves), Angela Thorne (Lady Hargreaves). Producer: Otto Preminger, for Wheel Productions (London), Sigma Productions (New York). Released by Metro-Goldwyn-Mayer.

Index